Analysis of Economics Data:
An Introduction to Econometrics

Contents

List of Figures   ix

List of Tables   xiii

Preface   xvii

1   Analysis of Economics Data   1
   1.1   Statistical Methods 1
   1.2   Types of Data 2
   1.3   Regression Analysis 4
   1.4   Key Concepts 5
   1.5   Exercises 6

2   Univariate Data Summary   7
   2.1   Summary Statistics for Numerical Data 7
   2.2   Charts for Numerical Data 15
   2.3   Charts for Numerical Data by Category 19
   2.4   Summary and Charts for Categorical Data 22
   2.5   Data Transformation 22
   2.6   Data Transformations for Time Series Data 24
   2.7   Key Concepts 28
   2.8   Exercises 29

3   The Sample Mean   35
   3.1   Random Variables 35
   3.2   Random Samples 38
   3.3   Sample Generated by an Experiment: Coin Tosses 39
   3.4   Properties of the Sample Mean 41
   3.5   Sampling from a Finite Population: 1880 Census 45
   3.6   Estimation of the Population Mean 47
   3.7   Nonrepresentative Samples 48
   3.8   Computer Generation of Random Samples 50
   3.9   Key Concepts 52

3.10 Exercises 54

4 Statistical Inference for the Mean   59
    4.1 Example: Mean Annual Earnings 59
    4.2 t Statistic and t Distribution 61
    4.3 Confidence Intervals 65
    4.4 Two-Sided Hypothesis Tests 69
    4.5 Two-sided Hypothesis Test Examples 73
    4.6 One-Sided Directional Hypothesis Tests 76
    4.7 Generalization of Confidence Intervals and Hypothesis Tests 79
    4.8 Proportions Data 81
    4.9 Key Concepts 83
    4.10 Exercises 85

5 Bivariate Data Summary   93
    5.1 Example: House Price and Size 93
    5.2 Two-way Tabulation 95
    5.3 Two-way Scatter Plot 96
    5.4 Sample Correlation 97
    5.5 Regression Line 100
    5.6 Measures of Model Fit 105
    5.7 Computer Output following OLS Regression 108
    5.8 Prediction and Outlying Observations 110
    5.9 Regression and Correlation 111
    5.10 Causation 112
    5.11 Computations for Correlation and Regression 113
    5.12 Nonparametric Regression 115
    5.13 Key Concepts 117
    5.14 Exercises 119

6 The Least Squares Estimator   125
    6.1 Population Model for Bivariate Regression 125
    6.2 Examples of Sampling from a Population 128
    6.3 Properties of the Least Squares Estimator 133
    6.4 Estimators of Model Parameters 138
    6.5 Key Concepts 140
    6.6 Exercises 141

7 Statistical Inference for Bivariate Regression   145
    7.1 Example: House Price and Size 145
    7.2 t Statistic 146
    7.3 Confidence Intervals 148
    7.4 Tests of Statistical Significance 150

7.5   Two-Sided Hypothesis Tests 153

7.6   One-Sided Directional Hypothesis Tests 156

7.7   Robust Standard Errors 158

7.8   Key Concepts 160

7.9   Exercises 161

8 Case Studies for Bivariate Regression   165

8.1   Health Outcomes across Countries 165

8.2   Health Expenditures across Countries 168

8.3   Capital Asset Pricing Model 170

8.4   Output and Unemployment in the U.S. 173

8.5   Exercises 176

9 Models with Natural Logarithms   179

9.1   Natural Logarithm Function 179

9.2   Semi-elasticities and Elasticities 181

9.3   Log-linear, Log-log and Linear-log models 182

9.4   Example: Earnings and Education 185

9.5   Further Uses of the Natural Logarithm 187

9.6   Exponential Function 190

9.7   Key Concepts 191

9.8   Exercises 192

10 Data Summary with Multiple Regression   197

10.1 Example: House Price and Characteristics 197

10.2 Two-way Scatter Plots 199

10.3 Correlation 200

10.4 Regression Line 201

10.5 Interpretation of Slope Coefficients 204

10.6 Model Fit 206

10.7 Computer Output Following Multiple Regression 209

10.8 Inestimable Models 210

10.9 Key Concepts 211

10.10 Exercises 213

11 Statistical Inference for Multiple Regression   217

11.1 Properties of the Least Squares Estimator 217

11.2 Estimators of Model Parameters 221

11.3 Confidence Intervals 222

11.4 Hypothesis Tests on a Single Parameter 223

11.5 Joint Hypothesis Tests 227

11.6 F Statistic under Assumptions 1-4 232

11.7 Presentation of Regression Results 235

11.8 Key Concepts 236
11.9 Exercises 237

12 Further Topics in Multiple Regression   241
12.1 Inference with Robust Standard Errors 241
12.2 Prediction 252
12.3 Nonrepresentative Samples 258
12.4 Best Estimation 260
12.5 Best Confidence Intervals 261
12.6 Best Hypothesis Tests 262
12.7 Data Science and Big Data: An Overview 264
12.8 Bayesian Methods: An Overview 265
12.9 A Brief History of Statistics, Regression and Econometrics 266
12.10 Key Concepts 267
12.11 Exercises 268

13 Case Studies for Multiple Regression   275
13.1 School Academic Performance 275
13.2 Cobb-Douglas Production Function 280
13.3 Phillips Curve 284
13.4 Automobile Fuel Efficiency 288
13.5 Rand Health Insurance Experiment 291
13.6 Access to Health Care and Health Outcomes 295
13.7 Gains from Political Incumbency 298
13.8 Institutions and Country GDP 301
13.9 From Raw Data to Final Data 303
13.10 Exercises 308

14 Regression with Indicator Variables   315
14.1 Example: Earnings, Gender, Education and Type of Worker 315
14.2 Regression on just a Single Indicator Variable 315
14.3 Regression on an Indicator Variable and Additional Regressors 319
14.4 Regression with Sets of Indicator Variables 322
14.5 Key Concepts 328
14.6 Exercises 329

15 Regression with Transformed Variables   333
15.1 Example: Earnings, Gender, Education and Type of Worker 333
15.2 Marginal Effects for Nonlinear Models 333
15.3 Quadratic Model and Polynomial Models 337
15.4 Interacted Regressors 340
15.5 Log-linear and Log-log Models 342
15.6 Prediction from Log-Linear and Log-Log Models 344

15.7 Models with a Mix of Regressor Types 346
15.8 Key Concepts 348
15.9 Exercises 349

16 Checking the Model and Data   355
16.1 Multicollinear Data 356
16.2 Model Assumptions Revisited 358
16.3 Incorrect Population Model 359
16.4 Regressors Correlated with Errors 362
16.5 Heteroskedastic Errors 363
16.6 Correlated Errors 364
16.7 Example: Democracy and Growth 365
16.8 Diagnostics 367
16.9 Key Concepts 371
16.10 Exercises 372

17 Special Topics   377
17.1 Cross-Section Data 377
17.2 Panel Data 380
17.3 Panel Data Example: NBA Team Revenue 384
17.4 Instrumental Variables 387
17.5 Causal Inference: An Overview 391
17.6 Nonlinear Regression Models 396
17.7 Time-Series Data 402
17.8 Time Series Example: U.S. Treasury Security Interest Rates 409
17.9 Further Reading 416
17.10 Key Concepts 416
17.11 Exercises 417

A Using Statistical Packages   429
A.1 General Issues 429
A.2 Stata Essentials 434
A.3 R Essentials 436
A.4 Gretl Essentials 440
A.5 Eviews Essentials 445
A.6 Excel and Google Sheets Spreadsheet Applications 449
A.7 Critical values and p-values 451

B Some Essentials of Probability Theory   453
B.1 Probability Theory for a Single Random Variable 453
B.2 Probability Theory for the Sample Mean 457
B.3 Probability Theory for Two Related Random Variables 459

C Properties of OLS, IV and ML Estimators   **463**
    C.1 OLS with Independent Homoskedastic Errors 463
    C.2 Robust Standard Errors 466
    C.3 Instrumental Variables Estimation 470
    C.4 OLS with Matrix Algebra 471
    C.5 Maximum Likelihood Estimation 473
    C.6 Exercises 474

D Solutions to Selected Exercises   **475**
    D.1 Solutions: Analysis of Economics Data 475
    D.2 Solutions: Univariate Data Summary 475
    D.3 Solutions: The Sample Mean 476
    D.4 Solutions: Statistical Inference for the Mean 477
    D.5 Solutions: Bivariate Data Summary 478
    D.6 Solutions: The Least Squares Estimator 479
    D.7 Solutions: Statistical Inference for Bivariate Regression 480
    D.8 Solutions: Case Studies for Bivariate Regression 481
    D.9 Solutions: Models with Natural Logarithm 481
    D.10 Solutions: Data Summary with Multiple Regression 482
    D.11 Solutions: Statistical Inference for Multiple Regression 483
    D.12 Solutions: Further Topics in Multiple Regression 484
    D.13 Solutions: Case Studies for Multiple Regression 485
    D.14 Solutions: Models with Indicator Variables 486
    D.15 Solutions: Models with Transformed Variables 486
    D.16 Solutions: Checking the Model and Data 487
    D.17 Solutions: Special Topics 489

E Tables for Key Distributions   **493**

F References   **501**

Index   **503**

List of Figures

1.1   Linear regression example   4

2.1   Normal distribution: Probability of being within one, two or three standard deviations of the mean.   12

2.2   Box Plot: Annual earnings of 30 year-old female full-time workers in 2010.   13

2.3   Histograms for symmetric, right-skewed and left-skewed data.   14

2.4   Histogram: Individual annual earnings with two different bin widths   17

2.5   Smoothed histogram: kernel density estimate for individual annual earnings with two different window widths   18

2.6   Line Chart: Real GDP per capita in U.S. (in 2012 dollars).   19

2.7   Column chart: U.S. health expenditures in 2018 (in billions of dollars)   20

2.8   Spatial Map: Average family size in each U.S. state in 2010.   21

2.9   Pie Chart: Fishing site used   23

2.10   Levels and natural logarithms: Histograms and kernel density estimates for individual annual earnings   24

2.11   Moving average and seasonal adjustment smoothing: Monthly sales of existing homes   25

2.12   Nominal and real data: U.S. GDP and per capita GDP in current dollars and in 2012 dollars.   27

3.1   Coin tosses histograms: for x in one sample (n = 30) and for mean of x in 400 samples (n = 30).   40

3.2   1880 Census histogram: Age for the entire U.S. population.   45

3.3   1880 Census histograms: Age in one sample (n = 25) and Mean age in 100 samples (n = 25).   46

4.1   Student's t distribution: $T(4)$ and $T(30)$ compared to the standard normal.   63

4.2   Student's t distribution: Critical values $t_{v,\alpha}$ and $t_{v,\alpha/2}$ for $v = 170$ and $\alpha = 0.05$. . .   65

4.3   Two-sided hypothesis test: p-value approach and critical value approach   71

4.4   One-sided directional hypothesis test (upper one-tailed alternative): p-value approach and critical value apporach   78

5.1   Scatterplot: House price and size with four quadrants defined by means of price and size   97

5.2   Correlation: Examples of different strengths and direction of correlation. 100
5.3   Residual: The vertical difference between the data point and the regression line. . . 102
5.4   House price and size: Regression. 103
5.5   R-squared: Total sum of squares and explained sum of squares for five observations. 106
5.6   Regression: Scatterplot and regression line computation example 114
5.7   House price and size: Nonparametric regression using local linear and lowess. . . . 117

6.1   Error u is difference between y and population line. Residual e is difference between
      y and fitted regression line. 127
6.2   Generated data: True population line and fitted regression line. 130
6.3   Generated data: Regression for three random samples (n = 30). 130
6.4   Generated data: Slopes and intercepts from 400 regressions (n=30). 131
6.5   1880 Census data: Slopes and intercepts from 400 regressions (n=200). 132

7.1   Two-sided hypothesis test: p-value approach and critical region approach. 154

8.1   Health outcomes: Life expectancy and infant mortality versus per capita health
      expenditures 167
8.2   Health expenditures per capita: Relationship with GDP per capita 169
8.3   CAPM Model: Coca Cola and market excess returns 173
8.4   Okun's Law: Percentage change in output and change in unemployment rate 175

9.1   Linear and log-linear models: Earnings and education 186
9.2   Levels and natural logarithm over time: Standard and Poors 500 index 189

10.1 Scatterplots: House price and various characteristics 199

11.1 F distribution: F(3,30) and F(10,30) 228

12.1 Prediction: Conditional mean and actual value 253

13.1 Academic Performance Index: Histogram and smoothed histogram 276
13.2 Academic Performance Index: Regression on parents' education 278
13.3 Cobb-Douglas production function: Plots of lnq and OLS residual over time 282
13.4 Cobb-Douglas production function: Predicted output and fitted isoquants 283
13.5 Phillips curve: 1949 to 1969. 285
13.6 Phillips curve: 1970 to 2014. 286
13.7 Automobiles fuel efficiency: Plot of fule conomy against horsepower 289
13.8 Gains from political incumbency: Regression discontinuity design plots 299
13.9 Institutions and country GDP: Plots of dependent variable against regressor and
      against instrument 302

14.1 Indicator variable: Inclusion as regressor and inclusion as interacted regressor. . . . 319

15.1 Marginal effect: Computation by calculus method and by finite difference method. . 335

15.2 Quadratic models: Examples of the possible shapes. 338

16.1 Democracy and growth: Scatter plot and fitted line. 366
16.2 Diagnostics: Actual values and OLS residuals plotted against fitted values. 369
16.3 Diagnostics: Residual, component plus residual and added variable plots 370

17.1 NBA team revenue: Scatterplot of natural logarithm against number of wins in previous season for 29 teams over 10 seasons. 385
17.2 Instrumental variables: Path diagrams for OLS and for IV 388
17.3 Nonlinear models: Predictions from logit, probit and OLS regression. 398
17.4 U.S. Treasury securities: Plot of 10-year and 1-year annualized returns from 1982 to 2015. 410
17.5 U.S. Treasury securities: Plots of monthly changes in 10-year and 1-year annualized returns from 1982 to 2015. 413

A.1 Stata: Sample output 437
A.2 R: Sample output 441
A.3 Gretl: Sample output 444
A.4 Eviews: Sample output. 448
A.5 Excel: Sample output. 450

B.1 Standard normal density: Graphs of $\Pr[X \leq 1.5]$ and $\Pr[0.5 \leq X \leq 1.5]$. 456

E.1 Standard normal distribution: Probabilities in the left tail 494
E.2 Student t distribution: Key critical values 495
E.3 $F(v1,v2)$ distribution: Critical values for a 10% significance test 496
E.4 $F(v1,v2)$ distribution: Critical values for a 5% significance test 497
E.5 $F(v1,v2)$ distribution: Critical values for a 1% significance test 498
E.6 $F(v1,\infty)$ and chi-squared(v1) distributions: Key critical values 499

List of Tables

1   Book Chapters. xviii

2.1   Summary statistics: Annual earnings of 30 year-old female full-time workers in 2010 (n=171). 8

2.2   Frequencies: Individual annual earnings in bins of width 15,000. 16

2.3   Numerical data by category: U.S. health expenditures in 2018 in billions of dollars . 20

2.4   Categorical data: Frequencies at each fishing site 22

2.5   Nominal and real data: U.S. GDP example 27

4.1   Summary statistics: Annual earnings of female full-time workers aged 30 in 2010 (n=171). 60

4.2   Confidence interval: Annual earnings. 60

4.3   Hypothesis test: Annual earnings have mean equal to 40000. 61

4.4   Student's t distribution: Critical values for various degrees of freedom and confidence levels. 68

4.5   Summary Statistics: Gasoline price per gallon at 32 gas stations. 74

4.6   Summary Statistics: Annual earnings of male full-time workers aged 30 in 2010. . . . 74

4.7   Summary Statistics: Annual growth rate in U.S. real GDP per capita using quarterly data from 1959 to 2020. 75

5.1   House price and size: Complete listing of data. 94

5.2   House price and size: Summary statistics (n=29). 94

5.3   House price and size: Cross tabulation with row and column sums 95

5.4   House price and size: Cross tabulation with expected frequencies. 96

5.5   House price and size: Computer output from regression. 109

5.6   Regression: Details for computation example. 113

6.1   Generated data: Model y = 1 + 2x + u where u is N(0, 4) distributed. 129

7.1   House price and size: Regression estimates with default standard errors. 145

7.2   Hypothesis tests: Summary for tests on the slope parameter. 158

8.1   Health outcomes: Variable definitions and summary statistics (n=34) 166

8.2   Health expenditures: Variable definitions and summary statistics (n=34) 169

xiii

8.3   CAPM data: Variable definitions and summary statistics (n=354) 172
8.4   Output and unemployment data: Variable definitions and summary statistics (n=59) 174

9.1   Change in ln(x) approximates proportionate change in x 181
9.2   Variable definitions and summary statistics: Annual Earnings of female full-time
      workers aged 25-65 in 2010. 185
9.3   Various regression models with logs: y is earnings and x is age 186
9.4   Approximating ln(1+x) by x for small x. 187
9.5   Rule of 72: Number of periods for investment at percentage rate r per period to
      double. 188

10.1 House price: Variable definitions and summary statistics (n=29) 197
10.2 House price: Complete listing of data. 198
10.3 House price: Correlations of variables 201
10.4 House price: Computer output from multiple regression. 209

11.1 Hypothesis tests on slope parameter: Summary for multiple regression. 224
11.2 House price: Computer output from multiple regression. 226
11.3 F distribution: Critical values for various degrees of freedom and confidence levels. . 229
11.4 Regression estimates: Various ways to report the results. 236

12.1 Robust standard errors: Leading examples. 242
12.2 Heteroskedastic-robust standard errors: House price example. 244
12.3 Hypothesis Tests: Type I and Type II Errors. 263

13.1 Academic Performance Index: Variable definitions and summary statistics (n=807) . 276
13.2 Academic Performance Index: Pairwise correlations 278
13.3 Academic Performance Index: Multiple regression estimates. 279
13.4 Cobb-Douglas data: Listing for U.S. from 1899 to 1922 (n=24). 281
13.5 Phillips curve data: Variable definitions and summary statistics (n=65) 284
13.6 Automobiles fuel efficiency: Summary Statistics (n=14,423) 288
13.7 Automobile fuel efficiency: Multiple regression estimates with cluster-robust stan-
      dard errors. 290
13.8 RAND Health Insurance Experiment: Year 1 summary statistics (n=5,639) 292
13.9 RAND Health Insurance Experiment: Year 1 regression estimates. 293
13.10 South African community clinics: Summary statistics (n=1,071) 297
13.11 South African community clinics: Difference-in-differences regression estimates. . . . 298
13.12 Gains from political incumbency: Regression discontinuity design regression estimates. 300
13.13 Institutions and country GDP: Summary statistics (n=64) 301
13.14 Institutions and country GDP: .OLS and IV regression estimates 302
13.15 Survey data: Format of raw data file. 304
13.16 Survey data: Summary statistics before data cleaning. 305
13.17 Survey data: Summary statistics after data cleaning. 307

14.1 Annual Earnings of full-time workers aged 25-65 in 2010: Summary statistics (n=872).316
14.2 Annual earnings: Summary statistics by gender 317
14.3 Indicator variable: Earnings regressions with an indicator for gender. 321
14.4 Sets of indicator variables: Earnings regression with indicators for type of worker . . 325

15.1 Annual Earnings of full-time workers aged 25-65 in 2010: Summary statistics (n=872).334

16.1 Democracy and growth: Variable definitions and summary statistics (n=131). 365

17.1 NBA team revenue: Variable definitions and summary statistics (n=29, T=10). . . . 384
17.2 NBA team revenue: Various robust standard error estimates for pooled OLS. 386
17.3 NBA team revenue: Pooled OLS, random effects and fixed effects estimates. 386
17.4 Rreturns to schooling: OLS and IV estimates in a log-wage regression 390
17.5 Nonlinear models: Leading examples for different data types. 401
17.6 US 10-year and 1-year Treasury securities monthly from January 1982 to January
    2015: Variable definitions and summary statistics (T=297) 410
17.7 US Treasury securities: Autocorrelations and residual autocorrelations. 411

A.1 Statistical packages: File-name extensions for script files and data files. 431
A.2 Statistical packages: Commands to calculate 5% critical values 451
A.3 Statistical packages: Commands to calculate p-values for a two-sided test. 452

Preface

Motivation

Data analysis and data literacy are important and valuable skills in today's data age. Students taking economics and related majors are well placed to take advantage of the demands for these skills, as their major places greater weight on mathematical and statistical training than many other majors.

This book is suited to the following uses.

1. A true first course in regression analysis, the statistical method most used in analysis of economics data and the field of econometrics. The book's main goal is to reach this audience.

2. A helpful inexpensive adjunct to "Introductory Econometrics" courses that use a more advanced text.

3. A stand-alone reference for any more advanced data analysis course or economics field course that presumes a basic knowledge of linear regression.

How to Use this Book

The book takes a learning-by-doing approach. The key requirement is use of an econometrics or statistical package. For the particular statistical package that is chosen to use with this book, the instructor and student can easily work through each chapter using the datasets and computer code that are all available at the book website. **This is by far the best way to learn the material.** The book itself is limited to presenting key summary tables; few specific commands and consequent computer output are provided as these vary with the package used in instruction.

The website cameron.econ.ucdavis.edu/aed provides the datasets as a Stata version 11 dataset, readable by most other packages, and as a comma-separated values text file, readable by all packages. Datasets are referred to in the book using capital letters without any prefix or file extension. For example, the dataset called HOUSE in the text is available as file AED_HOUSE.DTA, a Stata version 11 dataset, and as file AED_HOUSE.DTA.csv, a comma-separated values text file.

The book is written as much as possible to be usable with any statistical package. An appendix provides key details on using **Stata**, the free packages **R** and **Gretl,** and the commercial econometrics package **Eviews.** The datasets can be read into these packages. Selected parts of the main text provide additional details on use of these packages. The spreadsheet programs **Excel** and **Google Sheets** can also be used, but are more limited. Appendix A summarizes key commands for the various statistical packages. The book website provides computer code for repeating the analysis in the book using **Stata, R** and **Gretl.**

The book includes over three hundred end-of-chapter exercises that are mainly learning-by-doing empirical exercises. Many use a wide range of datasets that can be obtained from the book website. Overhead slides for each chapter are also available at the book website.

Table 1: Book Chapters.

PART	Ch.	Title	Essentials
I: UNIVARIATE	1	Analysis of Economics Data	x
(Single Series)	2	Univariate Data Summary	x
	3	The Sample Mean	
	4	Statistical Inference for the Mean	x
BIVARIATE	5	Bivariate Data Summary	x
(Two series)	6	The Least Squares Estimator	
	7	Statistical Inference for Bivariate Regression	x
	8	Case Studies for Bivariate Regression	x
	9	Models with Natural Logarithms	
MULTIVARIATE	10	Data Summary with Multiple Regression	x
(Several series)	11	Statistical Inference for Multiple Regression	x
	12	Further Topics in Multiple Regression	x
	13	Case Studies for Multiple Regression	x
	14	Regression with Indicator Variables	x
	15	Regression with Transformed Variables	
FURTHER TOPICS	16	Checking the Model and Data	x
	17	Special Topics	
APPENDICES	A	Using Statistical Packages	x
	B	Some Essentials of Probability Theory	
	C	Properties of OLS and IV Estimators	
	D	Solutions to Selected Exercises	x
	E	Tables for Key Distributions	
	F	Further Reading	

Book Outline

Table 1 provides a summary of the book, which is divided into four parts.

1. Analysis of a single variable that covers the key parts of material presented in an introductory probability and statistics class.

2. Analysis of the relationship between two variables, y and x, with emphasis on bivariate linear regression.

3. Analysis of the relationship between y and several other variables, with emphasis on multiple linear regression.

4. Model and data checking and brief overviews of the most commonly-used methods beyond OLS: fixed effects and random effects for panel data and clustered data, logit and probit for binary dependent variable, several methods for causal inference, and time series regression.

Book appendices cover statistical packages, more advanced material on probability and estimation theory, solutions to odd-numbered exercises, and statistical tables.

Course Outline

The book is intended to be suitable for three different introductory courses.

1. An essentials course places less emphasis on motivating the distribution of the sample mean and regression coefficient estimates, skipping chapters 3 and 7, and places less emphasis on various extensions, skipping chapters 9, 12.2-12.8, 15 and 17.

2. A fast-paced ten-week quarter-long course with two lectures a week can cover the key material in Chapters 1-16, including one case study in each of the two case studies chapters.

3. A semester-long course could cover most of chapters 1-16 and selected parts of chapter 17.

This book is additionally written to be used as a supplement to courses that use regression. There is enormous heterogeneity in students knowledge of regression even after taking a first course in regression. This book, one available at low cost, can be used as a supplement to fill gaps.

For the Instructor

The book is written to be suitable for students with a wide range of mathematical and statistical backgrounds. The book presents methods in the main text with minimal use of mathematics - the optional Appendices B-C provide greater mathematical detail. In particular, to be accessible to a wide range of students the book is deliberately written at a lower level than the excellent leading texts by Wooldridge (2019) and by Stock and Watson (2018).

Some use of mathematics is nonetheless necessary. The main text presents formulas using summation notation. Changes in one variable with respect to another are generally presented using delta notation, though at times connections to derivatives are made for the benefit of those with a calculus background. Less-prepared students may find it possible to gloss over much of the mathematics. The emphasis of the book is on the interpretation of statistical output rather than dexterity with mathematical and statistical formulas.

The book does provide the essentials of probability, so that students understand the distinction between sample and population, the distinction between estimate and parameter, and the concepts of confidence intervals and hypothesis tests. Ideally students have taken a prior course on probability and statistical inference for the population mean based on the sample mean. My own experience is that even if students have taken such a course, many do not understand or do not recall statistical inference. Accordingly students benefit greatly from seeing the material a second time. Furthermore, some instructors may prefer to teach this course to students with no background in probability and statistics. The essentials of probability are covered briefly in Chapter 3, and are presented in more detail in Appendix B. Basic statistical inference on the sample mean is covered in detail in Chapters 3 and 4. Derivations of the properties of the OLS estimator are provided in Appendix C.

Regression results presented in this book are generally based on default standard errors in earlier chapters, as these are identical across statistical packages. Appropriate robust standard errors are used especially from chapter 12 on. Note that formulas for computing robust standard errors can vary across statistical packages due to different finite sample adjustments; see Chapter 12.1.9.

An individual chapter can be covered in one or two seventy-five minute lectures. To simplify the exposition of methods, my approach is to work with the one data example throughout a chapter, or even across several chapters in the case of summarizing individual earnings and modeling the sale price of a house. At the same time many additional datasets are introduced throughout the book, most notably in the case studies chapters and in the many exercises at the end of each chapter. Some data examples come from empirical research articles published in leading economics journals that were deliberately chosen in the belief that the associated articles would be intelligible to undergraduate students.

As already noted, the exercises at the end of each chapter are mainly learning-by-doing empirical exercises. Solutions to most odd-numbered exercises are given in Appendix D. It is easy for an instructor to make variations on these exercises that lead to different answers. Variations include using alternative datasets, using the same dataset with some observations dropped, or using the same dataset with different variables.

Version History

The book is available as a pdf and as a hard copy at a modest price through Amazon's Kindle Direct Publishing.

Version 1.0 is dated December 2021 and was released January 5, 2022.

Version 1.1 is dated February 2022 and was released late February, 2022. It corrects errors in Version 1.0 and in places provides some rewording for clarity. Section numbering is unchanged and pagination is essentially unchanged.

This Edition compared to Earlier Drafts

This edition is a revision of the unpublished 2015 version. The basic progression of topics is unchanged. Compared to that earlier version the initial chapters are simplified. More difficult concepts such as power of tests and many uses of natural logarithms are pushed to later chapters. And there is less repetition of material across chapters. The goal is to emphasize basic statistical analysis. For details see a document provided at the book website `cameron.econ.ucdavis.edu/aed`.

Acknowledgements

The late Jack Repcheck, book editor at a commercial publisher, provided great encouragement for the writing of this ultimately self-published book.

I was fortunate to receive an unusually strong undergraduate education in econometrics at The Australian National University and subsequent graduate training at Stanford University. A list of teachers to whom I am indebted would be very long. This book is my attempt to in turn introduce econometrics to students.

I have benefitted greatly from research coauthors, most notably Pravin Trivedi and Doug Miller, and from the strong empirical economics community at U.C. Davis and my fellow econometricians Òscar Jordà, Shu Shen and Takuya Ura.

Finally I thank the Department of Economics in supporting the course on which this book is based, a course that is both a terminal course for some of our majors and a pre-requisite course to additional optional econometrics courses for other Economics majors.

Chapter 1

Analysis of Economics Data

Statisticians specialize in data analysis, and offer courses that cover many of the statistical techniques in this book. This chapter summarizes the main statistical methods used in analyzing economics data.

1.1 Statistical Methods

The starting point of statistical analysis is a dataset, a collection of measurements that most often come from a survey or from an experiment.

Statistical analysis begins with a **summary** or **description** of what can be a bewilderingly large set of numbers. There are several standard statistics that are used to summarize features of the data such as the central tendency of the data and the spread of the data. For example, given data on annual income of a number of individuals we may compute the average income for these individuals. This is relatively straightforward.

Most data analyses seek to go further and use such summary measures to extrapolate to the world beyond the particular dataset at hand. For example, if the average annual income in a sample of forty Californians is $60,000, what can we say about the average income of all Californians? Or if forty tosses of a coin lead to 18 heads and 22 tails, can we conclude whether or not the coin is fair coin?

This extrapolation entails the much more challenging methods of **statistical inference** - inferring details of a population from the sample at hand. The two main statistical tools used are **confidence intervals** and **hypothesis tests**; much of the book is focused on learning how to use these tools in a variety of settings.

Additionally, steps should be taken to ensure that a sample is representative and obtained in such a way that the phenomena of interest can be measured sufficiently precisely. Like other books at this level, these issues are only briefly considered; they are covered in detail in separate statistics courses on survey sampling and experimental design.

In some special cases the dataset may be large enough and precise enough that there is no need to control for randomness due to sampling. For example, this would be the case if we had a complete census of the population or if we could toss the coin a million times. While very large datasets are increasingly available, such as those from internet transactions, in typical economics applications one needs to control for uncertainty.

1.2   Types of Data

The discipline of statistics covers a wide range of data types and associated methods that are summarized in this section.

Within this wide range economists, and hence this book, focus on observational data on continuously measured variables analyzed using regression methods. An example is sale price data from a sample of individual house sales.

1.2.1   Economics Data

There are several types of data that may demand different statistical methods:

- Numerical data that are continuous.

- Numerical data that are discrete.

- Categorical data.

Economics data are usually **numerical data** that are naturally recorded and interpreted as numbers. Furthermore, they often potentially take so many different values that they are viewed to be **continuous numerical data**. Examples are individual annual income or national GDP.

Less often the data are **discrete numerical data** that take only integer values. Examples are the number of jobs held at a point in time or the number of patents awarded to a firm in a year.

Categorical data are an alternative to numerical data where the data are recorded as belonging to one of several possible categories, such as whether or not a person is employed. Such data may be coded as numbers, e.g. 1 if employed and 0 if not employed, but are not intrinsically numerical.

This book emphasizes the study of **economics data** that are continuous numerical data. Many examples will be provided, including leading relationships that are discussed in introductory microeconomics and macroeconomics courses. In many cases **economic theory** is used to guide in model selection. And in some cases economic data are used to test economic theory or to distinguish between economic theories.

Before analysis begins, data are often transformed to a more suitable form. For example, suppose interest lies in modelling improvements in living standards over time. A standard measure to use is the annual growth rate in real per capita gross domestic product (GDP). This entails transformations of the original GDP data to first adjust for inflation and population and to subsequently calculate year-to-year proportionate changes.

1.2.2   Observational Data

Economics data are most often **observational data**, meaning they are based on observations of actual behavior in an uncontrolled environment. A particular challenge of using observational data is that while it is easy to detect a relationship between two data series, it can be very difficult to determine cause and effect.

By contrast many physical and biological sciences in particular use **experimental data** that are observations on the results of experiments which can be controlled by the investigator. Experimental methods and quasi-experimental methods are increasingly used in econometrics. For pedagogical reasons these methods are deferred to Chapter 17.5 which presents various methods to determine **causal** relationship, the goal of many econometrics studies.

1.2.3 Types of Data Collection

Distinction is made between several types of data collection:

- Cross-section data on different individuals at a point in time.

- Time-series data on the same quantity at different points of time.

- Panel (or longitudinal) data on the same individuals at different points of time.

- Repeated cross-section data on different individuals at different points in time

Cross-section data are data on different entities, such as individuals, households, firms or countries, collected at a common point in time. Examples are earnings of individuals and output of firms. Such data are most often used in **microeconomics**. Standard notation is to use the subscript i to denote the typical observation. The sample of size n is denoted $x_1, ..., x_n$ with i^{th} observation x_i.

Time-series data are data on the same quantity collected at different points in time. Examples are gross domestic product and the interest rate on a 13-week Treasury bill. Such data are most often used in **macroeconomics** and **finance**. Standard notation is to use the subscript t to denote the typical observation. The sample of size T is denoted $x_1, ..., x_T$ with t^{th} observation x_t. In this book we use subscript i as much as possible, but revert occasionally to subscript t in some time series settings. In particular, the one-period change in a time series variable is $\Delta x_t = x_t - x_{t-1}$.

Panel data or **longitudinal data** are data on the same individuals, such as firms or people or countries, where each individual is observed at several points in time. Examples include analysis of individual income over several years, and analysis of GDP in several countries over time. Such data are used in both microeconomics and macroeconomics. The typical observation is x_{it}, data for the ith individual at time t.

Repeated cross-section data or **pooled data** are cross-section data collected in more than one time period, but in each time period different individuals are observed. Many surveys conducted on a regular basis sample different individuals in each survey.

The same basic statistical principles apply for all these types of data collections. However, each type of data collection also adds its own special considerations for statistical inference, such as computing confidence intervals, and for model specification. We focus on the simplest case of cross-section data.

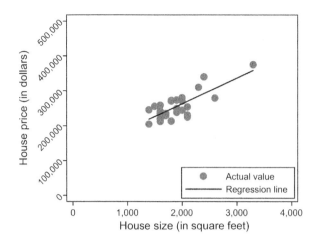

Figure 1.1: Linear regression example

1.3 Regression Analysis

Introductory statistics courses focus on data on a single variable considered in isolation, such as the individual income and coin toss examples. Some economic statistics such as the unemployment rate or the growth rate in real GDP or median earnings are also of interest on their own.

We first analyze **univariate data**, studying a single data series such as house price, with individual observations denoted x_i or denoted x_t. The treatment of univariate data is similar to that in an introductory statistics course.

Most economic data analysis, however, is focused on measuring the relationship between two or more variables. The statistical method used to measure such inter-relationships is called **regression analysis**. Most of this book studies regression analysis.

Bivariate data are data on two related data series, denoted y and x. For example, in Chapter 5 we consider the relationship between house price (in dollars) and house size (in square feet) for a sample of 29 house sales. Figure 1.1 presents a scatter plot of the data which suggests that, as expected, a higher price is associated with a higher price. Superimposed on this scatter plot is a line, called a **regression line**, that is the best fitting line for these data using a criterion given in Chapter 5. The regression line has slope coefficient equal to 74, approximately, so an increase in house size of one square foot is associated with an increase in house price of \$74.

Multivariate data methods consider three or more related series. Usually one of those variables, say y, is explained by several other variables, say x_1, x_2, ... using **multiple regression**. For example, we may consider the relationship between house price and several features of the house, such as size, number of bedrooms and lot size.

The term regression arises due to the phenomena of **regression towards the mean**. For example, consider the relationship between the height of a father (x) and the height of his son (y). If the father is of above average height, then the height of the son turns out to be on average also of above average height, though not as high as that of the father. Similarly the son of a below average height father is on average below average, but not as below average as the father. More generally the term regression refers to fitting a model of y as a function of x.

Regressions may be used to measure how an outcome variable (y) **changes** as one of the regressors (x) changes, or may be used to **predict** the outcome variable (y) for a given level of the regressors (x).

1.4 Key Concepts

1. There are two aspects to statistical analysis of data: description and inferential statistics. The latter attempts to extrapolate from the sample to the population, often using confidence intervals and/or hypothesis tests.

2. The analysis of economics data uses a subset of statistical methods, most notably regression analysis for continuous numerical data, and emphasizes economic interpretation of economics-related data.

3. Economics data are usually observational rather than experimental. This makes it difficult to establish causal effects. For pedagogical reasons this complication is deferred to Chapter 17.5, though much econometrics research seeks to estimate causal relationships, even with observational data.

4. Cross-section data (denoted x_i) are data on different individuals at a point in time; time-series data (denoted x_t) are data on the same quantity at different points of time; panel data or longitudinal data (denoted x_{it}) are data on the same individuals at different points of time; repeated cross-section data are cross-section data collected in more than one time period, but in each time period different individuals are observed.

5. The book covers, in turn, univariate data (single series), bivariate data (two series), and multivariate data (several series).

6. The key method of this book is regression analysis.

7. Key Terms: Summary statistics; sample; population; statistical inference; continuous numerical data; discrete numerical data; categorical data; observational data; experimental data, cross-section data; time series data; panel data; longitudinal data; univariate data; bivariate data; multivariate data; regression analysis; bivariate regression; multiple regression.

1.5 Exercises

1. For each of the following examples state whether the data are numerical or categorical, and state whether the data are cross-section, time series, panel or repeated cross-section data.

   (a) Quarterly data on the level of U.S. new housing construction from 2000 to 2018.
   (b) Data on number of doctor visits in 2018 for a sample of 192 individuals.
   (c) Data on annual health expenditures for each U.S. state from 2000 to 2018.
   (d) Data on usual mode of transportation used to commute to work for a sample of 151 individuals.
   (e) Data on individual income from an annual survey from 2000 to 2018 that surveys different individuals each year.

2. For each of the following examples state whether the data are numerical or categorical, and state whether the data are cross-section, time series, panel or repeated cross-section data.

   (a) Data on annual health expenditures in 2018 for the U.S. by use of funds.
   (b) Data for several days on whether the Dow Jones Index at the close of trading was at a higher or lower value than at the close of trading the preceding trading day.
   (c) Data on sales this quarter by each of 23 sales representatives.
   (d) Data on the price of 1 gigabyte of computer disk storage each year from 1980 to 2018.
   (e) Annual earnings of 153 individuals in each of the years 2010 to 2018.

3. For each of the following state whether the data are observational or experimental.

   (a) Data on earnings for individuals some of whom chose to participate in a training program and some who did not.
   (b) Data on earnings for individuals some of whom were randomly assigned to a training program and some who were not.
   (c) Data on school outcomes for charter schools and for traditional schools.

4. For each of the following state whether or not statistical inference is being used.

   (a) Recording the number of heads in 40 coin tosses.
   (b) Determining whether a coin is likely to be fair on the basis of the number of heads in 40 coin tosses.
   (c) Recording the annual earnings of 125 randomly chosen people and calculating the average.
   (d) Recording the annual earnings of 125 randomly chosen people and then determining how likely it is that mean annual earnings in the population exceed $40,000.

Chapter 2

Univariate Data Summary

Univariate data are a single series of data that are observations on one variable. A numerical data example is annual earnings for each person in a sample of women. A categorical data example is expenditures in each of a number of categories.

The chapter begins with presentation of summary statistics for numerical data. These are useful both in their own right and as a tool for checking that there are no obvious errors in data entry, such as negative values for a variable that should be nonnegative.

The chapter then presents charts that can provide a very quick way to grasp the essential features of univariate data. The graphical methods used vary with the type of data. While the key charts are given, there are many possible variations. The graphs presented here are quite basic. Presentation quality graphics entail much more preparation and are beyond the scope of this book. Useful resources for graph styles are leading publications such as *The Economist*, *The New York Times* and *The Wall Street Journal* that frequently present charts for economics data.

Statistical inference, using data from a sample to make inferences about the population from which the data is sampled, is introduced in Chapter 3.

2.1 Summary Statistics for Numerical Data

Summary statistics or **descriptive statistics** provide a summary of data on a numerical variable.

Consider data on the annual earnings of a sample of 171 women who are 30 years of age in 2010, all of whom worked full-time (35 or more hours per week and 48 or more weeks per year). The data are in dataset EARNINGS.

Table 2.1: Summary statistics: Annual earnings of 30 year-old female full-time workers in 2010 (n=171).

Statistic	Value
Mean	41,413
Standard deviation	25,527
Minimum	1,050
Maximum	172,000
Number of Observations	171
Variance	651,630,282
Upper quartile (75th percentile)	50,000
Median (50th percentile)	36,000
Lower quartile (25th percentile)	25,000
Skewness	1.71
Kurtosis	7.32

Table 2.1 presents various summary statistics, rounded to the nearest dollar, that are explained in this section. A summary statistics command in a statistical package usually automatically reports at least the first five of these.

As a quick check of the data we note that there are 171 observations that range from \$1,050 to \$172,000. The minimum value is surprisingly low as it implies earnings of less than \$1 per hour for this sample of full-time workers. From a more detailed check of the original survey data, this individual was self-employed, so such a low value is possible. The second lowest sample value of annual earnings is \$9,000.

The observations for a **sample** of size n are denoted

$$x_1, x_2, ..., x_n.$$

Here x_1 is the first observation, x_2 is the second observation, ... and x_n is the nth observation. For cross-section data the typical observation is the ith observation, denoted x_i, while for time series data it is more customary to use the subscript t, in which case x_t is the tth observation.

2.1.1   Central Tendency

A measure of **central tendency** or **central location** describes the center of the distribution of the data.

The most common measure is the **sample mean**, which is the arithmetic average of the data. For example, if the data take values 8, 3, 7 and 6, then the sample mean is $(8 + 3 + 7 + 6)/4 = 6$. More generally, for a sample of size n, the sample mean $\bar{x}$ is defined as

$$\bar{x} = \frac{x_1 + x_2 + \cdots + x_n}{n}.$$

A shorthand notation to present this formula, and many other formulas for summary statistics, uses **summation notation**. In general $\sum_{i=1}^{n} x_i$ denotes the sum of all the x_i from $i = 1$ to n, so that

$$\sum\nolimits_{i=1}^{n} x_i = x_1 + \cdots + x_n.$$

In the current example, $x_1 = 8$, $x_2 = 3$, $x_3 = 7$ and $x_4 = 6$ so $\sum_{i=1}^{4} x_i = 8 + 3 + 7 + 6 = 24$. As a second example, if $x_i = 5 + 2i^2$ then $\sum_{i=1}^{n} x_i = \sum_{i=1}^{3} (5 + 2i^2) = (5 + 2 \times 1^2) + (5 + 2 \times 2^2) + (5 + 2 \times 3^2) = 7 + 13 + 23 = 43$. For constant c that does not vary with i, $\sum_{i=1}^{n} c = n \times c$ and $\sum_{i=1}^{n} c x_i = c \times \sum_{i=1}^{n} x_i$. And $\sum_{i=1}^{n} (c x_i + d y_i) = c \sum_{i=1}^{n} x_i + d \sum_{i=1}^{n} y_i$.

Using summation notation, the sample mean can be written as

$$\bar{x} = \frac{1}{n} \sum\nolimits_{i=1}^{n} x_i.$$

The other leading estimate of central tendency is the **sample median**. The data are first ordered from the lowest value to the highest value, and the median is that value that divides the ordered data into two halves. This is directly obtained as the midpoint of the ordered data if there is an odd number of observations. For an even number of observations one chooses the average of the two observations in the middle. For sample 8, 3, 7 and 6, the ordered sample is 3, 6, 7 and 8, and the median equals $(6 + 7)/2 = 6.5$.

The median has the advantage of being more resistant to outliers than the mean. For example, mean income will change a lot if Bill Gates is included in the sample, whereas the median is essentially unchanged. And the median can be used if the highest values are top-coded, as is often the case for data on individual incomes. The mean is more often used, however, and this book focuses on statistical inference for the mean rather than the median.

A third measure, less commonly-used, is the **mid-range** which is the average of the smallest and largest values in the sample. This is very sensitive to outliers.

A fourth measure, the **mode**, is the most commonly occurring value. This is only useful when the data is discrete, or if the underlying data are intrinsically continuous but the observed data are greatly rounded, so that a given value can occur multiple times in the sample. Even then the mode is not necessarily a good measure of central tendency, especially if the distribution has more than one mode or if the distribution is asymmetric, defined below.

From Table 2.1, earnings are on average \$41,413. For these data with 171 observations the median is the 86th of the ordered observations, and this equals \$36,000. So half the women in the sample earn less than \$36,000 and half earn more than this amount. Note that mean earnings in this example are substantially greater than median earnings. This is often the case for data on incomes, earnings and prices. The midrange is $(172000 + 1050)/2$ or \$86,525; this is much higher than the mean and is not particularly meaningful here. The mode, not given in Table 2.1, is \$25,000. In practice it is unlikely that any two women in this sample of size 171 would have exactly the same earnings. Here, due to rounding in reporting, ten women reported earnings of exactly \$25,000.

2.1.2 Quartiles, Deciles and Percentiles

The median is the point that equally divides an ordered sample. One can consider other divisions of the ordered sample.

The **lower quartile** is that point where one-quarter of the ordered sample lies below and three-quarters of the ordered sample lies above. The **upper quartile** is that point where three-quarters of the ordered sample lies below and one-quarter of the ordered sample lies above. For example, with 9 observations the upper quartile is the 3rd highest, the median is the 5th highest and the lower quartile is the 3rd lowest. Adjustment, similar to that for the median with an even number of observations, is needed when more than one data point could be the quartile. The median is the middle quartile.

Even more detailed divisions of the sample are possible. **Percentiles** split the ordered sample into hundredths. The pth percentile is the value for which p percent of the observed values are equal to or less than the value. The upper quartile, median, and lower quartile are, respectively, the 75th, 50th, and 25th percentiles. **Deciles** split the ordered sample into tenths and are often used, for example, to summarize the distribution of individual income. A **quantile** is a percentile reported as a fraction of one rather than as a percentage. For example the .81 quantile is the 81st percentile.

From Table 2.1 the lower and upper quartiles of earnings are, respectively, \$25,000 and \$50,000, so the middle half of 30 year-old female full-time workers earned between \$25,000 and \$50,000 per year.

2.1.3 Data Dispersion or Spread

A measure of **dispersion** describes the **spread** or **variability** of the data. The most commonly-used measure is the standard deviation.

An obvious measure to use is the average of the deviations $(x_i - \bar{x})$ of the data x_i from the sample mean $\bar{x}$. But this can be shown to always equal zero, because in sum the negative deviations exactly balance the positive deviations. Instead these deviations are squared, before averaging, to get the **sample variance** s^2 where

$$s^2 = \frac{(x_1 - \bar{x})^2 + \cdots + (x_n - \bar{x})^2}{n-1} = \frac{1}{n-1}\sum_{i=1}^{n}(x_i - \bar{x})^2.$$

The division by $(n-1)$ rather than the more obvious n is explained in Chapter 3.2. A simpler computational formula for the sample variance is $s^2 = \frac{1}{n-1}\{(\sum_{i=1}^{n}x_i{}^2)-n\bar{x}^2\}$; see exercise 26 which shows that $\sum_{i=1}^{n}(x_i - \bar{x})^2 = (\sum_{i=1}^{n}x_i^2) - n\bar{x}^2$.

The sample variance is measured in units that differ from those in the original data, due to the squaring. For example, if the data were in units of dollars then the variance is in units of dollars squared. To return to the original units we take the square root. This yields the **sample standard deviation** s, defined as

$$s = \sqrt{s^2} = \sqrt{\frac{1}{n-1}\sum_{i=1}^{n}(x_i - \bar{x})^2}.$$

If one sample has a larger sample standard deviation than another then we view the sample as having greater variability.

As an example consider the sample 8, 3, 7 and 6 which has $n = 4$ and $\bar{x} = 6$. Then the sample variance

$$s^2 = \frac{(8-6)^2 + (3-6)^2 + (7-6)^2 + (6-6)^2}{4-1} = \frac{14}{3} \simeq 4.667,$$

and the sample standard deviation is $s = \sqrt{14/3} \simeq 2.16$.

In some cases it is useful to measure the variability of the data relative to the mean, using the **coefficient of variation**

$$CV = \frac{s}{\bar{x}}.$$

This measure is useful for comparing the relative variability in a variable across groups. For example, the sample of 171 women had $\bar{x} = 41413$ and $s = 25527$, while a similar sample of 191 men had $\bar{x} = 52345$ and $s = 65035$. So men have greater variability in earnings than women, but this may potentially just be an artifact of men also having higher earnings on average. The coefficient of variation controls for the different means. Since CV= $65035/52345 = 1.24$ for men exceeds CV= 0.62 for women, men have higher variability in earnings relative to mean earnings than do women.

Three other measures of variation in the data are the range, the interquartile range, and the average absolute deviation.

The **range** is the difference between the **maximum** and **minimum** values in the sample.

An **outlying observation**, or **outlier**, is an observation that is unusually large or small. The **interquartile range**, the difference between the upper quartile and the lower quartile, has the advantage of being more resistant to outliers than the standard deviation or the range.

The **average absolute deviation**, $\frac{1}{n}\sum_{i=1}^{n}|x_i - \bar{x}|$, is also more resistant to outliers than the standard deviation or the range.

From Table 2.1, the sample standard deviation of earnings is $25,527. The coefficient of variation is $25,527/41,413 = 0.62$, so the standard deviation of earnings is 62% of mean earnings. The range is $(172000 - 1050)$ or $170,950. The interquartile range is $(50000 - 25000)$ or $25,000.

For income and wealth data, interest lies in measuring relative shares and how these change over time. The **P90/P10 ratio** measures the ratio between the 90th percentile and the 10th percentile and is necessarily at least one. The P90/P10 ratio has the advantage that it does not require data on the richest individuals whose data may be top-coded for reasons of anonymity or unavailable due to survey nonresponse. If data on the entire distribution is available the **Gini coefficient** can be constructed. This measure ranges from zero with perfect equality to one if all goes to one individual. For wages and salaries of full-time full-year workers in the U.S. the P90/P10 ratio is in the range 5 to 6 while the Gini coefficient is around 0.35 to 0.40. Increases in these measures over time indicates rising **inequality**.

2.1.4 Interpretation of the Standard Deviation

The standard deviation is the commonly-used measure of variability, as is clear from subsequent chapters. It is not as easy to understand as the mean, which is simply the average.

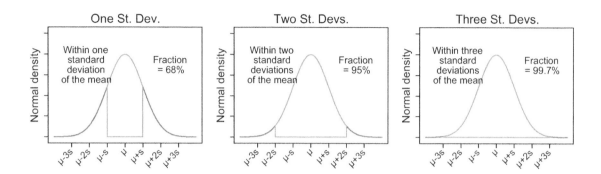

Figure 2.1: Normal distribution: Probability of being within one, two or three standard deviations of the mean.

A useful way to interpret the standard deviation is to use results for the normal distribution. For a random variable X that is normally distributed, the probability of being within one, two or three standard deviations of the mean is, respectively, 0.684, 0.955 and 0.997.

It follows that approximately two-thirds of the sample is within one standard deviation of the mean, 95% is within two standard deviations and 99.7% is within three standard deviations of the mean. These results can also provide an approximate guide for data that are not normally distributed.

This is illustrated in Figure 2.1, where the mean is denoted μ ("mu", the Greek letter for m), and the standard deviation is denoted σ ("sigma", the Greek letter for s).

Regardless of the actual distribution, a result called **Chebychev's inequality** implies that it always the case that at least three-quarters of a random sample is within two standard deviations of the mean, and at least eight-ninths is within three standard deviations of the mean.

As an example, consider the earnings data. These data have $\bar{x} = 41,413$ and $s = 25,527$, so the interval (15,886, 66,940) is within one standard deviation of the mean since, for example, $\bar{x} - s = 41,413 - 25,527 = 15,886$. For these data 77% of the observations are within this interval, compared to 68% predicted by the normal approximation. Similarly, for these data 96% of the observations are within two standard deviations of the mean, compared to 95% predicted by the normal approximation.

2.1.5 Box-and-Whisker Plot

A **box-and-whisker plot** or, more simply, a **box plot**, provides some of the key summary statistics for the data in a simple graphic.

All box-and-whisker plots give the lower quartile, median and upper quartile; these form the "box." Simple box-and-whisker plots additionally give the minimum and maximum; these form the "whiskers." More complicated box-and-whisker plots additionally plot outlying values. In that case

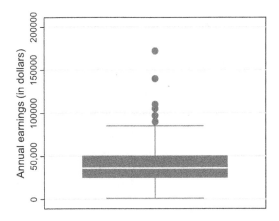

Figure 2.2: Box Plot: Annual earnings of 30 year-old female full-time workers in 2010.

the whiskers are data-determined lower and upper bounds, ones appropriate for data that are not too greatly dispersed, and outlying values are observations that exceed these bounds.

Figure 2.2 gives a box-and-whisker plot, of the more complicated form, for the earnings data. The solid shaded region ranges from the lower quartile of $25,000 to the upper quartile of $50,000. The solid white line within the shaded region is the median of $36,000. The upper bar equals the upper quartile plus 1.5 times the inter-quartile range. Here this equals $50,000 + 1.5 \times 25,000$ or $87,500. The six dots represent the six distinct values of earnings above $87,500 in the sample. (In fact due to one duplicate there are seven observations in excess of $87,500). The lower bar is the minimum sample value of $1,050, as in this example the minimum exceeds the lower quartile minus 1.5 times the inter-quartile range.

The plot clearly shows the right-skewness of the data. The difference between the upper quartile and the median is much greater than the difference between the median and the lower quartile. And there are quite a few outlying sample points that take large values.

2.1.6 Symmetry

A **symmetric distribution** is one whose shape is the same when reflected around the median. The normal distribution is an example.

Positive skewed or **right-skewed** data have a much longer tail on the right. Most of the data are bunched on the left, but there is a continued presence of high values on the right. **Negative skewed** or **left-skewed** data have a much longer left tail.

Skewness can sometimes be visually detected. Figure 2.3 presents histograms for symmetric, right-skewed and left-skewed data.

A formal measure of asymmetry is the **skewness statistic**, calculated as a scale-free measure by normalizing by the standard deviation. Different statistical packages can use slightly different formulae in computing the skewness statistic. The simplest measure, used by most econometrics

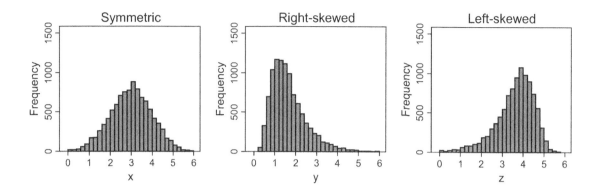

Figure 2.3: Histograms for symmetric, right-skewed and left-skewed data.

packages, is

$$\text{Skew} = \frac{\frac{1}{n}\sum_{i=1}^{n}(x_i - \bar{x})^3}{\left[\frac{1}{n}\sum_{i=1}^{n}(x_i - \bar{x})^2\right]^{3/2}}.$$

Some statistical packages, including Excel, multiply this measure by $\sqrt{n(n-1)}/(n-2)$, so Skew= $\frac{n}{(n-1)(n-2)}\sum_{i=1}^{n}\left(\frac{x_i-\bar{x}}{s}\right)^3$. This adjustment is felt to lead to a better measure in small samples. In large samples the difference between the two measures disappears and both approximately equal $\frac{1}{n}\sum_{i=1}^{n}\left(\frac{x_i-\bar{x}}{s}\right)^3$, where s is the sample standard deviation.

A zero value indicates symmetry since there is then no skewness. A positive value indicates positive or right-skewness and a negative value indicates negative skewness. There is no clear-cut rule for when data are highly skewed; a skewness measure in excess of one in absolute value indicates at least mild skewness. Note also that in small samples the skewness statistic is a less precise estimate of data skewness. For the three examples in Figure 2.3 the skewness measure equals, respectively, -0.04, 1.92, and -2.31.

Appreciable difference between the sample mean and sample median is also a sign of skewness. For right-skewed data the sample mean usually exceeds the sample median. For left-skewed data the sample mean usually is less than the sample median.

If economics data are skewed then they are usually right-skewed. For the earnings data, the histogram given below in Figure 2.4 clearly displays right skewness with a long right tail. For example, 94% of observations lie below the midrange of $85,475$ and only 6% lie above the midpoint. And, from Table 2.1, the mean of $41,413$ exceeds the median of $36,000$ and the skewness measure is 1.71.

Much economic analysis centers on modelling central tendencies. If skewness leads to an appreciable difference between the mean and the median, then both may be reported or, depending on the purpose, only one of the mean or median may be reported. For example, household income is right-skewed and government statistical reports emphasize median household income rather than mean household income. This reports the income of the household in the middle of the household income distribution. At the same time, other government reports emphasize real per capita GDP which is a mean. This is in part because in that case the median cannot be computed, as data are not collected on GDP at the individual level. But it is also because in measuring the resources available to the economy interest lies in how much is available per person rather than how much is available to the median person.

2.1.7 Kurtosis

The **kurtosis statistic** measures the relative importance of observations in the tail of the distribution.

Different statistical packages can use slightly different formulae in computing the **kurtosis statistic**. The simplest measure, used by most econometrics packages, is

$$\text{Kurt} = \frac{\frac{1}{n}\sum_{i=1}^{n}(x_i - \bar{x})^4}{\left[\frac{1}{n}\sum_{i=1}^{n}(x_i - \bar{x})^2\right]^2}.$$

Some statistical packages use an alternative measure of excess kurtosis that is felt to be better in small samples. One such measure, used by Excel, multiplies the kurtosis measure given above by $\frac{(n+1)(n-1)}{(n-2)(n-3)}$ and then computes excess kurtosis by subtracting $3\frac{(n-1)^2}{(n-2)(n-3)}$ rather than 3. In large samples the difference between different measures disappears and they approximately equal $\frac{1}{n}\sum_{i=1}^{n}\left(\frac{x_i - \bar{x}}{s}\right)^4$, where s is the sample standard deviation.

The normal distribution, with Kurt = 3, is often used as a benchmark, especially if the distribution is reasonably symmetric. **Excess kurtosis** measures kurtosis relative to the normal distribution, yielding

$$\text{ExcessKurt} \simeq \text{Kurt} - 3.$$

Positive excess kurtosis means that there is greater area in the tails than for the normal distribution with the same mean and variance, since $x_i - \bar{x}$ is raised to the fourth power. Some references state that the kurtosis statistic additionally measures the peakedness of the distribution, but this need not be the case especially if the distribution is asymmetric or bimodal.

The kurtosis measure is most often used for financial data. Fat tails are a feature of data on investment returns, and the greatest interest may lie in the tails since unusual events can provide the greatest opportunity to make a profit (or a loss).

From Table 2.1 the earnings data has kurtosis statistic (Kurt) of 7.32, substantially greater than 3, suggesting that the sample distribution has fatter tails than the normal distribution. For the three examples in Figure 2.3 the kurtosis measure equals, respectively, 3.04, 11.68, and 16.57.

2.2   Charts for Numerical Data

Histograms are the leading method for graphical inspection of cross-section numerical data. Histograms can also be useful for time series numerical data, provided that the data have been transformed to have little overall trend. As an example, histograms may be useful for summarizing real GDP growth rates or price inflation rates over time, but are of very limited use for describing GDP and price levels which trend upward over time.

Table 2.2: Frequencies: Individual annual earnings in bins of width 15,000.

Range (or bin)	Frequency	Relative frequency (%)
0-14,999	12	7.0
15,000-29,999	53	31.0
30,000-44,999	52	30.4
45,000-59,999	20	11.7
60,000-74,999	11	6.4
75,000-89,999	16	9.4
90,000-104,999	2	1.2
105,000-119,999	3	1.8
120,000-134,999	0	0.0
135,000-149,999	1	0.6
150,000-164,999	0	0.0
165,000-180,000	1	0.6

2.2.1 Histograms

Table 2.2 summarizes the earnings data grouped into intervals of width $15,000. Each interval is called a **bin**; here there are 13 bins, each of equal **bin width** of $15,000. The **frequency** is the number of observations that fall into a given bin, and the **relative frequency** is the proportion (or percentage) that fall into a given bin. For example, 53 observations or 31.0% of the sample have earnings between $15,000 and $29,999.

A **histogram** is a graph of the frequency distribution of the data where, for continuous data, the data are first grouped into bins. The horizontal axis has the values of the variable, while there are two variations for the vertical axis. One variation has the frequencies in each bin on the vertical axis. A second variation has the density (the relative frequency divided by the bin width) on the vertical axis – then the shaded area of the histogram has area one.

The first panel of Figure 2.4 presents the histogram corresponding to Table 2.2, with frequencies on the vertical axis. The second panel of Figure 2.4 provides a more detailed histogram that groups the data over a narrower range, with bin width $7,500.

The histogram varies with the number of bins, with a trade-off between few bins providing not enough detail and too many bins yielding a histogram that is very choppy. Given n observations, a common default choice for the number of bins is $\sqrt{n}$. The class intervals are then of width approximately equal to the highest value minus the lowest value divided by the number of bins, with possible modification for unusually small or large observations. For $n = 171$ this yields 13 bins of equal width $(172000 - 1050)/13 = 13,150$. Table 2.2 and the first panel of Figure 2.4 instead round these defaults to 12 bins of equal width $15,000 with a start value of $0. The second panel of Figure 2.4 doubles the number of bins, by halving the bin width to $7,500.

A variation on a histogram, one that gives more detail on the actual values taken by the data, is a **stem and leaf display**. This splits each data point into leading digits, called a stem, and remaining digits, called a leaf. For example for the earnings data the ten thousands may be the stem and the remaining digits the leaf. The data are then presented in tabular form where each

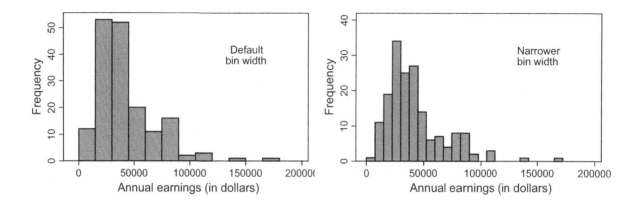

Figure 2.4: Histogram: Individual annual earnings with two different bin widths

row corresponds to a stem value and has first column the stem value and the second column the leaf values for that column.

Histograms can be used for numerical data that is either discrete or continuous. For **discrete data** that take low values, such as the number of different jobs held by a person during the year, each distinct value forms a bin so the bin width is one.

2.2.2   Smoothed Histograms (Kernel density estimate)

Data that take many different values, such as earnings data, have an underlying continuous probability density function rather than a discrete probability mass function. A classic example is the normal distribution which has a bell-shaped density. Probabilities are determined by areas under the curve and the total area under a density is one. It is then natural to directly estimate the density, using a smoothed histogram.

A **smoothed histogram** smooths the histogram in two ways. First, it uses rolling bins (or **windows**) that are overlapping rather than distinct. Second, in counting the fraction of the sample within each bin it gives more weight to observations that are closest to the center of the window and less to those near the ends of the window.

The smoothed histogram varies greatly with choice of **window width**, just as the histogram varies with the bin width. It varies less with the weights that are used. Different statistical packages may have different rules for choosing the default window width, and use different weights, called **kernel weights**, leading to different smoothed histograms.

The most commonly-used smoothed histogram is a **kernel density estimate**. Two kernel density estimates for the earnings data are presented in Figure 2.5. The first panel uses a window width close to the statistical package's default width, while the second is smoother as it uses a window width that is twice as large. The kernel density estimate is not bell-shaped, implying that the data are not normally distributed, and appears to be right-skewed. The vertical axis is scaled so that the area under the curve equals one.

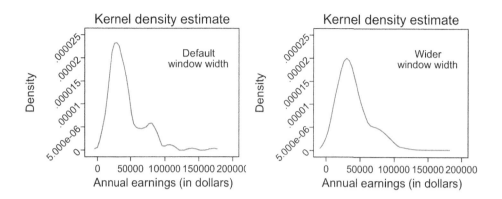

Figure 2.5: Smoothed histogram: kernel density estimate for individual annual earnings with two different window widths

2.2.3 Histograms and Smoothed Histograms using a Statistical Package

Histograms can be obtained using the `histogram` command in Stata, `hist` function in R, `hist` function in Gretl, and `distplot hist` command in Eviews. The default number of bins depends on the number of observations; as an alternative the number of bins can be specified.

Kernel density estimates can be obtained using the `kdensity` command in Stata, `density` function in R, `kdensity` function in Gretl and `distplot kernel` command in Eviews. The key option to consider changing from the default is the window width. More specialized is to change the kernel weight function from the default.

2.2.4 Line Charts for Ordered Data

A **line chart** plots the successive values $x_1, x_2, \ldots$ of the data against the successive index values $1, 2, \ldots$

The leading application is to time series data that are ordered by time. This leads to graphs that plot the variable of interest against time.

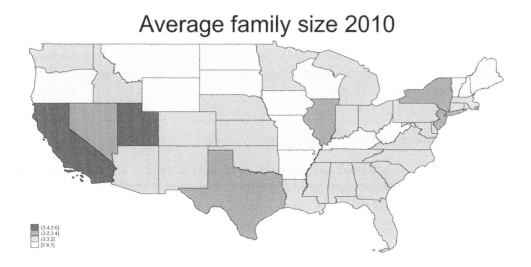

Figure 2.8: Spatial Map: Average family size in each U.S. state in 2010.

year college graduate) and 17 and above (postgraduate). Then give a bar chart of average income by schooling category. A histogram is just a column chart of frequencies plotted against the class boundaries.

2.3.2 Spatial Map

A **spatial map** for data that varies by geographic location plots the data against a geographic map.

As an example, consider average family size in each U.S. state in 2010 which ranges from 2.83 in Maine to 3.56. Figure 2.8 shows the average family in size in each state with darker shades corresponding to larger family size. The figure shows that southwest states tend to have larger families while north central states have smaller families. Spatial maps require more specialized software than that needed for the other graphs presented in this chapter.

2.4   Summary and Charts for Categorical Data

As an example of intrinsically categorical data consider choice of fishing site for a sample of 1,182 fishers given in dataset FISHING. There are four possibilities – fishing may be from a beach, pier, charter boat or private boat.

2.4.1   Data Summary using Tabulation

The fishing site data may be recorded as text, such as "beach", "pier", "charter" and "private". Or they may be recorded as numbers, such as 1, 2, 3 and 4. But even in the latter case the possibilities are intrinsically categorical. Furthermore there is no natural ordering of the categories.

For such data it is meaningless to compute summary statistics such as the sample mean. Instead the data are summarized using a **tabulation** of the **frequencies** for each category. For the fishing site data this is given in Table 2.4. It is clear that more people fished from a boat (private or charter) than from the shore (beach or pier).

Table 2.4: Categorical data: Frequencies at each fishing site

Category	Frequency	Relative frequency (%)
Beach	134	11.34
Pier	178	15.06
Private Boat	418	35.36
Charter Boat	452	38.24

2.4.2   Pie Charts

A **pie chart** splits a circle into slices, where the area of each slice corresponds to the relative frequency of observations in each category. Pie charts are most useful for visually representing each categories' share of the total, provided there are not too many categories.

Figure 2.9 presents a pie chart using the fishing site data. Again this makes clear that the largest categories are charter boat and private boat fishing.

The health expenditure data of Chapter 2.3 could be presented using a pie chart, if one was interested in the shares of each category of health spending. But this would be difficult to read as there are too many categories. Instead it would be best to aggregate the smallest categories. For example, one might use hospital, physician, drugs and supplies, and all other categories combined.

2.5   Data Transformation

Continuous numerical data are often transformed before analysis.

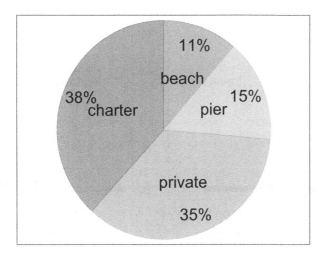

Figure 2.9: Pie Chart: Fishing site used

2.5.1 Natural Logarithms

Many cross-section data sets can be right-skewed. For example, data on income or wages of a sample of individuals are often right-skewed. The **natural logarithm** transformation can lead to a transformed data series that is more symmetrically distributed. It reduces especially large outlying values. Chapter 9.5 presents many uses of the natural logarithm.

The left panel of Figure 2.10 presents a histogram of earnings of female full-time workers aged 30 in 2010, along with a kernel density estimate, using data from dataset EARNINGS introduced at the start of this chapter. The data are clearly right-skewed. The second panel of Figure 2.10 shows the histogram after transformation to natural logarithms. The second panel histogram is close to symmetric, aside from one very small value (the sample included an observation with unusually low annual earnings of \$1,050 and corresponding low natural logarithm of 6.96), and is approximately normally distributed. In both cases the vertical axes are scaled so that the areas under the histograms and the kernel density estimates equals one.

If a variable x is such that $\ln x$ is normally distributed, then x itself is said to follow the **lognormal distribution**.

2.5.2 Standardized Scores (z-scores)

A **standardized score** is obtained by subtracting the mean and dividing by the sample standard deviation. Thus

$$z_i = \frac{x_i - \bar{x}}{s}, \quad i = 1, ..., n,$$

where x_i is the original value, $\bar{x}$ is the sample mean and s is the sample standard deviation. The resulting score has sample mean zero and sample standard deviation one.

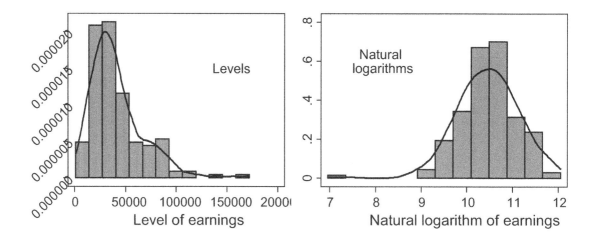

Figure 2.10: Levels and natural logarithms: Histograms and kernel density estimates for individual annual earnings

A standardized score is often called a **z-score** as its distribution may be well approximated by a standard normal distribution, which also has mean 0 and variance 1. Note also that the symmetry and kurtosis statistics approximately equal the sample averages of the standardized scores for each observation raised to, respectively, the third and fourth power.

A standardized score is immediately interpretable – a one unit increase in z_i equals a one standard deviation increase in the original score x_i.

Standardized scores are useful for comparing data series that are scaled differently. For example, suppose we wish to compare student performance on two tests with different total points or of different difficulty, so that the sample means and standard deviations differ across the tests. Then we compare the sample values of the standardized scores $z_{1i} = (x_{1i} - \bar{x}_1)/s_1$ and $z_{2i} = (x_{2i} - \bar{x}_2)/s_2$, where the subscripts 1 and 2 denote the first and second tests.

2.6   Data Transformations for Time Series Data

In this section we present some commonly-used transformations for time series data.

2.6.1   Moving Averages

A **moving average** or **rolling average** smooths data by taking the average of observations in several successive periods. This is especially useful for data that bounce around from period to period; averaging can smooth the data. Visual analysis of long-term trends in the data are easier to see, since period-to-period variation is reduced.

A **simple moving average** averages the current and immediate past observations. For exam-

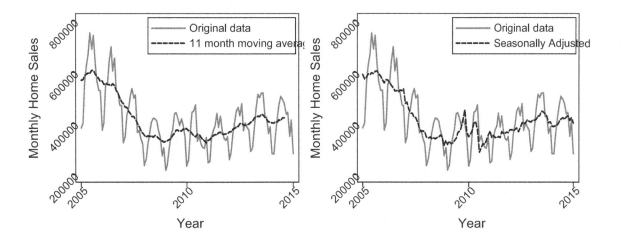

Figure 2.11: Moving average and seasonal adjustment smoothing: Monthly sales of existing homes

ple, a five-period moving average takes the average of the data over the current and preceding four periods, or $(x_t + x_{t-1} + x_{t-2} + x_{t-3} + x_{t-4})/5$.

If instead the current observation appears in the middle, then the moving average is a **centered moving average.** For example, a centered five-period moving average takes the average of the data two periods ago, one period ago, this period, next period, and the period after that, or $(x_{t-2} + x_{t-1} + x_t + x_{t+1} + x_{t+2})/5$. The centered moving average at time t has the disadvantage that it is not immediately available at time t as its computation also uses data from some future time periods.

A moving average can be used for several reasons, including reducing random noise in the data, smoothing out business cycle variation, and smoothing out seasonal variation.

As an example we consider smoothing out seasonal variation in U.S. monthly data from 2005 to 2014 on sales of existing homes, compiled by the National Association of Realtors. The data are in dataset MONTHLYHOMESALES.

The first panel of Figure 2.11 plots the original data along with an eleven-month centered moving average. The original data are relatively variable within a year, with a low point in January and February and a peak in summer. The data also indicate the large decrease accompanying the global financial crisis, with a thirty percent decline compared to 2005. The moving average smooths the data considerably. Note that centering the moving average comes at the expense of it not being computable for the most recent months as it requires data in future months.

2.6.2 Seasonal Adjustment

For data that fluctuate within the year due to seasonal influences specific methods have been developed to smooth out the seasonal variation that hopefully are better than simply using a moving average.

Seasonal adjustment smooths data to control for seasonal variation in the data. For example, monthly data are decreased in months that have relatively high values every year and are increased in months that have unusually low values every year.

The second panel of Figure 2.11 presents as a dashed line the published seasonally adjusted data for the existing homes sales series, using the widely-used X-11-ARIMA seasonal adjustment program developed by the U.S. Census Bureau. The seasonal adjusted series is much smoother than the original, and essentially eliminates the seasonal variation.

Many macroeconomics series are released as **seasonally adjusted data**. Analysts interpreting these data should be aware that there is no indisputable best way to seasonally adjust.

2.6.3   Real and Nominal Data

Economics data are often measured in dollars. Any meaningful interpretation of these data over time requires conversion to the purchasing power of a dollar in a benchmark year. The original data are called **nominal** data, measured in **current dollars**. Thus 1990 data are measured in 1990 dollars, 1991 data are measured in 1991 dollars, and so on. The data after conversion are called **real data**, measured in **constant dollars**. Then data in various years are reported in dollars of a given year, say 2012 dollars for example. Similar conversion using exchange rates or purchasing power parity indexes is needed to compare nominal data across countries with different currencies.

There is no perfect way to create a price index (or a quantity index) when both prices and quantities of the various goods and services that are components of the index change over time. The leading published indexes use methods that control partially for this problem.

As an example of use of real data rather than nominal data, consider U.S. Gross Domestic Product (GDP), the standard measure of the economy's total output. The solid line in the first panel of Figure 2.12 plots quarterly data on nominal GDP from 1959 to the first quarter of 2020. The data in dataset REALGDPPC are seasonally adjusted quarterly data, annualized by multiplying by four. Nominal GDP has increased 42 times, from \$510 billion to \$21,500 billion. The fall in GDP in the recession of 2007-2009 is most clearly visible.

Part of this large increase in nominal GDP reflects price inflation – a dollar in 1959 had much more purchasing power than a dollar in 2020. The conversion from nominal to real data is done by using a **price index,** which measures prices relative to a value of 100 in a base year. Here we use the GDP chain-type price index, normalized to equal 100 in 2012. The index in the first quarter of 1959 was 16.347, so a 1959 dollar was worth $100/16.347 = \$6.12$ in 2012 dollars, and 1959 first quarter nominal GDP of \$510.33 billion was worth \$3,121 billion ($510.33 \times 100/16.347$) in 2012 dollars. Similarly in the first quarter of 2020 the index was 113.502 and nominal GDP of \$21,539 billion was worth \$18,977 billion in 2012 dollars. Table 2.5 summarizes these calculations.

The dashed line in the first panel of Figure 2.12 plots real GDP from 1959 to 2020, measured in 2012 dollars. Real GDP increased 6.1 times, from \$3,121 billion to \$18,977 billion. This is still a substantial increase, but it is much less than the 42 times increase in nominal GDP. The difference is due to a 6.9 times ($113.502/16.347$) increase in prices over this period, leading to real GDP rising $42/6.9 = 6.1$ times.

The recessions in 1973-74, 1980, 1982 and 1991 become more pronounced using real GDP data, with more pronounced dips due to eliminating increases in nominal GDP that occur due to price

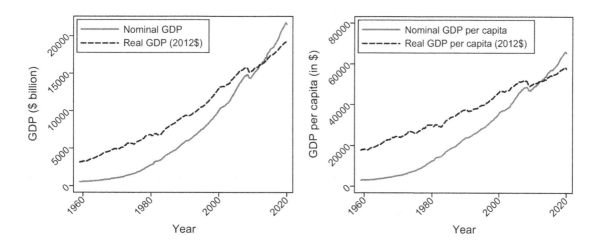

Figure 2.12: Nominal and real data: U.S. GDP and per capita GDP in current dollars and in 2012 dollars.

Table 2.5: Nominal and real data: U.S. GDP example

Time Period	Nominal Value	Index	Real Value
	Current \$ billions	2009=100	2009 \$ billions
1959 Q1	510.33	16.347	510.33×100/16.347=3,121
2020 Q1	21,539	113.502	21,539×100/113.502=18,977

inflation.

What if we used a year different from 2012 as the base year? Then the price index will differ and real GDP will differ as it is no longer measured in 2012 dollars. But the resultant proportionate changes will be unchanged, with a 6.9 times rise in prices and real GDP becoming 6.1 times larger over the 60 years.

2.6.4 Per Capita Data

Per capita data are data formed from an original series by dividing by the size of the population.

In some cases interest lies in aggregate data and in some cases per capita data. For example, to compare the size of the economy over time use real aggregate GDP, but to compare living standards over time use real per capita GDP.

As already noted, real GDP increased 6.1 times from 1959 to 2020. But the U.S. population is 1.87 times larger, with increase from 176 million to 329 million. Thus real per capita GDP has grown about 3.3 times, as $6.1/1.87 = 3.3$. This is illustrated in the second panel of Figure 2.12, with increase in real GDP per capita from \$17,700 to \$57,600. This is still an appreciable improvement over time, and is about 2.0 percent per annum, since $1.020^{60} \simeq 3.3$. But it is nowhere near as large as the initial starting point of a 42 times increase in nominal GDP.

Often U.S. real GDP growth is compared to that in western Europe or Japan. U.S. growth in real GDP is higher, but so too is its population growth. In fact the growth rate for per capita real GDP in the U.S. is similar to that in western Europe and Japan.

2.6.5 Growth Rates and Percentage Changes

If interest lies in changes over time it can be convenient to transform to **percentage changes** or **growth rates**. For example, to analyze changes in living standards we consider percentage changes in real per capita GDP over time.

The **one-period percentage change** in x_t is calculated as

$$\text{Percentage change in } x_t = 100 \times \frac{x_t - x_{t-1}}{x_{t-1}}.$$

In many cases this is converted to an **annualized rate**. For example, for quarterly data the quarterly change multiplied by four gives the annualized quarterly change. Alternatively, for quarterly data one can instead compute a four-period percentage change, $100 \times (x_t - x_{t-4})/x_{t-4}$, which also expresses the change as an annual rate. For data that are not already seasonally adjusted, this latter method can smooth out quarterly seasonal fluctuations. Similarly for monthly data we may use $100 \times (x_t - x_{t-12})/x_{t-12}$.

Potential confusion can arise when statements are made about changes in growth rates or interest rates. For example, suppose the growth rate increases from 3 percent in one year to 5 percent the next year. It is misleading to call this a 2 percent increase in the growth rate, since this literally means that an increase in the growth rate from 3.0 percent to $3.0 \times 1.02 = 3.06$ percent. Instead the correct term to use is that the growth rate increased by two **percentage points**. Very small changes are described in **basis points**, where a basis point is one-hundredth of a percentage point. For example, an increase from 3.0 percent to 3.15 percent is an increase of fifteen basis points.

An alternative calculation method for computing approximate percentage changes is to use

$$\text{Percentage change in } x_t \simeq 100 \times (\ln x_t - \ln x_{t-1}).$$

This result uses the calculus result that $d \ln x/dx = 1/x$, so $d \ln x = dx/x$. Thus $\Delta \ln x \simeq \Delta x/x$ or the change in $\ln x$ approximately equals the proportionate change in x. See Chapter 9.1 for further details.

2.7 Key Concepts

1. Commonly-used statistics for numerical data include the mean and median (for central tendency), the standard deviation, inter-quartile range and range (for dispersion), quartiles and percentiles, and symmetry and kurtosis statistics.

2. An outlying observation, or outlier, is an observation that is unusually large or small.

3. A box plot provides a visual summary of key sample statistics. Some box plots also plot outlying observations.

4. Commonly-used charts that can provide a useful visual presentation of the data are histograms, kernel density graphs, column charts, line charts, bar charts and pie charts. Which is best to use depends on whether the data is numerical (continuous or discrete) or categorical, and whether the data are cross-section or time series data.

5. Common transformations of economic data include the natural logarithm, standardized scores and (for time series data) moving averages, seasonal adjustment, real data, growth rates and percentage changes.

6. Key Terms: sample; summary statistics; central tendency; central location; summation notation; sample mean; median; mid-range; mode; quartile; decile; percentile; quantile; dispersion; sample variance; standard deviation; coefficient of variation; range; outlying observation; outlier; inter-quartile range; symmetry; skewness; right-skewed; positive skewed; kurtosis; normal distribution; box plot; histogram; frequency; relative frequency; stem and leaf display; smoothed histogram; kernel density estimate; line chart; horizontal bar chart; vertical bar chart; column chart; pie chart; standardized score; moving average; seasonal adjustment; nominal data; real data; growth rates; percentage changes; percentage points; basis points.

2.8   Exercises

1. Obtain $\sum_{i=1}^{n} z_i$ for the following cases with $n = 5$:

   (a) $z_i = 1$.   (b) $z_i = i$.   (c) $z_i = 2i^2$.   (d) $z_i = 1/i$.   (e) $z_i = (2 + 3i)$.

2. Calculate the following

   (a) $\sum_{i=1}^{6} 2$.   (b) $\sum_{i=1}^{4} 2/i$.   (c) $\sum_{i=1}^{3} 3i^3$.   (d) $\sum_{i=4}^{6} i$.   (e) $\sum_{i=1}^{4} (5 + 2i)$.

3. For the panel variable x_{it} that takes values $x_{11} = 5$, $x_{12} = 3$, $x_{13} = 7$, $x_{21} = 8$, $x_{22} = 6$, and $x_{23} = 4$:

   (a) Calculate $\sum_{t=1}^{3} x_{it}$ for $i = 1$ and for $i = 2$.
   (b) Calculate $\sum_{i=1}^{2} x_{it}$ for $t = 1$, for $t = 2$ and for $t = 3$.

4. For the panel variable x_{it} that takes values $x_{11} = 2$, $x_{12} = 5$, $x_{21} = 8$, $x_{22} = 4$, $x_{31} = 6$, and $x_{32} = 7$:

   (a) Calculate $\sum_{t=1}^{2} x_{it}$ for $i = 1$, for $i = 2$ and for $i = 3$.
   (b) Calculate $\sum_{i=1}^{3} x_{it}$ for $t = 1$ and for $t = 2$.

5. Compute from first principles (i.e. using the formula and a calculator) the mean, standard deviation, coefficient of variation, skewness statistic and kurtosis statistic for the sample 4, 2, 0, 2. Show all calculations.

6. Repeat the previous exercise when the observations are ten times larger, so the sample is now 40, 20, 0, and 20. Which of the measures are scale-free measures?

7. Repeat exercise 5 when the observations are translated by 2, so the sample is now 6, 4, 2, and 4. Which of the measures are unchanged by translation?

8. A sample of size 200 has mean of 20 and standard deviation of 5. If the data are normally distributed, what range of values do you expect 95% of the sample to lie in?

9. IQ scores have a mean of 100, standard deviation of 14 and are approximately normally distributed. What range of IQ scores do you expect 99.7% of the population lie in?

10. For a sample of size 1,000 the central two-thirds of the observations lie between 60 and 100. If these data are normally distributed, provide an estimate of the mean and standard deviation.

11. For each of the following situations state whether the median price or the mean price of cars sold is a more useful measure of central tendency.

    (a) You want to know the typical price of a car.
    (b) You also know the number of cars sold and want to calculate sales tax receipts when car sales are subject to a 5% tax.

12. In each of the following situations state whether or not the data are likely to be positively skewed, or whether there is not enough information to know.

    (a) The mean is 50 and the median is 20.
    (b) The skewness statistic is 0.1.
    (c) The excess kurtosis statistic is 5.
    (d) The 10th percentile is 20, the median is 50 and the 90th percentile is 200.

13. The dataset HOUSE has data on the price and size of houses sold in a small homogeneous community.

    (a) Read the data into your statistical package.
    (b) Obtain detailed summary statistics for price. Do the data appear to be skewed? Explain.
    (c) Obtain a histogram. Do the data appear to be normally distributed? Explain.
    (d) Obtain a kernel density estimate. Do the data appear to be normally distributed? Explain.

14. Repeat the previous exercise for house size.

15. A sample of 30 people had the following years of completed schooling: 12, 12, 14, 12, 12, 12, 12, 12, 16, 12, 14, 12, 12, 13, 14, 12, 17, 12, 12, 16, 12, 12, 8, 14, 16, 12, 12, 17, 12, 16.

    (a) Read the data into your statistical package.
    (b) Obtain summary statistics. Give the inter-quartile range. List the first five observations.
    (c) Obtain a table of frequencies for these data.
    (d) Give a histogram, with a bin width of one for these discrete data. Do the data appear to be normally distributed?
    (e) Provide a pie chart - what is the most common value of the variable?

16. Repeat the previous exercise for the following samples:

    (a) 20 people age 30 with the following number of annual doctor visits: 0, 0, 3, 4, 2, 5, 5, 2, 11, 2, 2, 2, 3, 0, 8, 0, 8, 1, 2, 4.
    (b) 25 families with the following number of family members: 3, 3, 4, 7, 4, 3, 5, 2, 2, 4, 7, 3, 4, 3, 3, 5, 3, 4, 4, 1, 6, 5, 4, 5, 5.

17. The unemployment rate for college graduates (bachelor's degree or higher) aged 25 to 34 years in April in each of the years 2000 to 2019 was 1.3, 2.0, 2.7, 2.9, 2.6, 2.1, 2.2, 1.9, 2.2, 4.3, 4.7, 3.9, 3.6, 3.6, 3.0, 2.5, 2.1, 2.3, 1.9, 2.2.

    (a) Read the data into your statistical package.
    (b) Obtain key summary statistics. Give the inter-quartile range. List the first five observations.
    (c) Order by increasing unemployment rate and give a line chart.

18. Repeat the previous exercise for high school graduates (no college) aged 25 to 34 years with April unemployment rates of 4.4, 5.2, 8.7, 7.9, 7.1, 6.4, 6.1, 5.5, 6.8, 13.6, 13.9, 13.7, 10.1, 9.9, 8.8, 7.8, 7.8, 6.0, 6.3, 4.8.

19. Obtain data from the website https://fred.stlouisfed.org/ (FRED - Federal Reserve Economic Data) on the unemployment rate for those 25 years and over with some college or an associate degree in April in each of the years 2000 to the present. Answer the same questions as in exercise.17

20. Table 2.3 gives U.S. health expenditures by category for 2018. For 2013 the corresponding amounts were, respectively, 937, 587, 111, 80, 148, 80, 156, 370, 37, 174, 75, 47, 118.

    (a) Give a column chart, ordered by the amount of expenditure.

    (b) Give a pie chart. Is this more or less useful than a column chart? Explain.

21. The dataset PRICEEARNINGSRATIO has annual data on the Shiller cyclically-adjusted price-earnings ratio (variable *cape*) in January for S&P500 firms from 1881 to 2020.

    (a) Obtain the summary statistics for *cape*. Do the data appear to be skewed? Do the data appear to have greater kurtosis than the normal distribution? Explain.

    (b) Plot the histogram. Do the data appear to be skewed?

    (c) Provide a time series plot of the data. Comment on any unusual features.

    (d) Do the data to be unusually high or low in 2020? Explain.

22. The dataset AUSREGWEALTH has data on average net worth of households in thousands of dollars in 517 regions in Australia in 2003-04.

    (a) Obtain the summary statistics. Do the data appear to be skewed? Do the data appear to have greater kurtosis than the normal distribution? Explain.

    (b) Plot the histogram. Do the data appear to be skewed?

    (c) If your software does this, plot the kernel density estimate. Do the data appear to be skewed?

    (d) Now take the natural logarithm of average net worth and repeat parts a-c.

23. Use quarterly data in dataset STOCKINDEX from January 1957 to November 2012.

    (a) Calculate the z-score for each of the Dow Jones, Nasdaq and S&P 500 indexes.

    (b) Do these z-scores have mean zero and standard deviation one?

    (c) Give histograms (or kernel density estimates) for each of the three z-scores. Do they appear to be normally distributed?

    (d) On the same graph give line plots of each of the three z-scores against time. Do the three series appear to move together?

24. Use data in dataset GDPAUSTRALIA from January 1960 to September 2013. The data are quarterly data on nominal GDP (at an annual rate in millions of Australian dollars), a price index (=100 in 2011) and population (in millions).

    (a) Plot nominal GDP and real GDP (which you need to create) against time. Comment.

    (b) Compute nominal GDP per capita and real GDP per capita and plot these against time. Comment.

25. Use data in dataset GDPAUSTRALIA, described in the previous exercise.

    (a) Compute a four period moving average for nominal GDP. Has this reduced seasonal variation?

    (b) Compute annual growth rate in real GDP as four times the proportionate change from one quarter to the next.

    (c) Compute annual growth rate in real GDP as the proportionate change over the last four quarters.

    (d) Compare the two growth rate measures and comment.

26. Derivation of the alternative computational formula for the sample variance.

   (a) Show that $(x_i - \bar{x})^2 = x_i^2 - 2x_i\bar{x} + \bar{x}^2$.

   (b) Hence show that $\sum_{i=1}^{n} (x_i - \bar{x})^2 = \sum_{i=1}^{n} x_i^2 - \sum_{i=1}^{n} 2x_i\bar{x} + \sum_{i=1}^{n} \bar{x}^2$.

   (c) Use the definition of $\bar{x}$ to show that $\sum_{i=1}^{n} x_i = n\bar{x}$.

   (d) Hence show that $\sum_{i=1}^{n} 2x_i\bar{x} = 2n\bar{x}^2$. (Hint: $\sum_{i=1}^{n} az_i = a\sum_{i=1}^{n} z_i$).

   (e) Substitute this result into part (b) and simplify to show that
       $\sum_{i=1}^{n} (x_i - \bar{x})^2 = \left(\sum_{i=1}^{n} x_i^2\right) - n\bar{x}^2$.

Chapter 3

The Sample Mean

Obtaining the sample mean $\bar{x}$, and other summary statistics, is straightforward. But different samples will yield different values of these sample statistics, due to the inherent randomness in the data. How can this randomness be controlled for if we want to make statements about the unchanging features of the distribution for the entire population? More simply, how can we extrapolate from the sample to the population?

For example, dataset EARNINGS introduced in Chapter 2 has data on individual annual earnings for a sample of 30-year-old female full-time workers. The sample mean from a random sample of size 171 was $41,413. What can be said about the likely range of values of mean earnings for all 30-year-old female full-time workers in the country? Are average earnings in this population really as high or as low as $41,413? Or is the observed sample mean of $41,413 just an artifact of this particular sample?

The chapter is relatively dense. While selecting only the essential material, it introduces a considerable amount of the probability theory covered in an introductory probability and statistics course. The focus is on the concepts of mean and variance of a single random variable, and the consequent distribution of the average of n random variables. The simplest material is presented in the text, with additional background material on probability and derivations for the sample mean presented in Appendix B.

For readers who skip this chapter, the essential properties of the sample mean are restated in Chapter 4.2.

3.1 Random Variables

Different samples take different values due to randomness. To account for this randomness we need to introduce random variables and define key properties of random variables, notably their mean, standard deviation and variance.

35

3.1.1 Random Variables

A **random variable** is a variable whose value is determined by the outcome of an experiment, where an **experiment** is an operation whose outcome cannot be predicted with certainty.

For example, the experiment may be tossing a coin and the random variable may take value 1 if heads and 0 if tails. As a second example, the experiment may be randomly selecting a person from the population and the associated random variable takes value equal to their annual earnings.

Standard notation is to denote the random variable in upper case, say X (or Y or Z), and to denote the values that the random variable can take in lower case, say x (or y or z).

3.1.2 Example: Coin Toss

The simplest example of a random variable is one that has only two possible values. We consider a coin toss with a fair coin and define the random variable X to take value 1 if heads and value 0 if tails. Because the coin is fair, there is equal probability of heads or tails.

The random variable is

$$X = \begin{cases} 0 & \text{with probability } 0.5 \\ 1 & \text{with probability } 0.5. \end{cases}$$

3.1.3 Mean of a Random Variable

Interest lies in summarizing the distribution of the random variable. Key measures used are the mean, to describe the average value that the random variable may take, and the variance and standard deviation, to measure the variability of the random variable.

The **expected value of the random variable** X is the long-run average value that we expect if we draw a value of X at random, draw a second value and so on, and then obtain the average of these values. Equivalently, calculate the probability-weighted average by weighting each value x that X may take by the probability of that value x occurring.

This expected value, denoted $\mathrm{E}[X]$, is called the **mean** of X.

Definition 1 *The mean $\mu = E[X]$ of the random variable X is the probability-weighted average of all values that the random variable X may take. The notation μ (or mu) is used to denote the man as μ is the Greek letter for m.*

Suppose our random variable may take values x_1, x_2, ... with potentially different probabilities $\Pr[X = x_1]$, $\Pr[X = x_2]$, ... These probabilities necessarily sum to one. Then **the mean of X is the probability-weighted average**

$$\begin{aligned} \mu \equiv \mathrm{E}[X] \quad &= x_1 \times \Pr[X = x_1] + x_2 \times \Pr[X = x_2] + \cdots \\ &= \textstyle\sum_x x \times \Pr[X = x], \end{aligned}$$

where $\sum_x$ denotes summation over all the possible distinct values that X may take.

As an example, for a fair coin toss where X can take values 0 or 1 with equal probabilities of 0.5 and 0.5 we have

$$
\begin{aligned}
\mu &= \sum_x x \times \Pr[X = x] \\
&= \Pr[X = 0] \times 0 + \Pr[X = 1] \times 1 \\
&= 0.5 \times 0 + 0.5 \times 1 \\
&= 0.5.
\end{aligned}
$$

As a second example, suppose the coin is not fair and X can take value 1 with probability 0.6 and value 0 with probability 0.4. Then $\mu = 0 \times 0.4 + 1 \times 0.6 = 0.6$.

3.1.4 Variance and Standard Deviation

The variance is the long-run average value that we expect if we draw a value of X at random, say x_1, and compute its squared deviation from the mean $(x_1 - \mu)^2$, draw a second value and compute $(x_2 - \mu)^2$, and so on, and then obtain the average of these values.

This **expected value** of $(X - \mu)^2$, denoted $\mathrm{E}[(X - \mu)^2]$, is called the **variance** of X and is also denoted σ^2 or σ_X^2.

Definition 2 *The variance* $\sigma^2 = E[(X - \mu)^2]$ *of the random variable* X *is the probability-weighted average of all values that* $(X - \mu)^2$ *may take. The standard deviation is* $\sigma = \sqrt{\sigma^2}$*. The notation* σ *(or sigma) is used to denote the standard deviation as* σ *is the Greek letter for s.*

For random variable X taking values x_1, x_2, ... the **variance of X is the probability-weighted average**

$$
\begin{aligned}
\sigma^2 \equiv \mathrm{E}[(X - \mu)^2] &= (x_1 - \mu)^2 \times \Pr[X = x_1] + (x_2 - \mu)^2 \times \Pr[X = x_2] + \cdots \\
&= \sum_x (x - \mu)^2 \times \Pr[X = x].
\end{aligned}
$$

The **standard deviation** σ is obtained by taking the square root of the variance.

Continuing the earlier fair coin toss example with $\mu = 0.5$

$$
\begin{aligned}
\sigma^2 &= \sum_x (x - \mu)^2 \times \Pr[X = x] \\
&= (0 - 0.5)^2 \times \Pr[X = 0] + (1 - 0.5)^2 \times \Pr[X = 1] \\
&= 0.25 \times 0.5 + 0.25 \times 0.5 \\
&= 0.25.
\end{aligned}
$$

The variance of X is 0.25 and the standard deviation of X is $\sqrt{0.25} = 0.5$.

3.1.5 Example: Best Three of Five

Suppose two evenly matched teams, with equal probabilities of winning any game, play in a series of up to five games, with the winner the first to win three games. How many games do we expect on average?

Let X denote the number of games, in which case X can take values 3, 4 or 5. It can be shown that $\Pr[X = 3] = \frac{1}{4}$, $\Pr[X = 4] = \frac{3}{8}$, and $\Pr[X = 5] = \frac{3}{8}$. Then

$$E[X] = 3 \times \tfrac{1}{4} + 4 \times \tfrac{3}{8} + 5 \times \tfrac{3}{8} = 4\tfrac{1}{8},$$

so on average we expect 4.125 games. Additionally

$$\mathrm{Var}[X] = (3 - 4\tfrac{1}{8})^2 \times \tfrac{1}{4} + (4 - 4\tfrac{1}{8})^2 \times \tfrac{3}{8} + (5 - 4\tfrac{1}{8})^2 \times \tfrac{3}{8} = \tfrac{39}{64}.$$

3.1.6   Some Key Properties of Random Variables

Further details on random variables are given in Appendix B. The mean of a constant a is that constant a. If we add a fixed amount a to a random variable then the mean is changed by the amount a. And if we multiply a random variable by a fixed multiple b then the mean is multiplied by b. Combining these results we have

Remark 1 $E[a + bX] = a + b \times E[X]$, *for constants a and b.*

The variance of a constant a is zero. If we add a fixed amount a to a random variable then the variance is unchanged. And if we multiply a random variable by a fixed multiple b then the variance is multiplied by b^2. Combining these results we have

Remark 2 $Var[a + bX] = b^2 \times Var[X]$, *for constants a and b.*

For example, if X has mean μ and variance σ^2, then $a + X$ has mean $a + \mu$ and variance σ^2 and bX has mean $b\mu$ and variance $b^2\sigma^2$. It follows that $a + bX$ has mean $a + b\mu$ and variance $b^2\sigma^2$. Applying these rules it follows that $Y = (X - \mu)/\sigma$ has mean 0 and variance 1; Y is called a **standardized random variable**.

3.2   Random Samples

For statistical inference we view our data as being a random sample with each observation being a random outcome.

3.2.1   Random Samples

A sample of size n takes values denoted $x_1, ..., x_n$. In Chapter 2 we focused on using various descriptive statistics and graphs to summarize these values. Now we recognize that each value is a random outcome: x_1 is the observed or realized or outcome value of the random variable X_1, x_2 is the observed or realized or outcome value of the random variable X_2, and so on.

For example, suppose we have a sequence of four coin tosses with consecutive results tails, heads, heads and heads. Then random variable X_1 has realized value $x_1 = 0$, X_2 takes value $x_2 = 1$, X_3 takes value $x_3 = 1$ and X_4 takes value $x_4 = 1$.

Definition 3 *A sample of size n has observed values $x_1, x_2, ..., x_n$ that are realizations of the random variables $X_1, X_2, ..., X_n$.*

3.2.2 The Sample Mean is a Random Outcome

The **sample mean** is the average of the n sample values $x_1, ..., x_n$, or

$$\bar{x} = \frac{x_1 + x_2 + \cdots + x_n}{n} = \frac{1}{n} \sum_{i=1}^{n} x_i.$$

For example, for four coin tosses that yield values 0, 1, 1 and 1, the sample mean is $\bar{x} = (0 + 1 + 1 + 1)/4 \simeq 0.75$.

The sample values $x_1, ..., x_n$ are realized outcomes of the random variables $X_1, X_2, ..., X_n$. It follows that **the sample mean $\bar{x}$ is a realization of the random variable**

$$\bar{X} = \frac{X_1 + X_2 + \cdots + X_n}{n} = \frac{1}{n} \sum_{i=1}^{n} X_i.$$

The random variable $\bar{X}$ is also called the **sample mean**. It should be clear from the context whether sample mean refers to the random variable $\bar{X}$ or its observed value $\bar{x}$.

Definition 4 *The observed sample mean $\bar{x}$ is the realized value of the random variable $\bar{X}$; $\bar{X}$ is also called the sample mean.*

3.2.3 Sample Variance and Standard Deviation

The **sample variance** is the average of the squared deviations of x around $\bar{x}$, rather than around μ, since μ is unknown. From Chapter 2

$$s^2 = \frac{1}{n-1} \sum_{i=1}^{n} (x_i - \bar{x})^2.$$

The divisor $(n-1)$ is called the **degrees of freedom** because only $(n-1)$ terms in the sum are free to vary since they are linked by the relationship $\bar{x} = \frac{1}{n} \sum_{i=1}^{n} x_i$. Taking the square root of s^2 yields the **sample standard deviation** s.

Like the sample mean, the sample variance is the realization of a random variable, namely

$$S^2 = \frac{1}{n-1} \sum_{i=1}^{n} (X_i - \bar{X})^2.$$

Similarly, the sample standard deviation s is a realization of the random variable S.

3.3 Sample Generated by an Experiment: Coin Tosses

We consider an example of a sample generated by an experiment where the values for the mean and standard deviation of the underlying random variable X are known and are specified.

We then take a series of samples, by running the experiment many times, and for each sample obtain the sample mean $\bar{x}$. We are interested in comparing the distribution of the many sample means to the distribution of X.

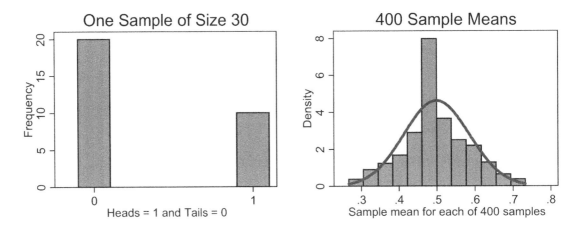

Figure 3.1: Coin tosses histograms: for x in one sample (n = 30) and for mean of x in 400 samples (n = 30).

3.3.1   Example: Coin Tosses

We consider the fraction of times that a fair coin lands heads in 30 tosses.

The random variable $X = 1$ if heads and $X = 0$ if tails. Given equal probabilities of heads and tails, X has mean $\mu = 0.5$ and standard deviation $\sigma = 0.5$.

The left panel of Figure 3.1 shows a histogram for one sample of 30 tosses. In this sample there were 10 heads and 20 tails, so $\bar{x} = 10/30 = 0.333$, and $s = 0.479$, values that due to randomness differ from $\mu = 0.5$ and $\sigma = 0.5$.

3.3.2   Many Samples

Now randomly draw 400 samples, each of 30 coin tosses. In this example the first three such samples have means $\bar{x}_1 = .333$, $\bar{x}_2 = .500$ and $\bar{x}_3 = .533$. Dataset COINTOSSMEANS has all 400 sample means.

The right panel of Figure 3.1 presents a histogram for the 400 sample means. The histogram is roughly centered on the individual mean; the average of the 400 means is 0.499 which is close to $\mu = 0.5$. The standard deviation of the 400 means equals 0.086. So there is much less variability in these 400 means than in the individual observations. Here the standard deviation of the 400 means is between one-fifth and one-sixth of $\sigma = 0.5$, the standard deviation of X. Finally, we superimpose the density for the normal distribution with mean 0.499 and standard deviation 0.086. It is clear that the histogram of the 400 means is roughly that of a normally distributed random variable.

In the preceding example we did not actually toss a coin 12,000 times to obtain the results for 400 samples, each with 30 coin tosses. Instead a computer was used to simulate the coin tosses. The method to do so is explained in Chapter 3.8.

3.4 Properties of the Sample Mean

The coin toss example yielded (1) sample mean that is on average close to the mean μ of the individual observations; (2) variability of the sample mean that is much less than that of the underlying individual observations; and (3) sample mean that is approximately normally distributed.

In this section these results are formalized in a general setting. The statistical properties of the random variable $\bar{X}$, the sample mean, are determined by the process generating the underlying individual random variables $X_1, X_2, ..., X_n$.

3.4.1 Assumptions

Standard basic assumptions about the individual random variables X_i are that

A. X_i has common mean μ: $E[X_i] = \mu$ for all i.

B. X_i has common variance σ^2: $\text{Var}[X_i] = \sigma^2$ for all i.

C. Different observations are statistically independent: X_i is statistically independent of $X_j, i \neq j$.

Here statistical independence implies, for example, that the value taken by X_2 is not influenced by the value taken by X_1; see Appendix B.2 for a more formal definition. For example, for a fair coin toss the probability of heads on the second coin toss is 0.5 regardless of whether the first coin toss yielded heads or tails.

Short-hand notation for assumptions A-B is that $X_i \sim (\mu, \sigma^2)$ for all i or, even more simply, that

$$X \sim (\mu, \sigma^2),$$

where $\sim$ means "**is distributed as**", and the terms in parentheses are, respectively, the mean and the variance of X_i.

Assumptions A-C are met when data are obtained from a **simple random sample**, often called more simply a **random sample**, where we make independent draws $X_1, ..., X_n$ from the same distribution. Chapter 3.4.6 discusses relaxing these assumptions.

3.4.2 Mean of the Sample Mean

The **mean of the sample mean** $\bar{X}$ is

$$\mu_{\bar{X}} \equiv E[\bar{X}] = \mu.$$

In words, the expected value of the sample mean equals the mean for each individual, so the average of $\bar{X}$ from many samples is expected to equal μ.

This result means that if we were able to obtain many random samples and for each sample obtain the sample mean, then on average the sample means equal the mean of a single variable X.

Only assumption A (common mean of X_i) is needed to obtain this result. The proof uses $\mathrm{E}[aX] = a\mathrm{E}[X]$ and $\mathrm{E}[X + Y] = \mathrm{E}[X] + \mathrm{E}[Y]$. Then

$$
\begin{aligned}
\mathrm{E}[\bar{X}] &= \mathrm{E}[\tfrac{1}{n}(X_1 + X_2 + \cdots + X_n)] \\
&= \tfrac{1}{n}\mathrm{E}[X_1 + X_2 + \cdots + X_n] \\
&= \tfrac{1}{n}\{\mathrm{E}[X_1] + \mathrm{E}[X_2] + \cdots + \mathrm{E}[X_n]\} \\
&= \tfrac{1}{n}\{\mu + \mu + \cdots + \mu\} = \mu.
\end{aligned}
$$

3.4.3   Standard Deviation of the Sample Mean

The variability of $\bar{X}$ around its mean of μ is measured using the variance and standard deviation of $\bar{X}$.

The **variance of the sample mean** $\bar{X}$ is

$$
\sigma_{\bar{X}}^2 = \; \mathrm{Var}[\bar{X}] \equiv \mathrm{E}[(\bar{X} - \mu_{\bar{X}})^2] = \frac{\sigma^2}{n},
$$

where σ^2 is the variance of X. The proof requires all of assumptions A-C (same mean, same variance and independence of X_i) and uses $\mathrm{Var}[aX] = a^2\mathrm{E}[X]$ and that for independent variables $\mathrm{Var}[X + Y] = \mathrm{Var}[X] + \mathrm{Var}[Y]$; see Appendix B.2 for complete details.

The **standard deviation of the sample mean** $\bar{X}$ is then

$$
\sigma_{\bar{X}} \equiv \sqrt{\frac{\sigma^2}{n}} = \frac{\sigma}{\sqrt{n}}.
$$

The variance result that $\sigma_{\bar{X}}^2 = \sigma^2/n$ implies that the sample mean is less variable than the underlying data, as demonstrated in Figure 3.1 for the coin toss example.

Furthermore the variability of the sample mean as an estimate of the mean of an individual variable X decreases greatly as the sample size increases, at rate n for the variance and at rate $\sqrt{n}$ for the standard deviation. Thus for the coin toss example the standard deviation of the 400 means was 0.086, close to the true standard deviation $\sigma/\sqrt{n} = 0.5/\sqrt{30} \simeq 0.091$.

As expected, **larger samples lead to greater precision** in estimating μ. Furthermore, $\sigma_{\bar{X}}^2 = \sigma^2/n \to 0$ as $n \to \infty$, so the sample mean will be very close to μ as the sample size $n \to \infty$.

Remark 3 *Under simple random sampling the sample mean $\bar{x}$ is the realization of a random variable $\bar{X}$ that has mean equal to the mean μ and standard deviation $\sigma/\sqrt{n}$ that gets smaller as the sample size increases.*

3.4.4   Normal Distribution and the Central Limit Theorem

From the right panel of Figure 3.1 the sample means appear to be approximately normally distributed, even though each observation is clearly not from the normal distribution. Remarkably this is the case in quite general settings, provided the sample size is sufficiently large.

The preceding results imply that the random variable

$$\bar{X} \sim (\mu,\, \sigma^2/n).$$

Subtracting the mean and dividing by the standard deviation leads to a standardized random variable that by construction has mean 0 and variance 1. Here we denote this standardized random variable by Z, so

$$Z = \frac{\bar{X} - \mu}{\sigma/\sqrt{n}} \sim (0,\, 1).$$

In general the distributions of $\bar{X}$ and of Z vary with the distribution of X and there is no simple formula for these distributions. One notable extension is that if X, the underlying variable for a single observation, is normally distributed then $\bar{X}$ is normally distributed and Z is standard normal distributed. Remarkably even if X is not normally distributed we obtain these results, provided the sample size is large.

In particular, if the sample satisfies assumptions A-C and, additionally, the sample size $n \to \infty$, then a result from statistics called the **central limit theorem**, states that Z has the **standard normal distribution**, so then

$$Z \sim N(0,\, 1) \text{ as } n \to \infty.$$

This remarkable result result is proved using advanced mathematical methods; there is no intuition for the result. The central limit theorem, first derived in 1733, gets its name because it is for the limit (as $n \to \infty$) of a measure of the center of the distribution.

It follows that for large n a good approximation to the distribution of $\bar{X}$ is

$$\bar{X} \sim N(\mu,\, \sigma^2/n).$$

Often $n > 30$ is sufficient for this to be a reasonable approximation. $\bar{X}$ is said to be **asymptotically normal** distributed, where the term **asymptotic** means as the sample size goes to infinity.

The wide applicability and usefulness of the central limit theorem cannot be understated. Regardless of the distribution of the underlying random variable X, if assumptions A-C hold then averaging leads to a standardized random variable that is standard normally distributed in large samples. It can also be extended to cases where not all of assumptions A–C hold; see Appendix B.2.

Remark 4 *Under assumptions A-C the central limit theorem implies that the standardized random variable $Z = (\bar{X} - \mu)/(\sigma/\sqrt{n})$ is standard normal distributed as the sample size goes to infinity. For large n a good approximation is that $\bar{X} \sim N(\mu,\, \sigma^2/n)$.*

3.4.5 Standard Error of the Sample Mean

The variance and standard deviation of $\bar{X}$ depend on the variance σ^2 which is unknown. Replacing σ^2 by its estimate s^2, leads to the following estimates.

The **estimated variance** of $\bar{X}$ is

$$s_{\bar{X}}^2 = \frac{s^2}{n} = \frac{\frac{1}{n-1}\sum_i (x_i - \bar{x})^2}{n}.$$

Taking the square root, the **estimated standard deviation** of $\bar{X}$, called the **standard error of the sample mean**, is

$$se(\bar{x}) = \frac{s}{\sqrt{n}} = \frac{\sqrt{\frac{1}{n-1}\sum_i (x_i - \bar{x})^2}}{\sqrt{n}},$$

where s is the sample standard deviation, the sample estimate of the standard deviation of X.

Note that in general the term "**standard error**" means **estimated standard deviation**. The various estimators considered in this book each have a distinct standard error. In many situations computer output will include a reported "standard error", but this is not necessarily the standard error of the sample mean $\bar{X}$.

Remark 5 *Under simple random sampling the standard error (the estimated standard deviation) of the sample mean $\bar{X}$ equals $s/\sqrt{n}$ where s is the sample standard deviation for a single observation.*

It can be shown that, under assumptions A-C, $S^2 = \frac{1}{n-1}\sum_{i=1}^{n}(X_i - \bar{X})^2$ has the desirable property that $E[S^2] = \sigma^2$. For this reason the formula for s^2 divides by $n-1$ rather than the more obvious n.

3.4.6   Relaxing assumptions A-C

The starting point is to assume simple random sampling, but methods can be adjusted to relax assumptions A-C.

Assumption A requires a common mean μ. Regression analysis generalizes this by allowing the mean to differ with individual characteristics. For example, expected earnings for an individual may vary with education.

Assumption B requires a common variance and assumption C requires independence of observations. If either of these assumptions fail, then $\bar{X}$ still has mean μ, provided assumption A holds, but the variance of $\bar{X}$ is no longer σ^2/n. In particular, if observations are correlated (assumption C fails) then alternative formulas to $s/\sqrt{n}$ are used to compute estimate $se(\bar{x})$, the standard error of the sample mean. The correct $se(\bar{x})$ is most easily obtained by least squares regression on just an intercept and using appropriate robust standard errors; see Chapter 12.1.

A greater complication arises if the sample is not representative of the population. This is discussed in Chapter 3.7.

3.4.7   Summary for the Sample Mean

The distinction between variability in X_i, the random variable leading to the ith sample value x_i, and the variability in $\bar{X}$, the random variable with observed value the sample mean $\bar{x}$, can cause confusion. A summary given simple random sampling is the following:

1. Sample values $x_1, ..., x_n$ are realized or observed values of the random variables $X_1, ..., X_n$.

2. Individual X_i are assumed to be independent have common mean μ and variance σ^2.

3. The average $\bar{X}$ of the n draws of X_i has mean μ and variance σ^2/n.

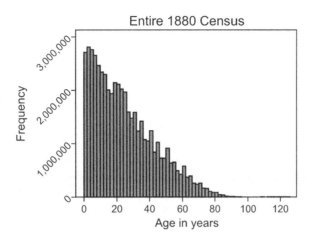

Figure 3.2: 1880 Census histogram: Age for the entire U.S. population.

4. The standardized statistic $Z = \frac{\bar{X} - \mu}{\sigma/\sqrt{n}}$ has mean 0 and variance 1.

5. Under assumptions A-C, Z is standard normal distributed as sample size $n \to \infty$, by the central limit theorem.

6. For large n a good approximation is that $\bar{X} \sim N(\mu, \sigma^2/n)$.

7. The standard error of $\bar{X}$ equals $s/\sqrt{n}$, where "standard error" is general terminology for "estimated standard deviation".

3.5   Sampling from a Finite Population: 1880 Census

As a second example of sampling we consider obtaining a sample from a finite population.

3.5.1   Example: 1880 U.S. Census

The 1880 Census provides a complete enumeration of the U.S. population in 1880. We consider one of the variables that was recorded, that on age in years.

3.5.2   Population

Figure 3.2 provides a histogram of age for all 50,169,452 people recorded as living in the U.S. in 1880. The distribution is basically declining in age. The blips are due to individuals rounding their age to the nearest five years or ten years.

For a complete census such as this, the observed distribution is actually the distribution of X, with the age of each person occurring with probability $1/N$, where $N = 50,169,452$. The population

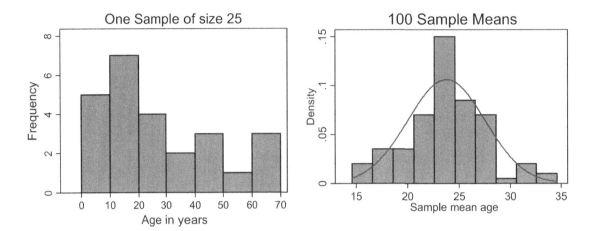

Figure 3.3: 1880 Census histograms: Age in one sample (n = 25) and Mean age in 100 samples (n = 25).

average age is 24.13 years, so $\mu = 24.13$, since $E[X] = \sum_x x \times \Pr[X = x] = \sum_{i=1}^{N} x_i \times \frac{1}{N} = 24.13$. Similarly, the population standard deviation of age is 18.61, so $\sigma = 18.61$.

3.5.3   Samples

Now consider taking one randomly-drawn **sample** of size $n = 25$ drawn from this population of size $N = 50{,}169{,}452$. The left panel of Figure 3.3 presents the histogram for this single sample of size $n = 25$. For this sample, the average age was 27.84 years, so $\bar{x} = 27.84$, and the standard deviation of age is 20.71, so $s = 20.71$. Due to the randomness of sampling, these are similar to, but not exactly equal to, μ and σ.

Now randomly draw 100 distinct samples of size 25, leading to 100 different sample means. The first three such samples turned out to have means $\bar{x}_1 = 27.84$, $\bar{x}_2 = 19.40$ and $\bar{x}_3 = 23.28$ years. The right panel of Figure 3.3 presents a histogram for these 100 sample means that are stored in dataset CENSUSAGEMEANS. Several things are apparent.

First, the histogram is roughly centered on the mean μ. In fact the average of the 100 means is 23.78, close to $\mu = 24.13$.

Second, there is much less variability in these 100 means than in the original population. Here the standard deviation of the 100 means is 3.76, roughly one-fifth of the standard deviation of $\sigma = 18.61$. In fact from theory already presented $\bar{X}$ has standard deviation $\sigma/\sqrt{n} = 18.61/\sqrt{25} = 3.72$.

Third, the histogram is roughly that of a normally distributed random variable. This is apparent by superimposing the density for the normal distribution with mean 23.78 and standard deviation 3.76.

3.6 Estimation of the Population Mean

In the examples given so far the distribution of X has been fully specified, so that we know the exact value of the **population mean** μ. In practice μ is unknown and we wish to estimate μ.

For example, if a coin is known to be fair then for a single coin toss $\mu = 0.5$. But suppose we do not know that the coin is fair. More generally let $\Pr[X = 1] = p$ in which case $\Pr[X = 0] = 1 - p$ and some simple algebra shows that $\mu = p$. Now we need to estimate p, which in this example is the same as estimating μ. The obvious estimator is $\bar{X}$, but in what sense is $\bar{X}$ a good estimator of μ?

Due to randomness, an estimator of μ will not exactly equal μ. Two desirable properties of an estimator of μ is that its distribution be centered on μ and that it has as little variability as possible around μ.

3.6.1 Parameter, Estimator and Estimate

The goal in estimation is to estimate one or more parameters, where a **parameter** is a constant that determines in part the distribution of X. Examples of parameters are the mean μ and the variance σ^2.

Definition 5 *A **parameter** is a constant that determines in part the distribution of X. An **estimator** is a method for estimating a parameter. An **estimate** is the particular value of the estimator obtained from the sample.*

For estimation of the mean of X using the sample mean, the parameter is μ, the estimator is the random variable $\bar{X}$, and the estimate is the sample value $\bar{x}$.

3.6.2 Unbiased estimators

The first goal of estimation is to have an estimator that is centered on the parameter we wish to estimate. One standard criteria used is **unbiasedness**.

Definition 6 *An **unbiased estimator** of a parameter has expected value equal to the parameter.*

The sample mean $\bar{X}$ is unbiased for μ under assumption A (a common mean) since, as already shown, $\mathrm{E}[\bar{X}] = \mu$.

Remark 6 *Under simple random sampling the sample mean is unbiased for μ, meaning that in repeated samples it will on average equal μ.*

3.6.3 Minimum Variance Estimators

Restricting attention to unbiased estimators still allows many potential estimators. For example, the sample median is an alternative estimator to the sample mean that is unbiased for μ if X is symmetrically distributed. In that case we discriminate between such estimators on the basis of the size of their variance.

Definition 7 *A **best estimator** or **efficient estimator** in a class of estimators has **minimum variance** among the class.*

Smaller variance is desired as then there will be less variability in the estimator from sample to sample. As an example of a poor choice for an unbiased estimator, suppose we just used the first observation in each sample of size n to estimate μ. Then this estimator is unbiased from sample to sample as $E[X_1] = \mu$. But it has variance σ^2 which is high relative to other possible unbiased estimators.

For simple random samples the sample mean $\bar{X}$ has variance σ^2/n. Whether alternative unbiased estimators for μ can have smaller variance than this depends on the distribution for X. For some common distributions of X, notably the normal, Bernoulli, binomial, Poisson and exponential, it can be shown that, given data from a simple random sample, no other unbiased estimator of μ has smaller variance.

Remark 7 *Under simple random sampling the sample mean has the smallest variance among unbiased estimators for some common distributions of X (including the normal, Bernoulli, binomial, Poisson and exponential) though not for all distributions of X.*

The sample mean is generally used, for simplicity and because even in situations where the sample mean is not the most efficient estimator, its variance is usually not much greater than the minimum possible variance, so the efficiency loss in using the sample mean is not great. The next chapter presents confidence intervals for μ and tests of hypotheses on μ that use the sample mean as the estimate of μ.

3.6.4   Consistent estimators

A more advanced concept considers **asymptotic properties** of an estimator, i.e. behavior as the sample size goes to infinity.

Definition 8 *A **consistent estimator** of a parameter is one that is almost certainly arbitrarily close to the parameter, as the sample size gets very large.*

A sufficient condition for **consistency** is that (1) any bias disappears as the sample size gets large, and (2) the variance of the estimator goes to zero as the sample size gets large. A more precise definition of **consistency** is given in Chapter 6.4.

The sample mean $\bar{X}$ is consistent for μ under simple random sampling (assumptions A-C) as it is unbiased and has variance σ^2/n which goes to zero as $n \to \infty$. This convergence of $\bar{X}$ to μ as the sample size gets large is an example of a so-called **law of large numbers**.

3.7   Nonrepresentative Samples

The standard assumption is that data are generated from a simple random sample. As already noted, for unbiased estimation of the mean the key assumption is assumptions A, that the sample has common mean μ; assumptions B-C can be relaxed.

Serious complications arise, however, if the sample is not representative of the population of interest. Then assumption A in Chapter 3.4 does not hold, and $\bar{X}$ may be biased and inconsistent for the population mean μ.

This issue is particularly relevant for samples based on a survey. It has become relatively inexpensive to conduct a survey by means such as telephone or the internet. Due to nonrepresentativeness of the grouped surveyed, or high nonresponse rates even if the group surveyed is representative, the sample may be a very skewed sample. If a sample reveals a surprising result, it may be an artifact of being nonrepresentative.

3.7.1 Examples of Nonrepresentative Samples

For example, a survey of readers of Golf Digest will provide an inconsistent estimate of the golfing habits of all Americans, since it oversamples active golfers. (The survey might, however, provide a consistent estimate of the golfing habits of all readers of Golf Digest. This would be of use to the advertising department of Golf Digest. In this latter case the population of interest is viewed to be readers of Golf Digest rather than all Americans.)

A famous example of a nonrepresentative sample is the incorrect prediction of the winner of the 1948 U.S. presidential election. Opinion polls predicted that the Republican candidate John Dewey would defeat the incumbent Democrat, President Harry Truman. Yet Truman won convincingly. The opinion polls were not representative for two reasons. First, the last opinion polls were taken well before the election, so a late surge to Truman meant that they were not representative of opinions on election day itself. Second, the opinion polls were not based on random sampling - the interviewers were given too much discretion as to who they interviewed.

3.7.2 Weighted Mean for Survey Data

Samples obtained from government surveys and from political polling surveys are often not representative of the population. Yet the leading national surveys can nonetheless be adjusted to provide valid estimates of the population mean.

For example, the unemployment rate in the United States is obtained from the Current Population Survey (CPS), a monthly survey of 60,000 households. This survey is not a simple random sample. For example, households in smaller states are oversampled to provide more reliable state-level data. Similarly, minority and disadvantaged populations are oversampled. And the surveyed households are clustered geographically to reduce interview costs.

To overcome these complications, surveys such as the CPS, provide sampling weights that make possible unbiased estimation of the population mean using a **weighted mean**

$$\bar{x}_w = \frac{\sum_{i=1}^{n} w_i x_i}{\sum_{i=1}^{n} w_i} = \frac{\frac{1}{n}\sum_{i=1}^{n} w_i x_i}{\frac{1}{n}\sum_{i=1}^{n} w_i},$$

where the **sample weights** w_i are the reciprocal of the **probability** that the ith individual in the population is included in the sample. This method requires correct specification of the weights w_i.

Most standard statistical software enables computation of the weighted mean and the standard error of the weighted mean, provided the sample weights are known. An example is given in exercise 19 of Chapter 12. Statistical software for **survey data** allows for additional complications of surveys.

3.8 Computer Generation of Random Samples

How are random samples generated on a computer?

The starting point is a **uniform random number generator** that creates values between 0 and 1 such that any value between 0 and 1 is equally likely and successive values appear to be independent of each other.

These random numbers are more properly called **pseudo random numbers**, as a deterministic rule is used to create the sequence of numbers $u_1, u_2, ...$ For example, one method given value j^{th} value u_j specifies the next value to be $u_{j+1} = (69069u_j + 1234567) \bmod 2^{32}$, where $a \bmod b$ is the remainder when a is divided by b. Remarkably this rule leads to u_{j+1} appearing to be unrelated to u_j and to the different possible values of u_j between 0 and 1 being equally likely.

The sequence depends on the starting value u_0, called the **seed**. For example, we might set the seed equal to 10101. When using random numbers it is always good practice to **set the seed**, as then results can be replicated exactly in future simulations.

3.8.1 Generating a Single Random Sample in a Statistical Package

In the coin toss example in Chapter 3.3 we did not actually toss a coin many times. Instead to simulate 30 coin tosses, say, we draw 30 uniform random numbers and let the result be heads if the uniform random number exceeds 0.5, and tails if the uniform random number is less than 0.5.

Similarly for the Census example, if the uniform random number is between 0 and $1/N$, where $N = 50,169,452$, we choose the first person. If the uniform random number is between $1/N$ and $2/N$ we choose the second person, and so on.

The uniform random numbers are also the basis for making draws from commonly-used distributions such as the binomial, Poisson and normal distributions. The following algorithm is used.

Remark 8 *To make n draws of the random variable X do the following: (1) set the sample size to n; (2) set the seed; and (3) make n draws of X from its specified distribution.*

For example, suppose we want to make 500 draws of variables x and y. Variable x is a draw from the uniform distribution on $(3, 9)$, so any value between 3 and 9 is equally likely. Equivalently variable x equals $3 + 6u$ where u is a draw from the uniform distribution on $(0, 1)$. Variable y is a draw from the $N(5, 2^2)$ distribution. Equivalently variable y equals $5 + 2z$ where z is a draw from the standard normal distribution.

In Stata give commands (1) `set obs 100`; (2) `set seed 10101`; (3) `generate x=runiform(3,9)`; and (4) `generate x=rnormal(5,2)`.

In R give the commands (1) `set.seed(10101)`; (2) `x=runif(100,min=3,max=9)`; and (3) `y=rnorm(100,5,2)`.

In Gretl give the commands (1) `nulldata 100`; (2) `set seed 10101`; (3) `genr x=uniform(3,9)`; and (4) `genr y=normal(5,2)`.

In Eviews give commands (1) `wfcreate mywf 100`; (2) `rndseed 10101`; (3) `series x=3+6*rnd`; and (4) `series y=5+2*rnd`.

Note that different packages will yield different results as they use different algorithms.

3.8.2 Computer Generation of Many Samples

The examples in Chapters 3.3 and 3.5 obtain the sample mean from each of many samples. This requires commands that allow repeated operations and saving the results of these repeated operations for subsequent analysis. These more advanced commands vary with statistical package.

The following Stata code obtains 400 sample means in the coin toss example of Chapter 3.3, as well as standard deviations and the sample size.

```
program onesample, rclass
    drop _all
    set obs 30
    generate u = runiform()
    generate x = u > 0.5
    summarize x
    return scalar xbar = r(mean)
    return scalar sd = r(sd)
    return scalar nobs = r(N)
end
simulate xbar=r(xbar) stdev=r(sd) nobs=r(nobs), seed(10101) reps(400): onesample
summarize
```

The program `onesample` simulates each of 30 fair coin tosses by first drawing a uniform number u between 0 and 1 and setting variable random x to 1 if u>0.5 and to 0 if u<=0.5. Some key results from command `summarize` are stored in `r()`, including $\bar{x}$ in `r(mean)`, s in `r(sd)`, s^2 in `r(Var)`, and N in `r(N)`. The `return scalar` commands generate variables that will be returned to command `simulate`. For example, the sample mean of the 30 x's will be returned in variable `xbar`. The command `simulate` runs the program `onesample` 400 times (the value in `reps()`), leading to 400 observations on variables `xbar`, `stdev` and `nobs`. The option `seed(10101)` provides a starting value for the initial draw of u, leading to the same results each time this code is run.

The following R code obtains 400 sample means in the coin toss example of Chapter 3.3, as well as standard deviations.

```
set.seed(10101)
result.mean=array(dim=400)
result.stdev=array(dim=400)
for(i in 1:400){
    x=rbinom(30,1,0.5)
    result.mean[i]=mean(x)
    result.stdev[i]=sd(x)
}
```

```
mean(result.mean)
sd(result.mean)
summary(result.mean)
```

The R code obtains 30 fair coin tosses by using the command `rbinom(30,1,0.5)` that 30 times makes 1 draw of a random variable equal to one with probability 0.5 (and hence equal to zero with probability 0.5). The `for` loop repeats this 400 times, and the resulting means for each sample are stored in the array `result.mean` and the standard deviations in the array `result.stdev`. The `set.seed(10101)` command provides a starting value for the initial draw of x, leading to the same results each time this code is run.

The following Gretl code obtains 400 sample means in the coin toss example of Chapter 3.3, as well as standard deviations.

```
# Mean of 400 coin toss samples each of size 30
nulldata 30
set seed 10101
loop 400 --progressive
    genr u = uniform(0,1)
    genr x = (u > 0.5)
    scalar tosses = nobs(x)
    scalar mean = mean(x)
    scalar stdev = sd(x)
    # print out results
    print tosses mean stdev
    # and save results in gretl dataset
    store aed03simresults.gdt tosses mean stdev
endloop
# Summarize the 400 means
clear
open aed03simresults.gdt
summary --simple
```

3.9   Key Concepts

1. A random variable is a variable whose value is determined by the outcome of an experiment.

2. Random variables X are denoted in upper case and realized values x are denoted in lower case.

3. The mean μ is the probability-weighted average of all values that the random variable X may take.

4. The variance σ^2 is the probability-weighted average of all values that $(X - \mu)^2$ may take.

5. The population standard deviation is σ.

6. If X has mean μ and variance σ^2 then $a + bX$ has mean $a + b\mu$ and variance $b^2\sigma^2$.

7. $Y = (X - \mu)/\sigma$ has mean 0 and variance 1.

8. Statistical inference seeks to infer properties of the distribution of X from the sample at hand.

9. A sample of size n has observed values $x_1, x_2, ..., x_n$ that are realizations of the random variables $X_1, X_2, ..., X_n$.

10. The sample statistics, such as the sample mean, are random variables whose statistical properties are determined by those of the random variables whose realizations produced the sample.

11. In particular, the sample mean $\bar{x}$ is a realization of the random variable $\bar{X}$.

12. We assume that (A) $\mathrm{E}[X_i] = \mu$, (B) $\mathrm{Var}[X_i] = \sigma^2$, and (C) X_i is statistically independent of X_j, $i \neq j$.

13. A simple random sample is one whose observations are independent draws from the same distribution with $X_i \sim (\mu, \sigma^2)$. Then assumptions A-C are satisfied.

14. Under assumptions A-C the sample mean $\bar{x}$ is the realization of a random variable $\bar{X}$ that has mean equal to the population mean μ and standard deviation $\sigma/\sqrt{n}$ that gets smaller as the sample size increases.

15. The estimated standard deviation of $\bar{X}$, called the standard error of $\bar{X}$, is denoted $se(\bar{x})$.

16. Under assumptions A-C, $se(\bar{x}) = s/\sqrt{n}$.

17. Under assumptions A-C the standardized random variable $Z = (\bar{X} - \mu)/(\sigma/\sqrt{n})$ is standard normal distributed as the sample size goes to infinity. For large n a good approximation is that $\bar{X} \sim N(\mu, \sigma^2/n)$.

18. A parameter is a constant that determines in part the distribution of X. An estimator is a method for estimating a parameter. An estimate is the particular value obtained from the sample.

19. An unbiased estimator of a parameter is a statistic whose expected value equals the parameter.

20. A consistent estimator of a parameter is a statistic that is almost certainly arbitrarily close to the parameter, as the sample size gets very large.

21. A best estimator or efficient estimator has minimum variance among the class of consistent estimators (or the class of unbiased estimators).

22. Under assumptions A-C, the sample mean is unbiased and consistent. Furthermore it is the best estimator in the special cases that the distribution of X is normal, Bernoulli, binomial, Poisson or exponential.

23. Adjustment to methods may be needed if the sample is not a simple random sample.

24. Key Terms: random variable; mean; variance; standard deviation; sample; assumptions A-C; simple random sample; sample mean; sample standard deviation; standard error of the sample mean; central limit theorem; normal distribution; standard normal distribution; asymptotically normal; parameter; estimate; estimator; unbiased; consistent; best estimator; minimum variance; nonrandom samples; weighted mean; random number generator.

3.10   Exercises

1. Let X denote annual health costs for an individual and suppose $X = 1000$ with probability 0.8 and $X = 5000$ with probability 0.2.

    (a) Obtain $\mu = E[X]$ from first principles.
    (b) Obtain $\sigma^2 = E[(X - \mu)^2]$ from first principles.
    (c) Hence find the standard deviation of X.

2. Repeat the previous exercise if $X = 0$ with probability 0.5, $X = 2000$ with probability 0.3 and $X = 12000$ with probability 0.2.

3. Suppose X has mean 5 and variance 4. For each of the following give the mean and variance.

    (a) $X + 3$.   (b) $2X$.   (c) $2X + 3$.   (d) $(X - 5)/2$.

4. Suppose X has mean μ and variance σ^2. For each of the following give the mean and variance.

    (a) $Y = (X - \mu)$.   (b) $Y = X/\sigma$.   (c) $Y = (X - \mu)/\sigma$.

5. Let $\bar{X}$ be the mean of a simple random sample of size 100 from a random variable that is distributed with mean 200, variance 400, and a distribution that is not the normal distribution.

    (a) Give the mean of $\bar{X}$.
    (b) Give the variance and standard deviation of $\bar{X}$.
    (c) Is $\bar{X}$ likely to be approximately normally distributed? Explain.

6. Repeat the previous exercise for a simple random sample of size 400 from a random variable that is distributed with mean 400, variance 200.

7. Use a computer and a random number generator to obtain 1000 random numbers between 0 and 1, setting the seed to 10101. These are generated in such a way that they can be viewed as independent draws of the uniform random variable X with mean $\mu = 0.5$ and variance $\sigma^2 = 1/12$.

   (a) Are the sample mean and sample variance approximately equal to μ and σ^2?

   (b) How many of the 1,000 random numbers do you expect to lie between 0.0 and 0.1, and between 0.1 and 0.2, etc.? Hint: Any value between 0 and 1 is equally likely.

   (c) Plot a histogram of the random numbers drawn, with starting value 0, 10 bins, and frequency on the vertical axis. Do you (approximately) get what you expected from part (b).

   (d) Give a scatter plot of the random numbers against the observation number. Do they appear to be randomly draws between 0 and 1?

   (e) Give a line plot of the random number against observation number for the first 50 observations. Do consecutive random numbers appear to be related to each other, or do they appear to be independent?

8. For random sampling from $X \sim (\mu, \sigma^2)$ state which of the following statements are true

   (a) $\bar{X} = \mu$.   (b) $\bar{X}$ has population mean μ.   (c) $\bar{X}$ has population variance σ^2.

9. Consider simple random sampling from $X \sim (\mu, \sigma^2)$. State what happens to the size of $E[\bar{X}]$, $Var[\bar{X}]$ and the standard deviation of $\bar{X}$ when the sample size is made four times as large.

10. For simple random sampling from $X \sim (\mu, \sigma^2)$ state which of the following statements are true

    (a) $E[\bar{X}] = E[X]$.   (b) $Var[\bar{X}] = Var[X]$.   (c) $\bar{X}$ has standard deviation σ/N.

11. Let $X = 1$ with $Pr[X = 1] = 1/6$ and $X = 0$ with $Pr[X = 0] = 5/6$. (One way this would arise is if we tossed a six-sided die and set $X = 1$ if a five, say is obtained, and let $X = 0$ otherwise.)

    (a) Obtain $\mu = E[X]$ from first principles.

    (b) Obtain $\sigma^2 = E[(X - \mu)^2]$ from first principles.

    (c) Now use a computer and a random number generator to obtain a sample of size 100 for this example. Hint: A random number is less than 1/6 with probability 1/6.

    (d) Compare the mean $\bar{x}$ and variance s^2 of this sample to your answers in parts a-b.

    (e) Obtain the histogram. Does X appear to be normally distributed?

12. The preceding computer experiment was run 400 times, yielding 400 samples of size 100. The sample mean $\bar{x}$ for each sample is given in dataset DIETOSS.

   (a) Obtain the descriptive statistics for the 400 values of $\bar{x}$. Are the mean and standard deviation what you expect? Explain.

   (b) Obtain the histogram (or better still the kernel density estimate). Is this what you expect? Explain.

13. Suppose X takes values 1, 2 and 3 with probabilities of, respectively, 0.4, 0.2 and 0.4.

   (a) Obtain $\mu = [X]$ from first principles.

   (b) Obtain $\sigma^2 = \mathrm{E}[(X - \mu)^2]$ from first principles.

   (c) Now use a computer and a random number generator to obtain a sample of size 1,000 for this example. Hint: Let u be the random number. Then $x = 1$ if $u < 0.4$, $x = 2$ if $0.4 \leq u < 0.6$, and $x = 3$ if $u \geq 0.6$.

   (d) Compare the mean and standard deviation of this sample to your answers in parts a-b.

14. The preceding computer experiment was run 400 times, obtaining 400 samples of size 100. The sample mean $\bar{x}$ for each sample is given in dataset ONETWOTHREE.

   (a) Obtain the descriptive statistics for $\bar{x}$. Are the mean and standard deviation what you expect? Explain.

   (b) Obtain the histogram (or better still the kernel density estimate). Is this what you expect? Explain.

15. An insurance company offers insurance to 10,000 people with independent loss distributions that have mean \$5,000 and standard deviation \$20,000. Let $\bar{X} = \frac{1}{10000} \sum_{i=1}^{10000} X_i$ denote the average loss per individual.

   (a) Find the mean and standard deviation of $\bar{X}$.

   (b) Suppose the insurance company sells insurance that provides complete coverage for \$5,400. For simplicity suppose that the insurance company has no costs aside from paying out any insurance claims. Is the insurance company likely to make a loss? Explain your answer. Hint: By the central limit theorem $\bar{X}$ is normally distributed.

16. Repeat the previous exercise when the insurance pool is 2,500 people with independent loss distributions that have mean \$10,000 and standard deviation \$30,000 with $\bar{X} = \frac{1}{2500} \sum_{i=1}^{2500} X_i$.

17. The dataset TDIST4 has the sample means $\bar{x}$ and corresponding standard standard deviations s from 1000 random samples of size 4 where $X \sim N(100, 16^2)$.

    (a) Obtain the descriptive statistics for $\bar{x}$. Are the mean and standard deviation what you expect? Explain.

    (b) Obtain the descriptive statistics for $se(\bar{x}) = s/\sqrt{n}$ for these data. Is the mean what you expect? Explain.

    (c) Compute $z = (\bar{x} - 100)/8$. Explain why z is standard normal distributed.

    (d) Obtain summary statistics for z, a histogram and a kernel density estimate.

    (e) For these data does z appear to be standard normally distributed? Explain using results in (d).

18. The dataset TDIST25 has the sample means $\bar{x}$ and and corresponding standard standard deviations s from 1000 random samples of size 25 where $X \sim N(200, 50^2)$.

    (a) Obtain the descriptive statistics for $\bar{x}$. Are the mean and standard deviation what you expect? Explain.

    (b) Obtain the descriptive statistics for $se(\bar{x})$ for these data. Is the mean what you expect? Explain.

    (c) Compute $z = (\bar{x} - 200)/10$. Explain why z is standard normal distributed.

    (d) Obtain summary statistics for z, a histogram and a kernel density estimate.

    (e) For these data does z appear to be standard normally distributed? Explain using results in (d).

19. State whether the following samples are likely to be representative or nonrepresentative of the population.

    (a) Every twentieth person is sampled. All people respond.

    (b) Every twentieth person is sampled. But only ten percent of those sampled respond.

    (c) Every person is sampled. Only ten percent of those sampled respond. We question every twentieth person who did respond.

20. Suppose we take a simple random sample from $X \sim (\mu, \sigma^2)$.

    (a) We estimate μ by X_1, the first value of X in the sample. Is this estimator unbiased for μ? Is this estimator consistent for μ? Explain.

    (b) We estimate μ by $\bar{X} + \frac{1}{n}$. Is this estimator unbiased for μ? Is this estimator consistent for μ? Explain.

    (c) Now suppose $X \sim N(\mu, \sigma^2)$ and we estimate μ by an estimator $\tilde{\mu}$ that has $\mathrm{E}[\tilde{\mu}] = \mu$ and $\mathrm{Var}[\tilde{\mu}] = 2\sigma^2/n$. Is this estimator a best unbiased estimator for μ? Explain.

21. The dataset AUSREGWEALTH has data on average net worth of households (x_i) in thousands of dollars in 517 regions in Australia in 2003-04. Calculate the weighted mean where weight by household size as follows. This is an example of weighting by frequency weights.

    (a) Let w_i equal number of households in each region. Compute $\sum_{i=1}^{n} w_i$.

    (b) Generate the variable $w_i x_i$ and hence the weighted mean $\bar{x}_w = \sum_{i=1}^{n} w_i x_i / \sum_{i=1}^{n} w_i$.

    (c) Compare the weighted mean to the unweighted mean.

    (d) Calculate the weighted variance as $\sum_{i=1}^{n} w_i (x_i - \bar{x}_w)^2 / \sum_{i=1}^{n} w_i$.

    (e) Compare the weighted standard deviation to the unweighted standard deviation.

    (f) If your software computes weighted means and standard deviation, reproduce these results using your software.

22. Repeat the previous exercise for the annual income per taxpayer (in dollars).

23. Repeat exercise 17 except generate the 1,000 sample means yourself. For Stata, use the Stata code in Chapter 3.8 except replace set obs 30 with set obs 4, replace commands generate u=runiform() and generate x=u>0.5 with generate x=rnormal(100,16), and replace reps(400) with reps(1000). For R use the R code in Chapter 3.8 except replace 400 with 1000 and replace x=rbinom(30,1,0.5) with x=rnorm(4,100,16).

24. Repeat exercise 18 except generate the 1,000 sample means yourself. For Stata, use the Stata code in Chapter 3.8 except replace set obs 30 with set obs 25 and replace commands generate u=runiform() and generate x=u>0.5 with generate x=rnormal(200,50), and replace reps(400) with reps(1000). For R use the R code in Chapter 3.8 except replace 400 with 1000 and replace x=rbinom(30,1,0.5) with x=rnorm(25,200,50).

Chapter 4

Statistical Inference for the Mean

The sample mean $\bar{x}$ is a random outcome – different samples lead to a different value of the sample mean. To deal with this randomness, the sample at hand is viewed as being one from sampling observations on a random variable X that has mean (or expected value) denoted by μ. The goal is to make inference on μ given the observed sample mean $\bar{x}$. For example, is the view that mean earnings in the population equal \$40,000, say, consistent with sample mean earnings equal to \$41,413?

This chapter analyzes inference based on the sample mean. It presents the fundamentals of statistical inference, notably confidence intervals and hypothesis tests. Confidence intervals give a range of plausible values of μ given the sample. Hypothesis tests are used to determine whether or not a specified value of μ or range of values of μ is plausible, given the sample.

While the focus is on statistical inference for the mean, these concepts carry over to other univariate statistics, such as the median, and to regression, the subject of most of this book. A good understanding of statistical inference is essential as it lies at the heart of analysis of economics data.

The chapter continues directly from the previous chapter. For readers who bypassed the details in Chapter 3, the key results for statistical inference on the mean are presented in Chapter 3.4.

4.1   Example: Mean Annual Earnings

The following example presents the methods of statistical inference that will be explained in this chapter.

Dataset EARNINGS introduced in Chapter 2 has data on individual annual earnings for a sample of 30 year-old full-time workers in 2010.

Table 4.1 presents several key sample statistics that are generated by a descriptive statistics command, such as the Stata `summarize` command.

The **sample mean** $\bar{x} = 41412.69$ and the **sample standard deviation** $s = 25527.05$.

The population considered is all 30 year-old female full-time workers in 2010 in the United States, with unknown population mean earnings denoted μ. We wish to make inference about the

Table 4.1: Summary statistics: Annual earnings of female full-time workers aged 30 in 2010 (n=171).

Variable	Obs	Mean	Std. Dev.	Min	Max
Earnings		41412.69	25527.05	1050	172000

mean μ, using data from the sample which is a simple random sample from the population. The standard tools of inference are confidence intervals and hypothesis tests.

Table 4.2 presents key results for inference on the mean produced by a command such as the Stata `mean` command.

Table 4.2: Confidence interval: Annual earnings.

Variable	Mean	Stand. Error	95% Conf. Interval	
Earnings	41412.69	1952.10	37559.21	45266.17

The entry Mean is the **sample mean** $\bar{x}$ and is the commonly-used estimate of μ. Here $\bar{x} = $ 41412.69, so the estimate of mean earnings in the population of all 30 year-old female full-time workers in 2010 is \$41,413.

The entry Stand. Error is the **standard error of the sample mean**, where standard error is the statistical term for estimated standard deviation. This measures the precision of the sample mean $\bar{x}$ as an estimate of μ. A smaller standard error means greater precision of $\bar{x}$ as an estimate of μ. Here the standard error of the sample mean equals \$1,952. This is much smaller than the sample standard deviation of \$25,227 for just one observation, because averaging reduces the variability. In fact, under simple random sampling the standard error equals the sample standard deviation of a single observation divided by the square root of the sample size. Here $s/\sqrt{n} = 25527/\sqrt{171} = 1952$.

The entry 95% Conf. Interval gives a 95% **confidence interval** that provides a range of values that includes the true (unknown) population mean μ with 95% confidence. Here the 95% confidence interval for population mean earnings is (\$37,559, \$45,266).

An **hypothesis test** is a test of whether or not the data support a hypothesized value or range of values for the population mean μ. As an example we test the hypothesis that $\mu = 40000$ against the alternative that $\mu \neq 40000$. A command such as the Stata command `ttest earnings=40000` produces the following output.

Some of the output in Table 4.3 repeats that from the command `mean earnings`. Additionally it provides t = 0.7237, called the t statistic, `degrees of freedom = 170`, and the results of three related hypothesis tests. For test of $\mu = 40000$ against $\mu \neq 40000$ the middle output with $\Pr(|T| < |t|) = 0.4703$ is relevant. This value of 0.4703 is called the p-value of the test. It is common to test at significance level 0.05, in which case we would not reject the hypothesis that $\mu = 40000$ since the p-value $0.4703 > 0.05$.

This example presents the key methods for statistical inference on the population mean based on the sample mean. The remainder of this chapter provides complete explanation.

Table 4.3: Hypothesis test: Annual earnings have mean equal to 40000.

Variable	Obs	Mean	Stand. Error	Stand. Dev.	95% Conf. Interval	
Earnings	171	41412.69	1952.03	25527.05	37559.21	45266.17
mean = mean(earnings)						t = 0.7237
Ho: mean = 40000						degrees of freedom = 170
Ha: mean < 40000			Ha: mean != 40000			Ha: mean > 40000
Pr(T < t) = 0.7649			Pr(|T| < |t|) = 0.4703			Pr(T > t) = 0.2351

4.2 t Statistic and t Distribution

Interest lies in estimating the mean μ, and we use the sample mean as the estimator. Chapter 3 detailed properties of the sample mean and why it is a good estimator of μ.

Now we wish to construct confidence intervals on μ, and perform hypothesis tests on μ, which requires knowledge of the distribution of the sample mean. As detailed in Chapter 3 and repeated below, under certain assumptions the sample mean is normally distributed with mean μ and variance σ^2/n; see Chapter 3.4.7 for a summary.

However, to immediately use this result requires knowledge of σ^2/n. In practice this is not known, so we instead estimate it by s^2/n where s is the sample standard deviation of X. Since s is an estimate this adds noise that leads to inference based on the t distribution, a distribution that has fatter tails than the standard normal. In this section we focus on how to obtain probabilities for the t distribution.

4.2.1 Normal distribution

A sample of size n has observed values $x_1, x_2, ..., x_n$ that are realizations of the random variables $X_1, X_2, ..., X_n$. Then $\bar{x}$ is the realization of the random variable $\bar{X} = (X_1 + \cdots X_n)/n$. The properties of $\bar{X}$ depend on the properties of $X_1, X_2, ..., X_n$.

We assume a simple random sample so that the underlying random variables X_i

A. have common mean μ: $\mathrm{E}[X_i] = \mu$ for all i.

B. have common variance σ^2: $\mathrm{Var}[X_i] = \sigma^2$ for all i.

C. are statistically independent: X_i is statistically independent of $X_j, i \neq j$.

Under these assumptions, the central limit theorem states that if additionally the sample size is large then $\bar{X}$ is normally distributed, regardless of the actual distribution of X, and the standardized random variable

$$Z = \frac{\bar{X} - \mu}{\sigma/\sqrt{n}} \sim N(0, 1) \text{ as } n \to \infty.$$

4.2.2   The t Statistic

In practice the sample standard deviation σ is unknown and we need to replace it by the standard deviation of X. Then the **distribution of the sample mean** $\bar{X}$ is defined in terms of the random variable

$$T = \frac{\bar{X} - \mu}{S/\sqrt{n}},$$

where $S^2 = \frac{1}{n-1} \sum_{i=1}^{n} (X_i - \bar{X})^2$.

The distribution of the random variable T is in general complicated. The standard approximation is to suppose that

$$T \sim T(n-1),$$

where $T(n-1)$ denotes the t **distribution** with $(n-1)$ degrees of freedom.

Different degrees of freedom correspond to different t distributions just as, for example, different means μ would correspond to different normal distributions. The term **degrees of freedom** is used because the relationship $\bar{X} = \frac{1}{n} \sum_{i=1}^{n} X_i$ implies that only $(n-1)$ terms in the sum are free to vary.

The reason for using the $T(n-1)$ distribution is that T can be shown to be exactly $T(n-1)$ distributed under assumptions A-C and the additional assumption that X is normally distributed. When X is not normally distributed a common rule-of-thumb is that the $T(n-1)$ distribution is generally a good approximation if $n > 30$.

We observe a single sample with sample mean $\bar{x}$, sample standard deviation s, sample standard error $se(\bar{x}) = s/\sqrt{n}$, and corresponding sample value of the t statistic. So the sample t statistic is a single realization of a $T(n-1)$ distributed random variable. For simplicity we write

$$t = \frac{\bar{x} - \mu}{se(\bar{x})} \sim T(n-1).$$

A common rule-of-thumb is that the approximation will be a good one if $n > 30$.

Remark 9 *From a **simple random sample** $x_1, ..., x_n$ calculate the **sample mean** $\bar{x}$, the sample standard deviation s and the **standard error of** $\bar{x}$, $se(\bar{x}) = s/\sqrt{n}$. The **t statistic***

$$t = \frac{\bar{x} - \mu}{se(\bar{x})} = \frac{\bar{x} - \mu}{s/\sqrt{n}}$$

*is a realization of a random variable that is approximately $T(n-1)$ distributed, where $T(n-1)$ denotes the **t distribution** with $n-1$ degrees of freedom.*

To form the t statistic the only summary statistics of the sample needed are the sample mean $\bar{x}$ and the sample standard deviation s. Additionally the t statistic depends on the population mean μ, which is unknown. The knowledge that the t statistic is $T(n-1)$ distributed is used to make statistical inference on μ, as detailed in subsequent sections of this chapter.

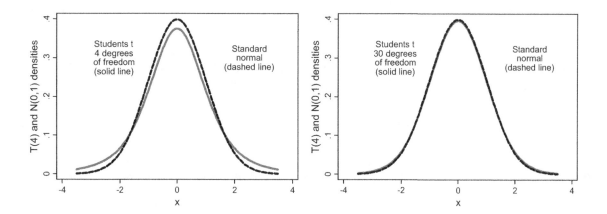

Figure 4.1: Student's t distribution: $T(4)$ and $T(30)$ compared to the standard normal.

4.2.3 The t Distribution

A t-distributed random variable is a continuous random variable. In that case probabilities are given by the area under the probability density function; see Appendix B.1. For example, $\Pr[a < T < b]$ is the area under the curve from a to b. The formula for the probability density function is complex and is not given here. Instead the properties of the t distribution are outlined.

The probability density function for the t **distribution**, or **Student's** t **distribution**, is a bell-shaped curve centered on zero, and symmetric about zero, that is a slightly squashed version of the standard normal. It has one parameter, denoted v here, called the **degrees of freedom**. The t distribution with v degrees of freedom, denoted $T(v)$, has mean 0, provided $v > 1$, and variance $v/(v - 2)$, provided $v > 2$. The standard normal has the same mean of 0, but smaller variance of 1.

Figure 4.1 presents, respectively, the $T(4)$ and $T(30)$ probability density functions and compares them in each case to the standard normal. The T distribution has bell-shaped curve similar to the standard normal distribution, except it has fatter tails reflecting increased randomness due to replacing the constant σ by the random variable S. The t distribution approaches the standard normal as v gets larger and the difference disappears as $v \to \infty$.

4.2.4 Probabilities for the t Distribution

There is no simple formula for **probabilities** for the t distribution; instead computation requires advanced numerical methods. Until recently statisticians needed to refer to published tables such as those given in Appendix E. Now one can directly use a computer.

For example, to compute $\Pr[T_{30} > 2]$, the probability that a $T(30)$ random variable exceeds 2, one can use the Stata function `ttail(30,2)` which returns a probability of 0.0273.

From the second panel of Figure 4.1 there is seemingly little difference between the $T(30)$ and the standard normal distributions. But there is still an appreciable difference in the tails of these distributions, with the t distribution having fatter tails. In fact $\Pr[|T_{30}| > 2] = 0.0546$. This is approximately 20% larger than $\Pr[|Z| > 2] = 0.0455$ for Z standard normal distributed.

Such differences can be large enough to matter for confidence intervals and hypothesis tests because they use tail probabilities. For this reason statistical packages and this book base inference on the t distribution rather than the standard normal distribution.

As the degrees of freedom $v \to \infty$, the difference disappears since the t distribution then collapses to the standard normal distribution. For example, for $T_{1000} \sim T(1000)$ we have $\Pr[|T_{1000}| > 2] = 0.0458$, very close to 0.0455 for the standard normal.

Remark 10 *The t distribution with v degrees of freedom, denoted $T(v)$, is like a squashed version of the standard normal distribution with fatter tails. As $v \to \infty$ the t distribution goes to the standard normal.*

4.2.5 Inverse Probabilities for the t Distribution

In some situations this computation needs to be inverted. The probability is set and we wish to calculate the associated value of t that gives this probability.

For example we may wish to find the value c such that the probability that a $T(170)$ distributed random variable exceeds c is equal to 0.05. Then, for example, one can use the Stata function `invttail(170,.05)` which returns a value of 1.6539. We have that $c = 1.6539$ solves $\Pr[T_{170} > c] = 0.05$. Appendix A of this book includes corresponding commands for various statistical packages other than Stata.

More generally the desired area is denoted α, the greek letter "alpha", and the **inverse probability**, called a **critical value**, $c = t_{v,\alpha}$ satisfies

$$\Pr[T_v > t_{v,\alpha}] = \alpha.$$

In words, the inverse probability or critical value $t_{v,\alpha}$ is that value such that a $T(v)$ distributed random variable exceeds $t_{v,\alpha}$ with probability α. Even more simply, **the area under the curve to the right of $t_{v,\alpha}$ equals** α.

The left panel of Figure 4.2 presents the example $\Pr[T_{170} > 1.654] = 0.05$. Then $\alpha = 0.05$ is the shaded area in the right tail, and the inverse probability $t_{v,\alpha} = t_{170,.05} = 1.654$ is given on the horizontal axis.

Definition 9 *The inverse probability or **critical value** $c = t_{v,\alpha}$ is that value for which a $T(v)$ distributed random variable exceeds $t_{v,\alpha}$ with probability α, i.e. $\Pr[T_v > t_{v,\alpha}] = \alpha$.*

Sometimes we want the **combined area** in left and right tails to equal α. Given the symmetry about 0 of the t distribution we have

$$\Pr[|T_v| > t_{v,\alpha/2}] = \Pr[T_v < -t_{v,\alpha/2}] + \Pr[T_v > t_{v,\alpha/2}] = \alpha/2 + \alpha/2 = \alpha.$$

The **combined area under the curve to the left of $-t_{v,\alpha/2}$ and to the right of $t_{v,\alpha/2}$ equals** α.

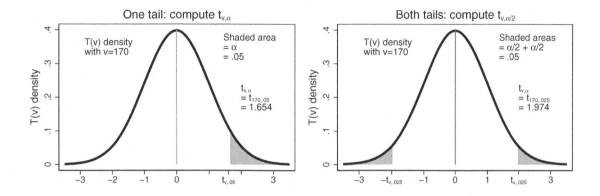

Figure 4.2: Student's t distribution: Critical values $t_{v,\alpha}$ and $t_{v,\alpha/2}$ for $v = 170$ and $\alpha = 0.05$.

For example, $\Pr[T_{170} > 1.974] = 0.025$, so $t_{170,.025} = 1.974$. Combining both tails of the t distribution it follows that $\Pr[|T_{170}| > 1.974] = 0.05$.

The right panel of Figure 4.2 presents the example $\Pr[|T_{170}| > 1.974] = 0.05$. Then the shaded area in each tail is 0.025, $\alpha = 0.05$ is the combined area in the two tails, and the critical value $t_{v,\alpha} = t_{170,.025} = 1.974$ is given on the horizontal axis.

Definition 10 *A t distributed random variable with v degrees of freedom exceeds **in absolute value** the **critical value** $t_{v,\alpha/2}$ with probability α, i.e.* $\Pr[|T_v| > t_{v,\alpha/2}] = \alpha$.

Note that some books define $t_{170,.05}$, for example, to be the .05 quantile or 5th percentile, so the area in the **left tail** of the distribution is .05. Throughout this book, however, $t_{170,.05}$ is that value for which the area in the **right tail** of the distribution is .05. This makes no difference in practice due to the symmetry of the t distribution about zero, for example, $t_{170,.95} = -t_{170,.05}$.

4.3 Confidence Intervals

Different samples will lead to different estimates of the population mean. A confidence interval for an unknown parameter, such as the population mean, gives a range of values that the parameter lies in with a certain "confidence level", defined next.

4.3.1 95% Confidence Interval

A confidence interval for the unknown population mean μ is a range of values that might contain μ with a pre-specified frequency. For example, a 95% confidence interval for μ is a range of values that may contain μ with 95% frequency, i.e. if we had infinitely many samples and constructed infinitely many confidence intervals then 95% of these confidence intervals will include the true value of μ.

Under assumptions 1-3 we have

Definition 11 *A **95 percent confidence interval for the population mean** is*

$$\bar{x} \pm t_{n-1,.025} \times se(\bar{x}),$$

*where $\bar{x}$ is the sample mean; $t_{n-1,.025}$ is that value (called a **critical value**) such that a $T(n-1)$ distributed random variable exceeds it in absolute value with probability 0.025; and $se(\bar{x}) = s/\sqrt{n}$ is the standard error of the sample mean.*

For derivation see Chapter 4.3.3. The confidence interval is centered around $\bar{x}$, the estimate of μ, the sample mean $\bar{x}$, and is symmetric. The use of the $T(n-1)$ distribution is exact under the additional assumption that X is normally distributed; otherwise it is a commonly-used approximation. The specific value $t_{n-1,.025}$ is used since with area 0.025 in each tail the area in the center of the $T(n-1)$ distribution is 0.95, corresponding to 95% confidence.

Intuitively the confidence interval is narrower the more precise is our estimate of μ. This is indeed the case, as from the formula the confidence interval is narrower the smaller is the standard error of $\bar{x}$. In particular, we have the following result.

Remark 11 *The confidence interval narrows as the sample size gets larger, since larger samples lead to a smaller standard error.*

4.3.2   Example: Mean Annual Earnings

For the female annual earnings data in dataset EARNINGS, introduced in Chapter 2, $n = 171$, $\bar{x} = 41413$, $s = 25527$, and $se(\bar{x}) = s/\sqrt{n} = 1952$. From T_{170} tables, $t_{170,.025} = 1.974$.

It follows that a 95% confidence interval for population mean earnings of thirty year-old female full-time workers is

$$\bar{x} \pm t_{n-1,.025} \times se(\bar{x}) = 41413 \pm 1.974 \times 1952 = 41413 \pm 3853 = (37560, 45266).$$

This is the 95% confidence interval that was given in Chapter 4.1.

4.3.3   Derivation of a 95% Confidence Interval

We derive a 95% confidence interval from first principles. For simplicity consider a sample with $n = 61$, in which case $n - 1 = 60$ and $t_{60,.025} = 2.0003$. Thus

$$\Pr[-2.0003 < T_{60} < 2.0003] = 0.95,$$

which we round to $\Pr[-2 < T < 2] = 0.95$. Substituting $T = \frac{\bar{X}-\mu}{S/\sqrt{n}}$ it follows that

$$\Pr\left[-2 < \frac{\bar{X} - \mu}{S/\sqrt{n}} < 2\right] = 0.95.$$

This interval can be converted to an interval that is centered on μ as follows

$$\Pr\left[-2 < \frac{\bar{X}-\mu}{S/\sqrt{n}} < 2\right] = 0.95$$
$$\Rightarrow \quad \Pr\left[-2S/\sqrt{n} < \bar{X}-\mu < 2S/\sqrt{n}\right] = 0.95 \quad \text{multiplying all terms by } S/\sqrt{n}$$
$$\Rightarrow \quad \Pr\left[-\bar{X}-2S/\sqrt{n} < -\mu < -\bar{X}+2S/\sqrt{n}\right] = 0.95 \quad \text{subtracting } \bar{X} \text{ from all terms}$$
$$\Rightarrow \quad \Pr\left[\bar{X}+2S/\sqrt{n} > \mu > \bar{X}-2S/\sqrt{n}\right] = 0.95 \quad \text{multiplying by } -1 \text{ reverses inequalities.}$$

Re-ordering the final inequality yields

$$\Pr\left[\bar{X} - 2 \times S/\sqrt{n} < \mu < \bar{X} + 2 \times S/\sqrt{n}\right] = 0.95.$$

Replacing random variables by their observed values, the interval $(\bar{x} - 2 \times s/\sqrt{n},\ \bar{x} + 2 \times s/\sqrt{n})$ is called a 95% confidence interval for μ.

More generally with sample size n the critical value is $t_{n-1;.025}$. Then a 95% confidence interval is $(\bar{x} - t_{n-1,.025} \times se(\bar{x}),\ \bar{x} + t_{n-1,.025} \times se(\bar{x}))$.

4.3.4 What Level of Confidence?

Ideally there is both a high level of confidence and a narrow confidence interval. For example, having 95% confidence that μ lies between 20 and 40 is preferred to having only 90% confidence that μ lies between 20 and 40. And having 95% confidence that μ lies between 20 and 40 is preferred to having 95% confidence that μ lies in the broader range of 10 to 50.

Unfortunately there is a trade-off between these two considerations. In order to have greater confidence the confidence interval needs to widen. For example, to be 100% confident we can only say that μ lies in the range $(-\infty, \infty)$.

So what value of confidence should be used? There is no best value in general, but **it is most common to use a 95% confidence interval**.

More generally, we consider confidence intervals with **confidence level** $100(1-\alpha)\%$, in which case the critical value is $t_{n-1,\alpha/2}$ since the area in each tail is then $\alpha/2$ leaving area $1-\alpha$ in the center of the $T(n-1)$ distribution.

Definition 12 *A* $100(1-\alpha)$ *percent confidence interval for the population mean is*

$$\bar{x} \pm t_{n-1,\alpha/2} \times se(\bar{x}).$$

The value $\alpha = 0.05$ corresponds to a 95% confidence interval since $100(1-.05) = 100\times0.95 = 95$. The other common choices are to use narrower 90% confidence intervals, with $\alpha = 0.10$, and wider 99% confidence intervals with $\alpha = 0.01$.

Table 4.4 presents the critical value $t_{v,\alpha/2}$ for various confidence levels, corresponding to different values of α, and for selected different numbers of observations, corresponding to different values of $v = n - 1$. The value $t_{v,\alpha/2}$ decreases as the sample size increases. For 95% confidence intervals, presented in bold, the t value is 2.042 for the t_{30} distribution falling to 1.960 for the t_∞ distribution which is equivalent to the standard normal distribution. A detailed table for the t distribution is provided in Table E.2 in Appendix E.

In typical econometrics applications the sample size $n > 30$, in which case from Table 4.4 the critical value $t_{n-1,.025}$ approximately equals 2. This leads to the following.

Table 4.4: Student's t distribution: Critical values for various degrees of freedom and confidence levels.

Confidence Level	$100(1 - \alpha)$	90%	95%	99%
Area in both tails	α	0.10	**0.05**	0.01
Area in single tail	$\alpha/2$	0.05	**0.025**	0.005
t value for $v = 10$	$t_{10,\alpha/2}$	1.812	**2.228**	3.169
t value for $v = 30$	$t_{30,\alpha/2}$	1.697	**2.042**	2.750
t value for $v = 100$	$t_{100,\alpha/2}$	1.660	**1.984**	2.626
t value for $v = \infty$	$t_{\infty,\alpha/2}$	1.645	**1.960**	2.576
standard normal value	$z_{\alpha/2}$	1.645	**1.960**	2.576

Remark 12 *It is most common, though arbitrary, to use a 95% confidence interval. An **approximate 95% confidence interval** for the population mean is a **two standard error interval**: the sample mean plus or minus two times the standard error.*

This is a useful guide. And it makes clear that if we are willing to tolerate an error range of plus or minus two standard errors, then a good choice of the confidence level is 95%. In any published work or in assignments, however, use the more precise interval $\bar{x} \pm t_{n-1,.025} \times se(\bar{x})$.

Confidence intervals at different levels of confidence are easily obtained using a statistical package. For example, a 90% confidence interval for earnings can be obtained using the Stata command `mean earnings, level(90)`.

4.3.5   Interpretation of Confidence Intervals

Interpretation of confidence intervals is conceptually difficult. With a given sample we can only form one confidence interval, which will either correctly include the true unknown mean μ or not include μ. A 95% confidence interval is constructed so that it includes μ with probability 0.95.

To understand this interpretation it is necessary to imagine that there are many separate samples of the population, each of size $n = 171$ in this example. From each sample we form a 95% confidence interval. Then we expect that on average 95% of such confidence intervals will include the true (unknown) mean μ.

For the 1880 Census example in Chapter 3.5 we know $\mu = 24.13$. Further analysis of the 100 samples of size 25 summarized in dataset CENSUSAGEMEANS yields a 95% confidence interval (19.29, 36.39) for the first sample, (12.79, 26.00) for the second sample, and so on. In total 91 of the 100 samples had 95% confidence intervals that included $\mu = 24.13$. For example, the 20th sample had 95% confidence interval (7.70, 22.38) that does not include $\mu = 24.13$. In theory we expect 95% of the 95% confidence intervals to include μ. The reason 91% rather than 95% included μ reflects randomness with just 100 confidence intervals, and that the $T(24)$ distribution for the t statistic is not exact for these right-skewed data. If we had obtained one million 95% confidence intervals, say, and the t statistic was exactly $T(24)$ distributed, then very close to 95% of these intervals would include μ. Similarly, for the coin toss example in Chapter 3.3, 388 of the 400 95% confidence intervals, or 97%, included the true parameter value $\mu = 0.5$.

As these examples demonstrate, a confidence interval will sometimes fail to include the population mean μ, due to the randomness inherent in sampling. A 95 percent confidence interval has the property that if we were able to obtain many separate random samples, then 95 percent of the resulting confidence intervals will include the population mean μ, and 5 percent will not.

In fact we have only one sample, and we say that the calculated 95 percent confidence interval from this sample includes the true population mean μ with probability 0.95. This probabilistic statement refers to the confidence interval, which is random, and not to μ which is fixed. It is **wrong** to instead interpret this confidence interval as meaning that with probability 0.95 the population mean μ lies inside (\$37,560, \$45,266) and with probability 0.05 it lies outside this range.

Remark 13 *A calculated 95 percent confidence interval for the population mean is an interval that if constructed for each of an infinite number of samples will include the true population mean μ 95% of the time (and will not include μ 5% of the time).*

4.4 Two-Sided Hypothesis Tests

4.4.1 Null and Alternative Hypotheses

The particular hypothesis under test is called the **null hypothesis** and is denoted H_0. The alternative to the hypothesis test is called the **alternative hypothesis** and is denoted H_a.

Here we consider test of whether μ takes a particular value. Let μ^* denote this value. Then the null hypothesis is $H_0 : \mu = \mu^*$, and the alternative hypothesis is $H_a : \mu \neq \mu^*$. Because the alternative hypothesis includes both $\mu < \mu^*$ and $\mu > \mu^*$ the test is called a two-sided test.

For example, consider the claim that population mean earnings equal \$40,000. To test this claim we test $H_0 : \mu = 40000$ against $H_a : \mu \neq 40000$.

Definition 13 *A **two-sided test** or **two-tailed test** for the mean μ is a test of the null hypothesis*

$$H_0 : \mu = \mu^*,$$

where μ^* is a specified value for μ, against the alternative hypothesis

$$H_a : \mu \neq \mu^*.$$

4.4.2 Significance Level of a Test

The result of a test is to either reject or not reject the null hypothesis.

This decision made may be in error. In particular, we may reject the null hypothesis when in fact it was true. This type of error is called a **type I error**.

For example, suppose the null hypothesis is that someone is innocent. Then a type I error is made if we reject the null and find the person guilty, when in fact the person was innocent. Similarly if the null hypothesis is that a person does not have a disease, then a type I error is to find disease when in fact none is present.

In the earnings example a type I error occurs if we reject $H_0 : \mu = 40000$ when in fact $\mu = 40000$.

Definition 14 *A **type I error** occurs if H_0 is rejected when H_0 is true.*

Ideally the probability of making a type I error is small. The following terminology is used.

Definition 15 *The **significance level** of a test or **test size**, denoted α, is the pre-specified maximum probability of a type I error that will be tolerated.*

The level of statistical significance to use is discussed in some length in a later section. It is most common to tolerate up to a 5% chance of making a type I error, in which case $\alpha = 0.05$.

Whatever the choice of α, we reject H_0 at significance level α if the probability of making a type I error is less than 0.05, and do not reject H_0 otherwise.

Note that if we do not reject the null hypothesis then we simply say that we "fail to reject the null hypothesis." We do not say that we "accept the null hypothesis." The reason for doing so is that there are other null hypotheses that we also fail to reject. For example, in the earnings example we show below that we do not reject $H_0 : \mu = 40000$. But for these data other null hypotheses, such as $H_0 : \mu = 41000$, will also be not rejected at level 0.05.

4.4.3 The t Statistic

The obvious decision rule is to reject the hypothesis that the mean equals μ^* if the sample mean $\bar{x}$ is far from μ^*. For example, we are much more likely to reject $H_0 : \mu = 40000$ if $\bar{x} = 80000$ than if, say, $\bar{x} = 45000$. So we form a test based on the difference $(\bar{x} - \mu^*)$.

Furthermore, the more precise $\bar{x}$ is as an estimate of μ, the more likely we are to reject H_0 for a given size of $(\bar{x} - \mu^*)$. The test statistic we use therefore normalizes by the standard error of $\bar{x}$. We therefore use the t statistic

$$t = \frac{\bar{x} - \mu^*}{se(\bar{x})}.$$

This has the additional advantage that we know t is the realization of a random variable that is $T(n-1)$ distributed.

Remark 14 *The t **statistic** for test of $H_0 : \mu = \mu^*$ against $H_a : \mu \neq \mu^*$ is $t = (\bar{x} - \mu^*)/se(\bar{x})$. Under $H_0 : \mu = \mu^*$, and assuming simple random sampling, t is the realization of a random variable that is approximately $T(n-1)$ distributed.*

For the data on earnings of 30 year-old female full-time workers in 2010 in the United States, $n = 171$, $\bar{x} = 41413$ and $se(\bar{x}) = 1952$.

For test of $H_0 : \mu = 40000$, the t statistic is therefore

$$t = \frac{\bar{x} - 40000}{se(\bar{x})} = \frac{41413 - 40000}{1952} = 0.724.$$

This is the value t=0.7237 obtained in Chapter 4.1. Under the null hypothesis, that $\mu = 40000$, the t statistic is a draw from the T_{170} distribution, since $n - 1 = 170$.

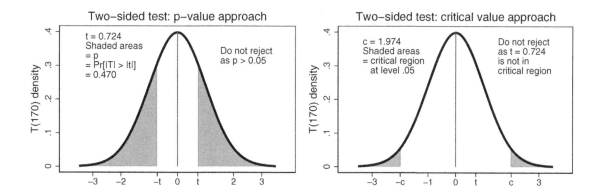

Figure 4.3: Two-sided hypothesis test: p-value approach and critical value approach

4.4.4 Rejection using p-values

We reject the null hypothesis if the t statistic is unusually large in absolute value. How unusual the value is can be determined since, under the null hypothesis, t is the realization of a $T(n-1)$ distributed random variable. If the value is so large as to be very unlikely to arise then our hypothesis that $\mu = \mu^*$ is most likely wrong and we reject the null hypothesis.

Definition 16 *The p-**value** is the probability of observing a t statistic at least as large in absolute value as that obtained in the current sample. For a two-sided test of $H_0 : \mu = \mu^*$ against $H_a : \mu \neq \mu^*$ the p-value is $p = \Pr[|T_{n-1}| \geq |t|]$.*

Definition 17 *H_0 is rejected at significance level α if $p < \alpha$, and is not rejected otherwise.*

Continuing immediately with the earnings example, we found that $t = 0.724$. Then

$$p = \Pr[|T_{170}| \geq 0.724] = 0.470.$$

This is the value `Pr(|T|>|t|)=0.4703` obtained in Chapter 4.1. There is high probability ($p = 0.470$) of observing a t value of 0.724 or larger in absolute value, even if the mean really is the hypothesized value of \$40,000. Since $p > 0.05$ we do not reject the null hypothesis that $\mu = 40000$ at significance level 0.05.

The left panel of Figure 4.3 displays the probability that $|T_{170}|$ exceeds the observed t statistic of 0.724.

We are more likely to reject the null hypothesis the larger is the absolute value of the t statistic. So, other things equal, we are more likely to reject the null hypothesis the smaller is $se(\bar{x})$, since computation of t entails division by $se(\bar{x})$. So a larger sample is better, as then $se(\bar{x})$ is smaller.

Remark 15 *More precise estimation of μ, such as through a larger sample size, makes it more likely that the null hypothesis is rejected.*

72 CHAPTER 4. STATISTICAL INFERENCE FOR THE MEAN

4.4.5 Rejection using Critical Regions

The p-value method requires access to a computer, in order to precisely compute the p-value for any possible value of t. Before widespread access to computers, an alternative method was used that, for given significance level α, leads to the same conclusion.

This **alternative method** defines a **critical region** or **rejection region**, which is the range of values of t that would lead to rejection of H_0 at the specified significance level α. Then reject H_0 if the computed value of t falls in this range.

Definition 18 *For a two-sided test of $H_0 : \mu = \mu^*$ against $H_a : \mu \neq \mu^*$, and for specified significance level α, the **critical value** c is such that $c = t_{n-1,\alpha/2}$; equivalently $\Pr[|T_{n-1}| \geq c] = \alpha$.*

Definition 19 *H_0 is rejected at significance level α if $|t| > c$, and is not rejected otherwise.*

Return to the female earnings example. For significance level 0.05 and $n - 1 = 170$, the critical value

$$c = t_{170,.025} = 1.974.$$

H_0 is not rejected at significance level 0.05, since $t = 0.724$ does not exceed 1.974 in absolute value. This conclusion is the same as that using the p-value approach.

The shaded region in the right panel of Figure 4.3 shows the rejection region, the range of values for which $|T_{170}|$ exceeds 1.974 since this occurs with probability 0.05. The sample t statistic equals 0.724 which does not fall in the shaded region. So we do not reject H_0.

It is important to note that the p-value and critical region approaches lead to the same conclusion, since $|t| > t_{n-1,\alpha/2}$ is equivalent to $p < \alpha$.

The critical value approach has the advantage that it does not require computing the p-value for any possible value of t. Instead one can refer to a reasonable-sized printed table for the t distribution at just a few selected probability values. Typically t tables are given for area in the right tail equal to 0.25, 0.10, 0.05, 0.01, and 0.005, and for all degrees of freedom from 1 to 30, every fifth integer from 30 to 60, then 70, 80, 90, 100 and ∞. To alternatively calculate p-values for a wide range of values of t would require many, many pages of tables.

The p-value approach is preferred as given p, the reader can easily test using his or her own preferred value of α. The alternative critical value method was developed for an earlier time when reliance on published tables made it difficult to accurately calculate p-values.

4.4.6 Which Significance Level?

Decreasing the significance level α makes it less likely that the null hypothesis is rejected. This should be clear from, for example, the second panel of Figure 4.3, where the rejection region will get smaller as the error α in the two tails gets smaller. What significance level should be used?

Remark 16 *It is most common to use $\alpha = 0.05$, called a test at the 5% significance level. Then a type I error is made 1 in 20 times.*

This is a convention and in many applications other values of α may be warranted. For example, in testing the null hypothesis that there will be no nuclear war the significance level may be chosen to be much higher than 0.05, since the consequence of incorrectly failing to reject the null hypothesis is so high. Reporting p-values allows the reader to easily test using their own preferred value of α.

4.4.7 Relationship to Confidence Interval

Two-sided tests can be implemented using confidence intervals. If the null hypothesis value μ^* falls inside the $100(1 - \alpha)$ percent confidence interval then do not reject H_0 at significance level α. Otherwise reject H_0 at significance level α.

For the female earnings data, from Table 4.2 the 95 percent confidence interval for population mean female earnings is $(37559, 45266)$. Since this interval includes 40000 we do not reject $H_0 : \mu = 40000$ at significance level 0.05.

4.4.8 Summary

A summary of the preceding earnings hypothesis test example is the following.

Hypotheses	$H_0 : \mu = 40000$, $H_a : \mu \neq 40000$
Significance level	$\alpha = 0.05$
Data	$\bar{x} = 41413$, $s = 25527$, $n = 171$
Test statistic	$t = (41413 - 40000)/(25527/\sqrt{171}) = 0.724$
(1) p-value approach	$p = \Pr[|T_{170}| \geq |0.724|] = 0.470$
(2) Critical value approach	$c = t_{170,.025} = 1.974$
Conclusion	Do not reject H_0 at level .05 as (1) $p > .05$ or (2) $|t| < c$.

The p-value and critical value approaches are alternative methods that for test at the same significance level always lead to the same conclusion.

4.5 Two-sided Hypothesis Test Examples

We consider three examples of two-sided hypothesis tests. Additionally we discuss complications that can arise – survey data should be from a representative sample and, for time series data, the standard error of the mean, $se(\bar{x})$, may no longer equal $s/\sqrt{n}$. The tests are computed manually here; more simply one can use a command such as the Stata `ttest` command.

4.5.1 Example: Gasoline Prices

Test the claim that the mean price of regular gasoline in Yolo County is neither higher nor lower than the norm for California.

The dataset GASPRICE comes from a website that provides daily data on gas prices. Data are available for 32 Yolo County gas stations on a day when the average price for all California gas stations was \$3.81. Descriptive statistics are given in Table 4.5. The standard error of the sample mean $se(\bar{x}) = s/\sqrt{n} = 0.1510/\sqrt{32} = .0267$.

Table 4.5: Summary Statistics: Gasoline price per gallon at 32 gas stations.

Variable	Obs	Mean	St. Dev.	Min	Max
Earnings	32	3.6697	0.1510	3.49	4.09

The null hypothesis is $\mu = 3.81$, tested against the alternative $\mu \neq 3.81$. The t statistic is

$$t = \frac{3.6697 - 3.81}{.0267} = -5.256.$$

Large values of t in absolute value favor the alternative, as then $\bar{x}$ is very different from 3.81. Using the p-value method we have

$$p = \Pr[|T_{31}| > |-5.256|] = 0.000.$$

We reject H_0 at level .05 since $p < .05$. Using the critical value method

$$c = t_{31,.025} = 2.040.$$

We reject H_0 at level .05 since $|t| = 5.256 > c = 2.040$. Therefore the claim that population mean Yolo County gas prices equal the California state-average price is rejected at significance level 0.05.

4.5.2   Example: Male Earnings

Test the claim that population mean earnings of male full-time workers in 2010 are $50,000.

The dataset EARNINGSMALE is a small subsample from the very large American Community Survey (ACS). The subsample is selected in such a way that it is a simple random sample of the population of 30 year-old male full-time workers in 2010. Descriptive statistics are given in Table 4.6. The minimum value of 1,000 is possible as the person was self-employed. The next lowest value was 8,000. The standard error of the sample mean $se(\bar{x}) = s/\sqrt{n} = 65034.74/\sqrt{191} = 4705.748$.

Table 4.6: Summary Statistics: Annual earnings of male full-time workers aged 30 in 2010.

Variable	Obs	Mean	St. Dev.	Min	Max
Earnings	191	52353.93	65034.74	1010	498000

The test is of $H_0 : \mu = 50000$ against $H_a : \mu \neq 50000$. The t statistic is

$$t = \frac{52353.93 - 50000}{4705.748} = .5002.$$

Large absolute values of t favor the alternative, as then $\bar{x}$ is much greater than 50000. Here

$$p = \Pr[|T_{190}| > .500] = 0.618.$$

We do not reject H_0 at level .05 since $p = .618$ is not less than .05. Alternatively, the critical value

$$c = t_{190,.025} = 1.973.$$

We do not reject H_0 at level .05 since $|t| = .500$ is not less than $c = 1.973$. The data do not support the claim that population mean earnings are more than \$50,000 at significance level .05.

Note that it is important that the sample be a representative sample. National government-sponsored surveys are usually not representative of the U.S. population, as they tend to oversample low population segments of interest to policy-makers, such as racial minorities, people with low income, and people in low population states. This is likely to lead to over-sampling of low-earnings individuals.

For **nonrepresentative samples** with sampling weights we should base inference on the sample mean $\bar{x}_w$ and its standard error $se(\bar{x}_w)$ that are defined in Chapter 3.7. Then the $100(1 - \alpha)\%$ confidence interval for μ is $\bar{x}_w \pm t_{n-1,\alpha/2} \times se(\bar{x}_w)$ and the t statistic becomes $t = (\bar{x}_w - \mu^*)/se(\bar{x}_w)$.

This issue was avoided in this illustrative example, however, by using the sampling weights to select a subset of the original ACS dataset in a way that ensured that the sample considered here is a representative sample of 30 year-old males. Similarly the female earnings data analyzed in Chapters 2-4 were selected in such a way as to be a representative sample.

4.5.3 Example: Growth in U.S. real GDP per capita

Test the claim that the annual growth rate in U.S. real GDP per capita averaged 2.0% over the period 1959 to 2020. Do the test at significance level $\alpha = .05$.

We use dataset REALGDPPC introduced in Chapter 2.6. Here we use the year-to-year percentage changes in real per capita GDP, calculated as $100 \times (y_t - y_{t-4})/y_{t-4}$ where y_{t-4} denotes the variable four periods earlier. Descriptive statistics are given in Table 4.7. Assuming observations are independent, the standard error $se(\bar{x}) = 2.1781/\sqrt{241} = 0.1403$.

Table 4.7: Summary Statistics: Annual growth rate in U.S. real GDP per capita using quarterly data from 1959 to 2020.

Variable	Obs	Mean	St. Dev.	Min	Max
Growth	241	1.9904	2.1781	-4.77	7.63

The null hypothesis is $\mu = 2.0$, tested against the alternative $\mu \neq 2.0$. The t statistic is

$$t = \frac{1.9904 - 2.0}{.1403} = -0.068.$$

Large absolute values of t favor the alternative hypothesis, as then $\bar{x}$ is very different from 2.0. Using the p-value method we have

$$p = \Pr[|T_{240}| > |-0.068|] = 0.946.$$

We do not reject H_0 at level .05 since $p > .05$. Using the critical value method

$$c = t_{240,.025} = 1.970.$$

We do not reject H_0 at level .05 since $|t| = 0.068 < c = 1.970$. Therefore we do not reject the claim that population mean growth rate was 2.0% at significance level 0.05.

An important caveat in this example is that the underlying theory assumes that observations in the sample are statistically independent or unrelated with each other. In fact for time series data there can be dependence as, for example, high growth in one quarter is likely to recur again the next quarter. Failure to control for this dependence can lead to an overestimate of the precision of estimation, i.e. the reported standard error is too small.

Inference for time series regression, introduced in Chapter 12.1, provide statistical methods that are valid even with such dependence. In this particular example there is very high dependence from one quarter to the next, and appropriate methods lead to much larger standard error of $\bar{x}$. From Chapter 12.1, allowing for this complication yields $se(\bar{x}) = 0.275$ which is about twice as large. Then $t = (1.9904 - 2.0)/.275 = -0.35$. With this adjustment H_0 is still not rejected at level .05.

4.6   One-Sided Directional Hypothesis Tests

A two-sided test is called two-sided as both $\mu < \mu^*$ or $\mu > \mu^*$ are included as alternatives to the null hypothesis. For a **one-sided hypothesis test** the alternative considered is only that $\mu < \mu^*$ or only that $\mu > \mu^*$.

A two-sided hypothesis test is non-directional, as rejection may be due to concluding that either $\mu > \mu^*$ or $\mu < \mu^*$. A one-sided test, by contrast, is directional. For example, we may test against the alternative that $\mu > \mu^*$.

For a one-sided directional hypothesis test care needs to be used in specifying the null and alternative hypotheses as the conclusion can differ according to which hypothesis is set up as the null and which is the alternative. As justified below, the following rule is used.

Remark 17 *For one-sided tests the statement being tested is specified to be the alternative hypothesis. And if a new theory is put forward to supplant an old, the new theory is specified to be the alternative hypothesis.*

For example, if we wish to test the claim that the population mean earnings exceed \$40,000, we should test $H_0 : \mu \leq 40000$ against $H_a : \mu > 40000$. By contrast, to test the claim that the population mean earnings are less than \$40,000, we should test $H_0 : \mu \geq 40000$ against $H_a : \mu < 40000$.

Definition 20 *An **upper one-tailed alternative test** is a test of $H_0 : \mu \leq \mu^*$, where μ^* is a specified value for μ, against $H_a : \mu > \mu^*$. A **lower one-tailed alternative test** is a test of $H_0 : \mu \geq \mu^*$ against $H_a : \mu < \mu^*$.*

Some textbooks instead define the null hypothesis of a one-sided test to be $H_0 : \mu = \mu^*$. For example, an upper one-tailed test is a test of $H_0 : \mu = \mu^*$ against $H_0 : \mu > \mu^*$. This alternative notation makes no difference to the subsequent analysis.

4.6.1 P-values and Critical Regions

Inference for both types of one-sided test is based on the same calculated test statistic

$$t = \frac{\bar{x} - \mu^*}{se(\bar{x})},$$

as used for two-sided hypothesis tests. As usual this statistic is viewed as being the realization of a $T(n-1)$ distributed random variable. What differs in the one-sided case is calculation of the p-values and critical values.

For an **upper** one-tailed alternative test, large positive values of t are grounds for rejection of H_0, since then $\bar{x}$ (the estimate of μ) is much larger than μ^*. Thus the p-value is the probability of being in the upper tail of the $T(n-1)$ distribution, so $p = \Pr[T_{n-1} \geq t]$. And the critical region for a test at significance level α is $t > c$ where c is such that $\Pr[T_{n-1} > c] = \alpha$ and is denoted $c = t_{n-1,\alpha}$. H_0 is rejected at significance level α if $p < \alpha$ or, equivalently, if $t > c$.

For a **lower** one-tailed alternative test large negative values of t lead to rejection of H_0, since then $\bar{x}$ is much smaller than μ^*, and the test procedure is appropriately modified.

Definition 21 *Let t be the usual t statistic. For an upper one-tailed alternative test the p-value is $p = \Pr[T_{n-1} \geq t]$, the critical value at significance level α is $c = t_{n-1,\alpha}$, and we reject H_0 if $p < \alpha$ or, equivalently, if $t > c$. For a lower one-tailed alternative test the p-value is $p = \Pr[T_{n-1} \leq t]$, the critical value at significance level α is $c = -t_{n-1,\alpha}$, and we reject H_0 if $p < \alpha$ or, equivalently, if $t < c$.*

A one-sided test is a more focused test that, at given significance level, requires less evidence to reject the null hypothesis, provided the test statistic t is in the correct tail of the distribution.

For example, consider an upper one-tail alternative test and suppose $t = 1.8$ and $n = 31$. We reject H_0 at significance level 0.05 since $p = \Pr[T_{30} > 1.8] = 0.041 < 0.05$, whereas with a two-sided test we would not reject as $p = \Pr[|T_{30}| > |1.8|] = 2 \times 0.041 = 0.082 > 0.05$.

4.6.2 Example: Mean Annual Earnings

Suppose we wish to evaluate the claim that the population mean exceeds \$40,000. A test of this claim is implemented as a test of $H_0 : \mu \leq 40000$ against $H_a : \mu > 40000$, an example of an upper one-tailed alternative test.

The t statistic has already been calculated as $t = 0.724$. Large positive values of t support rejection of H_0 since then $\bar{x}$ is much greater than the hypothesized population mean value of \$40,000.

The p-value, the probability that a t distributed random variable exceeds the observed t value of 0.724, is

$$p = \Pr[T_{170} \geq .724] = 0.235.$$

Since p is larger than 0.05, we do not reject H_0 at significance level 0.05. The p-value is the shaded region in the left panel of Figure 4.4.

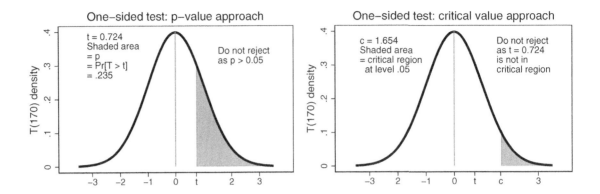

Figure 4.4: One-sided directional hypothesis test (upper one-tailed alternative): p-value approach and critical value apporach

Using the alternative equivalent critical value method instead, the critical value c solves $\Pr[T_{170} \geq c] = 0.05$ if testing is at the significance level 0.05. Then

$$c = t_{170,.05} = 1.654.$$

We do not reject H_0 at significance level 0.05, since $t = 0.724 \leq 1.654$. The critical region is the shaded area in the in the right panel of Figure 4.4.

Using either method we do not reject at significance level 0.05 the null hypothesis that the population mean earnings is less than or equal to \$40,000. There is not enough evidence to support the initial claim that mean earnings exceed \$40,000.

4.6.3 Specifying the Null Hypothesis for One-Sided Tests

This more difficult section explains why the statement being tested is specified as the alternative hypothesis.

Suppose the claim is made that population mean earnings are more than \$40,000. Should we perform an upper one-tailed alternative test or a lower one-tailed alternative test?

There are two potential ways to proceed, though only the first should be used as explained in what follows.

1. Test $H_0 : \mu \leq 40000$ against $H_a : \mu > 40000$.

2. Test $H_0 : \mu \geq 40000$ against $H_a : \mu < 40000$.

Suppose we take the first approach. The claim that $\mu > 40000$ is supported if H_0 is rejected. Rejection of H_0 requires a sample mean of considerably more than 40000, say $\bar{x} > 43000$. Suppose instead the second approach is taken. Then the claim is supported if H_0 is not rejected. Rejection of H_0 requires a sample mean of considerably less than 40000, say $\bar{x} < 37000$ (by symmetry). Non-rejection of H_0 then occurs if $\bar{x} > 37000$. Thus the claim that $\mu > 40000$ is supported if $\bar{x} > 37000$.

To summarize, the claim is that mean earnings exceed $40,000. The first specification of the null and alternative hypotheses leads to support of the claim if the sample average exceeds $43,000, while the second specification leads to support of the claim if the sample average exceeds $37,000. The philosophy of hypothesis testing is to require strong evidence to support a claim. The first specification is therefore used, with the claim made specified as the alternative hypothesis.

Remark 18 *For one-sided tests the claim being tested is specified to be the alternative hypothesis, as stronger evidence is then needed to support the claim than if the claim was set up as the null hypothesis.*

There can be considerable debate as to which hypothesis should be the null. For example, suppose we wish to determine whether women at a workplace have been discriminated against, a not unusual issue to be determined in court. One approach is to specify the alternative hypothesis to be that women are paid less than men (the claim made) while another approach is to specify this as the null hypothesis. Lawyers for the employer may favor the first approach, lawyers for the employee may favor the second approach, and the statistical methodology presented here selects the first approach.

4.7 Generalization of Confidence Intervals and Hypothesis Tests

Confidence intervals and hypothesis tests can be applied to parameters other than the population mean μ. Leading examples include the difference in two means $(\mu_2 - \mu_1)$, and the slope of a regression line, the subject of many later chapters. The approach for inference on μ extends easily to such settings.

4.7.1 Generalizations of Confidence Intervals

Inference on μ is based on $t = (\bar{x} - \mu)/se(\bar{x})$. In words, the t statistic equals the estimate minus the parameter divided by the standard error, where the standard error measures how precisely the parameter has been estimated. More generally we have the following result.

Remark 19 *For the estimators presented in this book, for sufficiently large sample size the statistic*

$$t = \frac{estimate - parameter}{standard\ error}$$

is a realization of a random variable that is approximately $T(v)$ distributed, where the degrees of freedom v for the t distribution varies with the application, and the standard error is the estimated standard deviation of the estimate.

A $100(1 - \alpha)\%$ confidence interval for μ is $\bar{x} \pm t_{v,\alpha/2} \times se(\bar{x})$. This generalizes as follows.

Remark 20 *A* $100(1 - \alpha)\%$ *confidence interval for the unknown parameter is*

$$estimate \pm t_{v,\alpha/2} \times standard\ error.$$

The most commonly-used confidence level is 95 percent and $t_{v,.025} \simeq 2$ for $v > 30$. This immediately leads to the following simple rule-of-thumb.

Remark 21 *An approximate 95% confidence interval for the unknown parameter is the two-standard error interval*

$$estimate \pm 2 \times standard\ error.$$

The term **margin of error** is used to describe the half-width of a confidence interval, or $t_{v,\alpha/2} \times se(\cdot)$. The term is most often used in the context of 95% confidence intervals, since these are the most commonly-used confidence intervals. Then since $t_{v,.025} \simeq 2$,

$$Margin\ of\ error = 2 \times Standard\ error.$$

As an example of the above, suppose the sample estimate of a parameter θ is 11 with standard error of the estimate equal to 3, and the sample size is large. Then an approximate 95% confidence interval for θ is $11 \pm 2 \times 3$ or $(5, 17)$. Since the standard error is 3, the margin of error is said to be $2 \times 3 = 6$, or ± 6.

4.7.2   Generalizations of Hypothesis Tests

For hypothesis testing we again use the more general form of the t statistic, assumed to be approximately $T(v)$ distributed.

Remark 22 *Consider a two-sided test at significance level* α *of the null hypothesis* (H_0) *that a parameter equals a hypothesized value against the alternative hypothesis* (H_a) *that it does not. Calculate the t statistic*

$$t = \frac{estimate - hypothesized\ parameter\ value}{standard\ error}.$$

Under the null hypothesis t is the sample realization of a random variable that is approximately $T(v)$ *distributed. The p-value approach is to reject* H_0 *if* $p < \alpha$ *where* $p = \Pr[|T_v| > |t|]$. *The critical value approach is to reject* H_0 *if* $|t| > c$ *where* $c = t_{v,\alpha/2}$ *satisfies* $\Pr[T_v > t_{v,\alpha/2}] = \alpha$. *For given* α, *the two methods lead to the same conclusion.*

This generalizes inference for the mean, where the estimate is $\bar{x}$, the parameter is μ, the standard error is $se(\bar{x}) = s/\sqrt{n}$, and $v = n - 1$.

Continuing the earlier example with estimate of θ equal to 11 and standard error of 3, for a test of whether or not $\theta = 20$ the t statistic is $t = (11 - 20)/3 = -3$. We will reject $H_0 : \theta = 20$ at level 0.05 since (for all but very small v) the $T(v)$ critical value is approximately 2 and $|-3| = 3 > 2$.

For both confidence intervals and hypothesis tests, the standard normal distribution is sometimes used rather than the $T(v)$ distribution. The difference between $T(v)$ and standard normal disappears as $v \to \infty$.

4.8 Proportions Data

As an example of adaptation or extension of methods for the sample mean, consider analysis of **proportions data** that are data on the fraction of times that a given event occurs. Economic examples are unemployment rates and employment rates, and a common example in the media are political opinion polls on the fraction intending to vote for a given political candidate.

4.8.1 Analysis using General Results for the Sample Mean

Statistical inference on these data can be done using the methods of this chapter. The sample proportion is viewed as the sample mean $\bar{x}$ of data that take only the value 0 or 1, such as 1 if an individual in the sample intends to vote Democrat and 0 otherwise.

The computational formula for the sample variance is $s^2 = \frac{1}{n-1}\{\sum_{i=1}^{n} x_i^2 - n\bar{x}^2\}$; see Chapter 2.1 Since x_i takes only values 0 or 1, $\sum_{i=1}^{n} x_i^2 = \sum_{i=1}^{n} x_i = n\bar{x}$, so $\sum_{i=1}^{n} x_i^2 - n\bar{x}^2 = n\bar{x}(1-\bar{x})$ and the sample variance equals $s^2 = n\bar{x}(1-\bar{x})/(n-1)$. It follows that the standard error of the sample mean $se(\bar{x}) = s/\sqrt{n} = \sqrt{\bar{x}(1-\bar{x})/(n-1)}$.

For proportions data the mean parameter μ is denoted p (for proportion). Then applying the results of this chapter for the sample mean, a $100 \times (1-\alpha)\%$ confidence interval for p is $\bar{x} \pm t_{\alpha/2;n-1} \times \sqrt{\bar{x}(1-\bar{x})/(n-1)}$. And a hypothesis test of whether or not $p = p^*$ can be based on the statistic $t = (\bar{x} - p^*)/\sqrt{\bar{x}(1-\bar{x})/(n-1)}$ which is viewed as the realization of a $T(n-1)$ distributed random variable.

4.8.2 Analysis using Results Specific to Proportions Data

Statistical packages often have procedures specific to proportions data that yield slightly different results to the preceding analysis. So we detail these procedures.

For proportions data the underlying random variable X for each surveyed individual is viewed as taking value 1 with probability p and value 0 with probability $1 - p$. This is the Bernoulli distribution with population mean $\mu = p$ and population variance $\sigma^2 = p(1-p)$; see Appendix B.1. For example, we may let $X = 1$ if the person intends to vote Democrat and $X = 0$ otherwise, so then p is the unknown population probability of voting for a Democrat candidate. The Bernoulli result that $\sigma^2 = p(1-p)$ implies that $Var[\bar{X}] = \sigma^2/n = p(1-p)/n$ which can be estimated by replacing p by an estimate.

For confidence intervals we estimate p by $\bar{x}$ leading to $se(\bar{x}) = \sqrt{\bar{x}(1-\bar{x})/n}$, rather than $\sqrt{\bar{x}(1-\bar{x})/(n-1)}$ given earlier. Furthermore it is most common to use critical values from the normal distribution. Then a $100 \times (1-\alpha)\%$ confidence interval for p is most often $\bar{x} \pm z_{\alpha/2} \times \sqrt{\bar{x}(1-\bar{x})/n}$.

For large n, often the case for proportions data such as political polling data, this confidence interval will be quite similar to that obtained using the earlier general result for the sample mean. First, the $z_{\alpha/2}$ and $t_{\alpha/2;n-1}$ critical values are very close for large n. Second, for large n the different estimates of $se(\bar{x})$ are very similar as division by n is then very similar to division by $n-1$.

For testing hypotheses on p it is most common to estimate $Var[\bar{X}] = p(1-p)/n$ by replacing p by the hypothesized value p^* (rather than by $\bar{x}$). Then $se(\bar{x}) = \sqrt{p^*(1-p^*)/n}$ and a two-sided hypothesis test of $H_0 : p = p^*$ against $H_a : p \neq p^*$ is based on the statistic $z = \frac{\bar{x}-p^*}{\sqrt{p^*(1-p^*)/n}}$ which is $N(0,1)$ distributed under H_0.

The standard normal approximation is felt to be good if both $np > 10$ and $n(1-p) > 10$. Thus for low p or high p considerably more than 30 observations are needed. For polling data and for most economics applications with proportions data there are many observations, so the approximation will be good. (If instead n is too small then hypothesis tests can use exact statistical inference on p based on the binomial distribution; this is not presented here.)

4.8.3 Example: Voting Intentions

Suppose we have a random sample of 921 voters of whom 480 intend to vote Democrat and 441 who intend to vote Republican. For statistical inference we use the special approach for proportions data.

For these data $\bar{x} = [480 \times 1 + 441 \times 0]/921 = 0.5212$ and $se(\bar{x}) = \sqrt{\bar{x}(1-\bar{x})/n} = 0.01646$. For the standard normal, $z_{.025} = 1.960$. So a 95% confidence interval for the population mean proportion of Democrat voters is $0.5212 \pm 1.960 \times 0.01646 = (0.4889, 0.5535)$. Equivalently, a 95% confidence interval for the population percentage of voters who intend to vote Democrat is (48.9%, 55.3%).

Now suppose we wish to test the belief that the Democrat candidate will win the election. This is a one-sided test with the belief specified to be the alternative hypothesis. Thus we test $H_0 : p \leq 0.5$ against $H_a : p > 0.5$. For hypothesis testing we use $se(\bar{x}) = \sqrt{p^*(1-p^*)/n}$, where $p^* = 0.5$, so the test statistic $z = \frac{0.5212-0.5}{\sqrt{0.5 \times (1-0.5)/921}} = 1.287$. Then $p = \Pr[|Z| > 1.287] = 0.198$ exceeds 0.05 so we do not reject the null hypothesis at significance level 0.05. Alternatively, the critical value $c = z_{.025} = 1.964$, and we do not reject H_0 at level .05 since $|z| = 1.287 < c$. We cannot conclude that the Democrat candidate will win the election at significance level 0.05.

4.8.4 Margin of Error of an Opinion Poll

The margin of error often reported alongside an opinion poll is two times the standard error, the approximate half-width of a 95% confidence interval. For proportions data $\bar{x}(1-\bar{x}) \leq 0.25$ since $\bar{x}(1-\bar{x})$ takes a maximum value of 0.25 when $\bar{x} = 0.5$. It follows that $se(\bar{x}) = \sqrt{\bar{x}(1-\bar{x})/n} \leq \sqrt{0.25/n} = 0.5/\sqrt{n}$, so the margin of error is at most $1/\sqrt{n}$.

Published opinion polls typically interview between 600 and 2,000 people. Then the corresponding maximum margin of error is, respectively, 4.1% and 2.2% since, for example, $100/\sqrt{600} \simeq 4.1$. For many purposes these margins of error are tolerable, but they will be too large for predicting the result of a close election.

4.9 Key Concepts

1. The key tools of statistical inference are confidence intervals and hypothesis tests.

2. For statistical inference on μ we use the t statistic $t = (\bar{x} - \mu)/se(\bar{x})$. This is the distance between $\bar{x}$ and μ, normalized by the standard error of the mean.

3. Under simple random sampling the t statistic t is the realization of a randomly variable that is $T(n-1)$ distributed, exactly if data are normally distributed and approximately for nonnormal data if n is sufficiently large.

4. In most cases for $n > 30$ it is reasonable to use the $T(n-1)$ distribution.

5. The $T(v)$ distribution, the t distribution with v degrees of freedom, is like a squashed version of the standard normal distribution with fatter tails. As $v \to \infty$ the t distribution goes to the standard normal.

6. T_v denotes a random variable that is $T(v)$ distributed.

7. The critical value $t_{v,\alpha}$ is that value such that a $T(v)$ distributed random variable exceeds $t_{v,\alpha}$ with probability α, i.e., $\Pr[T_v > t_{v,\alpha}] = \alpha$.

8. The critical value $t_{v,\alpha/2}$ is that value such that a $T(v)$ distributed random variable exceeds in absolute value $t_{v,\alpha/2}$ with probability α, i.e., $\Pr[|T_v| > t_{v,\alpha/2}] = \alpha$.

9. A $100(1-\alpha)\%$ confidence interval for μ is $\bar{x} \pm t_{n-1,\alpha/2} \times se(\bar{x})$. This interval will include μ with probability α.

10. A calculated 95 percent confidence interval for the population mean is an interval that if constructed for each of an infinite number of samples will include the true population mean μ 95% of the time (and will not include μ 5% of the time).

11. It is most common to use a 95% confidence interval, so $\alpha = 0.05$ and $\alpha/2 = 0.025$. A higher degree of confidence leads to a wider confidence interval.

12. An approximate 95% confidence interval for μ is the two standard error interval $\bar{x} \pm 2 \times se(\bar{x})$ where $se(\bar{x}) = s/\sqrt{n}$.

13. A two-sided hypothesis test is a test of $H_0 : \mu = \mu^*$ against $H_a : \mu \neq \mu^*$.

14. A type I error occurs if H_0 is rejected when H_0 is true.

15. The significance level or size of a test, denoted α, is the pre-specified maximum probability of a type I error that will be tolerated.

16. The t test statistic $t = (\bar{x} - \mu^*)/se(\bar{x})$ is the realization of a random variable that is approximately $T(n-1)$ distributed under $H_0 : \mu = \mu^*$.

17. The p-value is the probability of observing a t statistic at least as large in absolute value as that obtained in the current sample.

18. For a two-sided test $p = \Pr[|T_{n-1}| \geq |t|]$. H_0 is rejected at significance level α if $p < \alpha$, and is not rejected otherwise.

19. For a two-sided test the critical value $c = t_{n-1,\alpha/2}$. H_0 is rejected at significance level α if $|t| > c$, and is not rejected otherwise.

20. It is most common to test at significance level $\alpha = 0.05$.

21. For one-sided tests the statement being tested is specified to be the alternative hypothesis.

22. An upper one-tailed alternative test is a test of $H_0 : \mu \leq \mu^*$ against $H_a : \mu > \mu^*$. We reject H_0 if $p = \Pr[T_{n-1} \geq t] < \alpha$ or, equivalently, if $t > c = t_{n-1,\alpha}$.

23. A lower one-tailed alternative test is a test of $H_0 : \mu \geq \mu^*$ against $H_a : \mu < \mu^*$. We reject H_0 if $p = \Pr[T_{n-1} \leq t] < \alpha$ or, equivalently, if $t < c = -t_{n-1,\alpha}$.

24. For one-sided tests at significance level 0.05 a rough guide is to use as critical value 1.645 for an upper one-tail alternative and -1.645 for a lower one-tail alternative, as $t_{n-1,.025} = 1.645$ for large n.

25. In many settings the statistic $t = (\text{estimate}-\text{parameter})/(\text{standard error})$ can be viewed as the realization of a $T(v)$ distributed random variable where the degrees of freedom v varies with the application.

26. An approximate 95% confidence interval for a parameter is then the estimate plus or minus two times the standard error.

27. The half-width of a confidence interval is called the margin of error.

28. The margin of error for a 95% confidence interval is approximately two times the standard error.

29. Proportions data can be analyzed using the methods of this chapter, but are usually analyzed using a minor adaptation of these methods.

30. Key terms: t statistic; t distribution; degrees of freedom; confidence interval; two standard error interval; margin of error; hypothesis test; null hypothesis; alternative hypothesis; two-sided test; type I error; significance level; p-value; critical region; rejection region; critical value; one-sided test; upper one-sided alternative; lower one-sided alternative; margin of error.

4.10 Exercises

1. For a random variable T that is $T(22)$ distributed use a statistical package or a table of the $T(22)$ distribution to find

   (a) $\Pr[T > 2.0]$.   (b) $\Pr[T < -2.0 \text{ or } T > 2.0]$.   (c) t^* such that $\Pr[T > t^*] = .05$.
   (d) t^* such that $\Pr[T < -t^* \text{ or } T > t^*] = .05$.

2. Repeat the previous exercise for the $T(33)$ distribution.

3. For a standard normal distributed random variable Z, give the following (approximately) without using a computer or referring to a table. Hint: A normally distributed random variable lies within two standard deviations of its mean with approximate probability of 0.95.

   (a) $\Pr[Z > 2.0]$.   (b) $\Pr[Z < -2.0 \text{ or } Z > 2.0]$.   (c) z^* such that $\Pr[Z > z^*] = 0.025$.
   (d) z^* such that $\Pr[Z < -z^* \text{ or } Z > z^*] = 0.05$.

4. For a standard normal distributed random variable Z, give the following without using a computer or referring to a table. Hint: A normally distributed random variable lies within 1.645 standard deviations of its mean with approximate probability of 0.90.

   (a) $\Pr[Z > 1.645]$.   (b) $\Pr[Z < -1.645 \text{ or } Z > 1.645]$.   (c) z^* such that $\Pr[Z > z^*] = 0.05$.
   (d) z^* such that $\Pr[Z < -z^* \text{ or } Z > z^*] = 0.10$.

5. The dataset TDIST4 has the sample means $\bar{x}$ and corresponding standard standard deviations s from 1000 simple random samples of size 4 where $X \sim N(100, 16^2)$.

   (a) Compute $z = (\bar{x} - 100)/8$ for each of the 1,000 samples.
   (b) What mean, standard deviation and distribution do you expect for z? Explain.
   (c) Obtain detailed summary statistics for z. Compare these to your answers in (b).
   (d) Compute $t = (\bar{x} - 100)/se(\bar{x})$ where $se(\bar{x}) = s/\sqrt{N}$. Explain why t is t_3 distributed.
   (e) The t_3 distribution has mean 0 and variance 3 and for example, $\Pr[T_3 > 1.638] = 0.10$. Obtain detailed summary statistics for t and compare to these expected values.
   (f) On the same graph plot kernel density estimates for both z and t and comment on any differences.

6. The dataset TDIST25 has the sample means $\bar{x}$ and corresponding standard standard deviations s from 1000 simple random samples of size 25 where $X \sim N(200, 50^2)$.

    (a) Compute $z = (\bar{x} - 200)/10$ for each of the 1,000 samples.

    (b) What mean, standard deviation and distribution do you expect for z? Explain.

    (c) Obtain detailed summary statistics for z? Compare these to your answers in (b).

    (d) Compute $t = (\bar{x} - 200)/se(\bar{x})$ where $se(\bar{x}) = s/\sqrt{N}$. Explain why t is t_{24} distributed.

    (e) The t_{24} distribution has mean 0 and variance 1.091 and for example, $\Pr[T_{24} > 1.318] = 0.10$. Obtain detailed summary statistics for t and compare to these expected values.

    (f) On the same graph plot kernel density estimates for z and for t and comment on any differences.

7. For a random variable T that is $T(30)$ distributed, $\Pr[-1.3 < T < 1.3] = 0.80$. Using this result, obtain an 80% confidence interval for the population mean μ given a random sample with $n = 31$, $\bar{x} = 40$ and $s/\sqrt{n} = 10$.

8. Consider a random variable T that is $T(60)$ distributed.

    (a) Find $\Pr[|T| > 1.2]$. Show your answer on a hand-drawn graph similar to Figure 4.2.

    (b) Find $t_{60,.025}$. Show your answer on a hand-drawn graph similar to Figure 4.2.

9. Suppose we obtain a random sample with $\bar{x} = 10$, $s = 20$ and $N = 25$. Obtain a 95% confidence interval for μ using t critical values.

10. Repeat the previous exercise with $\bar{x} = 80$, $s = 60$ and $N = 100$.

11. The dataset HOUSE has data on the price and size of houses sold in a small homogeneous community.

    (a) Read the data into your statistical package.

    (b) Using a statistical package command obtain a 95% confidence interval for mean price.

    (c) Now manually calculate the same confidence interval using the sample mean, standard deviation, sample size and an appropriate t critical value.

12. Repeat the previous exercise for house size.

13. Suppose a sample yields a 95% confidence interval for μ of (20, 30). Do you expect a wider, narrower, or similar confidence interval in the following situations?

    (a) A 99% confidence interval is constructed;   (b) the sample size is much larger;

    (c) the sample mean is much larger;   (d) the standard deviation is much larger.

14. Suppose a sample yields a 95% confidence interval for μ of (20, 30). Which of the following is likely to lead to a narrower confidence interval?

   (a) A 90% confidence interval; (b) a smaller sample;

   (c) a sample that had the same mean but a larger standard deviation.

15. The dataset HOUSE has data on the price and size of houses sold in a small homogeneous community.

   (a) Read the data into your statistical package.

   (b) Using a statistical package command perform a two-sided test of whether or not for house price $\mu = 270000$ at significance level 0.05. State the null and alternative hypotheses and your conclusion.

   (c) Now manually perform the same test using the sample mean, standard deviation, sample size and an appropriate t critical value.

   (d) Repeat part (c) except compute the p-value. State your conclusion.

16. Repeat the previous exercise for house size and test of whether or not $\mu = 2000$.

17. Suppose a random sample of 25 economists forecast economic growth for the next year. The range of forecasts is from growth of -2.0 percent to growth of 3.5 percent with average 1.2 percent and with standard deviation of 2.0 percent.

   (a) Obtain the standard error of the sample mean forecast.

   (b) Give a 95 percent confidence interval for the population mean forecast.

   (c) Test at significance level 0.05 the claim that growth will be zero next year. State the null and alternative hypotheses and your conclusion.

   (d) Test at significance level 0.05 the claim that the next year will be a growth year, i.e. that growth will be positive. State the null and alternative hypotheses and your conclusion.

   (e) What distributional assumptions on the underlying forecasts are needed to justify the methods used in parts b to d?

   (f) You are told that the economists sampled are top advisors to the main opposition political party in the country. How, if at all, would the analysis in this exercise be affected?

18. The IQ score for a simple random sample of 88 people has sample mean 102 and sample standard deviation 14.

   (a) Give a 95% confidence interval for the population mean IQ. [Hint: Be sure to use the standard error of the sample mean and not the standard deviation].

   (b) Perform a test at significance level 0.05 of the null hypothesis that population mean IQ equals 100 against the alternative that it does not equal 100. Use the p-value approach.

   (c) Repeat part (b) using the critical value approach.

   (d) The claim is made that population mean IQ exceeds 100. Perform an appropriate hypothesis test at significance level 0.05 State clearly your conclusion.

19. Suppose we fail to reject H_0 at significance level 0.05. Do you expect it to be more likely that we reject H_0 in the following situations?

   (a) The test is at significance level 0.01.

   (b) The sample size is much larger.

20. For a random sample with $X_i \sim (\mu, \sigma^2)$ answer true or false to the following statements.

   (a) If we reject a hypothesis on μ at level 0.05 then we will necessarily also reject at level 0.01.

   (b) If a 95% confidence interval for μ includes zero then we will necessarily reject $H_0 : \mu = 0$ against $H_a : \mu \neq 0$ at level 0.05.

   (c) If $\bar{x} = 2$ leads to $p = 0.06$ in test of $H_0 : \mu = 0$ against $H_a : \mu \neq 0$ then we will reject $H_0 : \mu \leq 0$ against $H_a : \mu > 0$ at level 0.05.

21. The dataset TDIST4 has the sample means $\bar{x}$ and corresponding standard standard deviations s from 1000 random samples of size 4 where $X \sim N(100, 16^2)$.

   (a) For each of the 1,000 samples compute a 95% confidence interval for μ.

   (b) How many of these confidence intervals include 100. Is this what you expect? Explain.

   (c) For each of the 1,000 samples compute the t-statistic for test of $H_0 : \mu = 100$ against $H_a : \mu \neq 100$.

   (d) Count how many of these tests reject H_0 at level 0.05. Is this what you expect? Explain.

22. The dataset TDIST25 has the sample means $\bar{x}$ and corresponding standard standard deviations s from 1000 random samples of size 25 where $X \sim N(200, 50^2)$.

    (a) For each of the 1,000 samples compute separately the lower bound and upper bound of a 95% confidence interval for μ.

    (b) How many of these confidence intervals include 200. Is this what you expect? Explain.

    (c) For each of the 1,000 samples compute the t-statistic for test of $H_0 : \mu = 200$ against $H_a : \mu \neq 200$.

    (d) Count how many of these tests reject H_0 at level 0.05. Is this what you expect? Explain.

23. Repeat exercise 21 except generate the 1,000 sample means and standard deviations yourself. For example, use the Stata code in Chapter 3.7 except replace `set obs 30` with `set obs 4` and replace commands `generate u=runiform()` and `generate x=u>0.5` with `generate x=rnormal(100,16)`.

24. Repeat exercise 22 except generate the 1,000 sample means and standard deviations yourself. For example, use the Stata code in Chapter 3.7 except replace `set obs 30` with `set obs 25` and replace commands `generate u=runiform()` and `generate x=u>0.5` with `generate x=rnormal(200,50)`.

25. The summary statistics for usual hours worked per week (variable *hours*) for a simple random sample of women aged 30 years are the following

Variable	Obs	Mean	Std. Dev.	Min	Max
hours	109	32.81	19.73	0	90

    (a) Obtain the standard error of the sample mean.

    (b) Give a 95% confidence interval for population mean usual hours worked.

    (c) The claim is made that the population mean usual hours worked is 35 hours. Test this claim at significance level 0.01. State the null and alternative hypotheses and your conclusion.

    (d) The claim is made that the population mean usual hours worked is less than 35 hours. Test this claim at significance level 0.10. State the null and alternative hypotheses and your conclusion.

26. The summary statistics for educational level for a simple random sample of women aged 30 years who are full-time workers are the following

Variable	Obs	Mean	Std. Dev.	Min	Max
education	171	14.43	2.74	3	20

   (a) Obtain the standard error of the sample mean.

   (b) Give a 95% confidence interval for population mean usual hours worked.

   (c) The claim is made that the population mean education is 14 years. Test this claim at significance level 0.05. State the null and alternative hypotheses and your conclusion.

   (d) The claim is made that the population mean education is more than 14 year. Test this claim at significance level 0.05. State the null and alternative hypotheses and your conclusion.

27. A statistical package gives the following output. Use this output to answer the following questions in the easiest way.

One-sample t test

Variable	Obs	Mean	Std. Err.	Std. Dev.	[95% Conf. Interval]	
x	85	62.46812	10.07956	92.92892	42.42382	82.51242

```
    mean = mean(x)                                              t =    1.7330
Ho: mean = 45                                 degrees of freedom =        84

    Ha: mean < 45              Ha: mean != 45                 Ha: mean > 45
Pr(T < t) = 0.9566        Pr(|T| > |t|) = 0.0868          Pr(T > t) = 0.0434
```

   (a) Perform a test of whether or not $\mu = 0$ at significance level 0.05.

   (b) The claim is made that the population mean is positive. State the null and alternative hypotheses and perform a test at significance level 0.05

   (c) Calculate a 90% confidence interval for μ.

   (d) The claim is made that the population mean exceeds 35. State the null and alternative hypotheses and perform an appropriate test at significance level 0.05.

28. The dataset NAEP has scores for 51 U.S. states (including the District of Columbia) on the National Assessment of Educational Progress (NAEP) for eighth-grade mathematics for the years 2003, 2005, 2007 and 2009. Consider the change in the score for each state from 2003 to 2005 (which you need to calculate).

   (a) Generate data for the change in the score from 2003 to 2005.

   (b) Calculate a 95% confidence interval for the mean score change.

   (c) Test at significance level 0.95 the claim that there has been no change in the mean score. State the null and alternative hypotheses and your conclusion.

(d) Test at significance level 0.05 the claim that the mean score improved. State the null and alternative hypotheses and your conclusion.

29. Hospitals in the U.S. post very high charges, much higher than their costs. (Hospitals then discount off their posted prices with discount varying according to the power of the purchaser, such as an individual's health insurance company.) The dataset KNEEREPLACE has 2011 data for a number of New York hospitals on the average posted charge (*meancharge*) and average cost (*meancost*)of knee joint replacement for cases of moderate severity, where the average is over all such cases the hospital treated in 2011.

(a) Calculate the ratio of average posted charge to mean cost for each hospital.

(b) Calculate a 95% confidence interval for the mean of this ratio. Comment.

(c) Test at significance level 0.05 the claim that the mean ratio is equal to 2.5. State the null and alternative hypotheses and your conclusion.

(d) Test at significance level 0.05 the claim that the mean ratio is less than 2.5. State the null and alternative hypotheses and your conclusion.

30. The dataset SPOTFORWARD has data for the spot price (*niso*) and one-day ahead forward price (*npx*) in the California wholesale electricity market for the one hour period 5-6 p.m. for each day from April 1 1998 to February 12 2000. Restrict analysis to days in 1998.

(a) Generate daily data (for 1998) on the difference between the spot price and the one-day ahead price.

(b) Create a variable *dayofyear* and give a line plot of the difference against *dayofyear*. Comment.

(c) Calculate a 95% confidence interval for the mean difference.

(d) Test at significance level 0.95 the claim that there is no difference between the spot and one-day ahead price. State the null and alternative hypotheses and your conclusion.

(e) Test at significance level 0.05 the claim that the one-day ahead price exceeds the spot price. State the null and alternative hypotheses and your conclusion.

(f) If markets work fully efficiently then the day-ahead price should equal the spot price. Does this appear to be the case here?

31. Suppose the sample estimate of a parameter θ is 25 with standard error 4 and the sample size is large.

(a) Obtain an approximate 95% confidence interval for θ.

(b) Give the margin of error of the estimate.

(c) Perform a test whether or not $\theta = 15$ at significance level 0.05.

32. Repeat the previous exercise if the estimate is 10 with standard error 3.

33. Suppose a random sample of 1,025 potential voters of whom 550 plan to vote for candidate A and the remainder vote for candidate B. Use the methods of the section 4.8.3 example in answering the following.

    (a) Provide an estimate of the proportion voting for candidate A and the standard error of this estimate.

    (b) Provide a 95% confidence interval for the proportion voting for candidate A.

    (c) Give the margin of error for this opinion poll.

    (d) Perform a test at level 0.05 of whether candidate A will win the election.

34. A government survey of 5,283 people finds that the unemployment rate is 6.7%. Use the methods of the section 4.8.3 example in answering the following.

    (a) Compute the margin of error for the estimate of the unemployment rate.

    (b) Provide a 95% confidence interval for the unemployment rate.

    (c) Test at significance level 0.05 whether the population mean unemployment rate is 7.0%.

Chapter 5

Bivariate Data Summary

We now summarize the relationship between two variables, such as that between earnings and education or between house price and house size, rather than analyzing just one variable in isolation.

Without knowledge of the particular variables being analyzed, the two variables should be treated equally. In practice one variable is often viewed as being explained by another variable. The standard notation used follows that of mathematics, where y is a function of x. Thus the variable y is viewed as being explained by the variable x. It is important to note, however, that without additional information the roles of the two variables may in fact be reversed, so that it is x that is being explained by y. It is safest to say that we measure the association between variable y and variable x.

This chapter presents data summary using cross tabulation, a scatter plot, the correlation coefficient and, finally, least squares regression which is the key empirical method used in analysis of economics data. Statistical inference for regression is deferred to Chapters 6 and 7.

5.1 Example: House Price and Size

A common real-estate refrain is that the most important determinant of house price is "location, location, location." The data analyzed here already control for location by restricting analysis to houses within a small homogeneous community. The houses are of similar vintage and in the same school district. Given this control for location, it is reasonable to believe that house size will be the key determinant of house price.

Dataset HOUSE includes data on the price (in dollars) and size (in square feet) of 29 houses sold in a small homogeneous community. These data are used extensively in the next few chapters.

The complete listing of the data in Table 5.1 orders the observations by decreasing price, making interpretation easier. It does appear that larger houses are higher priced. For example, the five most expensive houses are all 2,000 square feet or more, while the four cheapest houses are all less than 2,000 square feet in size. The goal of this chapter is to better quantify this relationship.

Table 5.1: House price and size: Complete listing of data.

House Price	House Size	House Price	House Size	House Price	House Size
375,000	3,300	255,000	1,500	235,000	1,700
340,000	2,400	253,000	2,100	233,000	1,700
310,000	2,300	249,000	1,900	230,000	2,100
279,900	2,000	245,000	1,400	229,000	1,700
278,500	2,600	244,000	2,000	224,500	2,100
273,000	1,900	241,000	1,600	220,000	1,600
272,000	1,800	239,500	1,600	213,000	1,800
270,000	2,000	238,000	1,900	212,000	1,600
270,000	1,800	236,500	1,600	204,000	1,400
258,500	1,600	235,000	1,600		

Table 5.2 presents various summary statistics for these 29 observations. The house sale price ranges from \$204,000 to \$375,000 with mean \$253,910 and standard deviation \$37,391. House size ranges from 1,400 to 3,300 square feet with mean 1,883 square feet and standard deviation 398 square feet.

Table 5.2: House price and size: Summary statistics (n=29).

Statistic	House Price (in dollars)	House Size (in square feet)
Mean	253,910	1,883
Standard deviation (of x)	37,391	398
Standard error (of $\bar{x}$)	6,943	74
Maximum	375,000	3,300
Median (50th percentile)	244,000	1,800
Minimum	204,000	1,400
Skewness	1.56	1.73
Kurtosis	5.61	6.74

The standard visual method for bivariate data is a two-way scatter plot. For these data Figure 5.1 in Chapter 5.3 makes clear that house price tends to increase with house size.

The standard measure of association between two variables is the correlation coefficient. From Chapter 5.4 the correlation between house price and house size is 0.786 which indicates a strong positive association.

The standard method for estimating the average relationship between two variables is least squares regression. From Chapter 5.5 the resulting best fitting linear relationship is

$$\widehat{Price} = 115,017 + 73.77 \times Size.$$

It follows that an extra square foot of house is associated with a \$73.77 increase in house price.

5.2 Two-way Tabulation

A **two-way tabulation** or **cross tabulation** of the two variables x and y is a two-way frequency table that lists the number (or fraction) of observations equal to each of the distinct values taken by the pair (x, y).

A cross tabulation is easiest to read if the variables x and y take relatively few values. These values can be for data that are intrinsically categorical. For example, we might cross tabulate voting intentions (Democrat, Republican or Other) with race (White, Hispanic, ...). Or one or both variables may be numerical.

If either variable takes too many values then it is best to first aggregate the variable into a limited number of values. As an example, consider the house price and size data. Define the new variable *Pricerange* that takes a low value if *Price*<\$250,000 and a high value if *Price*≥\$250,000. And define the new variable *Sizerange* that takes the value small if *Size*<1,800, the value medium if 1,800≤*Size*<2,400, and the value large if *Size*≥2,400.

Table 5.3: House price and size: Cross tabulation with row and column sums

Price range	Size range			Total
	Small	Medium	Large	
Low	11	6	0	17
High	2	7	3	12
Total	13	13	6	29

Table 5.3 presents the two-way tabulation for these aggregated variables. The main entry is the number of observations with a given combination of price and size. For example, there were 11 houses that were of low price and small size. The table also includes **row sums** and **column sums**. For example in the row for low price range there are a total of $11 + 6 + 0 = 17$ observations. So 17 of the 29 houses sold were in the low price range. The table can also include a **row percentage**, that for each value of *Pricerange* gives the percentage of observations in each of the size ranges, and similarly constructed **column percentages**.

The table suggests that larger houses sell for a higher price. For example, 11 of the 13 small houses sold at a low price, while all 3 of the large houses sold for a high price.

Such comparisons can be formalized by including **expected frequencies**, created under the assumption that the two variables are statistically independent. If two variables are statistically independent then the joint probability of occurrence equals the product of each individual probability of occurrence. For example, a house is small with probability 13/29, since 13 out of the 29 prices are small, while a house is low priced with probability 17/29, since 17 of the 29 houses are low priced. Assuming independence, the joint probability of small size and low price then equals $(13/29) \times (17/29)$. Multiplying by 29 gives the expected frequency of $17 \times 13/29 = 7.62$. This is less than the observed frequency of 11.

Table 5.4 presents both the observed frequencies and the expected frequencies. For example, more of the small houses are low priced than would be expected if price and size were independent (11 versus 7.62) and more of the large houses are high priced than would be expected if price and size were independent (3 versus 1.24).

Table 5.4: House price and size: Cross tabulation with expected frequencies.

| | Size range | | | |
Price range	Small	Medium	Large	Total
Low	11	6	0	17
	7.62	7.62	1.76	17.00
High	2	7	3	12
	5.38	5.38	1.24	12.00
Total	13	13	3	29
	13.00	13.00	3.00	29.00

For data that are categorical, rather than numerical, comparing observed and expected frequency values provides a test for statistical independence. This formal test, Pearson's chi-squared goodness-of-fit test of statistical independence, is used extensively in many social sciences. It is much less used in economics as it does not extend easily to several variables, and is most useful for categorical variables.

Remark 23 *A **two-way tabulation** or **cross tabulation** of the two variables x and y is a two-way frequency table that lists the number (or fraction) of observations equal to each of the distinct values taken by the pair (x, y). It can include additional information including row percentages, column percentages and expected frequencies.*

5.3   Two-way Scatter Plot

The standard visual method for bivariate data is a **two-way scatter plot**. This is a plot of one variable on the vertical axis against the other variable on the horizontal axis. A major decision to make is which variable to place on the vertical axis and which to place on the horizontal axis. In many situations it is clear which variable it is that we want to explain, and this variable appears on the vertical axis. As expanded upon in Chapter 5.10, however, it need not be the case that the variable on the horizontal axis is causing the variable on the vertical axis.

The first panel of Figure 5.1 presents a scatter plot of the house price data. House price appears on the vertical axis and house size appears on the horizontal axis, since we wish to explain house price given house size. Each point represents a combination of sale price and size of house. For

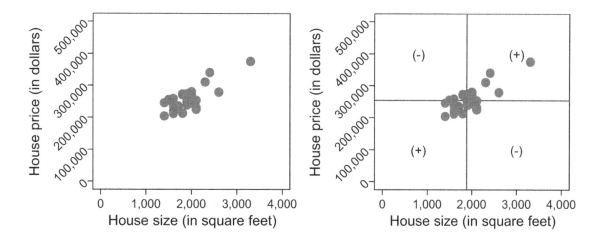

Figure 5.1: Scatterplot: House price and size with four quadrants defined by means of price and size

example, the upper right point is for a house that sold for $375,000 and was 3,300 square feet in size. The scatter plot clearly illustrates that, on average, larger houses sell for more.

Remark 24 *A two-way scatter plot is the standard tool for visualizing the relationship between two variables.*

When observation on y and/or x take only a few values multiple observations may take the same value of (x, y) making it difficult to read the scatterplot. In that case it can be useful to use a so-called jitter to add some random noise to the data before plotting.

5.4   Sample Correlation

The standard single measure of the association between two numerical variables is the **sample correlation coefficient**, defined as

$$r_{xy} = \frac{\sum_{i=1}^{n}(x_i - \bar{x})(y_i - \bar{y})}{\sqrt{\sum_{i=1}^{n}(x_i - \bar{x})^2}\sqrt{\sum_{i=1}^{n}(y_i - \bar{y})^2}}.$$

The sign of r_{xy} gives the direction of the association, the absolute size of r_{xy} gives the strength of the relationship, and by construction $-1 \leq r_{xy} \leq 1$.

The correlation between house price and house size is 0.786. This implies that increases in house size are associated with higher house price, since $r_{xy} > 0$, and this association is quite strong, since r_{xy} is fairly close to one.

The remainder of this section derives the correlation coefficient, which is based on the sample covariance.

5.4.1 Sample Covariance

Recall the formulas for the sample variances of x and y, respectively $s_x^2 = \frac{1}{n-1}\sum_{i=1}^n (x_i - \bar{x})^2$ and $s_y^2 = \frac{1}{n-1}\sum_{i=1}^n (y_i - \bar{y})^2$. The **sample covariance** between x and y is the analogous cross-product

$$s_{xy} = \frac{1}{n-1}\sum_{i=1}^n (x_i - \bar{x})(y_i - \bar{y}).$$

Note that the formula is symmetric in x and y, so $s_{yx} = s_{xy}$.

Also, the sample covariance between x and itself equals the variance of x. Algebraically, $s_{xx} = \frac{1}{n-1}\sum_i (x_i - \bar{x})(x_i - \bar{x}) = \frac{1}{n-1}\sum_i (x_i - \bar{x})^2 = s_x^2$.

The sign of the covariance is easily interpreted, with $s_{xy} > 0$ if there is positive association, $s_{xy} = 0$ if there is no association, and $s_{xy} < 0$ if there is negative association.

To see this, consider the case of positive covariance. Then $s_{xy} > 0$ if the cross-product $(x_i - \bar{x})(y_i - \bar{y})$ is mostly positive. Positive cross-product values arise if both $(x_i - \bar{x}) > 0$ and $(y_i - \bar{y}) > 0$, in which case both x_i and y_i are above average, or if both $(x_i - \bar{x}) < 0$ and $(y_i - \bar{y}) < 0$, in which case both x_i and y_i are below average. The association in this case is positive, since above-average values of x tend to be associated with above-average values of y, and below-average values of x tend to be associated with below-average values of y.

The second panel of Figure 5.1 indicates a positive covariance for the data on house price and size. The vertical line is the sample mean $\bar{x} = 1883$, and the horizontal line is the sample mean $\bar{y} = 253910$. The top-right quadrant, denoted $(+)$, has positive values of $(x_i - \bar{x})(y_i - \bar{y})$ since in this quadrant $(x_i - \bar{x}) > 0$ and $(y_i - \bar{y}) > 0$. Similar considerations lead to the signs in the other three quadrants. The covariance $s_{xy} = 11{,}701{,}613$ is positive, as most of the observations lie in the two quadrants with positive value for $(x_i - \bar{x})(y_i - \bar{y})$. Furthermore, for the observations in the two quadrants with negative value for $(x_i - \bar{x})(y_i - \bar{y})$, this negative cross product is relatively small in absolute value.

Remark 25 *The sample covariance s_{xy} is positive if x and y tend to move together in the same direction, and negative if x and y tend to move together in the opposite direction. A covariance of zero means there is no linear association between x and y.*

5.4.2 Sample Correlation

A weakness of the sample covariance is that its magnitude is not easily interpreted. For the house price and house size data $s_{xy} = 11{,}701{,}613$. This is a large number, but it does not necessarily imply that the association between x and y is large. Furthermore, s_{xy} changes with the units of measurement. For example, if house price is measured in thousands of dollars rather than dollars, the covariance is divided by one thousand since $(y_i - \bar{y})$ is then reduced by a factor of 1,000.

The **sample correlation coefficient** is a standardized measure, or unit-free measure, of association between x and y that standardizes the covariance by dividing by the standard deviations of x and y. Then

$$r_{xy} = \frac{s_{xy}}{s_x s_y} = \frac{\text{Covariance of } x \text{ and } y}{(\text{Standard deviation of } x) \times (\text{Standard deviation of } y)}.$$

Given the definitions of covariance and standard deviation,

$$r_{xy} = \frac{\sum_{i=1}^{n}(x_i - \bar{x})(y_i - \bar{y})}{\sqrt{\sum_{i=1}^{n}(x_i - \bar{x})^2}\sqrt{\sum_{i=1}^{n}(y_i - \bar{y})^2}},$$

since the multiplicative factor $1/(n-1)$ in the numerator and denominator cancels out.

It can be shown that this standardization leads to $-1 \leq r_{xy} \leq 1$. The sign of r_{xy} is the same as the sign of s_{xy}, since the denominator $s_x s_y > 0$. So a positive value for r_{xy} means a positive association, a negative value for r_{xy} means a negative association, and a zero value for r_{xy} means no association.

Remark 26 *The sample correlation coefficient r_{xy} lies between -1 and 1. It is positive if x and y tend to move together in the same direction and equals 1 if they move exactly together in the same direction. It is negative if x and y tend to move together in the opposite direction and equals -1 if they move exactly together in the opposite direction. It is zero if there is no linear association between x and y.*

For the house price and size data the covariance equals 11,701,613, and the standard deviations are given in Table 5.2 in Chapter 5.1. These lead to correlation coefficient $11701613/(398*37391) = 0.786$.

Some algebra shows that the sample correlation coefficient equals the sample covariance between the z-scores $(x_i - \bar{x})/s_x$ and $(y_i - \bar{y})/s_y$. It is also the sample correlation between these z-scores.

The formula for the correlation coefficient treats x and y symmetrically, so $r_{yx} = r_{xy}$. Thus while the correlation coefficient detects association, it is neutral on whether it is x that is causing y or y that is causing x.

There are several ways to measure association between two variables – the correlation coefficient is more completely called the **Pearson product moment correlation coefficient**. It measures linear association between two variables but can miss nonlinear association. As a result, while two variables that are statistically independent have zero correlation, zero correlation does not imply that the variables are statistically independent. In practice for most economics data the correlation coefficient is an adequate measure of association.

5.4.3   Strength of Correlation

Figure 5.2 illustrates, in turn, strong positive correlation ($r = .78$), moderate positive correlation ($r = .54$), almost no correlation ($r = .07$), and moderate negative correlation ($r = -.54$). While the terms "moderate" and "strong" correlation are used, there is no clear cutoff between "low", "moderate" and "strong".

5.4.4   Autocorrelations for Time Series Data

Time series data are often correlated over time, with this correlation reducing as observations become further apart in time.

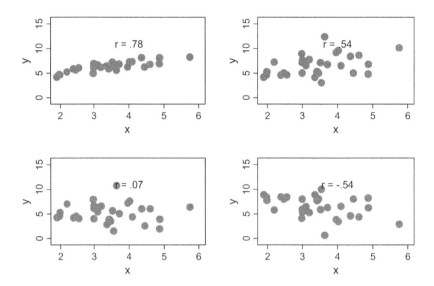

Figure 5.2: Correlation: Examples of different strengths and direction of correlation.

For a time series y_t, $t = 1, ..., T$, let y_{t-j} denote the data lagged j periods. Then the correlation between y_t and y_{t-j} is called the **autocorrelation at lag** j and is denoted ρ_j.

The simplest way to compute $\widehat{\rho}_j$ is to use the usual sample correlation coefficient between y_t and y_{t-j}. Note that this is computed using only $T - j$ observations since y_{t-j} is observed only for $t = j + 1, ..., T$. More specialized econometrics software uses a more refined formula for $\widehat{\rho}_j$ that leads to somewhat different estimates in finite samples but to the same value as the sample size gets very large.

As an example, consider quarterly data on the annual growth rate in U.S. real GDP per capita introduced in Chapter 4.5. The sample correlation coefficient yields autocorrelations at lags 1 to 3 of $\widehat{\rho}_1 = 0.868$, $\widehat{\rho}_2 = 0.660$, and $\widehat{\rho}_3 = 0.412$. A more specialized command to compute autocorrelations gives $\widehat{\rho}_1 = 0.866$, $\widehat{\rho}_2 = 0.657$, and $\widehat{\rho}_3 = 0.409$. Both sets of estimates indicate considerable correlation in annual growth rate over time.

Remark 27 *For time series data the autocorrelation at lag j is the correlation between current data and the data lagged j periods.*

5.5   Regression Line

The regression line is the data analysis tool most used by economists. It provides the best fitting linear relationship between y and x, where the criterion for best fit is explained below.

5.5.1 Regression Line

The **regression line** obtained from regression of y on x is denoted

$$\widehat{y} = b_1 + b_2 x.$$

The following terminology is used for the variables in this regression.

- y is called the **dependent variable.**

- $\widehat{y}$ is called the **fitted value** or **predicted value** of the dependent variable.

- x is called the **regressor variable** or **explanatory variable** or **independent variable** or **covariate.**

The data are used to estimate the coefficients b_1 and b_2, where b_1 is the estimated y-axis **intercept coefficient (or constant term)** and b_2 is the estimated **slope coefficient**.

5.5.2 The Residual

The difference between the actual value of y and its fitted value from the regression line is called the residual – the amount left over after fitting the line. Thus the **residual**

$$e = y - \widehat{y}.$$

Commonly-used alternative notation for the residual is $\widehat{u} = y - \widehat{y}$.

Figure 5.3 illustrates the residual for one observation. For the pictured observation the residual is negative, since $\widehat{y}$ exceeds y so $y - \widehat{y} < 0$.

For the first observation, with subscript 1, the residual is $e_1 = y_1 - \widehat{y}_1$. For the second observation the residual is $e_2 = y_2 - \widehat{y}_2$, and so on. For a representative observation, say the ith observation, the residual is given by

$$e_i = y_i - \widehat{y}_i = y_i - b_1 - b_2 x_i,$$

where the second equality uses $\widehat{y}_i = b_1 + b_2 x_i$.

If the regression line fitted the data perfectly then the residuals would all equal zero. This ideal rarely occurs in practice. Instead we seek to make the residuals as small as possible. There are several ways to proceed, depending on what penalty function is used for nonzero residuals.

The obvious method is to minimize the sum of the n residuals, $\sum_{i=1}^n e_i$. But there are too many ways to do so. For example if we let all fitted observations equal the sample mean (so $\widehat{y}_i = \bar{y}$ for all i), it can be shown that the sum of residuals always equals zero. The next most obvious method is to minimize the sum of absolute residuals, $\sum_{i=1}^n |e_i|$. This method is now feasible and is included in many statistical packages. But historically it was difficult to implement either mathematically or computationally.

Instead analysis is much simpler if the sum of squared residuals, $\sum_{i=1}^n e_i^2$, is minimized. Furthermore the least squares estimates have desirable properties presented in later chapters.

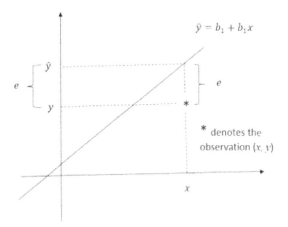

Figure 5.3: Residual: The vertical difference between the data point and the regression line.

5.5.3   Least Squares Regression

Given data $(y_1, x_1), ..., (y_n, x_n)$ the **least squares regression method** chooses b_1 and b_2 to **minimize the sum of squares of the residuals**,

$$\sum_{i=1}^{n} e_i^2 = \sum_{i=1}^{n} (y_i - \widehat{y}_i)^2 = \sum_{i=1}^{n} (y_i - b_1 - b_2 x_i)^2.$$

The resulting formula for the **least squares slope coefficient** is

$$b_2 = \frac{\sum_{i=1}^{n} (x_i - \bar{x})(y_i - \bar{y})}{\sum_{i=1}^{n} (x_i - \bar{x})^2},$$

and the **least squares intercept** is

$$b_1 = \bar{y} - b_2 \bar{x}.$$

These formulas for b_1 and b_2 are obtained using calculus methods. Differentiating with respect to b_1 and b_2 and setting the derivatives equal to zero gives two equations in two unknowns. These equations can be solved for b_1 and b_2 after considerable algebra.

A detailed example of computation by hand of b_1 and b_2 from these formulas is given in Chapter 5.11. These calculations are easily done by a computer. The estimates can always be computed, provided there are at least two observations and that there is some variation in the regressors, so that $\sum_{i=1}^{n} (x_i - \bar{x})^2 \neq 0$.

The origin of the term **regression** is given in Chapter 12.8. A more complete term for least squares regression is **ordinary least squares (OLS) regression**. The adjective "ordinary" is added as there are other variations on least squares; see Chapter 12.4.

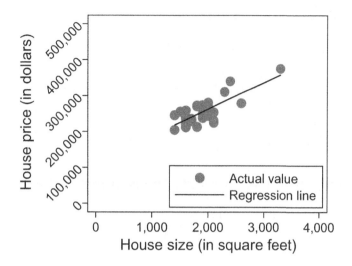

Figure 5.4: House price and size: Regression.

5.5.4 Interpretation of the Slope Coefficient

The slope coefficient b_2 can be directly interpreted as the change in the fitted value of y when x increases by one unit.

To see this, suppose the regressor changes by Δx from x to $(x + \Delta x)$. Then the fitted value $\widehat{y}$ changes from $b_1 + b_2 x$ to $b_1 + b_2(x + \Delta x) = b_1 + b_2 x + b_2 \Delta x$. This is a change of $b_2 \Delta x$. It follows that $\Delta \widehat{y} = b_2 \Delta x$, which implies

$$\frac{\Delta \widehat{y}}{\Delta x} = b_2.$$

For a one-unit change in x, $\Delta x = 1$ so $\Delta \widehat{y} = b_2$.

The same result can be obtained using calculus methods, since $\widehat{y} = b_1 + b_2 x$ has derivative $d\widehat{y}/dx = b_2$.

5.5.5 Example: House Price and Size

OLS regression of house sale price (variable *Price*) on house size (variable *Size*) using dataset HOUSE leads to fitted regression line

$$\widehat{Price} = 115,017 + 73.77 \times Size.$$

The slope coefficient of 73.77 implies that one more square foot in size is associated with a \$73.77 increase in the house price. Equivalently an additional small room of size ten feet by ten feet, or 100 square feet, is associated with a $100 \times \$73.77 = \$7,377$ increase in house price.

Figure 5.4 presents the regression line, superimposed on a scatter plot of the data.

5.5.6   Summary for the Regression Line

Combining the preceding results we have the following.

Remark 28 *The regression line is $\widehat{y} = b_1 + b_2 x$. The OLS estimates b_1 and b_2 are obtained by minimizing the sum of squared residuals, where the residual $e = y - \widehat{y}$ is the difference between the actual and predicted value of y. The slope coefficient b_2 gives the change in the fitted value of y when x changes by one unit.*

5.5.7   Intercept-only Regression yields the Sample Mean

Suppose we apply the least squares method to a model with only an intercept and no regressor x. Then we minimize $\sum_{i=1}^{n}(y_i - b_1)^2$ leading to estimate $b_1 = \bar{y}$.

Remark 29 *Regression of y on only an intercept yields the sample mean $\bar{y}$. Univariate statistics based on the sample mean is just a special case of OLS regression.*

This result provides a justification for using least squares regression – it can be viewed as an extension of the sample mean for univariate data. Going the other way, the methods presented for the sample mean are just a special case of least squares regression.

This result also provides a way to obtain a valid estimate of the standard error of the population mean when observations are correlated. Perform intercept-only OLS regression and obtain appropriate robust standard errors; see Chapter 12.1.

Intercept-only regression is an option available in most computer packages that have a command for OLS regression and yields estimated intercept equal to the sample mean. Alternatively, if the package has an option to run a regression with the intercept set to zero then create a new variable z equal to 1 for every observation and OLS regress y on z using the zero-intercept option.

5.5.8   Indicator Variable Regression yields the Difference in Means

An indicator variable or dummy variable is a variable that takes only values 0 or 1. For example exercise 20 defines the indicator variable *dsize* to equal to 1 if *size*> 1800 and equal to 0 if *size*≤ 1800. Then as explained in Chapter 14.2 we have the following.

Remark 30 *Regression of y on an intercept and an indicator variable d that takes just the values 0 or 1 yields intercept equal to the mean of y when $d = 0$ and slope coefficient equal to the difference in mean of y when $d = 1$ and mean of y when $d = 0$. Difference in means is just a special case of OLS regression.*

For example, suppose y has mean 20 when $d = 0$ and mean 30 when $d = 1$, so the difference in means is $30 - 20 = 10$. Then OLS regression of y on an intercept and d has intercept 20 and slope $30 - 20 = 10$. Then, as expected, $\widehat{y} = 20 + 10d$ equals 20 when $d = 0$ and equals 30 when $d = 1$.

5.6 Measures of Model Fit

Model fit is measured by the closeness of the data points to the fitted regression line. The standard error of the regression is a measure of the standard deviation of the model residuals. R-squared is a measure that is standardized to lie between 0 and 1, taking value 0 when x explains none of the variation in y and value 1 when the regression line perfectly fits the observed values of y.

5.6.1 Standard Error of the Regression

An obvious measure of how close the fitted values $\widehat{y}$ are to the actual values y is the standard deviation of the residual $\widehat{e} = y - \widehat{y}$. Instead a minor variation is used.

The **standard error of the regression** is

$$s_e = \sqrt{\frac{1}{n-2} \sum_{i=1}^{n} (y_i - \widehat{y}_i)^2}.$$

The measure s_e is essentially the standard deviation of the residual, except that division is by $n-2$ rather than $n-1$. The divisor $(n-2)$, called the **degrees of freedom**, is used because only $(n-2)$ terms in the sum are free to vary since computation of $\widehat{y} = b_1 + b_2 x$ is based on the two estimates b_1 and b_2 .

Lower values of s_e mean that the fitted values are closer to the actual values of y. Another name for s_e is the **root mean squared error (MSE) of the residual**. It is also sometimes called the **standard error of the residual**, and is most simply thought of as being the estimated standard deviation of the residual.

Remark 31 *The standard error of the regression measures the standard deviation of the residual, and hence the variability of the dependent variable around the regression line.*

The interpretation of s_e is very context specific. A very rough approximation is that 95% of y values may lie within two standard errors of the regression of the fitted line.

5.6.2 Definition of R-Squared

The standard error of the residual is not a scale free measure. For example, if we measured house price in thousands of dollars rather than dollars, then s_e after regression of house price on size would be 0.001 times as large. A scale-free measure is provided by R-squared.

R-Squared, denoted R^2, measures the **fraction of the variation of y (around the sample mean $\bar{y}$) that is explained by the regressor**.

Variability in y around the sample mean $\bar{y}$ is measured using the **total sum of squares**, denoted *TSS*, where

$$TSS = \sum_{i=1}^{n} (y_i - \bar{y})^2$$

is the sum of squared deviations of the dependent variable y around $\bar{y}$.

The left panel of Figure 5.5 presents the deviations $(y_i - \bar{y})$ for five data points with (x, y) equal to, respectively $(1, 4.7)$, $(2, 4.7)$, $(3, 4.5)$, $(4, 7.4)$, and $(5, 8.7)$.

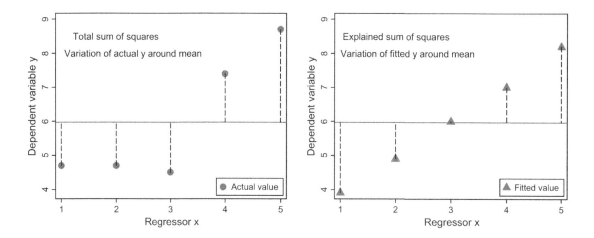

Figure 5.5: R-squared: Total sum of squares and explained sum of squares for five observations.

Variability around $\bar{y}$ after regression is measured using the **explained sum of squares**, denoted *ExpSS*, where

$$ExpSS = \sum_{i=1}^{n} (\widehat{y}_i - \bar{y})^2$$

is the sum of squared deviations of the fitted value $\widehat{y}$ around $\bar{y}$. The right panel of Figure 5.5 presents the deviations $(\widehat{y}_i - \bar{y})$ for the same data points, where the fitted regression was $\widehat{y} = 2.81 + 1.05x$, and the approximate fitted values are, respectively, 3.9, 4.9, 6.0, 7.0 and 8.1. The explained sum of squares is also referred to as the **regression sum of squares** or as the **model sum of squares**.

R-squared equals the explained sum of squares as a fraction of the total sum of squares

$$R^2 = \frac{ExpSS}{TSS} = \frac{\sum_{i=1}^{n} (\widehat{y}_i - \bar{y})^2}{\sum_{i=1}^{n} (y_i - \bar{y})^2},$$

and is also called the **coefficient of determination**.

For the five-observation example illustrated in Figure 5.5 the y values are, respectively, 4.7, 4.7, 4.5, 7.4 and 8.7. Since $\bar{y} = 6.0$, it follows that $TSS = (-1.3)^2 + (-1.3)^2 + (-1.5)^2 + 1.4^2 + 2.7^2 = 14.88$. The fitted $\widehat{y}$ values are, respectively, 3.9, 4.9, 6.0, 7.0 and 8.2. It follows that $ExpSS = (-2.1)^2 + (-1.1)^2 + (0.0)^2 + 1.0^2 + 2.2^2 = 11.46$. Thus $R^2 = 11.46/14.88 = 0.77$. So 77 percent of the variation in y is explained by regression on x.

R^2 is necessarily positive, since the two terms in the ratio are positive. Provided the regression includes an intercept, the explained sum of squares are at most equal to the total sum of squares, so $R^2 \leq 1$. If the regression does not include an intercept then R^2 should not be used.

Remark 32 *R^2 measures the fraction of the variation in the dependent variable explained by the regressor. Provided the regression includes an intercept, R^2 lies between 0 and 1. The minimum value occurs if there is no relationship between y and x, so $\widehat{y}_i = \bar{y}$ for all observations. $R^2 = 1$ if the regression line perfectly fits the dependent variable, so $\widehat{y}_i = y_i$ for all observations.*

5.6.3 Alternative Computation of R-Squared

The **residual sum of squares**, denoted *ResSS*, is defined by

$$ResSS = \sum_{i=1}^{n} (y_i - \widehat{y}_i)^2.$$

ResSS is the sum of squared deviations of the fitted value $\widehat{y}$ around the actual value y. The residual sum of squares is sometimes referred to as the **error sum of squares**.

It can be shown that for least squares regression including an intercept

$$TSS = ExpSS + ResSS.$$

It follows that **R-squared** can be equivalently defined as

$$R^2 = 1 - \frac{ResSS}{TSS} = 1 - \frac{\sum_{i=1}^{n}(y_i - \widehat{y}_i)^2}{\sum_{i=1}^{n}(y_i - \bar{y})^2}.$$

The least squares coefficients therefore maximize R^2, since they minimize the residual sum of squares.

For the five-observation example illustrated in Figure 5.5 the residuals $(y_i - \widehat{y}_i)$ are, respectively, $0.8, -0.2, -1.5, 0.4$ and 0.5. It follows that $ResSS = 0.8^2 + (-0.2)^2 + (-1.5)^2 + 0.4^2 + 0.5^2 = 3.34$. From previous calculation $TSS = 14.88$. So $R^2 = 1 - 3.34/14.88 = 0.77$. Again $R^2 = 0.77$.

5.6.4 R-Squared and the Correlation Coefficient

It can be shown that R^2 **equals the squared sample correlation coefficient between** y and x:

$$R^2 = r_{xy}^2.$$

Thus one by-product of regression analysis is to obtain the squared sample correlation coefficient. It follows that for the four datasets plotted in Figure 5.2, least squares regression leads to fitted models with R^2 of, respectively $0.61 \ (= 0.78^2)$, 0.29, 0.01, and 0.29. And since $r_{xy}^2 = r_{yx}^2$ this result also implies that R^2 from regression of y on x equals R^2 from regression of x on y.

It can be shown that the correlation coefficient is unchanged when data are subject to a linear transformation. Since $\widehat{y} = b_1 + b_2 x$ is a linear transformation of x it follows that $r_{\widehat{y}y}^2 = r_{xy}^2$. So R^2 equals the squared sample correlation coefficient between y and $\widehat{y}$.

Remark 33 *For bivariate regression R^2 equals the squared correlation between y and x. And R^2 equals the squared correlation between y and $\widehat{y}$.*

R^2, unlike r^2, can be easily extended to regression with additional regressors; see Chapter 10.6 which also introduces the adjusted R^2, denoted $\bar{R}^2$ that adjusts R^2 for the number of regressors.

5.6.5   Interpretation of R-Squared

It is clear that a value of $R^2 \simeq 0$ represents a poor fit and a value of $R^2 \simeq 1$ represents an excellent fit. But there is no rule for where R^2 becomes large enough that the fit moves from poor to good.

The value of R^2 increases as data become more aggregated. For example, R^2 will be quite low, around 0.1 to 0.4, for regression of earnings on education using individual-level data. If instead more aggregated data is used, such as analysis of state-average earnings across states or of national average earnings over time, R^2 will be much closer to 1.

For bivariate regression, R^2 can be used to compare models with the same dependent variable. Then models with higher R^2 are preferred. But it makes little sense to compare the R^2 across models with different dependent variable y, because then R^2 explains variation around different sample means $\bar{y}$. For example, a model explaining the level of annual GDP will in practice have a much higher R^2 than a model for the annual change in GDP.

Low values of R^2 do not mean that regression analysis is without merit. For example, regression of earnings on education usually indicates a substantial effect of education, such as one more year of education being associated with a six percent increase in annual earnings. At the same time the R^2 in earnings-education regressions using individual-level data is very low. These seemingly contradictory results can be explained as follows. There is a large effect of schooling on earnings, **on average**. But at the **individual level**, education is only one of many determinants of earnings and there is considerable variability in earnings even for people with the same level of education. If data analysis shows that, on average, schooling substantially raises earnings, then it is a worthwhile investment for government to encourage high levels of schooling. At the same time, however, there is great uncertainty as to whether any one given individual will necessarily increase their earnings given this additional education.

5.7   Computer Output following OLS Regression

Commands for OLS regression and examples of resultant output for several statistical packages are given in Appendix A. Different packages report results in somewhat different ways and provide different levels of detail. Here we present quite detailed regression results.

5.7.1   Computer Output for House Price Example

Table 5.5 presents fairly complete results from OLS regression of variable *Price* on variable *Size*.

The results can be broken into three parts – ANOVA table, regression coefficients, and diagnostic statistics – that are considered in turn.

5.7.2   ANOVA Table and R-squared

The analysis of variance (ANOVA) table is less important than the other results, and is for this reason not reported by all statistical packages.

In the column headed **SS** the total sum of squares is decomposed into the explained (or regression or model) sum of squares and the residual sum of squares. The column headed **df** gives the

Table 5.5: House price and size: Computer output from regression.

ANOVA Table

Source	SS	df	MS	F	p-value
Explained	2.4171×10^{10}	1	2.4171×10^{10}	43.58	0.000
Residual	1.4975×10^{10}	27	5.546×10^{8}		
Total	3.9146×10^{10}	28	1.3981×10^{9}		

Dependent Variable *Price*

Regressor	Coefficient	Standard Error	t statistic	p value	95% conf. int.	
Size	73.77	11.17	6.60	0.000	50.84	96.70
Intercept	115017	21489	5.35	0.000	70925	159110

Summary Statistics

Observations	29
F(1,27)	43.58
p-value for F	0.0000
R-squared	0.618
Adjusted R^2	0.603
St. error of regression	23551

associated degrees of freedom, the column headed **MS** gives the mean square which equals the sum of squares divided by its degrees of freedom. The remainder of the ANOVA table gives the F statistic and its p-value; see Chapter 11.6.

The ANOVA table provides data that is used to compute R-squared and the standard error of the regression.

The R-squared equals the explained sum of squares (2.4171×10^{10}) divided by the total sum of squares (3.9146×10^{10}) which equals 0.618, as given near the bottom of Table 5.5. Equivalently R-squared equals one minus the residual sum of squares (1.4975×10^{10}) divided by the total sum of squares (3.9146×10^{10}) which equals $1 - 0.382 = 0.618$.

The standard error of the regression (also called the standard error of the residual and the root mean square error) equals $\sqrt{\frac{1}{n-2} \sum_{i=1}^{n} (y_i - \widehat{y}_i)^2}$. Here the residual sum of squares $\sum_{i=1}^{n} (y_i - \widehat{y}_i)^2$ equals 1.4975×10^{10} or, more precisely, 14,975,101,655. Dividing by $n - 2 = 27$ yields value 5.546×10^8, which is the entry for residual mean square (MS) in the ANOVA table. Taking the square root yields $s_e = 23551$, which is the entry at the bottom of Table 5.5.

5.7.3 Regression Coefficients

The second block in Table 5.5 gives the main results. The intercept (or constant) equals 115017 and the slope coefficient (b_2) equals 73.77. Some statistical packages report the intercept last, as in Table 5.5, while others report the intercept first.

The remaining columns give the standard error, t statistic, p-value and 95% confidence interval for the intercept and slope estimates. These quantities are the subject of Chapter 7.

5.7.4   Regression Diagnostics

The third block in Table 5.5 gives key regression diagnostics. The F statistic, its p-value and the adjusted R^2 are relevant for multiple regression, rather than bivariate regression, so are presented in later chapters. Computation of R^2 and the standard error of the regression, from the results in the ANOVA table, has already been discussed.

$R^2 = 0.618$ can be viewed as a good fit. Note that R^2 equals the squared correlation coefficient, since $0.786^2 = 0.618$. The standard error of the regression equals 23551, substantially smaller than the standard deviation of variable *Price* which from Table 5.2 equals 37391.

5.8   Prediction and Outlying Observations

This section considers prediction following regression and detection of outlying observations.

5.8.1   Prediction

The regression line can be used to predict values of y for given values of x. For $x = x^*$ the **prediction** is

$$\widehat{y}^* = b_1 + b_2 x^*.$$

For example, for the house sales data a house of size 2000 square feet is predicted to sell for \$262,557, since $\widehat{y} = 115017 + 73.77 \times 2000 = 262557$.

Prediction can be **in-sample**, in which case $\widehat{y}_i = b_1 + b_2 x_i$ is called the **fitted value** of y_i, $i = 1, ..., n$. For in-sample prediction, a property of least squares regression is that on average the in-sample predictions equal the actual value of y. That is, $\frac{1}{n} \sum_{i=1}^{n} \widehat{y}_i = \frac{1}{n} \sum_{i=1}^{n} y_i = \bar{y}$. Equivalently, the **least squares residuals** $e_i = y_i - \widehat{y}_i$ **always sum to zero**. These results hold provided an intercept is included in the regression. (In practice these results may not hold exactly due to computer rounding error; see Appendix A.1).

Remark 34 *A property of OLS regression with an intercept is that the residuals sum to zero. Equivalently, the average of the in-sample fitted values is equal to the average of the sample values of y.*

Prediction can also be **out-of-sample**. In that case it can be tempting to extrapolate and make prediction for y for values of x beyond the range of the sample. Such predictions may not be very reliable.

Prediction at a particular value of x can be used for two purposes. First, it may be used to predict an **average outcome** such as the price on average for a house of size 2000 square feet. Second, it may be used to predict an **individual outcome** such as the price of one particular house of size 2000 square feet. It is much more difficult to predict the latter, though in both cases we use the prediction $b_1 + b_2 \times 2000$. Chapter 12.2 provides a detailed discussion of prediction.

5.8.2 Outlying Observations

An **outlier** or **outlying observation** is one that is a relatively large distance from the bulk of the data. In the bivariate context the outlier could have an unusual value of x, an unusual value of y, or an unusual combination of values of x and y. A scatter plot is a useful visual tool.

If the scatter plot includes the fitted regression line, then points far from the line correspond to observations with a large residual (recall $e = y - \hat{y}$). In such cases, the regression line is indicating that the actual value of y is unusual given the value of x.

Outlying observations can have an unusually large effect on the OLS estimates b_1 and b_2. From the numerator formula for b_2, an observation with a large value for $(x_i - \bar{x})(y_i - \bar{y})$ can have a big influence on b_2. This is the case for observations that are a long way from both $\bar{x}$ and $\bar{y}$. Chapter 16.8 provides further details.

5.9 Regression and Correlation

For bivariate data there is a very close connection between regression and correlation. The term $\sum_{i=1}^{n}(x_i - \bar{x})(y_i - \bar{y})$ appears in the definitions of both b_2 and r_{xy}. The slope coefficient can be re-expressed in terms of the sample correlation coefficient as

$$b_2 = r_{xy} \times \frac{s_y}{s_x}.$$

(To obtain this result, observe that $b_2 = s_{xy}/s_x^2$ upon cancellation of the common multiplicative factor $1/(n-1)$ in s_{xy} and s_x^2. Then multiplying by (s_y/s_y) and rearranging yields $b_2 = s_{xy}/s_x^2 = [s_{xy}/(s_x s_y)] \times (s_y/s_x)] = r_{xy} \times (s_y/s_x)$.)

Remark 35 *The slope coefficient is a multiple s_y/s_x of the sample correlation coefficient.*

It follows that if there is positive correlation, i.e. $r_{xy} > 0$, then the regression slope coefficient b_2 is positive, and similarly $r_{xy} < 0$ implies a negative regression slope coefficient. So the sample correlation coefficient and the slope coefficient always lead to the same conclusion regarding whether the association between the two variables is positive or negative.

Furthermore, it can be shown that if we **standardize** the data and regress the z-score $(y_i - \bar{y})/s_y$ on the z-score $(x_i - \bar{x})/s_x$, then the least squares slope coefficient equals r_{xy}. This implies the following.

Remark 36 *The correlation coefficient r_{xy} measures the number of standard deviations that y changes by when x changes by one standard deviation.*

This result provides a useful way to interpret the correlation coefficient. For example, if the correlation of income across generations, such as from father to son, is 0.3, then if the father's income increases by one standard deviation then the son's income will on average by 0.3 standard deviations higher.

In some other disciplines correlation analysis is extensively used, rather than regression. The two methods lead to the same conclusions regarding association between x and y. Regression can be extended to estimate the relationship between several variables.

5.10   Causation

There is an important distinction between correlation and regression analysis. The correlation coefficient always treats x and y neutrally, since $r_{xy} = r_{yx}$. Such symmetry is not the case for regression. As shown below, the slope coefficient from regression of y on x is not the reciprocal of that from reverse regression of x on y. Furthermore, without further information we can only measure association, and not causation. Thus even if there is an association between y and x, it could be that y causes x, x causes y, or that a third variable is causing both x and y.

5.10.1   Reverse Regression

The regression $\widehat{y} = b_1 + b_2 x$ is called **regression of** y **on** x. We could instead regress x on y, called a **reverse regression**, estimating

$$\widehat{x} = c_1 + c_2 y.$$

One might expect that one slope is the reciprocal of the other, so $c_2 = 1/b_2$, but this is not the case.

Using the formula for the slope coefficient with x and y reversed, the slope coefficient from the reverse regression is

$$c_2 = \frac{\sum_{i=1}^{n}(x_i - \bar{x})(y_i - \bar{y})}{\sum_{i=1}^{n}(y_i - \bar{y})^2},$$

and the intercept $c_1 = \bar{x} - b_2\bar{y}$. By inspection $c_2 \neq 1/b_2$. In fact the relationship between the two slope coefficients is

$$c_2 = b_2 \times \frac{s_x^2}{s_y^2}.$$

(To obtain this result, recall that $b_2 = r_{xy}s_y/s_x$. Similarly, $c_2 = r_{xy}s_x/s_y = [s_{xy}/s_x s_y] \times (s_x/s_y)$ given the definition of r_{xy}. Some rearrangement yields $c_2 = [s_{xy}/s_x^2] \times (s_x^2/s_y^2) = b_2 \times (s_x^2/s_y^2)$.)

Remark 37 *The slope coefficient from reverse regression of x on y does not equal the reciprocal of the slope coefficient from regression of y on x.*

For the house price regression, $b_2 = 73.77$. The reverse regression of house size on house price yields slope $c_2 = 0.0084$. This differs from the reciprocal $1/b_2 = 1/73.77 = 0.0136$.

5.10.2   Causation

The data alone cannot tell us which direction, if any, is the appropriate direction to run a regression, as the only information in the data is the size of the correlation. Thus given a fitted model $\widehat{y} = b_1 + b_2 x$, without further information we can only say that a one unit increase in x **is associated with** a b_2 increase in y. We **cannot** say that a one unit increase in x causes a b_2 increase in y.

For example, a medical study might find that alcohol consumption is associated with depression. But is it alcohol consumption that causes depression, or is it depression that leads to alcohol consumption?

Table 5.6: Regression: Details for computation example.

i	x_i	y_i	$(x_i - \bar{x})$	$(y_i - \bar{y})$	$(x_i - \bar{x})(y_i - \bar{y})$	$(x_i - \bar{x})^2$
1	1	1	-2	-1	2	4
2	2	2	-1	0	0	1
3	3	2	0	0	0	0
4	4	2	1	0	0	1
5	5	3	2	1	2	4
Sum	15	10	0	0	4	10
Mean	$\bar{x} = 3$	$\bar{y} = 2$				

With additional information we may be able to say that one causes the other. For example, for the relationship between parents' height and height of their fully-grown child, the direction of causation is clear. Indeed it is from this example that Francis Galton coined the term **regression** over one hundred years ago. Let y be child's height and x be midparent height (the average of mother's and father's height). Galton found that $y \simeq \bar{x} + b_2(x - \bar{x})$ where $b_2 = 0.33 < 1$. Thus if the parents have above average height, so that $(x - \bar{x}) > 0$, then the child will on average also be of above average height, but not as much above average as the parents. Galton termed this "regression towards mediocrity", where mediocrity is the average or mean.

Many examples exist where the direction of causation is questionable. Often it is due to a third variable that may be driving both y and x. For example, higher education is positively associated with higher earnings. But this may be due solely to unobserved innate ability that leads to both higher earnings, due to higher productivity, and higher education, due to ability to study more advanced material.

Remark 38 *Regression of y on x measures the association between y and x but does not on its own measure the direction of causation between y and x.*

Most of this book focuses merely on association. Methods to determine causation, in the absence of strong prior information, are presented in Chapter 17.5 and illustrated in Chapters 13.5–13.8.

5.11 Computations for Correlation and Regression

This section provides an example of manual computation of the sample covariance, sample correlation coefficient, OLS coefficients, the standard error of the regression and R-squared.

Consider artificial data on number of vehicles per household (y) and household size (x) measured by number of people of all ages. There are five sample observations: $(x_1, y_1) = (1, 1)$, $(x_2, y_2) = (2, 2)$, $(x_3, y_3) = (3, 2)$, $(x_4, y_4) = (4, 2)$, and $(x_5, y_5) = (5, 3)$. The data are plotted in Figure 5.6, along with the regression line that is calculated below.

To calculate the various quantities we compute the relevant component for each observation and sum over observations. These calculations are presented in Table 5.6.

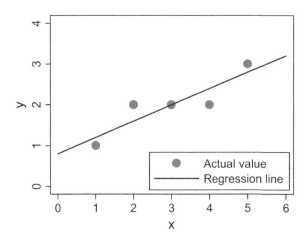

Figure 5.6: Regression: Scatterplot and regression line computation example

The sample covariance is $\frac{1}{n-1}\sum_{i=1}^{n}(x_i - \bar{x})(y_i - \bar{y}) = \frac{1}{4} \times 4 = 1$. It is positive indicating a positive association between cars and household size.

The sample correlation coefficient is computed as

$$r_{xy} = \frac{\sum_{i=1}^{n}(x_i - \bar{x})(y_i - \bar{y})}{\sqrt{\sum_{i=1}^{n}(x_i - \bar{x})^2 \times \sum_{i=1}^{n}(y_i - \bar{y})^2}} = \frac{4}{\sqrt{10 \times 2}} = \frac{2}{\sqrt{5}} = 0.894.$$

This is close to one and indicates strong positive association between cars and household size.

The OLS regression slope coefficient is

$$b_2 = \frac{\sum_{i=1}^{n}(x_i - \bar{x})(y_i - \bar{y})}{\sum_{i=1}^{n}(x_i - \bar{x})^2} = \frac{4}{10} = 0.4,$$

and the regression intercept is

$$b_1 = \bar{y} - b_2\bar{x} = 2 - 0.4 \times 3 = 0.8.$$

Thus the computed regression line is $\widehat{y} = 0.8 + 0.4x$.

The fitted values of $\widehat{y} = 0.8 + 0.4x$ for the five observations are, respectively, 1.2, 1.6, 2, 2.4, and 2.8. Then the residual sum of squares

$$ResSS = \sum_{i=1}^{n}(y_i - \widehat{y}_i)^2 = (1 - 1.2)^2 + (2 - 1.6)^2 + (2 - 2)^2 + (2 - 2.4)^2 + (3 - 2.8)^2 = 0.4.$$

The standard error of the regression is

$$s_e = \sqrt{\sum_{i=1}^{n}(y_i - \widehat{y}_i)^2/(n - 2)} = \sqrt{0.4/3} = 0.365148.$$

The explained sum of squares

$$ExpSS = \sum_{i=1}^{n} (\widehat{y}_i - \bar{y})^2 = (1.2-2)^2 + (1.6-2)^2 + (2-2)^2 + (2.4-2)^2 + (2.8-2)^2 = 1.6.$$

To compute the associated R^2 we also need to calculate the total sum of squares.

$$TSS = \sum_{i=1}^{n} (y_i - \bar{y})^2 = (1-2)^2 + (2-2)^2 + (2-2)^2 + (2-2)^2 + (3-2)^2 = 2.0.$$

Note that $ExpSS + ResSS = 0.4 + 1.6 = 2.0 = TSS$. So

$$R^2 = \frac{ExpSS}{TSS} = \frac{1.6}{2.0} = 0.8 \quad \text{or} \quad R^2 = 1 - \frac{ResSS}{TSS} = 1 - \frac{0.4}{2.0} = 0.8.$$

Thus 80% of the variation in number of cars is explained by household size. Note that the explained sum of squares is $2.0 - 0.4 = 1.6$. As expected, $r_{xy}^2 = (2/\sqrt{5})^2 = 4/5 = 0.8$ is equal to R^2.

5.12 Nonparametric Regression

The purpose of bivariate regression is to predict y given x. In this chapter we restrict attention to the linear model, with $\widehat{y} = b_1 + b_2 x$. Later chapters, notably Chapters 9 and 15, consider specific nonlinear models such as $\ln \widehat{y} = b_1 + b_2 \ln x$.

Nonparametric regression instead obtains fitted values $\widehat{y}$ without specifying (or parameterizing – hence the term nonparametric) a model for y given x.

Nonparametric regression would be straightforward if we had many values of y for each value of x, which can happen if the regressor takes a few discrete values. Then $\widehat{y}$ given x is simply the average of the values of y for each distinct value of x, called a **local average**. For example, if there were nine observations for which $x = 2$ then $\widehat{y}$ given $x = 2$ is simply the average of y for the nine observations for which $x = 2$.

There are two limitations to this approach. First, there may not be multiple observations for each potential value of x. Second, even if multiple observations are available, the local averages $\widehat{y}$ can vary considerably across adjacent values of x. This is analogous to forming a histogram with a very narrow bin width.

The standard nonparametric regression estimators smooth the local averages in a manner similar to kernel density estimation that leads to a smoother histogram. First, the averages are computed using rolling bins or windows of x that are overlapping rather than distinct. Second, in forming the average of y within each window of x more weight is given to observations that are closest to the center of the window and less to those near the ends of the window.

5.12.1 Local Constant, Local Linear and Lowess Regression

We briefly present the most commonly-used nonparametric estimators.

The **local constant estimator** or **Nadaraya-Watson estimator** smooths in a manner similar to kernel density estimation. First, local averages of y are computed using rolling bins or windows of x that are overlapping rather than distinct. Second, the local average of y within each window of x gives more weight to observations that are closest to the center of the window and less to those near the ends of the window. A local constant estimate of $\widehat{y}$ at the specific value $x = x_0$ is the following weighted average of y

$$\widehat{y}(x_0) = \sum_{i=1}^{n} w(x_i, x_0, h) y_i,$$

where the weights $w(x_i, x_0, h)$ sum over i to one and are greatest for x_i values closest to the evaluation point x_0. The weights depend on a **kernel function** $K(\frac{x_i - x_0}{h})$ where h is a bandwidth parameter that places more weight on x_i values closest to the evaluation point x_0 as h increases. The estimate is obtained at a series of evaluation points x_0.

The **local linear estimate** of $\widehat{y}$ at the specific value $x = x_0$ is obtained by local weighted regression. Specifically, $\widehat{y}(x_0) = a_0 + b_0 x_0$ where a_0 and b_0 minimizes the local weighted sum of squares

$$\sum_{i=1}^{n} K(\frac{x_i - x_0}{h}) \{y_i - a_0 - b_0(x_i - x_0)\}^2.$$

This provides better estimates of $\widehat{y}(x_0)$ for values of x_0 close to the minimum and maximum values of x.

The locally weighted scatterplot smoothing estimator (**lowess** or **loess**) is a variation of the local linear estimate that uses a variable bandwidth and downweights outlying values of y.

The less commonly-used kth **nearest neighbor estimate** of $\widehat{y}$ at the specific value $x = x_0$ uses just the k observations with x_i closest to x_0 and equally weights the k corresponding y_i observations.

5.12.2 Example: House Price and Size

Figure 5.7 illustrates two of the nonparametric regression estimation methods applied to the house price and size data. The solid curve is obtained by local linear regression. The dashed line is obtained by lowess estimation.

The two methods give similar results in this example, though in other cases there can be bigger differences, especially at the endpoints (low values and high values of *Size*) where estimation is noisier due to sparser data. The estimates vary with the window width, with wider windows leading to a smoother estimate, and to a lesser extent with the weighting function.

The two nonparametric regression estimates suggest that a linear model is a good model for these data. The linear model, assuming that it is a correctly specified model, has the advantages over the nonparametric regression of more precise estimation, and the possibility of prediction for values of x outside the range of sample values of x. Model-based methods also have the advantage of being more easily extended to regression with several regressors.

Nonparametric regression is most often used in exploratory data analysis, providing a visual summary of the relationship between two variables that can be useful in its own right and can aid in model specification and testing.

5.12.3 Nonparametric Regression Plots using a Statistical Package

The Stata `lpoly` command implements local constant and local linear regression and the `lowess` command implements lowess. For R, use the `ksmooth` function for local constant regression, `loess`

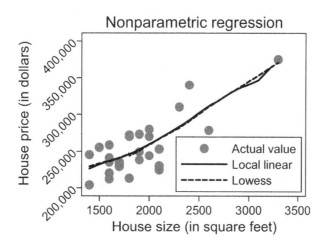

Figure 5.7: House price and size: Nonparametric regression using local linear and lowess.

for lowess; the `KernSmooth` package includes local linear regression. The Gretl `ndarwat` function provides local constant regression and `loess` implements lowess. For an Eviews `Scatterplot`, the `kernel fit` added element provides local constant and local linear regression and the `nearest neighbor fit` added element includes lowess.

The most important choice is the bandwidth. Different packages use different methods to specify the default bandwidth. Different packages can also use different kernel weighting functions. The most commonly-used kernels are Epanechnikov and Gaussian.

5.13 Key Concepts

1. A two-way tabulation or cross tabulation of two variables is a two-way frequency table that lists the number (or fraction) of observations equal to each of the distinct values taken by the pair of variables.

2. A two-way scatter plot is the standard tool for visualizing the relationship between two variables.

3. The sample correlation coefficient r_{xy} is a measure of association between two variables that lies between 1 (perfect positive association) and -1 (perfect negative association).

4. The autocorrelation at lag j of a time series is the correlation between current data and the data lagged j periods.

5. The least squares regression line is $\widehat{y} = b_1 + b_2 x$.

6. The residual $e = y - \widehat{y}$ is the difference between the actual and fitted values of the dependent variable.

7. The least squares coefficients b_1 and b_2 minimize the sum of squared residuals.

8. The least squares estimates can always be computed, provided there is some variation in the regressor value across observations.

9. The slope coefficient b_2 measures the change in the fitted value of y when x changes by one unit.

10. Regression on only an intercept yields the sample mean.

11. Regression of y on an intercept and an indicator variable yields the difference in means.

12. The standard error of the regression (s_e) measures the standard deviation of the residual, and hence the variability of y_i around the regression line.

13. R-squared (R^2) measures the fraction of the variation of y (around the sample mean $\bar{y}$) that is explained by the regressor.

14. For bivariate regression R-squared equals the squared correlation coefficient between x and y. And it equals the squared correlation between y and $\hat{y}$.

15. The slope coefficient is a multiple s_y/s_x of the sample correlation coefficient.

16. The correlation coefficient r_{xy} measures the number of standard deviations that y changes by when x changes by one standard deviation.

17. The slope coefficient from reverse regression of x on y does not equal the reciprocal of the slope coefficient from regression of y on x.

18. Least squares regression measures correlation, rather than causation. Without further information, we cannot say that a change in x causes y. The causal path may be reversed. Or both x and y may be associated with a third variable that is driving the association.

19. Nonparametric regression is a useful exploratory data analysis tool for providing a visual summary of the relationship between two variables.

20. Two commonly-used nonparametric methods are local linear regression and lowess.

21. Key Terms: two-way tabulation; cross tabulation; two-way scatter plot; sample covariance; sample correlation coefficient; positive correlation; negative correlation; autocorrelation; regression line; dependent variable; independent variable; explanatory variable; regressor variable; covariate; least squares regression; residual; fitted value; slope coefficient; ordinary least squares; intercept coefficient; prediction; in-sample prediction; out-of-sample prediction; standard error of the regression; intercept-only regression; R-squared; total sum of squares; explained (or regression or model) sum of squares; residual (or unexplained) sum of squares; error sum of squares; reverse regression; causation; nonparametric regression; local linear; lowess.

5.14 Exercises

1. Consider a dataset with three observations: $(x, y) = (2, 4)$, $(4, 10)$ and $(6, 28)$.

   (a) Provide a scatter plot of y against x. Is there a strong relationship? Explain.

   (b) From first principles calculate the covariance of y and x. Is there a strong relationship? Explain.

   (c) From first principles calculate the correlation of y and x. Is there a strong relationship? Explain.

   (d) Using a statistical package confirm your answer in part (c).

2. Repeat the previous exercise for observations $(x, y) = (2, 12)$, $(4, 12)$, $(6, 10)$ and $(8, 6)$.

3. Dataset DOCTORVISITS has individual-level data on the number of doctor visits in the past two weeks (*visits*) and the number of hospital admissions in the past 12 months (*hospadmi*).

   (a) Provide a cross tabulation of *visits* and *hospadmi*. Does there appear to be a relationship?

   (b) Provide a cross tabulation of *visits* and *hospadmi* that additionally includes the expected number of observations in each cell if *visits* and *hospadmi* are independent. Does there appear to be a relationship?

   (c) Obtain the correlation coefficient between *visits* and *hospadmi*. Does there appear to be a relationship?

4. Repeat exercise 3 for *visits* and *illness*, the number of illnesses in the past two weeks.

5. Consider a dataset with three observations: $(x, y) = (2, 4)$, $(4, 10)$ and $(6, 28)$.

   (a) From first principles calculate the slope coefficient from regression of y on an intercept and x.

   (b) Also compute the intercept coefficient.

   (c) Using a statistical package confirm your answers.

6. Repeat the previous exercise for observations $(x, y) = (2, 12)$, $(4, 12)$, $(6, 10)$ and $(8, 6)$.

7. Dataset HOUSE2015 has data on house sale price in dollars (*price*) and house size in square feet (*size*). Answer the following, and for each state whether there appears to be a relationship.

   (a) Provide a scatterplot of *price* against *size*. Does there appear to be a strong relationship?

   (b) Superimpose a regression line on your scatterplot of *price* against *size*.

   (c) Obtain the correlation coefficient between *price* and *size*.

   (d) Regress *price* on an intercept and *size*.

   (e) Provide a meaningful interpretation of the slope coefficient in part (d).

8. Repeat the previous exercise using dataset AUSREGWEALTH which has data on average net worth of households in thousands of dollars ($y = net\_worth\_per\_hh$) and average income per taxpayer in dollars ($x = income\_per\_taxpayer$) in 517 regions in Australia in 2003-04.

9. Variables x and y have variances of, respectively, 100 and 25, and their covariance is 10.

   (a) What is the sample correlation between the two variables?

   (b) What is the slope coefficient from regression of y on x?

   (c) If x increases by one standard deviation of x then on average by how many standard deviations of y will y change by?

10. Repeat the previous exercise when x and y have variances of, respectively, 400 and 16, and their covariance is 40.

11. Repeat exercise 7 using data in dataset REALGDPPC originally presented in Chapter 2.6 to analyze the relationship between real GDP per capita in dollars ($realgdppc$) and number of quarters since first quarter 1960 ($quarter$).

12. The dataset ANSCOMBE has 11 observations on variables x1–x4 and y1–y4.

   (a) Verify that x1–x4 have the same means and standard deviations.

   (b) Verify that y1–y4 have the same means and standard deviations.

   (c) Verify that the correlation between x1 and y1 equals that between x2 and y2, x3 and y3, and x4 and y4.

   (d) Verify that the intercept and slope coefficients from regression of y1 on x1 equals that from regression of y2 on x2, y3 on x3, and x4 on y4.

   (e) Now compare scatter plots of y1 on x1, y2 on x2, y3 on x3 and y4 on x4. Are you surprised? What is the lesson?

13. Consider a dataset with three observations on y equal to 2, 4 and 9. OLS regression of y on x leads to corresponding fitted values $\widehat{y}$ equal to 3, 5 and 7.

   (a) Obtain the OLS residuals. Do the residuals sum to zero?

   (b) Compute the residual sum of squares and the total sum of squares. Hence compute R^2.

14. Repeat the previous exercise if y equals 0, 4 and 5 and OLS regression of y on x leads to corresponding fitted values $\widehat{y}$ equal to 2, 3 and 4.

15. Consider a dataset with observations $(x, y) = (1, 7), (2, 1)$, and $(3, 1)$. From first principles as in Chapter 5.11 calculate the following.

   (a) The correlation coefficient between x and y.

   (b) Slope and intercept coefficients from least squares regression of y on x.

(c) The fitted values and residuals for the three observations. Do the residuals sum to zero?

(d) The standard error of the regression.

(e) The total sum of squares, explained sum of squares and the residual sum of squares. Does *ExpSS+ResSS= TSS*?

(f) R-squared. Compare R-squared to the squared correlation coefficient.

(g) The slope coefficient from reverse OLS regression of y on x. Compare this to your answer in part (b).

16. Repeat the previous exercise for a dataset with observations $(x, y) = (2, 4)$, $(4, 10)$ and $(6, 28)$.

17. Suppose regression of y on an intercept and x with 66 observations yields explained sum of squares 81 and total sum of squares 300.

(a) What is R^2?

(b) What is the correlation coefficient between y and x?

(c) What is the standard error of the regression?

18. You are given the following, where $\widehat{y}_i$ denotes fitted values after OLS regression. $\sum_{i=1}^{10}(x_i - \bar{x})^2 = 40$, $\sum_{i=1}^{10}(x_i - \bar{x})(y_i - \bar{y}) = 80$, $\sum_{i=1}^{10}(y_i - \bar{y})^2 = 360$, $\sum_{i=1}^{10}(y_i - \widehat{y}_i)^2 = 200$, $\bar{x} = 2$, $\bar{y} = 20$.

(a) Calculate the sample variance of y.

(b) Calculate the correlation coefficient between x and y.

(c) Calculate the OLS intercept and slope coefficients.

(d) Calculate the standard error of the regression.

(e) Calculate the R-squared of the regression.

19. Use dataset HOUSE to answer the following questions.

(a) Create the z-scores for *price* and *size*. (Recall: $z_i = (x_i - \bar{x})/s_x$).

(b) Use an appropriate command to verify that your new variables are standardized.

(c) Regress the z-score for *price* against the z-score for *size*.

(d) If house size increases by one standard deviation, by how many standard deviations does house price change?

(e) Compare the slope coefficient in part (c) to the correlation coefficient between *price* and *size*.

(f) Do reverse regression of *size* against *price*. Compare the slope coefficient and R^2 with that from regression of *price* against *size*. Comment.

20. Use dataset HOUSE to answer the following questions.

    (a) Regress *price* on just an intercept. Compare your answer with the sample mean of *price*.

    (b) Create an indicator variable *dsize* equal to 1 if *size* > 1800 and equal to 0 if *size* ≤ 1800.

    (c) Compute the mean of *price* for the two values of the indicator variable and compute the difference in means.

    (d) Regress *price* on an intercept and *size*. Compare your answer to that in c. (This result is explained in Chapter 14.2).

21. The dataset HOMEPRICEINDEX has monthly house price indices (=100 in January 2000) for twenty U.S. cities from January 1991 to September 2013.

    (a) Which city is least highly correlated with the composite10 index?

    (b) Which city is most highly correlated with the composite10 index?

    (c) Give a scatter plot for the price indices for the cities you found in parts (a)-(b), with the part a city on the vertical axis.

    (d) Regress the index for the part (a) city on that for the part (b) city. Explain in words the relationship between the two indices.

    (e) Find the squared correlation coefficient between the two cities. Compare this to R^2 from part (d).

22. The dataset ELECTRICITYPRICE has data for the California wholesale electricity market on the price of electricity (*price* in dollars per megawatt hour), and the volume of electricity (*volume* in megawatt hour) for the 3p.m.-4p.m. hourly period each day from January 1, 2000 to November 30, 2000.

    (a) Does the electricity price fluctuate very much over time? At what time of the year is it highest? Explain.

    (b) Does the volume of electricity fluctuate very much? At what time of the year is it highest? Explain.

    (c) Produce a scatter plot of price against volume, along with a fitted regression line.

    (d) Regress price against volume. Summarize your results.

    (e) Is this relationship estimating the supply curve or the demand curve? Hint: Electricity demand in California at this time was relatively price inelastic in the short run, but varied considerably with how hot it is. Short-run marginal costs increase with amount supplied as less efficient power plants come on line. Draw a price-quantity diagram with appropriate demand and supply curves.

23. The dataset KNEEREPLACE has 2011 data for many New York hospitals on the mean (the average over cases at each hospital) posted charge (*meancharge*) and mean cost (*meancost*) of knee joint replacement for cases of moderate severity. The actual amount paid is usually less than the posted charge with the difference varying according to the negotiating power of the hospital and the payer (usually an insurance company).

    (a) How much larger in relative terms is the average mean charge than the average mean cost?

    (b) Regress *meancharge* on *meancost*. Are you surprised by the value of the slope coefficient? Explain.

    (c) Now give a scatter plot of the data along with a fitted regression line. Note that two observations are outliers with the largest residual.

    (d) Using an appropriate computer command obtain the residuals and determine which two observations have the largest residual in absolute value.

    (e) Drop the largest outlier and regress mean charge on mean cost. Are you surprised by the value of the slope coefficient? Explain.

    (f) Additionally drop the second largest outlier and regress mean charge on mean cost. Are you surprised by the value of the slope coefficient? Explain.

24. This exercise requires precise calculation with new variables generated in double precision (see Appendix A.1). Some packages such as R do this automatically. If using Stata, however, for this exercise use the command `generate double` rather than `generate`, and use the command `predict double` rather than `predict`.

    (a) Run OLS regression of *price* on an intercept and *size* using dataset HOUSE.

    (b) Obtain the predicted *price* for each observation and compare the average of the predictions to the average *price*.

    (c) Obtain the residuals for each observation from this regression. Obtain the sample average of the residual. Comment.

    (d) Obtain the product of *size* times the residual for each observation. Obtain the sample average of this product. Comment.

25. Dataset HOUSE2015 has data on house sale price in dollars (*price*) and house size in square feet (*size*).

    (a) Provide a scatterplot of *price* against *size*.

    (b) Superimpose a regression line on your scatterplot of *price* against *size*.

    (c) Superimpose a nonparametric curve using any of local constant, local linear or lowess regression. You can use program defaults for these commands.

    (d) Does the relationship appear to be linear?

    (e) Redo part (c) using a window width is half that used in part (c). Comment on the difference.

26. Repeat the previous exercise for plot of *price* against *volume* using dataset ELECTRICITYPRICE.

Chapter 6

The Least Squares Estimator

Regression curve fitting is relatively easy. Now we consider the more difficult topic of extrapolation from the sample to the population.

Recall that in univariate statistics the sample mean was used to make inference about the population mean. Similarly the sample fitted regression line $\widehat{y} = b_1 + b_2 x$ can be used to make inference about the population line.

Different samples will lead to different fitted regression lines, due to different random departures in the data from the population conditional mean. Statistical inferential methods control for this randomness. For example, if the regression slope coefficient is greater than zero in our single sample, suggesting that y increases as x increases, does this necessarily hold in the population? Or is it just this particular sample that has this relationship?

This chapter presents the statistical properties of the least squares estimators. The subsequent chapter uses these properties to construct confidence intervals and perform hypothesis tests. For readers who skip this chapter, the essential properties of the least squares estimators are restated in Chapter 7.2.

6.1 Population Model for Bivariate Regression

For bivariate data we relate the sample fitted regression line to the population line, defined next. Interest lies especially in using the estimated slope coefficient of the fitted regression to make inference about the (unknown) slope of the population line.

6.1.1 Population Line or Conditional Mean

We wish to estimate the population relationship between y and x. That is, we would like to know what value of y to expect on average for each possible value that the regressor x might take.

Formally this is the **conditional mean** of Y given $X = x$, denoted $\mathrm{E}[Y|X = x]$, the **expected value** of Y given $X = x$. This is the probability-weighted average of all possible values of Y when X is restricted to taking the specific value x. The word "conditional" is added to indicate that the value of the mean of Y varies with the value x of the regressor.

125

Appendix B.3 provides more detail on conditional distributions and the conditional mean. It presents a specific example in which X can take two values (0 or 1) and the conditional mean of Y when $X = 1$ equals 40, whereas the conditional mean of Y when $X = 0$ takes the different value of 15.

For linear regression it is assumed that **conditional mean** of Y given $X = x$ is a **linear** function of x, so

$$\mathrm{E}[Y|X = x] = \beta_1 + \beta_2 x.$$

Here β is "beta", the Greek letter b. Then β_1 is the **population intercept parameter** and β_2 is the **population slope parameter**. The OLS coefficients b_1 and b_2 are the sample estimates of β_1 and β_2.

An example of a linear conditional mean is $\mathrm{E}[Y|X = 1] = 5$, $\mathrm{E}[Y|X = 2] = 7$, $\mathrm{E}[Y|X = 3] = 9$, since then $\mathrm{E}[Y|X = x] = 3 + 2x$ is linear in x. The conditional mean need not be linear, however. The example $\mathrm{E}[Y|X = 1] = 5$, $\mathrm{E}[Y|X = 2] = 7$, and $\mathrm{E}[Y|X = 3] = 12$ is nonlinear since there is an increase in the conditional mean of 2 from $X = 1$ to $X = 2$ but an increase of 5 from $X = 2$ to $X = 3$.

The linear function is a simplification as the conditional mean can in general be a quite complicated function of x. Some nonlinear relationships in the variables are studied in Chapters 9 and 15.

In the econometrics literature it is standard to write $\mathrm{E}[Y|X = x]$ more simply as $\mathrm{E}[y|x]$. Thus we write that the **conditional mean** or **conditional expectation** or **population line** is

$$\mathrm{E}[y|x] = \beta_1 + \beta_2 x.$$

The goal is to estimate the population line, as then we can make predictions and estimate the effect of changing x on the conditional mean $\mathrm{E}[y|x]$.

Remark 39 *$E[y|x]$ denotes the conditional mean of Y given $X = x$, the probability-weighted average of all possible values of Y given $X = x$. For linear regression $E[y|x] = \beta_1 + \beta_2 x$.*

6.1.2   Error Term

The dependent variable y does not exactly equal $\beta_1 + \beta_2 x$, it only equals $\beta_1 + \beta_2 x$ on average (more precisely, in expectation).

The difference between y and $\beta_1 + \beta_2 x$ is viewed as arising due to an **error term** or **disturbance term** that is denoted u. Thus we suppose that the data on y are generated by the **population model**

$$y = \beta_1 + \beta_2 x + u.$$

The notation u is used as the error is **unobserved**. Alternative notation for the error is ε, where ε is "epsilon", the Greek letter e. The error can be positive, leading to a y value above the population line, or negative, in which case the y value lies below the population line.

The first panel of Figure 6.1 shows a population line $\beta_1 + \beta_2 x$. The actual value of y is the value determined by the line plus the error u. For the displayed observation the error u is negative, leading to value y that is less than $\beta_1 + \beta_2 x$.

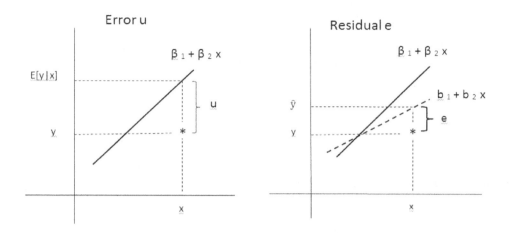

Figure 6.1: Error u is difference between y and population line. Residual e is difference between y and fitted regression line.

We assume that the **conditional mean of the error is zero**, so

$$E[u|x] = 0.$$

This means that for each value taken by the regressor variable x, on average the error term equals zero. For the model $y = \beta_1 + \beta_2 x + u$ the assumption that $E[u|x] = 0$ implies that the **conditional mean** of y given x

$$E[y|x] = \beta_1 + \beta_2 x.$$

6.1.3   Error Term versus Residual

The error term, denoted u, is not observed. It should not be confused with the residual, denoted e, which is observed and can be computed as the difference between y and the fitted value $\widehat{y} = b_1 + b_2 x$.

The second panel of Figure 6.1 adds a fitted regression line $b_1 + b_2 x$. Due to random sampling this will differ from the population line. The residual e is the difference between the fitted value $\widehat{y} = b_1 + b_2 x$ and the actual value y. For the displayed observation the residual is negative as the observed value y is less than $\widehat{y}$, and is smaller in absolute value than the error u.

More generally the residual may be smaller or larger in absolute value than the error and need not be of the same sign.

Remark 40 *The error term u is unobserved and equals the difference between y and the population line $\beta_1 + \beta_2 x$ where β_1 and β_2 are unknown population intercept and slope parameters. The residual e equals the difference between y and the fitted regression line $b_1 + b_2 x$ where b_1 and b_2 are intercept and slope coefficients estimated by OLS regression.*

6.1.4   Population Conditional Variance

The error term u provides the only variation in the distribution of Y given $X = x$. It follows that the **population conditional variance** of Y given $X = x$, denoted simply as $\text{Var}[y|x]$, equals the conditional variance of u given x. Thus

$$\text{Var}[y|x] = \text{Var}[u|x].$$

The simplest models assume that this variance does not vary with x. This means that for each value taken by the regressor variable x there is the same variation around the population line. This constant variance is denoted σ_u^2.

Remark 41 *The conditional variance of Y given $X = x$ is a measure of the variance of Y around the population line (for given $X = x$). This conditional variance equals $\sigma_u^2 = Var[u|x]$.*

6.1.5   Summary

In the univariate case it was assumed that $y_1, ..., y_n$ is a simple random sample from

$$Y \sim (\mu, \sigma^2),$$

and inference on μ is based on the sample mean $\bar{y}$.

For bivariate regression it is assumed that $(x_1, y_1), ..., (x_n, y_n)$ is a sample with data independent across observations and that

$$Y|X = x_i \sim (\beta_1 + \beta_2 x_i, \sigma_u^2).$$

Inference on β_1 and β_2 is based on the least squares estimates b_1 and b_2.

Remark 42 *Compared to univariate analysis, bivariate regression allows the population mean of Y to vary with the value taken by X, according to a linear relationship.*

6.2   Examples of Sampling from a Population

This section begins by generating a single example of five observations to make clear the difference between the population line and the sample line. This is followed by two examples that illustrate how different samples from the same population lead to different fitted regression lines. One example uses artificially generated data, while the other randomly draws observations from a well-defined finite population.

These examples demonstrate the more general result that

- the regression coefficients b_1 and b_2 on average are close to the population slope parameters β_1 and β_2

- the regression coefficients are approximately normally distributed, provided the sample size is sufficiently large.

Table 6.1: Generated data: Model y = 1 + 2x + u where u is N(0, 4) distributed.

Observation	x	E[y|x]=1+2x	u	y=1+2x+u
1	1	1+2×1=3	1.689889	4.689889
2	2	1+2×2=5	-.3187171	4.681283
3	3	1+2×3=7	-2.506667	4.493333
4	4	1+2×4=9	-1.63328	7.366720
5	5	1+2×5=11	-2.390764	8.609236

6.2.1 Single Sample Generated from an Experiment

Suppose that five observations on y and x are generated by the model

$$y_i = 1 + 2x_i + u_i, \quad i = 1, ..., 5$$
$$u_i \sim N(0, 4) \text{ independent over } i$$
$$x_1 = 1, \ x_2 = 2, ..., \ x_5 = 5.$$

Here the population line is $E[y|x] = 1 + 2x$ and the error term u has mean 0 and variance 4 that does not vary with x. There are five observations corresponding to values of x equal to $1, 2, ..., 5$.

Table 6.1 lists the generated data which are in dataset GENERATEDDATA. For the first observation, with $x_1 = 1$, suppose we draw error $u_1 = 1.689889$ from the $N(0, 4)$ distribution. Then $y_1 = 1 + 2 \times 1 + 1.689889 = 4.689889$. Other observations are similarly obtained.

The first panel of Figure 6.2 presents the true regression line $E[y|x] = 1 + 2x$ and the five generated observations for $y = 1 + 2x + u$. Note that the sample points deviate from the population regression line, due to the error term u. In this case the first observation $(x, y) = (1, 4.69)$ is above the line due to a positive error u, while the other four observations are below the population line due to negative draws of u.

The second panel of Figure 6.2 presents the fitted regression line $b_1 + b_2 x \simeq 2.81 + 1.05x$, obtain by OLS regression for the data listed in Table 6.1, along with the five data points. Clearly the fitted regression line differs from the population regression line.

The difference between the fitted regression line and the population regression line is due to sampling variability. The challenge is to make inference about the true regression line, which in practice is unknown, controlling for this sampling variability.

6.2.2 Many Samples Generated from an Experiment

Now suppose that many samples, each of 30 observations, are generated by the model

$$y_i = 1 + 2x_i + u_i \quad i = 1, ..., 30$$
$$u_i \sim N(0, 4) \text{ independent over } i$$
$$x_i \sim N(3, 1).$$

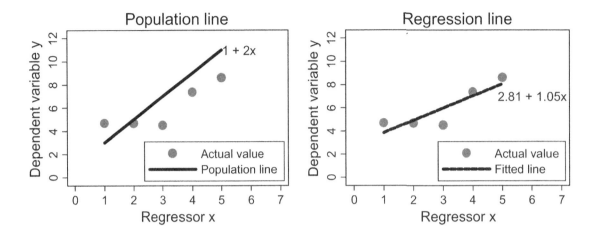

Figure 6.2: Generated data: True population line and fitted regression line.

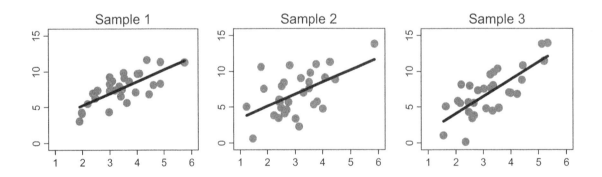

Figure 6.3: Generated data: Regression for three random samples (n = 30).

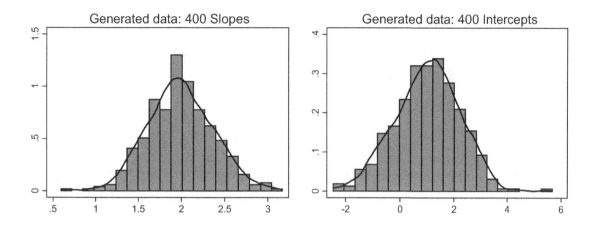

Figure 6.4: Generated data: Slopes and intercepts from 400 regressions (n=30).

Then $y = \beta_1 + \beta_2 x + u$ where $\beta_1 = 1$, $\beta_2 = 2$ and $\sigma_u^2 = 4$. This is similar to the preceding example, except now x takes a wider range of values than simply $1, 2, ..., 5$.

Figure 6.3 presents scatter plots of the data, and the associated fitted regression lines, for three randomly generated samples of size $n = 30$ from this population model. Clearly the data, and the consequent estimated intercept and slope coefficients b_1 and b_2, vary across the samples.

This exercise is repeated 400 times, yielding 400 samples of size 30 and hence 400 estimated slope coefficients and 400 intercepts that are in dataset GENERATEDREGRESSIONS.

The left panel of Figure 6.4 presents a histogram for the 400 estimated slope coefficients b_2. The histogram is roughly centered on the population slope coefficient $\beta_2 = 2$; in fact the average of the 400 estimated slopes is equal to 1.988.

The right panel of Figure 6.4 is a similar histogram for the 400 intercepts b_1, with average 1.018 close to the population value $\beta_1 = 1$.

It appears that on average the least squares coefficients are close to their population values. Furthermore, the histograms and kernel density estimates suggest that the least squares coefficients are approximately normally distributed.

6.2.3 Many Samples from a Finite Population: 1880 U.S. Census

The 1880 Census provides a complete enumeration of the U.S. population in 1880. We consider the relationship between labor force participation and age for males aged sixty to seventy years. The variable *Lfp* takes value 1 if in the labor force and value 0 if not in the labor force. The variable *Age* is age in years.

The Census gives the population. There are 1,058,475 males aged 60-70 years, of whom 89.45% were in the labor force. The population line is simply the regression line fitted using all 1,058,475

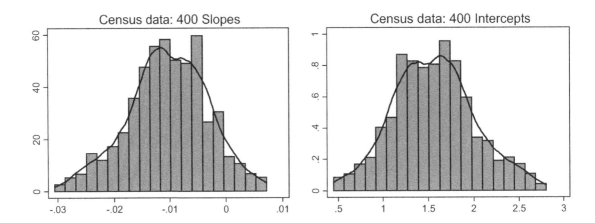

Figure 6.5: 1880 Census data: Slopes and intercepts from 400 regressions (n=200).

population values. This yields

$$\mathrm{E}[Lfp|Age] = 1.593 - 0.0109 \times Age,$$

so $\beta_1 = 1.593$ and $\beta_2 = -0.0109$. The negative coefficient on variable Age means that labor force participation declines with age, as expected. The population mean labor force participation rate is $1.593 - 0.0109 \times 60 = 0.939$ or 93.9% at age 60 and falls to 0.830 or 83.0% at age 70.

Now we take random samples of size 200 from this population and obtain estimates b_1 and b_2 for each sample. This corresponds to simple random sampling from the population. The larger sample size of 200 is used in this example because the fit for this regression is poor, with typical $R^2 \simeq 0.01$. The first three estimated samples yield regression estimates $1.708 - 0.0133 \times Age$, $1.535 - 0.0102 \times Age$, and $1.174 - 0.004 \times Age$.

400 samples of size 200 were randomly drawn from the Census data and fitted. This yields 400 fitted slopes and 400 intercepts that are given in dataset CENSUSREGRESSIONS.

The left panel of Figure 6.5 presents a histogram for the 400 estimated slope coefficients b_2. The histogram is roughly centered on the population slope coefficient $\beta_2 = -0.0109$; in fact the average of the 400 slopes is equal to -0.0104.

The right panel of Figure 6.5 is a similar histogram for the 400 intercepts b_1, with average 1.560 close to the population value $\beta_1 = 1.593$.

It again appears that on average the least squares coefficients are close to their population values. And the histograms and kernel density estimates suggest that the least squares coefficients are approximately normally distributed.

6.3 Properties of the Least Squares Estimator

From Chapter 5.5, the least squares slope and intercept estimates are

$$
\begin{aligned}
b_2 &= \frac{\sum_{i=1}^{n}(x_i - \bar{x})(y_i - \bar{y})}{\sum_{i=1}^{n}(x_i - \bar{x})^2} \\
b_1 &= \bar{y} - b_2\bar{x}.
\end{aligned}
$$

Alternative notation that is also commonly used is to denote b_1 and b_2 as $\widehat{\beta}_1$ and $\widehat{\beta}_2$, since they are viewed as estimators of β_1 and β_2 and a carat ($\widehat{\ }$) denotes an estimate.

In this section we detail the properties of b_1 and b_2 as estimators of the parameters β_1 and β_2. We present in order the mean, variance, standard deviation, standard error (the estimated standard deviation) and distribution of the slope coefficient b_2. Results are simply stated here. More detailed derivations are given in Chapter 16.2 and in Appendix C.1.

6.3.1 Data Assumptions

Throughout it is assumed that there is some variation in the regressors, so that $\sum_{i=1}^{n}(x_i - \bar{x})^2 \neq 0$. Otherwise it is not possible to compute the OLS coefficients b_1 and b_2. Additionally it is assumed that there are at least three observations. Otherwise it is not possible to compute the standard error of the regression.

The sampling process that yielded the sample $(x_1, y_1), \ldots, (x_n, y_n)$ can be simple random sampling, where (x_i, y_i) are jointly sampled from the population. Or the $x's$ may be fixed in advance, as is the case in a controlled experiment, with just the $y's$ randomly determined.

6.3.2 Population Assumptions

The statistical properties of the OLS coefficients depend crucially on the assumptions made about the population model. Since we are fitting a linear model, intuitively we need the population model to be linear, i.e. $E[y|x] = \beta_1 + \beta_2 x$. And the variability of estimates will depend on the variability of data around the population line, i.e. the variability of the error u.

The simplest and most restrictive assumptions, many of which are relaxed in later chapters, are

1. The **population model** is
$$
y_i = \beta_1 + \beta_2 x_i + u_i \text{ for all } i.
$$

2. The **error for the ith observation has zero mean conditional on the regressor**:
$$
E[u_i|x_i] = 0 \text{ for all } i.
$$

3. The **error for the ith observation has constant variance conditional on the regressor**:
$$
\text{Var}[u_i|x_i] = \sigma_u^2 \text{ for all } i.
$$

4. The **errors for different observations are statistically independent**

$$u_i \text{ is independent of } u_j \text{ for all } j \neq i.$$

Assumption 3 is called the assumption of conditionally **homoskedastic errors**, where the term "skedastic" is based on the Greek word for scattering and "homos" is the Greek word for same.

The following remark summarizes the relative importance of these assumptions.

Remark 43 *Population assumptions 1 and 2 are essential assumptions that imply that $E[y|x] = \beta_1 + \beta_2 x$. Population assumptions 3-4 are used to obtain an estimate of the precision of b_1 and b_2, and can be relaxed. Additionally it is assumed that there is some variation in the regressors and that $n \geq 3$.*

6.3.3   Mean and Variance of the Least Squares Slope Coefficient

Given assumptions 1-2 the **mean of the least squares slope coefficient** b_2 is

$$E[b_2] = \beta_2.$$

So b_2 is unbiased for β_2.

This result means that if we were able to obtain many random samples and for each sample estimate the slope coefficient, then the many different slope coefficients on average equal the population slope coefficient.

If we additionally make assumptions 3-4 then the **variance of the least squares slope coefficient** b_2 is

$$\text{Var}[b_2] \equiv \sigma_{b_2}^2 = \frac{\sigma_u^2}{\sum_{i=1}^{n}(x_i - \bar{x})^2}.$$

Assumptions 3-4 can be relaxed, in which case we get a different expression for $\text{Var}[b_2]$.

Remark 44 *Under assumptions 1-2 the estimated slope coefficient b_2 has mean equal to the population slope parameter β_2, so is unbiased. Under assumptions 1-4 the estimated slope coefficient b_2 has variance $\sigma_{b_2}^2 = \sigma_u^2 / \sum_{i=1}^{n}(x_i - \bar{x})^2$.*

6.3.4   Standard Error of the Least Squares Slope Coefficient

The standard deviation of b_2, denoted σ_{b_2}, depends on σ_u^2, the variance of the error term, which is unknown. The standard error of b_2, the estimated standard deviation of b_2, replaces σ_u^2 by an estimate.

Since $\sigma_u^2 = E[(y - \beta_1 - \beta_2 x)^2]$, an obvious estimator of σ_u^2 is the average of $(y_i - b_1 - b_2 x_i)^2 = (y_i - \hat{y}_i)^2$. Under assumptions 1-4 it can be shown that an unbiased estimator of σ_u^2 is obtained if the divisor in the average is $(n-2)$, rather than the more obvious division by n. Thus we estimate σ_u^2 by s_e^2 where

$$s_e = \sqrt{\frac{1}{n-2} \sum_{i=1}^{n}(y_i - \hat{y}_i)^2},$$

introduced in Chapter 5.6, is called the **standard error of the regression** or the **root mean square error**.

Replacing σ_u^2 by s_e^2 in the formula for $\text{Var}[b_2]$, and then taking the square root, the estimated standard deviation of b_2, called the **standard error of the slope coefficient**, is

$$se(b_2) = \frac{s_e}{\sqrt{\sum_{i=1}^{n}(x_i - \bar{x})^2}}.$$

Under assumptions 1-4, $\text{E}[se(b_2)^2] = \text{Var}[b_2]$, so $se(b_2)^2$ is unbiased for $\text{Var}[b_2]$.

As an example, consider the artificial data on a sample of size five, introduced in Chapter 5.11. Then the regression line was $\hat{y} = 0.8 + 0.4x$, $s_e = 0.365148$, and $\sum_{i=1}^{n}(x_i - \bar{x})^2 = 10$. It follows that $se(b_2) = 0.365148/\sqrt{10} = 0.115$.

6.3.5 When is the Slope Coefficient Precisely Estimated?

The standard error $se(b_2)$ measures the precision of b_2 as an estimate of β_2. Precision improves as $se(b_2)$ gets smaller. Since $se(b_2) = s_e/\sqrt{\sum_{i=1}^{n}(x_i - \bar{x})^2}$, it follows that the precision of estimation of β_2 is better

1. the closer the data are to the true regression line, as then s_e is small;

2. the larger is the sample size n, as then $\sum_{i=1}^{n}(x_i - \bar{x})^2$ has more terms and is larger;

3. the more widely scattered are the regressors x about their mean $\bar{x}$, as then $\sum_{i=1}^{n}(x_i - \bar{x})^2$ is larger.

The second property leads to an inverse square root rule for precision. If the sample size n quadruples, the sum $\sum_i(x_i - \bar{x})^2$ approximately quadruples, its reciprocal is approximately one-fourth as large and, taking the square root, $se(b_2)$ is approximately halved. More generally, if the sample is m times larger then the standard error of b_2 is approximately $1/\sqrt{m}$ times as large. Note that this is similar to the result for the sample mean which had standard error $s/\sqrt{n}$.

The third property suggests that precision is best if the regressors are widely scattered. This result is used in disciplines where the researcher can determine the regressor values, such as in the design of experiments.

Remark 45 *The standard error of b_2, the estimated standard deviation of b_2, is denoted $se(b_2)$ and equals $s_e/\sqrt{\sum_{i=1}^{n}(x_i - \bar{x})^2}$ under assumptions 1-4, where s_e is the standard error of the regression. Under assumptions 1-4 $se(b_2)^2$ is unbiased for the variance of b_2. Bigger samples are better – if the sample is m times larger then $se(b_2)$ is approximately $1/\sqrt{m}$ times as large. And wider dispersion of the regressor is better.*

6.3.6 Normal Distribution and the Central Limit Theorem

The histograms given in the left panels of Figures 6.4 and 6.5 suggest that the slope coefficients are approximately normally distributed. This is the case more generally, provided the sample size is sufficiently large.

The preceding results for the mean and variance of b_2 imply that under assumptions 1-4

$$b_2 \sim (\beta_2, \sigma_{b_2}^2).$$

Standardizing, by subtracting the mean and dividing by the standard deviation, yields a random variable with mean 0 and variance 1. Denoting this random variable by Z, we have

$$Z = \frac{b_2 - \beta_2}{\sigma_{b_2}} \sim (0, 1).$$

If additionally we assume that the sample size $n \to \infty$, then Z has the **standard normal distribution** by a **central limit theorem**. Thus

$$Z \sim N(0, 1) \text{ as } n \to \infty.$$

If follows that for large n a good approximation to the distribution of the least squares slope coefficient b_2 is

$$b_2 \sim N(\beta_2, \sigma_{b_2}^2).$$

We say that b_2 is **asymptotically normal** distributed.

How large should n be to use this result? In the univariate case it is felt that $n > 30$ is sufficient. For regression n should be larger, but there is no clear guide.

Remark 46 *Under assumptions 1-4 the standardized random variable $Z = (b_2 - \beta_2)/\sigma_{b_2}$ is standard normal distributed as the sample size goes to infinity. For large n a good approximation is that $b_2 \sim N(\beta_2, \sigma_{b_2}^2)$.*

In practice σ_{b_2} is unknown as it depends on the error variance σ_u^2 which is unknown. Instead we replace σ_{b_2} by the standard error s_{b_2}, leading in Chapter 6 to the t statistic and use of the t distribution rather than the standard normal distribution.

6.3.7   The Least Squares Intercept Coefficient

The preceding results consider the slope coefficient. Similar results, including the following, can be obtained for the intercept.

Under assumptions 1-2 the intercept estimate $b_1 = \bar{y} - b_2\bar{x}$ has the property that $E[b_1] = \beta_1$. So b_1 is unbiased for β_1.

Given assumptions 1-4 the variance of b_1 is $\text{Var}[b_1] = \sigma_u^2 \sum_{i=1}^n x_i^2 / [n \sum_{i=1}^n (x_i - \bar{x})^2]$. The standard error of the intercept estimate b_1 is then

$$se(b_1) = \sqrt{\frac{s_e^2 \sum_{i=1}^n x_i^2}{n \sum_{i=1}^n (x_i - \bar{x})^2}},$$

where s_e is the standard error of the regression.

If additionally $n \to \infty$ then $Z = (b_1 - \beta_1)/\sigma_{b_1} \sim N(0, 1)$, where $\sigma_{b_1}^2$ is the variance of b_1.

6.3.8 Relaxing Assumptions 1-4

Assumptions 1 and 2 are necessary for the OLS estimators to be unbiased. Assumptions 3-4 regarding the error variance and the independence of errors lead to the formula for $\text{Var}[b_2]$ being $\sigma_u^2 / \sum_{i=1}^n (x_i - \bar{x})^2$. Variants to assumptions 3-4 on the error term, presented later, lead to alternative formulas for $\text{Var}[b_2]$ and hence different values for standard errors, confidence intervals and t-statistics.

Assumption 1 specifies the basic relationship to be **linear**. Least squares regression can be adapted to nonlinear relationships, however; see Chapters 9 and 15.

Assumption 2 is crucial, even in more general models than the single regressor linear model of assumption 1. It means that for any value of x, the error u on average equals zero. This crucial assumption rules out, for example, the possibility of high values of x being associated with high values of u.

To investigate the reasonableness of assumption 2, consider regression of earnings on years of schooling. In that case the error term includes all things other than schooling that may effect the level of earnings, such as innate ability. People with high ability might be expected to have, on average, higher levels of schooling (x). But even given their level of schooling, they might be expected to have an additional boost to their earnings due to innate activity, in which case the error (u) is positive. This suggests that, for larger values of x, $\text{E}[u|x] > 0$. This is a violation of assumption 2.

It can be shown that assumption 2 implies that the error term u is uncorrelated with the regressor x (see Appendix B.3.6), so

$$\text{Cor}[u_i, x_i] = 0.$$

So an alternative way to state assumption 2 is that the **error term is uncorrelated with the regressor**.

Assumption 2 can be accommodated somewhat by adding additional regressors in the model, in the hope that after doing so the remaining error is uncorrelated with the regressors. In the earnings-schooling example we could include as an additional regressor a variable measuring innate ability, if such data were available, and use multiple regression presented in later chapters. Then the remaining error may be uncorrelated with the regressors.

Throughout most of this text it is assumed that assumption 2 holds. Chapter 16.4 provides further discussion. Chapters 17.4 and 17.5 on causal methods discusses relaxation of assumption 2, and Chapters 13.5–13.8 provide some applications of causal methods.

Assumption 3 implies that regardless of the value taken by x, the error term u has conditional (on x) variance that does not vary with x. This rules out, for example, that in a regression of earnings on schooling, the variability in earnings is greater for those with high levels of schooling than it is for low levels of schooling. Assumption 3 is called the assumption of conditionally **homoskedastic errors**, where the term "skedastic" is based on the Greek word for scattering and "homos" is the Greek word for same.

Note that there is an asymmetry. Assumptions 1-2 imply that the conditional mean varies with x while assumption 3 is that the conditional variance does not vary with x. Assumption 3 can easily be relaxed, however; see Chapters 7.7 and 12.1.

Assumption 4 means that the value taken by the error u for one observation is unrelated to the value of the error for other observations. This rules out, for example, a time series model for GDP where, say, a positive error in one period (so GDP is unusually high given the regressor) is quite likely to be followed by a positive error in the subsequent period. Assumption 4 can be relaxed, however; see Chapters 7.7 and 12.1.

6.3.9   Summary for the Least Squares Slope Coefficient

A summary given assumptions 1-4 is the following.

1. Individual observations y_i given x_i are assumed to have conditional mean $\beta_1 + \beta_2 x_i$ and conditional variance σ_u^2.

2. The slope coefficient b_2 from a sample of size n has mean β_2 and variance $\sigma_{b_2}^2 = \sigma_u^2 / \sum_{i=1}^n (x_i - \bar{x})^2$.

3. The standard error of the slope coefficient b_2 is s_{b_2} where $s_{b_2}^2 = s_e^2 / \sum_{i=1}^n (x_i - \bar{x})^2$ and $s_e^2 = \frac{1}{n-2} \sum_{i=1}^n (y_i - \widehat{y}_i)^2$.

4. The standardized statistic $Z = (b_2 - \beta_2)/\sigma_{b_2}$ has mean 0 and variance 1.

5. As sample size $n \to \infty$, Z is standard normal distributed by the central limit theorem.

6.4   Estimators of Model Parameters

Desirable properties of an estimator of a parameter were defined and explained in Chapter 3.6, and are not repeated here. In this section we apply these same concepts to the OLS estimates b_1 and b_2 of the population model parameters β_1 and β_2.

6.4.1   Unbiased Estimator

Under assumptions 1-2, $E[b_1] = \beta_1$ and $E[b_2] = \beta_2$, so the least squares estimators are **unbiased estimators**. This means that if we obtain many samples and hence many estimates b_1 and b_2, on average these estimates will equal β_1 and β_2.

Remark 47 *The OLS estimators b_1 and b_2 are unbiased for β_1 and β_2 under assumptions 1-2; essentially under sampling such that $E[y_i|x_i] = \beta_1 + \beta_2 x_i$.*

6.4.2   Minimum Variance Estimator

The least squares estimates b_1 and b_2 are not the only unbiased estimators of β_1 and β_2. As in Chapter 3.6, ideally we should use the **best estimator** or **efficient estimator,** which is the estimator with **minimum variance** in the class of estimators under consideration; here unbiased estimators.

First, restrict attention to slope estimators that are weighted averages of the dependent variable y, of the form

$$b_2 = \sum_{i=1}^{n} w_i y_i,$$

where the weights w_i can depend on the regressor values. The least squares slope coefficient is a special case with $w_i = (x_i - \bar{x}) / \sum_{j=1}^{n} (x_j - \bar{x})^2$. It can be shown that under assumptions 1-4, the least squares estimator has the smallest variance of all such weighted average estimators. These weighted averages are linear combinations of $y_1, ..., y_n$. So under assumptions 1-4 the least squares estimator b_2 is called the **best linear unbiased estimator** (or **BLUE**) of β_2. A similar result holds for b_1 as an estimator of β_1.

Second, if we make assumptions 1-4 and the additional assumption that the errors are normally distributed, then the least squares estimates of b_1 and b_2 can be shown to have the lowest variances of any unbiased estimators of β_1 and β_2. So under assumptions 1-4 and the assumption of normal errors the least squares estimators are the **best unbiased estimators** (or **BUE**) .

Remark 48 *The OLS estimators b_1 and b_2 are best linear unbiased under assumptions 1-4, and best unbiased if additionally the errors are normally distributed.*

6.4.3 Consistent Estimator

The estimator b_2 is consistent for β_2 if its distribution collapses on the point β_2 as the sample size gets large. A sufficient condition for consistency of an unbiased estimator is that additionally the variance of the estimator goes to zero as $n \to \infty$. Now $\text{Var}[b_2] = \sigma_u^2 / [\sum_{i=1}^{n} (x_i - \bar{x})^2]$ under assumptions 1-4, so all we need is that the regressors are such that $\sum_{i=1}^{n} (x_i - \bar{x})^2$ goes to infinity as progressively more observations are added. Similarly b_1 is consistent for β_1 under these assumptions.

Remark 49 *The OLS estimators b_1 and b_2 are consistent for β_1 and β_2 under assumptions 1-2 plus any additional assumptions, such as assumptions 3-4, that ensure that the variances of b_1 and b_2 exist and go to zero as $n \to \infty$.*

Furthermore, it can be shown that in standard settings the OLS estimator has smallest variance among consistent estimators given assumptions 1-4.

6.4.4 Least Squares in Practice

Assumptions 1-2 are essential for the least squares estimators to be unbiased and consistent. These assumptions are sufficient for unbiasedness, and not much more is needed for consistency. If these assumptions fail then alternative estimation methods are needed. Examples include failure of assumption 1 due to a nonlinear relationship, and failure of assumption 2 due to regressors correlated with the error.

This introductory text focuses on settings where at least assumptions 1-2 hold, so least squares is a valid procedure. But the formulas presented for the standard errors, and hence the values of the resultant confidence intervals and test statistics, depend on the additional assumptions 3-4. In Chapters 7.7 and 12.1 we discuss alternative formulas for the standard errors under variations of assumptions 3-4 that are often more reasonable assumptions for the economics data analyzed in practice.

6.5   Key Concepts

1. The conditional mean of Y given $X = x$, denoted, $E[Y|X = x]$ denotes the conditional mean of Y given $X = x$, the probability-weighted average of all possible values of Y in the population given $X = x$.

2. The simpler notation $E[y|x]$ is typically used in the econometrics literature.

3. For linear regression $E[y|x] = \beta_1 + \beta_2 x$.

4. Statistical inferential methods extrapolate the sample OLS estimates b_1 and b_2 of the regression line to the population parameters β_1 and β_2.

5. The error term u leads to randomness of y around the population line $\beta_1 + \beta_2 x$.

6. The sample must be such that there is some variation in the regressors.

7. The key population assumptions are (1) $y = \beta_1 + \beta_2 x + u$, and (2) $E[u|x] = 0$.

8. Additional population assumptions are needed to obtain the standard error and distributions of the estimates.

9. The simplest additional assumptions are (3) $\text{Var}[u|x] = \sigma_u^2$ does not vary with x (homoskedasticity), and (4) the errors u are uncorrelated across observations.

10. The slope coefficient standard error $se(b_2)$ is smaller the better the regression line fits the data, the larger the sample, and the greater the variability of the regressors in the sample.

11. Under assumptions 1-4 the standardized random variable $Z = (\beta_2 - b_2)/\sigma_{b_2}$ is standard normal distributed as the sample size goes to infinity. A good approximation is that $b_2 \sim N(\beta_2, \sigma_{b_2}^2)$.

12. Under assumptions 1 and 2, b_1 and b_2 are unbiased estimator of β_1 and β_2. With additional assumptions such as assumptions 3 and 4, b_1 and b_2 are consistent estimators of β_1 and β_2.

13. Under assumptions 1-4, least squares is the best linear unbiased estimator. If additionally the errors are normally distributed then least squares is the best unbiased estimator.

14. Key Terms: Population line; parameter; conditional mean; conditional variance; error term; disturbance term; assumptions 1-4; homoskedastic errors; ordinary least squares; standard error of the slope coefficient; standard error of the regression; asymptotically normal; degrees of freedom; unbiased; consistent; best linear unbiased; BLUE; best unbiased.

6.6 Exercises

1. Suppose the population model is $y = 1 + 2x + u$ and $E[u|x] = 0$. We obtain a sample with $(x, y) = (1, 3.78), (2, 6.69), (3, 7.56)$ leading to fitted regression line $\hat{y} = 2.23 + 1.89$. For each of the three observations give the following.

   (a) The conditional mean of y given x.   (b) The error term.   (c) The fitted value of y.

   (d) The residual term.

2. Repeat exercise 1 with $y = -1 + 3x + u$ and $(x, y) = (1, 4.92), (2, 4.99), (3, 8.12)$, and $\hat{y} = 2.81 + 1.60x$.

3. Suppose $y = 3 + 5x + u$ with $u \sim (0, 4)$.

   (a) Give the conditional mean of y given x.   (b) Give the conditional variance of y given x.

4. For each of the following state when the slope coefficient is likely to be more precisely estimated, holding other things constant.

   (a) The sample size is 100 or the sample size is 400.

   (b) The regressor ranges from 30 to 40 or the regressor ranges from 0 to 70.

   (c) The error term has variance 2 or the error term has variance 10.

5. You are given the following, where $\hat{y}_i$ denotes fitted values after OLS regression. $\bar{x} = 2$, $\bar{y} = 10$, $\sum_{i=1}^{20}(x_i - \bar{x})^2 = 80$, $\sum_{i=1}^{20}(x_i - \bar{x})(y_i - \bar{y}) = 120$, $\sum_{i=1}^{20}(y_i - \bar{y})^2 = 900$, $\sum_{i=1}^{20}(y_i - \hat{y}_i)^2 = 450$.

   (a) Compute the OLS slope and intercept estimates.

   (b) Compute the standard error of the OLS slope coefficient.

6. Repeat the previous exercise if $\sum_{i=1}^{10}(x_i - \bar{x})^2 = 40$, $\sum_{i=1}^{10}(x_i - \bar{x})(y_i - \bar{y}) = 80$, $\sum_{i=1}^{10}(y_i - \bar{y})^2 = 360$, $\sum_{i=1}^{10}(y_i - \hat{y}_i)^2 = 200$, $\bar{x} = 2$, $\bar{y} = 20$.

7. For each of the following state which is expected to lead to a more precise OLS estimate of the slope coefficient.

   (a) $n = 50$ or $n = 100$.   (b) $\sigma_u^2 = 10$ or $\sigma_u^2 = 20$.   (c) $\sum_{i=1}^{30}(x_i - \bar{x})^2 = 40$ or $= 80$.

8. For each of the following state the expected approximate change in the standard error of the OLS estimate of the slope coefficient.

   (a) n increases from 50 to 200.   (b) σ_u^2 increases from 10 to 90.

   (c) $\sum_{i=1}^{30}(y_i - \hat{y}_i)^2$ increases from 25 to 100.

9. The population model is $y_i = 1 + 2x_i + u_i$ where the error term has conditional mean 0 and conditional variance $4x_i^2$.

   (a) Will the OLS estimator be unbiased? Explain.

   (b) Will the OLS estimator most likely be consistent? Explain.

   (c) Will the OLS estimator of the slope coefficient have variance $\sigma_u^2 / \sum_{i=1}^n (x_i - \bar{x})^2$? Explain.

10. Suppose an estimator $b \sim (\beta, \sigma^2)$. State true or false to the following.

   (a) $(b - \beta)/\sigma \sim (0, 1)$ necessarily.   (b) $(b - \beta)/\sigma \sim N(0, 1)$ necessarily.

   (c) $(b - \beta)/\sigma \sim N(0, 1)$ is likely in large samples.

11. Suppose $y_i = \beta_1 + \beta_2 x_i + u_i$. For each of the following situations state whether the OLS slope coefficient b_2 can be consistently estimated using $se(b_2) = s_e / \sqrt{\sum_{i=1}^n (x_i - \bar{x})^2}$.

   (a) u_i independent over i with $u_i | x_i \sim (0, 4)$. Explain.

   (b) u_i independent over i with $u_i | x_i \sim (0, 4e^{x_i})$. Explain.

   (c) u_i is correlated with u_j for $j \neq i$ and $u_i | x_i \sim (0, 4)$. Explain.

12. Suppose $y_i = \beta_1 + \beta_2 x_i + u_i$. For each of the following situations state whether the OLS slope coefficient b_2 is unbiased for β_2.

   (a) u_i independent over i with $u_i | x_i \sim (0, 4)$.

   (b) u_i independent over i with $u_i | x_i \sim (0, 4e^{x_i})$.

   (c) $u_i | x_i$ is correlated with u_j for $j \neq i$ and $u_i \sim (0, 4)$.

   (d) u_i independent over i with $u_i | x_i \sim (0.2x_i, 4)$.

13. The following Stata code generates a sample with 10 observations where $y_i = 1 + 2x_i + u_i$ where x_i is uniformly distributed on $(0, 2)$ and $u_i \sim N[0, 4^2]$.

   (a) Run this code.

   (b) Is the slope coefficient close to what you expect? Explain.

```
clear
set seed 10101
set obs 10
generate x = runiform(0,2)
generate u = rnormal(0,4)
generate y = 1 + 2*x + u
regress y x
```

If using R then instead use the following code.

```
set.seed(10101)
x=runif(10,0,2)
u=rnorm(10,0,4)
y = 1 + 2*x + u
ols = lm(y~x)
summary(ols)
```

14. Now increase the sample size to 1,000 observations.

    (a) Is the slope coefficient close to what you expect? Explain.

    (b) A rule of thumb is that if you increase the sample size m times then the standard error of the estimate is roughly $1/\sqrt{m}$ times as large. Does that appear to be the case here?

15. The following Stata code estimates the model of exercise 13 400 times where each sample has 10 observations. See Chapter 3.8 for explanation of some of the commands used below.

    (a) Run this code.

    (b) Does the OLS slope coefficient appear to be unbiased? Explain.

    (c) Does the OLS slope coefficient appear to be normally distributed? Explain. (Hint: The normal distribution has skewness 0 and kurtosis 3).

```
program onesample, rclass
    drop _all
    quietly set obs 10
    generate x = runiform(0,2)
    generate u = rnorm(0,4)
    generate y = 1 + 2*x + u
    regress y x
    return scalar slope = _b[x]
end
simulate slope=r(slope), seed(10101) reps(400): onesample
summarize slope, detail
histogram slope
```

If using R then instead use the following code.

```
set.seed(10101)
result.bslope=array(dim=400)
for(i in 1:400){
    x=runif(10,0,2)
    u=rnorm(10,0,4)
    y = 1 + 2*x + u
    ols = lm(y~x)
    summary(ols)
    result.bslope[i]=coef(summary(ols))[2,1]
}
summary(result.bslope)
install.packages("moments")
library(moments)
skewness(result.bslope)
kurtosis(result.bslope)
hist(result.bslope)
```

16. Continue with the preceding code but instead generate the error using Stata command `generate u = sqrt(8)*(rchi2(1)-1)` or R command `u=sqrt(8)*(rchisq(100,1)-1)`. This generates an error with mean 0 and standard deviation 4, but the error is no longer normally distributed and is right-skewed.

    (a) Does the OLS slope coefficient appear to be normally distributed? Comment.

    (b) Now increase the sample size in part (a) to 100. Does the OLS slope coefficient appear to be normally distributed? Comment.

Chapter 7

Statistical Inference for Bivariate Regression

As explained in Chapter 6, the OLS intercept and slope coefficients are random outcomes – different samples lead to different estimates. The sample at hand is viewed as being one from a population, where the conditional mean of y given x is $\beta_1 + \beta_2 x$.

The goal is especially to make inference on the population slope parameter β_2 given the estimated slope parameter b_2. For example, is the view that house prices increase with house size consistent with the slope estimate of 73.77 obtained for the house price and size dataset HOUSE analyzed in Chapter 5.

The chapter continues directly from the previous chapter. For readers who bypassed the details in Chapter 6, the key results for statistical inference on β_2 are reproduced in Chapter 7.2.

7.1 Example: House Price and Size

Table 7.1 presents key output for statistical inference following regression of house price (in dollars) on size (in square feet) using data in dataset HOUSE.

The slope and intercept coefficients (73.77 and 115017) were discussed in Chapter 5.5. The standard errors of the coefficients, introduced in Chapter 6.3, are $se(b_2) = 11.17$ and $se(b_1) = 21489$. These are the estimated standard deviations of b_2 and b_1.

The table description uses the term **default** standard errors because they are computed under assumptions 1-4. Chapter 7.7 introduces alternative standard errors that are obtained when

Table 7.1: House price and size: Regression estimates with default standard errors.

Variable	Coefficient	Standard Error	t statistic	p-value	95% confidence interval	
Size	73.77	11.17	6.60	0.000	50.84	96.70
Intercept	115017.30	21489.36	5.35	0.000	70924.76	159109.8

assumptions 3 and 4 are relaxed.

The remainder of the table is explained briefly here, with detailed explanation provided in the rest of the chapter.

The t statistic for the slope coefficient is for test of $H_0 : \beta_2 = 0$ against $H_a : \beta_2 \neq 0$. The reason for testing specifically whether $\beta_2 = 0$ is that if this is indeed the case, then there is no (linear) association between house price and house size. Given $\beta_2 = 0$, the t statistic simplifies to $t = b_2/se(b_2) = 73.77/11.17 = 6.60$. The p-value is the probability of observing a $T(n-2)$ distributed random variable that is larger than the observed t statistic in absolute value; here $p = \Pr[|T_{27}| > |6.60|] = 0.0000004$ from t tables or statistical package. Since $p < 0.05$ we reject H_0 at significance level 0.05.

The 95% confidence interval for β_2 is (50.84, 96.70). There is a 95% chance that this interval will correctly include the unknown β_2.

The sample size is $n = 29$, a small sample size so the $T(n-2)$ distribution may not necessarily be a good approximation. This approximation may nonetheless be reasonable since the model fits the data well with $R^2 = 0.618$.

7.2   t Statistic

Statistical inference on the population slope parameter is based on the t statistic, a transformation of the estimated slope coefficient, rather than the estimated slope coefficient itself.

7.2.1   Model Assumptions

To obtain the statistical properties of the OLS coefficients we need to make assumptions about the population model and the sampling process that yielded the sample $(x_1, y_1), ..., (x_n, y_n)$. We begin by summarizing key results from Chapter 6.

The population model is assumed to satisfy the following assumptions

1. The population model is: $y_i = \beta_1 + \beta_2 x_i + u_i$ for all i.

2. The error terms have zero mean conditional on the regressor: $E[u_i|x_i] = 0$ for all i.

3. The error terms have constant variance conditional on the regressor: $Var[u_i|x_i] = \sigma_u^2$ for all i.

4. The errors for different observations are statistically independent: u_i is independent of u_j for all $j \neq i$.

Assumptions 1-2 imply that the population line for y is linear in the regressor x, with $E[y_i|x_i] = \beta_1 + \beta_2 x_i$. The OLS coefficients b_1 and b_2 are estimators of the unknown intercept and slope parameters β_1 and β_2 of this population line. The additional assumptions 3-4 determine the formulas for the variances of b_1 and b_2.

Under assumptions 1-4, and the additional assumption that the sample size is large, b_1 and b_2 are normally distributed by the central limit theorem. This result does not require an assumption about the exact distribution of the error term u (and hence the distribution of y). The result is that the standardized variable

$$Z = \frac{b_2 - \beta_2}{\sigma_{b_2}} \sim N(0, 1) \text{ as } n \to \infty,$$

where $\sigma_{b_2}^2 \equiv \text{Var}[b_2] = \sigma_u^2 / \sum_{i=1}^{n} (x_i - \bar{x})^2$.

7.2.2 The t Statistic

The development of the t statistic for inference on β_2 is qualitatively similar to development of the t statistic for inference on μ given in Chapter 4.2. The preceding normal distribution result for Z requires knowledge of σ_{b_2}, the standard deviation of b_2. In practice this is not known, as it depends in part on σ_u, the standard deviation of the error.

As a result σ_{b_2} needs to be replaced by its estimate, the standard error $se(b_2) = s_e / \sqrt{\sum_i (x_i - \bar{x})^2}$, where sle is an estimate of σ_u. This adds noise, leading to the statistic

$$T = \frac{b_2 - \beta_2}{se(b_2)}$$

that is approximately $T(n-2)$ distributed, a distribution that has fatter tails than the standard normal.

The following result considers the slope parameter. A similar result exists for the intercept.

Remark 50 *From a sample* $(x_1, y_1), ..., (x_n, y_n)$ *calculate the* **OLS intercept and slope coefficients** b_1 *and* b_2, *the standard error of the regression,* s_e, *and hence the standard error of* b_2, $se(b_2) = s_e / \sqrt{\sum_{i=1}^{n} (x_i - \bar{x})^2}$. *Given assumptions 1-4, the t* **statistic**

$$t = \frac{b_2 - \beta_2}{se(b_2)}$$

is a realization of a random variable that is approximately $T(n-2)$ *distributed, where* $T(n-2)$ *denotes the* **t distribution** *with* $n-2$ *degrees of freedom.*

The $T(n-2)$ distribution is exact if additionally the error term is normally distributed; otherwise it is an approximation that improves as the sample size gets larger.

The t distribution, discussed in detail in Chapter 4.2, is bell-shaped and coincides with the standard normal distribution as $n \to \infty$. One departure from Chapter 4 is that for bivariate regression the $T(n-2)$ distribution is used rather than the $T(n-1)$ for the mean. The intuition is that two degrees of freedom are lost due to estimation of two parameters (β_1 and β_2), whereas only one parameter (μ) was estimated in the univariate case.

To form the t statistic the only sample statistics needed are the fitted slope b_2 and its standard error $se(b_2)$. Additionally the t statistic depends on the population slope parameter β_2, which is unknown. The knowledge that the t statistic is $T(n-2)$ distributed is used to make statistical inference on β_2, as detailed in subsequent sections of this chapter.

7.3 Confidence Intervals

Different samples yield different regression lines with different slopes. A confidence interval for β_2 gives a range of values that, with a specified probability or level of confidence, includes β_2.

7.3.1 Confidence Interval for the Slope Parameter

Construction of a confidence interval for β_2 mimics that for the population mean given in Chapter 4.3 and the generalization given in Chapter 4.7.

A t statistic that is t_v distributed yields a $100(1-\alpha)$ percent confidence interval for a parameter that is of form *estimate* $\pm t_{v,\alpha/2} \times$ *standard error*. Applying this general result to β_2 estimated by b_2 yields the following.

Remark 51 *A* $\mathbf{100(1-\alpha)}$ *percent confidence interval for the slope parameter* β_2 *is*

$$b_2 \pm t_{n-2,\alpha/2} \times se(b_2),$$

where b_2 is the OLS slope coefficient, $t_{n-2,\alpha/2}$ is that value such that a $T(n-2)$ distributed random variable exceeds it in absolute value with probability $\alpha/2$, and $se(b_2)$ is the standard error of the slope coefficient estimate b_2.

This confidence interval is exact under assumptions 1-4 if additionally the data are normally distributed; otherwise it is an approximation that improves as the sample size gets larger.

The confidence interval is centered around b_2, the estimate of β_2. It is narrower the more precisely b_2 estimates β_2, as $se(b_2)$ is then smaller. Thus the confidence interval should narrow as the sample size gets larger.

A $100(1-\alpha)\%$ confidence interval for β_2 is one that with probability $1-\alpha$ includes the true (and unknown) population slope coefficient β_2. Higher levels of confidence arise if the confidence interval is wider; in the formula above $T(n-2)$ becomes larger as α becomes smaller.

7.3.2 What Level of Confidence?

There is no best choice for the confidence level. The trade-offs between high level of confidence and narrow confidence interval are the same as those discussed at length for confidence intervals for the population mean; see Chapter 4.3.

The standard choice is to form a 95% confidence interval, so $\alpha = 0.05$. This is the default level used in output from a regression package. Most regression packages allow the user the option to select a different level of confidence. The other most common choices are 90% and 99% confidence intervals.

From Table 4.4, $t_{n-2,.025} \simeq 2$ for most values of $n > 30$. Then an approximate 95% confidence interval is $b_2 \pm 2 \times se(b_2)$.

Remark 52 *It is most common, though arbitrary, to use a 95% confidence interval.* **An approximate 95% confidence interval** *for* β_2 *is the* **two-standard error interval**, *the estimate b_2 plus or minus two times the standard error $se(b_2)$.*

In any published work or in assignments, however, use the more precise interval $b_2 \pm t_{n-2,.025} \times se(b_2)$.

7.3.3 Example: House Price and Size

As an example, consider the house price and size data. Regression on a sample of size $n = 29$ yields coefficient $b_2 = 73.77$ and standard error $se(b_2) = 11.17$. And $t_{n-2,\alpha/2} = t_{27,.025} = 2.052$ from a statistical package or from a table. So the 95% confidence interval for β_2 is

$$b_2 \pm t_{n-2,\alpha/2} \times se(b_2) = 73.77 \pm 2.052 \times 11.17 = 73.77 \pm 22.93 = (50.84, 96.70).$$

This is the confidence interval given in Table 7.1.

7.3.4 Example: Artificial Data

As a second example, consider artificial data on a sample of size $n = 5$, where y is the number of cars in a household and x is the number of people in the household. The sample values of (x, y) are $(1, 1)$, $(2, 2)$, $(3, 2)$, $(4, 2)$ and $(5, 3)$.

From Chapter 5.11, $b_1 = 0.8$ and $b_2 = 0.4$, and $se(b_2) = s_e / \sqrt{\sum_{i=1}^{n}(x_i - \bar{x})^2} = 0.365148 / \sqrt{10} = 0.115$. For a 95% confidence interval from a sample of size 5 we use critical value $t_{3,.025} = 3.182$. A 95% confidence interval for the slope coefficient β_2 is

$$b_2 \pm t_{3,.025} \times se(b_2) = 0.4 \pm 3.182 \times 0.115 = 0.4 \pm 0.367 = (0.033, 0.767).$$

Given the small sample size this inference requires the additional assumption that the error term u is normally distributed.

7.3.5 Interpretation of Confidence Intervals

Interpretation of confidence intervals is conceptually difficult. For this reason the discussion in Chapter 4.3 for the population mean is repeated, with adaptation to the regression case.

Consider the house price example with 95% confidence interval $(50.84, 96.70)$ for the population slope β_2. The correct interpretation of this confidence interval is that **the calculated 95 percent confidence interval** from this sample **includes β_2 with probability 0.95.**

To understand this interpretation it is necessary to imagine that there are many separate samples of the population, each of size $n = 29$ in the house price and size example. For concreteness suppose the true population slope coefficient is $\beta_2 = 70.0$. The first sample may yield a confidence interval of, say, $(40.7, 75.8)$. A second sample will have a different slope estimate and associated standard error and hence a different confidence interval of, say, $(56.7, 95.3)$. And so on. Some samples will have unusually large or small estimated values of the slope coefficient. For example, one sample might have an unusually high value $b_2 = 98.7$ with standard error $se(b_2) = 11.3$, say, so that $t_{27,.025} \times se(b_2) = 23.2$, leading to a 95% confidence interval of $(75.5, 121.9)$. This confidence interval, unlike the preceding ones, does not include the population slope parameter which is 70.0.

Thus the confidence interval will sometimes fail to include the population value β_2, due to the randomness inherent in sampling. A 95% confidence interval has the property that if we were able to obtain many separate random samples, 95 percent of the resulting confidence intervals will include β_2, and 5 percent will not.

In fact we have only one sample, and we say that the calculated 95% confidence interval from this sample includes the true population slope coefficient β_2 with probability 0.95. Note that it is wrong to instead interpret this confidence interval as meaning that with probability 0.95 the population parameter β_2 lies inside $(50.84, 96.70)$ and with probability 0.05 it lies outside this range.

Remark 53 *A calculated 95 percent confidence interval for the population slope parameter β_2 is an interval that includes β_2 with probability 0.95.*

7.4   Tests of Statistical Significance

Hypothesis tests are used to decide whether a specified value of β_2 is plausible, given the sample estimate b_2. Before providing a general treatment of hypothesis testing for the slope coefficient, building on Chapter 4.4 for tests on the population mean, we briefly consider the most common test, that of whether or not $\beta_2 = 0$.

7.4.1   Tests of Statistical Significance

For linear regression, the most common hypothesis test is a test of whether or not the population slope parameter equals zero. The reason for this test is that if $\beta_2 = 0$ then there is no relationship between y and x in the population.

This test is called a test of the statistical significance of a regressor. It answers the question of whether or not there is an association between x and y. If there is no association, then clearly $\beta_2 = 0$ and the population regression model $y = \beta_1 + \beta_2 x + u$ reduces to $y = \beta_1 + u$, so that y bounces around a mean value of β_1.

Remark 54 *A **two-sided test** or **two-tailed test** of the statistical significance of a regressor for the population mean μ is a test of the null hypothesis*

$$H_0 : \beta_2 = 0,$$

against the alternative hypothesis

$$H_a : \beta_2 \neq 0.$$

The test of whether $\beta_2 = 0$ is based on how far the sample estimate b_2 is from zero. If b_2 was very precisely estimated, then even small departures of b_2 from 0 lead to the conclusion that $\beta_2 \neq 0$, while if b_2 is very imprecisely estimated then large departures of b_2 from 0 are needed to conclude $\beta_2 \neq 0$. The precision or imprecision of b_2 is controlled for by using the t statistic, $T = (b_2 - \beta_2)/se(b_2)$, evaluated here at the null hypothesis value of $\beta_2 = 0$. Thus we use the t statistic, also called the t-ratio $t = \frac{b_2}{se(b_2)}$. H_0 is rejected if the observed t is far from zero.

Remark 55 *The t **statistic** for test of $H_0 : \beta_2 = 0$ against $H_a : \beta_2 \neq 0$ is the **t-ratio***

$$t = b_2/se(b_2).$$

Under H_0, and given assumptions 1-4, t is the realization of a random variable that is approximately $T(n-2)$ distributed.

From Chapter 4.4 the **p-value** is the probability of observing a t statistic at least as large in absolute value as that obtained in the current sample. Here $p = \Pr[|T_{n-2}| \geq |t|]$. This p-value is compared to the **significance level** α that is a preset cutoff value for the p-value.

Regression packages automatically print out both the t statistic for test of $H_0 : \beta_2 = 0$ against $H_a : \beta_2 \neq 0$ and the associated p-value. Since the p-value is the probability that the observed t occurs by chance, if in fact $\beta_2 = 0$, small p-values are evidence against the null hypothesis and in favor of the alternative hypothesis.

Remark 56 *Let $p = \Pr[|T_{n-2}| \geq |t|]$ be the p-value for test of $H_0 : \beta_2 = 0$ against $H_a : \beta_2 \neq 0$. If $p < \alpha$ then H_0 is rejected at significance level α, and the regressor is said to be **statistically significant at significance level** α. If instead $p > \alpha$ then H_0 is not rejected and the regressor is said to be **statistically insignificant at level** α.*

For example if $p = 0.03$ then the regressor is statistically significant at significance level 0.05, since $0.03 < 0.05$. But the regressor is statistically insignificant at significance level 0.01, since $0.03 \not< 0.01$. The most common choice of α is 0.05, followed by 0.01 and 0.10.

The **critical region** approach, see Chapter 4.4, provides an alternative approach to using p-values that leads to the same conclusion. This defines a range of values for the t statistic that leads to rejection at the specified significance level α. For regression with a single regressor and test at significance level α, the **critical value** is $c = t_{n-2,\alpha/2}$ and we reject H_0 if $|t| > t_{n-2,\alpha/2}$.

As demonstrated in Table 4.4, $t_{n-2,.025} \simeq 2$ for $n > 30$. So, approximately, a test will conclude that the regressor is statistically significant at level 0.05, the most common choice of α, if $|t| > 2$. This leads to the following:

Remark 57 *A regressor is (approximately) statistically significant at level 0.05 if $|b_2|$ exceeds two times the standard error of b_2.*

7.4.2 Example: House Prize and Size

For the house price and size data, Table 7.1 gives $t = 6.60$ with $p = 0.000$ to three decimal places. (More precisely, $p = \Pr[|T_{27}| > 6.60] = 0.000000441$). So, at the usual significance level of $\alpha = 0.05$, H_0 is rejected and there is a statistically significant relationship between *Price* and *Size*. Indeed, here *Size* is a highly statistically significant regressor since p is so low.

7.4.3 Economic Significance versus Statistical Significance

For a regressor to be useful in explaining the dependent variable it should be both statistically significant and economically significant.

Remark 58 *A regressor is of **economic significance** if its coefficient is of large enough value for it to matter in practice. Economic significance depends directly on b_2, while statistical significance depends directly on t which is the ratio $b_2/se(b_2)$.*

Determining economic significance requires subjective interpretation that varies with the application. Suppose house price (in dollars) is regressed on number of bedrooms. A slope coefficient of $b_2 = 100$ has little economic significance, as then another bedroom is associated with only a \$100 increase in price, while a slope coefficient of 100,000 has great economic significance. Even this interpretation might change if the data pertain to Afghanistan, rather than the U.S., as Afghanistan has per capita GDP of less than US \$1,000.

The fact that a regressor is statistically significant does not necessarily mean that it is of economic significance. With enough data any regressor that is even very mildly associated with the dependent variable is likely to be statistically significant, since the standard error of b_2 falls as the sample size increases.

Going the other way, the fact that a regressor is statistically insignificant does not necessarily mean that it is of no economic significance. It may just be that imprecise estimation, often due to a small sample size or little variation in the regressor, leads to a standard error that is too large for the variable to be statistically significant.

It is easy to be overly reliant on tests of statistical significance. For a two-sided test at level 0.05 statistical significance is determined, approximately, according to whether or not $|t| = |b_2|/se(b_2) > 2$, or equivalently whether $|b_2| > 2 \times se(b_2)$. Economic significance is instead determined by whether $|b_2|$ is "small" or "large", a subjective judgement that is context specific.

7.4.4   Tests Based on the Correlation Coefficient

The **population correlation coefficient** ρ_{xy}, defined in Appendix B.3, measures the correlation between X and Y in the population. An alternative way to test whether there is a relationship between y and x is to test whether $\rho_{xy} = 0$, based on the sample correlation coefficient r_{xy} defined in Chapter 5.4.

Some algebra shows that if $se(b_2)$ is computed under assumptions 1-4, then $t = b_2/se(b_2)$ can be re-expressed in terms of r_{xy} as

$$t = \frac{r_{xy}\sqrt{n-2}}{\sqrt{1-r_{xy}^2}}.$$

So the two tests are closely related, and the t statistic is larger in absolute value the larger in absolute value is the sample correlation between y and x.

In some disciplines association between y and x is tested using the sample correlation coefficient rather than the regression slope coefficient. In large samples tests of statistical significance based on $b_2/se(b_2)$ lead to the same conclusions as tests of $H_0 : \rho_{xy} = 0$ against $H_a : \rho_{xy} \neq 0$ based on r_{xy}. In smaller samples the conclusions can differ somewhat.

This link between the t statistic and the sample correlation coefficient provides two insights. First, the correlation coefficient measures only linear association, since the regression model is linear. Second, statistically significant correlation between two variables means merely that the association is statistically significant; it need not be economically important.

Economists test association between two variables using regression based tests of $\beta_2 = 0$ rather than tests of zero correlation. One reason for doing so is that tests of correlation require that assumptions 1-4 hold, whereas regression-based tests using $t = b_2/se(b_2)$ can relax assumptions 3-4 leading to different ways to compute $se(b_2)$. A second reason is that economists usually estimate models with additional regressors.

7.5 Two-Sided Hypothesis Tests

The preceding section presented a simple way to test whether or not $\beta_2 = 0$. More generally we may wish to test whether β_2 equals other values. Then regression packages no longer automatically print out the relevant test statistic and its p-value. Instead some additional manual computation is needed, unless the regression package provides a separate command to perform such tests following regression.

Extension of hypothesis testing from μ to β_2 is almost immediate. To reinforce the methods, however, a fairly complete treatment is given here, despite obvious duplication of Chapter 4.4.

Let β_2^* denote a hypothesized value for β_2, such as $\beta_2^* = 0$ or $\beta_2^* = 90$.

Remark 59 *A **two-sided test** or **two-tailed test** for the population slope β_2 is a test of the null hypothesis*

$$H_0 : \beta_2 = \beta_2^*,$$

where β_2^* is a specified value for β_2, against the alternative hypothesis

$$H_a : \beta_2 \neq \beta_2^*.$$

The term two-sided is used as the alternative hypothesis covers both the case that $\beta_2 < \beta_2^*$ and the case that $\beta_2 > \beta_2^*$.

The following discussion builds on Chapter 4.4 for tests on the population mean. As in Chapter 4.4 we have

Definition 22 *A **type I error** occurs if H_0 is rejected when H_0 is true. The **significance level** of a test or **test size**, denoted α, is the pre-specified maximum probability of a type I error that will be tolerated.*

7.5.1 Example: House Price and Size

As an example, consider the claim that the population mean sale price of a house increases by \$90 per additional square foot in size, so $\beta_2^* = 90$. This would be a natural value to test if enlarging an existing house costs \$90 per square foot. From Table 7.1, the regression slope coefficient $b_2 = 73.77$ for a sample of $n = 29$ houses. Is this far enough away from 90 to reject the hypothesis that $\beta_2 = 90$? Or could this difference from 90 be merely an artifact of sampling variability?

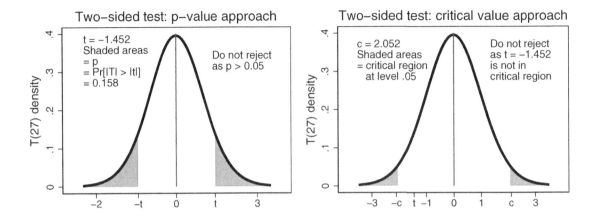

Figure 7.1: Two-sided hypothesis test: p-value approach and critical region approach.

To test $H_0 : \beta_2 = 90$ we evaluate the t statistic when $\beta_2 = 90$, yielding

$$t = (b_2 - 90)/se(b_2) = (73.77 - 90)/11.17 = -1.452.$$

If indeed $\beta_2 = 90$ this is a draw from the $T(27)$ distribution, since $n - 2 = 27$.

How likely are we to obtain a draw from the $T(27)$ distribution equal to or greater than -1.45 in absolute value? This probability is the p-value

$$p = \Pr[|T_{27}| \geq |-1.452|] = 0.158.$$

The first panel of Figure 7.1 illustrates the p-value. There is a somewhat low probability (0.158) of observing a t statistic value as large or larger than -1.45 in absolute value than if in fact $\beta_2 = 90$, suggesting that the null hypothesis that $\beta_2 = 90$ may be wrong. If we use the common convention to reject H_0 if this probability is less than 0.05, however, then we do not reject $H_0 : \beta_2 = 90$ since $p = 0.158 > 0.05$.

An alternative equivalent method bases rejection or non-rejection directly on the value of the t statistic. Suppose we require that $p < 0.05$ in order to reject H_0. This would require that $|t| > 2.052$ since $\Pr[|T_{27}| \geq 2.052] = 0.05$. The second panel of Figure 7.1 illustrates the rejection region, which does not include $t = -1.45$. Again $H_0 : \beta_2 = 90$ is not rejected at significance level 0.05.

7.5.2   Test Statistic

The test of whether $\beta_2 = \beta_2^*$ is based on the closeness of the sample estimate b_2 to the population slope β_2^*. But b_2 may differ from β_2^* for two reasons that lead to polar opposite conclusions. It may be that $\beta_2 \neq \beta_2^*$, so the null hypothesis should be rejected. Or it may be that $\beta_2 = \beta_2^*$ but $b_2 \neq \beta_2^*$ due to sampling variability in b_2. Then the null hypothesis should not be rejected.

The obvious decision rule is to reject $H_0 : \beta_2 = \beta_2^*$ if the OLS slope estimate b_2 is far from the hypothesized β_2^*. It is convenient to transform from this difference $(b_2 - \beta_2^*)$ to $(b_2 - \beta_2^*)/se(b_2)$, since the latter is known to have a t distribution.

Remark 60 *The t statistic for test of $H_0 : \beta_2 = \beta_2^*$ against $H_a : \beta_2 = \beta_2^*$ is $t = (b_2 - \beta_2^*)/se(b_2)$. Under H_0 and assumptions 1-4, t is the realization of a random variable that is approximately $T(n-2)$ distributed.*

7.5.3   Rejection using p-values

The p-**value** is the probability of observing a t statistic at least as large in absolute value as that obtained in the current sample, under the assumption that H_0 is correct so that $\beta_2 = \beta_2^*$.

Remark 61 *For a two-sided test of $H_0 : \beta_2 = \beta_2^*$ against $H_a : \beta_2 \neq \beta_2^*$ the p-**value**, the probability of observing a t statistic at least as large in absolute value as that obtained in the current sample, is $p = \Pr[|T_{n-2}| \geq |t|]$. H_0 is rejected at significance level α if $p < \alpha$, and is not rejected otherwise.*

The standard testing approach is to take the conservative stance of rejecting H_0 only if the p-value is low. The most common choice of significance level is $\alpha = .05$. The next most common choices are .10 and .01.

7.5.4   Rejection using Critical Regions

The p-value approach requires access to a computer, in order to precisely compute the p-value for any given value of t. An alternative approach requires only tables of the t distribution for selected values of α, and was the method used before the advent of ready access to computers.

This alternative approach defines a **critical region** or **rejection region** that gives the range of values of the t statistic that lead to rejection of H_0 at the specified significance level α. H_0 is rejected if the computed value of t falls in this range.

Remark 62 *For a two-sided test of $H_0 : \beta_2 = \beta_2^*$ against $H_a : \beta_2 \neq \beta_2^*$, and for specified α, the **critical value** c is such that $c = t_{n-2,\alpha/2}$; equivalently $\Pr[|T_{n-2}| \geq c] = \alpha$. H_0 is rejected at significance level α if $|t| > c$, and is not rejected otherwise.*

Many textbooks provide tables to compute c for selected values of α, as already noted. Alternatively one can use a function provided in a statistical package.

7.5.5   Relationship to Confidence Interval

Two-sided tests can be implemented using confidence intervals.

Remark 63 *If the null hypothesis value β_2^* falls inside the $100(1 - \alpha)$ percent confidence interval then do not reject H_0 at significance level α. Otherwise reject H_0 at significance level α.*

For the house price data, the 95% confidence interval for β_2 is $(50.84, 96.70)$. Since this interval includes 90 we do not reject $H_0 : \beta_2 = 90$ at significance level 0.05.

7.5.6　Summary: House Price Summary

A summary of the house price hypothesis test example is the following.

Hypotheses	$H_0 : \beta_2 = 90$, $H_a : \beta_2 \neq 90$
Significance level	$\alpha = 0.05$
Data	$b_2 = 73.77$, $se(b_2) = 11.17$, $n = 29$
Test statistic	$t = (73.77 - 90)/11.17 = -1.452$
(1) p-value approach	$p = \Pr[|T_{27}| \geq |-1.452|] = 0.158$
(2) Critical value approach	$c = t_{27,.025} = 2.052$
Conclusion	Do not reject H_0 at level .05 as (1) $p > .05$ or (2) $|t| < c$.

The p-value and critical value approaches are alternative methods that, for given significance level α, always lead to the same conclusion.

7.6　One-Sided Directional Hypothesis Tests

A one-sided hypothesis test is used to test a one-sided claim such as that the population slope parameter in the house sale example exceeds 90. A one-sided test uses the same test statistic as a two-sided test but the p-value and critical value are calculated differently, leading to a different rejection region. This section adapts to regression the lengthier treatment in Chapter 4.6.

7.6.1　One-Sided Directional Hypotheses

A two-sided hypothesis test is non-directional, as rejection may be due to concluding that either $\beta_2 < \beta_2^*$ or $\beta_2 > \beta_2^*$. A one-sided test, by contrast, is directional. For example, we may test against the alternative that $\beta_2 > \beta_2^*$.

For a **one-sided directional hypothesis test** care needs to be used in specifying the null and alternative hypotheses as the conclusion can differ according to which hypothesis is set up as the null and which is the alternative.

Remark 64 *For one-sided tests the statement being tested is specified to be the alternative hypothesis. And if a new theory is put forward to supplant an old, the new theory is specified to be the alternative hypothesis.*

For example, if we wish to test the claim that the population slope parameter exceeds 90, we should test $H_0 : \beta_2 \leq 90$ against $H_a : \beta_2 > 90$. By contrast, to test the claim that the population slope parameter is less than 90, we should test $H_0 : \beta_2 \geq 90$ against $H_a : \beta_2 < 90$.

Remark 65 *An **upper one-tailed alternative test** is a test of $H_0 : \beta_2 \leq \beta_2^*$, where β_2^* is a specified value for β_2, against $H_a : \beta_2 > \beta_2^*$. A **lower one-tailed alternative test** is a test of $H_0 : \beta_2 \geq \beta_2^*$ against $H_a : \beta_2 < \beta_2^*$.*

Some texts use a different notation for the null hypothesis in one-sided tests, defining it to be $H_0 : \beta_2 = \beta_2^*$ rather than $H_0 : \beta_2 \leq \beta_2^*$ (or $H_0 : \beta_2 \geq \beta_2^*$). This alternative notation makes no difference to the subsequent analysis as the alternative hypothesis remains the same.

7.6.2 P-values and Critical Regions

Inference for both types of one-sided test is based on the same calculated test statistic

$$t = (b_2 - \beta_2^*)/se(b_2),$$

as used for two-sided hypothesis tests. As usual this statistic is viewed as being the realization of a $T(n-2)$ distributed random variable. What differs in the one-sided case is calculation of the p-values and critical values.

For an **upper** one-tailed alternative test large positive values of t are grounds for rejection of H_0, since then b_2 (the estimate of β_2) is much larger than β_2^*. For a **lower** one-tailed alternative test large negative values of t lead to rejection of H_0, since then b_2 is much smaller than β_2^*.

Remark 66 *Let t be the usual t statistic. For an upper one-tailed alternative test the p-value is $p = \Pr[T_{n-2} \geq t]$, the critical value at significance level α is $c = t_{n-1,\alpha}$, and we reject H_0 if $p < \alpha$ or, equivalently, if $t > c$. For a lower one-tailed alternative test the p-value is $p = \Pr[T_{n-2} \leq t]$, the critical value at significance level α is $c = -t_{n-2,\alpha}$, and we reject H_0 if $p < \alpha$ or, equivalently, if $t < c$.*

Note that for a one-sided test $p = \Pr[T_{n-2} \leq t]$ which is one-half of $p = \Pr[|T_{n-2}| \leq t]$ for a two-sided test. We are therefore more likely to reject, at given significance level α, if we use a one-sided test.

Remark 67 *Provided $t > 0$ for an upper one-tailed alternative test, or $t < 0$ for an lower one-tailed alternative test, the p-value for a two-sided test can be calculated as one-half the p-value for a two-sided test.*

7.6.3 Example: House Price and Size

Suppose the claim is made that house prices increase by less than \$90 per additional square foot. Then the appropriate test is a lower one-sided test of $H_0 : \beta_2 \geq 90$ against $H_a : \beta_2 < 90$; as explained in Chapter 4.6.3 we make the claim the alternative.

The t statistic is the same as in the two-sided case, so $t = -1.45$. Now $p = \Pr[T_{27} \leq -1.45] = \Pr[T_{27} \geq 1.45] = 0.079$, where we have used the symmetry of the t distribution. H_0 is not rejected at significance level 0.05, since $p > 0.05$. Equivalently, the critical value $c = t_{27,.05} = -1.70$. $H_0 : \beta_2 > 90$ is again not rejected since $t = -1.45 > -1.70$. At significance level 0.05 there is not enough evidence to support the initial claim that house prices increase by less than \$90 per additional square foot.

Note that compared to the similar two-sided test at level $\alpha = 0.05$ the p-value is lower in the one-sided test (0.079 versus 0.158), making rejection of H_0 more likely. This is because it is easier to determine that β_2 lies in the narrower alternative hypothesis region $\beta_2 < 90$ than in the broader region $\beta_2 \neq 90$.

Table 7.2: Hypothesis tests: Summary for tests on the slope parameter.

	Two-sided Test	One-sided Upper alternative	One-sided Lower alternative
Null hypothesis	$H_0 : \beta_2 = \beta_2^*$	$H_0 : \beta_2 \leq \beta_2^*$	$H_0 : \beta_2 \geq \beta_2^*$
Alternative Hypothesis	$H_a : \beta_2 \neq \beta_2^*$	$H_a : \beta_2 > \beta_2^*$	$H_a : \beta_2 < \beta_2^*$
t statistic	$t = (b_2 - \beta_2^*)/se(b_2)$	$t = (b_2 - \beta_2^*)/se(b_2)$	$t = (b_2 - \beta_2^*)/se(b_2)$
Rejection region	Both tails	Right tail	Left tail
p-value	$p = \Pr[|T_{n-2}| \geq t]$	$p = \Pr[T_{n-2} \geq t]$	$p = \Pr[T_{n-2} \leq t]$
Rejection rule	$p < \alpha$	$p < \alpha$	$p < \alpha$
Critical value	$c = t_{n-2,\alpha/2}$	$c = t_{n-2,\alpha}$	$c = -t_{n-2,\alpha}$
Rejection region	$|t| > c$	$t > c$	$t < c$

7.6.4   One-sided Tests of Statistical Significance

When testing statistical significance of a regressor there may be a prior belief that the slope coefficient is positive or that it is negative. In that case an appropriate one-sided test should be used. For example if we believe the coefficient is positive we test $H_0 : \beta_2 \leq 0$ against $H_a : \beta_2 > 0$. This requires halving the printed p-value for a two-sided test. In addition one needs to verify that $b_2 > 0$ for tests against $H_a : \beta_2 > 0$ or that $b_2 < 0$ for tests against $H_a : \beta_2 < 0$.

Unfortunately there can be ambiguity in the statement that "the regressor is statistically significant at significance level 0.05" as it will not always be clear whether a one-sided or two-sided test was performed. Usually a two-sided test is reported. If a one-sided test is used it is clearer is to say that a regressor is **positively statistically significant** if the prior belief that β_2 is positive is supported by an upper one-tailed alternative test, and a regressor is **negatively statistically significant** if the prior belief that β_2 is negative is supported by a lower one-tailed alternative test.

7.6.5   Summary for One-Sided and Two-Sided Tests

Table 7.2 summarizes one-sided and two-sided hypothesis tests on the population slope coefficient. The p-value approach is the simplest testing approach, though some care is needed for one-sided tests.

While we have focused on computing $se(b_2)$ under assumptions 1-4, Table 7.2 continues to be used if alternative formulas for $se(b_2)$, presented in the next section, are used.

7.7   Robust Standard Errors

Standard errors for OLS coefficients obtained under assumptions 3-4 are called **default standard errors**. Those obtained under assumptions on the model errors weaker than assumptions 3-4 are called **robust standard errors**. Throughout it is assumed that sufficient assumptions are made to ensure that OLS is unbiased and consistent.

There are several different formulas for robust standard errors. These vary according to the alternative assumptions on the model errors which depends on the type of data being analyzed.

Most statistical packages, though not R and not Excel, will compute these alternative standard errors as an option to the basic OLS regression command. Chapter 12.1.9 and Appendix A present commands to compute robust standard errors in various statistical packages.

Given a robust standard error of b_2, denoted $se_{rob}(b_2)$, confidence intervals and hypothesis tests are based on using

$$T = \frac{b_2 - \beta_2}{se_{rob}(b_2)}.$$

The distribution of T is approximated by the $T(v)$ distribution, where the degrees of freedom v vary with the robust standard error that is used.

In this chapter we only present heteroskedastic-robust standard errors which are the most commonly-used example of robust standard errors for cross-section data. The other leading examples of cluster-robust standard errors for clustered data (such as panel data) and HAC-robust standard errors for time series data are presented in Chapter 12.1. An essential part of any regression analysis is knowing which particular robust standard error method should be used.

7.7.1 Heteroskedastic Robust Standard Errors

For **cross-section data** it is often reasonable to assume that model errors are independent across observations (assumption 4), but model errors may have variance whose size varies across observations. For example, the error variance may increase as the value of the regressor x increases. Then the errors are said to be **heteroskedastic** and assumption 3 is replaced with the assumption that $\text{Var}[u_i|x_i] = \sigma_i^2$, $i = 1, ..., n$, where σ_i^2 varies with i.

Provided assumptions 1-2 and 4 still hold, the OLS estimates remain unbiased and consistent. The one change is that the usual formula for the standard error of b_2, called the **default standard error**, is replaced by the **heteroskedasticity-robust standard error**

$$se_{het}(b_2) = \sqrt{\frac{n}{n-2}} \times \frac{\sqrt{\sum_{i=1}^n e_i^2 (x_i - \bar{x})^2}}{\sum_{i=1}^n (x_i - \bar{x})^2},$$

where e_i is the OLS residual. Appendix C.2 provides a derivation. Heteroskedasticity-robust standard errors are often within 20% of default standard errors, sometimes larger and sometimes smaller. The distribution of the t statistic is then approximated by the $T(n-2)$ distribution.

Most statistical packages provide this as an option for OLS regression. It is standard to use heteroskedastic-robust standard errors rather than default standard errors whenever model errors can be assumed to be independent across observations (assumption 4). These standard errors are often called **White robust standard errors**, after the econometrician Halbert White who introduced them in a seminal 1980 research article.

Remark 68 *Heteroskedastic-robust standard errors are used if assumptions 1-2 and 4 hold, but model errors are heteroskedastic rather than homoskedastic. These are routinely used for cross-section data.*

7.7.2   Example: House Price and Size

For the house price example the default standard errors for the slope and intercept coefficients are, respectively, 11.17 and 21489. The heteroskedastic-robust standard errors are, respectively, 11.33 and 20298, so the difference is very small in this example.

Then a 95% confidence interval for β_2 becomes $73.77 \pm t_{27,.025} \times 11.33 = (50.53, 97.01)$, compared to $(50.84, 96.70)$ when default standard errors are used.

And for test of $H_0 : \beta_2 = 0$, the test statistic $t = 73.77/11.17 = 6.51$, rather than 6.60 using default standard errors. Again $p = \Pr[|T_{27}| > 6.51] = 0.000$ and we reject the null hypothesis at level 0.05.

7.8   Key Concepts

1. Confidence intervals and hypothesis tests on the population slope β_2 are based on the t statistic $t = (b_2 - \beta_2)/se(b_2)$.

2. The t statistic is treated as being $T(n-2)$ distributed. This is an approximation that improves as $n \to \infty$. If assumptions 1-4 hold and additionally the errors are normally distributed then the t statistic is exactly $T(n-2)$ distributed.

3. A $100(1-\alpha)\%$ confidence interval for β_2 is $b_2 \pm t_{n-2,.\alpha/2} \times se(b_2)$. This interval will include β_2 with probability $1 - \alpha$.

4. It is most common to use 95%, 90% and 99% confidence intervals, corresponding to α equal to .05, .10 and .01.

5. An approximate 95% confidence interval for β_2 is $b_2 \pm 2se(b_2)$.

6. A two-sided hypothesis test of $H_0 : \beta_2 = \beta_2^*$ against $H_a : \beta_2 \neq \beta_2^*$ can be computed using either p-values or critical values.

7. A test of statistical significance is the special case that $\beta_2^* = 0$.

8. A statistically significant variable can be of little economic significance, and a statistically insignificant variable can still be of considerable economic significance.

9. For a two-sided test, the p-value is the probability of observing a $T(n-2)$ distributed random variable at least as large as the observed t in absolute value, i.e., $p = \Pr[|T_{n-2}| \geq |t|]$. H_0 is rejected at significance level α if $p < \alpha$.

10. For a two-sided test at significance level α, the critical value c is that value for which there is probability α of observing a $T(n-2)$ distributed random variable at least as large as c, so c is such that $\Pr[|T_{n-2}| \geq c] = \alpha$. We reject H_0 at level α if $|t| < c$.

11. An approximate two-sided test at level 5% is to reject H_0 if $|t| > 2$, or equivalently if $|b_2 - \beta_2^*| > 2se(b_2)$.

12. For one-sided tests we make the claim the alternative hypothesis.

13. An upper one-tailed test is a test of $H_0 : \beta_2 \leq \beta_2^*$ against $H_a : \beta_2 > \beta_2^*$.

14. A lower one-tailed test is a test of $H_0 : \beta_2 \geq \beta_2^*$ against $H_a : \beta_2 < \beta_2^*$.

15. Robust standard errors are used when assumptions 3 and/or 4 do not hold.

16. Heteroskedasticity-robust standard errors are used when model errors are heteroskedastic and independent (assumption 3 does not hold).

17. Key Terms: t statistic; confidence interval; null hypothesis; alternative hypothesis; significance level; statistical significance; economic significance; two-sided test; one-sided test; rejection; p-value; critical value; critical region; rejection region; heteroskedasticity; robust standard errors; heteroskedastic-robust standard errors; presentation of regression results.

7.9 Exercises

1. Dataset HOUSE2015 has data on house sale price in dollars (*price*) and house size in square feet (*size*).

   (a) Regress *price* on *size* and hence say how much house price increases on average when house size increases by one square foot.

   (b) Give the 95% confidence interval for the slope coefficient.

   (c) Perform a two-sided test at level 0.05 of the null hypothesis that house size is statistically significant.

   (d) Verify your answer in (b) using only the estimated slope coefficient, its standard error and critical values from the t distribution.

   (e) Verify your answer in (c) using only the estimated slope coefficient, its standard error and critical values or probability values for the t distribution.

2. Repeat the previous exercise except regress *price* on number of bedrooms (*bedrooms*).

3. Dataset SALARYSAT.DTA has data on 876 individuals aged 26-28 years observed in 2010. (The data are from the 2010 round for the representative sample of the National Longitudinal Survey of Youth 1997, an annual survey of the same individuals that began in 1997 when the youth were aged 12-18 years.) The variables include *salary* (annual in dollars), *satmath*, *satverb*, and *highgrade* (highest grade completed). Variables *satmath* and *satverb* are scores on the mathematics and verbal components of the SAT, a standardized test used for college admission in the U.S. Scores can range from 200 to 800; for confidentiality reasons the scores in this survey were rounded to increments of 100.

   (a) Obtain summary statistics. Do you see any strange values in the data?
   (b) Obtain the correlation between *salary* and *satmath*.
   (c) Regress *salary* on *satmath*. Interpret the slope coefficient.
   (d) Compare R^2 from this regression with the correlation coefficient obtained earlier.
   (e) Is the slope coefficient statistically significant at 5%?
   (f) Test at 5% the hypothesis that a 100 point increase in the SAT math score is associated with a $3,000 increase in salary. (Note: be careful with units here).

4. Repeat the previous exercise except consider the relationship between *salary* and *satverb*.

5. Consider the model $y = \beta_1 + \beta_2 x + u$. Regression of y on an intercept and x with a sample of 40 observations leads to slope coefficient equal to 7 with standard error equal to 3. Hint: For inference on β_2 the t statistic is $(b_2 - \beta_2)/se(b_2)$ and is t_{n-2} distributed.

   (a) Provide a 95 percent confidence interval for β_2.
   (b) Test the hypothesis that $\beta_2 = 0$ against the alternative that $\beta_2 \neq 0$ at significance level 0.05.
   (c) Test the hypothesis that $\beta_2 \leq 0$ against the alternative that $\beta_2 > 0$ at significance level 0.05.
   (d) Test the hypothesis that $\beta_2 = 10$ against the alternative that $\beta_2 \neq 10$ at level 0.05.
   (e) Which of assumptions 1-4 in the notes are necessary for this analysis to be valid?

6. Repeat the previous exercise for a sample of 86 observations with slope coefficient equal to 54 and standard error equal to 30. In part (d) test whether or not $\beta_2 = 100$.

7. Based on a very large sample we obtain estimate $\widehat{\theta} = 39$ with standard error of $\widehat{\theta} = 10$.

   (a) Obtain a 95% confidence interval for θ.
   (b) Do we reject $H_0 : \theta = 20$ against $H_a : \theta \neq 20$ at significance level 5%? Explain.
   (c) Now suppose the claim is made that θ exceeds 20. Perform a test of this claim at 5%, stating clearly the null and alternative hypotheses and your conclusion.

8. Repeat the previous exercise with $\widehat{\theta} = 75$, standard error of $\widehat{\theta} = 20$ and tests of $\theta = 50$.

9. Use dataset AUSREGWEALTH which has data on average net worth of households in thousands of dollars ($y = net\_worth\_per\_hh$) and average income per taxpayer in dollars ($x = income\_per\_taxpayer$) in 517 regions in Australia in 2003-04.

   (a) Provide a scatterplot of *net_worth_per_hh* against *income_per_taxpayer*. Does there appear to be a relationship?

   (b) Regress *net_worth_per_hh* on an intercept and *income_per_taxpayer*. Provide a verbal summary of the relationship between income per taxpayer (in dollars) and net worth per household (in dollars). Note: You need to pay attention here to the units of measurement.

   (c) Is *income_per_taxpayer* statistically significant at 5%?

   (d) Test at significance level 0.05 the claim that a $1 increase in income per taxpayer is associated with a $12 increase in net worth per household. State the null and alternative hypotheses and your conclusion. Note: You need to pay attention here to the units of measurement.

   (e) Test at significance level 0.05 the claim that a $1 increase in income per taxpayer is associated with a more than $12 increase in net worth per household. State the null and alternative hypotheses and your conclusion.

10. Repeat the previous exercise using as dependent variable assets of households in thousands of dollars ($y = assets\_per\_hh$).

11. Hospitals in the U.S. post very high charges, much higher than their costs. (Hospitals then discount off their posted prices with discount varying according to the power of the purchaser, such as an individual's health insurance company.) The dataset KNEEREPLACE has 2011 data for a number of New York hospitals on the average posted charge (*meancharge*) and average cost (*meancost*) of knee joint replacement for cases of moderate severity, where the average is over all such cases the hospital treated in 2011.

   (a) Provide a scatterplot of *meancharge* against *meancost*. Does there appear to be a relationship?

   (b) Regress *meancharge* on an intercept and *meancost*. Is *meancost* statistically significant at 5%?

   (c) Test at significance level 0.05 the claim that a $1 increase in the mean cost is associated with a $2 increase in the mean charge. State the null and alternative hypotheses and your conclusion.

   (d) Test at significance level 0.05 the claim that a $1 increase in the mean cost is associated with less than a $2 increase in the mean charge. State the null and alternative hypotheses and your conclusion.

12. Use dataset EARNINGS introduced in chapter 2.

    (a) Provide a scatterplot of *earnings* against *education*. Does there appear to be a relationship?

    (b) Regress *earnings* on an intercept and *education*. Is *education* statistically significant at 5%?

    (c) Test at significance level 0.05 that one more year of education is associated with annual earnings that are $4,000 higher. State the null and alternative hypotheses and your conclusion.

    (d) Test at significance level 0.05 that one more year of education is associated with annual earnings that are more than $4,000 higher. State the null and alternative hypotheses and your conclusion.

13. You are given the following partial OLS output. Provide (A) to (H)

```
    Source |      SS        df        MS              Number of obs =        21
-----------+----------------------------------        F(  2,    19) =
     Model |     270                                  Prob > F      =
  Residual |      90                                  R-squared     =        (B)
-----------+----------------------------------        Adj R-squared =
     Total |     (A)                                  Root MSE      =        (C)
------------------------------------------------------------------------------
         y |    Coef.   Std. Err.      t    P>|t|     [95% Conf. Interval]
-----------+------------------------------------------------------------------
         x |       6       3.0       (D)    (E)        (F)           (G)
     _cons |      -8       (H)      -1.6
------------------------------------------------------------------------------
```

14. Repeat the previous exercise for the following partial OLS output.

```
    Source |      SS        df        MS              Number of obs =        26
-----------+----------------------------------        F(  2,    24) =
     Model |     648                                  Prob > F      =
  Residual |     (A)                                  R-squared     =        (B)
-----------+----------------------------------        Adj R-squared =
     Total |    1080                                  Root MSE      =        (C)
------------------------------------------------------------------------------
         y |    Coef.   Std. Err.      t    P>|t|     [95% Conf. Interval]
-----------+------------------------------------------------------------------
         x |       9       6.0       (D)    (E)        (F)           (G)
     _cons |      10       (H)        4
------------------------------------------------------------------------------
```

Chapter 8

Case Studies for Bivariate Regression

This chapter provides four detailed examples of bivariate data analysis. The first and second examples analyze cross-country data on, respectively, health outcomes and health expenditures. The third example analyses monthly data on the returns on Coca-Cola stock compared to returns on the market portfolio, using the capital asset pricing model. The final example analyses the relationship between real GDP growth and changes in unemployment using annual macroeconomic data for the U.S.

In these examples the initial analysis uses default standard errors for the regression coefficients. Then consideration is given to using alternative robust standard errors, introduced in Chapter 7.7 and presented in greater detail in Chapter 12.1.

8.1 Health Outcomes across Countries

The two most widely-used measures of country health outcomes, available for most countries, are life expectancy and infant mortality. These are expected to improve as more resources are devoted to health care, as measured by health expenditures per capita. Qualitatively similar results are obtained if instead the regressor is health expenditure as a percentage of GDP or the regressor is GDP per capita.

8.1.1 Application

Dataset HEALTH2009 has 2009 data for the 34 wealthy and relatively wealthy nations in the Organization of Economic Cooperation and Development (OECD). The countries, ordered alphabetically, are Australia, Austria, Belgium, Canada, Chile, Czech Republic, Denmark, Estonia, Finland, France, Germany, Greece, Hungary, Iceland, Ireland, Israel, Italy, Japan, Korea, Luxembourg, Mexico, Netherlands, New Zealand, Norway, Poland, Portugal, Slovak Republic, Slovenia, Spain, Sweden, Switzerland, Turkey, United Kingdom, and United States.

Table 8.1 provides some summary statistics. There is wide variation in annual health expenditures per capita, ranging from \$923 in Mexico to \$7,990 in the United States. Life expectancy at birth of males ranges from 69.8 years in Estonia to 79.9 years in Switzerland. Infant mortality

Table 8.1: Health outcomes: Variable definitions and summary statistics (n=34)

Variable	Definition	Mean	St. Dev.	Min	Max
Hlthpc	Annual health expenditure per capita (in US $)	3256	1494	923	7990
Lifeexp	Life expectancy at birth of males (in years)	76.7	2.94	69.8	79.9
InfMort	Infant mortality per 1,000 live births	4.45	2.72	1.8	14.7

(death in the first year of life) ranges from 1.8 per one thousand live births in Iceland to 14.7 in Mexico.

A useful way to compare variation across different series, measured on different scales, is to use the coefficient of variation. This normalizes by the average of the series, since it equals the standard deviation divided by the sample mean. This makes clear that there is much less variation in life expectancy (CV = 0.04) across countries than there is in the other two measures.

8.1.2 Life Expectancy

Life expectancy at birth in 2009 is calculated by assuming that someone born in 2009 will face the same death rates as they age as the death rates computed for each year of age in 2009.

OLS regression yields

$$Lifeexp = \underset{(71.36)}{73.08} + \underset{(3.88)}{0.00111} \times Hlthpc, \quad R^2 = 0.320, \quad s_e = 2.46, \quad n = 34,$$

where t statistics based on default standard errors are given in parentheses. Here life expectancy is for males, but qualitatively similar results are obtained for females or for both genders combined.

The relationship between health spending and life expectancy is quantitatively significant. A $1,000 increase in per capita health spending, a two-thirds of a standard deviation change, is associated with an increase in life expectancy of 1.11 years.

The relationship is highly statistically significant, as $t = 3.88$. Since the prior belief is that $\beta_2 > 0$ in this example, it is most appropriate to perform a one-sided test of $H_0 : \beta_2 \leq 0$ against $H_a : \beta_2 > 0$. Then $c = t_{32,.05} = 1.69$ and we reject H_0 at significance level 0.05 since $t = 3.88 > c$. The p-value, not listed, is $p = \Pr[T_{32} > 3.88] = 0.000$ to three decimal places.

The first panel of Figure 8.1 plots the data and regression line. The country codes are generally the first three letters of the country name, exceptions being AUT for Austria, CHL for Chile, NZ for New Zealand, SLR for Slovak Republic, UK for the United Kingdom, and USA for the United States. The scatter plot suggests that the relationship is curvilinear rather than linear, and that the U.S. has much lower life expectancy (six years lower) than expected given its high level of health spending.

8.1.3 Heteroskedastic-robust Standard Errors

With cross-section data, model errors may be heteroskedastic and it is now common econometric practice to use heteroskedastic-robust standard errors.

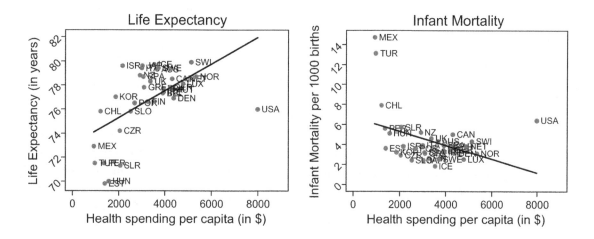

Figure 8.1: Health outcomes: Life expectancy and infant mortality versus per capita health expenditures

For the linear regression the slope coefficient has default standard error 0.000287, while the heteroskedastic-robust standard error is 0.000464, so the t statistic falls considerably from 3.88 to 2.40 when heteroskedastic-robust standard errors are used. The regressor *Hlthpc* nonetheless remains statistically significant at level 0.05.

The observed substantial difference between default and heteroskedastic-robust standard errors (60% larger) is unusual. It arises because the USA residual e_i is very large, see the first panel of Figure 8.1. As a result $e_i^2(x_i - \bar{x})^2$ is unusually large for this observation and hence $se_{het}(b_2) = \sqrt{\sum_{i=1}^{n} e_i^2(x_i - \bar{x})^2 / \sum_{i=1}^{n}(x_i - \bar{x})^2}$ is large. Dropping the U.S. observation, the default standard error is 0.000299 and the heteroskedastic-robust standard error is 0.000301, essentially the same.

8.1.4 Infant Mortality

For **infant mortality** qualitatively similar results are obtained. The linear regression slope coefficient is -0.000693, so a \$1,000 increase in health spending per capita is associated with a reduction of 0.693 in infant mortality per 1,000 live births, a substantial reduction given sample mean infant mortality of 4.45. The default standard error is 0.000298 and the heteroskedastic-robust standard error is 0.000515, so the t statistic falls considerably from -2.33 to -1.35 when heteroskedastic-robust standard errors are used. From the second panel of Figure 8.1 the U.S. is again an outlier.

8.1.5 Discussion

This cross-country comparison example indicates that two key health outcome measures improve on average as health expenditures are increased.

The analysis also indicates that the U.S. is a clear outlier among OECD countries. From a statistical perspective, should we include this outlier in the analysis? If the U.S. observation is dropped the slope coefficient in the linear model for lie expectancy increases substantially from 0.00111 to 0.00169. The practice in economic analysis is to not drop outliers, unless there is a compelling reason for doing so. In the current setting it is standard to include the U.S. in the analysis, though perhaps it might be mentioned as an aside that it is an outlying observation.

From the scatter plots in Figure 8.1 the health outcome relationships appear to be nonlinear in health spending. Nonlinear relationships estimated using log-linear and log-log models are presented in Chapter 9.3 and exercise 13 in Chapter 9 applies the log-log models to the data studied here. For example a log-log model finds that a 10% increase in health spending per capita is associated with a substantial 4.58% decrease in infant mortality. The predicted value for the U.S. from the log-log model is 2.7 deaths per 1,000 live births, using an adjustment detailed in Chapter 15.6, much less than the observed 6.4 deaths. Again the U.S. appears to be an outlier with worse health outcomes than predicted. Even in the raw data it has the fourth highest infant mortality rate.

These nonlinear relationships show that the improvements in health outcomes with health spending are much greater for poorer countries. While Mexico is the poorest country in this sample of OECD countries, it should be noted that its per capita GDP exceeds the world average and exceeds that of the median country. The world's poorest countries in 2009 had GDP per capita of $500, life expectancy of 50 years and infant mortality of 100 per one thousand live births.

From an economic policy perspective it is clear that health outcomes in the U.S. are much lower than predicted given the high level of health expenditures. Health economists have determined that these high expenditures are particularly due to the high price of health goods and services, rather than the volume of health care. Explanations for the poorer than expected health outcomes include the greater heterogeneity in income, race and immigrant status of the U.S. population compared to many countries, the lack of universal health insurance cover, and a higher rate of teenage pregnancy which increases infant mortality rates. Many studies have looked at these issues.

8.2   Health Expenditures across Countries

Here we analyze the relationship between health expenditures and income using aggregate data for a number of developed nations. Similar analysis can also be done using individual level data, if this is available.

8.2.1   Application

The analysis uses the dataset HEALTH2009 introduced in Chapter 8.1. This has 2009 data for the 34 wealthy and relatively wealthy nations in the Organization of Economic Cooperation and Development (OECD).

Table 8.2 provides some summary statistics. Health expenditure is measured per capita, and income is measured using GDP per capita. There is considerable variation in GDP per capita, measured in current US dollars at current exchange rates, ranging from $13,807 for Mexico to $82,901 for Luxembourg, a small European country with population of half a million.

Table 8.2: Health expenditures: Variable definitions and summary statistics (n=34)

Variable	Definition	Mean	St. Dev.	Min	Max
Gdppc	GDP per capita (in US $)	33054	12918	13807	82901
Hlthpc	Health expenditure per capita (in US $)	3256	1494	923	7990

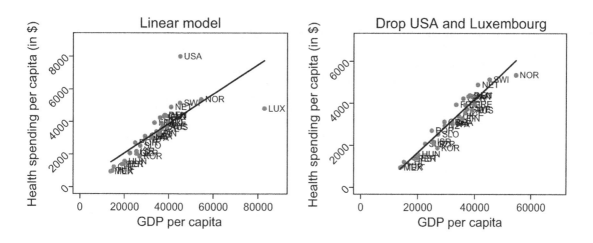

Figure 8.2: Health expenditures per capita: Relationship with GDP per capita

8.2.2 Linear Regression

If health expenditure is a normal good, then there is a positive relationship between per capita health expenditures (*Hlthpc*) and per capita GDP (*Gdppc*).

OLS regression yields

$$Hlthpc = \underset{(0.63)}{285} + \underset{(6.99)}{0.0899} \times Gdppc, \quad R^2 = 0.604, \quad s_e = 954, \quad n = 34,$$

where t statistics based on default standard errors are given in parentheses.

The slope coefficient estimate implies that an extra $1,000 in per capita GDP is associated with an $89.90 increase in per capita health expenditures. The relationship is highly statistically significant, as $t = 6.99$. Since the prior belief is that $\beta_2 > 0$ in this example, it is most appropriate to perform a one-sided test of $H_0 : \beta_2 \leq 0$ against $H_a : \beta_2 > 0$. Then $c = t_{32,.05} = 1.69$ and we reject H_0 at significance level 0.05 since $t = 6.99 > c$.

The first panel of Figure 8.2 plots the data and regression line. There are two notable outlying observations. First the U.S. spends almost two times as much on health given its per capita GDP as predicted by the OLS regression. Second, Luxembourg has unusually high per capita GDP while its health spending per capita is similar to that of the other wealthiest European countries.

These two observations are so far from the line that they warrant further investigation. A check reveals that the data have not been entered incorrectly. The right panel of Figure 8.2 shows the effect of dropping the two countries – the slope coefficient increases to 0.1267, the fit is much better with $s_e = 3.38$ and $R^2 = 0.928$, leading to a much higher $t = 19.69$. Despite his improvement, econometrics practice is to retain all observations unless the data are clearly miscoded or there are other strong reasons for dropping an observation. We prefer that the analysis be of all OECD countries rather than an analysis of OECD countries excluding the U.S. and Luxembourg.

8.2.3   Heteroskedastic-robust Standard Errors

With cross-section data, model errors may be heteroskedastic and it is now common econometric practice to use heteroskedastic-robust standard errors. For the original linear regressor the heteroskedastic-robust standard error for the slope coefficient increases substantially from 0.0129 to 0.0293, so the t statistic falls considerably from 6.99 to 3.08.

This substantial difference between default and heteroskedastic robust standard errors is very unusual. It arises because for Luxembourg and the USA the residuals e_i are very large, see the first panel of Figure 8.2, so $e_i^2(x_i - \bar{x})^2$ is large and hence $se_{het}(b_2) = \sqrt{\sum_{i=1}^{n} e_i^2(x_i - \bar{x})^2} / \sum_{i=1}^{n}(x_i - \bar{x})^2$ defined in Chapter 7.7.1 is large.

8.3   Capital Asset Pricing Model

The **capital asset pricing model** (CAPM) is a workhorse model for finance. It formalizes the relationship between the return on a given stock and the return on the market portfolio.

8.3.1   Theory of CAPM

We consider the relationship between the return on a risk-free asset, the return on the market portfolio, and the return on a (risky) investment asset.

The analysis uses the dataset CAPM. Let RF denote the **risk-free interest rate**. In the example below RF is the interest rate on a one-month U.S. Treasury bill. And let RM denote the **overall market return** on stocks. In the example below RM is the value-weighted return on all stocks listed on the New York Stock Exchange (NYSE), American Stock Exchange (AMEX) and NASDAQ. The difference $(RM - RF)$ is called the **market excess return** or the **equity market premium** as it gives the additional return received by investing in the market compared to holding a riskless asset.

Now consider individual investments. Let RA denote the return on the **investment asset** A, such as an individual stock or a stock portfolio. In the example below we focus on stock in Coca-Cola.

The CAPM links the returns on individual investments to the market return, according to the relation

$$\mathrm{E}[RA_t - RF_t] = \beta_A \mathrm{E}[RM_t - RF_t],$$

where the subscript t denotes time. The expected return on an individual investment in excess of the risk-free rate, $E[RA - RF]$, is just a multiple of the expected excess return in the market. The investment-specific coefficient $\beta_A = \text{Cov}[RA_t, RM_t]/\text{Var}[RA_t]$ and is a measure of the correlation of the investment with the market portfolio.

The multiple β_A varies across investments. In aggregate individual investments sum to the market so on average β_A equals one. Some stocks have $\beta_A > 1$ and are often called **growth stocks** as they will outperform the market when the equity premium $RM_t - RF_t$ is positive. At the same time they will underperform the market when the equity premium is negative. Other stocks have $\beta_A < 1$ and are often called **value stocks**. Utilities are an example. Cash has $\beta_A = 0$. An investment with $\beta_A < 0$ is viewed as a **hedge** or insurance policy.

8.3.2 Estimation of CAPM

The population values of $E[RA_t - RF_t]$, $E[RM_t - RF_t]$ and β_A are unknown. Using time series data we instead estimate by OLS for investment A the model

$$RA_t - RF_t = \alpha_A + \beta_A(RM_t - RF_t) + u_t,$$

where the error term u_t is assumed to have zero mean and to be uncorrelated with the regressors, so that $E[u_t|(RM_t - RF_t)] = 0$.

The estimated slope coefficient b_A is called the stock's **beta**. The estimated intercept a_A is called the stock's **alpha**. According to the CAPM $\alpha_A = 0$. If instead $\alpha_A > 0$, then the investment has performed better than is to be expected given its variability and correlation with the market portfolio as measured by β_A. Warren Buffett's company Berkshire Hathaway has for many years had an alpha that is both positive and high, though this is not a guarantee of future performance.

8.3.3 Application

The dataset CAPM has monthly data on the returns to holding stock in Coca-Cola, Target and Walmart from May 1983 to October 2012. It also includes the one-month U.S. Treasury bill rate and a market return that is the value-weighted return on all stocks listed on the NYSE, AMEX and NASDAQ. The data are summarized in Table 8.3.

The market return and individual stock returns substantially exceed the risk-free rate, reflecting a reward for holding a riskier asset. The average market excess return is 0.55% per month, an annual compounded return of 6.8% ($= 100 \times (1.0055^{12} - 1)$). The average returns on individual stocks are higher than the market return, reflecting the greater risk due to less diversification – the standard deviations of returns on the three individual stocks are 35% to 65% higher than the standard deviation of the market return.

The first panel of Figure 8.3 is a time series plot of the market excess return and the excess return to Coca-Cola stock from January 2007 to September 2012; for readability this uses just the last 20% of the sample period. It is clear that the Coca-Cola stock excess return does follow the market excess return, though not perfectly. The financial crash in late 2008 is also apparent.

The second panel of Figure 8.3 displays a scatter plot of the Coca-Cola excess return against the market excess return for the entire 1983-2013 period. A nonparametric regression line estimated

Table 8.3: CAPM data: Variable definitions and summary statistics (n=354)

Variable	Definition	Mean	St. Dev.	Min	Max
RM	Market return	.0091	.0456	-.2254	.1285
RF	One-month U.S. Treasury Bill rate	.0035	.0022	.0000	.0100
RKO	Return on Coca-Cola	.0137	.0618	-.1909	.2227
RTGT	Return on Target	.0138	.0842	-.4781	.2673
RWMT	Return on Walmart	.0156	.0703	-.2698	.2644
RM-RF	Excess Market Return (equity premium)	.0055	.0456	-.2314	.1243
RKO-RF	Excess Return on Coca-Cola	.0102	.0616	-.1952	.2188
RTGT-RF	Excess Return on Target	.0103	.0842	-.4840	.2629
RWMT-RF	Excess Return on Walmart	.0121	.0702	-.2758	.2612

by local linear methods, see Chapter 5.12, is very close to linear, with departure from linearity only for the very extreme low and high excess returns. So a linear model, implied by the CAPM model, seems appropriate for these data.

OLS regression gives fitted CAPM model for Coca-Cola (RKO)

$$(RKO - RF) = \underset{(0.00295)}{0.00681} + \underset{(0.0644)}{0.6063} \times (RM - RF), \quad R^2 = 0.201, \quad s_e = 0.055, \quad n = 354,$$

where default standard errors are given in parentheses.

The slope coefficient, the stock's beta, is statistically different from zero, since $t = 0.6063/0.0644 = 9.41 > t_{352,.025} = 1.967$. The slope coefficient is also statistically different from one, since $t = (0.6063 - 1)/0.0644 = -6.11$ and $|-6.11| > t_{32,.025} = 1.967$. Since Coca-Cola's beta lies between 0 and 1 it is viewed to be a value stock. Large companies such as Coca-Cola generally move less than the market as a whole, leading to $\beta < 1$. (Note that to test whether Coca-Cola is a value stock we should perform a lower tail alternative one-sided test of $H_0 : \beta_2 \geq 1$ against $H_a : \beta_2 < 1$. Again $t = -6.111$ and we reject H_0 as $-6.11 < -t_{352,.05} = -1.649$.)

The intercept coefficient, the stock's alpha, is a risk-adjusted measure of stock performance that measures the return in excess of that expected given the riskiness of the stock. The CAPM model in its purest form restricts $\alpha = 0$. This restriction is rejected here at significance level 0.05, since $t = 0.00681/0.00295 = 2.31 > t_{0.025,352} = 1.967$. Furthermore the alpha is large in magnitude. The monthly return for Coca-Cola stock is 0.68 basis points higher than expected given its beta, leading to a compounded annual return that is 8.5 percentage points $(= 100 \times (1.0068^{12} - 1))$ higher. Such high alpha arises in part due to survivor bias. A company whose stock has a large negative alpha will eventually face bankruptcy or a takeover. Since on average alpha is expected to be zero, companies such as Coca Cola that do survive for a long time can be expected to have a positive alpha in a time series analysis such as this.

Analyses of the monthly excess returns of stock in Target and Walmart are left as exercises.

8.3.4 Heteroskedastic-robust Standard Errors

The preceding statistical inference uses default standard errors based on model assumptions 1-4.

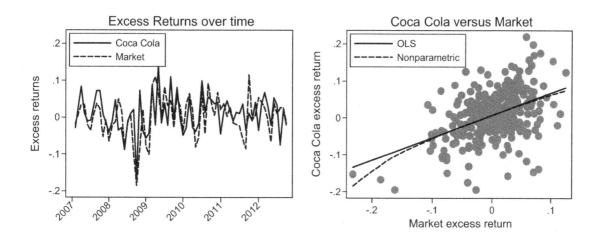

Figure 8.3: CAPM Model: Coca Cola and market excess returns

It is likely that when the regressor $(RM - RF)$ is large in absolute value the error in the linear model for the dependent variable $(RKO - RF)$ is also large in absolute value. In that case the errors are heteroskedastic rather than homoskedastic. When heteroskedastic-robust standard errors are computed there is little change in the standard error for the intercept. The standard error of the slope coefficient increases from 0.0644 to 0.0770, so again the estimated beta is statistically significantly different from both zero and one. For these data there is little difference between default and heteroskedastic-robust standard errors.

For time series data the model errors may be correlated over time, in which case model assumption 4 is incorrect. For financial data, however, excess returns are intrinsically not forecastable if markets are efficient. So the error term should be uncorrelated. This is the case for these data. Let e_t be the fitted residual from the original OLS regression. Then the correlation between e_t and e_{t-1} is -0.039, very close to zero.

To nonetheless guard against possible model error autocorrelation we use heteroskedastic- and autocorrelation-consistent (HAC) standard errors, see Chapter 12.1, allowing for the errors to be potentially correlated for up to 13 months. Then there is little change in the standard error for the intercept, while the HAC standard error of the slope coefficient is 0.0885, fifteen percent higher than the heteroskedastic-robust standard error of 0.0770.

More generally for data on financial returns it is often sufficient to use heteroskedastic-robust standard errors.

8.4 Output and Unemployment in the U.S.

Over the business cycle there is a negative relationship between unemployment and GDP growth rates, with unemployment falling as GDP growth rises.

8.4.1 Okun's Law

Furthermore, unemployment fluctuates less than GDP growth. Each percentage point increase in the unemployment rate is associated with an approximate two percentage point decrease in the GDP growth rate. This phenomenon is called **Okun's law**, after Okun who first proposed it in a 1962 journal article. A better term is "Okun's rule-of-thumb" as it is an empirical relationship rather than an ironclad law.

8.4.2 Application

We investigate this relationship using more recent annual U.S. data from 1961 to 2019. The dataset GDPUNEMPLOY has data on *Rgpgrowth*, the annual percentage growth in real GDP, and on *URATEchange*, the annual change in the percentage unemployment rate for the civilian population aged 16 years and older. For example, if the unemployment rate expressed as a percentage increases from 5.3% to 6.5% then *URATEchange* equals 1.2.

Table 8.4 summarizes the data. Over this period real GDP grew on average 3.05% per year and was approximately twice as volatile as the annual change in the unemployment rate, with standard deviation 2.04 compared to 0.99.

Table 8.4: Output and unemployment data: Variable definitions and summary statistics (n=59)

Variable	Definition	Mean	St. Dev.	Min	Max
Rgdpgrowth	Annual percentage growth in real GDP	3.059	2.038	-2.537	7.237
URATEchange	Annual change in the unemployment rate	-0.032	0.987	-2.143	3.530

The first panel of Figure 8.4 presents a scatter plot of the data. A nonparametric regression line estimated by local linear methods, see Chapter 5.12, is very close to linear.

OLS regression yields

$$Rgdpgrowth = \underset{(0.171)}{3.008} - \underset{(0.175)}{1.589} \times URATEchange, \quad R^2 = 0.592, \quad s_e = 1.313, \quad n = 59,$$

where default standard errors are given in parentheses. A useful approximation is that U.S. real GDP growth has averaged 3.008 percent per year since 1960, and declines by 1.589 percentage points for each 1 percentage point increase in the unemployment rate. The slope coefficient of 1.589 is less than Okun's earlier estimate of 2.

The slope coefficient is highly statistically significant with $t = -1.589/.175 = -9.09$. A more interesting test is whether the data confirm Okun's law. For a test of $H_0 : \beta_2 = -2.0$ against $H_a : \beta_2 \neq -2.0$, $t = (1.589 - 2.0)/0.175 = -2.35$, so $p = \Pr[|T_{23}| \geq 2.35] = 0.022$. The null hypothesis is rejected at significance level 0.05, though the estimate of -1.59 is not too different from -2.0.

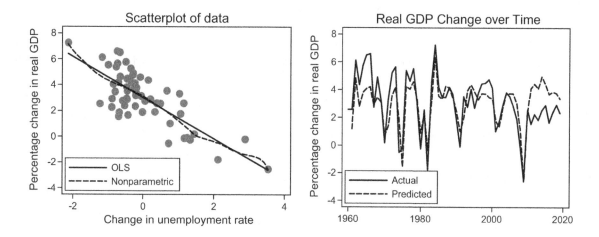

Figure 8.4: Okun's Law: Percentage change in output and change in unemployment rate

8.4.3 Prediction

How well does this estimated model fit the economic downturn following the global financial crisis? In the two years 2007 to 2009 the unemployment rate rose from 4.7 to 9.4 percent. The model predicts that real GDP would change over these two years by $2 \times 3.008 - 1.589 \times (9.4 - 4.7) = -1.5$ percent. This is reasonably close to the actual fall in real GDP from 2007 to 2009 of 2.7 percent.

The model does not do so well for the subsequent recovery. From 2009 to 2019 the unemployment rate fell from 9.4% to 3.7%. The model predicts that real GDP would increase over these ten years by $10 \times 3.008 - 1.5894 \times (3.7 - 9.4) = 39$ percent. But in fact real GDP grew by only 25 percent from 2009 to 2019.

The second panel of Figure 8.4 plots both the actual change in real GDP growth rate and the change predicted from the regression model. The predictions track the actual changes reasonably well, but there is considerable overprediction of the real GDP growth rate in the most recent years, confirming the preceding numerical analysis. Okun's rule of thumb performs poorly in explaining the economic recovery following the recent global financial crisis. This slower economic growth is a subject of ongoing macroeconomic research.

8.4.4 Robust Standard Errors

For time series data the model errors may be correlated over time, called autocorrelation. Then model assumption 4 is incorrect and default standard errors or heteroskedastic-robust should be used. Instead one should use heteroskedastic and autocorrelation robust (HAC) standard errors, presented in Chapter 12.1, that control for both autocorrelation and heteroskedasticity in the error.

For a model with the dependent variable measured as a change rather than a level, however, error autocorrelation is greatly reduced. For example, for these data the autocorrelation between real GDP and previous year's real GDP is 0.95, while the correlation between real GDP growth and previous year's real GDP growth in the previous year is only 0.34.

In fact the HAC robust standard error of the coefficient of *URATEchange* is 0.211, allowing for the errors to be potentially correlated for up to five years. This is somewhat larger than default standard error of 0.175.

For macroeconomics data it is safest to use HAC standard errors. This can make a big difference when the dependent variable is measured in levels. It makes a smaller difference when the dependent variable is a change, as was the case for this example.

8.5   Exercises

1. Using dataset HEALTH2009 regress infant mortality (*infmort*) on per capita health expenditures (*hlthpc*).

   (a) Provide a scatterplot with fitted regression line of *infmort* against *hlthpc*.

   (b) By how much does infant mortality change when per capita health expenditures increase by $1,000?

   (c) Is this effect statistically significant at level 0.05?

   (d) Drop the two countries with the lowest health spending and repeat parts (b) to (c). What do you conclude?

2. Using dataset HEALTH2009 answer the following.

   (a) Regress life expectancy at birth (*lifeexp*) on per capita GDP (*gdppc*).

   (b) By how much does life expectancy change when GDP per capita increases by $1,000?

   (c) Is this effect statistically significant at level 0.05?

   (d) What single variable best explains life expectancy at birth: *gdppc* or *hlthpc*? Are you surprised?

   (e) Now drop the observations for the United States and repeat part (d). Comment.

3. Repeat exercise 1 using dataset HEALTH2018.

4. Repeat exercise 2 using dataset HEALTH2018.

5. Go to the OECD Health Statistics website (https://www.oecd.org/health/health-statistics.htm at the time of writing) and choose OECD Health Statistics 202x: Frequently Requested Data, where by 202x I mean the latest year.

   (a) Download data for the year 2017 on life expectancy at birth (both sexes) and per capita health expenditures. If data are unavailable for a country in that year use data from the closest year.

   (b) Regress life expectancy at birth on per capita health expenditures.

   (c) By how much does life expectancy change when health spending per capita increases by $1,000?

   (d) Compare life expectancy in the U.S. with the predicted value from this regression.

6. Using dataset CAPM, analyze the returns to holding stock in Target using only data beginning with the 565th observation.

   (a) Produce a figure similar to the first panel in Figure 8.3. Compare to Figure 8.3.

   (b) Regress the stock return in excess of the risk-free rate on an intercept and the market return in excess of the risk-free rate and obtain heteroskedastic-robust standard errors.

   (c) Does Target earn a return in excess of that expected given the riskiness of the stock? Perform an appropriate test at level 0.05.

   (d) Is Target a value stock? Perform appropriate tests at level 0.05.

7. Repeat the previous exercise using data on the returns to holding stock in Walmart.

8. This exercise is based on the data used in the article Francis Galton (1886), "Regression towards Mediocrity in Hereditary Stature," *The Journal of the Anthropological Institute of Great Britain and Ireland*, 15, 246–263. (JSTOR 2841583). This article introduced the term "regression towards the mean". Actually Galton used the term "mediocrity" rather than the mean. Galton defined a deviate to be the deviation from the mean (i.e. $y_i - \bar{y}$ and $x_i - \bar{x}$). He then wrote "By the use of this word and that of 'mid-parentage' we can define the law of regression very briefly. It is that the height-deviate of the off-spring is, on the average, two-thirds of the height-deviate of its parentage." The comma-separated values dataset GALTON.CSV has Galton's data for 928 adult children who had 205 unique sets of parents. The variables are *child* (height of adult child in inches where female height has been multiplied by 1.08) and *midparent* (average of mother and father's height where mother's height has been multiplied by 1.08). The original data were in tenths of an inch but the available data from Table I of Galton's paper grouped the data to intervals of one inch.

   (a) Calculate the difference between mean sample mean of child's height and sample mean of mean midparents' height. Is there a substantial difference?

   (b) From summary statistics the child height is much more variable than the midparent height. Explain why this is the case. (Hint: consider the definition of midparent height).

(c) Provide a scatterplot of *child* on *midparent*. Do you see a problem?

(d) Now provide a scatterplot of the data that jitters the data. Is this an improvement?

(e) Regress *child* on an intercept and *midparent* and interpret the regression coefficients.

(f) What fraction of the variation in child's height is explained by midparents height?

(g) Generate deviations from the mean for variables *child* and *midparent* and regress the child deviate on the midparent deviate. Compare the estimated slope coefficient to that in (c).

(h) Galton used a method other than least squares to conclude that "the height-deviate of the off-spring is, on the average, two-thirds of the height-deviate of its parentage." Given your answer in (e) do you agree with his results?

(i) Galton noted that the reverse regression of *midparent* on *child* does not have slope that is the reciprocal of that from regression of *child* on *midparent*. Instead he says that "a midparental deviate of one unit implies a mid-generational deviate of 1/3". Do you agree?

Chapter 9

Models with Natural Logarithms

The standard linear regression model has the attraction of simplicity. The slope coefficient is readily interpretable as it gives the change in the dependent variable as the regressor changes by one unit.

But often economists are interested in measuring proportionate changes. For example, a price elasticity of demand measures the proportionate change in demand for a good or service in response to a given proportionate change in price. As another example, a semi-elasticity of earnings with respect to education measures the proportionate change in earnings with respect to one more year of education.

In this chapter we present ways to estimate elasticities and semi-elasticities by OLS estimation of models in which key variables are first transformed by taking the natural logarithm.

Additional uses of the natural logarithm are also presented in this chapter. In particular many macroeconomic time series exhibit compounding or exponential growth that becomes linear when the data are transformed to the natural logarithm. The exponential function is also briefly presented.

9.1   Natural Logarithm Function

A **logarithmic function** is the reverse operation to raising a number to a power. For example, $10^2 = 100$ implies that $\log_{10} 100 = 2$. In words, if 10 raised to the power 2 equals 100 then the logarithm to the base 10 of 100 is 2. More generally, if $a^b = x$ then $\log_a x = b$, i.e., the logarithm to the base a of x equals b.

There are many possible choices of the base for logarithms. In economics analysis it is common to use the **natural logarithm**, or **logarithm to base** e.

Definition 23 *The natural logarithm of x, denoted* $\ln x$ *where* $\ln$ *denotes log natural, is*

$$\ln x = \log_e x, \quad x > 0,$$

where $e \simeq 2.7182818...$ *is an irrational and transcendental number (like* $\pi \simeq 3.1415927...$*).*

Properties of the natural logarithm include $\ln x^a = a \ln x$, and $\ln(xy) = \ln x + \ln y$. For those familiar with calculus $d \ln x/dx = 1/x$.

As noted in Chapter 2.5, taking the natural logarithm can greatly reduce skewness in right-skewed data such as individual income, earnings or prices, and it can also reduce the impact of outlying observations.

The natural logarithm has many other desirable properties. One that economists use extensively, and one that is the focus of this chapter, is the following.

9.1.1   Approximating Proportionate Changes

Let $\Delta x = x_1 - x_0$ define the change in x when x changes from x_0 to x_1. Then the **proportionate change** in x is

$$\frac{\Delta x}{x_0} = \frac{x_1 - x_0}{x_0}.$$

For example, consider a change from $x_0 = 40$ to $x_1 = 40.4$. Then $\Delta x = 40.4 - 40 = 0.4$, and the proportionate change in x is $\Delta x/x_0 = 0.4/40 = 0.01$. Equivalently the percentage change in x is 1% ($= 100 \times 0.01$).

For small proportionate changes we can use the following approximation.

Remark 69 *The natural logarithm function has the property that the change in the natural logarithm of x approximately equals the proportionate change in x, for small proportionate changes in x. That is*

$$\frac{\Delta x}{x} \simeq \Delta \ln x \text{ for small } \frac{\Delta x}{x}.$$

Letting $\%\Delta x = 100 \times \frac{\Delta x}{x}$ denote the percentage change in x, it follows that

$$\%\Delta x \simeq 100 \times \Delta \ln x \text{ for small } \%\Delta x.$$

For readers familiar with calculus, this property arises because the natural logarithm has derivative $d \ln x/dx = 1/x$, so $\Delta \ln x/\Delta x = 1/x$ for very small proportionate changes in x. Manipulating leads to $\Delta \ln x = \Delta x/x$.

For example, when x changes from $x_0 = 40$ to $x_1 = 40.4$, then the approximation yields $\Delta \ln x = \ln(40.4) - \ln(40) = 3.69883 - 3.68888 \simeq 0.00995$, close to $\Delta x/x = (40.4 - 40)/40 = 0.01000$.

Table 9.1 compares $\Delta \ln x$ to $\Delta x/x$. The approximation under-estimates the actual proportional change by a small amount for small changes, say $\Delta x/x < 0.10$, and by increasing amounts as $\Delta x/x$ increases. For $\Delta x/x$ as large as 0.2 the approximation yields 0.1823 rather than 0.20, a difference of 8.8%.

Table 9.1: Change in ln(x) approximates proportionate change in x

		"Small" $\Delta x/x$			"Large" $\Delta x/x$	
		$\Delta x/x = 0.01$	$\Delta x/x = 0.05$	$\Delta x/x = 0.10$	$\Delta x/x = 0.15$	$\Delta x/x = 0.20$
True Value	$\Delta x/x$	0.01	0.05	0.10	0.15	0.20
Approximation	$\Delta \ln x$	0.00995	0.0488	0.0953	0.1398	0.1823
Percentage difference		-0.5%	-2.4%	-4.7%	-6.8%	-8.8%

Many economic analyses are of data with small proportionate changes, so the approximation can be reasonably accurate. For example, for the U.S. in recent years annual inflation rates, annual returns on government bonds, and annual growth rates in real GDP have been less than five percent, a proportionate change of less than 0.05.

For this reason, and because regressions with variables transformed to natural logarithms yield coefficients that can be interpreted as semi-elasticities or elasticities, it is common for economic analyses to use the natural logarithm.

9.2 Semi-elasticities and Elasticities

The regression examples to date have measured how many units y changes by when x changes by one unit. For example, OLS regression lead to estimates of the change in house price (in dollars) associated with a one square foot increase in house size.

In some applications it can be more useful to consider proportionate changes. For example, in modelling earnings it can be more natural to think that one more year of education or one more year of aging leads to a certain percentage increase in earnings, rather than a certain dollar increase in earnings. Such proportionate changes are measured using semi-elasticities and elasticities, widely used in economics and seldom used in many other areas of applied statistics. The natural logarithm transformation greatly simplifies computation of semi-elasticities and elasticities.

9.2.1 Definition of Semi-Elasticity and Elasticity

A semi-elasticity gives the proportionate response in y, $\Delta y/y$, to a change in levels in x.

Definition 24 *The **semi-elasticity of** y **with respect to** x is the ratio of the proportionate change in y to the change in the level of x :*

$$Semi\text{-}elasticity_{yx} = \frac{\Delta y/y}{\Delta x}.$$

Multiplying by 100, yields the percentage change in y when x changes by one unit.

For example, if the semi-elasticity of earnings with respect to years of schooling is 0.08, then one more year of schooling is associated with a 0.08 proportionate increase in earnings, or an 8% increase in earnings.

An elasticity gives the ratio of proportionate responses.

Definition 25 *The **elasticity of** y **with respect to** x is the ratio of the proportionate change in y to the proportionate change in x :*

$$Elasticity_{yx} = \frac{\Delta y/y}{\Delta x/x}.$$

The elasticity equals the percentage change in y when x changes by one percent.

For example, if the price elasticity of demand for a good is -2.0, then a one percent increase in price leads to a 2.0 percent decrease in demand. And if the income elasticity of demand for a good is 0.4, then a one percent increase in income leads to a 0.4 percent increase in demand.

Semi-elasticities and elasticities can be obtained from a linear model, but they are difficult to interpret as they take different values at different data points. For example, an elasticity can also be written as $(\Delta y/\Delta x) \times x/y$, so it equals the slope $\Delta y/\Delta x$ multiplied by x/y. For a fitted linear model $\widehat{y} = b_1 + b_2 x$ the slope $\Delta \widehat{y}/\Delta x = b_2$ so the elasticity equals $b_2 x/\widehat{y}$. This will vary across observations since x and $\widehat{y}$ will vary across observations.

9.2.2 Approximation of Semi-Elasticity and Elasticity

Since $\Delta x/x \simeq \Delta \ln x$, and $\Delta y/y \simeq \Delta \ln y$ similarly, we have the following result.

Remark 70 *Semi-elasticities and elasticities can be approximated as follows.*

$$
\begin{aligned}
Semi\text{-}elasticity_{yx} &= \frac{\Delta y/y}{\Delta x} \simeq \frac{\Delta \ln y}{\Delta x} \\
Elasticity_{yx} &= \frac{\Delta y/y}{\Delta x/x} \simeq \frac{\Delta \ln y}{\Delta \ln x}.
\end{aligned}
$$

These approximations can be used to directly obtain semi-elasticities and elasticities that do not vary across observations by OLS regression of models that first transform variables to natural logarithms.

9.3   Log-linear, Log-log and Linear-log models

Log-linear and log-log models provide a simple way to estimate, respectively, a semi-elasticity and an elasticity.

9.3.1 Log-linear Model

A log-linear model is one that has dependent variable the natural logarithm of y, while the regressor appears in levels. The fitted OLS model is then $\widehat{\ln y} = b_1 + b_2 x$. The slope coefficient b_2 gives the change in the dependent variable, here $\ln y$, of a one unit change in x. It follows that $b_2 = \Delta \ln y / \Delta x$, a semi-elasticity.

Remark 71 *The **log-linear or log-level model** regresses* $\ln y$ *on* x *with fitted value*

$$\widehat{\ln y} = b_1 + b_2 x.$$

*The slope coefficient b_2 is an estimate of the **semi-elasticity of** y **with respect to** x.*

The log-linear model can only be applied if $y > 0$, since only then is $\ln y$ defined.

9.3.2 Log-log Model

A log-log model is one that has dependent variable the natural logarithm of y and regressor the natural logarithm of x. The fitted OLS model is then $\widehat{\ln y} = b_1 + b_2 \ln x$. The slope coefficient b_2 gives the change in the dependent variable, here $\ln y$, of a one-unit change in $\ln x$. It follows that $b_2 = \Delta \ln y / \Delta \ln x$, an elasticity.

Remark 72 *The **log-log model** regresses* $\ln y$ *on* $\ln x$ *with fitted value*

$$\widehat{\ln y} = b_1 + b_2 \ln x.$$

*The slope coefficient b_2 is an estimate of the **elasticity of** y **with respect to** x.*

The log-log model can only be applied if $y > 0$ and $x > 0$.

9.3.3 Linear-log Model

A linear-log model is one that has as dependent variable the level of y and regressor the natural logarithm of x. The fitted OLS model is then $\widehat{y} = b_1 + b_2 \ln x$. The slope coefficient b_2 gives the change in the dependent variable, here y, of a one-unit change in $\ln x$. It follows that $b_2 = y / \Delta \ln x$.

A one-unit change in $\Delta \ln x$ is a very large change. It is better to consider a one percent change in x, in which case $\Delta \ln x \simeq 0.01$. Then $b_2/100$ measures the change in y when x changes by one percent.

Remark 73 *The **linear-log model** or **level-log** regresses* y *on* $\ln x$ *with fitted value*

$$\widehat{y} = b_1 + b_2 \ln x.$$

$b_2/100$ *is an estimate of the change in y in response to a one percent change in x.*

The linear-log model can only be applied if $x > 0$.

9.3.4   Log-log Model Example

In Chapter 8.2 we regressed per capita health expenditures (*Hlthpc*) on an intercept and per capita GDP (*Gdppc*) for a sample of 34 OECD countries.

OLS regression yields

$$Hlthpc = \underset{(0.63)}{285} + \underset{(6.99)}{0.0899} \times Gdppc, \quad R^2 = 0.604, \quad s_e = 954, \quad n = 34,$$

where t statistics based on default standard errors are given in parentheses.

The slope coefficient estimate implies that an extra \$1,000 in per capita GDP is associated with an \$89.90 increase in per capita health expenditures. The OLS regression confirms that health is a **normal good**, since $\beta_2 > 0$. A more interesting question is whether health is a **superior good**, meaning that the income elasticity of health exceeds unity. On average the income elasticity of a good is unity, since if income doubles so too will consumption on average (ignoring savings). Here we ask whether health is a superior good, with income elasticity in excess of one.

This is important to policy makers as if health is a superior good, and GDP rises over time, then we expect that health expenditures as a fraction of GDP will rise over time (in the case of the U.S. from an already high 17.7% of GDP).

Definition and estimation of elasticities is detailed in Chapter 9.3, where it is shown that an elasticity can be obtained from OLS regression where the dependent variable and regressor are first transformed to natural logarithm (a log-log model). Specifically, if $\widehat{\ln y} = b_1 + b_2 \ln x$, then b_2 measures the elasticity of $\widehat{y}$ with respect to x.

OLS regression in natural logarithms yields

$$\ln(Hlthpc) = \underset{(-5.27)}{-5.010} + \underset{(13.66)}{1.256} \times \ln(Gdppc), \quad R^2 = 0.853, \quad s_e = 0.199, \quad n = 34,$$

where t statistics based on default standard errors are given in parentheses. The estimated income elasticity of health spending is 1.256, so a 10% increase in GDP per capita is associated with a 12.56% increase in health spending per capita.

A superior good is one for which the income elasticity exceeds one. So we test $H_0 : \beta_2 \leq 1$ against $H_a : \beta_2 > 1$. The output listed here does not include $se(b_2)$ but it can still be computed. The reported t statistic is for test of $\beta_2 = 0$, so $t = b_2/se(b_2)$ leading to $se(b_2) = t/b_2 = 1.256/13.66 = 0.092$. Then for test of test $H_0 : \beta_2 \leq 1$ against $H_a : \beta_2 > 1$, $t = (1.256 - 1)/.0920 = 2.78$. We reject H_0 at level 0.05 since $p = \Pr[T_{32} > 2.68] = 0.009 < 0.05$, or since $c = t_{32,.05} = 1.69$ and $t = 2.78 > c$. The data support the view that health is a superior good.

The data, in natural logarithms, and the regression line are illustrated in the second panel of Figure 8.2. The model fit appears to be good, as already known since $R^2 = 0.853$.

Comparing the first and second panels of Figure 8.2, the residuals for the U.S. and Luxemburg are not as large (relatively) in the log-log model. As a result, in the log-log model the heteroskedastic-robust standard error of 0.174 is closer to the default standard error of 0.0912 than was the case following linear regression.

9.4 Example: Earnings and Education

The data in dataset EARNINGS introduced in Chapter 2 includes data on annual earnings (*Earnings*) and years of completed schooling (*Education*) for 171 full-time female workers in 2010 aged 30 years. Summary statistics for the data are given in Table 9.2. Mean earnings are \$63,476 per year and mean age is 42.84 years. Table 9.2 additionally includes transformations of variables *Earnings* and *Age* that are used in this chapter.

Table 9.2: Variable definitions and summary statistics: Annual Earnings of female full-time workers aged 25-65 in 2010.

Variable	Definition	Mean	Standard Deviation	Min	Max
Earnings	Annual earnings in \$	41413	25527	1050	172000
Lnearnings	Natural logarithm of *Earnings*	10.46	0.62	6.96	12.06
Education	Years of schooling	14.43	2.73	3	20
Lneduc	Natural logarithm of *Education*	2.65	0.22	1.10	3.00
n	171				

9.4.1 Linear model estimates

Least squares regression of *Earnings* (y) on *Education* (x) yields fitted model

$$\widehat{y} \underset{(-3.49)}{=} -31056 + \underset{(8.30)}{5021}x, \quad R^2 = .290$$

where t statistics based on default standard errors are given in parentheses. (The t statistic based on heteroskedastic-robust standard errors is 7.66 for the slope coefficient). One additional year of schooling is associated with a \$5,021 increase in annual earnings, and this estimate is statistically significant at the 5% level.

The first panel of Figure 9.1 presents a scatter plot and the fitted line for the linear model.

9.4.2 Natural Logarithm Model Estimates

Table 9.3 summarizes key results for the linear, log-linear, log-log and linear-log models.

Because variables have been transformed it is more meaningful to compare across models the t statistic of the regressor, rather than the standard error, so t statistics (based on default standard errors) are given in parentheses. For all models the regressor was statistically significant at significance level 0.05.

The economic significance of the coefficients is substantial. The linear model suggests that one additional year of schooling is associated with a \$5,021 increase in annual earnings.

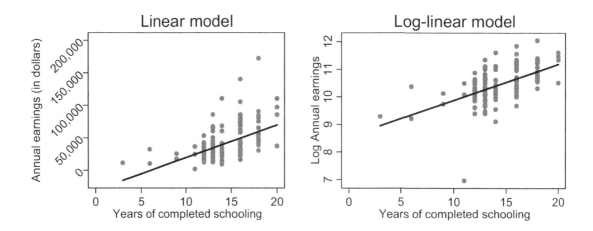

Figure 9.1: Linear and log-linear models: Earnings and education

Table 9.3: Various regression models with logs: y is earnings and x is age

Model	Estimates	R^2	Slope	Semi-elasticity	Elasticity
Linear	$\widehat{y} = -31056 + 5021x$ (−3.49) (8.30)	0.290	5021		
Log-linear	$\widehat{\ln y} = 8.561 + 0.131x$ (40.83) (9.21)	0.334	-	0.131	
Log-log	$\widehat{\ln y} = 6.543 + 1.478 \ln x$ (13.70) (8.23)	0.286	-	-	1.478
Linear-log	$\widehat{y} = -102767 + 54452 \ln x$ (−5.05) (7.11)	0.230	-	-	-

The second panel of Figure 9.1 presents a scatter plot and the fitted line for the log-linear model. The log-linear model slope estimate of 0.131 implies that aging one year is associated with a 0.131 proportionate increase in earnings, or a 13.1 percent increase in annual earnings.

The log-log model slope estimate of 1.478 implies that a one percent increase in schooling is associated with a 1.478 percent increase in annual earnings.

The linear-log model slope estimate of 54452 implies that a one percent increase in schooling is associated with a \$544 (= 54452/100) increase in annual earnings.

The R^2 can be directly compared across models with the same dependent variable and with the same number of regressors. So the linear model fits substantially better than the linear-log model, and the log-linear model provides a substantially better fit than the log-log model.

Comparing the linear model to the log-linear model is complicated by the models having different dependent variable. Transforming the dependent variable to $\ln y$ also complicates prediction of y. These issues are pursued in more detail in Chapter 15.6.

More generally economic theory and policy can guide in determining which model to use. For example, a production function of Cobb-Douglas form can be estimated using a log-log model; see Chapter 13.2. And, as already noted, in different settings direct estimates of a semi-elasticity or an elasticity may be desired.

9.5 Further Uses of the Natural Logarithm

Many economic time series entail compounding or exponential growth. For example, an investment of $100 invested at an annual interest rate of 2 percent will be worth 100×1.02^{10} after 10 years of compounding. Appropriate use of the natural logarithm can simplify analysis.

9.5.1 Approximating the Natural Logarithm

A property of the natural logarithm is that

$$\ln(1+x) = \sum_{n=1}^{\infty} (-1)^{n+1} \frac{x^n}{n} = x - \frac{x^2}{2} + \frac{x^3}{3} - \cdots .$$

If we use just the first term then $\ln(1+x) \simeq x$.

For example, $\ln(1.1) = \ln(1+0.1) = 0.10 - 0.1^2/2 + 0.1^3/3 - \cdots = 0.10 - 0.005 + 0.00033 - \cdots$ If we just use the first term then $\ln(1.1) \simeq 0.1$, reasonably close to $\ln(1.1) = 0.09531$, though not as close as $\ln(1.1) \simeq 0.09533$ if we sum the first three terms.

Table 9.4 compares the approximation x to $\ln(1+x)$. The approximation works quite well for small x, though x increasingly overestimates $\ln(1+x)$. For $x < 0.10$ the approximation is within five percent of $\ln(1+x)$, whereas the approximation $x = 0.2$, for example, is ten percent larger than $\ln 1.2 = 0.1823$. For many purposes the approximation is adequate for $x < 0.1$.

Table 9.4: Approximating ln(1+x) by x for small x.

		"Small" x			"Large" x	
		x=0.01	x=0.05	x=0.10	x=0.15	x=0.20
True Value	ln(1+x)	0.00995	0.0488	0.0953	0.1398	0.1823
Approximation	x	0.01	0.05	0.10	0.15	0.20

Remark 74 *For small x we can approximate $\ln(1+x)$ by x. For many purposes this approximation is adequate for $x < 0.10$.*

9.5.2 Compounding and the Rule of 72

Suppose money is invested at three percent per annum, a proportionate rate of 0.03. After n years the investment is $1.03 \times \cdots \times 1.03 = 1.03^n$ times larger. For example, $100 invested for ten years is worth 100×1.03^{10} or $134.39 after ten years.

How many years will it take for this investment to double in value? Similarly if inflation averages three percent a year, in how many years will price levels double?

The number of periods n that it takes to double is the solution to $(1.03)^n = 2$. Then

$$
\begin{aligned}
1.03^n &= 2 \\
\Rightarrow \quad \ln(1.03^n) &= \ln 2 \qquad \text{taking the natural logarithm of both sides} \\
\Rightarrow \quad n \ln(1.03) &= \ln 2 \qquad \text{as } \ln x^b = b \ln x \\
\Rightarrow \quad n &= \ln 2 / \ln 1.03 \quad \text{solving for } n
\end{aligned}
$$

More generally, suppose money is invested at **proportionate rate** r per period. Then by similar algebra the number of periods that it takes for money to double is $n = \ln 2 / [\ln(1 + r)]$. We make the following approximations. First, $\ln(1 + r) \simeq r$ for small r. Second, $\ln 2 = 0.6931 \simeq 0.72$. So $n \simeq 0.72/r$.

It is more convenient to work with growth rates expressed as a percentage. Then for money invested at **percentage rate** r per period it takes approximately $n = 72/r$ for the investment to double.

Remark 75 *The **rule of 72** states that it takes approximately $n = 72/r$ periods for a series to double if it is growing at the percentage rate r.*

Table 9.5 gives the number of years that it takes for money to double when invested at r percent per annum, using the exact result and using the rule of 72 approximation. For our three percent return example it takes approximately 24 years for the investment to double. The approximation for $r < 10\%$ is very good, only slightly overestimating the number of periods to double.

Table 9.5: Rule of 72: Number of periods for investment at percentage rate r per period to double.

		r=1%	r=2%	r=3%	r=4%	r=6%	r=8%	r=9%
True Value	$\ln 2 / \ln(1 + r/100)$	69.66	35.00	23.45	17.67	11.90	9.01	8.04
Rule of 72	$72/r$	72	36	24	18	12	9	8

While $\ln 2 \simeq 0.6931$, it is more convenient to use the cruder approximation $\ln 2 \simeq 0.72$ as the integers 2, 3, 4, 6, 8 and 9 all divide exactly into 72. Variations of this rule that are more precise for low r but not for moderate r are the **rule of 70**, using $70/r$, and even the **rule of 69**, using $69/r$.

9.5.3   Linearizing Exponential Growth

Many economic quantities grow over time according to a power law, or exponentially. Examples include investments and price levels.

As an example consider the Standard and Poors 500 Stock Market Index. Annual data (at close of trading December 1 of each year) are in dataset **SP500INDEX**. These data give the index with no inflation adjustment and do not include any returns from dividends.

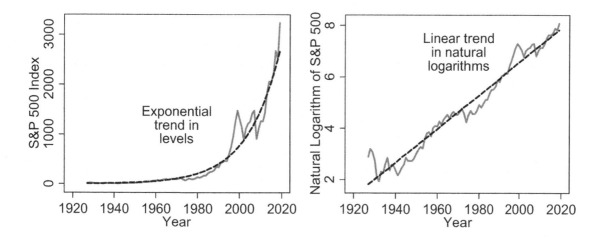

Figure 9.2: Levels and natural logarithm over time: Standard and Poors 500 index

Figure 9.2 plots the data for the period 1927-2019. There growth is exponential and the recent data show peaks at 1999, 2007 and 2019. The two dips are the "tech wreck" in 2000, when greatly inflated technology stocks lost much of their value, and the global financial crisis in 2008.

Let x_t be a variable with **growth rate** that is constant over time. Then an **exponential time trend** with initial value x_0 at time 0 and growth rate r leads to value $x_0(1 + r)$ after one period, value $x_0(1 + r) \times (1 + r) = x_0(1 + r)^2$ after two periods, and so on. In the tth period

$$x_t = x_0(1 + r)^t.$$

When $r > 0$ there is **exponential growth**, while for $r < 0$ there is **exponential decay** such as in the case of depreciation of an asset.

The smoother curve in the left panel of Figure 9.2 is an exponential time trend for the S&P 500 data, a line of the form $x_0(1 + r)^t$ where $r \simeq 0.065$.

Taking the natural logarithm of both sides of the preceding equation yields

$$
\begin{aligned}
\ln x_t &= \ln(x_0(1 + r)^t) \\
&= \ln x_0 + \ln(1 + r)^t & \text{using } \ln(ab) = \ln a + \ln b \\
&= \ln x_0 + \ln(1 + r) \times t & \text{using } \ln(a^b) = (\ln a) \times b.
\end{aligned}
$$

It follows that the **natural logarithm** of x_t is a **linear function** of t.

Furthermore, for small r, $\ln(1 + r) \simeq r$, so

$$\ln x_t \simeq \ln x_0 + r \times t.$$

The slope approximately equals r for small r.

The right panel of Figure 9.2 plots the natural logarithm of the S&P 500 index against time. Superimposed is a **linear time trend**, a line of the form $a + rt$. This graph more clearly shows departures from trend than does the left panel of Figure 9.2. It shows the great depression of the 1930's and another major dip in the early 1970's, a consequence of the first OPEC oil shock in 1973-74. And it indicates that stocks were rising much above trend rates in the late 1990's.

The slope of the linear trend in logs is $r = .065$, so the index grew at a compound rate of 6.5 percent per year. This gain is a nominal gain that overstates real gains; complete analysis should go further and convert to a real return. At the same time the index understates nominal gains as it fails to include stock dividends.

Remark 76 *For an exponential time trend with constant growth rate the natural logarithm is linear in time. The slope approximately equals r if $x_t = x_0(1 + r)^t$. Going the other way, if the natural logarithm is linear in time then growth in the original series is exponential.*

9.6   Exponential Function

The natural logarithm is the reverse operation to exponentiation. The exponential function is denoted

$$\exp(x) = e^x,$$

where $e \simeq 2.7182818...$ For completeness we present some properties of the exponential function.

In the physical sciences, exponential growth at rate r is often best represented as $x_t = \exp(a+rt)$. Then taking the natural logarithm yields immediately that $\ln x_t = a + r \times t$. The natural logarithm is linear in time with slope exactly equal to r.

A property of the exponential function is that

$$\exp(x) = \sum_{n=0}^{\infty} \frac{x^n}{n!} = 1 + x + \frac{x^2}{2} + \frac{x^3}{6} - \cdots .$$

If we use just the first term then

$$\exp(x) \simeq 1 + x, \quad \text{for, say, } |x| < 0.1.$$

While this approximation also works well for small $|x|$, it increasingly underestimates e^x as $x > 0$ increases and increasingly overestimates e^x as $x < 0$ decreases.

The exponential function has the property that for any x its slope equals its value. For example at $x = 2$ the function takes value e^2 and its curve has slope e^2. For those familiar with calculus this is because $d\exp(x)/dx = \exp(x)$.

9.6.1   Compound Interest Rates

Interest rates are often reported as annual interest rates, even though interest on the investment may be calculated more frequently than annually, such as monthly or even daily. In that case one needs to be careful in defining the annual interest rate.

Suppose that an interest rate is compounded monthly at a monthly interest rate of 1 percent. Then the nominal annual interest rate is defined to be the monthly interest rate times the number of months, or $12 \times 1 = 12$ percent. The effective annual interest rate is more than 12 percent, due to compounding. Compounding over twelve months, $(1 + .01)^{12} = 1.12683$, leading to an effective annual interest rate of 12.683 percent. If compound is daily rather than monthly, then the annual effective interest rate becomes 12.750 percent, since $(1 + 0.12/365)^{365} = 1.12747$.

In general if the nominal annual interest rate is r and there are n compounding periods per year then the effective annual interest rate is

$$r_{effective} = (1 + r/n)^n - 1.$$

The nominal annual interest rate is also called the **annual percentage rate** (APR) while the effective annual interest rate is called the **annual percentage yield** (APY).

If one **continuously compounds** an interest rate at progressively smaller intervals, then

$$(1 + r/n)^n \to e^r \quad \text{as } n \to \infty.$$

In the current example $\exp(0.12) = 1.12750...$, which equals the earlier result for daily compounding to four decimal places and the earlier result for monthly compounding to three decimal places.

9.7 Key Concepts

1. The change in $\ln x$ approximately equals the proportionate change in x, for small proportionate changes in x. And $100 \times \Delta \ln x$ approximately equals the percentage change in x.

2. The semi-elasticity of y with respect to x equals $(\Delta y/y)/\Delta x$, the ratio of the proportionate change in y to the change in the level of x.

3. The log-linear model gives a direct estimate of the semi-elasticity.

4. The elasticity of y with respect to x equals $(\Delta y/y)/(\Delta x/x)$, the ratio of the proportionate change in y to the proportionate change in x.

5. The log-log model gives a direct estimate of the elasticity.

6. The level-log model yields slope coefficient b_2 where $b_2/100$ is an estimate of the change in units of y in response to a one percent change in x.

7. For small x we can approximate $\ln(1 + x)$ by x. For many purposes this approximation is adequate for $x < 0.10$.

8. The rule of 72 states that it takes approximately $n = 72/r$ periods for a series to double if it is growing at the percentage rate r.

9. For an exponential time trend with constant growth rate the natural logarithm is linear in time. The slope approximately equals r if $x_t = x_0(1+r)^t$. Going the other way, if the natural logarithm is linear in time then growth in the original series is exponential.

10. The exponential function is denoted $\exp(x) = e^x$, where $e \simeq 2.7182818...$ The natural logarithm is the reverse operation to exponentiation.

11. For small x we can approximate $\exp x$ by $(1 + x)$. For many purposes this approximation is adequate for $|x| < 0.10$.

12. Key Terms: Data transformation; natural logarithm function; proportionate changes; semi-elasticity; elasticity; log-linear model, log-log model; linear-log model; rule of 72; linearizing exponential growth; exponential function; continuous compounding.

9.8   Exercises

1. Answer the following.

    (a) Suppose $y = \exp(a + bx)$. What is $\ln y$?

    (b) Suppose $\ln y = (c + dx)$. What is e^y?

    (c) Suppose $y = (a + bx)^c$. What is $\ln y$?

    (d) Suppose $y = x \times z$. What is $\ln y$?

2. For the time series variable x_t that takes consecutive values 5, 3, 7, 8 for $t = 1, ..., 4$:

    (a) Calculate $\sum_{t=1}^{4} x_t$.

    (b) Calculate Δx_t for $t = 2, 3, 4$ and hence $\sum_{t=2}^{4} \Delta x_t$.

3. Suppose x increases from 500 to 520.

    (a) What is the proportionate change in x?

    (b) What is the change in $\ln x$?

    (c) Compare your answers in parts a and b and comment.

    (d) Repeat parts a-c if x increases from 500 to 1000.

4. Repeat exercise 3 for x changing from 20 to 21 in parts a-c and from 20 to 30 in part (d).

5. For each of the following models provide the simplest possible explanation of the extent to which EARNS (annual earnings in $) changes as IQ (intelligent quotient has mean of 100) changes.

    (a) $earns = 20000 + 200 \times iq$.

    (b) $\ln(earns) = 10 + 0.009 \times iq$.

    (c) $\ln(earns) = 10 + 0.8 \times \ln(iq)$.

    (d) $earns = 18000 + 15000 \times \ln(iq)$.

6. Repeat exercise 5 where HOURS is annual hours worked for

   (a) *earns* = -18000 + 17×*hours*; (b) ln(*earns*) = 10 + 0.02×*hours*;
   (c) ln(*earns*) = 6 + 1.2×ln(*hours*); (d) *earns* = -300000 + 90000×*hours*;

7. For each of the following say whether b measures an elasticity or semi-elasticity or neither.

   (a) $y = a + b \ln x$;   (b) $y = a + bx$;   (c) $\ln y = a + b \ln x$.

8. For each of the following say what model leads to the given interpretation of the slope coefficient.

   (a) A one unit change in x is associated with a 0.3 unit change in y.

   (b) A one unit change in x is associated with a 0.3 percent change in y.

   (c) A one percent change in x is associated with a 0.3 percent change in y.

   (d) A one percent change in x is associated with a 0.3 unit change in y.

9. A detailed description of dataset SALARYSAT.DTA is given in exercise 3 of Chapter 7. We consider the relationship between salary (*salary*) and the score on the mathematics portion of the SAT (*satmath*). Use heteroskedastic-robust standard errors.

   (a) Regress *lnsalary* on an intercept and *satmath*. Interpret the slope coefficient.

   (b) Regress *lnsalary* on *lnsatmath* (a variable you need to create). Interpret the slope coefficient.

   (c) Test at 5% the hypothesis that a 1% increase in the *satmath* score is associated with a 1% increase in *salary*. Use heteroskedastic-robust standard errors.

   (d) Which model do you prefer - that in (a) or that in (b)? Explain.

10. Repeat the previous exercise with the score on the verbal portion of the SAT (*satverb*) rather then *satmath*.

11. In Chapter 8.1 we explored the relationship between life expectancy at birth (*Lifeexp*) and per capita health expenditures (*hlthpc*). Using dataset HEALTH2009 answer the following.

    (a) Estimate a linear model.

    (b) Estimate a linear-log model. Provide an interpretation of the slope coefficient as a semi-elasticity.

    (c) Which model do you prefer? That in part (a) or that in part (b)? Explain.

    (d) Provide a graph with (1) a scatterplot of *lifeexp* against *hlthpc*; (2) predicted values from the linear model against *hlthpc*; (3) predicted values from the linear-log model against *hlthpc*. Which model seems to fit best?

12. Continuing with the previous exercise we now consider models with ln(*lifeexp*) as the dependent variable.

    (a) Estimate a log-linear model. Provide an interpretation of the slope coefficient as a semi-elasticity.

    (b) Estimate a log-log model. Provide an interpretation of the slope coefficient as an elasticity.

    (c) Which model do you prefer? That in part (a) or that in part (b)? Explain.

    (d) Provide a graph with (1) a scatterplot of ln(*lifeexp*) against *hlthpc*; (2) predicted values of ln(*lifeexp*) from the log-linear model against *hlthpc*; (3) predicted values of ln(*lifeexp*) from the log-log model against *hlthpc*. Which model seems to fit best?

13. In Chapter 8.2 we regressed per capita health expenditures (*hlthpc*) on an intercept and per capita GDP (*gdppc*) for a sample of 34 OECD countries. The relationship is well fitted by a linear model, and from figure 8.2 the intercept is essentially 0. We have a linear model $y \simeq 0.09x$.

    (a) Take the natural logarithm of both sides of $y \simeq 0.09x$. Is the model linear in logs? What is the approximate intercept and slope coefficient.

    (b) Plot ln(*hlthpc*) against ln(*gdppc*). Does the relationship appear to be linear?

    (c) Give the estimates from OLS regression of ln(*hlthpc*) on an intercept and ln(*gdppc*). Are the coefficients close to what you expect from part (a).

    (d) Provide an interpretation of the slope coefficient in part (c) as an elasticity or semi-elasticity.

    (e) Perform at level 0.05 a two-sided test of the hypothesis that the slope coefficient equals one. Use heteroskedastic-robust standard errors.

14. Suppose $x_t = x_0 \times 1.04^t$ and $x_0 = 100$.

    (a) Plot x_t against t for $t = 1, ..., 100$. Comment on the shape of the curve.

    (b) Plot $\ln x_t$ against t for $t = 1, ..., 100$. Comment on the shape of the curve.

15. Monthly data for various stock indexes are given in dataset STOCKINDEX.

    (a) Plot the Dow Jones index (*dowjones*) against time from January 1957 to November 2012. Does the growth appear to be (approximately) linear or exponential?

    (b) Which period had the greatest absolute decrease in the index?

    (c) Now take the natural logarithm of the index and plot against time. Do you think the original index grows (approximately) exponentially? Explain.

    (d) State which decade(s) had relatively high proportionate growth in the index.

    (e) Given the value of the natural logarithm at the start and end dates, what do you think is the approximate average monthly rate of growth in the index? Explain.

    (f) Now run a regression to give an estimate of the average monthly rate of growth.

16. Repeat the analysis of the previous exercise using the following stock indexes in dataset STOCKINDEX.

    (a) Nasdaq index (*nasdaq*) from February 1971 to November 2012.

    (b) Russell index (*russell*) from September 1987 to November 2012.

    (c) Harder: Dow Jones index from January 1901 to December 1956 using monthly data that you obtain from the web.

17. Give the approximate annual rate of return to the following

    (a) An investment doubled in 9 years.

    (b) An investment quadrupled in 16 years. What was the approximate annual rate of return?

    (c) Over twenty years the natural logarithm of a stock price index increases from 11.35 to 11.75.

18. Suppose x_t grows exponentially at 6% per year with initial value $x_0 = 80$.

    (a) Give the formula for x_t.

    (b) Exactly how many years (or part thereof) will it take before $x_t = 160$?

    (c) Give the formula for $\ln x_t$.

    (d) Using the rule of 72, approximately how many years will it take before $x_t = 160$?

    (e) Compare your answers in parts b and d and comment.

19. Suppose $y = \ln x$ and that x changes by Δx. Use the properties of the natural logarithm given in Chapter 9.1 to answer the following.

    (a) Show that $\Delta y = \ln(x + \Delta x) - \ln x$.

    (b) Hence show that $\Delta y = \ln[(x + \Delta x)/x]$.

    (c) Hence show that $\Delta y = \ln[1 + \Delta x/x]$.

    (d) Hence show that $\Delta y \simeq \Delta x/x$ for small $\Delta x/x$.

    (e) Hence conclude that $\Delta \widehat{y}/\Delta x = 1/x$ as $\Delta x \to 0$. This is the derivative dy/dx.

20. For the exponential function $y = e^x$:

    (a) Find y when x changes by Δx to $x + \Delta x$.

    (b) Hence show that $\Delta y = e^x(e^{\Delta x} - 1)$. Hint: $e^{a+b} = e^a e^b$.

    (c) Hence find $\Delta y/\Delta x$.

    (d) Simplify using the result that $e^{\Delta x} \simeq (1 + \Delta x)$ for small Δx to obtain $\Delta y/\Delta x$ as $\Delta x \to 0$. This is the derivative dy/dx.

Chapter 10

Data Summary with Multiple Regression

This chapter presents the leading statistical method used in analysis of economics data, multiple regression of one variable on an intercept and several other variables. For example, we consider how house sale price is related to various features of the house such as house size, number of bedrooms, lot size and age.

This chapter considers summary of the relationship between variables in the sample. Chapter 11 presents statistical inference for the population and Chapter 12 presents additional details.

10.1 Example: House Price and Characteristics

We consider the same dataset HOUSE for 29 houses as that analyzed in Chapters 5-7, except now additional variables are included in the analysis.

Table 10.1 presents variable descriptions and summary statistics for these data on houses sold in a homogeneous community in a single year. A half bathroom is a lavatory without bath or shower. Precise data on lot size are unavailable; instead the lot size is coded as 1 for small, 2 for medium

Table 10.1: House price: Variable definitions and summary statistics (n=29)

Variable	Definition	Mean	Standard deviation	Min	Max
Price	Sale Price in dollars	253910	37391	204000	375000
Size	House size in square feet	1883	398	1400	3300
Bedrooms	Number of bedrooms	3.79	0.68	3	6
Bathrooms	Number of bathrooms	2.21	0.34	2	3
Lotsize	Size of lot (1, 2 or 3)	2.14	0.69	1	3
Age	House age in years	36.4	7.12	23	51
Monthsold	Month of year house was sold	5.97	1.68	3	8

and 3 for large.

Interest lies in the extent to which house price is explained by the other variables. For this example the dataset is small, so we can make some preliminary conclusions by simply listing the data.

Table 10.2: House price: Complete listing of data.

Price	Size	Bedrooms	Bathrooms	Lot Size	Age	Month Sold
375,000	3,300	4	2.5	2	39	3
340,000	2,400	4	3	2	34	6
310,000	2,300	4	2.5	2	28	5
279,900	2,000	4	2	2	31	7
278,500	2,600	6	2	3	38	8
273,000	1,900	5	2	2	37	7
272,000	1,800	4	2.5	2	46	3
270,000	2,000	4	2.5	3	39	5
270,000	1,800	4	2	3	31	3
258,500	1,600	3	2	1	39	8
255,000	1,500	4	2	3	47	7
253,000	2,100	4	2	3	47	6
249,000	1,900	4	3	3	37	6
245,000	1,400	4	2	2	30	8
244,000	2,000	4	2	1	29	7
241,000	1,600	4	2	2	34	8
239,500	1,600	3	2	3	34	6
238,000	1,900	4	2	2	29	7
236,500	1,600	3	2	3	23	8
235,000	1,600	3	2	3	35	5
235,000	1,700	4	2	2	29	7
233,000	1,700	3	2	1	40	6
230,000	2,100	4	2	2	34	8
229,000	1,700	4	2.5	2	35	3
224,500	2,100	4	2.5	2	47	6
220,000	1,600	3	2	1	49	4
213,000	1,800	3	2	2	51	4
212,000	1,600	3	3	2	33	5
204,000	1,400	3	2	1	31	7

Table 10.2 gives a listing, ordered by house price, and suggests that price increases with house size as already noted in Chapter 5. House price increases with number of bedrooms as, for example, the four highest priced houses have one more bedroom than the four lowest priced houses. There appears to be little relationship with number of bathrooms, lot size, age of house and month of the year in which the house was sold.

A more systematic analysis is needed, for several reasons. First, for many datasets the data listing is so large as to make interpretation impossible. Second, it is desirable to quantify the relationship between the different series. For example, what is the estimated change in house price associated with an increase in house size of one hundred square feet? Third, we wish to extrapolate

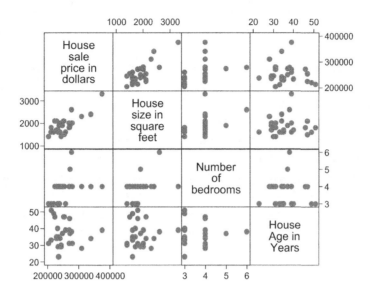

Figure 10.1: Scatterplots: House price and various characteristics

from the sample to the population, in which case confidence intervals and hypothesis tests are used. All of these points have already been raised in the preceding chapters on bivariate regression.

Multiple regression departs from bivariate regression by controlling for several variables simultaneously. This allows isolation of the effect of one regressor after controlling for other regressors.

For example, consider the relationship between house price and both number of bedrooms and house size. Bivariate regression with *Bedrooms* as the only regressor yields fitted model

$$\widehat{Price} = 164138 + 23667 \times Bedrooms.$$

This suggests a large association between price and number of bedrooms, with an increase in price of \$23,667 per bedroom. If instead we perform multiple regression with both *Bedrooms* and *Size* as regressors, then

$$\widehat{Price} = 111691 + 1553 \times Bedrooms + 72.41 \times Size.$$

Now an extra bedroom is associated with only a \$1,553 increase in the price of the house. So bedrooms actually have relatively small association with house price, once house size is controlled for.

10.2 Two-way Scatter Plots

Graphical methods for displaying the data are necessarily restricted to plots in two or three dimensions.

Figure 10.1 presents an **array of separate two-way scatter plots** for four of the variables in the house price dataset. The top row has house price on the vertical axis. The first scatterplot in the top row is of house price against size, the relationship studied in the bivariate regression. The second scatterplot in the top row shows a modest positive relationship of price with number of bedrooms, and the final scatterplot shows little relationship with house age. The second row has house size on the vertical axis. The first scatterplot in the second row shows that size has a strong positive relationship with house size; this is the reverse plot of the price-size plot given in the first row. The scatter plots also show no data points that are unusually large outliers.

In general for k series there are potentially $k \times (k-1)$ separate plots, where for each pair of series there are two plots depending on which variable is on the vertical axis, and there is no point in plotting a series against itself. It can be simpler to read a variant of Figure 10.1 that provides only one-half of the possible scatter plots by not including scatter plots with the axes reversed.

Twoway scatter plots are especially useful for plotting related series where separate two-way comparisons are of intrinsic interest. For example, this can be the case for related financial data series such as interest rates at various maturities. And the scatter plots may show unusual outlying data points, possibly due to data coding error.

Three-dimensional graphs (or surface plots) plot the relationship between three series. These are used much less than two-way scatterplots.

10.3   Correlation

Pairwise correlations can be useful for exploratory data analysis.

10.3.1   Pairwise Correlation

From Chapter 5.4, the **sample correlation coefficient** between variables y and x is

$$r_{xy} = \frac{\sum_{i=1}^{n}(x_i - \bar{x})(y_i - \bar{y})}{\sqrt{\sum_{i=1}^{n}(x_i - \bar{x})^2} \times \sqrt{\sum_{i=1}^{n}(y_i - \bar{y})^2}},$$

where $-1 \leq r_{xy} \leq 1$. The sign of r_{xy} gives the direction of the association, strictly speaking the linear association, between x and y, and the association is stronger the larger is $|r_{xy}|$.

In multivariate analysis several variables are considered. Then we can construct **pairwise correlations** that are correlations for each unique pair of variables. If there are k variables then there are potentially k^2 pairwise correlations. Not all of the correlations need to be computed and reported, however, since $r_{xx} = 1$ and $r_{xy} = r_{yx}$ as the correlations are symmetric.

10.3.2   Example: House Price

Table 10.3 presents pairwise correlations for the data summarized in Table 10.1, with asterisks denoting that the sample correlation coefficient is statistically different from zero at significance level 0.05. The table lists correlations only in the lower half – the upper half is just the mirror image as $r_{yx} = r_{xy}$. For example the entry for row *Price* and column *Size* would be 0.79.

Table 10.3: House price: Correlations of variables

	Price	*Size*	*Bedrooms*	*Bathrooms*	*Lotsize*	*Age*	*Monthsold*
Price	1						
Size	.79*	1					
Bedrooms	.43*	.52*	1				
Bathrooms	.33	.32	.04	1			
Lotsize	.15	.11	.29	.10	1		
Age	-.07	.08	-.03	.03	-.02	1	
Monthsold	-.21	-.21	.18	-.39*	-.06	-.37	1

Since we ultimately wish to explain *Price*, the first column of Table 10.3 is of greatest relevance. The most highly correlated variable with *Price* is *Size* ($r = .79$), followed by *Bedrooms* ($r = .43$). From the second column, however, *Size* and *Bedrooms* are fairly highly correlated ($r = .52$) so, for example, *Bedrooms* may not add much more explanatory power than *Size* alone. Regression of *Price* on *Size* and *Bedrooms* permits determination of the independent effect on price of the number bedrooms, controlling for house size.

10.4 Regression Line

The regression line for multiple regression is similar to that for bivariate regression, except additional variables are added. The least squares estimates again minimize a sum of squared residuals.

10.4.1 Regression Line

The **regression line** from regression of y on several variables $x_2, ..., x_k$ is denoted

$$\widehat{y} = b_1 + b_2 x_2 + b_3 x_3 + \cdots + b_k x_k.$$

The terminology is the same as that for bivariate regression. The variable y is called the **dependent variable**, $\widehat{y}$ is the **fitted value** or **predicted value**, $x_2, .., x_k$ are **regressor** (or independent or explanatory) variables or covariates, b_1 is the estimated y-axis intercept and $b_2, ..., b_k$ are the estimated slope parameters.

Note that the first regressor variable is denoted x_2 rather than x_1; implicitly $x_1 = 1$ for the intercept. There are k regression coefficients, including the intercept, and hence $n - k$ degrees of freedom. (Some other texts denote the first regressor after the intercept as x_1 and specify $\widehat{y} = b_0 + b_1 x_1 + b_2 x_2 + b_3 x_3 + \cdots + b_k x_k$. Then there are $k + 1$ regression parameters, and hence $n - k - 1$ degrees of freedom. In that case wherever $n - k$ appears below, these other texts would use $n - k - 1$.)

The fitted model for the ith observation is written as

$$\widehat{y}_i = b_1 + b_2 x_{2i} + b_3 x_{3i} + \cdots + b_k x_{ki},$$

where the first subscript for regressors denotes the variable and the second subscript denotes the observation. For example, x_{ji} is the ith observation for the jth regressor.

10.4.2   Least Squares Estimation

For multiple regression the **residual** e, the difference between the actual and fitted values of y, is

$$e_i = y_i - \widehat{y}_i = y_i - b_1 - b_2 x_{2i} - b_3 x_{3i} - \cdots - b_k x_{ki}.$$

As for bivariate regression, **least squares regression** computes the regression coefficients, here $b_1, ..., b_k$, to make as small as possible the **residual sum of squares**,

$$\sum_{i=1}^{n} e_i^2 = \sum_{i=1}^{n} (y_i - \widehat{y}_i)^2 = \sum_{i=1}^{n} (y_i - b_1 - b_2 x_{2i} - \cdots - b_k x_{ki})^2.$$

The **ordinary least squares (OLS) estimates** $b_1, ..., b_k$ are the solution to k equations in k unknowns. These equations, called the **normal equations** or **first-order conditions** are that

$$\sum_{i=1}^{n} x_{ji}(y_i - b_1 - b_2 x_{2i} - b_3 x_{3i} - \cdots - b_k x_{ki}) = 0, \quad j = 1, ..., k,$$

where x_{ji} is the jth regressor and $x_{1i} = 1$ for all i.

The sample size must exceed the number of regressors (including the intercept), since there are k equations in k unknowns. Additionally there must be enough **variation in the sample regressors** so that the regressors are not perfectly correlated with each other, or with linear combinations of each other. For example, if $x_3 = 2x_2$ then it is not possible to regress y on x_2 and x_3 and disentangle the combined influence of x_2 and x_3.

Definition 26 *The multiple regression line is* $\widehat{y} = b_1 + b_2 x_2 + b_3 x_3 + \cdots + b_k x_k$. *The OLS estimates* $b_1, b_2, ..., b_k$ *are obtained by minimizing the sum of squared residuals where the residual* $e = y - \widehat{y}$ *is the difference between the actual and predicted value of* y.

Given the definition of the residual e_i, the normal equations can be rewritten as

$$\sum_{i=1}^{n} x_{ji} e_i = 0, \quad j = 1, ..., k.$$

So the sum over observations of the regressor times the residual equals zero. The mathematical terminology for this property is that **each regressor is orthogonal to the residual**.

The intercept term is $x_{1i} = 1$ for all i, so the preceding result with $j = 1$ implies that $\sum_{i=1}^{n} e_i = 0$. Thus the residuals sum to zero, and their in-sample average is zero. Since $e_i = y_i - \widehat{y}_i$, it follows that $\frac{1}{n} \sum_{i=1}^{n} (y_i - \widehat{y}_i) = 0$, so the sample mean of the fitted values equals the sample mean of the dependent variable.

Remark 77 *A property of OLS regression is that residuals are orthogonal to the regressors, so that the sum over observations of the cross product of any regressor with the residuals equals zero. Furthermore, if an intercept is included in the regression then the residuals sum to zero and average zero. This in turn implies that the average of the in-sample fitted values is equal to the average of the sample values of the dependent variable.*

10.4.3 Least Squares Estimates

The complete formula for the OLS estimates from multiple regression cannot be expressed directly in summation notation, unlike bivariate regression.

The simplest representation is the following. Consider the coefficient b_j of the jth regressor x_j. Let $\widehat{x}_{ji}$ be the fitted value from the auxiliary multiple regression of x_j on an intercept and all regressors other than x_j, and let $\widetilde{x}_{ji} = x_{ji} - \widehat{x}_{ji}$ be the residual from this auxiliary regression. Then $\widetilde{x}_{ji}$ captures the additional information provided by the ith observation of the jth regressor beyond that already captured by the other regressors in the model.

It can be shown that b_j from the original model multiple regression of y_i on an intercept and $x_{2i}, ..., x_{ki}$ can be calculated as the slope estimate from bivariate OLS regression of y_i on an intercept and the residual $\widetilde{x}_{ji}$. Then the **estimated slope coefficient** for the jth regressor is

$$b_j = \frac{\sum_{i=1}^{n} \widetilde{x}_{ji}(y_i - \bar{y})}{\sum_{i=1}^{n} \widetilde{x}_{ji}^2}.$$

Simplification to the usual bivariate slope coefficient formula has occurred because by construction $\overline{\widetilde{x}_j} = \frac{1}{n}\sum_{i=1}^{n} \widetilde{x}_{ji} = 0$, since $\widetilde{x}_{ji}$ is an OLS residual from a regression that includes an intercept.

This representation of the OLS slope coefficient b_j from multiple regression makes clear that b_j measures the effect of x_j, after controlling for the other regressors in the regression.

Remark 78 *The OLS coefficient b_j from multiple regression can be calculated by bivariate regression of y on an intercept and $\widetilde{x}_j$, where $\widetilde{x}_j$ is the residual from regressing x_j on an intercept and all regressors other than x_j.*

This result includes as a special case bivariate regression. Then x_2 is the only regressor, the residual $\widetilde{x}_2$ is obtained by regressing x_2 on just an intercept, so $\widehat{x}_{2i} = \overline{x}_2$ and $\widetilde{x}_{2i} = x_{2i} - \overline{x}_2$. It follows that $b_2 = \sum_i (x_{2i} - \overline{x}_2)(y_i - \bar{y})/\sum_i (x_{2i} - \overline{x}_2)^2$.

In more advanced courses that use matrix algebra there is a simple formula for the OLS estimates from multiple regression. For completeness this matrix formula is given in an Appendix C.4.

10.4.4 Example: House Price

OLS regression of house sale price (variable *Price*) on the variables listed in Table 10.1 leads to the fitted regression line

$$\widehat{Price} = 137791 + 68.37 \times Size + 2685 \times Bedrooms + 6833 \times Bathrooms$$
$$+2303 \times Lotsize - 833 \times Age - 2089 \times Monthsold.$$

The coefficient of 68.37 for variable *Size* implies that one more square foot in size is associated with a \$68.37 increase in the house price after controlling for the number of bedrooms, number of bathrooms, the lot size, house age and the month the house was sold. By "controlling for" we mean that *Size* changes while none of the other features of the house change.

By contrast bivariate regression of *Price* on *Size* does not hold these other features constant and leads to a different coefficient of 73.77 for variable *Size*. In other examples the difference between the bivariate regression and multiple regression coefficients can be much larger; see Chapter 10.1 for an example. This distinction is fundamentally important and is pursued in the next section.

More complete output for this regression is given in Table 10.4. It includes p-values for tests of the statistical significance of each of the variables in the regression; see Chapter 11.4. Only *Size* is statistically significant at 5%. So while the remaining regressors may have the expected signs, it needs to be borne in mind that the coefficients are imprecisely estimated and these regressors are statistically insignificant at 5%.

10.5   Interpretation of Slope Coefficients

As regressors are added in the model the slope coefficient of any specific regressor will generally change.

10.5.1   Estimated Partial Effect

Suppose x_2 is changed by Δx_2, while holding all other regressors at their current values. Then the predicted value of y becomes

$$
\begin{aligned}
\widehat{y}_{new} &= b_1 + b_2(x_2 + \Delta x_2) + b_3 x_3 + \cdots + b_k x_k \\
&= b_2 \Delta x_2 + b_1 + b_2 x_2 + b_3 x_3 + \cdots + b_k x_k \\
&= b_2 \Delta x_2 + \widehat{y}_{old}.
\end{aligned}
$$

It follows from subtraction that $\Delta \widehat{y} = b_2 \Delta x_2$, so that $\Delta \widehat{y}/\Delta x_2 = b_2$.

This result is the **estimated partial effect** of x_2 on $\widehat{y}$, and is expressed as

$$
\left. \frac{\Delta \widehat{y}}{\Delta x_2} \right|_{x_3,...,x_k} = b_2,
$$

where the notation means that only x_2 is changed, while the other regressors $x_3, ..., x_k$ are held constant. The effect is also called the effect of x_2 **ceteris paribus**, where the Latin phrase "ceteris paribus" means all other things equal or held constant.

For convenience the simpler notation $\Delta \widehat{y}/\Delta x_2 = b_2$ may be used in place of the more formal notation $\Delta \widehat{y}/\Delta x_2|_{x_3,...,x_k} = b_2$.

Remark 79 *The slope coefficient b_2 in the multiple regression $\widehat{y} = b_1 + b_2 x_2 + \cdots + b_k x_k$ gives the partial effect on the predicted value of y when x_2 changes by one unit, holding the remaining regressors $x_3, ..., x_k$ constant.*

10.5.2   Estimated Total Effect

In the house price example, the partial effect corresponds to an experiment where one feature of the house is changed in isolation, while all other features are held constant.

In practice, however changes in one feature of the house may also be associated with changes in other features of the house. For example, an extra bedroom may be associated with a larger house

– both features may effect the price of the house. The **total effect** on $\widehat{y}$ of a change in x_2 includes all the secondary effects through $x_3, ..., x_k$ also changing.

For simplicity, consider multiple regression on two regressors x_2 and x_3, with fitted model $\widehat{y} = b_1 + b_2 x_2 + b_3 x_3$. Suppose changing x_2 by Δx_2 is associated with a change in x_3 of Δx_3. Then the total effect on y of changing x_2 by Δx_2 equals $\Delta \widehat{y} = b_2 \Delta x_2 + b_3 \Delta x_3$. Dividing by Δx_2, it follows that the total effect of a change in x_2 on $\widehat{y}$ equals $\Delta \widehat{y}/\Delta x_2 = b_2 + b_3 \Delta x_3/\Delta x_2$.

This leads to the following more general result.

Remark 80 *For multiple regression of y on an intercept and $x_2, ..., x_k$, the estimated total effect of a change in x_2 allows for the secondary effect that the remaining regressors change when x_2 changes. The estimated total effect is*

$$\frac{\Delta \widehat{y}}{\Delta x_2}\bigg|_{Total} = b_2 + b_3 \frac{\Delta x_3}{\Delta x_2} + \cdots + \frac{\Delta x_k}{\Delta x_2}.$$

For those familiar with advanced differential calculus, the partial effect is the partial derivative of $\widehat{y}$ with respect to x_2, denoted $\partial \widehat{y}/\partial x_2$. The total effect is the total derivative of $\widehat{y}$ with respect to x_2, denoted $d\widehat{y}/dx_2$.

One consequence of this result is that the difference between the partial and total effects of a variable x are likely to be greater the more highly x is correlated with the other variables included in a multiple regression. In the extreme case that $\frac{\Delta x_3}{\Delta x_2} = 0, ..., \frac{\Delta x_k}{\Delta x_2} = 0$, the two effects are equal. This also makes clear when inclusion of an additional regressor is likely to change coefficient estimates.

Remark 81 *The addition of a regressor that is perfectly uncorrelated with the other variables in the model will lead to no change in the slope coefficients of those variables.*

10.5.3 Estimated Partial and Total Effects for OLS

There is a mechanical relationship between estimated partial and total effects when models are estimated by OLS regression.

The slope coefficient from bivariate regression of x_3 on x_2 is an estimate of $\Delta x_3/\Delta x_2$. More generally, the slope coefficient from bivariate regression of x_j on x_2 is an estimate of $\Delta x_j/\Delta x_2$.

Using these $k - 2$ bivariate slope estimates for the $k - 2$ changes $\Delta x_j/\Delta x_2$ in the preceding formula yields a value for the estimated total effect $\Delta \widehat{y}/\Delta x_2$ that, remarkably, exactly equals the slope coefficient from bivariate regression of y_2 on x_2 alone. Exercise 3 provides an example.

Remark 82 *When regression is by OLS, the total effect on the predicted value of y when x_2 changes by one unit from a multiple regression of y on $x_2, ..., x_k$ equals the slope coefficient from bivariate regression of y on x_2 alone.*

10.5.4 Partial versus Total Effects

In many regression applications it is the partial effect that we are interested in. For example, consider how earnings vary with education. Rather than the simple bivariate relationship between earnings and education, interest often lies in the size of any difference in earnings by educational level after controlling for individual characteristics such as age, gender and socioeconomic background.

10.5.5   Causation

While the term "effect" has been used in the preceding discussion, it is important to realize that OLS regression measures association between y and the regressors $x_2, ..., x_n$, but not necessarily causation.

For example, regression of earnings on education and other regressors such as age and gender may find that even after inclusion of these other variables, higher earnings are associated with more education. But it is not necessarily the case that more education causes higher earnings. Instead it may be that the positive association is due to a variable such as unobserved ability, not included as a regressor, that causes both higher earnings and more education.

As a second example, a regression of a measure of individual health status on income and other regressors such as age and gender may find that lower income is associated with poorer health. But it may be that it is poor health that leads to lower income due to limiting an individual's ability to work, rather than lower income that leads to poorer health.

For this reason, unless there is clear a priori information about the direction of causality one should merely say that in a fitted multiple regression model a one unit change in x_j is **associated with** a b_j change in $\widehat{y}$, holding all other regressors constant. Methods to determine causation are presented in Chapters 17.4 and 17.5, and Chapters 13.5–13.8 provide some applications of these causal methods.

Remark 83 *In a fitted multiple regression model a one unit change in x_j is associated with a b_j change in $\widehat{y}$, holding all other regressors constant. The association need not imply causation.*

10.6   Model Fit

For OLS estimation the sum of squared residuals necessarily decreases, or at worse remains unchanged, as more regressors are added to a model. Some, but not all, measures of model fit compensate for this by penalizing larger models.

10.6.1   Standard Error of the Regression

For multiple regression the **standard error of the regression** is

$$s_e = \sqrt{\frac{1}{n-k} \sum_{i=1}^{n} (y_i - \widehat{y}_i)^2}.$$

Now division is by $n-k$ **degrees of freedom**, rather than $n-2$ in the bivariate case, as k degrees are lost since computation of $\widehat{y} = b_1 + b_2 x + \cdots + b_k x_k$ is based on the k estimates $b_1, ..., b_k$.

As was the case for bivariate regression, other names for s_e are the **root mean squared error (MSE) of the residual** and the **standard error of the residual**. And s_e is most simply thought of as being the standard deviation of the residual. Lower values of s_e indicate better fit.

Adding regressors cannot increase the sum of squared residuals, since if another regressor is added we can always leave the sum of squared residuals unchanged by giving the new regressor a coefficient of zero and leaving the coefficients of the other regressors unchanged. So as regressors are added $\sum_{i=1}^{n}(y_i-\widehat{y}_i)^2$ falls. At the same time k is now higher, so the term $1/(n-k)$ is higher, leading to a penalty for model size. Combining these two effects, s_e can either rise or fall as regressors are added to the model.

Remark 84 *The standard error of the regression measures the standard deviation of the residual, and hence the variability of the dependent variable around the regression line. As regressors are added to a model s_e may decrease or may increase, though when n is large it is more likely to increase.*

10.6.2 R-Squared

As in the bivariate case the **total sum of squares** $\sum_{i=1}^{n}(y_i-\bar{y})^2$, denoted *TSS*, can be decomposed as

$$TSS = ExpSS + \ ResSS,$$

where the **explained sum of squares** (*ExpSS*) equals $\sum_{i=1}^{n}(\widehat{y}_i-\bar{y})^2$ and the **residual sum of squares** (*ResSS*) equals $\sum_{i=1}^{n}(y_i-\widehat{y}_i)^2$.

The coefficient of determination, or **R-squared**, is defined exactly as in the bivariate case as

$$R^2 = \frac{ExpSS}{TSS} = \frac{\sum_{i=1}^{n}(\widehat{y}_i-\bar{y})^2}{\sum_{i=1}^{n}(y_i-\bar{y})^2},$$

where *ExpSS*, the **explained sum of squares**, is also referred to as the **regression sum of squares** or as the **model sum of squares**. The only change is that $\widehat{y}_i$ is the prediction from a model with additional regressors. R^2 takes a maximum value of 1 if the residual sum of squares is zero, in which case the actual data y_i are perfectly fit by the regression line. And $R^2 \geq 0$ provided an intercept term is included in the regression. If there is no intercept in the regression then R^2 is a meaningless concept and $R^2 < 0$ is possible.

As in the bivariate case, **R-squared** can also be expressed as

$$R^2 = 1 - \frac{ResSS}{TSS} = 1 - \frac{\sum_{i=1}^{n}(y_i-\widehat{y}_i)^2}{\sum_{i=1}^{n}(y_i-\bar{y})^2},$$

where *ResSS* is the **residual sum of squares** and is sometimes referred to as the **error sum of squares**.

It can be shown that R^2 equals the squared correlation coefficient between the fitted values $\widehat{y}_i$ and the actual values y_i.

Remark 85 R^2 *measures the fraction of the variation in the dependent variable explained by the regressor. Provided the regression includes an intercept, R^2 lies between 0 and 1. R^2 can equivalently be measured as the squared correlation coefficient between y and $\widehat{y}$, and as one minus the residual sum of squares divided by the total sum of squares.*

10.6.3 Adjusted R-squared

A weakness of R^2 is that it necessarily increases, or at worse remains unchanged, as more regressors are added to a model. This is because the sum of squared residuals will at most be unchanged as regressors are added, so $R^2 = 1 - ResSS/TSS$ is at the least unchanged.

To compare the fit across models with different numbers of regressors it is better to use a measure that penalizes larger models. The **adjusted R-squared**, denoted $\bar{R}^2$, is defined by

$$\bar{R}^2 = 1 - \frac{ResSS/(n-k)}{TSS/(n-1)} = 1 - \frac{\sum_{i=1}^{n}(y_i - \widehat{y}_i)^2/(n-k)}{\sum_{i=1}^{n}(y_i - \bar{y})^2/(n-1)}.$$

The motivation is that k regression coefficients are estimated to form $\widehat{y}_i$, so the residual sum of squares is divided by the degrees of freedom, $n - k$. For similar reason the total sum of squares is divided by $n - 1$ due to the estimate $\bar{y}$.

Given the above definition of $\bar{R}^2$, it follows immediately that

$$\bar{R}^2 = 1 - \frac{s_e^2}{s_y^2},$$

where s_e^2/s_y^2 is the ratio of the squared standard error of the regression to the sample variance of y. It follows that as regressors are added to the model, $\bar{R}^2$ will increase or decrease according to whether or not the standard error of the regression decreases as regressors are added.

$\bar{R}^2$ is related to R^2 by the formula

$$\bar{R}^2 = R^2 - \frac{k-1}{n-k}(1 - R^2).$$

Clearly $\bar{R}^2 \leq R^2$. It can be shown that the difference between R^2 and $\bar{R}^2$ is greater the larger is the number of regressors (k) and the smaller is the sample size (n).

Remark 86 *The adjusted R^2, denoted $\bar{R}^2$, is less than R^2 due to a modest penalty for the number of regressors in the model. As regressors are added $\bar{R}^2$ will increase if s_e decreases and $\bar{R}^2$ will decrease if s_e increases.*

While $\bar{R}^2$ is better than R^2, it may still err on the side of favoring models with many regressors. In particular, the penalty that $\bar{R}^2$ gives to larger models is not as large as the penalty imposed using hypothesis tests at the standard significance levels; see Chapter 11.5.

10.6.4 Information Criteria

For basic multiple regression the standard goodness-of-fit measures that provide a penalty for model size are $\bar{R}^2$ and s_e.

For completeness we present three **information criteria** (IC) that also penalize model size. The measures in order of increasing penalty for model size are as follows.

Criteria		General formula
Akaike IC	AIC	$= n \times \ln \widehat{\sigma}_e^2 + n(1 + \ln 2\pi) + 2k$
Bayesian (or Schwarz) IC	BIC	$= n \times \ln \widehat{\sigma}_e^2 + n(1 + \ln 2\pi) + k \times \ln(n)$
Hannan-Quinn IC	$HQIC$	$= n \times \ln \widehat{\sigma}_e^2 + n(1 + \ln 2\pi) + 2k \times \ln(\ln(n)).$

Table 10.4: House price: Computer output from multiple regression.

Summary Statistics						
Observations	29					
R-squared	0.651					
Adjusted R^2	0.555					
St. error of regression	24936					

Dependent Variable *Price*						
Regressor	**Coefficient**	**Standard Error**	**t statistic**	**p value**	**95% conf. int.**	
Size	68.37	15.39	4.44	0.000	36.45	101.29
Bedrooms	2685	9193	0.29	0.773	-16379	21749
Bathrooms	6833	15721	0.43	0.668	-25771	39437
Lot Size	2303	7227	0.32	0.753	-12684	17290
Age	-833	719	-1.16	0.259	-2325	659
Monthsold	-2089	3521	-0.59	0.559	-9390	5213
Intercept	137791	61465	2.24	0.035	10321	265261

ANOVA Table					
Source	**SS**	**df**	**MS**	**F**	**p-value**
Explained	2.5466×10^{10}	6	4.2444×10^9	6.83	0.0003
Residual	1.3679×10^{10}	22	0.6218×10^9		
Total	3.9146×10^{10}	28	0.1398×10^9		

Here $\widehat{\sigma}_e^2 = \frac{1}{n}\sum_{i=1}^{n}(y_i - \widehat{y}_i)^2$ is the sample average of the squared residuals. This is similar to s_e^2 except there is no degrees of freedom correction, so division is by n rather than $n - k$. The term $n(1 + \ln 2\pi)$ is common to all three IC measures, so some statistical packages drop $n(1 + \ln 2\pi)$ in computing the information criteria. Models with low information criterion are preferred.

The information criteria favor models with smaller sum of squared residuals, but add a penalty for models with more regressors. *AIC* provides a penalty for model size that is too light in practice. *BIC* provides a larger penalty and is most often used.

10.7 Computer Output Following Multiple Regression

As an example we consider regression of house sale price on several regressors. The example is illustrative. We use default standard errors that presume errors are homoskedastic. For these data it is standard to instead use heteroskedastic-robust standard errors; these are presented in Table 12.2. And a better way to incorporate the variable *Lotsize*, one that takes the three arbitrary values 1, 2 and 3, is to use a set of indicator variables, presented in Chapter 14.4.

The top part of Table 10.4 presents measures of the overall fit of the model. $R^2 = .651$, an increase compared to $R^2 = .618$ for the model with just *Size* as regressor. The adjusted R^2 can be computed as $\bar{R}^2 = .651 - (6/22) \times .349 = .555$. This is actually lower than $\bar{R}^2 = .603$ for the regression with just *Size* as regressor, suggesting that the additional regressors have not added enough to the model fit to compensate for the extra five slope coefficients that are estimated. The standard error of the regression equals 24936. This is substantially smaller than the standard deviation of variable *Price* which from Table 5.2 equals 37391. At the same time it is larger than $s_e = 23551$ for the regression with just *Size* as regressor, again confirming that the additional regressors added little to model fit. The F statistic and its associated p-value are used to test the joint statistical significance of all the regressors; see Chapter 11.5.

The middle part of Table 10.4 presents the key regression output. We have $b_2 = 68.37$ and so on, with fitted model

$$\widehat{Price} = 137791 + 68.37 \times Size + 2685 \times Bedrooms + 6833 \times Bathrooms$$
$$+2303 \times Lot\ Size - 833 \times Age - 2089 \times Month\ Sold.$$

Controlling for other likely determinants of house price, the estimated partial effect of an increase in the size of the house by one square foot is an increase in house price of \$68.37. This is not very different from the earlier bivariate regression slope estimate of \$73.77, which gives the estimated total effect.

The t statistics and p-values given are for tests of statistical significance of each regressor. These and the confidence intervals can be interpreted in the same way as for bivariate regression. Details on hypothesis testing for multiple regression are presented in Chapter 11. The regressor *Size* has $p < .05$, so it is the only regressor that is statistically significant at level 0.05. We conclude that house size is the primary determinant of house price in this market.

The bottom part of Table 10.4 gives the analysis of variance table that may be included in computer output if inference is based on the assumption of independent homoskedastic errors. Given the definition of R^2, we have $R^2 = 2.5466 \times 10^{10}/(3.9146 \times 10^{10}) = 0.651$. And given the definition of the standard error of the regression, $s_e = \sqrt{1.3679 \times 10^{10}/22} = 24936$. These values are those already given at the top of Table 10.4.

10.8 Inestimable Models

It is not always possible to estimate all k regression coefficients in the regression of y on an intercept and regressors $x_2, ..., x_k$.

A simple example of this is where there is no variation in the values taken by a regressor. For example, suppose all houses in the sample have exactly two bathrooms. Then in regression of *Price* (y) on an intercept, *Size* (x_2), *Bedrooms* (x_3) and *Bathrooms* (x_4),

$$\widehat{y} = b_1 + b_2 x_2 + b_3 x_3 + b_4 x_4$$
$$= b_1 + b_2 x_2 + b_3 x_3 + b_4 \times 2$$
$$= (b_1 + 2b_2) + b_2 x_2 + b_3 x_3.$$

In that case the coefficient of *Bathrooms* (x_4) cannot be estimated (it is absorbed in the intercept), though the coefficients of *Size* and *Bedrooms* can still be estimated.

A second example of an inestimable is where regressors are **perfectly collinear**, meaning that there is an exact linear relationship among regressors. For example suppose for all houses in the sample the sum of the number of bedrooms and bathrooms equals six. Continuing with the previous example, $x_3 + x_4 = 6$ so $x_4 = (6 - x_3)$ and

$$
\begin{aligned}
\widehat{y} &= b_1 + b_2 x_2 + b_3 x_3 + b_4 x_4 \\
&= b_1 + b_2 x_2 + b_3 x_3 + b_4 (6 - x_3) \\
&= (b_1 + 6b_4) + b_2 x_2 + (b_3 - b_4) x_3.
\end{aligned}
$$

We cannot obtain a coefficient for *Bathrooms* (x_4). Furthermore the coefficient of *Bedrooms* (x_3) is no longer simply b_3. The only meaningful estimate is that of b_2, the coefficient of *Price*.

When a coefficient of a regressor cannot be estimated the coefficient is said to be **not identified.** In these two examples it is only the coefficients of regressors with inadequate variation or that are linearly related that are not identified. The coefficients of the remaining regressors are still identified.

In such cases computer output such as that in the middle of Table 10.4 will have no entries for one or more regressors, and may include the word omitted. While dropping regressors solves the problem, it is still good practice to determine why a computer package is dropping regressors.

For more discussion see Chapter 14.4 on the dummy variable trap, and Chapter 16.1.

10.9 Key Concepts

1. Least squares regression with many regressors is no more difficult to perform than regression with just one regressor.

2. The multiple regression line is $\widehat{y} = b_1 + b_2 x_2 + b_3 x_3 + \cdots + b_k x_k$.

3. The residual $e = y - \widehat{y}$ is the difference between the actual and fitted values of the dependent variable.

4. The least squares coefficients $b_1, ..., b_k$ minimize the sum of squared residuals.

5. The least squares estimates can always be computed, provided there is sufficient variation in the regressor values across observations.

6. OLS residuals are orthogonal to the regressors, so for the jth regressor, $\sum_{i=1}^{n} x_{ji} e_i = 0$.

7. If an intercept is included in the regression then OLS residuals sum to zero, average to zero, and the average of in-sample fitted values equals the sample average of the dependent variable.

8. The coefficient b_j in a multiple regression can be calculated by bivariate regression of y on $\widetilde{x}_j$, where $\widetilde{x}_j = x_j - \widehat{x}_j$ is the residual from regressing x_j on an intercept and all regressors other than x_j.

9. The slope coefficient b_j measures the partial effect of a change in the fitted value of y when x_j changes by one unit and all other regressors are unchanged.

10. The total effect on the predicted value of y when x_j changes by one unit additionally allows for the secondary effect that the remaining regressors may change when x_j changes. When regression is by OLS, this total effect simply equals the slope coefficient from bivariate regression of y on x_j.

11. OLS regression measures association or correlation, rather than causation. Without further information we can only say that a one-unit increase in x_j is associated with, rather than is caused by, a b_j increase in y, holding all other variables constant.

12. The standard error of the regression (s_e) measures the standard deviation of the residual, and hence the variability of y around the regression line.

13. R-squared (R^2) measures the fraction of the variation of y (around the sample mean $\bar{y}$) that is explained by the regressor. It should only be used if the regression includes an intercept.

14. R-squared equals the squared correlation between y and $\hat{y}$.

15. The adjusted R^2, denoted $\bar{R}^2$, is less than R^2 due to a modest penalty for the number of regressors in the model.

16. As regressors are added, R^2 cannot decrease, $\bar{R}^2$ will often increase but can also decrease, and s_e will often decrease but may also increase.

17. Information criteria, used less often than $\bar{R}^2$, apply a penalty for model size to the sample average of the squared residuals.

18. If regressors have inadequate variation or are perfectly collinear then not all coefficients are identified.

19. Key terms: Two-way scatter plot; correlation; regression line; dependent variable; ordinary least squares regression; residual; fitted value; slope coefficient; intercept coefficient; causation; standard error of the residual; R-squared; adjusted R-squared; total sum of squares; residual (or error) sum of squares; explained (or regression or model) sum of squares; information criteria; inestimable model; not identified model; perfectly collinear regressors.

10.10 Exercises

1. Use dataset SALARYSAT, described in exercise 3 of Chapter 7.

    (a) Obtain the correlations between *salary* (annual in dollars) and the SAT scores *satverb* and *satmath*. Which variable do you think better explains salary?

    (b) Regress *salary* on an intercept and *satverb*. Provide an interpretation of the slope coefficient.

    (c) Regress *salary* on an intercept, *satverb* and *satmath*. Provide an interpretation of the coefficient of *satverb*.

    (d) Can the correlation between *satverb* and *satmath* explain this result? Explain.

2. Repeat the previous exercise, replacing *satverb* with *highgrade*.

3. Use dataset HOUSE.

    (a) Regress *price* on an intercept and *bathrooms*. Provide an interpretation of the slope coefficient.

    (b) Now regress house price on an intercept, *bathrooms* and *size*. Provide an interpretation of the coefficient of *bathrooms*.

    (c) Which regressor has a bigger effect on house price? Hint: Consider the effect of a one standard deviation change for each regressor.

    (d) Regress *bathrooms* on an intercept and *size*, calculate the residuals from this regression, then regress house price on an intercept and the residual. Compare the slope coefficient with that for *bathrooms* in part (b). Comment.

    (e) Denote the estimates in part (b) as $\widehat{price} = b_1 + b_2 \times bathrooms + b_3 \times size$. Compute the *total effect* on house sale price of adding a bathroom as $b_2 + b_3 \times \frac{\Delta size}{\Delta bathrooms}$, where $\frac{\Delta size}{\Delta bathrooms}$ is estimated by the slope coefficient from regression of *size* on an intercept and *bathrooms*. Compare your answer to that in part (a). Comment.

4. Repeat the previous exercise using dataset HOUSE2015.

5. Dataset ADVERTISING as data from 200 markets on sales in number of units and TV, radio and newspaper advertising in thousands of dollars.

    (a) Which form of advertising is used the most? Explain.

    (b) Which form of advertising is most correlated with sales? Explain.

    (c) Which form of advertising has the biggest sole impact on sales? Perform three separate bivariate regressions.

    (d) Now regress *sales* on an intercept, *tv*, *radio* and *newspaper*. Which variable do you think has the biggest impact on sales?

6. Continue with dataset ADVERTISING and consider regression of sales on an intercept, TV advertising and radio advertising. For each of the following say what change you expect on the fitted intercept and slope coefficients.

   (a) Sales are now measured in thousands of units rather than number of units.

   (b) TV and radio advertising are measured in dollars rather than thousands of dollars.

   (c) Verify your answer in part (a) by OLS regression using dependent variable *sales* divided by 1,000..

   (d) Verify your answer in part (b) by OLS regression using dependent variable *sales* and regressors 1,000 times *tv* and 1,000 times *radio*.

7. Use dataset HOUSE. We consider the effect of adding an extra regressor on existing estimates.

   (a) Regress *price* on an intercept and *bedrooms*. What is the slope coefficient?

   (b) Now add *size* as a regressor. Has the coefficient of *bedrooms* changed much?

   (c) Instead add *age* as a regressor. Has the coefficient of *bedrooms* changed much?

   (d) Obtain the correlation of *bedrooms* with *size* and with *age*. Hence explain your answers in parts (b) and (c).

8. Dataset COVIDFALL2020 has data for the 50 U.S. states on average daily cases in the past seven days per 100,000 (*cases*) on November 9, 2020. This was a time when the number of cases was growing rapidly (over 50% every two weeks) as weather grew colder. It was also a time when the response to corona virus was politicized, with Republican leaning states less aggressive than Democratic leaning states in responding to the virus. The dataset also has historical data on average daily temperature in Fall (*avetemp*), and the presidential vote for the Republican candidate Donald Trump in 2016 (*voterep*).

   (a) Obtain the correlations between the variables. Are these what you expect? Explain.

   (b) Obtain scatterplots of *cases* against *avetemp* and of *cases* against *voterep*. Are these what you expect? Explain.

   (c) Obtain separate regressions (with intercept) of *cases* against *avetemp* and of *cases* against *voterep*. Do the slope coefficients have the sign you expect?

   (d) Now regress *cases* against an intercept, *avetemp* and *voterep*. Do the slope coefficients have the signs you expect?

   (e) Have the slope coefficients changed much compared to those in part (c). Are you surprised given your answer in part (a)?

9. This exercise requires precise calculation with new variables generated in double precision (see Appendix A.1). Some packages such as R do this automatically. If using Stata, however, for this exercise use the command `generate double` rather than `generate`, and use the command `predict double` rather than `predict`.

   (a) Run OLS regression of *price* on an intercept, *size* and *bedrooms* using dataset HOUSE.

   (b) Obtain the predicted *price* for each observation and compare the average of the predictions to the average *price*.

   (c) Obtain the residuals for each observation from this regression. Obtain the sample average of the residual. Comment.

   (d) Obtain the product of *size* times the residual for each observation. Obtain the sample average of this product.

10. Repeat the previous exercise using dataset HOUSE2015. Comment.

11. You are given the following OLS regression on an intercept and three variables: $\sum_{i=1}^{20}(y_i - \bar{y})^2 = 500$ and $\sum_{i=1}^{20}(y_i - \widehat{y}_i)^2 = 400$.

    (a) Calculate the standard deviation of y.

    (b) Calculate the R-squared of the regression.

    (c) Calculate the standard error of the regression.

    (d) Calculate the adjusted R-squared of the regression.

    (e) Calculate the correlation between y and $\widehat{y}$.

12. Repeat the previous exercise following OLS regression on an intercept and five variables with $\sum_{i=1}^{46}(y_i - \bar{y})^2 = 900$ and $\sum_{i=1}^{46}(y_i - \widehat{y}_i)^2 = 400$.

13. Using dataset HOUSE, run OLS regression of *price* on an intercept, *size* and *bedrooms* where analysis is restricted to houses with exactly three bedrooms. Explain your results.

14. For OLS regression answer true or false to each of the following.

    (a) R-squared can fall as regressors are added.

    (b) Adjusted R-squared can fall as regressors are added.

    (c) The standard error of the regression can fall as regressors are added.

    (d) The correlation between y and $\widehat{y}$ can fall as regressors are added.

Chapter 11

Statistical Inference for Multiple Regression

Different samples will lead to different fitted regression lines, due to different random departures in the data from the population conditional mean. Statistical inferential methods control for this randomness.

This chapter presents the statistical properties of the least squares estimates and uses these properties to construct confidence intervals and perform hypothesis tests on the population parameters.

11.1 Properties of the Least Squares Estimator

The assumptions and their consequences for multiple regression are essentially the same as those for bivariate regression detailed in Chapter 7, except the population model now includes additional regressors and conditioning is on these extra regressors. A more abbreviated treatment is given here for multiple regression.

In this chapter we make the strong assumptions that model errors are independent and homoskedastic, in which case inference is based on default standard errors. These assumptions can be relaxed, in which case inference is based on robust standard errors that are presented in Chapter 12.1 and that lead to different t statistics, p-values and confidence intervals.

11.1.1 Data Assumptions

Throughout it is assumed that all the OLS coefficients can be computed. This requires that the sample size exceeds the number of regressors (including the intercept), that there is variation in the sample values taken by each regressor, and that there is no exact linear relationship between the regressors.

If these conditions are not met then regression output from most statistical packages will not report coefficients for all regressors. Instead the computer output will indicate that one or more regressors (or the intercept) are omitted, or will simply have no entry for one or more regressors.

217

11.1.2 Population Line or Population Conditional Mean

The population relationship between y and $x_2, ..., x_n$ is defined by $\mathrm{E}[Y|X_2 = x_2, ..., X_k = x_k]$, the **population conditional mean** of Y given $X_2 = x_2, ..., X_k = x_k$. This is the probability-weighted average of all possible values of Y in the population given $X_2 = x_2, ..., X_k = x_k$. In the econometrics literature it is standard to write the population conditional mean more simply as $\mathrm{E}[y|x_2, ..., x_k]$.

For linear regression it is assumed that **conditional mean** is a **linear** function of the regressors. Thus we write that the **conditional mean** or **conditional expectation function** or **population line** is

$$\mathrm{E}[y|x_2, ..., x_k] = \beta_1 + \beta_2 x_2 + \cdots + \beta_k x_k.$$

The goal is to estimate the population parameters $\beta_1, \beta_2, ..., \beta_k$ as then we can make predictions, and we can estimate the effect on the conditional mean of changing one or more of the regressors.

Remark 87 *$E[y|x_2, ..., x_k]$ denotes the conditional mean of Y given $X_2 = x_2, ..., X_k = x_k$, the probability-weighted average of all possible values of Y in the population given $X_2 = x_2, ..., X_k = x_k$. For linear regression $E[y|x_2, ..., x_k] = \beta_1 + \beta_2 x_2 + \cdots + \beta_k x_k$.*

11.1.3 Population Assumptions

To obtain the statistical properties of the OLS coefficients we need to make assumptions about the population model and the sampling process that yielded the sample $(x_1, y_1), ..., (x_n, y_n)$.

We introduce the **error term** u and make the standard assumptions are that:

1. The **population model** is

$$y_i = \beta_1 + \beta_2 x_{2i} + \beta_3 x_{3i} + \cdots + \beta_k x_{ki} + u_i \text{ for all } i.$$

2. The **error for the ith observation has zero mean conditional on all regressors:**

$$\mathrm{E}[u_i|x_{2i}, ..., x_{ki}] = 0 \text{ for all } i.$$

3. The **error for the ith observation has constant variance conditional on the regressors:**

$$\mathrm{Var}[u_i|x_{2i}, ..., x_{ki}] = \sigma_u^2 \text{ for all } i.$$

4. The **errors for different observations are statistically independent**

$$u_i \text{ is independent of } u_j, \text{ for all } i \neq j.$$

Assumptions 1-2 are the crucial assumptions that ensure that the population relationship between y and the regressors is a linear relationship. Specifically the population mean is then

$$\mathrm{E}[y_i|x_{2i}, ..., x_{ki}] = \beta_1 + \beta_2 x_{2i} + \beta_3 x_{3i} + \cdots + \beta_k x_{ki},$$

so that the data are generated by a linear population relationship. In that case it makes sense to fit the data with a regression line.

Assumptions 3 and 4 are additional assumptions that are used in determining the precision and distribution of the estimates b_1 and b_2. Assumption 3 implies that the error term is homoskedastic, so the conditional variance of y is the same across observations, with

$$\text{Var}[y_i | x_{2i}, ..., x_{ki}] = \sigma_u^2.$$

More detailed discussion of these assumptions was given in Chapter 6.3. See also Chapter 16.

11.1.4 Mean and Variance of a Least Squares Slope Coefficient

Let the typical regressor be the jth regressor x_j. Then inference on its coefficient β_j is based on the OLS estimate b_j. The following results are simply stated here. Proofs in the case of a single regressor are given in Appendix C.1; see also Chapter 16.2.

The **mean of the least squares estimate** b_j is

$$\text{E}[b_j] = \beta_j, \quad j = 1, ...k,$$

given assumptions 1-2. So b_j is unbiased for β_j. If many samples were available, yielding many estimates b_j, the average of the b_j equals β_j.

If we additionally make assumptions 3-4 then the **variance of the least squares slope coefficient** b_j can be shown to be

$$\text{Var}[b_j] = \sigma_{b_j}^2 = \frac{\sigma_u^2}{\sum_{i=1}^{n} \widetilde{x}_{ji}^2},$$

where $\widetilde{x}_{ji}$ denotes the residual from regressing x_{ji} on an intercept and all regressors other than x_{ji}.

Remark 88 *Under assumptions 1-2 the estimated slope coefficient b_j has mean equal to the population slope parameter β_j. Under assumptions 1-4 the estimated slope coefficient b_j has variance $\sigma_{b_j}^2 = \sigma_u^2 / \sum_{i=1}^{n} \widetilde{x}_{ji}^2$, where $\widetilde{x}_{ji}$ denotes the residual from regressing x_{ji} on an intercept and all regressors other than x_{ji}.*

The variable $\widetilde{x}_j$ is a residual that measures the net information that the regressor x_j adds beyond that obtained from the other regressors. Smaller values of $\widetilde{x}_j$ mean less net information is conveyed and $\sum_{i=1}^{n} \widetilde{x}_{ji}^2$ will be smaller. At the same time σ_u^2 will decrease as the other regressors improve model fit. So on balance $\text{Var}[b_j]$ may be bigger or smaller and b_j may be less or more precisely estimated as additional regressors are added to the model.

11.1.5 Standard Error of a Least Squares Slope Coefficient

The variance of b_j depends in part on σ_u^2, the variance of the error term, which is unknown. Under assumptions 1-4, an unbiased estimator of σ_u^2 is the **standard error of the regression**

$$s_e^2 = \frac{1}{n-k} \sum_{i=1}^{n} (y_i - \widehat{y}_i)^2.$$

The **standard error of** b_j, the estimated standard deviation of b_j, is obtained by replacing σ_u^2 in the formula for $\sigma_{b_j}^2$ by s_e^2 and then taking the square root. Then

$$se(b_j) = \frac{s_e}{\sqrt{\sum_{i=1}^n \widetilde{x}_{ji}^{\,2}}}.$$

11.1.6   When is a Slope Coefficient Precisely Estimated?

Given the formula for $se(b_2)$ the precision of estimation of β_2 is better the closer the data are to the true regression line (then s_e is small) and the larger is the sample size n (then there are more terms in the sum). This is the same as in bivariate regression.

Additionally $se(b_j)$ is smaller the **less** x_j is explained by the other regressors $x_2, ..., x_{j-1}, x_{j+1}, ..., x_k$. The simple intuition is that the coefficient of x_j will be more precisely estimated the more x_j adds an independent piece of information, rather than duplicating information already contained in the other regressors.

Algebraically, $se(b_j)$ is small if $|\widetilde{x}_{ji}|$ is large since then $\sum_{i=1}^n \widetilde{x}_{ji}^{\,2}$ is large. Since $\widetilde{x}_{ji} = x_{ji} - \widehat{x}_{ji}$ where $\widehat{x}_{ji}$ is the fitted value from regressing x_{ji} on an intercept and all regressors other than x_{ji}, $|\widetilde{x}_{ji}|$ is large when $\widehat{x}_{ji}$ does a poor job of predicting x_{ji}.

Remark 89 *The standard error of b_j is $se(b_j) = s_e / \sqrt{\sum_{i=1}^n \widetilde{x}_{ji}^{\,2}}$, where s_e is the standard error of the regression. Under assumptions 1-4 $se(b_j)^2$ has mean equal to the variance of b_j. Bigger samples are better – if the sample is m times larger then $se(b_j)$ is approximately $1/\sqrt{m}$ times as large. And wider dispersion of x_j, after controlling for the other regressors, leads to greater precision.*

11.1.7   The t Statistic

The t-statistic for multiple regression is the exact analog of that for bivariate regression, with the one change that the degrees of freedom are now $n - k$ rather than $n - 2$.

Under assumptions 1-4, $b_j \sim (\beta_j, \sigma_{b_j}^2)$, so the standardized statistic $Z = (b_j - \beta_j)/\sigma_{b_j} \sim (0, 1)$. By the central limit theorem, Z is standard normal distributed as $n \to \infty$. However, σ_{b_j} depends on the unknown parameter σ_u^2. Replacing σ_{b_j} by its estimate $se(b_j)$ leads to the t statistic.

Remark 90 *For OLS regression on k regressors including the intercept, under assumptions 1-4 the t statistic*

$$t = \frac{b_j - \beta_j}{se(b_j)},$$

is a realization of a randomly variable that is approximately $T(n - k)$ distributed, where $T(n - k)$ denotes the t distribution with $(n - k)$ degrees of freedom.

The $T(n - k)$ approximation is exact if additionally the errors are normally distributed or if $n \to \infty$.

11.1.8 How Large Should the Sample Be?

In general errors are not normally distributed and the $T(n-k)$ distribution is an approximation, one that gets more reasonable as the sample size gets large. Unfortunately, there is no simple way to determine whether the sample size for a particular data set and regression is adequate for the $T(n-k)$ approximation to be good, though more advanced analysis using simulations can provide some guidance. Thus there is no hard and fast rule for how large the sample size should be.

For bivariate regression with a single regressor many authors feel that there should be at least thirty observations, though this is by no means sufficient for all types of data. For example, suppose the dependent variable y takes only two values, such as a variable for whether or not an individual is employed. Then a larger sample size will be needed since it is very unlikely that the error term u has a continuous normal distribution when the dependent variable y is discrete and takes only two values.

For multiple regression, as more regressors are added the sample size should be even larger.

If the sample size is too small then the distribution of the t statistic generally has fatter tails than the $T(n-k)$. As a consequence, confidence intervals based on the $T(n-k)$ will be too narrow, and hypothesis tests will tend to reject the null hypothesis too often.

The house price example used in several chapters of this book has only 29 observations. This has the pedagogical advantage of, for example, making it easy to list the complete data. In practice, however, it would be better to have a larger sample.

Aside from considerations of approximating the distribution of the t statistic, another reason for not using samples that are too small is that estimation may be very imprecise, so that statistical analysis is too noisy to be useful.

11.2 Estimators of Model Parameters

The first goal of inference is to obtain estimates of the population parameters $\beta_1, ..., \beta_k$. This is called **point estimation**, to distinguish it from interval estimation using confidence intervals.

11.2.1 Optimal Properties of OLS Estimators

The desirable properties of OLS in bivariate regression, presented in Chapter 6.4, carry over to multiple regression.

First, the estimated OLS coefficients b_j are **unbiased** for the population slope parameters β_j, provided the population model satisfies assumptions 1 and 2 since then $E[b_j] = \beta_j$.

Second, the estimated OLS coefficients b_j are **consistent** for the population slope parameters β_j, if additionally $\text{Var}[b_j]$ goes to zero as $n \to \infty$. This is the case under the additional assumptions 3 and 4, and under alternative assumptions such as those given in Chapter 7.7.

Third, under assumptions 1-4, the OLS estimates b_j are **best linear unbiased (BLUE)**. They have smallest variance among unbiased estimators that are a weighted average of y_i of the form $b_j = \sum_{i=1}^{n} w_i y_i$ where the weights will depend on the regressors. This result is called the **Gauss-Markov Theorem**.

Fourth, if additionally the errors are normally distributed then the OLS estimates b_j are **best unbiased**, meaning the have minimum variance among unbiased estimators. OLS is also the best estimator among those estimators that are consistent and asymptotically normal, even if the errors are not normally distributed.

Remark 91 *The OLS estimators $b_1, ..., b_k$ are unbiased for $\beta_1, ..., \beta_k$ under assumptions 1-2, best linear unbiased under assumptions 1-4, and best unbiased if additionally the more errors are normally distributed. In large samples the OLS estimators $b_1, ..., b_k$ are consistent for $\beta_1, ..., \beta_k$ under assumptions 1-2, plus assumptions(s) such as assumptions 3-4 that ensure the estimators have finite variance, and are best among consistent and asymptotically normal estimators under assumptions 1-4.*

11.2.2   Relaxing Assumptions 1-4

The slope parameter estimates b_j will usually be **biased** and **inconsistent** if assumptions 1 and/or 2 are not satisfied. In that case alternative analysis is needed.

Often interest lies in the coefficient of a single regressor, say the coefficient of years of schooling in an earnings-schooling regression that includes additional control variables. Alternative analysis that may lead to consistent estimation of the key parameter of interest may entail using a different functional form for the conditional mean, including additional control variables in the regression, using data from a different source, and using an estimation method other than OLS (see Chapter 17).

Assumptions 3-4 generally effect only the estimation of the precision of b_j. These assumptions can be relaxed. First, one can continue to estimate by OLS but use an alternative formula to compute the standard errors of the OLS coefficient estimates; see Chapters 7.7 and 12.1. Second, one can use alternative estimation methods that may lead to coefficient estimates that are more precise than the OLS estimates; see Chapter 12.4 for further discussion.

11.3   Confidence Intervals

11.3.1   Confidence Intervals

As usual, the confidence interval is the estimate plus or minus the relevant critical value times the standard error of the estimate.

Remark 92 *A $100(1-\alpha)$ **percent confidence interval for the slope parameter** β_j is*

$$b_j \pm t_{n-k, \alpha/2} \times se(b_j),$$

where b_j is the OLS slope coefficient, $t_{n-k, \alpha/2}$ is that value such that a $T(n-k)$ distributed random variable exceeds it in absolute value with probability α, and $se(b_j)$ is the standard error of the slope coefficient estimate b_j.

This confidence interval is exact only if assumptions 1-4 hold and the errors are normally distributed.

The interpretation of the confidence interval is the same as that detailed in Chapter 7.3 for bivariate regression. A 95% confidence interval for β_j is interpreted as an interval that has probability 0.95 of including β_j. That is, if we had many repeated samples leading to many different confidence intervals, 95% of these confidence intervals will include the true unknown value of β_j and 5% will not.

11.3.2 Example: House Price and Size

As an example, consider the house price data in dataset HOUSE. Output from regression of house price on an intercept and six other regressors was presented in Table 10.4. For regressor *Size*, the output lists the 95 percent confidence interval to be $(36.45, 100.29)$.

This confidence interval can be computed from first principles as follows. The output gives $b_{Size} = 68.37$, from the coefficient column, and $se(b_{Size}) = 15.39$, from the standard error column. And here $t_{n-k,\alpha/2} = t_{22;.025} = 2.074$. Then a 95% confidence interval for β_{Size} is

$$b_{Size} \pm t_{n-k,\alpha/2} \times se(b_{Size}) = 68.37 \pm 2.074 \times 15.39 = 68.37 \pm 31.92 = (36.45, 100.29).$$

11.4 Hypothesis Tests on a Single Parameter

The presentation here is brief. Chapter 12.6 provides a more detailed discussion of the issues involved in hypothesis testing.

11.4.1 Tests on Individual Parameters

Consider tests on the jth regression parameter β_j. A **two-sided test** or **two-tailed test** on the parameter β_j is a test of $H_0 : \beta_j = \beta_j^*$ against $H_a : \beta_j \neq \beta_j^*$, where β_j^* is a specified value for β_j.

The null hypothesis is rejected when b_j is far from β_j^*. Equivalently the null hypothesis is rejected if the t statistic $t = (b_j - \beta_j^*)/se(b_j)$ is large. Under the null hypothesis that $\beta_j = \beta_j^*$ and under assumptions 1-4, the t statistic is approximately a draw from the $T(n-k)$ distribution (and exactly a draw from the $T(n-k)$ distribution if additionally model errors are normally distributed). The null hypothesis is rejected if the observed value $|t|$ is so large that it is very unlikely to have observed this value, if indeed H_0 was true so that the t statistic was indeed a draw from the $T(n-k)$.

Similar to the bivariate case, this leads to the following.

Remark 93 *For a **two-sided test** of $H_0 : \beta_j = \beta_j^*$ against $H_a : \beta_j \neq \beta_j^*$ the t statistic*

$$t = \frac{b_j - \beta_j^*}{se(b_j)}$$

*is a draw from the $T(n - k)$ distribution, approximately, if H_0 is true. The p-**value** is $p = \Pr[|T_{n-k}| \geq |t|\,]$ and H_0 is rejected if $p < \alpha$, where α is the desired **significance level** of the*

Table 11.1: Hypothesis tests on slope parameter: Summary for multiple regression.

	Two-sided Test	One-sided Upper alternative	One-sided Lower alternative
Null hypothesis	$H_0 : \beta_j = \beta_j^*$	$H_0 : \beta_j \leq \beta_j^*$	$H_0 : \beta_j \geq \beta_j^*$
Alternative Hypothesis	$H_0 : \beta_j \neq \beta_j^*$	$H_0 : \beta_j > \beta_j^*$	$H_0 : \beta_j < \beta_j^*$
t statistic	$t = (b_j - \beta_j^*)/se(b_j)$	$t = (b_j - \beta_j^*)/se(b_j)$	$t = (b_j - \beta_j^*)/se(b_j)$
p-value	$p = \Pr[|T_{n-k}| \geq t]$	$p = \Pr[T_{n-k} \geq t]$	$p = \Pr[T_{n-k} \leq t]$
Rejection rule	$p < \alpha$	$p < \alpha$	$p < \alpha$
Critical value	$c = t_{n-k,\alpha/2}$	$c = t_{n-k,\alpha}$	$c = -t_{n-k,\alpha}$
Rejection region	$|t| > c$	$t > c$	$t < c$

*test. The **critical value** c is such that $c = t_{n-k,\alpha/2}$, equivalently $\Pr[|T_{n-k}| \geq c] = \alpha$, and H_0 is rejected at significance level α if $|t| > c$.*

It is also possible to perform a **one-sided** or **one-tailed test.** In that case the claim to be tested is set as the alternative hypothesis. Table 11.1 summarizes one-sided and two-sided hypothesis tests on the population parameter slope coefficient.

11.4.2   Relationship between t test and Adjusted R-Squared

It can be shown that the adjusted R-squared, $\bar{R}^2$, increases as one regressor is added to the model if and only if a test for statistical significance of this regressor, one based on default standard errors, yields $|t| > 1$.

By contrast a hypothesis test at the usual significance level of 0.05 has a much higher threshold such as $|t| > 1.96$ for a large sample size. It follows that an increase in $\bar{R}^2$ does not necessarily imply statistical significance of the additional regressor(s) at conventional levels of significance such as $\alpha = 0.05$. While $\bar{R}^2$ provides a penalty for large model size, the penalty is weak.

11.4.3   Tests of Individual Statistical Significance

A special case of tests on an individual parameter is a **test of statistical significance**, in which case the hypothesized value of β_j is $\beta_j^* = 0$.

Regression packages print out the necessary statistics to automatically test this hypothesis, including both the t statistic and the p-value for the test of $H_0 : \beta_j = 0$ against $H_a : \beta_j \neq 0$. An example is given in Table 10.4. H_0 is rejected at statistical significance level α if $p < \alpha$. If instead $p > \alpha$ we do not reject H_0, and conclude that there is no statistically significant relationship or equivalently, that the regressor is statistically insignificant. The most common choice of α is 0.05, followed by 0.01 and 0.10.

It is most common to perform two-sided tests of statistical significance, so computer output reports the p-value for a two-sided test. If we have prior beliefs about the sign of β_j, however, then this prior belief can be employed by performing a one-sided test. The prior belief is setup as the alternative hypothesis, as explained in Chapter 4.6. For example, since we believe that house price increases with size, a one-tailed test of significance of house size may be a test of $H_0 : \beta_j \le 0$ against $H_a : \beta_j > 0$. In that case we halve the printed p-value, provided the estimate b_j is positive.

There can be ambiguity in the statement that "the regressor is statistically significant at significance level 0.05", as it is not always made clear whether a one-sided or two-sided test was performed. Most often tests of statistical significance are performed as two-sided tests, even if there are strong prior beliefs on the direction of the relationship.

Statistical significance by itself does not imply automatically that the regressor has **economic significance**. As discussed in Chapter 7.4.3, an economically significant regressor has coefficient b_j that is large enough that changing x_j is associated with meaningful changes in the dependent variable. Statistical significance is determined by the size of the t statistic which is the coefficient b_j scaled by $se(b_j)$. Economic significance is instead determined only by whether the coefficient b_j is "small" or "large". This is a subjective judgement that is context specific.

11.4.4   Example: House Prices

As an example we consider regression of house sale price on several regressors using dataset HOUSE. The example is illustrative. We use default standard errors that presume errors are homoskedastic. For these data it is standard to instead use heteroskedastic-robust standard errors; these are presented in Table 12.2. And a better way to incorporate the variable *Lotsize*, one that takes the three arbitrary values 1, 2 and 3, is to use a set of indicator variables, presented in Chapter 14.4.

Results are given in Table 11.2, which repeats Table 10.4.

The only regressor that is statistically significant at significance level 0.05 is *Size* with $p = 0.000$. The next most statistically significant regressor is *Age* with a p-value of 0.259 that is much higher than 0.05.

Suppose that instead of a test of statistical significance we wish to test whether an increase in house size of one square foot is associated with a \$50 increase in house price. For test of $H_0 : \beta_{Size} = 50$ against $H_0 : \beta_{Size} \ne 50$, $t = (68.37 - 50)/15.39 = 1.194$. Then $p = \Pr[|T_{22}| > |1.194|] = 0.245$ so we do not reject H_0 at significance level 0.05.

Looking at the magnitude of the coefficients, the estimate $b_{Size} = 68.37$ means that a 100 square foot increase in size, equivalent to a small room that is ten feet by ten feet, is associated with a \$6,837 increase in house price, an economically meaningful effect. An additional bathroom is also associated with a substantial increase in house price, but this estimate is so imprecise (the 95% confidence interval is from −\$25,771 to \$39,437) that no attention should be paid to it.

We conclude that house size is the primary determinant of house price in this market.

One reason for the lack of importance of the other regressors may be that, aside from size, the houses are quite homogeneous as they are of similar vintage and are in a small part of a small city. A real estate maxim is "location, location, location", and here location has already been controlled for by choosing to focus on a fairly homogenous region.

A second reason for statistical insignificance of the other regressors may be the small sample size.

A third reason may be that in fact collectively the house attributes other than size may matter, even if individually each attribute is not statistically significant. This can be tested using the F test presented below.

Table 11.2: House price: Computer output from multiple regression.

Summary Statistics

Observations	29
R-squared	0.651
Adjusted R^2	0.555
St. error of regression	24936

Dependent Variable *Price*

Regressor	Coefficient	Standard Error	t statistic	p value	95% conf. int.	
Size	68.37	15.39	4.44	0.000	36.45	101.29
Bedrooms	2685	9193	0.29	0.773	-16379	21749
Bathrooms	6833	15721	0.43	0.668	-25771	39437
Lot Size	2303	7227	0.32	0.753	-12684	17290
Age	-833	719	-1.16	0.259	-2325	659
Monthsold	-2089	3521	-0.59	0.559	-9390	5213
Intercept	137791	61465	2.24	0.035	10321	265261

ANOVA Table

Source	SS	df	MS	F	p-value
Explained	2.5466×10^{10}	6	4.2444×10^9	6.83	0.0003
Residual	1.3679×10^{10}	22	0.6218×10^9		
Total	3.9146×10^{10}	28	0.1398×10^9		

11.4.5   Tests of a Single Hypothesis on more than One Parameter

The t test can be extended to test a single hypothesis that involves more than one parameter. The following example can be adapted to other cases of a single hypothesis.

Suppose we want to test whether or not $\beta_2 = \beta_3$. Equivalently we want to test $H_0 : \beta_2 - \beta_3 = 0$ against $H_0 : \beta_2 - \beta_3 \neq 0$. This difference can be estimated by $b_2 - b_3$ which has standard error $se(b_2 - b_3)$, leading to the t statistic

$$t = \frac{b_2 - b_3}{se(b_2 - b_3)}.$$

We reject H_0 at level 0.05 if $p = \Pr[|T_{n-k}| < |t|] < 0.05$.

This test requires calculating $se(b_2 - b_3) = \sqrt{se^2(b_2) - 2c_{23} + se(b_3)^2}$, where c_{23} is the estimated covariance between b_2 and b_3. But c_{23} is not automatically provided in standard regression output.

Fortunately, many statistical software packages provide a command to implement such tests, yielding the t statistic (or in some cases the square of the t statistic) and the associated p-value.

If this is not the case then the test can be implemented as follows. Rewrite the model as

$$\begin{aligned} y &= \beta_1 + \beta_2 x_2 + \beta_3 x_3 + \beta_4 x_4 + \cdots + \beta_k x_k + u \\ &= \beta_1 + (\beta_2 - \beta_3) x_2 + \beta_3 (x_2 + x_3) + \beta_4 x_4 + \cdots + \beta_k x_k + u. \end{aligned}$$

Then regress y on an intercept, x_2, $(x_2 + x_3)$, $x_4, ..., x_k$ and perform a regular t test of whether the coefficient of x_2 equals zero.

As an example, suppose we want to test whether the coefficient of *Bedrooms* equals that of *Bathrooms*. We create a variable *Bedplusbath* equal to the sum of *Bedrooms* and *Bathrooms* and regress *Price* on *Size, Bedrooms, Bedplusbath, Lotsize, Age* and *Monthsold*. The regressor *Bedrooms* has coefficient -4148, standard error 17806, $t = -0.233$ and $p = 0.818$. We do not reject at level 0.05 the null hypothesis that $\beta_{Bedrooms} = \beta_{Bathrooms}$.

11.5 Joint Hypothesis Tests

For multiple regression we often wish to test more than one restriction on the parameters. For example we may wish to test whether or not both $\beta_2 = 0$ and $\beta_3 = 0$. A more complicated example is a test that both $\beta_2 = -\beta_3$ and $2\beta_4 + \beta_6 = 9$.

There are two reasons for performing such tests. One reason is to determine which regressors should be included in the regression model. Models with fewer regressors are often preferred, for reasons of simplicity and because more precise estimates can be obtained if unnecessary regressors are excluded from the model. A second reason is to test restrictions implied by economics theory.

These joint hypothesis tests use test statistics that are most often F distributed, rather than the t distributed. (A variation using the chi-squared distribution is presented later in this section). The test statistics take only positive values so rejection of the null hypothesis occurs if the test statistic takes large positive values.

For joint hypotheses the test statistics are in general a complicated function of coefficient estimates and their associated standard errors and estimated covariances. Many statistical packages provide a command to implement joint tests, and all statistical packages provide as output a joint test of whether or not the regressors are jointly statistically significant, a test of $H_0 : \beta_2 = 0$, $\beta_3 = 0, ..., \beta_k = 0$.

In the special case of independent, homoskedastic errors (assumptions 1-4) it is possible to calculate F test statistics using residual sums of squares. Such calculation does not generalize to inference based on robust standard errors, such as heteroskedastic robust. But it provides useful insights and it is presented in Chapter 11.6.

11.5.1 The F Distribution

The F**distribution** is a continuous right-skewed distribution for a random variable that takes only positive values. The distribution depends on two parameters, called the first and second degrees of freedom, and is denoted $F(v_1, v_2)$ where the degrees of freedom v_1 and v_2 are positive integers.

Note that the order of the degrees of freedom matters, as $F(v_1, v_2) \neq F(v_2, v_1)$. The mean exists if $v_2 > 2$ and equals $v_2/(v_2 - 2)$, so the mean approaches one as v_2 gets large which is the case in regression samples when the sample size gets large. When $v_1 = 1$ the F distribution reduces to the square of the t distribution, i.e. $F_{1,v_2} = (T_{v_2})^2$.

In regression applications v_1 is the number the number of parameter restrictions being tested, so is small, and $v_2 = n - k$, the regression degrees of freedom.

Figure 11.1 presents the probability density function of the F distribution for $(v_1, v_2) = (3, 30)$ and $(v_1, v_2) = (10, 30)$.

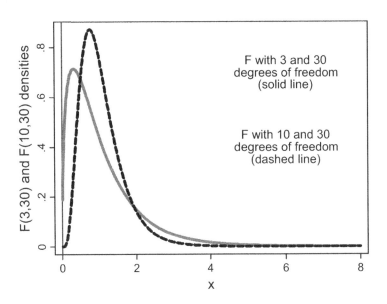

Figure 11.1: F distribution: F(3,30) and F(10,30)

Remark 94 *The $F(v_1, v_2)$ distribution is a right-skewed distribution, with degrees of freedom v_1 and v_2, for a random variable that takes only positive values. $F_{v1,v2,\alpha}$ denotes the value for which the area in the right tail of the distribution equals α.*

11.5.2 Probabilities and Inverse Probabilities for the F Distribution

Probabilities for the F distribution are given by the area under the curve and require use of an appropriate computer command. For example, in Stata $\Pr[F_{10,30} > 2] = $ `Ftail(10,30,2)`.

Inverse probabilities or **critical values** for the $F(q, n-k)$ distribution can be obtained form an appropriate computer command. For example, in Stata $F_{10,30,.05} = $ `invFtail(10,30,.05)`. Alternatively, tables give these at different degrees of freedom and at key significance levels such as 0.10, 0.05 and 0.01. The critical values decrease as the number of restrictions (q) increases, the degrees of freedom in the unrestricted model ($n-k$) increases, and as test significance level (α) increases. Table 11.3 provides some examples and Appendix E provides more detailed tables.

Unlike t critical values, F critical values are difficult to interpret directly and it is much easier to rely on p-values computed by a statistical package. If these are unavailable note that if $n - k > 10$ then H_0 is always rejected at level 0.05 if $F > 5$, regardless of the size of q.

For tests of a single restriction we use the $F(1, n-k)$ distribution which is the square of the $T(n-k)$ distribution. Since the 5% critical value for the $T(\infty)$ distribution is 1.96, it follows that the 5% critical value for the $F(1, \infty)$ distribution is $1.96^2 = 3.84$.

Table 11.3: F distribution: Critical values for various degrees of freedom and confidence levels.

Test size		$q = 1$	$q = 2$	$q = 3$	$q = 10$	$q = 20$
10%	$n - k = 30$	2.88	2.49	2.28	1.82	1.67
	$n - k = \infty$	2.71	2.30	2.08	1.60	1.42
5%	$n - k = 30$	4.17	3.32	2.92	2.16	1.93
	$n - k = \infty$	3.84	3.00	2.60	1.83	1.57
1%	$n - k = 30$	7.56	5.39	4.51	2.98	2.55
	$n - k = \infty$	6.64	4.61	3.78	2.32	1.88

11.5.3 The F Statistic

The F statistic applies to models that are nested in each other.

The more general model, called the **unrestricted model** or **complete model**, is a model with k regressors, so

$$y = \beta_1 + \beta_2 x + \beta_3 x_3 + \cdots + \beta_k x_k + u.$$

The **restricted model** or **reduced model** is a model that places restrictions on the parameters $\beta_1, \beta_2, ..., \beta_k$. Most often this restricted model is one that omits some of the regressors, so that some of the $\beta's$ are set to zero.

Let q denote the number of restrictions imposed by the restricted models. If just one regressor is dropped then $q = 1$ while if all regressors but the intercept are dropped then $q = k - 1$.

In general the formula for the F statistic is complicated. As an example, suppose we wish to test the two restrictions $\beta_2 = 0$ and $\beta_3 = 0$. So we test $H_0 : \beta_2 = 0$, $\beta_3 = 0$ against $H_a :$ at least one of $\beta_2 \neq 0$, $\beta_3 \neq 0$. Then it can be shown that

$$F = \frac{[b_2 se(b_2)^2 - 2b_2 b_3 c_{23} + b_2 se(b_2)^2]/2}{se(b_2)^2 se(b_3)^2 - c_{23}^2}$$

where c_{23} is the estimated covariance between b_2 and b_3.

For the moment we assume that computer output provides the desired F statistic. In the subsequent section we present formulas in the special case that errors are independent and heteroskedastic so that assumptions 1-4 hold and we can use default standard errors.

11.5.4 F Tests

The main use of the F statistic is in hypothesis testing.

Definition 27 *An F **test** is a **two-sided test** of H_0 : The q parameter restrictions implied by the restricted model are correct, against the alternative hypothesis H_a : At least one of the q parameter restrictions implied by the restricted model is incorrect.*

The F statistic is necessarily positive and large values of the F statistic lead to rejection of H_0.

Remark 95 *The p-**value** for the F test of q restrictions is $p = \Pr[F_{q,n-k} \geq F]$, and H_0 is rejected if $p < \alpha$, where α is the desired **significance level** of the test. The **critical value** c is such that $c = F_{q,n-k,\alpha}$, equivalently $\Pr[|F_{q,n-k}| \geq c] = \alpha$, and H_0 is rejected at significance level α if $F > c$.*

Note that the F test is a **two-sided test**. It is true that the F test p-value or critical value is calculated using only **one tail**, the right tail, of the F distribution. But the test itself is a two-sided test because in the case of testing exclusion of several regressors, for example, the alternative hypothesis can only be that parameters are not equal to zero rather than, for example, greater than zero. A one-sided F test is not possible.

The leading examples of the F test are now presented.

11.5.5   Test of Overall Significance

The first test, called as **test of overall significance**, is a test of whether or not the regressors taken together add substantially to predictive ability compared to an intercept-only model. The null hypothesis is that only an intercept is needed, so all the slope parameters equal zero, while the alternative hypothesis is that at least one of the slope coefficients differs from zero.

Remark 96 *A **test of overall significance** is a **two-sided test of** $H_0 : \beta_2 = 0, ..., \beta_k = 0$, against the alternative hypothesis $H_a :$ At least one of $\beta_2 \neq 0, ..., \beta_k \neq 0$.*

Most statistical packages automatically print out the F statistic for test of overall significance, along with its associated p-value. If $p < 0.05$, for example, then the regressors are said to be jointly statistically significant at significance level 0.05.

For the house price example $k = 7$ and $n = 29$, so a test if overall significance tests $q = 6$ restrictions and $n - k = 22$. The output in Table 11.2 includes $F(6, 22) = 6.83$ with $p = 0.0003$. Since $p < 0.05$ we conclude that the regressors are jointly statistically significant at level 0.05.

Note that the F test is merely a test of whether at least one regressor is statistically significant, not that all regressors are statistically significant. In this example from Table 11.2 only one of the regressors, *Size*, is individually statistically significant at level 0.05.

11.5.6   Test of Subsets of Regressors

Tests of a subset of regressors or of **exclusion restrictions** compare two models with one model a reduced version of the other and test whether the additional regressors in the unrestricted model are jointly statistically significant. This test is often used to test the joint statistical significance of sets of indicator variables, such as for geographic region or for ethnic background, that are presented in Chapter 14.4.

The unrestricted model or complete model with k regressors is specified to be

$$y = \beta_1 + \beta_2 x_2 + \cdots \beta_g x_g + \beta_{g+1} x_{g+1} + \cdots + \beta_k x_k + u.$$

The restricted model or reduced model is specified to include only the first g regressors so

$$y = \beta_1 + \beta_2 x_2 + \cdots \beta_g x_g + u.$$

The restricted model is therefore obtained by setting $k - g$ slope coefficients to zero.

Remark 97 *Let the last $q = k - g$ regressors be omitted in the restricted model. Then a **test of a subset of regressors** is a **two-sided test of** $H_0 : \beta_{g+1} = 0, ..., \beta_k = 0$, against the alternative hypothesis H_a : At least one of $\beta_{g+1} \neq 0, ..., \beta_k \neq 0$.*

Return to the house price example. We have shown that house size is the only one of the six regressors that is individually statistically insignificant. A natural question to ask is whether the five regressors when taken together are statistically significant, or whether a model with just house size as a regressor is adequate. This is a test of five restrictions. Using a specialized test command yields $F = 0.417$ with $p = 0.832 > 0.05$ so we do not reject $H_0 : \beta_3 = 0, ..., \beta_7 = 0$ at significance level 0.05. We conclude that the additional five regressors are jointly statistically insignificant. It is best to just include *Size* as a regressor.

Statistical packages that provide a post-estimation test command that computes this F test may additionally enable test of more complicated hypotheses, such as a test of $H_0 : \beta_2 + \beta_3 = 1$, $\beta_4 = 2$ against H_0 : At least one of $\beta_2 + \beta_3 \neq 1$, $\beta_4 \neq 2$.

11.5.7 Test of a Single Regressor

The F test for subsets of regressors can be used to test whether a single regressor is statistically significant, in which case $q = 1$. This F test yields exactly the same result as that from a two-sided t test of statistical significance.

First, it can be shown algebraically that for $q = 1$ the F test statistic is the square of the usual t test statistic, so $F = t^2$. Second, a random variable with $T(n - k)$ distribution when squared is $F(1, n - k)$ distributed.

It follows that when $q = 1$, the F-test critical value equals the square of the critical value for a two-sided t test. So a two-sided t-test critical value of 1.96 corresponds to an F-test critical value of $1.96^2 = 3.84$.

Remark 98 *The F test for statistical significance of a single regressor is equivalent to a two-sided t test, since $F = t^2$ and $\Pr[|T_{n-k}| > t] = \Pr[F_{1,n-k} > t^2]$.*

For example, using a specialized test command to test whether *Bedrooms* is statistically significant yields $F = 0.085$ with $p = \Pr[F_{1,n-k} > 0.085] = 0.773$. From Table 11.2 the regressor *Bedrooms* has $t = 0.292$, so $t^2 = 0.292^2 = 0.085 = F$, and the same $p = 0.773$.

11.5.8 Computation of Tests in a Statistical Package

OLS regression output includes tests of statistical significance for each regressor and the test of overall significance. For more complicated tests such as tests of subsets of regressors in Stata one uses the `test` and `testparm` commands; see Appendix A.2 for an example. In R one can use the `linearHypothesis` function in the `car` package; see Appendix A.3 for an example. In Gretl use the `restrict` command with option `wald`. In Eviews use the `wald` view.

11.5.9   Chi-squared Distribution

The t distribution goes to the standard normal distribution as the degrees of freedom go to infinity, that is the $T(\infty)$ distribution is the $N(0, 1)$ distribution.

A similar limit result exists for the F distribution. A random variable that has an $F(q, \infty)$ distribution when multiplied by q has the chi-squared distribution with q degrees of freedom, denoted $\chi^2(q)$. The $\chi^2(q)$ distribution has mean q and variance $2q$.

Some statistical commands report a χ^2 statistic that is χ^2 distributed rather than an F statistic that is F distributed. In that case note that a $\chi^2(q)$ random variable divided by its degrees of freedom q has the $F(q, \infty)$ distribution. For example, a $\chi^2(10)$-distributed test statistic of 40 corresponds to an $F(10, \infty)$-distributed test statistic of $40/10 = 4$.

11.5.10   Separate Tests of Many Hypotheses

This section has considered jointly testing several hypotheses, such as whether the regressors are jointly statistically significant. What if instead we perform a series of separate tests?

Suppose we run twenty independent hypothesis tests at significant level 0.05 when in all twenty cases the null hypothesis is correct and there is no relationship. Then there is very high probability that at least one of the twenty tests rejects and obtains a spurious result. To see this, note that for a test of size 0.05 the probability of an individual test not rejecting when there is indeed no relationship is $1 - 0.05 = 0.95$. The probability of none of the twenty tests not rejecting is therefore $0.95^{20} = 0.358$. So the probability of at least one of the twenty tests rejecting is $1 - 0.358 = 0.642$.

Thus if we do many tests of statistical significance there is a high chance of finding relationships even where they do not exist.

One should therefore be sceptical about claims that, for example, eating fish has beneficial effects for the heart if it is likely that the study did a battery of separate tests on models that included a range of foods as regressors, or included a range of health outcomes, and used the usual critical values for each test. Similarly one should be sceptical of claims that a particular investment strategy is a winning strategy because it has historically outperformed the market. Many researchers will have tested many strategies using the same data and there is a bias to reporting only the historically best strategies.

What can be done to avoid erroneously finding results? More advanced methods for **multiple testing** that are beyond the scope of this text can provide an estimate of test size when multiple tests are performed. There are also simpler versions of these methods but unfortunately these are too conservative as they actually over-estimate the size in the common case that the tests are positively correlated rather than independent.

The simplest solution is to minimize the use of separate tests and as much as possible use joint hypothesis tests that simultaneously test several hypotheses.

11.6   *F* Statistic under Assumptions 1-4

We now specialize to the special case of independent, homoskedastic errors (assumptions 1-4). It is then possible to calculate F test statistics using residual sums of squares.

Intuitively if the fit of the restricted model is very close to that of the unrestricted model we should favor the restricted model since it is a smaller model, whereas if the difference is great then the cost of imposing the restrictions is too high and we should favor the unrestricted model.

Under assumptions 1-4 this intuition can be formalized, using the residual sum of squares, $\sum_{i=1}^{n}(y_i - \widehat{y}_i)^2$, as a measure of model fit. Let $ResSS_r$ denote the residual sum of squares in the restricted model, and $ResSS_u$ denote the residual sum of squares in the unrestricted model. Then $ResSS_r > ResSS_u$ since OLS minimizes the residual sum of squares and this minimum will be lower in the more general unrestricted model. A large value for $ResSS_r - ResSS_u$ indicates that the restricted model has much worse fit, so we should not use the restricted model. The F statistic uses an appropriate rescaling of $ResSS_r - ResSS_u$.

Remark 99 *Under assumptions 1-4 the **F statistic** can be computed as*

$$F = \frac{(ResSS_r - ResSS_u)/q}{ResSS_u/(n-k)},$$

where ResSS denotes residual sum of squares, subscripts r and u denote the restricted and unrestricted models, q is the number of parameter restrictions, n is the number of observations, and k is the number of regressors in the unrestricted model.

This statistic is exactly $F(q, n-k)$ distributed if additionally the data are normally distributed.

11.6.1   Test of Overall Significance under Assumptions 1-4

For tests of overall significance we have the following simplifications. First, there are $q = k - 1$ restrictions. Second, the restricted model is regression of y on an intercept that yields $b_1 = \bar{y}$, so $ResSS_r = \sum_{i=1}^{n}(y_i - \bar{y})^2$. But this is just TSS, the total sum of squares in the unrestricted model. So $ResSS_r - ResSS_u = TSS - ResSS = ExpSS$, since the total sum of squares in the unrestricted model can be decomposed as $TSS = ExpSS + ResSS$.

Remark 100 *Under assumptions 1-4 A **test of overall significance** is a **two-sided test of** $H_0 : \beta_2 = 0, ..., \beta_k = 0$, against the alternative hypothesis H_a : At least one of $\beta_2 \neq 0, ..., \beta_k \neq 0$. Then the general formula simplifies to*

$$F = \frac{(ExpSS)/(k-1)}{ResSS/(n-k)},$$

where ExpSS and ResSS are, respectively, the explained and residual sum of squares in the unrestricted model.

The F statistic can be directly calculated from an ANOVA table. For the house price example it is the ratio of the first two terms in the last column in Table 11.2. From the MS column of that table, $(ExpSS)/(k-1) = 4.244 \times 10^9$ and $(ResSS)/(n-k) = 0.6218 \times 10^9$. The ratio is then 6.83, which was given as the entry $F(6, 22) = 6.83$.

The F statistic can also be expressed in terms of R^2 as

$$F = \frac{R^2/(k-1)}{(1-R^2)/(n-k)}.$$

This implies that F necessarily increases as R^2 increases. The F statistic essentially provides a threshold for the increase in R^2 before we can say that the regressors lead to a statistically significant improvement in model fit.

Returning to the house price example, $R^2 = 0.6506$ and the formula for F in terms of R^2 yields $F = (.6506/6)/(.3494/22) = 6.83$.

11.6.2   Test of Subsets of Regressors under Assumptions 1-4

For tests of subsets of regressors we need the restricted sum of squares in restricted and unrestricted models.

For the house price example consider test of whether the five regressors other than house size when taken together are statistically significant, or whether a model with just house size as a regressor is adequate.

From Table 11.2, $ResSS_u = 1.3679 \times 10^{10}$ in the unrestricted model that includes all six regressors. The restricted model is a bivariate regression of house price on house size. From Table 5.5 in Chapter 5.7, $ResSS_r = 1.4975 \times 10^{10}$. Then

$$F = \frac{(1.4975 \times 10^{10} - 1.3679 \times 10^{10})/5}{1.3679 \times 10^{10}/22} = 0.417.$$

Since $p = \Pr[F_{5,22} > 0.417] = 0.832 > 0.05$, we do not reject $H_0 : \beta_3 = 0, ..., \beta_7 = 0$ at significance level 0.05.

11.6.3   Relationship between F test and Adjusted R-Squared

Under assumptions 1-4 it can be shown that the adjusted R-squared, $\bar{R}^2$, increases as one or more regressors are added to the model if and only if the F statistic for these additional regressors exceeds one.

By contrast an F test at the usual significance level of 0.05 has a much higher threshold than $F > 1$. It follows that an increase in $\bar{R}^2$ does not necessarily imply statistical significance of the additional regressors at conventional levels of significance such as $\alpha = 0.05$. While $\bar{R}^2$ provides a penalty for large model size, the penalty is weak.

Remark 101 *As regressors are added the adjusted R-squared increases if and only if $F > 1$ where F is the test statistic for test of joint statistical significance of the additional regressors computed under assumptions 1-4.*

11.7 Presentation of Regression Results

Published articles differ in the method of presentation of regression results due to a desire to economize on space used in reporting results. Key slope coefficients are always reported, though not necessarily all coefficients if there are many regressors. R^2 is usually reported and the F statistic for overall significance is usually reported.

There is great variation in the extent to which combinations of the standard error, t statistic (for test that the population coefficient equals zero), and its associated p-value are reported. Given knowledge of one of these three, and knowledge of the slope coefficient, it is always possible to compute the other two. For example, for the jth regressor given b_j and $se(b_j)$, we can compute $t_j = b_j/se(b_j)$ and $p_j = \Pr[|T_{n-k}| \leq t_j]$ where $T_{n-k} \sim T(n-k)$. Similarly, given b_j and t_j we can compute $se(b_j) = b_j/t_j$. Finally confidence intervals can be computed given b_j and $se(b_j)$.

It is easiest if all four of b_j, $se(b_j)$, t_j and p_j are reported, along with confidence intervals. Indeed these are all given in typical computer output. But for space reasons, especially if there are several different models estimated or if the models have additional regressors, it is quite common for published studies to report only b_j and one of $se(b_j)$, t_j and p_j.

Thus for regression of house price on house size and the number of bedrooms, using default standard errors, we might report the coefficients and standard errors

$$\widehat{Price} = \underset{(27589)}{111691} + \underset{(13.30)}{72.41} \times Size + \underset{(7846)}{1553} \times Bedrooms \qquad R^2 = 0.618.$$

Alternatively we may report the coefficients, along with t statistics for whether the population coefficients equal zero

$$\widehat{Price} = \underset{(4.05)}{111691} + \underset{(5.44)}{72.41} \times Size + \underset{(0.20)}{1553} \times Bedrooms \qquad R^2 = 0.618.$$

Or just the coefficients and p-values (for test of $\beta_j = 0$) may be reported

$$\widehat{Price} = \underset{(0.000)}{111691} + \underset{(0.000)}{72.41} \times Size + \underset{(0.845)}{1553} \times Bedrooms \qquad R^2 = 0.618.$$

A fourth possibility is to report the 95% confidence intervals, possibly also with the coefficients

$$Price = \underset{(54980,168401)}{111691} + \underset{(45.07,99.75)}{72.41} \times Size + \underset{(-14576,17683)}{1553} \times Bedrooms \qquad R^2 = 0.618.$$

And yet another possibility, one that takes less space, is to report just coefficients along with asterisks that indicate the level of statistical significance. Then one, two, or three asterisks are used for statistical significance levels of, respectively, 10%, 5%, and 1%. Thus

$$Price = 111691^{***} + 72.41 \times Size^{***} + 1553 \times Bedrooms \qquad R^2 = 0.618.$$

Table 11.4 presents results reported using these various methods of presentation. Since there are various ways to compute the standard errors it is good practice to additionally include a table footnote stating the method used.

Using any of these alternatives we can verify that the slope coefficient is statistically significant at level 0.05. And while we have focused on the slope coefficient it is clear from this output that the intercept is also statistically significant at level 0.05.

Table 11.4: Regression estimates: Various ways to report the results.

In parentheses:	Results 1 Standard errors	Results 2 t statistics	Results 3 p-values	Results 4 95% Conf. int.	Results 5
Size	72.41	72.41	72.41	72.41	72.41***
	(13.30)	(5.44)	(0.000)	(45.07,99.75)	
Bedrooms	1553	1553	1553	1553	1553
	(7847)	(0.20)	(0.845)	(-14576,17682)	
Intercept	11691	11691	11691	11691	11691***
	(27589)	(4.05)	(0.000)	(54981,168401)	
R^2	0.618	0.618	0.618	0.618	0.618
F(2,26)	21.93	21.93	21.93	21.93	21.93
n	29	29	29	29	29

Note: Default standard errors are used.

11.8   Key Concepts

1. The methods of statistical significance are generally similar to those used in the bivariate case, except the population model includes additional regressors and conditioning is on these additional regressors.

2. It is assumed that there is sufficient variation in the regressor values across observations to enable computing the OLS coefficients.

3. For linear regression $E[y|x] = \beta_1 + \beta_2 x_2 + \cdots + \beta_k x_k$.

4. Population Assumptions 1-4 now condition on $x_2, ..., x_k$ and not just x.

5. Under assumptions 1 and 2, $b_1, ..., b_k$ are unbiased estimators and, with additional assumptions such as assumptions 3 and 4, consistent estimators of $\beta_1, ..., \beta_k$.

6. Under assumptions 1-4, least squares is the best linear unbiased estimator. If additionally the errors are normally distributed then least squares is the best estimator.

7. The slope coefficient standard error $se(b_j)$ is smaller the better the regression line fits the data, the larger the sample, and the greater the variability of the regressors in the sample, after controlling for the other regressors.

8. Statistical inference on β_j is based on $t = (\beta_j - b_j)/se(b_j)$ that is treated as being $T(n-k)$ distributed.

9. Confidence intervals for β_j and hypothesis tests on β_j are similar to the bivariate case except that the $T(n-k)$ distribution is used.

10. Joint hypothesis tests on several parameters can be implemented using an F test.

11. A test of overall significance is a test of whether $\beta_2 = 0, ..., \beta_k = 0$.

12. A test of subset of regressors is a test of whether a subset of $\beta_{g+1}, ..., \beta_k$ is equal to zero.

13. F is approximately $F(q, n - k)$ distributed under the null hypothesis that the q parameter restrictions are correct.

14. In general the formula for F is complicated.

15. In the special case of inference under assumptions 1-4, $F = [(ResSS_r - ResSS_u)/q]/ResSS_u/(n-k)]$ where $ResSS$ is the residual sum of squares and subscripts r and u denote, respectively, the restricted and unrestricted models.

16. Regression results given in published articles usually give the estimated coefficients along with just one of the following: standard error, t statistic, p-value and 95% confidence interval.

17. Key terms: population model; error term; disturbance term; assumptions 1-4; standard error of the regression coefficient; standard error of the regression; t statistic; t distribution; degrees of freedom; parameter; unbiased; best unbiased; best linear unbiased; confidence interval; confidence region; null hypothesis; alternative hypothesis; one-sided test; two-sided test; rejection; p-value; critical value; critical region; F distribution; F test; test of overall significance; test of subsets of regressors.

11.9 Exercises

1. Suppose the population model is $y = 1 + 2x_2 + 3x_3 + u$ and $E[u|x] = 0$. We obtain a fitted regression line $\hat{y} = 1.7 + 2.5x_2 + 1.7x_3$. For an observation with $(x_2, x_3, y) = (2, 4, 17.8)$ give each of the following.

   (a) The conditional mean of y given x.   (b) The error term.   (c) The fitted value of y.

   (d) The residual term.

2. Repeat exercise 1 with $y = 2 + 2x_2 + 3x_3 + u$ and $\hat{y} = 2.5 + 1.2x_2 + 3.7x_3$ and observation $(x_2, x_3, y) = (3, 2, 12)$.

3. Suppose $y = 3 + 5x_2 + 14x_3 + u$ with $u \sim (0, 9)$.

   (a) Give the conditional mean of y given x.   (b) Give the conditional variance of y given x.

4. For each of the following state when the slope coefficient is likely to be more precisely estimated, holding other things constant.

   (a) The sample size is 100 or the sample size is 400.

   (b) The regressor of interest ranges from 30 to 40 or the regressor ranges from 0 to 70.

   (c) The error term has variance 2 or the error term has variance 10.

5. The population model is $y_i = 1 + 2x_{2i} + 4x_{3i} + u_i$ where the error term has conditional mean 0 and conditional variance $4x_i^2$.

   (a) Will the OLS estimator of β_2 be unbiased? Explain.

   (b) Will the OLS estimator of β_3 be unbiased? Explain.

   (c) Will the OLS estimator of β_2 have the variance given in Chapter 11.1? Explain.

6. For each of the following situations state whether the OLS estimator of a slope coefficient is unbiased and whether its variance is that given in Chapter 11.1.

   (a) Assumptions 1-4 hold.

   (b) Assumptions 1-2 hold but assumptions 3-4 do not hold.

   (c) Assumptions 1-2 do not hold but assumptions 3-4 do hold.

7. A detailed description of dataset SALARYSAT is given in exercise 3 of Chapter 7. We consider the relationship between salary (*salary*) and *satmath, satverb, age* and *highgrade*. Use heteroskedastic-robust standard errors.

   (a) Obtain the correlations between the variables. Which variable is most highly correlated with *salary*?

   (b) Regress *salary* on the other variables. Which variables are statistically significant at 5%?

   (c) Do any of the regressors have coefficients with unexpected sign? Explain.

   (d) Provide an interpretation of the coefficient of *satmath*.

   (e) Are the regressors jointly statistically significant at 5%? Explain.

   (f) Which model has better fit: this model or the model with just *satmath* as a regressor? Explain.

   (g) Are the variables other than *satmath* jointly statistically significant at 5%? Explain.

8. Repeat the previous exercise using dataset HOUSE2015 described in exercise 7 of Chapter 5. Regress *price* on an intercept, *size, bedrooms, bathrooms* and *daysonmarket*. Compare models with just *size* as a regressor with the models with all the regressors.

9. A detailed description of dataset SALARYSAT is given in exercise 3 of Chapter 7. We consider the best fitting relationship between salary (*salary*) and most of the other variables. Use heteroskedastic-robust standard errors.

   (a) Regress *salary* on *satmath*, *satverb*, *highgrade*, *age*, *sex*, *minority*, *height*, *weight* and *genhealth*.

   (b) Sequentially drop the least statistically significant variable until you have a model where all included regressors are statistically significant at 5%. List the variables in the order dropped, and list the retained variables.

   (c) Now separately add back into your preferred model each of the dropped variables. Do any of them become statistically significant at 5%?

10. Repeat the previous exercise using dataset HOUSE2015. Regress *price* on an intercept, *size*, *bedrooms*, *bathrooms* and *daysonmarket*.

11. Consider regression with $n = 50$ observations, $k = 7$ regressors including the intercept and test at 5% of the overall statistical significance of the regressors.

   (a) If $F = 3.0$ do you reject the null hypothesis? Explain.

   (b) If $p = 0.05$ what was the value of F?

   (c) Now suppose a chi-squared test is used. If $\chi^2 = 12.0$ do you reject the null hypothesis? Explain. (Hint: See Figure E.6 or Table A.2 or A.3).

   (d) If $p = 0.05$ what was the value of the χ^2 statistic.

12. Repeat the previous exercise with $n = 70$, $k = 8$, $F = 2.7$, $p = 0.14$, and $\chi^2 = 13.0$.

13. Suppose we add a regressor. For each of the following state whether the regressor is definitely statistically significant at level 0.05 using default standard errors.

   (a) A t test of statistical significance of the variable has $p = 0.04$.

   (b) The inclusion of the regressor increased R^2.

   (c) The inclusion of the regressor increased adjusted R^2.

   (d) The inclusion of the regressor decreased s_e.

   (e) The F statistic comparing the model without this additional regressor and with this additional regressor had $p = 0.04$.

14. Consider tests of overall statistical significance under assumptions 1-4. Then $F = [ExpSS/(k-1)]/[ResSS/(n-k)]$.

   (a) Show that this implies $F = [R^2/(k-1)]/[(1-R^2)/(n-k)]$. Hint: Divide numerator and denominator by TSS and use the definitions of R^2.

   (b) Will F necessarily increase as R^2 increases, holding n and k fixed?

   (c) Will F necessarily increase as n increases, holding R^2 and k fixed?

15. You are given the estimates $\widehat{y} = \underset{(6)}{10} + \underset{(40)}{72}\,x_2 + \underset{(5)}{16}x_3$ where standard errors are given in parentheses. The sample size is large so you can use standard normal critical values.

   (a) Obtain the t statistic for b_2, the coefficient of x_2.

   (b) Is x_2 statistically significant at 5%?

   (c) Provide a 95% confidence interval for β_2.

16. Repeat the previous exercise if $\widehat{y} = \underset{(28)}{110} + \underset{(8)}{18}x_2 + \underset{(10)}{24}\,x_3$.

17. You are given the estimates $\widehat{y} = \underset{(2.5)}{10} + \underset{(3)}{72}x_2 + \underset{(5)}{16}x_3$ where t **statistics** are given in parentheses. The sample size is large so you can use standard normal critical values.

   (a) Is x_2 statistically significant at 5%?

   (b) Obtain the standard error for b_2, the coefficient of x_2.

   (c) Provide a 95% confidence interval for β_2.

18. Repeat the previous exercise if $\widehat{y} = \underset{(3.5)}{110} + \underset{(12)}{18}\,x_2 + \underset{(10)}{24}\,x_2$.

Chapter 12

Further Topics in Multiple Regression

This lengthy chapter begins with three essential topics, followed by some more advanced material.

First, any application of regression requires the user to choose the appropriate method for computing standard errors (and hence t statistics, p-values and confidence intervals). The preceding chapters have emphasized statistical inference under the assumption of independent and homoskedastic errors (assumptions 3 and 4). In practice these assumptions are too strong, in which case the default standard errors are invalid and robust standard errors, such as heteroskedastic-robust standard errors, need to be used.

Second, obtaining a prediction from a fitted regression is straightforward. But the precision of the prediction depends on whether the prediction is of an average outcome or is of an individual outcome. For example, a regression model may predict well earnings on average for a given level of schooling and other characteristics, but may predict very poorly the earnings of any given individual.

Third, samples used in regression are often not representative of the population. OLS regression can continue to be fine if the nonrepresentative sampling is on variables that are regressors, but OLS estimates are biased and inconsistent if the nonrepresentative sampling is on the dependent variable.

The chapter then presents some further details on statistical inference - estimation, confidence intervals and hypothesis tests - for regression. Once assumptions 3-4 are relaxed methods other than OLS can yield more precise estimates, though in practice OLS with appropriate robust standard errors is still used. Hypothesis testing involves a trade-off between test size and test power.

The chapter concludes with a brief overview of recent advances in data science for better prediction methods, Bayesian methods that are an alternative to the statistical methods of this book, and the history of statistics and regression.

12.1 Inference with Robust Standard Errors

Model assumptions 1-4 lead to standard errors for the regression coefficients that are called **default standard errors**.

In almost any application the model assumptions 3 and 4 need to be are relaxed, in which case statistical inference needs to be based on alternative standard errors, called **robust standard**

errors, that were introduced in Chapter 7.7. This leads to different numerical values for standard errors and the associated confidence intervals, t statistics and F statistics, but they are then used in the same way as detailed in preceding chapters. An essential part of any regression analysis is knowing which particular robust standard error method should be used.

Remark 102 *Standard errors for the least squares coefficients obtained under assumptions weaker than assumptions 3-4 are called* **robust standard errors.**

The three leading examples of robust standard errors are given in Table 12.1 and explained in detail in this section. All three relax assumption 3 and allow errors to be heteroskedastic. Heteroskedastic-robust standard errors maintain assumption 4 of independence. Cluster-robust and HAC standard errors additionally relax assumption 4 to allow error correlation.

Table 12.1: Robust standard errors: Leading examples.

Error Dependence Structure	**Robust Standard Error Type**	**Data Type**
Errors independent	Heteroskedasticity robust	Most Cross section
Errors correlated within cluster and independent across clusters	Cluster robust	Some Cross section Most Panel
Errors autocorrelated over time and independent after m lags	Heteroskedasticity and autocorrelation (HAC) robust	Most Time Series

All statistical packages other than Excel provide robust standard errors. There are different ways to compute a particular robust standard error, however, so that different packages may give different heteroskedasticity-robust, cluster-robust or HAC standard errors; see Chapter 12.1.9. The formulas given here, ones that include a degrees-of-freedom correction, are the default formulas used by the various `vce()` options of the Stata `regress` command; any robust standard errors computed in this text use the Stata defaults. Variations additionally attempt to control for bias and for leverage of observations.

12.1.1   How To Use Robust Standard Errors

For statistical inference on a **single parameter** the main change is to replace the default standard error with the appropriate robust standard error. Thus given a robust standard error of b_j, denoted $se_{rob}(b_j)$, confidence intervals and hypothesis tests are based on the t statistic

$$t = \frac{b_j - \beta_j}{se_{rob}(b_j)}.$$

The distribution of t is asymptotically normal and is approximated by the $T(n - k)$ distribution in most cases. For clustered errors, defined below in Chapter 12.1.4, one instead uses the $T(G - 1)$ distribution where G is the number of clusters and G must be large, rather than the usual requirement that the number of observations n is large.

For tests on **several parameters** with robust standard errors, the formulas for the F statistic given under assumptions 1-4 in Chapter 11.6 no longer hold – the F statistic is no longer simply determined by the residual sums of squares. The adjusted formulas for the robust F statistic use matrix algebra, that is not presented here. The robust F statistic is treated as being $F(q, n-k)$ distributed, or as $F(q, G-1)$ distributed in the case of clustered errors with G clusters. A statistical package that has a robust option will calculate and report the appropriate F statistic for joint statistical significance of the regressors and, if available, a post-estimation test command will also compute the F statistic for tests of more complicated joint hypotheses.

For statistical inference on the **population mean** using univariate data, one should also use robust standard errors if observations are not independent; leading examples are autocorrelated time series and data from a clustered sample. This is rarely done or mentioned in textbooks, and statistical packages do not have an obvious command to do this, but it should be done. A robust standard error for the sample mean $\bar{y}$ can be easily computed by OLS regression of y on just an intercept, since then the intercept estimate $b_1 = \bar{y}$, with standard errors computed as HAC-robust or cluster-robust. Failure to make this correction can lead to large underestimation of the standard error of the sample mean. This correction is not necessary when there is heteroskedasticity as in the intercept-only case heteroskedastic-robust standard errors equal default standard errors. For further details see Chapter 12.1.6.

Remark 103 *If assumptions 3 and 4 do not hold then the appropriate robust standard errors should be computed and used to calculate confidence intervals, t statistics and F statistics.*

The formulas given below for various robust standard errors for the slope coefficient in bivariate OLS regression are derived in Appendix C.2. These formulas extend to multiple regressors but then require use of matrix notation.

12.1.2 Heteroskedastic-Robust Standard Errors

For many examples with cross-section data it is reasonable to assume that model errors are independent (assumption 4), but model errors may be heteroskedastic rather than homoskedastic (assumption 3). For example, the error variance may increase as the value of a regressor increases.

Assumption 3 of homoskedastic errors is then replaced with the assumption of heteroskedastic errors.

3.*het* The **error for the** i^{th} **observation has varying variance conditional on the regressors**:

$$Var[u_i | x_{2i}, ..., x_{ki}] = \sigma_i^2, \quad i = 1, ..., n,$$

where σ_i^2 varies with the values of $x_{2i}, ..., x_{ki}$.

The OLS estimates are unchanged, while the standard errors are computed by a different method. For the simplest case of bivariate regression a common formula for **heteroskedastic-robust standard errors** is

$$\{se_{het}(b_2)\}^2 = \frac{n}{n-k} \times \frac{\sum_{i=1}^{n}(x_i - \bar{x})^2 e_i^2}{\{\sum_{i=1}^{n}(x_i - \bar{x})^2\}^2},$$

Table 12.2: Heteroskedastic-robust standard errors: House price example.

Variable	Coefficient	Robust se	t statistic	p value	95% conf. int.	
Size	68.37	15.36	4.44	0.000	36.52	100.22
Bedrooms	2685	8286	0.32	0.749	-14498	19868
Bathrooms	6833	19284	0.35	0.726	-33159	46825
Lot Size	23020	5329	0.43	0.670	-8748	13355
Year Built	-833	763	-1.09	0.287	-2415	749
Age	-2089	3738	-0.56	0.582	-9841	5664
Intercept	137791	65545	2.10	0.047	1856	273723
Summary Statistics						
n	29					
F(6,22)	6.41					
p-value for F	0.0005					
R^2	0.651					
St. error	24936					

where $k = 2$, e_i is the OLS residual, and it is assumed that the sample size goes to infinity. A derivation of this formula, called HC1, is given in Appendix C.2.

The heteroskedastic-robust standard errors are valid even if errors are homoskedastic, whereas default standard errors are invalid if errors are heteroskedastic. For cross-section data with independent errors it is common practice to automatically use heteroskedastic-robust standard errors, rather than default standard errors, as they relax assumption 3 at the expense of relatively minor additional assumptions that are necessary for theoretical validity.

In many applications these standard errors are within 20% or 30% of each other. While this may seem a small difference it can mean, for example, the difference between a t statistic of 1.8 and t statistic of 2.2, or a difference between a p-value of 0.07 and a p-value of 0.03.

12.1.3   Example: Heteroskedastic-Robust Standard Errors

Table 12.2 presents results for the house price example using dataset HOUSE when heteroskedastic-robust standard errors are used rather than default standard errors. The estimated coefficients are the same as those given in Table 11.2, while the standard errors increase or decrease by as much as 30 percent compared to the default standard errors given in Table 11.2. In this example, despite these changes the variable *Size* remains the only statistically significant regressor at significance level 5%.

The F statistic for overall statistical significance of all regressors is now 6.41 with $p = 0.0005$, compared to 6.83 with $p = 0.0003$ when default standard errors are used. Again the regressors are jointly statistically significant at significance level 5%.

From analysis not presented in Table 12.2, the F statistic for tests that all coefficients other than the variable *Size* have coefficient equal to zero is now 0.457 with $p = 0.804$, compared to 0.417 with $p = 0.832$ when default standard errors are used. Again these regressors are jointly statistically insignificant at significance level 5%.

Remark 104 *Heteroskedastic-robust standard errors are used if assumptions 1-2 and 4 hold, but model errors are heteroskedastic rather than homoskedastic (assumption 3.het). These are routinely used for cross-section data, provided observations are independent of each other.*

12.1.4 Cluster-Robust Standard Errors

In many applications observations can be grouped into clusters where the errors for observations in the same cluster are correlated with each other while errors for observations in different clusters are independent. The idea is that if the model overpredicts (or underpredicts) for one observation in the cluster it is also more likely to overpredict (or underpredict) for other observations in the same cluster. In that case model errors are said to be **clustered**.

For example, individuals may be grouped into villages, with errors for individuals in the same village being correlated, while errors for individuals in different villages are independent. Or we may have panel data (with individuals observed in several time periods), where observations are independent across individuals but are correlated over time for a given individual.

To ensure that OLS remains consistent assumption 2 needs to be strengthened to assume that the error has zero mean conditional on the regressors of all observations in the cluster. We again also allow for the errors to be heteroskedastic. So assumptions 2-4 are replaced by

2.*clu* The **error for the** i^{th} observation **has zero mean conditional on all regressors in the same cluster** (and the nonzero covariances similarly can vary with the regressors):

$$E[u_i | x_{2i}, ..., x_{ki}, x_{2j}, ..., x_{kj}] = 0, \quad i \text{ and } j \text{ in same cluster.}$$

3.*clu* The **error for the** i^{th} observation **has varying variance conditional on the regressor**:

$$\text{Var}[u_i | x_{2i}, ..., x_{ki}] = \sigma_i^2, \quad i = 1, ..., N.$$

4.*clu* The **errors for observations in the same cluster are correlated**:

$$\text{Cor}[u_i, u_j | x_{2i}, ..., x_{ki}, x_{2j}, ..., x_{kj}] \begin{cases} \neq 0 & i \text{ and } j \text{ in same cluster} \\ = 0 & i \text{ and } j \text{ in different clusters.} \end{cases}$$

The resulting standard errors, denoted $se_{clu}(b_2)$, are called **cluster-robust standard errors**, though more precisely they are both heteroskedastic-robust and cluster-robust.

For OLS regression with an intercept and a single-regressor the cluster-robust standard error of the slope coefficient is defined by

$$\{se_{clu}(b_2)\}^2 = \frac{G}{G-1} \frac{n-1}{n-k} \frac{\sum_{i=1}^{n} \sum_{i=1}^{n} \delta_{ij}(x_i - \bar{x})(x_j - \bar{x})e_i e_j}{\{\sum_{i=1}^{n}(x_i - \bar{x})^2\}^2},$$

where δ_{ij} equals 1 if observations i and j are in the same cluster and G is the number of clusters. The term $G/(G-1)$ is a degrees-of-freedom adjustment and the term $(n-1)/(n-k)$ is a finite-sample adjustment. A derivation of this formula, called HC1 or CR1, is given in Appendix C.2.

The cluster-robust standard errors simplify to heteroskedastic-robust standard errors if there is just one observation per cluster, and cluster-robust standard errors are valid even if model errors are independent and/or homoskedastic.

Remark 105 *Cluster-robust standard errors are used if assumptions 1-2 hold, but model errors are correlated within clusters, uncorrelated across clusters, and possibly heteroskedastic. The t statistic is then treated as $T(G-1)$ distributed, rather than $T(n-k)$ distributed, where G is the number of clusters and G needs to be large. F tests of q restrictions should use the $F(q, G-1)$ distribution.*

Cluster-robust standard errors are usually larger than default or heteroskedastic-robust standard errors. This difference can be exceptionally large, so it is especially important that cluster-robust standard errors be used if the model errors are clustered. The intuition is that for data correlated within cluster, each additional observation in a cluster provides less than a complete piece of new information. This information loss, which cluster-robust standard errors control for, leads to less precise estimation and hence larger standard errors.

Econometrics packages that have a cluster-robust option require the user to provide a variable that identifies which of the G clusters each observation falls in. Determining the clusters is not always obvious. A common setting is the following. Interest lies in a regressor x_k that is a policy variable that is the same for everyone in a group, so the intracluster correlation $\rho_{x_k} = 1$, and there is also reason to be that there is some error correlation within the group, even if this correlation is very small. In such examples the groups are the cluster. For example, everyone in a village (or state) benefits from a policy so we cluster on village (or state).

It is important to note that the validity of cluster-robust standard errors relies on having many clusters, not just many observations, as the theory assumes $G \to \infty$. In many applications there are enough observations within each cluster that estimators are reasonably precise, but there are only a few clusters. With G small, the $T(G-1)$ and $F(q, G-1)$ distributions do not provide a good approximation, leading to confidence intervals whose width is under-estimated and test statistics that reject the null hypothesis too often. Several alternative methods, beyond the scope of this book, have been recently proposed. One such method is the Wild cluster bootstrap; see the end of Chapter 12.1.8.

How wrong are the default standard errors? A rough guide is that if model errors are clustered then for the OLS coefficient of the kth regressor the default standard error should be inflated by

$$\tau_k \simeq \sqrt{1 + \rho_{x_k}\rho_u((n/G) - 1)},$$

where ρ_{x_k} is a measure of the within-cluster correlation of x_k, ρ_u is the within-cluster error correlation, G is the number of clusters and n/G is the average number of observations per cluster. The difference is especially great if ρ_{x_k} is large. In particular, $\rho_{x_k} = 1$ in the extreme case that a regressor may take the same value for everyone in the same cluster. For example, if $\rho_{x_k} = 1$, $\rho_u = 0.1$ and $n/G = 81$, then $\tau_k \simeq \sqrt{1 + 1 \times 0.1 \times 80} = 3$, so the true standard error is three times the default. For an example see Chapter 17.3.1.

12.1.5 HAC-Robust Standard Errors for Time Series

For **time series data**, we might expect that the error in one time period is correlated with the error in the preceding time period, in which case the errors are said to be **autocorrelated** or **serially correlated**. For example, if y given regressors is unusually high last period, so $u_{t-1} > 0$, then we might expect that y_t given regressors is also likely to be unusually high with $u_t > 0$. This situation is common for time-series data; see Chapter 17.7 for additional discussion.

To ensure that OLS remains consistent with autocorrelated time series data, assumption 2 is strengthened to the assumption that $\mathrm{E}[u_t | x_t, x_{t-1}, ..., x_1] = 0$ for all t. Now the error must be uncorrelated with not just the current value of the regressor but also with past regressors.

This assumption means that HAC standard errors cannot be used if the regressors include a lagged dependent variable and the errors are autocorrelated. For simplicity suppose $y_t = \beta_1 + \beta_2 y_{t-1} + u_t$. Then the regressor y_{t-1} depends in part on u_{t-1}, since lagging the model one period yields $y_{t-1} = \beta_1 + \beta_2 y_{t-2} + u_{t-1}$. But if u_t is correlated with u_{t-1}, and y_{t-1} depends in part on u_{t-1}, then u_t is correlated with y_{t-1}. As a result OLS in the original model $y_t = \beta_1 + \beta_2 y_{t-1} + u_t$ is inconsistent as the regressor y_{t-1} is correlated with the error term. Essentially $\mathrm{E}[u_t | y_{t-1}, y_{t-2}, ...] \neq 0$ and the strengthened assumption 2 is not met. If lagged dependent variables appear in the model one should include sufficient lags to ensure that the model errors are not autocorrelated.

While model errors can be autocorrelated, the HAC-robust method requires that this autocorrelation eventually disappears. Specifically it is assumed that errors are only autocorrelated up to m periods apart.

For some data this assumption is not met. A leading example is a random walk process, with $y_t = y_{t-1} + u_t$. In that case a simple approach is to then instead analyze the differenced data Δy_t. The more complicated approach of directly analyzing the level of y_t for a random walk process is beyond the scope of this text. A brief discussion is given in Chapter 17.7.

Finally, the errors u_t are also allowed to be heteroskedastic.

Replacing subscript i by subscript t for time-series data, assumptions 2-4 are replaced by

2.*hac* The **error for the** t^{th} observation **has zero mean conditional on current and past regressors values**

$$\mathrm{E}[u_t | x_{2t}, x_{2t-1}, ..., x_{21}, ... x_{kt}, x_{kt-1}, ... x_{k1}] = 0, \quad t = 1, ..., T.$$

3.*hac* The **error for the** t^{th} observation **has varying variance conditional on the regressor**:

$$\mathrm{Var}[u_t | x_{2t}, ..., x_{kt}] = \sigma_t^2, \quad t = 1, ..., T.$$

4.*hac* The **errors for observations are correlated up to at most** m **periods apart**

$$\mathrm{Cor}[u_t, u_s | x_{2t}, ..., x_{kt}, x_{2s}, ..., x_{ks}] \begin{cases} \neq 0 & |t - s| \leq m \\ = 0 & |t - s| > m. \end{cases}$$

The standard errors, denoted $se_{HAC}(\cdot)$, are called **heteroskedastic- and autocorrelation-robust (HAC) standard errors**. In the simplest case of regression on a single regressor, so

$y_t = \beta x_t + u_t$, the HAC variance estimate assuming that the error term u_t is correlated for no more than m lags, is

$$\{se_{HAC}(b_2)\}^2 = \left\{ \sum_{t=1}^T x_t^2 e_t^2 + 2\sum_{j=1}^m \frac{m+1-j}{m+1} \left(\sum_{t=j+1}^m x_t x_{t-j} e_t e_{t-j} \right) \right\} / (\sum_{t=1}^T x_t^2)^2.$$

If $m = 0$ this reduces to $\left\{ \sum_{t=1}^T x_t^2 e_t^2 \right\} / (\sum_{t=1}^T x_t^2)^2$ which is the heteroskedastic-robust estimate. A derivation of these HAC standard errors, called Newey-West standard errors after the econometricians who developed this formula, is given in Appendix C.2.

HAC standard errors are usually larger than default or heteroskedastic-robust standard errors. The intuition is that for data correlated over time, each additional observation provides less than a complete piece of new information. This information loss, which HAC standard errors control for, leads to less precise estimation and hence larger standard errors. The HAC standard errors simplify to heteroskedasticity-robust standard errors if $m = 0$.

Remark 106 *Heteroskedastic- and autocorrelation consistent (HAC) robust standard errors are used if assumptions 1 and 2.hac hold, model errors are autocorrelated up to at most m periods apart and are possibly heteroskedastic (assumptions 3.hac and 4.hac).*

The HAC standard errors differ with the value of m, and there is no single standard method for choosing m. As a result different researchers and/or different statistical packages can obtain different HAC standard errors given the same data and OLS estimates.

Some specialized software determines m automatically, though usually the user must specify a value for m that ideally is the smallest value for which residuals are no longer autocorrelated. For moderately correlated errors with $Cor[u_t, u_{t-1}] < 0.5$, rules of thumb include letting m equal the first integer larger than $0.75T^{1/3}$ or larger than $T^{1/3}$. If the error correlation is higher then a larger m, possibly a much larger m, is needed. A useful guide is to let $m + 1$ be the lag at which the autocorrelations (see Chapter 5.4) of the OLS residual become small, say less than 0.1 or 0.2 in value.

12.1.6   Robust Standard Errors for the Sample Mean

For statistical inference on the **population mean** using univariate data, one should also use robust standard errors if observations are from an autocorrelated time series or from a clustered sample. This is rarely done or mentioned in textbooks, and statistical packages do not have an obvious command to do this, but it should be done. A robust standard error for the sample mean $\bar{y}$ can be easily computed by OLS regression of y on just an intercept, since then the intercept estimate $b_1 = \bar{y}$, with standard errors computed as HAC-robust or cluster-robust. Failure to make this correction can lead to large underestimation of the standard error of the sample mean. This correction is not necessary when there is heteroskedasticity as in the intercept-only case heteroskedastic-robust standard errors equal default standard errors.

OLS regression of y on just an intercept yields fitted value $\hat{y} = b_1$ where $b_1 = \bar{y}$; see Chapter 5.5.7. So regression on an intercept only is equivalent to estimating the sample mean. The associated population model is $y_i = \beta_1 + u_i$ and $\mu = E[y_i] = \beta_1$ under the standard assumption that $E[u_i]$. So using b_1 for inference on β_1 is equivalent to using $\bar{y}$ for inference on μ.

In Chapter 4 inference on the population mean was limited to the case where y_i had common mean and variance and was independent. This is equivalent to making assumptions 2-4 for the model $y_i = \beta_1 + u_i$. But we can relax assumptions 3-4 and use robust standard errors.

For intercept-only regression it can be shown that heteroskedastic-robust standard errors equal default standard errors. For observations that are correlated, however, we should use the appropriate robust standard errors.

Remark 107 *For inference on the population mean from samples where observations are not statistically independent, valid inference can be obtained by regression on only an intercept and using appropriate robust standard errors, such as cluster-robust standard errors or HAC standard errors.*

Intercept-only regression is an option available in most computer packages that have a command for OLS regression. Giving the OLS command with dependent variable y and no regressor yields estimated intercept equal to the sample mean. Alternatively, if the package has an option to run a regression with the intercept set to zero then create a new variable z equal to 1 for every observation and OLS regress y on z using the zero-intercept option.

12.1.7 Example: HAC Standard Errors for the Sample Mean

As an example of inference on the mean with correlated regressors, return to the quarterly data on the annual growth rate in U.S. real GDP per capita studied in Chapter 4.5 using dataset REALGDPPC. The sample mean growth rate was 1.990 with standard error of the mean equal to $2.1781/\sqrt{241} = 0.140$. This sample standard deviation was based on the assumption that observations were independent, when in fact growth this quarter is correlated with growth in preceding quarters.

Since the sample mean can be obtained by regression of y on just an intercept, we regress growth on just an intercept. As expected, the estimated intercept is 1.990, equal to the sample mean. And the default standard error is 0.140, equal to the standard sample standard deviation. To compute the HAC standard error we need to specify the maximum lag length m.

The OLS residual for this intercept-only regression is $e_t = y_t - \bar{y}$ and is autocorrelated. The first five autocorrelations are, respectively, 0.868, 0.660, 0.442, 0.168 and 0.030. We set $m = 5$ as the autocorrelations have died down by then. Then the HAC standard error is 0.276, almost twice the default 0.140, and the 95% confidence interval for population mean growth is $(1.45, 2.54)$ compared to $(1.71, 2.27)$ using default standard errors.

12.1.8 Bootstrapped Standard Errors

The **bootstrap** is a computational method for obtaining statistics such as a standard error by appropriate random sampling of the original data.

Let β denote a single parameter of interest in a linear model with k regressors and assume that model errors are independent. Using the **pairs** (or x-y) **bootstrap** method, the bootstrap standard error of the OLS estimate b of β is obtained as follows. Obtain a new sample of size n from the original sample by randomly sampling observations with replacement. For example, the original dataset observation 1 might appear twice, the original dataset observation 2 might not appear, the original dataset observation 3 might appear twice once, and so on. Perform OLS on this new dataset to obtain a new estimate denoted b_1. Repeat this process S times to obtain S OLS estimates $b_1^*, ..., b_S^*$ where, for example, $S = 400$. Then the bootstrap estimate of the variance of b is simply the sample variance of these S estimates

$$\widehat{V}_{boot}[b] = \frac{1}{S-1} \sum_{s=1}^{S} (b_s^* - \overline{b^*})^2,$$

where $\overline{b^*} = \frac{1}{S} \sum_{s=1}^{S} b_s^*$ is the average of the S bootstrap estimates. The bootstrap standard error of b, denoted $se_{boot}[b]$, is the square root of $\widehat{V}_{boot}[b]$.

The resampling means that $se_{boot}[b]$ will vary with the number of resamples and with the way random resamples are generated. This variation diminishes as $S \to \infty$ and $S = 400$ might be viewed as a minimum. The bootstrap resampling is based on a random number generator, so one should always set the seed before bootstrapping to ensure that results are reproducible. Exercise 13 provides an example.

The preceding bootstrap standard error can be shown to be asymptotically equivalent to the heteroskedastic-robust standard error, where by asymptotically equivalent we mean that $n \to \infty$.

For model errors that are clustered the resampling is instead over clusters rather than individual observations. Then the cluster bootstrap standard error can be shown to be asymptotically equivalent to the cluster-robust standard error, where by asymptotically equivalent we mean that the number of clusters goes to infinity.

For model errors that are correlated over time the resampling is more difficult as it needs to preserve the dependence structure over time.

For OLS regression there is generally no benefit to using bootstrap standard errors as computer output provides default and robust standard errors. The bootstrap is useful when simple formulas are no longer available. For example, if interest lies in a parameter $\alpha = \beta_2 \times \beta_3$ we can perform S bootstraps leading to S estimates $a_1^*, ..., a_S^*$ where, for example $a_1^* = b_{2,1}^* \times b_{3,1}^*$ and the bootstrap standard error is the square root of $\frac{1}{S-1} \sum_{s=1}^{S} (a_s^* - \overline{a^*})^2$.

There are many ways to bootstrap. For basic regression the bootstrap is rarely needed. The one notable exception is cluster-robust inference with few clusters, in which case the usual cluster-robust methods tend to result in confidence intervals that are two narrow and hypothesis tests that over-reject. In that case one better method is the more specialized Wild cluster bootstrap. This advanced method can be implemented using the Stata user-written command `boottest` or using the `vcovBS` function in the R `sandwich` package.

12.1.9 Computing Robust Standard Errors using Different Statistical Packages

The formulas given previously are those used by Stata. Other packages may use more recently developed variations that lead to somewhat different standard errors. At the level of this book these differences are of secondary importance, but can explain why a different software package may give the same coefficient estimates but slightly different standard errors (and hence t statistics and confidence intervals) to those presented in this text.

For Stata, heteroskedastic-robust standard errors are obtained using the `vce(robust)` option of the `regress` command that computes the so-called HC1 formula; available variations are HC2 and HC3. For cluster-robust standard errors one uses the `vce(cluster cvar)` option, where `cvar` is the variable identifying clusters, to obtain CR1 standard errors. (Note that if the estimation command used is an `xt` command, rather than `regress`, then the `vce(robust)` option actually computes cluster-robust standard errors where clusters are determined by the variable given in the `xtset` command). HAC standard errors for OLS are not available using the `regress` command. Instead one needs to first use the `tsset` command to give the variable that defines the time periods, and then obtain OLS estimates using the `newey` command with the lag length specified in the `lag()` option; e.g., `tsset year` followed by `newey y x, lag(3)`.

Robust standard errors in R can be obtained using the R package `sandwich` which provides a wide range of ways to compute robust standard errors. Heteroskedastic-robust standard errors are obtained using the `vcovHC` function. HC1 standard errors, the method used by Stata, are obtained with `type="HC1"`. To reproduce the Stata heteroskedastic standard errors use the command `vcovHC(name, type="HC1")` where `name` is the label given to the previously obtained OLS estimates. Variations include HC2 and HC3 and the default is actually the variation `type="HC3"`. Cluster-robust standard errors are obtained using the `vcovCL` function and the default `type="HC1"` uses the same formula as that used by Stata. To reproduce the Stata HAC standard errors use the command `NeweyWest(name, lag=3, prewhite=FALSE)` where in this example the lag length is three. Alternative HAC standard errors are computed using the `vcovHAC` function that includes methods to automatically determine the lag length. For R code that implements robust standard errors and performs subsequent hypothesis tests see Appendix A.3.

Gretl supports a range of methods for computing standard errors. The defaults give the same standard errors as those used by Stata. The default for the `robust` option of the `ols` command gives HC1 heteroskedastic-robust standard errors, and the `cluster=cvar` option gives HC1 cluster-robust standard errors. To obtain HAC-robust standard errors one must first declare the data to be time series data using the `time-series` option of the `setobs` command. There are then several options. The command `set hac_length 3`, for example, yields the same simplest Newey-West standard errors for lag length three as those obtained by Stata. Variations on these defaults can be obtained using specific `set` commands. Finally, give command `set force_hc off` so that subsequent use of the `robust` option of the `ols` command yields HAC-robust standard errors. (If heteroskedastic-robust standard errors are subsequently needed then give command `set force_hc on`).

Eviews also computes a range of standard errors. The default for heteroskedastic-robust standard errors is HC2, rather than Stata's HC1, and the default for cluster-robust is CR1, the same as for Stata. To reproduce the Stata HAC standard errors choose no whitening, a Bartlett kernel, user-specified kernel, and set the bandwidth to $m + 1$ where m is the maximum lag length.

12.1.10   When to Use Robust Standard Errors

When model errors are independent, so assumption 4 holds, it is now standard in econometrics practice to use heteroskedastic-robust standard errors rather than default standard errors, even if it might be felt reasonable to assume that errors are homoskedastic. Model errors are often independent, though not always so, when cross-section data is used. And in some time series applications with financial returns data, model errors may be independent (see Chapter 8.3).

Clustered standard errors are commonly used in two settings. One is cross-section data where individuals are grouped, for example into villages, and model errors are correlated within group; see Chapter 17.1. A second setting is panel data on individuals (people or firms or county) over time, where errors are independent across individuals but are autocorrelated over time for a given individual; see Chapter 17.2.

HAC standard errors need to be used in most time series regressions, though not all. HAC standard errors should not be used if the lagged dependent variable is a regressor. HAC standard errors are not necessary if errors are not autocorrelated; a leading example is some financial returns regressions as under the efficient markets hypothesis the current price reflects all information.

Beyond model specification, part of the practitioner's art is using appropriate standard errors. In the case of clustered standard errors this requires determining the variable to cluster on. For HAC standard errors this requires determining the lag length m; some methods automatically pick the length. Even with the same OLS model coefficient estimates different researchers may make different choices, and/or use different statistical packages, leading to different standard errors, confidence intervals, test statistics and p-values.

12.2   Prediction

A key distinction in prediction is that between predicting an average outcome and predicting an individual outcome. For example in predicting the price of a house with a given set of observable characteristics it is much easier to predict what on average such a house will sell for than to predict the price of a given individual house with those characteristics. Similarly it is much easier to predict average earnings at various levels of education than earnings for any individual.

Multiple regression and more data can greatly improve the precision of such prediction, but especially for individual predictions of most outcomes of interest to economists there can still be considerable prediction error.

12.2.1   Prediction Example: House Price and Size

Figure 12.1 presents predictions from the fitted model of house price (y) for house size (x^*) ranging from 1400 to 3300 square feet. The center line in each panel gives the point prediction, $\widehat{y} = b_1 + b_2 x^* = 115017 + 73.771 x^*$.

The first panel gives the 95% confidence interval (based on default standard errors) for the prediction of the average outcome, more precisely the condition mean, at various values of x^*. The 95% confidence interval is narrowest at the sample mean $\bar{x} = 1883$ and widens as the regressor value x^* moves away from $\bar{x}$.

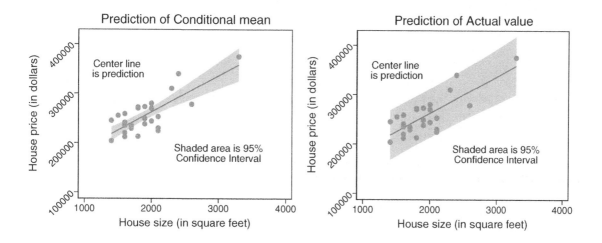

Figure 12.1: Prediction: Conditional mean and actual value

The second panel gives the 95% confidence interval (also based on default standard errors) for the actual price of the house given house size. In this example the interval is so wide that it is of little use for someone trying to select an appropriate price for a particular house using information on size alone.

The remainder of this section provides details on these two different uses of prediction.

12.2.2 Prediction of an Average Outcome

Interest may lie in prediction of an average outcome, such as what price a house may sell for on average. In that case we wish to predict the **conditional mean** of y given specified values $x_2^*, ..., x_k^*$ of the regressors:

$$E[y|x_2^*, ..., x_k^*] = \beta_1 + \beta_2 x_2^* + \cdots + \beta_k x_k^*.$$

Replacing the parameters by their estimates, the **prediction of the conditional mean** is

$$\widehat{y}_{cm} = b_1 + b_2 x^* + \cdots + b_k x_k^*,$$

where the subscript cm denotes conditional mean.

Since $\widehat{y}_{cm}$ is a linear combination of $b_1, ..., b_k$, its statistical properties follow from those of $b_1, ..., b_k$. The prediction is unbiased under assumptions 1-2 since then $b_1, ...b_k$ are unbiased for $\beta_1, ..., \beta_k$. The variance of $\widehat{y}_{cm}$ is

$$\text{Var}(\widehat{y}_{cm}) = \text{Var}(b_1 + b_2 x^* + \cdots + b_k x_k^*).$$

This variance depends on the precision of the estimates of $b_1, ...b_k$.

Let $se(\widehat{y}_{cm})$ denote the standard error of $\widehat{y}_{cm}$, the square root of the estimate of $\mathrm{Var}(\widehat{y}_{cm})$. A $100(1-\alpha)\%$ confidence interval for the conditional mean is

$$\mathrm{E}[y|x_2^*, ..., x_k^*] \in \widehat{y}_{cm} \pm t_{n-k,\alpha/2} \times se(\widehat{y}_{cm}).$$

With many observations the regression parameters can be precisely estimated, leading to $se(\widehat{y}_{cm})$ being potentially quite small and hence quite narrow confidence intervals for the conditional mean when the sample size is large.

12.2.3   Prediction of an Actual Value

Alternatively, interest may lie in predicting the **actual value** of y given specified values of the regressors:

$$y|x_2^*, ..., x_k^* = \beta_1 + \beta_2 x^* + \cdots + \beta_k x_k^* + u^*.$$

This has an additional term, the error term about which little is known aside from its mean of zero given assumption 2.

Replacing the parameters by their estimates, and replacing the unknown error u^* by its unbiased estimate of 0, the **prediction of the actual value**, or **forecast**, is

$$
\begin{aligned}
\widehat{y}_f &= b_1 + b_2 x^* + \cdots + b_k x_k^* + 0 \\
&= b_1 + b_2 x^* + \cdots + b_k x_k^*,
\end{aligned}
$$

where the subscript f denotes forecast. While $\widehat{y}_f = \widehat{y}_{cm}$ it should be clear that it is being used for the different and more difficult purpose of predicting the actual value.

The forecast $\widehat{y}_f$ is used to predict $\beta_1 + \cdots + \beta_k x_k^* + u$, not just $\beta_1 + \cdots + \beta_k x_k^*$. Since u is pure noise that is unpredictable and is uncorrelated with $b_1, ..., b_k$, it follows that the variance of the forecast is the sum of the variance of $\widehat{y}_{cm}$ and the error variance.

$$\mathrm{Var}[\widehat{y}_f] = \mathrm{Var}[\widehat{y}_{cm}] + \mathrm{Var}[u|x_2^*, ..., x_k^*].$$

As before $\mathrm{Var}(\widehat{y}_{cm})$ is estimated by $se^2(\widehat{y}_{cm})$. Let $s_{u^*}^2$ denote the estimate of $\mathrm{Var}[u|x_2^*, ..., x_k^*]$. Then the estimated variance of $\widehat{y}_f$ is $se^2(\widehat{y}_{cm}) + s_{u^*}^2$, so the standard error of $\widehat{y}_f$ is

$$se(\widehat{y}_f) = \sqrt{se(\widehat{y}_{cm})^2 + s_{u^*}^2}.$$

A $100(1-\alpha)\%$ confidence interval for the actual value is then

$$y|x_2^*, ..., x_k^* \in \widehat{y}_f \pm t_{n-k,\alpha/2} \times se(\widehat{y}_f).$$

With a large amount of data the regression parameters can be precisely estimated, leading to $se(\widehat{y}_{cm})$ being potentially quite small. But $se(\widehat{y}_f) > s_{u^*}^2$ always, and a 95% confidence interval for the actual value of y is at least $\widehat{y}_f \pm 1.96 \times s_{u^*}^2$.

12.2.4 Prediction using a Statistical Package

Statistical packages differ in the extent to which they enable statistical inference for prediction. Many packages will compute $se(\widehat{y}_{cm})$, based on both default and robust standard errors for $b_1, ..., b_k$.

More problematic is computation of s_{u*}^2, the variance of the error term which is needed to compute $se(\widehat{y}_f)$. Under assumptions 1-4 the errors are homoskedastic and we can use $s_{u*}^2 = s_e^2$, where s_e is the standard error of the regression or root mean squared error that is provided in standard regression output. If errors are heteroskedastic the simplest solution is to assume that $\text{Var}[u|x_2^*, .., x_k^*]$ equals the sample average error variance, in which case we again use s_e^2. Richer methods instead use an estimate from a fitted model for $\text{Var}[u|x_2^*, .., x_k^*]$.

As an example, consider OLS regression of y on a single regressor x followed by out-of-sample prediction for $x = 2000$ and $x = 2500$. The general procedure is to first obtain OLS estimates using the initial sample and then apply a prediction command to a separate dataset with the two values of x of interest, using a prediction command that gives not only $\widehat{y}$ but also $se(\widehat{y}_{cm})$.

For concreteness consider Stata and inference based on heteroskedastic-robust standard errors. First give command `regress y x, vce(robust)`. Then create a dataset with the two new regressor values using the following five commands: `clear, input x, 2000, 2500` and `end`. The two predictions $\widehat{y}_{cm}$ can be obtained using command `predict ycm, xb` followed by `list`. The corresponding standard errors $se(\widehat{y}_{cm})$ can be obtained using command `predict seycm, stdp` followed by `list`. The forecasts $\widehat{y}_f$ are again `ycm` while the associated standard errors $se(\widehat{y}_f) = \sqrt{se(\widehat{y}_{cm})^2 + s_{u*}^2}$ and, as already noted, it is simplest to let $s_{u*}^2 = s_e^2$.

For R with default standard errors give command `model<-lm(y~x)`. Then create a data frame `new.x` with the two new x values using command `new.x <- data.frame(x=c(2000,2500))`. The ensuing command `predict(model,newdata=new.x,interval="confidence",level=0.95)` gives the two predictions $\widehat{y}_{cm}$ and an associated 95% confidence interval. The argument `se.fit=TRUE` gives the standard errors $se(\widehat{y}_{cm})$. For inference based on robust standard errors, instead use the `predict.lm` function in the `car` package which adds the argument `vcov`. For example, if the robust variance matrix is stored as `vrobust` then add the argument `vcov=vrobust`.

12.2.5 Example: House Price given Multiple House Characteristics

Suppose based on OLS estimates using dataset HOUSE we wish to make predictions for a 2000 square foot house with four bedrooms, two bathrooms and medium lot size that is forty-years old and is sold in June. Then the predicted value is

$$\widehat{y} = b_1 + 2000b_2 + 4b_3 + 2b_4 + 2b_5 + 40b_6 + 6b_7 = 257691.$$

First, consider prediction of the conditional mean assuming assumptions 1-4 hold. Using statistical software that includes commands for prediction after OLS regression, we find that $se(\widehat{y}_{cm}) = 6488$, using default standard errors. Since $t_{22,.025} = 2.074$, the 95% confidence interval for the conditional mean house price, given the regressor values stated above, ranges from \$244,235 to \$271,146.

Second, consider forecasting the actual value assuming assumptions 1-4 hold. Here $s_e = 24936$, so $se(\widehat{y}_f) = \sqrt{6488^2 + 24936^2} = 25766$. The 95% confidence interval for the actual house price, given the regressor values stated above, ranges from \$204,255 to \$311,126, a much broader range.

Now suppose instead that model errors are heteroskedastic. Using statistical software that includes commands for prediction after OLS regression and use of heteroskedastic-robust standard errors, we obtain $se(\widehat{y}_{cm}) = 6631$ and the 95% confidence interval for the conditional mean is \$243,939 to \$271,442. For forecasting the actual value we additionally need an estimate of $\mathrm{Var}[u|x^*, ..., x_k^*]$. It is simplest to again use $s_e^2 = 24936^2$, in which case $se(\widehat{y}_f) = \sqrt{6631^2 + 24936^2} = 25803$ and the 95% confidence interval is \$204,176 to \$311,206.

While both the conditional mean and actual value of a 2,000 square foot house are estimated to be \$257,691, the actual value is much less precisely estimated with a standard error that is four times that of the estimate for the conditional mean. As a result, in this example the 95% confidence interval for the actual value of y given $x = 2000$ is of width over \$100,000, so wide as to be of little practical use. It is much more difficult to forecast accurately the actual value than it is to predict the average value.

12.2.6   Prediction for Bivariate Regression under Assumptions 1-4

In the special case of bivariate regression under assumptions 1-4 there exists a simple formula for $se(\widehat{y}_{cm})$, one that gives insights into when predictions and forecasts are likely to be more precise. We have

Remark 108 $\widehat{y}_{cm} = b_1 + b_2 x^*$ *is an estimate of* $E[y|x^*] = \beta_1 + \beta_2 x^*$, *the conditional mean of* y *given* $x = x^*$. *When model assumptions 1-4 hold, so default standard errors for the OLS estimates are used, the **standard error** for the predicted conditional mean is*

$$se(\widehat{y}_{cm}) = s_e \times \sqrt{\frac{1}{n} + \frac{(x^* - \bar{x})^2}{\sum_{i=1}^{n}(x_i - \bar{x})^2}},$$

where $s_e = \frac{1}{n-2}\sum_{i=1}^{n}(y_i - b_1 - b_2 x_i)^2$ *is the standard error of the regression.*

The formula for $se(\widehat{y}_{cm})$ implies that the predicted conditional mean is more precise in the following situations.

1. The data points y are less scattered around the regression line, as then s_e is smaller.

2. The greater the variation in regressors, as then $\sum_{i=1}^{n}(x_i - \bar{x})^2$ is larger.

3. The closer x^* is to the sample mean as then $(x^* - \bar{x})^2$ is smaller.

4. The larger the sample size, as then $1/n$ is smaller and $(x^* - \bar{x})^2 / \sum_{i=1}^{n}(x_i - \bar{x})^2$ is smaller.

An approximate 95% confidence interval for the predicted conditional mean is $\widehat{y}_{cm} \pm 2 \times se(\widehat{y}_{cm})$. Note that $se(\widehat{y}_{cm}) \to 0$ as the sample size $n \to \infty$, so the confidence interval becomes very tight.

Moving to forecasting an individual outcome, the result that $se(\widehat{y}_f) = \sqrt{se(\widehat{y}_{cm})^2 + s_e^2}$ yields

Remark 109 $\widehat{y}_f = b_1 + b_2 x^*$ *is an estimate of* $y|x^* = \beta_1 + \beta_2 x^* + u$, *the actual value of* y *given* $x = x^*$. *When model assumptions 1-4 hold, so default standard errors for the OLS estimates are used, the* **standard error** *for the* **actual value (or forecast)** *is*

$$se(\widehat{y}_f) = s_e \times \sqrt{1 + \frac{1}{n} + \frac{(x^* - \bar{x})^2}{\sum_{i=1}^{n}(x_i - \bar{x})^2}}.$$

It is important to note that $se(\widehat{y}_f) \geq s_e$, regardless of the sample size. This makes sense since the model error is unforecastable and has standard deviation of σ_u that is estimated by s_e. So an approximate 95% confidence interval for the actual value is at least of width $\widehat{y}_{cm} \pm 2 \times s_e$.

12.2.7 Bivariate Regression Example: House Price given House Size

We manually compute predictions and associated standard errors using the preceding formulas for the bivariate case with default standard errors.

Consider prediction of the conditional mean price of a house that is 2000 square feet in size, based on OLS regression of *Price* on *Size* using dataset HOUSE. Then

$$\widehat{y}_{cm} = b_1 + b_2 x^* = 115017 + 73.771 \times 2000 = 262559.$$

The conditional mean price is predicted to be \$262,559.

The standard error of $\widehat{y}_{cm}$ using default standard errors is computed as follows. From regression output, $n = 29$ and $s_e = 23551$, and from summary statistics $\bar{x} = 1882.76$. The final piece needed is $\sum_i (x_i - \bar{x})^2$. This is not directly given in output. Instead it can be calculated as $(n - 1) \times s_x^2$ since the estimated variance of x is $s_x^2 = \frac{1}{n-1} \sum_i (x_i - \bar{x})^2$. From summary statistics, *size* has standard deviation $s_x = 389.2721$, so $\sum_i (x_i - \bar{x})^2 = 28 \times 398.2721^2 = 4441379$. Combining, $se(\widehat{y}_{cm}) = 23551 \times \sqrt{\frac{1}{29} + \frac{(2000-1882.76)^2}{4441379}} = 4565$.

Next consider forecast of the actual value of the price of a house that is 2000 square feet in size. Then again $\widehat{y}_f = b_1 + b_2 x^* = 262559$. Since $se(\widehat{y}_{cm}) = 4565$ and $s_e = 23551$, the standard error of the forecast is $se(\widehat{y}_f) = \sqrt{4565^2 + 23551^2} = 23989$. This is more than five times $se(\widehat{y}_{cm}) = 4565$.

The resulting 95% confidence interval for $E[y|x = 2000]$ is $262559 \pm 2.052 \times 4565 = (253192, 271927)$, since $t_{27,.025} = 2.052$. And the 95% confidence interval for the actual value of y given $x = 2000$ is much wider, equalling $262559 \pm 2.052 \times 23989 = (213338, 311781)$.

12.2.8 Are Poor Forecasts a Problem?

Econometric models, especially those estimated using individual-level cross-section data, can have low R^2, and consequently relatively large error variance. This can lead to very noisy forecasts of the actual value for an **individual observation**. But the predictions can still be very informative about **average behavior**. Recall that the standard error for the conditional mean is much smaller than that for a forecast, and can approach zero as the sample size gets large.

For example, many studies find that on average education has a statistically significant impact on earnings, and furthermore this impact is large in magnitude. This is the case even though for an individual the confidence interval for forecast earnings given years of education is very wide.

Knowing that on average high levels of education are predicted to lead to high earnings is very useful information for policy makers, as it suggests it is worthwhile subsidizing education as it will lead on average to higher earnings and hence higher output and tax receipts in the future.

At the same time knowing that we cannot predict well for an individual means that an individual cannot be sure of getting a return on further schooling, so they may be unwilling to pay up front for university education, for example. Government subsidy will make it more likely that individuals will take further education. Such subsidy may pay off down the line for the government through increased tax revenues given higher earnings.

12.3   Nonrepresentative Samples

Samples used in regression are not always simple random samples. Instead, some units in the population may be oversampled or undersampled. Then, as discussed in Chapter 3.7, the population mean of a single variable needs to be estimated using a weighted mean, rather than an unweighted mean.

In this section the regression case is considered. An important distinction is whether the non-representative sampling is on variables that are regressors or is on the dependent variable.

12.3.1   Nonrepresentative Sampling on Regressors

If the nonrepresentative sampling is solely on variables that are regressors then OLS can still be used, provided that enough regressors are included in the regression model and the model is sufficiently flexible so that the remaining error in the model has zero mean conditional on the regressors. Then model assumptions 1-2 are still satisfied.

For example, for the house price dataset small houses will be oversampled, since small houses are sold more frequently than large houses. As a result, the sample mean price understates the population mean price for all houses in the community. By contrast, the regression model for house price includes house size as a regressor, thereby controlling for the unrepresentative sample.

More specifically, the sample mean corresponds to the regression model $y = \beta_1 + u$ and in this example we feel $E[u] < 0$, so assumption 2 does not hold, because our sample oversamples smaller homes that will on average sell for less. A weighted mean needs to be used. But in the regression model $y = \beta_1 + \beta_2 \times Size + u$ it is reasonable to assume that $E[u|Size] = 0$, so now assumption 2 holds and OLS can be used.

As a second example, consider an earnings regression based on data from a complex survey such as the American Community Survey. If smaller states and minority populations are deliberately oversampled, then this will also lead to oversampling of people with low earnings, since earnings tend to be lower in smaller states and for minorities. So we should use a weighted mean in estimating population mean earnings. For regression analysis, however, we can include sufficient controls for minority status and state of residence and estimate using regular OLS.

Economic studies using survey data often include many regressors, in addition to the regressor(s) of intrinsic interest, to yield a model that satisfies

$$y = \beta_1 + \beta_2 x_2 + \cdots + \beta_k x_k + u$$
$$\mathrm{E}[u|x_2, ..., x_k] = 0,$$

when nonrepresentative sampling is solely on the regressors. Then estimation can be by OLS.

Remark 110 *For nonrepresentative sampling on variables other than the dependent variable, OLS estimation is possible if appropriate regressors are included as controls.*

12.3.2 Nonrepresentative Sampling on the Dependent Variable

If the nonrepresentative sampling is on variables that are dependent variables then OLS is inconsistent and cannot be used.

For example, suppose high-priced houses are over-sampled and we estimate the model $y = \beta_1 + \beta_2 \times Size + u$. Then a high price arises because size is large, given $\beta_2 > 0$. But it can also arise due to unusually large values of the error term. But this implies that $\mathrm{E}[u|Size] > 0$ so assumption 2 does not hold.

As a second example, consider an earnings regression when people with low earnings are deliberately oversampled. Then people with negative values of the error term will have been over-sampled, so $\mathrm{E}[u|x_2, ..., x_k] < 0$.

Sampling on the dependent variable, rather than just the regressor variables, is called **sample selection**. This is much more problematic as the nonrepresentative sampling is partly on the error term, and no data are available for the error term. Models for sample selection exist, but they generally rely on strong assumptions about the error process and are inconsistent if any of these strong assumptions do not hold.

Remark 111 *For nonrepresentative sampling on the dependent variable, OLS yields biased and inconsistent estimates for the population.*

In some cases population weights are available. In that case, considered next, analysis is straightforward.

12.3.3 Weighted Least Squares

It is not always possible to ensure that $\mathrm{E}[u|x_2, ..., x_k] = 0$ when the sample is not representative of the population. One example is nonrepresentative sampling on the dependent variable. A second example is nonrepresentative sampling on variables other than the dependent variable, but data on these variables is not available. In the house price example it may be that houses that were substantially remodelled in the past ten years were oversampled, but this variable is not known to the data analyst.

If $\mathrm{E}[u|x_2, ..., x_k] \neq 0$, unbiased estimation is still possible if **sample weights** w_i are available. Sample weights can be directly given as population weights, in which case w_i equals the number of individuals in the population represented by the ith observation. Or we may have the **probability**

weight π_i that gives the probability that the ith observation is included in the sample, in which case the sample weight $w_i = 1/\pi_i$. In either case the **weighted least squares estimates** minimize the weighted sum of squares

$$\sum_{i=1}^{n} w_i(y_i - b_1 - b_2 x_{2i} - \cdots - b_k x_{ki})^2.$$

This downweights the squared residual for oversampled observations by w_i.

Weighted least squares with weights w_i can be implemented by OLS regression of $\sqrt{w_i} y_i$ on $\sqrt{w_i}, \sqrt{w_i} x_{2i}, ..., \sqrt{w_i} x_{ki}$ where the intercept is not included and inference should be based on robust standard errors. Exercise 17 provides an example.

More simply, some statistical packages have weighted least squares as an option and will then compute the correct standard errors, t statistics, p-values and confidence intervals. But care is needed in providing the correct weights as, for example, it is easy to specify that $w_i = \pi_i$ rather than $1/\pi_i$.

Remark 112 *For nonrepresentative samples with sample weights provided, population weighted least squares can be used.*

12.4   Best Estimation

When assumptions 3-4 are relaxed the OLS estimator is no longer the most efficient estimator of the linear regression model and more precise estimation than OLS is possible. Different best estimators, meaning minimum variance among consistent estimators, are obtained depending on how assumptions 3-4 are changed.

For completeness we briefly review these better estimators. In practice most economic studies continue to use OLS estimation with analysis based on appropriate robust standard errors to ensure that inference is valid. Reasons for continued use of OLS are that the more efficient estimators often have only a small gain in efficiency and any gain is dependent on correct specification of the alternative model for the errors.

12.4.1   Feasible Generalized Least Squares Estimator

As an example, suppose errors are heteroskedastic and independent and for simplicity consider bivariate regression, so $y_i = \beta_1 + \beta_2 x_i + u_i$. Suppose we knew $\sigma_i^2 = \text{Var}[u_i]$. Then the transformed model $(y_i/\sigma_i) = \beta_1(1/\sigma_i) + \beta_2(x_i/\sigma_i) + (u_i/\sigma_i)$ has error that (u_i/σ_i) that is independent and homoskedastic (with constant variance 1), so the best estimators of β_1 and β_2 are obtained by OLS in this transformed model that by construction satisfies assumptions 1-4. In practice σ_i^2 is unknown and to implement this procedure we need to first specify a model for σ_i^2, such as $\sigma_i^2 = \exp(\alpha_1 + \alpha_2 x_i)$, estimate α_1 and α_2, and then perform OLS estimation of the transformed equation with σ_i replaced by $\widehat{\sigma}_i$ where $\widehat{\sigma}_i^2 = \exp(\widehat{\alpha}_1 + \widehat{\alpha}_2 x_i)$.

The preceding estimator is an example of the **feasible generalized least squares (FGLS) estimator**. It requires specifying a model for the error variances (and error covariances if relevant) and consistently estimating the parameters of this model. If it is assumed that the error model is correctly specified, then the FGLS estimator is BLUE and hence is more precise than OLS.

Different feasible GLS estimators are used for different types of data that have different types of model error variances and correlations. For cross-section data with independent heteroskedastic errors the FGLS estimation method is the weighted least squares method presented above. For cross-section data with clustered errors and short panel data the most commonly-used FGLS estimator is the random effects estimator; see Chapter 17.1 and 17.2. For time series data the most commonly-used FGLS estimator is the Cochrane-Orcutt estimator; see Chapter 17.7.

Remark 113 *If assumptions 3-4 do not hold then feasible generalized least squares estimation may lead to more precise estimates than OLS regression. Different FGLS estimators are used in different settings.*

12.4.2 Robust Standard Errors for FGLS

FGLS is guaranteed to be more efficient than OLS only if the model for the error variances (and error covariances if relevant) is correctly specified. If instead this model is incorrectly specified then FGLS remains consistent in the case of weighted least squares and random effects estimation, but not for Cochrane-Orcutt for time series autocorrelation. In the first two cases one should use appropriate robust standard errors after GLS estimation to ensure valid inference if the model for the errors is misspecified. Then it is no longer guaranteed that FGLS is fully efficient, though FGLS is still likely to be more efficient than OLS.

In practice OLS, with appropriate robust standard errors, is used more often than FGLS. This is partly because the efficiency gains to FGLS can be small in some applications, notably for weighted least squares.

12.5 Best Confidence Intervals

The OLS estimators are not the only estimators of $\beta_1, ..., \beta_k$ in the linear regression model. The preceding section introduced generalized least squares estimators when assumptions 3-4 are relaxed. And another possible estimator is the least absolute deviations (LAD) estimator that minimizes $\sum_{i=1}^{n} |y_i - \widehat{y}_i|$, the sum of the absolute value of the residuals.

This section considers which estimators are best to use to construct confidence intervals and hypothesis tests. The bottom line is that it is best to use the most efficient estimator, that with the smallest variance.

12.5.1 Best Confidence Intervals

The best confidence interval is the shortest confidence interval.

Let $\widehat{\beta}_j$ be generic notation for an estimator of β_j, such as OLS, FGLS and LAD. For these estimators the distribution of the associated t statistic is symmetric and unimodal, in which case the shortest $100(1 - \alpha)\%$ confidence interval for β_j is $\widehat{\beta}_j \pm t_{n-k,\alpha/2} \times se(\widehat{\beta}_j)$. The width of the confidence interval is therefore $2 \times t_{n-k,\alpha/2} \times se(\widehat{\beta}_j)$ which is minimized for estimator $\widehat{\beta}_j$ that has the smallest standard error $se(\widehat{\beta}_j)$.

Thus the best confidence interval is one based on the most efficient estimator, essentially FGLS for the models considered in this book. In practice it is common to instead use OLS with robust standard errors. While this does not provide the shortest confidence intervals, the increase in confidence interval width is often not great.

12.6   Best Hypothesis Tests

For test of $H_0 : \beta_j = \beta_j^*$ against $H_a : \beta_j \neq \beta_j^*$ based on $t = (\widehat{\beta}_j - \beta_j^*)/se(\widehat{\beta}_j)$ the best tests are those that can best discriminate between the null hypothesis value β_j^* and values under the alternative hypothesis such as $\beta_j^* + \Delta$ for various values of Δ such as 0.1, 0.2, ...

Intuitively this discrimination will be easiest the more precise is the estimator $\widehat{\beta}_j$. Thus the best hypothesis test is one based on the most efficient estimator.

The remainder of this section provides more detail and introduces terminology that is used in more advanced courses.

12.6.1   Type I and II errors

Consider a medical test of whether or not someone has a disease. A positive test result indicates disease while a negative result indicates the absence of disease.

Medical tests are not always perfect. A **false positive** occurs when the test finds disease when in fact there is none. And a **false negative** occurs when the test fails to find disease that is present.

Ideally a medical test leads to both few false positives and few false negatives. But there is a trade-off between the two. A more sensitive test will detect disease more often leading to fewer false negatives, but this will be at the expense of more false positives. And if there are many positive false positives, leading to expensive and stressful false alarms, it may not even be worthwhile doing the test.

Similar issues arise in hypothesis testing. Let the null hypothesis (H_0) be that there is no disease and the alternative hypothesis (H_1) be that disease is present. Then a false positive corresponds to rejecting the null hypothesis (and finding disease) when we should not reject (there was actually no disease), a type I error introduced in Chapter 4.4. A false negative corresponds to failing to reject the null hypothesis when we should reject. The standard terminology is the following.

Remark 114 *A **type I error** (or false positive) occurs if H_0 is rejected when H_0 is true. A **type II error** (or false negative) occurs if H_0 is not rejected when H_0 is false.*

The situation is summarized in Table 12.3 where, for example, a false positive is rejecting $H_0 : \beta_2 = \beta_2^*$ when in fact $\beta_2 \neq \beta_2^*$.

Table 12.3: Hypothesis Tests: Type I and Type II Errors.

Decision	Truth	
	H_0 really true: No disease	H_0 really false: Disease
Do not reject H_0 : Find no disease	Correct decision	**Type II error** (false negative)
Reject H_0 : Find disease	**Type I error** (false positive)	Correct decision

12.6.2 Test Size and Test Power

Ideally both type 1 and type II errors occur with low probability. But unfortunately decreasing the probability of one type of error means increasing the probability of the other. For example, we can reduce the probability of a type I error by rarely rejecting H_0, but then the type II error probability will rise as we then are unlikely to reject even if we should.

The following terminology is used.

Definition 28 *Test size or significant level of a test*, *denoted α, is the pre-specified maximum* *probability of a type I error* *that will be tolerated.*

The test procedures we have presented set test size at some prespecified level α, the significance level of the test. Most often $\alpha = 0.05$. Computer output automatically reports a p-value that can be compared to the desired test size.

Definition 29 *Test power is one minus the probability of a type II error.*

Ideally test power is high as then the probability of a type II error is low. Computer output (and studies) rarely report power because it varies with the parameter value under the alternative hypothesis. For example, we are very likely to erroneously fail to reject $H_0 : \beta_2 = 40$ against $H_a : \beta_2 = 40.001$, while we are much less likely to reject $H_0 : \beta_2 = 40$ against $H_a : \beta_2 = 60$. The further apart the H_0 and H_a values, the easier it is to discriminate, and the less likely we are to make a type II error.

12.6.3 Most Powerful Tests

Ideally we want test procedures that have both as small test size as possible (close to 0) and as high test power as possible (close to 1). But decreasing size comes at the expense of decreasing power, and increasing power comes at the expense of increasing size.

The usual response to this conundrum is to set test size at a specified low level such as 0.05, and then use testing procedures that keep the probability of a type II error as small as possible, and hence test power as high as possible, for the specified probability of a type I error.

These best tests, those with the most power for a given test size, are called **most powerful tests**. For the tests presented in this book such tests are based on the unbiased estimator (or consistent estimator) with minimum variance.

For tests of hypotheses on the population mean μ based on a simple random sample, the t test is the most powerful test if the data are identically and independently distributed (assumptions A-C) and are normally distributed. And for tests on regression parameters $\beta_1, ..., \beta_1$ the t test and F test are the most powerful test under assumptions 1-4 and the additional assumption that data are normally distributed.

The standard choices of α are 0.05 or 0.01 or 0.10, reflecting a reluctance to make the error of unwarranted rejections of the null hypothesis. But this comes with the potential cost of a high probability of failing to reject the null hypothesis when we should have rejected.

Furthermore there is an asymmetry. As sample size gets larger, leading to more precise estimation, it is possible to simultaneously improve both test size and power. Instead, standard practice is to keep test size at the usual 0.05 level, and only test power improves.

The most powerful tests are based on the most efficient estimator, essentially FGLS for the models considered in this book. In practice it is common to instead use OLS with robust standard errors; the decrease in test power is often not great.

12.7 Data Science and Big Data: An Overview

There has been a recent explosion in the availability of enormous amounts of data and the computer power to store and analyze these data. Economic examples include shopper scanner data, web click data, real-time financial trading data, and Google search terms.

This has led to terms such as the following. **Data science** or **data analytics** is the science of discerning patterns in data. **Machine learning** or **statistical learning** is a branch of **artificial intelligence** that attempts to algorithmically learn from data, rather than specifying a model based on expert knowledge of the particular application. In the popular media it is common to refer to almost any data analysis as big data, but to data scientists the term **big data** refers to datasets that are enormously large, so large that the commonly-used software tools such as the standard statistical and econometric packages are inadequate and more specialized tools are needed.

Often the goal of big data is **prediction**. Large amounts of data can lead to improved prediction with smaller prediction error $y - \hat{y}$ as it enables estimation of models with many explanatory variables and models and estimation methods, such as lasso, neural networks, deep nets, regression trees and random forests, that can be very complex. And with large amounts of data not all the data needs to be used in determining the model; some of the data can be set aside for out-of-sample model testing that reduces the chance of model overfitting. The machine learning methods can predict better than simpler methods such as OLS.

The use of big data methods to predict is ubiquitous. For example, the first few letters typed in a Google search automatically lead to several possible completions of the search; these are instantaneous predictions.

In some cases predictions can be very accurate even at the individual level. For example, this is the case with software that uses a digital image to determine the numbers and letters in a vehicle license plate.

In many other cases predictions can be quite inaccurate at the individual level but still be useful if they perform well on average. For example, high frequency traders are repeatedly making predictions and can make a very substantial profit by on average predicting better than the competition even if on any given trade the prediction is poor. Similarly web browsing history is used to predict what banner advertisements any given individual is exposed to. The prediction may led to low probability of any individual clicking on an ad, but if a sufficiently large proportion click on an ad then the predictions are profitable.

Care is needed in applying these methods to predicting individual human behavior. Predicting whether a baseball player should be drafted appears to be a positive and benign use of data. But similar tools can be used to predict, for example, the probability that a prisoner will re-offend upon release from prison, given observable prisoner characteristics such as the neighborhood they will return to and their closeness to family. A good prediction model obtained by an algorithmic machine learning method will be a black box that is impossible to explain. The model may predict average behavior well but may have low R-squared, so that individual behavior is poorly predicted. Yet if the model predicts that a given individual has a relatively high probability of re-offence then early release is ruled out and the person may remain in prison for many more years.

As another example, an algorithm may determine whether or not someone receives an expensive life-saving medical treatment that is the only available treatment for their medical condition.

Is society willing to allow such major decisions to be made by a black box? The era of data science opens up many such societal questions.

12.8 Bayesian Methods: An Overview

The statistical inference methods in this book are those of classical statistics. Given data and a model for the data we obtain an estimate $\widehat{\theta}$ of an unknown fixed parameter θ that is random due to sampling error since different samples yield different estimates $\widehat{\theta}$. A resulting 95% confidence interval is interpreted as one that with repeated sampling of the population will include θ 95% of the time.

Bayesian methods provide an alternative approach to statistical inference. Knowledge of the unknown fixed parameter θ is obtained by combining sample information, specifically a model for the distribution of the data given θ, with prior information on θ. This yields a distribution, called the **posterior distribution**, for the possible values that θ might take. A point estimate of θ is the mean of the posterior distribution. A resulting 95% Bayesian credible region can be directly interpreted as being an interval that θ lies in with probability 0.95.

Until recently Bayesian methods were infrequently used due in part to analytical intractability in all but the simplest models. **Markov chain Monte Carlo** (MCMC) computational methods, developed in the 1980's, provide many draws from the posterior distribution even in models that are analytically intractable. Modern computing power has made feasible implementation of these MCMC methods. Consequently Bayesian methods have become widely used in applied statistics.

Bayesian methods are particularly useful when there is good **prior information** on parameters. In many econometrics settings such as regression with many regressors and hence many parameters this is often not the case. In such cases one can with care specify a weak or uninformative prior; then Bayesian methods give similar results to those of classical statistical methods such as OLS regression.

As an example, consider regression of house price (measured in thousands of dollars) on an intercept and house size. Analysis used program defaults for the data (a normal distribution), for the prior distribution of the parameters (intercept, slope and variance of the error term), and for the MCMC computational method. This led to 10,000 draws from the posterior distribution. For the slope parameter (the coefficient of *Size*) the mean of these 10,000 draws was 0.0767, the standard deviation of these draws was 0.0115, and the 95% credible region range was $(0.0540, 0.1003)$ since the 2.5 and 97.5 percentiles of these 10,000 draws were 0.0340 and 0.1003. Since the priors here were relatively uninformative these are similar to the regular regression estimates of slope coefficient 0.0738, standard error 0.0112 and 95% confidence interval $(0.0508, 0.0967)$.

Great care is needed in the use of Bayesian methods. First, an appropriate density for the data needs to be specified, such as the normal for linear regression. Second, a prior distribution for the parameters needs to be specified. This is particularly difficult for econometrics applications where prior information can be weak for some or all model parameters. In that case the specified prior needs to be one that is **uninformative**, meaning it has very little effect on the results. It can be easy to mistakenly specify an informative prior, especially if program defaults are used. For example, the preceding analysis was repeated with house price measured in dollars, rather than thousands of dollars. Then the mean of the posterior draws was 132.3, quite different from the OLS slope estimate of 76.7, so the prior had substantial impact on the resulting posterior distribution. Finally, one always needs to confirm that the MCMC iterative procedure has converged to the posterior distribution.

12.9   A Brief History of Statistics, Regression and Econometrics

Statistical inference initially focused on the sample mean. An early version of the law of large numbers was proved by Jacob Bernoulli in 1713. An early version of the central limit theorem was obtained by Abraham de Moivre in 1733. The term "standard deviation" was introduced by Karl Pearson in 1894. Pearson also popularized the term "normal distribution" which previously was known by several names including the Laplace-Gaussian curve. The exact $T(n-1)$ distribution for the t statistic for random sampling of normals was obtained by William Sealy Gosset in 1908. Gosset's employer, the Guinness brewery, did not allow the research findings of its employees to be published lest they aided its competitors. Guinness made an exception for Gosset's result, but so other employees did not know of this exception the result was published under the pseudonym "Student".

Visual description of the sample distribution using histograms was proposed by Karl Pearson in 1895. Kernel density estimates (a smoothed histogram) were introduced independently by Murray Rosenblatt in 1956 and by Emanuel Parzen in 1962.

The method of least squares was introduced by Pierre Laplace in 1805 and Carl Friedrich Gauss in 1809 as a numerical method to find an approximate solution to a system of equations when there were more equations than unknowns. Specifically, it was used to summarize astronomical observations on the movement of the planets about the sun when there were more observations than variables in the system and these observations were measured with error.

The term "regression" was introduced by Francis Galton in 1885. Galton also introduced the term "co-relation" (now correlation). The modern statistical formulation of correlation and the linear regression model was well established by the 1920's, with significant contributions by Francis Galton, Francis Ysidro Edgeworth, Karl Pearson, George Udney Yule, and Ronald A. Fisher. The F distribution, an important generalization of the t distribution used in multiple regression, is named after Fisher who introduced a variant of the F distribution in a 1924 paper.

More flexible kernel regression (a nonparametric regression method) was introduced by Elizbar A. Nadaraya and Geoffrey S. Watson in 1964. Robust standard errors for OLS regression were introduced in the 1980's by Halbert White (heteroskedastic-robust), Whitney Newey and Kenneth West (HAC) and Kung-Yee Liang and Scott Zeger (cluster-robust).

A leading case where estimators other than OLS are used is when samples are not representative of the population but population weights are available and the weighted least squares estimator is used.

The recent development of regression methods has moved in tandem with improvements in computer technology. The first electronic computers were developed in the 1940's. Much smaller and faster mainframe computers based on transistors (rather than vacuum tubes) and integrated circuits were introduced in the 1960's. Even with these initial advances, the exercises in this book if done in the 1970's would have required state-of-the-art mainframe computers.

Personal computers were introduced in the 1970's. Apple's Macintosh with a mouse and graphical user interface was introduced in 1984. The 1989 Macintosh had 8 megabytes of RAM and ran at 16 MHZ; personal computers today run more than 1,000 times faster and the gains in memory and storage are even greater than this. This increased computational power, and accompanied development of statistical software, has made the methods covered in this text simple to implement.

Increased computational power has also led to development of new statistical methods, most notably machine learning for prediction and MCMC methods for Bayesian analysis.

Econometrics uses the previously mentioned tools, applied to problems of economic policy and business interest and using the insights of economics such as the important role of prices. Econometrics applications have especially focused on causal inference, estimating the causal effect of a change in a key variable x on an outcome of interest y. Many of the causal methods developed and used by econometricians are for observational data, though increasingly economists are also running experiments or discovering observational settings that can be interpreted as natural experiments. A brief overview is given in Chapter 17.5, and some applications are given in Chapters 3.5–3.8.

12.10 Key Concepts

1. Robust standard errors are used when assumptions 3-4 do not hold.

2. Heteroskedasticity-robust standard errors are used when model errors are heteroskedastic and independent (assumption 3 does not hold).

3. Cluster robust standard errors are used when model errors are heteroskedastic, correlated within cluster and uncorrelated across clusters (assumptions 3 and 4 do not hold).

4. Heteroskedastic- and autocorrelation-consistent (HAC) robust standard errors are used when model errors are heteroskedastic and correlated over time (assumptions 3 and 4 do not hold).

5. Distinction needs to be made between prediction of an average outcome (the conditional mean) and prediction of an actual value (forecasting). The latter is more imprecise.

6. For nonrepresentative sampling on variables other than the dependent variable, OLS estimation is possible if appropriate regressors are included as controls.

7. For nonrepresentative sampling on the dependent variable, OLS cannot be used.

8. For nonrepresentative samples with sample weights provided, population weighted least squares can be used.

9. Generalized least squares estimators may be more precise than OLS when assumptions 3-4 do not hold.

10. The best confidence intervals and best tests for linear regression model parameters are those based on the most efficient estimators.

11. A type I error (or false positive) occurs if H_0 is rejected when H_0 is true.

12. A type II error (or false negative) occurs if H_0 is not rejected when H_0 is false.

13. Test size is the probability of a type I error.

14. Test power is one minus the probability of a type II error.

15. The best tests are the most powerful tests that maximize power for given test size.

16. Key terms: Robust standard errors; heteroskedastic-robust standard errors; cluster-robust standard errors; HAC standard errors; bootstrap standard errors; prediction of conditional mean; prediction of actual value; nonrepresentative sample; sample selection; sample weights; weighted least squares; feasible generalized least squares; type I error; type II error; test size; test power; most powerful test.

12.11   Exercises

1. For each of the following state what standard errors are most appropriate.

    (a) Errors are independent and heteroskedastic.

    (b) Errors are independent and homoskedastic.

    (c) Errors are correlated over time.

    (d) Errors are correlated within groups and uncorrelated across groups.

2. For each of the following state what standard errors are most likely to be appropriate.

    (a) Data are time series data.
    (b) Data are cross-section data on individuals.
    (c) Errors are cross-section data on individuals within various villages.

3. A detailed description of dataset SALARYSAT is given in exercise 3 of Chapter 7. We consider OLS regression of *salary* on an intercept and *satmath*, *satverb*, *age* and *highgrade*.

    (a) Obtain OLS estimates with default standard errors.
    (b) Obtain OLS estimates with heteroskedastic-robust standard errors.
    (c) Compare the OLS estimates in part (b) to those in part (a).
    (d) Compare the standard errors of the OLS estimates in part (b) to those in part (a).
    (e) Compare the overall F test of statistical significance in part (b) to that in part (a).

4. Repeat the previous exercise using dataset HOUSE2015. Regress *price* on an intercept, *size*, *bedrooms*, *bathrooms* and *daysonmarket*.

5. Dataset PHARVIS has data from the 1997-98 World Bank Vietnam Living Standards Survey. The survey covers 27,753 people in 5,739 households and 194 communes (villages). We consider OLS regression of *pharvis* (number of direct pharmacy visits) on an intercept, *hhexp* (total household expenditure), *age* (age in years), *illness* (number of illnesses in past year), and *hlthins* (equals one if have health insurance cover). We will compute cluster-robust standard errors that control for potential correlation of errors within household or within village.

    (a) Obtain OLS estimates with heteroskedastic-robust standard errors. Are the signs of coefficients what you expect? Explain.
    (b) Obtain OLS estimates with cluster-robust standard errors that cluster on household (variable *hhid*). Compare the standard errors to those in part (a).
    (c) Obtain OLS estimates with cluster-robust standard errors that cluster on commune (variable *commune*). Compare the standard errors to those in part (b).

6. Repeat the previous exercise for OLS regression of *pharvis* on an intercept, *age* (age in years), *gender* (1 if male), *illdays* (number of illness days), and *actdays* (number of days of reduced activity).

7. Use dataset PHARVIS described in exercise 5. Here we obtain various estimates of the standard error of the sample mean of *pharvis* (number of direct pharmacy visits).

    (a) Use univariate statistics methods to find the sample mean and its standard error.
    (b) Regress *pharvis* on only an intercept with default standard error. Compare your answer to that in part (a).

(c) Regress *pharvis* on only an intercept with heteroskedastic-robust standard error. Compare your answer to that in parts (a) and (b).

(d) Regress *pharvis* on only an intercept with cluster-robust standard error that cluster on *commune*. Compare your answer to that in part (a) and comment.

8. Repeat the previous exercise for *illness* (number of illnesses in past year).

9. Use dataset GDPUNEMPLOY detailed in Chapter 8.4 for OLS regression of *Rgdpgrowth* (annual percentage growth in real GDP) on an intercept and *uratechange* (annual change in the unemployment rate).

(a) Obtain OLS estimates with heteroskedastic-robust standard errors.

(b) Obtain the OLS residual and the first six autocorrelations of the residuals. Do the residuals appear to be autocorrelated?

(c) Obtain OLS estimates with HAC-robust standard errors with lag length set to six (see Chapter 12.1.9). Compare the standard error of the slope coefficient to that in part (a).

10. Repeat the previous exercise using dataset PHILLIPS detailed in Chapter 13.3 for OLS regression of *inflgdp* (annual price inflation rate) on an intercept, *urate* (unemployment rate) and *inflgdp1yr* (forecast of one year ahead inflation).

11. A good source for macroeconomic and financial data is FRED (Federal Reserve Economic Data) provided by the Federal Reserve Bank of St. Louis. The data are available at the website https://fred.stlouisfed.org/. Data can be downloaded directly from Stata using the import fred command, and from R using the fredr package. We will instead separately download two series in separate spreadsheet files, merge within the spreadsheet, and then read into our statistical package. The two series are monthly data on 1 year (GS1) and 20 year (GS20) constant maturity U.S. treasury interest rates.

(a) In Fred search type GS1, GS20.

(b) Separately download each series as a comma-separated values (csv) file.

(c) Merge the two series to create a single file with variables *date*, *gs1*, and *gs20*.

(d) From now on use data from 1993.10 to 2019.10. This will yield the same answers as given in the solutions. Give the mean of *gs1* and *gs20*.

(e) Which series is more volatile: *gs1* or *gs20*? Explain.

(f) Create a line chart with both *gs1* and *gs20* plotted against month. Do *gs1* and *gs20* appear to move together?

(g) Create a scatterplot with *gs20* plotted against *gs1* along with a fitted regression line. Do *gs1* and *gs20* appear to move together?

(h) Give the intercept and slope coefficients and R^2 from OLS regression of *gs20* on *gs1*. Comment.

12. Continue with the same data as obtained in the previous exercise.

    (a) Regress *gs20* on *gs1* and obtain default standard errors.

    (b) Now obtain heteroskedastic-robust standard errors and compare these to the default standard errors.

    (c) Obtain the OLS residuals. Are these serially correlated? Explain.

    (d) Regress *gs20* on *gs1* and obtain Newey-West HAC standard errors with the lag length set to 24 months. Compare to the other standard errors and comment.

    (e) Note that a similar example is studied in more detail in Chapter 17.7.

13. This exercise implements the pairs bootstrap presented in Chapter 12.1.8. With many bootstraps and $n \to \infty$ the bootstrap standard errors are equivalent to heteroskedastic-robust standard errors. Use dataset SALARYSAT described in exercise 3 of Chapter 7 and consider OLS regression of *salary* on an intercept and *satmath, satverb, age* and *highgrade*.

    (a) Obtain bootstrap standard errors with 2,000 bootstrap replications and the seed set to 10101. In Stata this is option `vce(boot, reps(2000) seed(10101))`. In R first `set.seed(10101)` then use command `vcovBS(name, R=2000)` in the `sandwich` package.

    (b) Compare the bootstrap standard errors to the heteroskedastic-robust standard errors.

    (c) Compare the bootstrap standard errors to the default standard errors.

14. Repeat the previous exercise using dataset ADVERTISING described in exercise 5 of Chapter 10. Regress *sales* on an intercept, *tv, radio* and *newspaper*.

15. Use dataset HOUSE and OLS regress *price* on an intercept, *size* and *bedrooms* with default standard errors. Consider predicting the price of a 2,000 square foot house with three bedrooms.

    (a) Obtain the predicted conditional mean of *price*.

    (b) Obtain the standard error of the predicted conditional mean price.

    (c) Hence give a 95% confidence interval for the conditional mean price.

    (d) Obtain the standard error of the forecast actual price.

    (e) Hence give a 95% confidence interval for the forecast price.

    (f) Repeat parts (b) and (d) with heteroskedastic-robust standard errors.

16. Repeat the previous exercise using dataset HOUSE2015 and predicting the price of a 2,500 square foot house with four bedrooms.

17. This exercise and the subsequent three exercises use dataset SURVEYDATA, an extract from the U.S. American Community Survey. The sample is not purely random as some types of individuals are over-sampled and other types are under-sampled. The dataset includes the variable *perwt* (person weight) that records how many people in the population a single observation represents. For example, if *perwt* equals 67 then the observation represents 67 people in the population. The extract used is of 191 full-time year-round 30 year-old female workers. Throughout use heteroskedastic-robust standard errors.

    (a) Summarize the variable *perwt*. Is there great variability in *perwt* across observations?

    (b) Regress *earnings* on an intercept and *educ* (years of completed schooling). This summarizes the relationship in the sample.

    (c) Perform weighted OLS (add [pw=perwt] in Stata or weights=perwt in R) to estimate the relationship in the U.S. population. Compare the slope coefficient and its standard error to your answer in part (b).

    (d) Now manually implement weighted OLS by regular OLS on transformed variables. First construct the variables *trearnings*, *trintercept* and *treduc* by premultiplying, respectively, *earnings*, the intercept (one) and *educ* by the square root of *perwt*. Then regress *trearnings* on *trintercept* and *treduc*, using the no constant or no intercept option of OLS. You should obtain the same results as in part (c).

18. Repeat the previous exercise, except consider the relationship between *uhrswork* (usual hours worked per week) and *educ*.

19. Use dataset SURVEYDATA described in exercise 17. Here we compute the weighted mean (introduced in Chapter 3.7.2) of *earnings* using *perwt* as the weight.

    (a) Obtain the unweighted mean and its standard error.

    (b) Compute the weighted mean directly using your computer software. (Command mean with [pw=perwt] in Stata or use weighted.mean in R). Compare the estimate and its standard error to your answer in part (a).

    (c) Compute the weighted mean manually using the formula in Chapter 3.7.2. So compute the sum (or average) of *earnings* and divide by the sum (or average) of *perwt*. Compare the estimate to your answer in part (b).

    (d) Recall that the mean can be estimated by regression on just an intercept. Similarly the weighted mean can be estimated by weighted regression on an intercept. Perform weighted OLS (add [pw=perwt] in Stata or weights=perwt in R) to estimate the mean in the U.S. population. Compare your answer to that in part (b).

20. Repeat the previous exercise for *educ* (years of completed schooling).

21. Suppose OLS regression with robust standard errors leads to the standard error of a slope coefficient being larger than if default standard errors had been used. Answer true or false to the following.

    (a) The t statistic for statistical significance will then be larger.
    (b) The p-value for statistical significance will then be larger.
    (c) The 95% confidence interval will be wider.

22. Consider two alternative estimation methods for the same regression, both of which lead to valid statistical inference. Answer true or false to each of the following.

    (a) The method with largest standard error is preferred.
    (b) The method with widest confidence interval is preferred.
    (c) The method with highest power for a given size is preferred.

23. Consider test of $H_0 : \theta = 0$ against $H_a : \theta = 1$. Suppose the probability of rejecting $H_0 : \theta = 0$ equals 0.05 if $\theta = 0$ and equals 0.20 if $\theta = 1$.

    (a) Give the probability of a type I error.
    (b) Give the size of the test.
    (c) Give the probability of a type I error.
    (d) Give the power of the test.

24. Consider test of $H_0 : \theta = 0$ at level 0.05 against either $H_a : \theta = 1$ or $H_a : \theta = 2$. Answer true or false to each of the following.

    (a) The size of the test is the same against either $H_a : \theta = 1$ or $H_a : \theta = 2$.
    (b) The power of the test is higher under $H_a : \theta = 2$.
    (c) The probability of a type II error is higher under $H_a : \theta = 2$.

Chapter 13

Case Studies for Multiple Regression

This chapter presents several case studies. These illustrate the multiple regression methods presented in Chapters 10 and 11, as well as the earlier univariate analysis and bivariate regression. For all examples we use the appropriate robust standard errors, see Chapter 12.1, rather than default standard errors. The second and fourth examples use regression with natural logarithms, for which the material in Chapter 9.3 provides sufficient background.

For most examples the material covered so far is sufficient background. An exception is the fifth example, on the Rand Health Insurance Experiment, that uses regression with sets of indicator variables presented in Chapter 14.4. A second exception is the last example, on the effect of institutions on country growth rates, that uses instrumental variables regression explained in Chapter 17.4. The chapter concludes with an example of cleaning a dataset before analysis.

13.1 School Academic Performance

California, and many other states, introduced tests to measure individual student performance and overall performance. The goal was to improve student performance overall and especially in "low performing" schools. A complication is that the performance of students in schools depends not only on the quality of teaching but also the socioeconomic background of students.

Here we analyze school performance data for California high schools in 1999.

13.1.1 Data Description

California schools were assessed using the annual Academic Performance Index (API) from 1999 to 2013. The API score for each school was determined by the performance of all students at the school in a standardized test, the STAR test, that varied by grade level.

The lowest possible API score was 200 and the highest possible score was 1000. The goal was for schools to attain a score of at least 800. Schools in California are organized and managed at the local district level (often city), rather than the state level. Schools with API below 800 were expected to increase their score each year, with the threat of state intervention if they failed to do so.

Table 13.1: Academic Performance Index: Variable definitions and summary statistics (n=807)

Variable	Definition	Mean	Standard deviation	Min	Max
Api	Academic Performance Index	620.94	107.44	355	966
Edparent	Average years of schooling of parents	12.84	1.23	9.62	16
Meals	% of students in lunch program	21.92	23.67	0	98
Englearn	% of students English learners	14.00	12.79	0	66
Yearround	= 1 if multi-track year-round school	0.02	0.15	0	1
Credteach	% of teachers with full credentials	89.84	8.44	33	100
Emerteach	% of teachers with emergency credentials	10.47	8.21	0	56

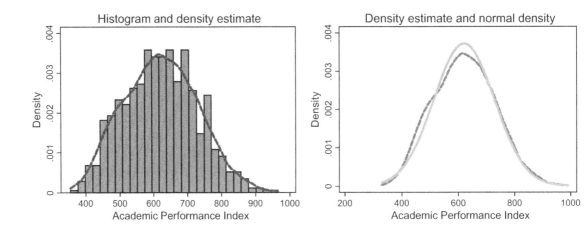

Figure 13.1: Academic Performance Index: Histogram and smoothed histogram

Dataset API99 has data for 807 high schools in California in 1999 on the API and on factors that may affect school performance on the API. The data are summarized in Table 13.1. The variables *Edparent*, *Meals* and *Englearn* measure the socioeconomic background of students – variable *Meals* gives the percentage of students in a free or reduced price lunch program which is available only to students from poorer families. The variables *Credteach* and *Emerteach* measure the extent to which teachers have passed state teacher credentialing requirements and may be a crude measure of teacher quality.

The first panel of Figure 13.1 gives a histogram for *Api*, along with the kernel density estimate. *Api* appears to be normally distributed. Often scaled scores such as the API are constructed in such a way as to follow the normal distribution bell curve. As an aside we pursue the question of normality further.

The second panel of Figure 13.1 gives both the kernel density estimate and a normal density with mean and standard deviation equal to the sample mean and standard deviation (621 and 107). The data do appear to be quite close to being normally distributed. In output not given, the symmetry statistic for Api is 0.121, close to 0, the median is 621, close to the mean of 620.9, and the kurtosis statistic is 2.61, close to 3 for the normal. Finally, if Api is normally distributed then we expect 5% of the sample, or 40 observations, to be more than 1.96 standard deviations from the mean. In fact 35 observations lie outside this range.

The standard error for the sample mean is $107.44/\sqrt{807} = 3.78$. A 95 percent confidence interval for the population mean school API is $620.94 \pm 1.96 \times 3.78 = (613, 628)$.

13.1.2 Bivariate Regression

To what extent is school performance simply a result of the socioeconomic characteristics of students, rather than distinctive special attributes of the schools and teachers?

To answer this question we regress student performance on the educational attainment of parents as many studies find these to be highly correlated. OLS regression of Api on $Edparent$ yields estimates

$$\widehat{Api} = \underset{(15.99)}{-400.31} + \underset{(1.22)}{79.53} \times Edparent, \quad s_e = 43.674, \quad R^2 = 0.835, \quad \bar{R}^2 = 0.835,$$

where, since observations are independent, heteroskedastic-robust standard errors are given in parentheses.

$Edparent$ is highly statistically significant, with $t = 79.53/1.219 = 65.25$. Furthermore it is economically very significant. A one year increase in average parental schooling is associated with an 80 point increase in Api, which is a three-quarter of a standard deviation in Api ($79.53/107.44 = 0.74$).

Figure 13.2 presents a scatter plot of Api against $Edparent$ and the fitted regression line. This confirms visually the strength of the relationship, with $R^2 = 0.83$. Much of the variation in school scores is explained by parents' education. While the range in scores is $966 - 355 = 611$, from Figure 13.2 the maximum deviation between an actual and predicted API score is only approximately 200.

A fitted nonparametric regression, obtained using local linear regression, is almost indistinguishable from the OLS fitted line, confirming that the relationship is linear.

Deviations of sample observations from the fitted line appear unrelated to the level of the regressor $Edparent$, so there is no real sign of heteroskedasticity. And in fact the default standard error for $b_{Edparent}$ is 1.25, very close to the heteroskedastic-robust standard error of 1.22. Nonetheless it is standard with independent observations to use heteroskedastic-robust standard errors.

13.1.3 Multiple Regression

It is possible that parent education level is simply picking up the effect of other variables associated with parent education level, including other socioeconomic variables and school input variables such as teacher quality.

Table 13.2 presents pairwise correlations for the data. The asterisk indicates statistical significance at significance level 0.05. Here all correlations are statistically significantly different from zero.

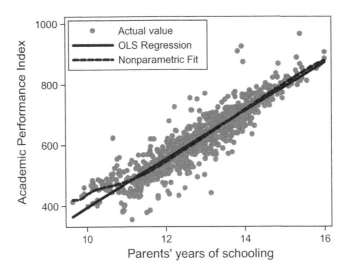

Figure 13.2: Academic Performance Index: Regression on parents' education

Table 13.2: Academic Performance Index: Pairwise correlations

	Api	*Edparent*	*Meals*	*Englearn*	*Yrrd*	*Cred*	*Emer*
Api	1						
Edparent	.91*	1					
Meals	-.54*	-.60*	1				
Englearn	-.66*	-.71*	.56*	1			
Yearround	-.19*	-.25*	.29*	.22*	1		
Credteach	.46*	.40*	-.27*	-.26*	-.18*	1	
Emerteach	-.45*	-.37*	.22*	.20*	.09*	-.82*	1

From the first column of Table 13.2, school API is positively correlated with parents' education, negatively associated with children who receive free and reduced price lunches or are English learners, positively associated with teachers having full credentials and negatively correlated with teachers having emergency credentials. All correlations have the expected sign and are at least of moderate size, aside from variable *Yearround* with correlation −0.19.

The second column of Table 13.2 indicates that parents' education is strongly correlated with the other socioeconomics and school teacher variables. Perhaps the strong association of parents' education with API is merely picking up the effect of these other variables.

Table 13.3 lists results from multiple regression of *Api* on *Edparent* and the other variables, with homoskedastic-robust standard errors. Even including the other variables, *Edparent* has a large impact, with coefficient lowered only slightly from 79.5 in bivariate regression to 73.9. There is a modest improvement in adjusted R^2 from 0.834 to 0.852. The regressors are jointly highly

Table 13.3: Academic Performance Index: Multiple regression estimates.

Dependent Variable *API*						
Variable	Coefficient	Standard Error	t statistic	p value	95% conf. int.	
Edparent	73.942	1.835	40.29	0.000	70.339	77.545
Meals	0.079	0.092	0.86	0.390	-0.102	0.260
Englearn	-0.358	0.177	-2.02	0.044	-0.706	-0.010
Yearround	25.956	10.752	2.41	0.016	4.850	47.062
Credteach	0.387	0.349	1.11	0.268	-0.298	1.073
Emerteach	-1.470	0.358	-4.11	0.000	-2.174	-0.767
Intercept	-345.328	44.027	-7.84	0.000	-431.750	-258.905
Observations	807					
F(6,22)	801.0					
p-value for F	0.000					
R-squared	0.853					
Adjusted R^2	0.852					
St. error of regression	41.4					

statistically significant since the overall F test $p = 0.000$.

The regressors *Englearn* and *Credteach* are statistically significant at 5%, and have the expected negative sign. The coefficient of *Englearn* implies that, after controlling for the other regressors, a one standard deviation change (12.79 from Table 13.1) in the proportion of English learners is associated with a 4.6 point decrease ($-0.358 \times 12.79 = -4.58$) in API, which is a relatively small effect. Similarly a one standard deviation change in the percentage of teachers with emergency credential is associated with a modest twelve point decrease in the API. The regressors are highly jointly statistically significant with $F = 801.0$ with $p = 0.000$

The joint statistical significance of the additional regressors is a test of $H_0 : \beta_3 = 0, ..., \beta_7 = 0$ against H_a :at least one of $\beta_3, ..., \beta_7 \neq 0$. A specialized test command gives $F = 14.80$ with $p = 0.000$ with $p = 0.000$ so the null hypothesis is rejected.

As an aside we note that default standard errors are within fifteen percent of the heteroskedastic-standard errors for all regressors. Using default standard errors the F statistic for test of the subset regressors (Chapter 12.6) can be computed as follows. The residual sum of squares ($ResSS$) in the (restricted) bivariate regression model equals 1535468 and $ResSS$ in the (unrestricted) full model equals 1371154. (While $ResSS$ was not listed in the bivariate regression output, s_e was listed, and we can use $ResSS = (n-2) \times s_e^2 = 805 \times 43.674^2$). The remaining numbers are provided in Table 13.3. Then $F = [(1535468 - 1371154)/(7-2)]/[1371154/(807-7)] = 19.17$.

The performance of a high school on the Academic Performance Index is very highly correlated with the average educational attainment of the parents of the school children. This association is of large economic magnitude. The association remains high even after controlling for several variables that also measure student socioeconomic background and crude variables for teacher quality. This strong association makes it difficult to calculate the separate role of other educational inputs, such as teacher quality.

To control for dependence of the API score on socioeconomic characteristics the state of California additionally provided a ranking of each school relative to 100 other schools that have similar "opportunities and challenges" based on measures that include student mobility, race, ethnicity, parental education and English learners.

13.2   Cobb-Douglas Production Function

A production function models output as a function of capital and labor, and possibly additionally inputs such as land. the benchmark functional form is the Cobb-Douglas production function. We use data from the classic 1928 study that proposed and analyzed the Cobb-Douglas production function,

13.2.1   Cobb-Douglas Production Function and Natural Logarithm Transformation

Let Q be the number of units of output, K be the number of units of capital and L be the number of units of output. Then the **Cobb-Douglas production function** specifies

$$Q = \alpha K^{\beta_2} L^{\beta_3}.$$

Of particular interest is testing whether the returns to scale are constant, so that doubling both inputs leads to exactly doubling output. For the Cobb-Douglas this is the case if $\beta_2 + \beta_3 = 1$. Returns to scale are increasing if $\beta_2 + \beta_3 > 1$ and are decreasing if $\beta_2 + \beta_3 < 1$. For example, we might have $Q = 10K^{0.4}L^{0.5}$. Then returns to scale are decreasing since $0.4 + 0.5 = 0.9 < 1$.

The model for Q is nonlinear in K and L, making multiple regression seemingly impossible. But standard regression is possible as the model for $\ln Q$ is linear in $\ln K$ and $\ln L$. Taking the natural logarithm of both sides, some algebra yields

$$\begin{aligned} \ln Q &= \ln(\alpha K^{\beta_2} L^{\beta_3}) \\ &= \ln \alpha + \ln(K^{\beta_2}) + \ln(L^{\beta_3}) \\ &= \ln \alpha + \beta_2 \ln K + \beta_3 \ln L \\ &= \beta_1 + \beta_2 \ln K + \beta_3 \ln L, \end{aligned}$$

where $\beta_1 = \ln \alpha$. This result uses the properties of natural logarithm that $\ln(a \times b) = \ln a + \ln b$ and $\ln a^b = b \ln a$.

It follows that the Cobb-Douglas production function can be estimated by OLS regression of $\ln Q$ on an intercept, $\ln K$ and $\ln L$. This is a special case of the log-log model with two regressors; see Chapter 9.3 for the bivariate case.

13.2.2   Data Description

Dataset COBBDOUGLAS has U.S. aggregate data on manufacturing for the 24 years from 1899 to 1922. These data come from, respectively, Tables VI, II and III of Cobb and Douglas (1928).

Table 13.4: Cobb-Douglas data: Listing for U.S. from 1899 to 1922 (n=24).

Year	Q	K	L	Year	Q	K	L
1899	100	100	100	1911	153	216	145
1900	101	107	105	1912	177	226	152
1901	112	114	110	1913	184	236	154
1902	122	122	118	1914	169	244	149
1903	124	131	123	1915	189	266	154
1904	122	138	116	1916	225	298	182
1905	143	149	125	1917	227	335	196
1906	152	163	133	1918	223	366	200
1907	151	176	138	1919	218	387	193
1908	126	185	121	1920	231	407	193
1909	155	198	140	1921	179	417	147
1910	159	208	144	1922	240	431	161

Table 13.4 presents the data on output (Q), capital (K) and labor (L) that are normalized to equal 100 in 1899. From the data in Table 13.4, over this period output more than doubled, capital input quadrupled, and labor input less than doubled. The capital/output ratio (K/Q) increased, the labor/output ratio (L/Q) decreased, and the capital/labor ratio (K/L) increased (it more than doubled). So production has become more capital intensive.

The variables are highly correlated, with the pairwise correlations between $\ln Q$, $\ln K$ and $\ln L$ all in excess of 0.90. The variables are also highly autocorrelated.

The first panel of Figure 13.3 plots the dependent variable over time and it is clear that the data are autocorrelated. The first-order autocorrelation, the correlation between $\ln Q$ and $\ln Q$ in the previous year, equals 0.89.

After inclusion of regressors some of the autocorrelation may disappear. The second panel of Figure 13.3 presents a plot of the OLS residual from regression of $\ln Q$ on an intercept and $\ln K$ and $\ln L$. The residuals are not very autocorrelated, and in fact the first three autocorrelations of the residual are $\widehat{\rho}_1 = 0.11$, $\widehat{\rho}_2 = -0.16$, and $\widehat{\rho}_3 = -0.16$.

Given this low autocorrelation of the residuals it might be reasonable to just use heteroskedastic-robust standard errors. However, we follow the standard approach of using HAC standard errors, see Chapter 12.1.5, with lag length 3 since $0.75T^{1/3} = 0.75 \times 24^{1/3} = 2.16$.

13.2.3 Multiple Regression

The regression results (with Newey-West HAC standard errors computed with lag length 3) are

$$\widehat{\ln Q} = -0.177 + 0.233 \times \ln K + 0.807 \times \ln L, \ s_e = 0.0581, \ R^2 = 0.957.$$
$$\underset{(0.398)}{} \quad \underset{(0.062)}{} \quad \underset{(0.134)}{}$$

By comparison heteroskedastic-robust standard errors are, respectively, 0.548, 0.105 and 0.216, and default standard errors are, respectively, 0.434, 0.064 and 0.145.

The model fits the data very well, with high R^2, and the coefficients of $\ln K$ and $\ln L$ are reasonably precisely estimated and are highly statistically significant at level 0.05.

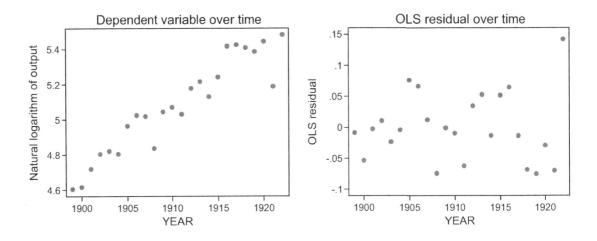

Figure 13.3: Cobb-Douglas production function: Plots of lnq and OLS residual over time

13.2.4   Test of Constant Returns to Scale

To test whether returns to scale are constant we test $H_0 : \beta_2 + \beta_3 = 1$ against $H_a : \beta_2 + \beta_3 \neq 1$. Since $b_2 + b_3 = 0.233 + 0.807 = 1.040$ the estimates sum to close to one. Using a specialized test command we obtain $F = 0.23$ with $p = 0.64$ so the null hypothesis is not rejected at significance level 0.05. The data support constant returns to scale.

13.2.5   Test of the Specified Parameter Values

Cobb and Douglas did not estimate this model by linear regression, but instead set $\beta_2 = 0.25$ and $\beta_3 = 0.75$. The estimated coefficients, $b_2 = 0.233$ and $b_3 = 0.807$, are individually not statistically different from these values. For example, for test of $H_0 : \beta_3 = 0$ the test statistic $t = (0.807 - 0.75)/0.134 = 0.43$.

The joint test of $H_0 : \beta_2 = 0.25$, $\beta_3 = 0.75$ against H_0 : at least one of $\beta_2 \neq 0.25$, $\beta_3 \neq 0.75$ does not lead to rejection of the parameter values specified by Cobb and Douglas, since a specialized test command yields $F = 0.89$ with $p = 0.889$.

13.2.6   Predicted Output

To predict the level of output we cannot simply predict $\ln q$ and then exponentiate. As explained in Chapter 15.6 for fitted log-linear model $\widehat{\ln y} = b_1 + b_2 x$ we use as prediction in levels $\widehat{y} = \exp(s_e^2/2)\exp(b_1 + b_2 x)$, where s_e is the standard error of the $\ln y$ regression and the additional

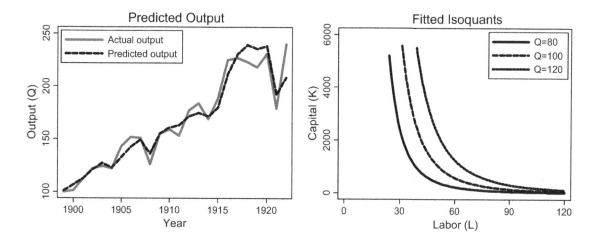

Figure 13.4: Cobb-Douglas production function: Predicted output and fitted isoquants

term $\exp(s_e^2/2)$ arises due to transformation from predicting $\ln y$ to predicting y. It follows that

$$
\begin{aligned}
\widehat{Q} &= \exp(s_e^2/2) \times \exp(-0.177 + 0.233\ln K + 0.807 \times \ln L) \\
&= \exp(0.0581^2/2) \times \exp(-0.177) \times K^{.233} \times L^{.807} \\
&= 1.0017 \times 0.838 \times K^{.233} \times L^{.807} \\
&= 0.839 \times K^{.233} L^{.807}.
\end{aligned}
$$

The potential retransformation bias here is small as $\exp(0.0581^2/2) = 1.0017$ is close to 1. Using the estimated coefficients yields $\widehat{Q}$ with mean 166.0, quite close to Q with mean 165.9.

The first panel of Figure 13.4 plots actual Q and predicted Q against time. The fit is quite good, though in the final year (1922) actual output was much higher than that predicted given the 1922 levels of capital and labor.

13.2.7 Fitted Isoquants

An isoquant plots capital (K) as a function of labor (L) for a given level of output (Q).

In general the isoquants can be obtained from the Cobb-Douglas production function using

$$
\begin{aligned}
Q &= \alpha K^{\beta_2} L^{\beta_3} \\
\Rightarrow \quad K^{\beta_2} &= Q/(\alpha L^{\beta_3}) \\
&= \alpha^{-1} Q L^{-\beta_3} \\
\Rightarrow \quad K &= \alpha^{-1/\beta_2} Q^{1/\beta_2} L^{-\beta_3/\beta_2}.
\end{aligned}
$$

For the estimated Cobb-Douglas function this yields $K = 2.144 \times Q^{4.29} \times L^{-3.46}$. (This ignores the log transformation bias, for simplicity.

The second panel of Figure 13.4 plots three isoquants with output set to $Q = 80$, $Q = 100$, and $Q = 120$, and with labor varying from $L = 30$ to $L = 120$. As expected the isoquants do not cross so that increasing both capital and labor necessarily increases output.

13.3 Phillips Curve

The **Phillips curve** is a curve that plots price inflation against unemployment. The curve was proposed by Phillips (1958) who found a negative relationship. The explanation is that an increase in money supply may stimulate the economy in the short-run, leading to lower unemployment accompanied by some increase in wages. While Phillips considered wage inflation it subsequently became standard to analyze the relationship between price inflation and unemployment.

The relationship observed by Phillips had a strong effect on macroeconomic policy, especially in the 1960's, as it offered the possibility of lowering unemployment at the mild expense of somewhat higher price inflation. At the same time it spawned a fierce debate as to whether this relationship held in the long-run.

13.3.1 Data Description

Table 13.5 presents variable definitions and summary statistics for dataset PHILLIPS that has annual U.S. data from 1949 to 2014. We focus on inflation measured by the GDP implicit price deflator. The more extended analysis uses expectations of future price inflation, specifically the median across forecasters of the one-year ahead expectations of inflation measured by the GDP implicit price deflator. The series comes from the Survey of Professional Forecasters conducted by the Federal Reserve Bank of Philadelphia, and is available only from 1970 on.

Table 13.5: Phillips curve data: Variable definitions and summary statistics (n=65)

Variable	Definition	Obs	Mean	Standard deviation	Min	Max
Urate	Civilian unemployment rate (percentage)	66	5.87	1.63	2.70	10.80
Inflgdp	Annual inflation rate in GDP implicit price deflator	66	3.20	2.32	-1.97	10.51
Inflpgdp1yr	Forecast of one-year ahead *Inflgdp*	45	3.31	2.05	1.14	8.67

13.3.2 Bivariate Regression - Phillips Curve pre-1970

Figure 13.5 presents both a time series plot (first panel) and a scatter plot of CPI inflation and unemployment (second panel) for the period 1949 to 1969. It is clear that there is a negative relationship between the two series.

OLS regression using data from 1949 to 1969 yields

$$\widehat{Inflgdp} = 7.106 - 1.030 \times Urate, \ s_e = 1.315, \ R^2 = 0.454, \ n = 21,$$
$$\underset{(4.49)}{} \ \underset{(-3.17)}{}$$

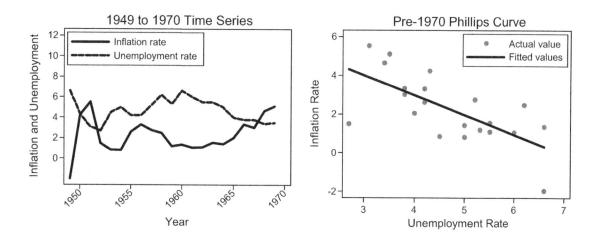

Figure 13.5: Phillips curve: 1949 to 1969.

where t statistics given in parentheses are based on HAC standard errors with lag length set at 3 since $0.75 \times 21^{1/3} = 2.07$; see Chapter 12.1.5.

There is a negative relationship between inflation and the unemployment, and the regressor is statistically significant at level 0.05 since $|t| = 2.91 > t_{19,.025} = 2.09$. A lowering in the unemployment rate of one percentage point is associated with a 1.03 percentage point increase in annual inflation, which might be viewed as a reasonable trade-off.

The errors in this time series model are potentially correlated over time, so HAC standard errors have been used. The residuals are not highly correlated here, as the first three autocorrelations are $\widehat{\rho}_1 = 0.11$, $\widehat{\rho}_2 = -0.18$, and $\widehat{\rho}_3 = 0.04$. Heteroskedastic-robust standard errors yield t statistic for *Urate* equal to -2.91 and default standard errors yield $t = -3.97$. In all cases *Urate* is statistically significant at significance level 0.05.

13.3.3 Bivariate Regression - Phillips Curve post-1970

The pre-1970 estimates suggest that by running an expansionary monetary policy one can enjoy low unemployment at the cost of a modest increase in price inflation. The monetarist economist Milton Friedman in a 1968 paper objected to this line of reasoning, arguing that people would eventually adapt their expectations to higher price inflation so that the expansionary monetary policy would have no real effect. His predictions were borne out and led to richer models.

The first panel of Figure 13.6 presents time series plots for the period 1970 to 2014. If anything it appears that the two series often move in the same direction.

OLS regression using data from 1970 to 2014 yields

$$\widehat{Inflgdp} = \underset{(1.87)}{1.928} + \underset{(0.81)}{0.266} \times Urate, \ s_e = 2.442, \ R^2 = 0.028, \ n = 45,$$

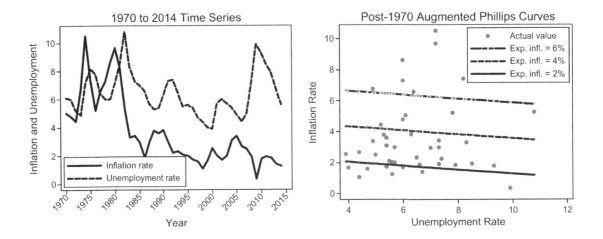

Figure 13.6: Phillips curve: 1970 to 2014.

where t statistics given in parentheses are based on HAC standard errors with lag length set at 5.

The residuals for the post-1970 period are now highly autocorrelated, with the first three autocorrelations being $\widehat{\rho}_1 = 0.84$, $\widehat{\rho}_2 = 0.62$, and $\widehat{\rho}_3 = 0.53$. So the HAC robust standard errors are computed with lag length five, greater than the Chapter 12.1.5 rule-of-thumb value of three $(0.75 \times 21\,\hat{}\,(1/3) = 2.67)$. Heteroskedastic standard errors lead to $t = 1.14$, and default standard errors yield $t = 1.11$.

There is a now a surprising positive relationship between inflation and the unemployment, though the regressor is statistically insignificant at level 0.05 since $|t| = 1.11 < t_{43,.025} = 2.02$.

13.3.4 Multiple Regression - Augmented Phillips Curve

Clearly the Phillips curve relationship broke down, beginning in the 1970's.

One possible explanation is that the stimulatory effect of an increase in money supply varies according to whether inflationary expectations are high or low. If people expect high price inflation, then an increase in money supply of 5%, say, would merely support these expectations and provide no stimulatory effect. But if people expect little price inflation, then an increase in money supply of 5% may have a major stimulatory effect with a lower increase in price inflation and a decrease in the unemployment rate.

The **augmented Phillips curve** includes an additional regressor, the **expected inflation rate**, in the regression of the inflation rate on the unemployment rate.

The practical problem is to obtain a measure of expected inflation. One way to determine this is through a survey of inflationary expectations of randomly chosen individuals or of professional business cycle forecasters. Such surveys are done, though generally they are available in more recent years. One of the oldest available measures is the series on one-year ahead expectations of inflation measured by the GDP implicit price deflator. This forecast comes from the Survey of Professional

Forecasters conducted by the Federal Reserve Bank of Philadelphia, and is available from 1970.
OLS regression using data from 1970 to 2014 yields

$$\widehat{Inflgdp} = \underset{(0.43)}{0.270} - \underset{(-1.58)}{0.128} \times Urate + \underset{(13.48)}{1.146} \times Inflgdp1yr, \quad s_e = 0.86, \ R^2 = 0.881, \ n = 45,$$

where t statistics given in parentheses are based on HAC standard errors with lag length set at 5.

The coefficient of expected price inflation is close to one, so there is approximately a one-to-one relationship between expected inflation and inflation. The standard error of b_3 equals 0.085, so a 95% confidence interval for b_3 is $1.146 \pm t_{42,.025} \times .085 = (0.97, 1.32)$. This is close to containing the value one, but since it does not we marginally reject $H_0 : \beta_3 = 1$ against $H_0 : \beta_3 \neq 1$ at significance level 5%.

After controlling for expected price inflation the coefficient of the unemployment rate is now negative, as in the original Phillips curve. But the coefficient is not statistically significant at 5%, as $|t| = 1.58 < t_{43,.025} = 2.02$.

The residuals have first four autocorrelations of $\widehat{\rho}_1 = 0.59$, $\widehat{\rho}_2 = 0.37$, $\widehat{\rho}_3 = 0.41$ and $\widehat{\rho}_4 = 0.35$, so we have used HAC robust standard errors.

We conclude that the breakdown in the Phillips curve can be attributed to the omission of expected price inflation as a regressor. After controlling for inflationary expectations, there is an inverse relationship between price inflation and the unemployment rate.

13.3.5 Predictions

The augmented Phillips curve relationship can be represented by a series of regular Phillips curves, where each curve is given for a different expected inflation rate. For example, for an expected inflation rate of 2.0% we have

$$\widehat{Inflgdp} = 0.270 - 0.128 \times Urate + 1.146 \times 2 = 2.562 - 0.128 \times Urate.$$

The second panel of Figure 13.6 plots augmented Phillips curves for expected inflation rates of 2%, 4% and 6%. It is clear that as inflationary expectations increase, the Phillips curve shifts up and out.

13.3.6 Omitted Variables Bias

The observed sign reversal for the coefficient of $Urate$ is a classic example of omitted variables bias. The true model is

$$Inflgdp = \beta_1 + \beta_2 \times Urate + \beta_3 \times Inflgdp1yr + u_t.$$

Mistakenly running a regression of $Inflgdp$ on $Urate$ alone yields estimate $Inflgdp = b_1 + b_2 \times Urate$. Omitted variables bias is presented in Chapter 16.3, where it is stated that

$$E[b_2] = \beta_2 + \beta_3 \gamma,$$

where γ is the coefficient of $Urate$ in a regression of the omitted variable $Inflgdp1yr$ on $Urate$.

Table 13.6: Automobiles fuel efficiency: Summary Statistics (n=14,423)

Variable	Definition	Mean	Standard deviation	Min	Max
year	Year	-	-	1980	2006
idmfr	Unique numeric identifier for manufacturer	-	-	1	45
mpg	Miles per gallon	27.90	6.43	8.7	76.4
curbwt	Unloaded wight of vehicle in pounds	3019.53	593.64	1450	6200
hp	Horsepower	157.10	76.96	48	660
torque	Torque	238.68	105.13	69.4	1001
d_truck	= 1 if light (pickup) truck, = 0 if car	0.00	0.00	0	0
d_manual	= 1 if manual transmission, = 0 otherwise	0.38	0.49	0	1
time_d_manual	d_manual times (year - 1979)	5.10	8.04	0	27
d_diesel	= 1 if uses diesel fuel, = 0 otherwise	0.03	0.18	0	1
d_turbo	= 1 if turbocharged, = 0 otherwise	0.11	0.31	0	1
d_super	= 1 if supercharged, = 0 otherwise	0.01	0.11	0	1

From the multiple regression we have estimates of β_2 and β_3 of -0.128 and 1.146. Separate bivariate regression of *Inflgdp1yr* on *Urate*, not detailed here, yields a slope estimate of γ of 0.343. Then $\widehat{E[b_2]} = -0.128 + 1.146 \times 0.343 = 0.266$, which is the previously obtained estimated coefficient of *Urate* from regression of *Inflgdp* on just *Urate*.

13.4   Automobile Fuel Efficiency

A major goal of public policy has been to improve the fuel efficiency of automobiles. The study, reproduced in part below, shows that there has been considerable improvement in fuel efficiency but that much of this has been undone by a consumer switch to bigger and more powerful vehicles.

13.4.1   Data Description

Dataset AUTOSMPG has annual data on most models of cars and light trucks on sale in the U.S. from 1980 to 2006. The original source is the article by Knittel (2012). The original dataset had 27,871 observations. Dataset AUTOSMPG follows the original study and does not include 876 observations that are dropped due to missing data or obvious coding errors. The remaining 26,995 observations are on 14,423 cars (*d_truck*= 0) and 12,572 trucks (*d_truck*= 1) that weigh less than 8,500 pounds. In this section only cars are analyzed.

Table 13.6 presents variable definitions and summary statistics for cars.

13.4.2   Graphical Analysis

Key determinants of fuel efficiency are engine power and vehicle weight.

The first panel of Figure 13.7 provides a plot of *mpg* against *hp* for cars in the years 1980 and 2006 along with Lowess nonparametric regression curves, Note that this figure restricts attention

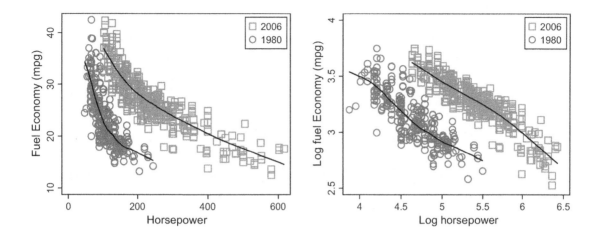

Figure 13.7: Automobiles fuel efficiency: Plot of fule conomy against horsepower

to cars that are fueled by gasoline (about 96% of the cars). The curves show a strong negative relationship. There is marked improvement in fuel efficiency over the 26 years, with an increase of approximately ten miles per gallon for a given level of horsepower. Finally note that horsepower has increased markedly over this period, and the purpose of the article by Knittel was to establish that virtually all the gains in efficiency were negated by a movement to more powerful and larger vehicles.

The second panel of Figure 13.7 is a variation that plots the natural logarithms of *mpg* and *hp*. Comparing the two curves, the fuel efficiency over the 26 years has increased by about 0.5 on a log scale, or by around 65% ($= 100 \times (\exp(0.5) - 1)$).

The second panel of Figure 13.7 indicates a relationship that is close to linear in logs. Similar graphs for *mpg* against *curbwt* and *lmpg* against *lcurbwt* again show a negative relationship that is also close to linear in logs. Thus a log-log regression model is estimated below.

13.4.3 Regression Analysis

The basic model is a log-log model with dependent variable *lmpg* and regressors *lcurbwt*, *lhp* and *ltorque* that control for car weight and engine size. Additional variables are whether the car has a manual transmission (*d_manual*), a time trend in this variable (*d_manual_time*), and various engine features (*d_diesel, d_turbo* and *d_super*).

For all regressions standard errors are clustered on manufacturer. This is essential as a given car model often changes little from year to year, so an additional year's data is not adding much new independent information. And even within a given year some car models are very minor variations on a closely-related model. The correct cluster-robust standard errors are approximately five times incorrect heteroskedastic-robust standard errors; see Chapter 13.4.4.

The first model presented in Table 13.7 adds a linear time trend. All regressors except *lcurbwt*

Table 13.7: Automobile fuel efficiency: Multiple regression estimates with cluster-robust standard errors.

Dependent Variable *lmpg* (ln(*mpg*))						
	Time trend		Time dummies		Mfr fixed effects	
Variable	Coefficient	St. Error	Coefficient	St. Error	Coefficient	St. Error
lcurbwt	-0.415	0.052	-0.398	0.046	-0.383	0.032
lhp	-0.294	0.046	-0.324	0.047	-0.268	0.039
ltorque	-0.047	0.039	-0.019	0.038	-0.064	0.030
d_manual	0.084	0.013	0.087	0.013	0.101	0.013
time_*d_manual*	-0.004	0.001	-0.004	0.001	-0.004	0.001
d_diesel	0.191	0.019	0.196	0.018	0.212	0.017
d_turbo	0.028	0.011	0.025	0.010	0.051	0.010
d_super	0.049	0.019	0.055	0.017	0.034	0.011
year	0.017	0.001	-	-	-	-
intercept	-25.914	1.843	7.857	0.254	7.686	0.200
time dummies	No		Yes		Yes	
manufacturer FEs?	No		No		Yes	
R-squared	0.824		0.838		0.883	
Observations	14423		14423		14423	

are statistically significant at 5%. The coefficients are meaningfully large. Controlling for other regressors, a 10% increase in vehicle weight is associated with a 4.1% decrease in fuel efficiency, and a 10% increase in engine horsepower is associated with a 2.9% decrease in fuel efficiency.

Controlling for the various vehicle attributes there has been a very substantial improvement in fuel efficiency. The coefficient of the time trend is 0.0172, so over the 26 years from 1980 to 2006 car miles per gallon has increased by $26 \times 0.0172 = 0.447$ on a log scale, or by 56 percent $(= \exp(0.447) - 1)$!

The second fitted model in Table 13.7 estimated replaces the linear time trend (variable *year*) with a more flexible set of indicator variables for each year, with a dummy for 1980 the omitted dummy. There is little change in coefficient estimates, which are exactly the same as those for Model 1 in table 2 of the Knittel paper. The dummies increase in an approximately linear fashion. The omitted category is 1980 and the dummy for 2006 has coefficient with 0.522, a difference of 0.522 that is consistent with the linear time trend estimate of a 0.447 increase from 1980 to 2006.

The final model in Table 13.7 adds a set of indicator variables for each manufacturer. Again there is little change in coefficient estimates. The manufacturer dummy coefficients range from -0.401 for Lamborghini to 0.068 for Toyota and can be compared to the omitted manufacturer which was AMC.

13.4.4   Cluster-robust Standard Errors

A given car model often changes little from year to year, so an additional year's data is not adding much new independent information. And even within a given year some car models are very minor variations on a closely-related model. We therefore obtained cluster-robust standard errors with clustering on car manufacturer. This assumes that errors for observations on different manufacturers are uncorrelated, but for different observations (car model and/or year) from the same manufacturer there can be arbitrary correlation and heteroskedasticity.

In this example there are 14,423 observations and 38 manufacturers, so the average cluster size is $14423/38 = 379.6$ observations. Consider, for example, the estimated OLS coefficient of *lhp* in the first fitted model in Table 13.7. Specialized commands provide the within-cluster correlation of the OLS residual, $\widehat{\rho}_e = 0.267$, and the within-cluster correlation of *lhp*, $\widehat{\rho}_{lhp} = 0.301$. The approximate standard error inflation formula given in Chapter 12.1.4 yields $\tau_{lhp} \simeq \sqrt{1 + 0.301 \times 0.267 \times (379.6 - 1)} = 5.61$. In fact variable *lhp* had cluster-robust standard error of 0.04552 that was 5.75 times the heteroskedastic-robust standard error of 0.00792 and 7.75 times the default standard error of 0.00587.

13.5 Rand Health Insurance Experiment

Health insurance, like any other form of insurance reduces an individual's exposure to risk. This leads to welfare gain as consumers are usually risk-averse. At the same time health insurance reduces the effective price or net price paid by the consumer. This may lead to a welfare loss due to overconsumption of health services, just as a subsidy on a good can lead to welfare loss.

A big issue in health care policy is therefore measuring how price responsive is the use of health care services. A simple method regresses health care use on the level of health insurance. In countries with universal health insurance all consumers have the same basic insurance, so such analysis is restricted to measuring the effect of supplemental insurance that provides increased cover beyond the basic cover. In the U.S. this approach is less restrictive as there is a very wide range of health insurance policies across individuals (including no insurance).

13.5.1 Experiment and Data Description

In either case, however, regression of health care use on the level of health insurance that is chosen by the individual measures only association, and not causation. Individuals with greater demand for health care can be expected to self select into choosing a higher level of health insurance. A finding that a higher level of health insurance is associated with higher use of health care services combines increase due to self selection and increase due to lower prices. The self selection can be partly controlled for by including as regressors various health status measures, such as the number of chronic conditions, and demographic variables, such as age and education. But there remain unobservable factors that are correlated with health insurance level, so OLS is biased and inconsistent as assumption 2 is violated.

As a result, the U.S. government funded the Rand Health Insurance Experiment conducted in the 1970s. This was a large social experiment where different families were randomly assigned health insurance policies with different levels of insurance cover. Specifically, different policies had different coinsurance rates where the coinsurance rate is the percentage of health costs paid by the individual. For example, with 25% coinsurance the insured pays 25% and the insurance company pays 75%. Experiment details and results are given in Manning, Newhouse, Duan, Keeler,

Table 13.8: RAND Health Insurance Experiment: Year 1 summary statistics (n=5,639)

Variable	Definition	Mean	Standard deviation	Min	Max
plan	Insurance plan	-	-	1	6
year	Year of plan	1	0	1	1
coins0	= 1 if 0% coinsurance (free) and = 0 otherwise	0.332	0.471	0	1
coins25	= 1 if 25% coinsurance and = 0 otherwise	0.113	0.317	0	1
coinsmixed	= 1 if 25/50% coinsurance and = 0 otherwise	0.085	0.279	0	1
coins50	= 1 if 50% coinsurance and = 0 otherwise	0.066	0.249	0	1
coinsindiv	= 1 if 0% coinsurance and = 0 otherwise	0.216	0.411	0	1
coins95	= 1 if 95% coinsurance and = 0 otherwise	0.187	0.390	0	1
coinsrate	modified coinsurance rate	0.394	0.351	0	1
mde	maximum deductible expenditure	418.5	381.2	0	1000
spending	Inpatient and outpatient spending (in 2011 \$)	1679.5	4968.1	0	175831
oop	Out-of-pocket expenditure	228.6	463.2	0	4341

Leibowitz, and Marquis (1987). The dataset used here comes from the reanalysis by Aron-Dine, Einav and Finkelstein (2013).

Dataset HEALTHINSEXP has 20,203 individual-year observations on 5,915 individuals in 2,205 families that were mostly in the experiment for either three years or five years. Some variables change from year to year, while others were collected at the start of participation in the experiment and do not change from year to year. Spending is measured in 2011 dollars.

In this chapter we use just data for the first year of the experiment and use only selected variables. We analyze variable *spending* which is total spending, the sum of outpatient (outside hospital) and inpatient (in hospital) spending.

There were six different insurance plans ranging from 0% coinsurance (free care) to 95% coinsurance. For plans with positive coinsurance the coinsurance rate reverted to 0% once the annual maximum deductible (*mde*) was reached. A mixed plan (*coinsmixed*) had 25% coinsurance except for 50% mental and dental care and is calculated to have an average coinsurance rate of 31.897%. The sixth plan (*coinsindiv*=1) had 95% coinsurance for outpatient services (up to a low MDE) and 0% for inpatient services for an average 57.67825% coinsurance rate.

Table 13.8 presents summary statistics for these variables. The coinsurance indicator variables are ordered in terms of increasing coinsurance rate of the plan, so *coinsindiv* (plan 6) appears before *coins95* (plan 5).

13.5.2   Variation in Spending with Health Insurance Plan

Interest lies in measuring the extent to which health spending varied with the generosity of the health insurance plan. Here we analyze data for just the first year of the experiment.

Simple summary statistics give average spending of \$2,154, \$1,397, \$1,702, \$1,786, \$1,697 and \$1,046 in, respectively, the 0%, 25%, mixed, 50%, individual deductible and 95% plans. So on balance health spending is higher with more generous health insurance.

Table 13.9: RAND Health Insurance Experiment: Year 1 regression estimates.

Dependent Variable *spending*						
Variable	Coefficient	St. Error	p value	Coefficient	St. Error	p value
coins25	-757	190	.000	-742	191	.000
coinsmixed	-452	239	.059	-440	240	.067
coins50	-368	618	.552	-324	635	.610
coinsindiv	-546	162	.001	-584	166	.000
coins95	-1108	150	.000	-1103	153	.000
intercept	2154	118	.000	1129	153	.000
age				40.0	4.4	.000
gender				-355	134	.008
badhealth				852	253	.001
goodhealth				322	162	.047
Observations		5639			5380	
F(5,n-k)		11.39			10.9	
p-value for F		0.000			0.000	
R-squared		0.007			0.031	
Adjusted R^2		0.006			0.029	
St. error of regression		4954			4973	

To test for joint statistical significance, and to enable appropriate robust inference, we regress *spending* on an intercept and a set of indicator variables for insurance type, choosing free care (0% coinsurance) as the omitted category. Inference is based on cluster-robust standard errors, with clustering on family.

Table 13.9 presents OLS estimates. Interpretation of results of regression on a set of mutually exclusive indicator variables is presented in Chapter 14.4. The intercept gives the sample average of y for the omitted category. So spending was on average \$2,154 for those with free care. The remaining coefficients give the deviation from the omitted category. For example, those with 25% coinsurance spent on average \$757 less than those in the omitted category; equivalently they spent on average \$1,397 (= 2154 − 757). The insurance policies in terms of decreasing generosity were, in order, 0% coinsurance, 25% coinsurance, 25%/50% mixed, 50% coinsurance, individual deductible and 95% coinsurance. All coefficients of the corresponding indicator variable are negative, as expected given that 0% coinsurance is the omitted category. But they do not exactly decline with increasing coinsurance. For example, the coefficient of *coins50* is less negative than that of *coins25*, but this should not be taken too literally as the coefficient is very imprecisely estimated with a standard error of 618.

The F statistic for overall statistical significance of the five insurance indicator variables takes value 11.39 with $p = 0.000$, so health care use does respond to prices. This key takeaway from the experiment might be obvious to economists but was not so obvious to all health professionals.

Note that the insurance indicator variables explain very little of the variation in spending, as $R^2 = 0.007$ and the standard error of the regression is \$4,954 which is very large compared to mean spending of \$1,679.

13.5.3 Adding Control Variables

To improve model fit we add as regressors *age* (age in years), *gender* (equals 1 if male and 0 if female), and indicator variables for *badhealth* and for *goodhealth* (with excellent health the omitted category).

The estimates are given in the second set of results in Table 13.9. The sample size reduces from 5,639 to 5,380 observations as the health indicators aren't available for all observations. The coefficients of the health insurance indicators are little changed. This is expected as this was a randomized experiment, so by design the additional control variables are essentially uncorrelated with the randomly assigned health insurance policies. The highest correlation between any of the coinsurance indicator variables and any of the four additional regressors is 0.0221 for correlation between *coins0* and *badhealth*.

The model fit is improved somewhat, but $R^2 = 0.031$ is still very low and the standard error of the regression is basically unchanged. As a result there is no real gain in precision, and indeed the standard errors are actually a little larger due to the reduced sample size.

The coefficients of the control variables are all statistically significant at 5%. On average, spending increases by $400 with ten years of aging, is $355 lower for men, and is $852 higher for those in bad health and $322 higher for those in good health compared to those with excellent health.

The reason for the poor fit of the model is that spending is exceptionally right skewed; the 50th, 75th, 95th and 99th percentiles are, respectively, $480, $1,385, $7,012 and $16,206. The large expenditures are due to health incidents such as cancer or heart attack that are difficult to predict. In theory it would be better to model the natural logarithm of expenditure, but 15% of the sample had zero spending and the log of zero is undefined. (The original RAND study additionally included a more complex model that first modeled whether or not spending was positive and then modeled log spending for those with positive spending).

13.5.4 Measuring the Price Elasticity

The simple summary statistics show very clearly substantial price responsiveness. At the extremes, average spending increased from $1,046 on the 95% coinsurance plan to $2,154 on the free plan.

Economists prefer to use the price elasticity to measure price responsiveness. From Chapter 9.2, the elasticity $(\Delta y/y)/(\Delta x/x)$ gives the percentage change in y in response to a one percent change in x.

Elasticity estimates can be obtained by pairwise comparison of plans. For example, the biggest response was between $2,154 for the 0% plan and $1,046 for the 95% plan. The arc elasticity evaluates at midpoint values of y and x and yields

$$Elasticity = \frac{(2154 - 1046)/\frac{(2154+1046)}{2}}{(0 - 95)/\frac{(0+95)}{2}} = -0.346.$$

A one percent increase in price to the consumer (measured by the coinsurance rate) leads to a 0.35 percent reduction in health spending.

From Chapter 9.3 the elasticity can be computed by OLS estimation of a log-log model. This is problematic here due to zero values for both spending and coinsurance rate. An ad hoc method sometimes used for log regression with some zero values of y is to instead use as dependent variable $\ln(y + 1)$. The problematic zero values for the regressor are easily handled by dropping those observations; then the price elasticity estimate is restricted to those individuals who did not have completely free care. OLS regression of $\ln(spending+1)$ on $\ln(coinsrate)$ for the 3,766 observations with positive coinsurance rate yields slope coefficient -0.577 with cluster-robust standard error of 0.148 that is highly statistically significant.

An alternative measure of price is the average out-of-pocket share in each plan (*aveoopshare*), computed as *oop/spending* for each individual with positive spending and then averaged across all individuals in each plan. OLS regression of $\ln(spending+1)$ on $\ln(aveoopshare)$ for the 3,766 observations with positive coinsurance rate yields slope coefficient of -0.566 with cluster-robust standard error of 0.156.

An alternative more advanced regression estimate of the elasticity can be obtained by Poisson regression of *spending* on $\ln(coinsrate)$ or on $\ln(aveoopshare)$; see Chapter 17.6.3 and exercise 27. This yields smaller estimated elasticities of, respectively, -0.224 and -0.175.

While there is a range of estimates, there clearly is a price response and one that is large enough to be important for policy.

13.6 Access to Health Care and Health Outcomes

To what extent does greater access to health care improve health status?

The study by Tanaka (2014) analyzed the effect of improved access in South Africa on the health of very young children.

In 1994 health care use fees in South Africa were abolished for pregnant women and children under the age of six. This substantially increased access for poor black South Africans. The resulting increase in access to health care was greater for children in communities with clinics (a "high-treatment" region) than for those in communities without a clinic (a "low-treatment" region).

This provides a natural experiment, and Tanaka applied a difference-in-differences (DID) strategy to compare the changes in child weight between the communities with and without health clinics, before and after the policy change. We first explain the DID method and then apply it to data from the study.

13.6.1 Difference in Differences

Suppose we have data on two sets of individuals over two periods of time. Both groups are untreated in the first period, while in the second period only one of the groups is treated.

A **treatment-control comparison** compares the outcomes for treated and untreated groups in the second period. So the treatment effect equals $\bar{y}$ for the treated group less $\bar{y}$ for the untreated group. This comparison is misleading if the treated and untreated groups differ in their characteristics.

A **before-after comparison** compares the outcome over time for just the group who were treated in the second period. So the treatment effect equals $\bar{y}$ for the treated group after treatment less $\bar{y}$ for the treated group before treatment. This comparison is misleading if other changes over time also effect the outcome for the treated.

Difference in differences combines these two methods. It uses change over time for the untreated group to control for changes over time that are unrelated with treatment. Let $\Delta\bar{y}_{tr}$ denote the change over time in the average outcome for those in the treated group and $\Delta\bar{y}_{untr}$ denote the change over time in the average outcome for those untreated. Then the treatment effect equals $\Delta\bar{y}_{tr} - \Delta\bar{y}_{untr}$, which is a difference in a difference.

Given individual-level data it can be shown that the DID estimate can be computed as the estimate of β_4 in the OLS regression

$$y_i = \beta_1 + \beta_2 T_i + \beta_3 d_i + \beta_4 T_i \times d_i + u_i,$$

where $d_i = 1$ if in the treatment group and $d_i = 0$ otherwise, and $T_i = 1$ one in the second period and $T_i = 0$ zero in the first. This is often written as

$$y_i = \beta_1 + \beta_2 Post_i + \beta_3 Treat_i + \beta_4 Post_i \times Treat_i + u_i,$$

where *Post* is an indicator equal to one in the post-treatment period.

The key assumption for the validity of this method is that the treated and untreated groups would have the same trend (or **parallel trend**) over time in the absence of treatment.

The regression formulation of the DID method enables inference to be based on robust standard errors. And additional regressors can be included that may make the assumption of parallel trends more reasonable and may improve estimator precision by reducing the standard error of the regression. The model can be extended to more than two time periods.

13.6.2   Data Description

The sample is of young African children (where African means not white, colored or Indian) with data from a longitudinal household survey in the KwaZulu-Natal province of South Africa. Households were surveyed in 1993 and again in 1998 (with an 85% follow-up rate). The households were in 54 communities of which 26 had access to a health care clinic in 1993 (the high-treatment group) and 28 were without a health care clinic in 1993 (the low-treatment group).

Table 13.10 presents variable definitions and summary statistics for dataset HEALTHACCESS that has data restricted to those children less than four years old.

The outcome variable we use is the weight-for-age z-score (variable *waz*) which is standardized to have mean 0 and variance 1 for a benchmark U.S. population of children.

13.6.3   Non-regression Estimate

The following table gives the mean values of *waz* for the high treated and low treated children, before and after the expansion in free health care.

Table 13.10: South African community clinics: Summary statistics (n=1,071)

Variable	Definition	Mean	Standard deviation	Min	Max
idcommunity	Identifier for community	-	-	59	244
year	= 93 if 1993 and = 98 if 1998	-	-	93	98
hightreat	= 1 if in community with clinic in 1993	0.428	0.495	0	1
post	= 1 if year = 98 and = 0 if year=93	0.467	0.499	0	1
postXtreat	*post* times *treat*	0.198	0.399	0	1
waz	Weight-for-age z-score	-0.206	1.588	-5.88	4.94
whz	Weight-for-height z-score	0.639	2.120	-9.89	9.99
fedu	Father's education	1.76	3.10	0	12
medu	Mother's education	4.73	3.64	0	12
hhsizep	Household size	11.17	5.13	2	34
lntotminc	Log Monthly household income	6.83	1.02	3.55	9.85
nonclinic	# of other types of health infrastructure	0.108	0.427	0	3
immuniz	Immunization campaign	0.491	0.547	0	2
age	Precise age in fractions of years	2.145	1.057	0	3.992

	High treated	Low treated
Before (1993)	-0.545 ($n = 246$)	-0.414 ($n = 325$)
After (1998)	0.322 ($n = 212$)	-0.069 ($n = 288$)
Change over time	0.867	0.345
Difference in differences		0.522

Before the treatment the weight-for-age measure was half a standard deviation below the benchmark. The increased access to free care led to *waz* increasing on average from -0.545 to 0.322 for the high treated children, a gain of 0.867. For low treated children there was also a gain, from -0.414 to -0.069, a gain of 0.345. The average gain for the high treated was greater, and leads to a DID estimate of $0.867 - 0.345 = 0.522$. This is a very substantial effect.

13.6.4 Regression Estimates

Table 13.11 presents OLS regression estimates for several models with dependent variable *waz* and cluster-robust standard errors clustered on community. These reproduce results given in Table 3 of the Tanaka paper.

The first OLS regression reproduces the preceding manual calculations and yields a DID estimate of 0.522, given in the first row of the table. The standard error is 0.235, so $t = 2.22$ and the effect is statistically significant at 5%. The second regression adds six regressors as control variables. These variables have the expected signs and increase R^2 from 0.040 to 0.061 and lead to little change in the DID estimate.

The two remaining columns include two sets of indicator variables as regressors. First, a set of eight mutually exclusive age indicators are added: four yearly age dummies (for ages 0, 1, 2 and 3)

Table 13.11: South African community clinics: Difference-in-differences regression estimates.

Variable	Basic	Add controls	Indicators	Indicators + Controls
postXhigh	0.522	0.516	0.571	0.638
	(0.235)	(0.227)	(0.250)	(0.268)
post	0.345	-0.823		
	(0.137)	(0.262)		
hightreat	-0.131	-0.142		
	(0.197)	(0.191)		
fedu		0.019		0.016
		(0.016)		(0.019)
medu		0.000		-0.014
		(0.016)		(0.016)
hhsizep		-0.008		-0.014
		(0.010)		(0.010)
lntotminc		0.145		0.155
		(0.055)		(0.055)
immuniz		1.070		0.925
		(0.220)		(0.302)
nonclinic		-0.167		-0.330
		(0.141)		(0.182)
intercept	-0.414	-1.302	-0.222	-2.059
	(0.115)	(0.351)	(0.148)	(0.407)
Age indicators	No	No	Yes	Yes
Community fixed effects	No	No	Yes	Yes
R-squared	0.040	0.061	0.197	0.211

in each of the pre-period 1993 and the post-period 1998. Usually only one of these eight dummies needs to be dropped to avoid the dummy variable trap; see Chapter 14.4. Here the variable *post* is 0 in 1993 and 1 in 1998 so a second age dummy needs to be dropped. We drop the dummy for age 0 in 1993 and the dummy for age 0 in 1998. Second, a set of 54 mutually exclusive community indicators are added, with the first community the omitted dummy. These models led to estimated effects of, respectively, 0.571 and 0.638 that are again statistically significant at 5%.

13.7   Gains from Political Incumbency

If a political party just wins a seat there is a substantial bump in the probability of retaining the seat in a subsequent election compared to if they just lose this seat. This advantage arises due to incumbency benefits such as increased staff support, press coverage, political donations, name recognition, and so on.

We estimate this incumbency advantage for the U.S. Senate, using dataset INCUMBENCY on 1,390 Senate seat elections from 1914 to 2010 due to Calonico, Cattaneo, Farrell, and Titiunik (2017). Senators hold office for six years in overlapping terms so that one-third of the Senate (which currently has 100 members) is up for election every two years. Additional elections are held if a

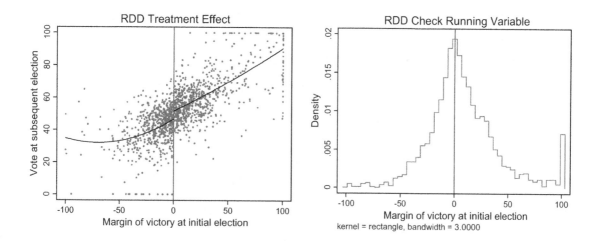

Figure 13.8: Gains from political incumbency: Regression discontinuity design plots

Senator leaves office prematurely.

This setup is an example of **regression discontinuity design** (RDD), where an outcome y depends on a running variable s and a treatment ($d = 1$) occurs if the running variable s crosses a threshold; see also Chapter 17.5.7 for a brief discussion.

Here the outcome y is the Democratic Party vote share (variable *vote*) in the subsequent election, the running or forcing variable s is the Democratic Party margin of victory (variable *margin*) in the previous Senate seat election, and the treatment d is variable *wins* that is a binary variable that takes value 1 if *margin* > 0 and value 0 if margin < 0. Variables *vote* and *margin* are measured as a percentage of the total vote and have sample means equal to, respectively, 52.67 and 7.17, so the Democratic Party had an edge over the Republican Party over this period.

13.7.1 Graphical Analysis

RDD applications lend themselves well to an initial graphical analysis.

The first panel of Figure 13.8 presents a scatter plot of *vote* against *margin*. The two fitted lines are obtained by separate quadratic regressions for *margin* < 0 and *margin* > 0. The gap at zero is an estimate of the treatment effect, and suggests an incumbent advantage of around five percent which is quite substantial.

One should check that the running variable s changes as expected at the threshold value. For example, in some settings individuals may be able to manipulate the running variable enough to nudge over the threshold and receive a desirable treatment. This is unlikely here.

The second panel of Figure 13.8 provides a simple visual check using a kernel density plot of *margins* that uses a narrow bandwidth and rectangular kernel to plot the fraction of observations in each bin of width 3. (The plot is equivalent to a histogram with a bin width of 3.) It shows no aberrant behavior around the threshold of *margins* $= 0$.

Table 13.12: Gains from political incumbency: Regression discontinuity design regression estimates.

Variable	No treatment	Linear	Quadratic	Local
win	–	4.785	4.935	6.750
		(0.860)	(1.129)	(1.712)
margin	0.397	0.348	0.421	0.169
	(0.013)	(0.017)	(0.079)	(0.277)
marginsq			0.003	-0.003
			(0.001)	(0.011)
win × margin			-0.095	0.283
			(0.097)	(0.355)
win × marginsq			-0.002	-0.007
			(0.001)	(0.015)
intercept	49.537	47.331	46.740	45.299
	(0.341)	(0.526)	(0.842)	(1.334)
Sample	All	All	All	|margin|<25
Observations	1297	1297	1297	845
R-squared	0.569	0.578	0.591	0.290

13.7.2 Regression Analysis

Table 13.12 presents OLS regression estimates of various models with heteroskedastic-robust standard errors; cluster-robust standard errors that cluster on state lead to similar standard errors for the treatment variable *win*.

The first regression excludes the treatment variable. There is a highly statistically significant positive effect of the running variable, with regression towards the mean as the slope coefficient is less than one.

The second model fits the simple model $y_i = \beta_1 + \gamma d_i + \beta_2 s_i + u_i$. This model uses all the data and is linear in the running variable s with the same slope either side of the zero threshold. It yields an estimated treatment effect of 4.785 that is highly statistically significant.

The third model fits separate quadratic relationships either side of the zero threshold; recall that variable *win* takes value 0 and 1. The treatment effect estimate is 6.630. This fitted model is exactly the same as that plotted in the first panel of Figure 13.8.

The final model restricts attention to closer elections, those with $|margin|< 25$, leading to use of 65% of the sample and a treatment effect estimate of 6.750. We conclude the incumbency advantage is substantial, at least five percent of the vote.

The RDD model is conceptually simple but involves several decisions, particularly how flexible a model to use and whether to use all the data or use only data in the neighborhood of the treatment.

Table 13.13: Institutions and country GDP: Summary statistics (n=64)

Variable	Definition	Mean	Standard deviation	Min	Max
logpgp95	Log GDP per capita in 1995 (at PPP)	8.06	1.04	6.11	10.22
avexpr	Average protection against appropriation risk	6.52	1.47	3.5	10.0
logem4	Log settler mortality	4.66	1.26	2.15	7.99

13.8 Institutions and Country GDP

Countries with weaker institutions tend to be economically less prosperous. But is this lower prosperity due to weaker institutions? Perhaps the causality is the reverse, with economic prosperity determining the strength of institutions.

The study by Acemoglu, Johnson and Robinson (2001) used instrumental variables estimation to address this issue. We reproduce part of that study.

13.8.1 Data Description

Dataset INSTITUTIONS has data for 64 countries colonized by Europeans. The outcome variable is the logarithm of GDP per capita in 1995 (*logpgp95*). The measure of institutions used is an index produced by Political Risk Services on the protection against "risk of appropriation" (*avexpr*). Higher values of *avexpr* indicate stronger institutions.

Table 13.13 presents summary statistics for *logpgp95*, *avexpr*, and a third variable (*logem4*) that is explained below.

The first panel of Figure 13.9 plots *logpgp95* against *avexpr*. Stronger institutions are clearly related to higher GDP growth. The fitted regression line has slope 0.522. This implies a very large effect of institutions, as a one standard deviation change in *avexpr* is associated with a $0.522 \times 1.47 = 0.767$ increase in log GDP per capita or a 115% increase in GDP per capita ($= 100 \times (e^{0.767} - 1)$).

At this stage only association is being measured as causation could run the other way, with higher GDP per capita leading to stronger institutions.

13.8.2 Instrumental Variables Regression

To find a causative effect of institutions the study uses instrumental variables (IV) estimation, detailed in Chapter 17.4. As explained there, in the regression model $y = \beta_1 + \beta_2 x + u$ we want an instrument z that (1) is uncorrelated with the error u; and (2) is correlated with the regressor x. The first assumption is an exclusion restriction that z does not directly effect y after inclusion of x as a regressor. This is a nontestable assumption that instead needs to be justified by a priori argument.

The current study proposed using log settler mortality (*logem4*) as an instrument for *avexpr*. The paper on page 1371 states that "The exclusion restriction implied by our instrumental variable regression is that, conditional on the controls included in the regression, the mortality rates of

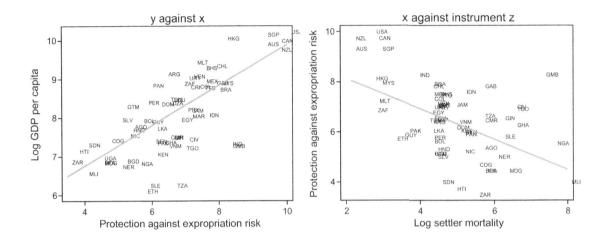

Figure 13.9: Institutions and country GDP: Plots of dependent variable against regressor and against instrument

Table 13.14: Institutions and country GDP:.OLS and IV regression estimates

Variable	OLS	IV	OLS	IV
avexpr	0.522	0.944	0.372	0.713
	(0.050)	(0.176)	(0.084)	(0.147)
Intercept	4.660	1.910	5.074	3.686
	(0.320)	(1.174)	(1.275)	(1.279)
Instrument	No	*logem4*	No	*logem4*
24 additional controls	No	No	Yes	Yes
Observations	64	64	64	64
R-squared	0.540	0.187	0.849	0.738

European settlers more than 100 years ago have no effect on GDP per capita today, other than their effect through institutional development." This is a nontestable assumption.

The second panel of Figure 13.9 shows a strong association between the instrument *logem4* and the regressor *avexp*. The correlation coefficient between *logem4* and *avexpr* equals -0.52.

Table 13.14 presents OLS and IV regression coefficients and their heteroskedastic-robust standard errors.

The OLS results, already mentioned, are given in the first column and are the same as the results given in column 2 of Table 2 of the Acemoglu et al. paper. The second column gives the instrumental variables estimates, that are the same as the results given in column 1 of Table 4 of the Acemoglu et al. paper. The coefficient of *avexpr* has increased to 0.944. As is common, IV estimates are much less precise than OLS and the standard error is 3.5 times higher. Nonetheless the coefficient remains highly statistically significant.

The third and fourth columns adds regressors that are included in Table 6 of the Acemoglu et al. paper. These 24 variables control for malaria (*humid1-humid5* and *temp1-temp5*), agricultural potential (six soil type indicators), natural resource extraction (five mineral indicators), the extent of European descent and ethnocentric fractionalization, and latitude and whether landlocked. This leads to a reduction in the OLS and IV coefficients of *avexpr*, but there is still a large and highly statistically significant effect of institutions on GDP per capita.

13.9 From Raw Data to Final Data

This text, like most texts, analyzes and provides datasets that can be immediately used for data analysis.

In practice data come in a raw form. Going from this raw form to a final dataset ready for analysis can require considerable work, a task that has been recently labelled as **data carpentry.**

The first task is **reading** any sort of data into a statistical package. Easy-to-read examples include Excel spreadsheets (with extension .xls or .xlsx), a plain text file with comma-separated values or character-separated values (with extension .csv), or a data file formatted for a commonly-used statistical package. Somewhat less convenient is data that appear in a table in a PDF document (with extension .pdf). Hardcopy data may be scanned and digitized using an optical character recognition program such as that in Adobe Acrobat. Or web data may be obtained using a web scraping program.

The second task can be **combining data** that come from multiple sources. Merging data requires care to ensure that data from different sources are correctly matched to the same individual. Merging can be especially tricky if names are misspelled or have variations (such as with or without middle initial), or if the data are time series observed at different frequencies and with different formats for recording dates.

The third task is **cleaning** the data. This entails recoding data and detecting data that are in error.

This section provides a simple example. The data are downloaded from the web in a form that can be immediately read into a statistical package. There is just a single dataset. The emphasis is on then cleaning the data so that it is ready for analysis.

13.9.1 Downloaded Data in Fixed Format

The data come from the Michigan Panel Survey of Income Dynamics (PSID) which tracks thousands of people who are surveyed every year for many years. The PSID is a major data set for research by academic economists especially in labor economics and public economics.

The data are on age, number of children, education, annual hours worked, annual labor income (earnings), marital status and sex for women from aged 30 to 50 years from the PSID. These data were directly downloaded using a web interface provided by the PSID. This interface has changed since the data were downloaded, so the many steps used to obtain the data are not repeated here. The download created two files.

The data are in file psid3050.dat that has fixed width data on 4856 observations on nine variables. The first two lines of the data are

```
4 43912 7725029402 21
4 63512 1200020402 24
```

These data could be mistakenly viewed as being on just four variables, separated by spaces. Instead there are nine variables in fixed format, without separators. Especially for large datasets this is common as the size of the data file is reduced by not having separators. To read the data we need to know the formatting.

The second file, psidf3050.sas, is a SAS command file to read the data using SAS. If we are using SAS we can immediately run this program to read in file psidf3050.dat. If we are using other software, we can adapt the information in file psidf3050.sas to read in the file. For example, file psid3050.sas includes the lines

```
V30809 8-9
V30809="AGE OF INDIVIDUAL 93"
```

which means that the 8th and 9th columns in each line of file psidf3050.dat contain data on variable V30809 which is the person's age. Table 13.15 summarizes the variables in file psidf3050.dat and the file format.

Table 13.15: Survey data: Format of raw data file.

Code	Columns	Variable Name
V30001	1-4	1968 INTERVIEW NUMBER
V30002	5-7	PERSON NUMBER
V30809	8-9	AGE OF INDIVIDUAL 93
V30820	10-11	G90 HIGHEST GRADE COMPLETED 93
V30821	12-17	TOTAL LABOR INCOME 93
V30823	18-21	1992 ANNUAL WORK HOURS 93
V32000	22	SEX OF INDIVIDUAL
V32022	23-24	LIVE BIRTHS TO THIS INDIVIDUAL
V32049	25	LAST KNOWN MARITAL STATUS

13.9.2 Read Data into Statistical Package

Using the information in Table 13.15 the data were read into a statistical package, the variables were renamed, and the results saved as dataset PSIDRAW. Summary statistics are given in Table 13.16.

There are 4856 observations. Most variables have sensible descriptive statistics, except that variables *Educatn*, *Kids* and *Married* have unusually high mean values, due to the unrealistic maximum values of 99 and 9.

Table 13.16: Survey data: Summary statistics before data cleaning.

Name	Obs	Mean	St. Dev.	Min	Max
Intnum	4856	4958.10	2761.97	4	9306
Persnum	4856	59.21	79.75	1	205
Age	4856	38.46	5.59	30	50
Educatn	4856	16.38	18.45	0	99
Earnings	4856	14244.51	15985.45	0	240000
Hours	4856	1235.33	947.18	0	5160
Sex	4856	2.00	0.00	2	2
Kids	4856	4.48	14.49	0	99
Married	4856	1.92	1.50	1	9

Variable *Age* is between 30 and 50 as selected. Variable *Earnings* has a maximum value of 240000, so presumably this is annual earnings in dollars. Variable *Hours* has a maximum of 5160 which is 14 hours per day seven days a week, a value that is unusually high but physically possible. Variable *Sex* is always 2, which presumably is the code for women.

13.9.3 Read the Codebook

Variables *Educatn*, *Kids* and *Married* have the unrealistic maximum values of 99 and 9. This is most likely due to missing values for these variables.

Not all questions in an interview survey are answered, and responses can include don't know or a deliberate nonresponse. A given question may deliberately be asked of just a subset of individuals. Even when questions are answered, they may need to be recoded. For example, it is standard to define a variable equal to 1 if married and 0 otherwise, but the survey data may be more detailed than this with responses such as widowed.

Tabulation of the variables in dataset PSIDRAW reveals that variable *Educatn* takes values 0-17 and then 98 and 99; variable *Kids* takes values 0-10 and then 98 and 99; and variable *Married* takes values 1-5 and then 8 and 9. We need to find out what values 98 and 99 mean for variables *Educatn* and *Kids*, and what the values for variable *Married* mean.

This requires looking at the **codebook** for the data, available from the PSID website. We find that for *Educatn* the value 98 corresponds to "don't know" and 99 corresponds to "inappropriate", for variable *Kids* the value 98 means "don't know" or "inappropriate" and 99 means "no birth history"; and for variable *Married* value 8 corresponds to "don't know" and 9 corresponds to "no history".

13.9.4 Missing Data

Missing data are often given a distinctive value to indicate that the data are missing. The current example used values 8, 9, 98 and 99. Commonly-used values to indicate missing data include -999, -99, -9, NA, N/A, * and even a blank entry. Yet another missing data code can be 0, as in some situations a value of 0 may simply mean that the respondent was not asked the question. When characters are used for missing values this can make numeric data harder to read in as it is now a mix of numbers and characters.

Once a data point is viewed to be missing, a command is given to assign a missing value to that data point. Statistical packages usually assign a particular value for missing and have a particular way of displaying the missing data. Stata displays missing data as "." R uses NA, Gretl uses " "and Eviews uses "NA"Excel does not provide this option.

The missing data point is given a particular value internally, often a very large number. This can cause problems when transforming data. For example a command to recode all data values greater than 1000 to 1000 will also erroneously recode missing values to 1000 if the missing value is stored internally as a number greater than 1000.

It is best to code missing data as missing, rather than drop an observation entirely, as this enables analysis using as much of the data as is available. Suppose there are 100 observations and some are missing so that there are 80 nonmissing observations on x, 70 nonmissing observations on y, and only 60 observations have nonmissing data for both x and y. Then deleting all 40 observations that are incompletely observed is not a good idea if analysis is only on x, for which 80 observations available. Going the other way, if interest lies in regression of y on x that uses only the 60 observations for which data on both x and y are available then it may be best to first report descriptive statistics on x and y using just the same 60 observations, rather than all observable data.

When data are missing it is possible to impute the missing value. This yields a larger sample but imputation relies on strong assumptions about the process generating the data. Imputation methods are beyond the scope of this book. The data provided in large national surveys such as the Current Population Survey may include imputed values for key variables such as income that some respondents refuse to answer.

13.9.5   Recode Data

The main variable in this example that needs recoding is variable *Married*. From the codebook, in addition to the missing values (8 and 9) already encountered, we have that 1 = married, 2 = never married, 3 = widowed, 4 = divorced or annulment, 5 = separated. Here we recode 2-5 as not married (0), so the marital status variable here equals one if currently married and not separated and 0 otherwise.

The variable *Educatn* is topcoded at 17, which corresponds to one year of graduate school since 16 corresponds to completed four years of college. The value 17 could possibly be recoded to 18 as some master's degrees take two years and some of the people will have received a Ph.D. which is 20 years of schooling. This is not done here.

Analysis of earnings will be influenced by outlying observations. For example, should a value of $240,000 for annual earnings be included, dropped on grounds of being suspiciously high (perhaps due to a coding error) or should it be top-coded at a value of, say $100,000. By using other years of data for the same individual, if available, one can ascertain in most cases whether the data appears reasonable. Here we do not recode the variable.

13.9.6 Transform Data

Some new variables may be created, such as the natural logarithm of earnings or hourly wage which here is calculated as annual earnings divided by annual hours . Before doing such transformations, however, one needs to be sure that the variables fall into the allowable range. For example, one cannot take the logarithm of zero or a negative number.

Here we define variable *Wage* to be the hourly wage, equal to *Earnings* divided by *Hours*. The variable *Wage* is set to missing if the person had zero earnings. Many studies using self-reported data to construct wage will delete observations that have unusually low or unusually high wage.

13.9.7 Inspect the Data

After coding missing values, recoding variable *Married* and creating variable *Wage* we have dataset PSIDFINAL.

Table 13.17 presents summary statistics. Note that the number observations varies across variables, due to missing values or, for the last two variables, due to no earnings.

Table 13.17: Survey data: Summary statistics after data cleaning.

Name	Obs	Mean	St. Dev.	Min	Max
Intnum	4856	4958.10	2761.97	4	9306
Persnum	4856	59.21	79.75	1	205
Age	4856	38.46	5.60	30	50
Educatn	4630	12.36	3.05	0	17
Earnings	4856	14244.51	15985.45	0	240000
Hours	4856	1235.33	947.18	0	5160
Sex	4856	2.00	0.00	2	2
Kids	4738	2.14	1.43	0	10
Married	4804	0.64	0.48	0	1
Wage	3652	13.05	17.77	0.01	364.23
Lnwage	3652	2.22	0.84	-5.07	5.90

Before proceeding to analysis we should ask for each variable whether the summary statistics make sense? In particular, are the sample mean, minimum and maximum reasonable? How does the sample size compare to the original sample size? Does it seem that too many observations were lost for reasons such as missing data?

For the data set here the variables mostly make sense, except perhaps that only 63% of women between age 35 and 39 are married. The minimum of 0 year of schooling is very low. The hourly wage varies from $0.01, which seems too low, to $364.23 which may be too high.

A box plot can also be a useful aid in detecting outliers. While a complete listing of the data is not practical for large datasets, it can be good practice to at least inspect a partial listing, such as listing all variables for several of the observations.

In some cases data are obviously miscoded. For example, an age of 178 years is clearly miscoded. In other cases it is a judgement call. For example, unusually low and unusually large values of hourly wage may be dropped, but this requires determining what is unusual. Additional information may help in determining what is unusual. For example, an hourly-paid employee in a job covered by the minimum wage law should not have a wage of $1, whereas this is possible for a self-employed person. When data are viewed as miscoded ist is most common to treat the variable as missing.

13.9.8 Data Analysis

Some variables are missing data, and in analysis we would need to decide whether to restrict analysis to a dataset where data are available for all the variables. This throws away data but has the advantage that the sample size and mix does not vary according to which variables are analyzed.

Large data sets such as the PSID are not random samples of the U.S. population. They are instead clustered samples from select geographic areas, to reduce interview costs. Furthermore these data sets oversample groups of particular interest to policy-makers, namely minorities and low-income groups. A thorough analysis would recognize this and do analysis weighted by the so-called sampling weights, possibly dropping observations from the deliberately over-sampled groups. We ignore this complication here.

For these data regression of *Lnwage* on *Educatn* yields $b_{Educatn} = 0.11$, so one additional year of education is associated with an 11% increase in hourly wage.

13.10   Exercises

1. The comma-separated values file API2006.CSV has data similar to that in Chapter 13.1, except for the year 2006, from 773 California senior high schools with more than 500 students. Key variables are *api06* (2006 Academic Performance Index), *avgedyrs* (average years of parents education), *meals* (percentage of students in free or reduced price lunch program), *englearn* (percent English learners), *full* (percent of teachers at school with full credential), and *emer* (percent of teachers at school with emergency credential). Use heteroskedastic-robust standard errors throughout.

    (a) Obtain summary statistics for *api06*, *avgedyrs*, *meals*, *englearn*, *full* and *emer*.

    (b) Obtain a scatterplot of *api06* on *avgedyrs* with fitted regression line.

    (c) Comment on the magnitude of the effect of one more year of average parental education.

    (d) Is the relationship between API and parental education statistically significant at 5%?

    (e) Calculate the predicted value of API for a school with *avgedyrs* = 16.78.

    (f) Give a 95% confidence interval for the population conditional mean of API for a school with *avgedyrs* = 16.78.

    (g) Give a 95% confidence interval for the actual value of API for a school with *avgedyrs* = 16.78. Why is this wider than the interval in part (e)?

    (h) Davis Senior High School has *avgedyrs* = 16.78. Does the school perform as well as predicted? Use relevant data from parts (e)-(g) in your answer.

2. Continue with the same data as the previous exercise and use heteroskedastic-robust standard errors.

   (a) Are *avgedyrs*, *meals*, *englearn*, *full* and *emer* individually highly correlated with the API?

   (b) Regress API on *avgedyrs*, *meals*, *englearn*, *full* and *emer*.

   (c) Which variables are statistically significant using a two-sided test at 5%?

   (d) State which, if any, of *meals*, *englearn*, *full* and *emer* do not have the sign you expect a priori, and give an explanation for why you expected a different sign.

   (e) Compared to regression with just *avgedyrs* as a regressor, do the regressors *meals*, *englearn*, *full* and *emer* add much to the explanation of API? Explain your answer.

   (f) Are these additional variables jointly statistically significant at 5%.

3. Dataset USMANUFACTURING has data for 51 U.S. states (including D.C.) for each of the years 2012-2014 on output (q), capital (k) and labor (l), measured in millions of dollars, and their natural logarithms (*lnq*, *lnk* and *lnl*). For this exercise use 2014 data and heteroskedastic-robust standard errors throughout.

   (a) Regress *lnq* on an intercept and *lnk*. Provide an interpretation of the coefficient of *lnk* in terms of elasticities.

   (b) Using just the regression output, manually test at level 0.05 the claim that the coefficient of *lnk* equals 1.

   (c) Regress *lnq* on an intercept and *lnl* and *lnk*. Are the regressors *lnk* and *lnl* jointly statistically significant at level 0.05?

   (d) Test at level 0.05 whether returns to scale are constant; i.e., test whether the coefficients of *lnl* and *lnk* sum to one. This requires a special post-regression test command; see Chapter 11.5.8.

   (e) The more general translog production function additionally includes quadratic and interaction terms. Regress *lnq* on an intercept, *lnk*, *lnl*, $(lnk)^2$, $(lnl)^2$ and $(lnl \times lnk)$. Has there been much improvement in model fit compared to part (d)? Explain.

   (f) Perform a test of whether the additional regressors $(lnk)^2$, $(lnl)^2$ and $(lnl \times lnk)$ are jointly statistically significant at level 0.05. State your conclusion.

4. Repeat the previous exercise using data for 2012.

5. Use dataset PHILLIPS detailed in Chapter 13.3. Here we use an alternative measure of inflation - the CPI (*inflcpi*). For parts (a)-(d) restrict analysis to before 1970.

   (a) Plot *inflcpi* against *urate*. Is there the expected relationship?

   (b) Regress *urate* on an intercept and *inflcpi*, using heteroskedastic-robust standard errors. Is the relationship statistically significant at 5%?

   (c) Obtain the first three autocorrelations of the residuals from part (b). Do the residuals appear to be autocorrelated?

   (d) Obtain HAC-robust standard errors allowing for up to three years of error correlation. Is the relationship in part (b) statistically significant at 5%?

   (e) Now restrict analysis to the period from 1970 on. Plot *inflcpi* against *urate*. Is there the expected relationship?

   (f) Regress *inflcpi* on an intercept and *urate*. Comment.

6. Use dataset PHILLIPS detailed in Chapter 13.3. Here we use an alternative measure of inflation - the CPI (*inflcpi*). Throughout restrict analysis to the period from 1970 on.

   (a) Regress *inflcpi* on an intercept and *urate*, using heteroskedastic-robust standard errors. Comment.

   (b) Now add a measure of the expected inflation rate (*inflgdp1yr*) to the regression in part (a). Comment on how your results have changed.

   (c) Obtain the first three autocorrelations of the residuals from part (b). Do the residuals appear to be autocorrelated?

   (d) Obtain HAC-robust standard errors allowing for up to three years of error correlation. Is the relationship in part (b) statistically significant at 5%?

   (e) Repeat part (b) using variable *pastinflcpi*, an ad hoc measure that is the weighted average of inflation over the past four years ($\dot{p}_t^e = 0.4\dot{p}_{t-1} + 0.3\dot{p}_{t-2} + 0.2\dot{p}_{t-3} + 0.1\dot{p}_{t-1}$), where $\dot{p}_t$ denotes the inflation rate in year t.

7. Use dataset AUTOSMPG detailed in Chapter 13.4. Here we analyze pickup trucks ($d\_truck=1$) rather than cars.

   (a) Provide a scatterplot, along with a nonparametric regression curve, of *mpg* against *hp* in 1980. Does fuel efficiency decline with increased horsepower?

   (b) Provide similar analysis to that in part (a) in 2006. Has fuel efficiency improved over time?

   (c) Repeat part (a) using natural logarithm of *mpg* against natural logarithm of *hp*. Does the relationship appear to be linear in logs?

   (d) Regress *lmpg* against an intercept and *lhp* in 1980. By how much does fuel efficiency decline with a 10% increase in truck horsepower?

(e) Fit the time trend model of Table 13.7 for pickup trucks rather than for cars. By how much does fuel efficiency decline with a 10% increase in truck horsepower?

(f) For the model in part (e) and variable *lhp* compare heteroskedastic-robust standard errors to cluster-robust standard errors with clustering on *idmfr*. Comment.

(g) Fit the time dummies model of Table 13.7 for pickup trucks rather than per cars. By how much does fuel efficiency decline with a 10% increase in truck horsepower?

8. Repeat exercise 7 for the relationship between fuel efficiency (*mpg*) and truck weight (*curbwt*). So in parts (a)-(d) use *curbwt* and *lcurbwt* rather than *hp* or *lhp*, and in parts (e)-(g) consider a 10% increase in weight.

9. Use dataset HEALTHINSEXP detailed in Chapter 13.5. Analyze outpatient spending (*outpat*) in year 1 and use cluster-robust standard errors that cluster on family (*idfamily*).

   (a) Obtain average outpatient spending by each plan, ordered by increased coinsurance rate. Does spending appear to decrease as insurance becomes less generous?

   (b) Regress *outpat* on an intercept and the set of mutually exclusive coinsurance indicator variables, with *coins0* the omitted base category. Are the indicator variables jointly statistically significant at 5%?

   (c) Now add as regressors *age*, *gender*, *badhealth* and *goodhealth*. Do these additional variables have the expected signs? Are these variables jointly statistically significant at 5%.

   (d) Have the additional variables in part (c) led to much change in your results in part (b)? Are you surprised? Explain.

10. Repeat the previous exercise, except analyze total spending (*spending*) in year 3.

11. Use dataset HEALTHACCESS detailed in Chapter 13.6. In this exercise the dependent variable analyzed is *whz*, the weight-for-height z-score.

    (a) Obtain the means of the dependent variable for the four groups - treated 1993, untreated 1993, treated 1998 and untreated 1998.

    (b) Perform a before-after comparison for the treated group. Does this suggest an improvement?

    (c) Perform a treatment-control comparison for 1998. Does this suggest an improvement?

    (d) Obtain the difference-in-difference estimate using the means in part (a). Does there seem to be an improvement?

    (e) Now perform an appropriate OLS regression to reproduce your answer in part (d). Using cluster-robust standard errors is there a statistically significant effect at 5%?

12. Use dataset HEALTHACCESS detailed in Chapter 13.6. In this exercise the dependent variable analyzed is *waz*, the weight-for-age z-score.

   (a)-(e) Repeat parts (a)-(e) of the previous exercise, except with variable *waz* and analysis restricted to children with age less than two years.

   (f) Repeat part (e) but for children with age greater than or equal to two years. Comment.

13. Use dataset INCUMBENCY detailed in Chapter 13.7. Restrict attention to the period from 1965 on. Use heteroskedastic-robust standard errors.

   (a) Obtain summary statistics for *margin* and *win*. Did the Democratic Party appear to have an advantage over the Republican party over this period? Explain.

   (b) Reproduce a figure similar to the first panel of Figure 13.8. Does there appear to be an incumbency advantage?

   (c) Reproduce a figure similar to the second panel of Figure 13.8. Does there appear to be manipulation around the zero threshold? Explain. (If obtaining a suitable kernel density estimate is a problem then use a histogram with a bin width of 3).

   (d) Regress *margin* on an intercept and *win*. Is there an incumbency advantage? If so, is it statistically significant at 5%.

   (e) Estimate the model listed as Quadratic in Table 13.12. Is there an incumbency advantage? If so, is it statistically significant at 5%.

   (f) Repeat part (e) but restricted analysis to observations with $|margin| < 25$.

14. Repeat the previous exercise for the period before 1965.

15. Use dataset INSTITUTIONS detailed in Chapter 13.8. Exclude New Zealand, Australia, Canada and the USA from analysis (use variable *shortnam*). Use heteroskedastic-robust standard errors.

   (a) Provide a scatter plot of *logpgp95* against *avexpr*. Does there seem to be a relationship.

   (b) OLS regress *logpgp95* on an intercept and *avexpr*. Is there a statistically significant positive relationship?

   (c) Consider use of *logem4* as an instrument for *avexpr*. Is *logem4* reasonably correlated with *avexpr*.

   (d) Obtain IV estimates from regression of *logpgp95* on an intercept and *avexpr* with instrument *logem4*. Is the slope coefficient statistically significant at 5%?

   (e) Has IV estimation led to a great loss of estimator precision compared to OLS? Explain.

   (f) Does the result in part (d) imply a very large effect of institutions on GDP per capita? Explain.

16. Repeat the previous exercise using data for all countries, but do analysis in levels. So replace *logpgp95* with *pgp95* = exp(*logpgp95*).

17. Use dataset NBA detailed in Chapter 17.3. Obtain a good OLS regression model for predicting *wins*, using as potential regressors all the variables in the dataset. Explain how you arrived at your final model and why you think it is a good model. Note: This exercise is deliberately quite open-ended and there is no single correct answer.

18. This exercise provides an example of economic research. Consider the article by Nollenberger, Rodríguez-Planas and Sevilla (2016). Depending on access privileges you can obtain this via Google scholar or JStor (http://www.jstor.org). The paper also has a data appendix, which you do not need to download, that includes the following information. Across the countries the mathematics gender gap has mean -15.70 and standard deviation 26.04 and the gender gap index (*GGI*) has mean 0.69 and standard deviation 0.05. Across individuals *Female* has mean 0.52 and standard deviation 0.08, *Age* (in years and months) has mean 15.77 and standard deviation 0.06, and the indicator variable *Different_grade* (equals one if student's grade $\neq$ modal grade for other children at the children's age in the host country) has mean 0.35 and standard deviation 0.17.

   (a) Given the information in the first sentence of the second paragraph of Section I: Data, for all students how much does the math score change by with one more month of schooling?

   (b) What range of values can the gender gap index take?

   (c) From Figure 1 which country has the best performance of girls relative to boys?

   (d) From Figure 1 which country has the worst performance of girls relative to boys?

   (e) Given the line fitted in Figure 1, by how much does the mathematics gender gap change by if the gender gap index changes from 0 to 1? (Hint: Guesstimate the ends of the fitted line and calculate the slope).

19. Now consider Table 1 of the same article.

   (a) Which of the variables in column 1 of Table 1 are statistically significant at level 0.05?

   (b) How many fixed effects are included in the model of column 1? Hint: The data are for 2003, 2006, 2009 and 2012, for 35 countries of ancestry and for 9 host countries. For each set of dummies we need to drop one category.

   (c) Given your answer in (b) compute an overall test of statistical significance for the model of column 1, assuming we can use the simplest F-test for OLS with independent homoskedastic errors. Hint: Don't forget that an intercept is included in the regression.

   (d) For the estimates in Table 1, by how much does the math gender gap score change by when the gender gap index changes by one standard deviation? Translate this change into months of schooling.

(e) The model in column 1 of Table 1 does not include the variable GGI. It only includes the variable GGI×Female. Why is this? Hint: This model includes dummy variables for each ancestry country.

(f) Ignoring column 3, the R^2 increases (or is unchanged at the two significant digit level) across the columns. Are you surprised? Explain.

Chapter 14

Regression with Indicator Variables

This chapter presents multiple regression in the special case that the regressors include one or more indicator variables, which are variables that indicate which category an observation falls into and for simplicity are coded as take only the values zero or one. For example, an indicator variable for gender may equal one if female and zero if male.

As a regression application, consider the determinants of annual earnings of individuals. This may depend on indicator variables that may appear individually, such as gender, or as sets of mutually exclusive indicator variables, such as three indicator variables for the type of job (self-employed, private sector or public sector). Furthermore, the indicator variables may be interacted with other regressors, such as an interaction between gender and years of schooling.

This topic warrants a separate chapter as economic models often include indicator variables and the interpretation of estimated coefficients is not always straightforward.

14.1 Example: Earnings, Gender, Education and Type of Worker

This chapter uses the dataset EARNINGS_COMPLETE on male and female full-time workers aged 25 to 65 years surveyed in 2010.

Table 14.1 presents summary statistics for the dependent variable *Earnings* and the other variables used in this chapter. Mean earnings are $56,639 per year, mean age is 43.31 years, 43.3% of the sample are female, and mean education is 13.85 years of schooling. The type of worker is broken into three categories – self-employed, employed in private sector and employed in government sector.

14.2 Regression on just a Single Indicator Variable

An **indicator variable** or **categorical variable** is a variable that indicates whether or not an observation falls into a particular category. For simplicity such variables are coded as 1 if in the category and 0 if not in the category. An indicator variable is also called a **dummy variable** where the term "dummy" means that it used as a substitute for the category.

Table 14.1: Annual Earnings of full-time workers aged 25-65 in 2010: Summary statistics (n=872).

Variable	Definition	Mean	Standard Deviation	Min	Max
Earnings	Annual earnings in $	56369	51516	4000	504000
Gender	= 1 if female	0.433	0.496	0	1
Education	Years of schooling	13.85	2.88	0	20
Genderbyeduc	*Gender* times *Education*	6.08	7.17	0	20
Age	Age in years	43.31	10.68	25	65
Genderbyage	*Gender* times *Age*	19.04	22.87	0	65
Hours	Usual hours worked per week	44.34	8.50	35	99
Genderbyhours	*Gender* times *Hours*	18.56	21.76	0	80
d1 or dself	= 1 if self-employed	0.091	0.287	0	1
d2 or dpriv	=1 if private sector employee	0.760	0.427	0	1
d3 or dgovt	=1 if government sector employee	0.149	0.356	0	1
n	872				

Common notation for an indicator variable is d. For example the indicator variable may indicate gender, with $d = 1$ if a person is female and $d = 0$ if a person is male. Or for data from an experiment $d = 1$ if the subject is in the treatment group and $d = 0$ if the subject is in the control group.

In this section we consider the simplest setting where interest lies in how an outcome variable of interest y varies according to whether $d = 1$ or $d = 0$.

14.2.1   Regression on an Indicator Variable yields the Difference in Means

Linear regression of y on an intercept and the indicator variable d yields fitted values

$$\widehat{y} = b + ad.$$

Then $\widehat{y}_i$ takes one of only two possible values

$$\widehat{y}_i = \begin{cases} b + a & \text{if } d_i = 1 \\ b & \text{if } d_i = 0. \end{cases}$$

It follows that the marginal effect $(\Delta\widehat{y}/\Delta x)$ of changing d from 0 to 1, a one unit increase in d, is to change $\widehat{y}$ by a. Thus the slope coefficient a measures the difference in the predicted value of y when $d = 1$ rather than $d = 0$.

Let $\bar{y}_1$ denote the sample average of y for observations with $d = 1$ and let $\bar{y}_0$ denote the sample average of y for observations with $d = 0$. Then it can be shown that OLS regression of y on an intercept and d yields $b = \bar{y}_0$ and $b + a = \bar{y}_1$, so the intercept and slope coefficients are

$$b = \bar{y}_0 \text{ and } a = \bar{y}_1 - \bar{y}_0.$$

Remark 115 *The slope coefficient from OLS regression of y on an intercept and an indicator variable d equals the difference in the mean of y across the two categories defined by d.*

For statistical inference the corresponding population model is

$$y = \beta + \alpha d + u.$$

A test of statistical significance of the indicator variable d provides a test of whether the mean of y differs across the two categories.

14.2.2 Example: Earnings and Gender

Table 14.2 presents summary statistics for earnings by gender. On average women earn \$16,397 ($= 47080 - 63476$) less than men.

Table 14.2: Annual earnings: Summary statistics by gender

Gender	Sample size	Mean	Standard Deviation	Min	Max
Male Earnings (Gender=0)	494	63476	61713	5000	504000
Female earnings (Gender=1)	378	47080	31597	4000	322000

OLS regression of earnings on gender yields estimates

$$\widehat{Earnings} = \underset{(2776)}{63476} - \underset{(3217)}{16396} \times Gender \qquad R^2 = 0.025, \; s_e = 50900.$$

The intercept equals average male ($d = 0$) earnings and the slope equals the difference between male ($d = 0$) earnings and female ($d = 1$) earnings. The earnings difference of \$16,396 per year is very substantial.

The standard errors given in parentheses are heteroskedastic-robust as the variability in earnings varies by gender – from Table 14.2 the standard deviation of earnings for men is twice that for women.

Gender is highly statistically significant with $t = -16396/3217 = -5.10$, so a two-sided t test has $p = \Pr[|T_{870}| > 5.10] = 0.000$. And a 95% confidence interval for the difference in mean earnings is $(-22711, -10081)$.

14.2.3 Basic Difference in Means Test

In many areas of applied statistics the preceding example is performed using a problem specific method, called difference in means, that does not use OLS regression. Then the same estimate of the difference in means is obtained, while a slightly different standard error is computed and the t distribution used can have degrees of freedom other than $n - 2$. For completeness we present this method.

The sample with $d = 1$ has sample mean $\bar{y}_1$, sample variance s_1^2 and standard error of $\bar{y}_1$ equal to $s_1/\sqrt{n_1}$ where n_1 is the number of observations in the sample with $d = 1$. Similarly for $d = 0$ define

$\bar{y}_0$, s_0^2, n_0 and $se(\bar{y}_0) = s_0/\sqrt{n_0}$. The difference in means is $(\bar{y}_1 - \bar{y}_0)$ and, given the assumption of independent samples and unequal variances in the two samples, has standard error

$$se(\bar{y}_1 - \bar{y}_0) = \sqrt{(s_1^2/n_1) + (s_0^2/n_0)}$$

since the two samples are independent so that $\text{Var}[\bar{y}_1 - \bar{y}_0] = \text{Var}[\bar{y}_1] + \text{Var}[\bar{y}_0]$ (see Appendix B.3) with estimate $se^2(\bar{y}_1) + se^2(\bar{y}_0)$. This formula for the standard error is slightly different from the heteroskedastic-robust standard error of the slope coefficient if estimation is by OLS, leading to slightly different confidence intervals and test statistics.

A 95% confidence interval of the difference in means is then

$$(\bar{y}_1 - \bar{y}_0) \pm t_{v;.025} \times se(\bar{y}_1 - \bar{y}_0)$$

and the t statistic for test of equality of means ($H_0 : \mu_1 - \mu_0 = 0$) is $t = (\bar{y}_1 - \bar{y}_0)/se(\bar{y}_1 - \bar{y}_0)$. The t statistic is viewed as a draw from the $T(v)$ distribution. A simple approach sets $v = n_0 + n_1 - 2 = n - 2$ as the estimates s_0^2 and s_1^2 in total use two degrees of freedom. A more advanced approach, often used by statistical packages, uses a complicated formula called Satterthwaite's approximation that yields a value of v less than $n_0 + n_1 - 2$.

For the earnings by gender example, $se(\bar{y}_1 - \bar{y}_0) = \sqrt{(31596^2/378) + (61713^2/494)} = 3217$ using data in Table 14.2. To four significant digits this standard error is the same as that obtained using OLS with heteroskedastic-robust standard errors, so the t statistics are essentially the same.

Calculation to seven significant digits using a computer package yields exactly the same estimate of the difference in means (as expected), with standard error 3217.251 compared to 3217.429 using OLS, and Satterthwaite's degrees of freedom equals 770.407 rather than $n - 2 = 870$.

The regression approach is more general than the preceding more specialized approach as it can measure the effect of the indicator variable after controlling for additional regressors, and inference can be based on various robust standard errors.

14.2.4   Difference in Means Tests in Different Statistical Packages

Basic difference in means tests can be implemented using the `ttest` command in Stata, the `t.test` function in R, and mean equality tests in Eviews.

These commands include a more restrictive variation that assumes the variances are the same in the two samples. In that case the resulting standard error of the difference is identical to that obtained from OLS regression with default standard errors.

When the data y are binary (taking values 0 and 1), an alternative test is the difference in proportions test which again uses $(\bar{y}_1 - \bar{y}_0)$ but with $se(\bar{y}_1 - \bar{y}_0) = \bar{y}(1 - \bar{y})(\frac{1}{n_1} + \frac{1}{n_2})$, where $\bar{y}$ is the overall proportion. When data are paired, such as weights of the same individuals measured at two points in time, a paired test is used. And especially when sample sizes are small, and data are not well approximated by the normal distribution, the Wilcoxon rank test is used.

These alternative tests are not used often in econometrics applications. Instead, especially with large samples, it is enough to use the basic difference-in-means test with unequal variances or its indicator variable OLS regression implementation with heteroskedastic-robust standard errors.

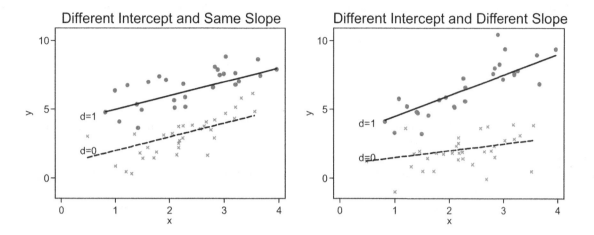

Figure 14.1: Indicator variable: Inclusion as regressor and inclusion as interacted regressor.

14.3 Regression on an Indicator Variable and Additional Regressors

For the earnings by gender example the difference in average earnings may be due to other characteristics of the workers, such as hours worked or age or educational level. This complication is easily handled by OLS regression.

14.3.1 Single Indicator Variable plus other Regressors

Consider the population model

$$y = \beta_1 + \beta_2 x + \alpha d + u,$$

where α is the coefficient of the indicator variable d. For simplicity only one regressor other than d is included, but results carry through immediately if $\beta_2 x$ is replaced with $\beta_2 x_2 + \cdots + \beta_k x_k$. A two-sided test of a difference in the conditional mean of y across the two categories, controlling for the other regressors, is a test of $H_0 : \alpha = 0$ against $H_a : \alpha \neq 0$.

In the fitted model

$$\widehat{y}_i = \begin{cases} b_1 + b_2 x_i + a & \text{if } d_i = 1 \\ b_1 + b_2 x_i & \text{if } d_i = 0. \end{cases}$$

The coefficient a of the indicator variable regressor measures the change in $\widehat{y}_i$ when $d_i = 1$ rather than $d_i = 0$, holding all other regressor(s) constant.

The first panel of Figure 14.1 illustrates that the indicator variable shifts the intercept in the regression of y on an intercept, d and x according to whether $d = 1$ or $d = 0$, while keeping the slope coefficients the same.

Remark 116 *In multiple regression the coefficient on an indicator variable acts as an intercept shifter. A test of the statistical significance of the indicator variable is a test of the difference in means after controlling for the other regressors.*

14.3.2   Interacted Indicator Variables

An **interacted indicator variable** is a regressor that is the product of an indicator variable and another regressor. Consider the model

$$y = \beta_1 + \beta_2 x + \alpha_1 d + \alpha_2 d \times x + u,$$

where d is an indicator variable taking values 0 or 1 and x is another regressor. Then in the fitted model

$$\widehat{y}_i = \begin{cases} (b_1 + a_1) + (b_2 + a_2)x_i & \text{if } d_i = 1 \\ b_1 + b_2 x_i & \text{if } d_i = 0. \end{cases}$$

As before a_1 measures the difference in the intercept term between the case $d = 1$ and the case $d = 0$. Additionally a_2 gives the difference in the slope coefficient of the regressor x between the case $d = 1$ and the case $d = 0$.

The second panel of Figure 14.1 shows that if regressors include both an indicator variable and the same indicator variable interacted with x then both the intercept and the slope coefficient of x differ according to whether $d = 1$ or $d = 0$.

Remark 117 *An interacted indicator variable is a regressor that is the product of an indicator variable and another regressor. This enables slope coefficients to vary according to the value of the indicator variable.*

Tests of statistical significance of an indicator variable that is additionally interacted become joint tests. A test of whether d is statistically significant is a test of whether or not both $\alpha_1 = 0$ and $\alpha_2 = 0$. Similarly, a test of whether x is statistically significant is a test of whether or not both $\beta_2 = 0$ and $\alpha_2 = 0$.

For marginal effects in an interacted regressor model see Chapter 15.4.

14.3.3   Example: Earnings and Gender with Additional Controls

Returning to the earnings and gender example, we consider the difference in earnings by gender after controlling for other characteristics of the worker. To begin with we control for educational level, then allow for interaction of education with gender, and finally add age and hours worked as additional control variables.

Table 14.3 presents the results with t statistics based on heteroskedastic-robust standard errors reported in parentheses. The first column gives the earlier difference-in-means regression.

The second column of Table 14.3 shows little change in the effect of gender once education is included as a control, even though education has a considerable effect with earnings increasing on average by $5,907 with each year of education.

Table 14.3: Indicator variable: Earnings regressions with an indicator for gender.

Variable / Model	d only	d and Ed	d, Ed and d × Ed	More controls	Fully interacted
d (gender)	-16396	-18258	20219	19022	57129
	(-5.10)	(-5.82)	(1.32)	(1.27)	(1.79)
Education	-	5907	6921	6417	6315
	-	(9.03)	(7.31)	(7.24)	(7.19)
d × Education	-	-	-2765	-2456	-2124
	-	-	(-2.37)	(-2.19)	(-1.94)
Age	-	-	-	526	549
	-	-	-	(3.63)	(2.41)
Hours	-	-	-	1325	1621
	-	-	-	(3.76)	(3.22)
d × Age	-	-	-	-	-49
	-	-	-	-	(-0.18)
d × Hours	-	-	-	-	-930
	-	-	-	-	(-1.68)
Intercept	63476	-17552	-31451	-107340	-120432
	(22.86)	(-2.20)	(-2.66)	(-4.83)	(-4.17)
F(q,n-k) for indicator(s)	25.97	33.89	17.18	15.22	8.14
p-value for F	.000	.000	.000	.000	.000
n	872	872	872	872	872
R^2	.025	.134	.140	.198	.203
Adjusted R^2	.024	.132	.137	.193	.196
St. error	50900	47997	47870	46272	46183
Overall F	25.97	41.77	31.92	23.32	21.25
p-value for overall F	.000	.000	.000	.000	.000

The third column adds an interaction between education and earnings. The statistically significant (at 5%) coefficient of the interaction term means that each year of education leads to an increase in earnings that is $2,765 dollars less for women than the $6,921 benefit it brings to men. A test of the statistical significance of gender is now a joint test that the coefficient of gender is zero and the coefficient of gender times education is zero. This test has $F = 17.18$ with $p = 0.000$, so gender is statistically significant at 5%.

The fourth column adds age and hours as regressors. Both variables are statistically significant (at 5%) with the expected positive signs. There is relatively little change in the coefficients for the gender variables.

The final column in Table 14.3 is a model in which all variables are interacted with gender. It can be shown that separate OLS regression for the male-only ($d = 0$) sample of earnings on an intercept, education, age and hours yields the same coefficients as those in the final column, while a similar separate OLS regression for the female-only ($d = 1$) sample yields coefficients that are equal to the sum of the coefficients of the original and interacted variables in the final column. For example education has coefficient 6315 in the male-only sample regression, while education has coefficient $4191 = 6315 + (-2124)$ in the female-only sample regression. A joint test that the coefficients of gender and its interactions with education, age and hours all have zero coefficients has $F = 8.14$ with $p = 0.000$. So gender is statistically significant at 5%.

14.3.4   Dependent Variable is an Indicator Variable

In some applications the dependent variable is an indicator variable. For example, we may wish to model whether or not an individual is employed, in which case $y = 1$ if a person works and $y = 0$ if a person does not.

   If estimation is by OLS regression of y on regressors then robust standard errors must be used. OLS slope coefficients are interpreted as measuring the average effect over the sample of a change in regressor values, rather than the effect for any given individual.

   For a dependent variable that is an indicator variable it is better to use logit or probit models presented in Chapter 17.6.

14.4   Regression with Sets of Indicator Variables

In some cases a categorical variable may have several categories.

   If these categories are **ordered** it can be convenient to create a single regressor with a distinct value for each category. For example, in the house price example of Chapter 10 the lot sizes of small, medium and large were given values of 1, 2 and 3. This method has the limitation of restricting the predicted change in house price when moving from a small lot to a medium lot to equal the predicted change when moving from a medium lot to a large lot, an assumption that may not be reasonable.

   Furthermore this expedient approach is not possible when the categories are **unordered**, such as a variable for color that has categories blue, red and green.

   Instead when a categorical variable includes several categories we form a **set of indicator variables**, one for each category where each indicator variable takes value 0 or 1. These indicator variables are included as regressors, with one of the indicator variables omitted if the regression also includes an intercept, for reason given below.

14.4.1   Sets of Indicator Variables

For simplicity, consider a variable that lies in one of three categories. Then we create three indicator variables, one for each category. The example considered in this chapter is type of worker that has three categories – self-employed, employed in the private sector and employed in the government sector.

   Then three indicator variables are defined as

$$d1 = \begin{cases} 1 & \text{if self-employed} \\ 0 & \text{otherwise,} \end{cases}$$

$$d2 = \begin{cases} 1 & \text{if employed in private sector} \\ 0 & \text{otherwise.} \end{cases}$$

$$d3 = \begin{cases} 1 & \text{if employed in government sector} \\ 0 & \text{otherwise.} \end{cases}$$

A set of indicator variables is **mutually exclusive** if any individual in the sample falls into exactly one of the categories. This is the case for this example. Then for any individual observation only one of the indicator variables takes value 1, while the remaining indicator variables take value 0. Thus for every observation the indicator variables sum to one

$$d1 + d2 + d3 = 1.$$

One way to establish mutual exclusivity is to verify that each indicator variable takes only values 0 or 1 and that the sum of the sample means of the indicator variables equals one. Here $0.091 + 0.760 + 0.149 = 1$.

OLS regression of y on a complete set of mutually exclusive indicators, with the intercept excluded and no other regressors included, yields coefficients that give the sample mean of y in each category.

14.4.2 Dummy Variable Trap

Due to the relationship between the three indicators, not all three indicators can be included in the regression if an intercept is also included. Erroneous inclusion of the complete set of indicator variables is called the **dummy variable trap.**

To see this problem, note that $d1 + d2 + d3 = 1$ implies that $d1 = 1 - d2 - d3$. Making this substitution

$$
\begin{aligned}
y &= \beta_1 + \beta_2 x + \alpha_1 d1 + \alpha_2 d2 + \alpha_3 d3 + u \\
&= \beta_1 + \beta_2 x + \alpha_1(1 - d2 - d3) + \alpha_2 d2 + \alpha_3 d3 + u \\
&= (\beta_1 + \alpha_1) + \beta_2 x + (\alpha_2 - \alpha_1)d2 + (\alpha_3 - \alpha_1)d3 + u.
\end{aligned}
$$

We can only identify four coefficients (those of the intercept, x, $d2$ and $d3$) but have five parameters to estimate (β_1, β_2, α_1, α_2 and α_3). The solution is to drop one of the indicator variables or to drop the intercept.

Remark 118 *The dummy variable trap arises if the set of indicator variables included exhausts all possibilities so that their sum equals one for every observation. Then one of the indicator variables or the intercept needs to be dropped. These solutions lead to equivalent estimates of the difference in y across the categories, and equivalent slope coefficients of other regressors.*

14.4.3 Base Category

For the current example suppose $d1$ is dropped. Then from the preceding equation the coefficient $(\alpha_2 - \alpha_1)$ of $d2$ measures the difference between earnings for a private sector worker ($d2 = 1$) and a self-employed worker ($d1 = 1$) after controlling for the other regressors. Similarly the coefficient $(\alpha_3 - \alpha_1)$ of $d3$ measures the difference between earnings for a government sector worker ($d3 = 1$) and a self-employed worker ($d1 = 1$) after controlling for other regressors. So the coefficients of the included indicator variables measure the marginal effect of being in those categories compared to the omitted category.

The **omitted category** is called the **base category** or **reference category**. Interpretation of coefficients is simplest if the base category is a meaningful category. For example, in the type of worker example it might be most natural to use employment in the private sector as the base category, as most workers are in this category.

Remark 119 *Suppose a categorical variable has C categories. Form a set of C mutually exclusive indicator variables d1, d2,..., dC. To avoid the dummy variable trap drop one of the indicator variables, called the omitted or base category. The coefficient of an included indicator variable measures the marginal effect of being in that category compared to the base category, after controlling for the other regressors.*

Note that for similar reasons in the earlier gender example we created only an indicator variable for female, and did not create a second indicator variable for male. Male became the base category.

14.4.4 Hypothesis Tests on Indicator Variables

Care is needed in interpreting hypothesis tests. When $d1$ is the omitted category the coefficient of $d2$ measures $(\alpha_2 - \alpha_1)$, so a test of statistical significance of $d2$ is a test of $H_0 : \alpha_2 = \alpha_1$ against $H_a : \alpha_2 \neq \alpha_1$. In the earnings example it is a test of whether private sector workers earn the same on average as self-employed workers after controlling for the other regressors. It is important to note that it is not a test of whether or not $\alpha_2 = 0$. And if instead $d3$ was dropped, say, then by similar reasoning the coefficient of d_2 measures $(\alpha_2 - \alpha_3)$.

Remark 120 *A t test of the statistical significance of a single indicator variable is a test of whether the marginal effect of that category differs from that for the base category. It is not a test of whether the marginal effect of that category is zero.*

To test whether collectively the set of indicator variables is statistically significant we use the F test for a subset of regressors. If $d1$ is the base category then we test whether the coefficients of $d2$ and $d3$ are jointly statistically significant. Similarly if $d2$ is the base category, say, then we test whether the coefficients of $d1$ and $d3$ are jointly statistically significant.

Remark 121 *An F test of the joint statistical significance of the C-1 included indicator variables is a test of whether the set of indicator variables is statistically significant. This joint F test leads to the same result regardless of the category that is dropped.*

14.4.5 Example: Earnings and Type of Worker

Regressing earnings on all three categorical variables for type of worker, and excluding the constant,

$$\hat{y} = \underset{(9637)}{72306}d1 + \underset{(1898)}{54521}d2 - \underset{(2825)}{56105}d3 \qquad R^2 = 0.550, \ s_e = 51325,$$

where heteroskedastic-robust standard errors are given in parentheses. Since the three categories are mutually exclusive, and estimation is by OLS, the coefficients are just the sample averages for each category. For example, average earnings for the self-employed are $72,306 with a standard error of $9,636.

Table 14.4 presents the results of several regressions that vary in how the sets of indicators are introduced in the model. Heteroskedastic-robust standard errors are given in parentheses and t statistics are given in square brackets.

Table 14.4: Sets of indicator variables: Earnings regression with indicators for type of worker

Variable	No Indicators	Drop d1	Drop d2	Drop d3	Drop intercept
Age	525	488	488	488	488
	(151)	(150)	(150)	(150)	(150)
	[3.47]	[3.26]	[3.26]	[3.26]	[3.26]
Education	5811	5865	5865	5865	5865
	(641)	(652)	(652)	(652)	(652)
	[9.06]	[8.99]	[8.99]	[8.99]	[8.99]
d1 (self-employed)	-	-	17098	19123	–30151
	-	-	(9342)	(9586)	(13140)
	-		[1.83]	[1.99]	[-2.29]
d2 (private sector)	-	-17098	-	2025	-47249
	-	(9342)	-	(3099)	(11377)
	-	[-1.83]	-	[0.65]	[-4.15]
d3 (government sector)	-	-19123	-2025	-	-49274
	-	(9586)	(3098)	-	(12132)
	-	[-1.99]	[-0.65]	-	[-4.00]
Intercept	-46875	-30151	-47249	-49274	-
	(11306)	(13140)	(11377)	(12312)	-
	[-4.15]	[-2.29]	[-4.15]	[-4.00]	-
F(2,n-k) for indicators	-	2.01	2.01	2.01	-
p-value for F	-	.135	.135	.135	-
n	872	872	872	872	872
R^2	.115	.125	.125	.125	.601
Adjusted R^2	.113	.121	.121	.121	.599
St. error	48519	48312	48312	48312	48312
Overall F	42.85	22.12	22.12	22.12	313.06
p-value for overall F	.000	.000	.000	.000	.000

The first regression simply regresses earnings on education and age, without any of the indicator variables. Education has a large effect, one more year of schooling is associated with a $5,811 increase in annual earnings, and is highly statistically significant. One more year of aging is associated with a $525 increase in earnings and is statistically significant at level 0.05.

The next three columns of Table 14.4 present results when the indicator variables for type of worker are included as regressors and the base category is, in turn, self-employed ($d1 = 1$), private sector ($d2 = 1$) and government sector ($d3 = 1$).

From columns 2-4, many of the entries in Table 14.4 are invariant to the choice of omitted category. The coefficients, standard errors and t statistics for the other regressors, *Education* and

Age, do not change. The goodness of fit measures, namely R^2, $\bar{R}^2$, s_e and the F statistic for overall significance, do not change. Additionally the F statistics for the joint significance of the two included indicator variables, given after the coefficient estimates do not change. These $F(2, 867)$ tests all have $F = 2.01$ and $p = .135$ so we conclude that the type of worker is jointly statistically insignificant at significance level 0.05.

From columns 2-4, change in the omitted category does lead to change in the estimated intercept and the estimated coefficients for the included indicator variables. From the second column, when $d1$ is omitted $d2$ has estimated coefficient -17098 and $d3$ has estimated coefficient -19123. So after controlling for age and education, private sector workers earn \$17,098 less than self-employed workers and government workers earn \$19,123 less than self-employed workers.

From column 3, with $d2$ instead omitted, $d1$ has estimated coefficient 17098, so self-employed sector workers earn \$17,098 more than those in the private sector. This is consistent with the results with $d1$ omitted that found that private sector workers earn \$17,098 less than self-employed workers. And $d3$ has estimated coefficient -2025, so government workers earn \$2,025 less than those in the private sector. This is consistent with the results with $d1$ omitted that found that private sector workers earn \$17,098 less than self-employed workers and government workers earn \$19,123 less than self-employed workers, since $17098 - 19123 = -2025$.

The t tests of individual coefficients differ according to which indicator variable is omitted since they are tests of the significance compared to the reference group. For example, using the base category of private worker, so $d2$ is omitted, we see from column 3 that the difference between earnings of self-employed workers and private sector workers is statistically insignificant at level 0.05, since $t = 1.83$. Similarly the difference between earnings of government workers and private sector workers is not statistically significant since $t = -0.65$.

The choice of omitted category is one of convenience. If, for example, we are interested in measuring earnings of workers relative to those in the private sector then drop the indicator variable for the private sector.

Another way to avoid the dummy variable trap is to include all the indicator variables but drop the intercept. The final column of Table 14.4 gives results using this alternative method. Again the coefficients, standard errors and t statistics for the other regressors, *Age* and *Education*, do not change. The coefficients of the indicator variables now directly estimate the coefficients α_1, α_2 and α_3 (at the expense of being unable to estimate the intercept β_1). Since $a_1 = -30151$ and $a_2 = -47249$, the difference in earnings between self-employed workers and private sector workers equals $a_1 - a_2 = -30151 - (-47249) = 17098$. This equals the estimated coefficient of $d2$ in the model with $d1$ omitted, given in column 3 of Table 14.4.

From the last column of Table 14.4, dropping the intercept has led to a change in the overall goodness of fit measures – R^2, $\bar{R}^2$, s_e and the F statistic for overall significance. The reason is that these statistics are inappropriate in regressions that do not include an intercept. Recall that R^2 measures explained variation relative to the total sum of squares, which is regression with just an intercept. Similarly the F test presumes that the restricted model includes an intercept. This is one reason for omitting an indicator variable rather than the intercept.

14.4.6 Difference in Several Means

Suppose we simply want to test whether earnings vary across the type of worker, without inclusion of any controls. Regressing earnings on an intercept, $d2$ and $d3$ yields

$$\widehat{y} = \underset{(7.50)}{72306} - \underset{(-1.81)}{17785d2} - \underset{(-1.61)}{16201d3} \qquad R^2 = 0.010, \; s_e = 51325,$$

where t statistics based on heteroskedastic-robust standard errors are given in parentheses. Then earnings are \$72,306 for self-employed workers, the omitted category, and are \$17,785 less than this for private sector workers and \$16,201 lower for government sector workers. The F statistic for joint statistical significance of $d2$ and $d3$ equals 1.68 with $p = 0.188$ so at significance level 0.05 there is no statistically significant difference in earnings across the three types of workers.

Note that the OLS estimates imply that earnings are on average \$72,306 for the self-employed, \$54,521 ($= 72306 - 17785$) for government workers, and \$56,105 ($= 72306 - 16201$) for private sector workers. These quantities equal the sample mean of earnings in each of the three categories of worker, and can also be directly obtained from OLS regression of *Earnings* on $d1$, $d2$ and $d3$ with the intercept omitted.

In areas of applied statistics that do not use regression methods, the difference in means across categories is tested using **analysis of variance (ANOVA) methods** that are an extension of the t test for difference in two means and assume independent homoskedastic errors. ANOVA is implemented using the `anova` command in Stata and Gretl, the `aov` function in R and mean equality tests in Eviews. The advantages of using regression methods, rather than ANOVA, are that robust standard errors can be used and that additional regressors can be easily included.

14.4.7 More Complex Indicators and Interactions

More complex models can include several sets of indicator variables. Then it is simplest to include the intercept while one indicator variable is dropped from each of the sets of indicator variables.

As increasingly more complex models are estimated, care is needed to avoid inadvertently running into the dummy variable trap. For example, suppose the regressors include an indicator for female, an indicator for married, and an interaction between these two indicators. Then problems will arise if there are, for example, no married men in the sample.

When the dummy variable trap does arise a statistical package will drop one of the regressors, or more than one regressor if the dummy variable trap occurs more than once. This can change the way that the coefficients of indicator variables are interpreted. Special care is needed if a statistical package drops one or more regressors.

14.4.8 Creating Sets of Indicator Variables in a Statistical Package

Creating a single indicator variable is straightforward. For example, suppose the text variable HOURS takes values ZERO, PART and FULL. Then in Stata the command `generate dpart = HOURS=="PART"` creates a variable `dpart` equal to one if part-time and zero otherwise. And in R one can use the command `dpart<-ifelse(HOURS="PART",1,0)` to create the same variable.

When we wish to create a set of indicator variables for a variable that takes many values, the preceding can be repeated for each value of the variable which is tedious. In Stata a shortcut uses the `generate` option of the `tabulate` command. For the current example, `tabulate HOURS, generate(dhours)` generates three dummy variables: `dhours1` (=1 if `HOURS="FULL"`, 0 otherwise), `dhours2` (=1 if `HOURS="PART"`, 0 otherwise) and `dhours3` (=1 if `HOURS="ZERO"`, 0 otherwise). The ordering is alphabetical. In R one uses the `factor` function, in Gretl use the `dummify` command, and in Eviews use `@expand`. The same methods can be used for a variable that takes several numerical values.

One can directly use factor variable notation in statistical commands that obviates the need to create the indicator variables. Consider the variable *lotsize* in dataset HOUSE that takes three numerical values. The Stata command `regress price i.lotsize` regresses `price` on an intercept and two indicator variables, with the lowest category automatically omitted. In R the corresponding command is `lm(price~factor(lotsize))`. In Eviews the corresponding OLS model is `price @expand(lotsize, @dropfirst)` where `@dropfirst` drops the first indicator variable.

Stata factor variables, unlike R, are limited to underlying variables that take numerical values. However, one can use the `encode` command to convert a string variable to a numeric variable. For example, `encode HOURS, generate(hours2)` creates a variable *hours2* that takes values 1 (if FULL), 2 (if PART) and 3 (if ZERO). Then one can use command `regress price i.hours2`. To subsequently test joint statistical significance give command `testparm i.hours2*`.

14.5 Key Concepts

1. In multiple regression the coefficient on an indicator variable acts as an intercept shifter.

2. An interacted indicator variable is a regressor that is the product of an indicator variable and another regressor. This enables slope coefficients to vary according to the value of the indicator variable.

3. For a categorical variable that takes one of several possible values we form a set of indicator variables, one for each category.

4. The dummy variable trap arises if two or more mutually exclusive indicator variables are included and they exhaust all possibilities so that their sum equals one for every observation. Then one of the indicator variables or the intercept needs to be dropped. These solutions lead to equivalent estimates of the difference in y across the categories, and equivalent slope coefficients of other regressors.

5. The coefficient of an included indicator variable measures the marginal effect of being in that category compared to the base category (the omitted category) after controlling for the other regressors.

6. For sets of mutually exclusive indicator variables, a t test of the statistical significance of a single indicator variable is a test of whether the marginal effect of that category differs from

that for the base category. It is not a test of whether the marginal effect of that category is zero.

7. An F test of the joint statistical significance of the included indicator variables is a test of whether the set of indicator variables is statistically significant. This joint F test leads to the same result regardless of the category that is dropped.

8. Key Terms: indicator variable; dummy variable; interacted indicator variable; categorical variable; sets of indicator variables; mutually exclusive; dummy variable trap; base category; reference category; no intercept; difference in means; joint F test; difference in several means.

14.6 Exercises

1. Consider data on an outcome variable y_i and an indicator variable d_i.

   (a) Suppose $\bar{y} = 30$ for the subsample with $d_i = 1$ and $\bar{y} = 20$ for the subsample with $d_i = 0$. Give the fitted model from OLS regression of y_i on d_i using the full sample.

   (b) Suppose OLS regression using all data yields fitted model $\widehat{y}_i = 3 + 5d_i$. Give $\bar{y}$ for the subsample with $d_i = 0$ and $\bar{y}$ for the subsample with $d_i = 1$.

2. Repeat the previous exercise where in part (a) $\bar{y} = 30$ for $d_i = 1$ and $\bar{y} = 50$ for $d_i = 0$, and in part (b) $\widehat{y}_i = 5 - 3d_i$.

3. Suppose a sample of 400 women has mean monthly earnings of \$2,500 with a standard deviation of \$2,000, and a sample of 300 men has mean monthly earnings of \$2,800 with a standard deviation of \$3,000. Is the difference in mean earnings statistically different at 5\%?

4. Consider a desirable medical screening test. One health system has a screening test rate of 0.75 with a standard error of 0.02 based on a sample of 469 members. A second health system has a screening test rate of 0.80 with a standard error of 0.01 based on a sample of 1,600 members. Is the difference in screening test rates statistically significant at 5\%? Explain. (Note: Here the standard error is given, not the standard deviation).

5. Use dataset HOUSE.

    (a) Create the indicator variable *dlater* equal to one if the house is sold after June (*month-sold> 6*) and equal to zero otherwise. Give the mean of *dlater*.

    (b) Compute the average of *price* when *dlater*= 1 and when *dlater*= 0, and the difference in the means.

    (c) OLS regress *price* on an intercept and *dlater* and use heteroskedastic-robust standard errors. Compare the slope coefficient to your answer in part (b). Is the difference in means statistically significant at 5%?

    (d) Now use a statistical package difference-in-mean command to test the difference in means assuming unequal variances. Compare the estimate, standard error and degrees of freedom to your answer in part (c).

    (e) Repeat part (c) but use default standard errors.

    (f) Repeat part (d) assuming equal variances and compare to your answer in part (e).

6. Repeat the previous exercise for outcome *size* rather than *price*.

7. Let d_i be an indicator variable and define $dx_i = d_i \times x_i$.

    (a) Suppose OLS regression using all data yields fitted model $\widehat{y}_i = 3 + 5d_i + 6x_i + 7dx_i$. Give the predictions for the subsample with $d_i = 1$ and the subsample with $d_i = 0$.

    (b) Suppose $\widehat{y}_i = 2 + 5x_i$ for the subsample with $d_i = 1$ and $\widehat{y}_i = 6 + 7x_i$ for the subsample with $d_i = 0$. Give the predictions for the combined model of form $\widehat{y}_i = b_1 + b_2 d_i + b_3 x_i + b_4 dx_i$.

8. Repeat the previous exercise where in part (a) $\widehat{y}_i = 5 - 3d_i + 4x_i + 2dx_i$ and in part (b) $\widehat{y}_i = 5 + 2x_i$ when $d_i = 1$ and $\widehat{y}_i = 3 + 6x_i$ when $d_i = 0$.

9. Use dataset HOUSE.

   (a) Create the indicator variable *dlater* equal to one if the house is sold after June (*month-sold*> 6) and equals zero otherwise. Create the variable *dlatersize* = *dlater*×*size*. Give the mean of *dlater* and *dlatersize*.

   (b) Prepare scatterplots with a fitted regression line of *price* against *size* for *dlater*= 1 and for *dlater*= 0. Does the relationship appear to differ with *dlater*?

   (c) OLS regress *price* on an intercept, *size*, *dlater* and *dlatersize* with heteroskedastic-robust standard errors. Report the fitted model.

   (d) Test at 5% the null hypothesis that the relationship between *price* and *size* is the same for the two different values of *dlater*. State the null hypothesis and your conclusion.

   (e) Test at 5% the null hypothesis that the relationship between *price* and *size* is statistically significant. State the null hypothesis and your conclusion.

   (f) Perform separate OLS regression of *price* against *size* for *dlater*= 1 and for *dlater*= 0. Show how your coefficient estimates are consistent with those from part (c).

10. Repeat the previous question using indicator variable *dlarge* equal to one if the house is on a larger lot (*lotsize*= 3) and equals zero otherwise, and the interaction variable *dlarge* = *dlarge*×*size*.

11. You obtain OLS estimates $\widehat{y} = 1 + 2x + 4d1 + 7d2$, with $R^2 = 0.5$, where $d1$, $d2$ and $d3$ are a set of mutually exclusive dummy variables and $d3$ is omitted. For each of the following OLS regressions give the fitted model. If R^2 will change in any of the following parts then state so.

    (a) Regress y on an intercept, x, $d1$ and $d3$.

    (b) Regress y on an intercept, x, $d2$ and $d3$.

    (c) Regress y on x, $d1$, $d2$ and $d3$.

12. Repeat the previous exercise for $\widehat{y} = 1 + 2x + 4d2 + 7d3$ with $d1$ the omitted category.

13. Use data in dataset HOUSE and heteroskedastic-robust standard errors.

    (a) Create three separate dummy variables *d1*, *d2*, *d3* for *lotsize* equal to 1, 2 and 3.

    (b) Verify that these dummy variables are mutually exclusive.

    (c) Regress *price* on *size* and *lotsize*.

    (d) Regress *price* on *size*, *d2* and *d3*. Are *d2* and *d3* jointly statistically significant?

    (e) Which model do you prefer, that in (b) or that in (c)? Explain.

    (f) Redo part (d) with *d1* and d2 rather than *d2* and *d3*. How have your answers changed?

    (g) Regress *price* on *size*, *d1*, *d2* and *d3*. Explain what has happened.

    (h) Regress *price* on *size*, *d1*, *d2* and *lotsize*. Explain what has happened.

14. A detailed description of dataset SALARYSAT is given in exercise 3 of Chapter 7. The variable *genhealth* measures health status and takes values 1=Excellent, 2=VeryGood, 3=Good, 4=Fair and 5=Poor.

    (a) Create five dummy variables *dhealth1* to *dhealth5* corresponding to the five values taken by *genhealth*.

    (b) Verify that the dummies are mutually exclusive.

    (c) Regress *salary* on *dhealth1* to *dhealth5* with no intercept in the regression. Compare the OLS coefficients to the mean of salary for each value of *genhealth*. Comment.

    (d) Now regress *salary* on an intercept and *dhealth2* to *dhealth5*. Compare the coefficient of *dhealth2* to the difference in the mean of *salary* when *dhealth2*=1 and the mean of *salary* when *dhealth1*=1. Comment.

    (e) Are the health status dummies jointly statistically significant at 5% in part (d)?

    (f) Now instead regress *salary* on an intercept and *dhealth1* to *dhealth4*. Provide an interpretation of the coefficient of *dhealth1*.

Chapter 15

Regression with Transformed Variables

The linear model can be made more flexible by including as regressors variables that are nonlinear transformations of the underlying regressors (or the dependent variable) such as powers, natural logarithms and interactions of variables.

As an example, consider the determinants of annual earnings of individuals. Age may appear quadratically rather than linearly. Variables may be interacted, such as an interaction between age and education. And variables may have multiplicative effects, in which case the dependent variable and/or regressors may appear as natural logarithms.

Estimation by OLS remains straightforward, as long as the model remains linear in the coefficients $b_1, b_2, ..., b_k$. But the interpretation of the coefficients becomes more complicated as it is no longer the case that a slope coefficient measures the change in $\widehat{y}$ when x changes by one unit.

15.1   Example: Earnings, Gender, Education and Type of Worker

This chapter uses the dataset EARNINGS_COMPLETE on male and female full-time workers in 2010 aged 25 to 65 years.

Table 15.1 presents summary statistics for the dependent variable *Earnings* and the other variables used in this chapter. Mean earnings are $56,369 per year, 43.3% of the sample are female, mean age is 43.31 years and mean education is 13.85 years of schooling. The type of worker is broken into three categories – self-employed, employed in private sector and employed in government sector.

15.2   Marginal Effects for Nonlinear Models

In nonlinear models the interpretation of coefficient estimates becomes more complicated as it is no longer the case that a coefficient measures the change in $\widehat{y}$ when x changes by one unit.

333

Table 15.1: Annual Earnings of full-time workers aged 25-65 in 2010: Summary statistics (n=872).

Variable	Definition	Mean	Standard Deviation	Min	Max
Earnings	Annual earnings in $	56369	51516	4000	504000
Lnearnings	Natural logarithm of *Earnings*	10.69	0.68	8.29	13.13
Age	Age in years	43.31	10.68	25	65
Agesq	*Age* squared	1989.7	935.7	625	4225
Education	Years of schooling	13.85	2.88	0	20
AgebyEduc	*Age* times *Education*	598.8	193.69	0	1260
Gender	= 1 if female	0.433	0.496	0	1
d1 or dself	= 1 if self-employed	0.091	0.287	0	1
d2 or dpriv	=1 if private sector employee	0.760	0.427	0	1
d3 or dgovt	=1 if government sector employee	0.149	0.356	0	1
Hours	Usual hours worked per week	44.34	8.50	35	99
Lnhours	Natural logarithm of *Hours*	3.78	0.16	3.56	4.60
n	872				

15.2.1 Marginal Effects in a Nonlinear Model

In many studies interest lies in the effect on the dependent variable of a change in an explanatory variable. This is called the marginal effect.

Remark 122 *The **marginal effect (ME)** on the predicted value of the dependent variable of a change in a regressor is defined as the ratio of the change in $\widehat{y}$ to the change in x, so $ME_x = \Delta\widehat{y}/\Delta x$.*

For the linear regression model $y = b_1 + b_2 x$ the ME is simply the slope coefficient b_2.

For a nonlinear model, however, this is no longer the case. Instead, the marginal effect depends in part on b_2 but it also varies with the evaluation point x. Furthermore, there is more than one way to calculate the marginal effect at a given point x.

Figure 15.1 plots the nonlinear curve $y = 12 - 2 \times (x - 3)^2$ whose slope (the marginal effect) clearly varies with x. The two panels present two different ways to compute the marginal effect at $x = 2$.

The first panel of Figure 15.1 evaluates the marginal effect at $x = 2$ as being the **slope of the tangent** to the curve at $x = 2$. The tangent line passes through $y = 10$ at $x = 2$ and $y = 14$ at $x = 3$, so the slope of the tangent equals $14 - 10 = 4$. This method is called the **calculus method** as the slope of the tangent is the **derivative** of the curve. It computes the ratio $\Delta y/\Delta x$ for a very small change in x (the tangent to the curve) and then extrapolates this to a one unit change in x. For those familiar with calculus, the plotted curve $y = 12 - 2 \times (x-3)^2$ has derivative $dy/dx = 12 - 4x$ which equals 4 at $x = 2$.

The second panel of Figure 15.1 evaluates the marginal effect at $x = 2$ as being the change in y when x increases by one unit, from $x = 2$ to $x = 3$. Since $y = 10$ at $x = 2$ and $y = 12$ at $x = 3$, the marginal effect equals $12 - 10 = 2$. This method is called the **finite difference method**. It computes the ratio $\Delta y/\Delta x$ for a one unit change in x.

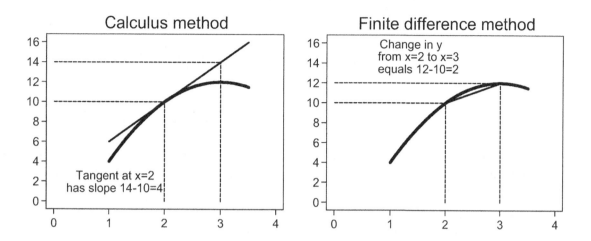

Figure 15.1: Marginal effect: Computation by calculus method and by finite difference method.

Economists most often use the first method, the calculus method. When the finite difference method is used it is most often used for an indicator variable regressor. For example for an indicator variable $d = 1$ if female and $d = 0$ if male it is more natural to consider a change from $d = 0$ to $d = 1$ than it is to consider a very small change.

Remark 123 *Marginal effects at a given value of x are most often computed exactly at x (the* **calculus method***). In some cases marginal effects at x are instead computed for a discrete change from x such as a one-unit change (the* **finite difference method***).*

Using either method the marginal effect will change as x changes. For example, using the finite difference in the current example the marginal effect at $x = 1$ equals 6 (since $y = 4$ at $x = 1$ and $y = 10$ at $x = 2$, a change of $10 - 4 = 6$) whereas the ME at $x = 2$ equals $12 - 10 = 2$.

15.2.2 AME, MEM and MER

There are three commonly-used methods to summarize the marginal effect on y of a change in x. We begin with the simplest case where the ME depends only on x and does not depend on other variables.

1. Average marginal effect (AME): the average over the sample of the marginal effect for each individual (so evaluate the ME at each x_i and then average).

2. Marginal effect at the mean (MEM): the marginal effect evaluated at the sample mean $\bar{x}$.

3. Marginal effect at a representative value (MER): the marginal effect evaluated at a representative value x^*.

So AME equals $\frac{1}{n}\sum_{i=1}^{n}\mathrm{ME}_i$, MEM equals ME at $x = \bar{x}$ and MER equals ME at $x = x^*$.

Remark 124 *Three alternative measures of the marginal effect are the average marginal effect (AME), the marginal effect at the mean (MEM), and the marginal effect at a representative value (MER).*

For a linear model all three ME's are the same and equal the slope coefficient of x. In nonlinear models the three measures differ. It is most common to use the AME which gives the sample average of the ME's. The MEM gives the ME for the average regressor value. The MER is used if interest lies in evaluation at particular values of x, such as computing the ME of schooling on earnings at twelve years of schooling.

15.2.3   Computation of AME, MEM and MER

Some statistical packages provide post-estimation commands to calculate AME, MEM and MER. These commands can additionally provide standard errors and confidence intervals for these estimates.

Care is needed in use of these commands due to the additional complication that in nonlinear models the ME of a change in x can depend on variables other than x.

For example, if $\widehat{y} = 1 + x^3 + xz^2$ then using the calculus method $\mathrm{ME}_x = 3x^2 + z^2$, so ME_x additionally depends on variable z.

For the AME it is standard to again evaluate for each individual and average, so $\mathrm{AME}_x = \frac{1}{n}\sum_{i=1}^{n}(3x_i^2 + z_i^2)$.

For the MEM all variables are usually set at their means, so $\mathrm{MEM}_x = 3\bar{x}^2 + \bar{z}^2$.

For MER we may just be interested in evaluation at a particular value x^* of x, with z taking the values for each individual, in which case $\mathrm{MER}_x = 3(x^*)^2 + \frac{1}{n}\sum_{i=1}^{n}z_i^2$. Or we may additionally specify evaluation at a particular value z^* of z, in which case $\mathrm{MER}_x = 3(x^*)^2 + (z^*)^2$.

15.2.4   Nonlinear Models in Practice

Several issues arise when the relationship is nonlinear, in addition to computation of marginal effects.

The first issue is how to estimate a nonlinear relationship. OLS can be used if the coefficients in the model still appear linearly and only the explanatory variable (or the dependent variable) appear nonlinearly. For example, a linear-log model $\mathrm{E}[y|x] = \beta_1 + \beta_2 \ln x$ can be estimated by least squares regression of y on $\ln x$, rather than y on x.

For some other nonlinear models, however, such as $\mathrm{E}[y|x] = \exp(\beta_1 + \beta_2 x)$ standard least squares estimation is not possible as the parameters do not appear linearly. Then alternative more advanced estimation methods are needed; see Chapter 17.6.

A second issue is whether a direct interpretation of slope coefficients is possible. In some cases it is possible, such as in log-linear, log-log and linear log models as detailed in Chapter 9.3.

A third issue is prediction of y when y is transformed before regression. For example, if the model is $\mathrm{E}[\ln y|x] = \beta_1 + \beta_2 x$, then how do we retransform to predict the level of y?

Finally, how do we choose the appropriate nonlinear model? For a bivariate model we can plot y against x and get some idea of the relationship. This is more difficult for a model that includes additional regressors. In many applications economic theory and the experiences of other studies that use similar data can provide a good guide.

15.3 Quadratic Model and Polynomial Models

A leading example of a nonlinear relationship is a model where y is a quadratic function of x rather than a linear function of x. More generally polynomial models include powers of x as regressors.

15.3.1 Quadratic Models

A **quadratic model** is the model

$$\widehat{y} = b_1 + b_2 x + b_3 x^2.$$

This is a polynomial model of degree two, and reduces to a linear model if $b_3 = 0$.

The model defines a parabola, though often only one side of the parabola appears for the sample range of x. Figure 15.2 presents various possible shapes for the relationship between y and x for a quadratic model.

The top three panels of Figure 15.2 show examples where b_3, the coefficient of x^2, is positive. For the parabola in the top left panel it can be shown that the minimum value of y occurs when $x = -b_2/(2b_3)$. For the middle panel in the top row $x < -b_2/(2b_3)$, so the data include only the left half of the parabola, while for the right panel in the top row $x > -b_2/(2b_3)$.

The bottom three panels of Figure 15.2 show examples where $b_3 < 0$. The parabola in the left panel y takes its maximum value when $x = -b_2/(2b_3)$, for the middle panel $x < -b_2/(2b_3)$ and for the right bottom panel $x > -b_2/(2b_3)$.

A quadratic model is estimated as follows. First, create a variable called, say, xsq, where $xsq = x^2$. Then do least squares regression of y on x and xsq.

Remark 125 *The parabola $\widehat{y} = b_1 + b_2 x + b_3 x^2$ has turning point $-b_2/(2b_3)$ at a minimum if $b_3 > 0$ and at a maximum if $b_3 < 0$.*

15.3.2 Marginal Effects for Quadratic Model

Begin with fitted quadratic model

$$\widehat{y} = b_1 + b_2 x + b_3 x^2 + b_4 z,$$

where an additional regressor z has been added.

If x increases by the amount Δx, leading to evaluation at $x + \Delta x$, then $\widehat{y}$ becomes

$$\begin{aligned} \widehat{y}_{new} &= b_1 + b_2(x + \Delta x) + b_3(x + \Delta x)^2 + b_4 z \\ &= b_1 + b_2 x + b_2 \Delta x + b_3 x^2 + 2b_3 x \Delta x + b_3(\Delta x)^2 + b_4 z. \end{aligned}$$

Examples of Quadratic Model

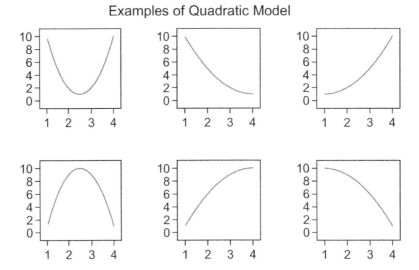

Figure 15.2: Quadratic models: Examples of the possible shapes.

On subtraction of $\widehat{y}_{old} = b_1 + b_2 x + b_3 x^2 + b_4 z$ it follows that $\Delta \widehat{y} = b_2 \Delta x + 2 b_3 x \Delta x + b_3 (\Delta x)^2$, so the **marginal effect** on y of changing x by Δx, computed by the **finite-difference method** is

$$\mathrm{ME}_x = \frac{\Delta \widehat{y}}{\Delta x} = b_2 + 2 b_3 x + b_3 \Delta x.$$

Note that the size of ME varies with both x, through the term $2 b_3 x$, and Δx, through the term $b_3 \Delta x$.

For a finite change, the usual choice is to consider a **one-unit change** in x, so $\Delta x = 1$ and $\mathrm{ME}_x = b_2 + 2 b_3 x + b_3$.

It is more common to use the **calculus method** that computes the ME when Δx is very small. When $\Delta x \to 0$ the third term $b_3 \Delta x \to 0$ and $\mathrm{ME}_x = b_2 + 2 b_3 x$. For those familiar with calculus this result can be obtained immediately, as the derivative of $\widehat{y} = b_1 + b_2 x + b_3 x^2$ with respect to x is $d\widehat{y}/dx = b_2 + 2 b_3 x$.

Remark 126 *The marginal effect in the fitted quadratic model $\widehat{y} = b_1 + b_2 x + b_3 x^2$ equals $b_2 + 2 b_3 x$ using calculus methods.*

For the quadratic model the AME is

$$\mathrm{AME}_x = \frac{1}{n} \sum\nolimits_{i=1}^{n} (b_2 + 2 b_3 x_i) = b_2 + 2 b_3 \times \frac{1}{n} \sum\nolimits_{i=1}^{n} x_i = b_2 + 2 b_3 \bar{x}.$$

For the quadratic model this equals the MEM; for other nonlinear models such as a cubic model the AME and MEM differ.

15.3.3 Hypothesis Tests for a Quadratic Model

Consider the corresponding population model

$$y = \beta_1 + \beta_2 x + \beta_3 x^2 + \beta_4 z + u.$$

A test of $H_0 : \beta_3 = 0$ against $H_a : \beta_3 \neq 0$ is a test of whether the quadratic term is necessary.

To test whether variable x is statistically significant we perform an F test of $H_0 : \beta_2 = 0$, $\beta_3 = 0$ against $H_a :$ at least one of $\beta_2 \neq 0$, $\beta_3 \neq 0$, since variable x appears as both regressor x and regressor x^2.

15.3.4 Quadratic Example: Earnings and Age

We consider an example with a quadratic in age. Least squares regression of *Earnings* (y) on *Age* (x), *Agesq* (x^2), and *Education* (z), is

$$\widehat{Earnings} = \underset{(-4.02)}{-98620} + \underset{(2.86)}{3105} \times Age - \underset{(-2.38)}{29.66} \times Agesq + \underset{(8.94)}{5740} \times Education, \quad R^2 = 0.120,$$

where the t statistics given in parentheses are based on heteroskedastic-robust standard errors. A quadratic term is warranted as it is statistically significant at level 0.05 since $|t| = 2.38 > t_{868,.025} = 1.963$.

In general the turning point for the quadratic is at $x = -b_2/2b_3$. Here the turning point is at $Age = -3105/(2 \times (-29.66)) = 52.3$. Controlling for education, earnings on average increase with age to a maximum at 52.3 years and then decline with additional age.

The estimated ME$= 3105 + 2 \times (-29.66)x - 29.66\Delta x$ by the finite difference method, so for a one-unit change, with $\Delta x = 1$, ME$= 3075 - 59.32x$.

We focus on using the calculus method, with ME$= 3105 - 59.32x = 3105 - 59.32 \times Age$. The AME$= \frac{1}{n}\sum_{i=1}^{n}(3105 - 59.32 \times Age_i) = 3105 - 59.32 \times \overline{Age} = 3105 - 59.32 \times 43.31 = 536$. The MEM$= 3105 - 59.32\overline{Age} = 5153 - 105.56 \times 43.31 = 536$. As already noted, for the quadratic model the MEM equals the AME. The MER at $Age = 25$, for example, is $3105 - 59.32 \times 25 = 1622$.

The AME of \$536 is similar to that of \$525 for the linear model. The advantage of the quadratic model is that it allows for variation in the ME at different ages. The ME is highest at \$1,622 for 25-year-olds and lowers substantially to a minimum of -\$751 at age 65 years.

The joint test that the coefficients of x and x^2 equal zero has $F = 9.29$ with $p = 0.0001$, so age is statistically significant at 5%.

15.3.5 Polynomial Model

A generalization of the quadratic model is a **polynomial model of degree** p that includes powers of x up to x^p. Then the fitted model is

$$\widehat{y} = b_1 + b_2 x + b_3 x^2 + \cdots + b_{p+1} x^p.$$

This model has up to $p - 1$ turning points. The order of the polynomial can be determined by progressively adding terms x^2, x^3, ... in a multiple regression until additional terms are no longer statistically significant.

By calculus methods it can be shown that the marginal effect is

$$\text{ME}_x = b_2 + 2b_3 x + 3b_4 x^2 + \cdots + p b_{p+1} x^{p-1},$$

which again will vary with the point of evaluation x.

15.4 Interacted Regressors

An **interacted regressor** is a regressor that is the product of other regressors that appear in the model. Estimation by OLS regression remains straightforward, but adjustment is needed in testing statistical significance of a variable and in interpreting estimated coefficients.

15.4.1 Interacted Regressors

Consider the model

$$\widehat{y} = b_1 + b_2 x + b_3 z + b_4 xz,$$

where $xz = x \times z$ is an interacted regressor.

Interpretation of regressors is more difficult, however, as the variable x is a component of two regressors, the regressor x and the regressor xz. Similarly the variable z appears in the two regressors z and xz.

To compute the marginal effect (ME) on $\widehat{y}$ of a change in x, holding z constant, we need to consider the combined effect of change in any regressor that depends on x, here the regressors x and xz. Then

$$\text{ME}_x = \frac{\Delta \widehat{y}}{\Delta x} = b_2 + b_4 z.$$

To see this, note that if x changes by Δx to $x + \Delta x$, then $\widehat{y}$ changes to $\widehat{y} = b_1 + b_2(x + \Delta x) + b_3 z + b_4(x + \Delta x) \times z$, which is an increase of $\beta_2 \Delta x + \beta_4 \Delta x \times z$. Dividing by Δx yields ME_x. This result can also be obtained by directly taking the derivative of $\widehat{y}$ with respect to x, holding z constant. The marginal effect varies with the level of variable z.

Similar algebra for the marginal effect on $\widehat{y}$ of a change in z, holding x constant, yields $\text{ME}_z = \frac{\Delta \widehat{y}}{\Delta z} = b_3 + b_4 x$.

15.4.2 Hypothesis Tests for an Interacted Regressor

Consider the corresponding population model

$$y = \beta_1 + \beta_2 x + \beta_3 z + \beta_4 x \times z + u.$$

A test of $H_0 : \beta_4 = 0$ against $H_a : \beta_4 \neq 0$ is a test of whether the interaction term term is necessary.

To test whether variable x is statistically significant we need to perform a test of the joint statistical significance of all regressors that depend on the variable x, here the regressors x and xz. Thus we perform an F test of $H_0 : \beta_2 = 0$, $\beta_4 = 0$ against H_a : at least one of $\beta_2 \neq 0$, $\beta_4 \neq 0$.

Similarly to test whether variable z is statistically significant we perform an F test of $H_0 : \beta_3 = 0$, $\beta_4 = 0$ against H_a : at least one of $\beta_3 \neq 0$, $\beta_4 \neq 0$.

Remark 127 *When a variable appears directly as a regressor and additionally as an interacted regressor the marginal effect of the variable includes an effect through the interaction term. A test of the statistical significance of the variable is an F test of the joint statistical significance of the regressor and the interaction term. A t test of statistical significance of the interacted regressor is a test of whether the interaction term is needed.*

15.4.3 Interactions Example: Earnings, Education and Age

OLS regression of *Earnings* on *Age* (x) and *Education* (z) yields estimates

$$\widehat{Earnings} = \underset{(-4.15)}{-46875} + \underset{(3.47)}{525} \times Age + \underset{(9.06)}{5811} \times Education, \ R^2 = 0.115,$$

where t statistics based on heteroskedastic-robust standard errors are given in parentheses. Both regressors are highly statistically significant and have economically meaningful coefficients.

Now suppose we wish to allow for the possibility that the returns to schooling vary with age. To test this we introduce an interaction term *AgebyEduc* ($x \times z$) that equals *Age* times *Education*. The fitted model is now

$$\widehat{Earnings} = \underset{(-0.94)}{-29089} + \underset{(0.18)}{127} \times Age + \underset{(1.88)}{4515} \times Education + \underset{(0.52)}{29.04} \times AgebyEduc, \ R^2 = 0.115,$$

where t statistics based on heteroskedastic-robust standard errors are given in parentheses.

The interaction term is statistically insignificant at 5%, with $t = 0.52$, so the data do not support inclusion of an interaction term.

Furthermore, the regressor *Age* is now individually statistically insignificant at significance level 0.05, with $t = 0.18$, whereas it is statistically significant in a model without the interaction term. So at first glance it appears that now age has no statistically significant effect on earnings, since regressor *Age* has $t = 0.18$. But this conclusion would be wrong. A joint test of the statistical significance of the regressor *Age* (x) and the age-education interaction term ($x \times z$), here a test of $H_0 : \beta_2 = 0, \ \beta_4 = 0$, has $F = 6.49$ with $p = 0.002$, so age is highly statistically significant.

Similarly *Education* (z) appears to be individually statistically insignificant at 5% with $t = 1.88$, but a joint test of *Education* (z) and age-education ($x \times z$), yields $F = 43.00$ with $p = 0.000$.

Why have the variables *Age* and *Education* become individually statistically insignificant with inclusion of the interaction term? The interaction variable *AgebyEduc* is quite highly correlated with *Age* ($\hat{\rho} = 0.73$) and *Education* ($\hat{\rho} = 0.64$). When regressors are highly correlated with each other their individual contributions are measured much less precisely. Thus the standard errors of *Age* and *Education* more than triple from, respectively, 151 to 719 and 641 to 2401, with inclusion of variable *AgebyEduc*. As already noted, joint F tests that include the interaction term show that education and age remain statistically significant. This increase in imprecision when regressors are highly correlated is an example of multicollinearity, studied in Chapter 16.1.

Now consider interpretation of the regression coefficients, allowing for inclusion of the interaction term. The marginal effect of one more year of schooling is

$$ME_{Ed} = 4515 + 29.04 \times Age.$$

So the returns to education increase as one ages. For example the marginal effect is \$5,240 at age 25 years and \$6,403 at age 65 years. The average marginal effect (AME) is $\text{AME}_{Ed} = \frac{1}{n}\sum_{i=1}^{n}[4515 + 29x_i] = 4515 + 29.04\bar{x} = 5773$. The AME equals the marginal effect at the mean (MEM), a result that holds more generally whenever the interaction term is of multiplicative form $x \times z$.

Some statistical packages provide a command that directly computes the AME or MEM of a variable that appears as in interaction in the regression, allowing for the complication that the variable appears in more than one regressor, as in the preceding example. Such a command will also compute the standard error of the marginal effect, which in the previous example equals $\sqrt{se(b_3)^2 + 2\bar{x} \times \widehat{cov}(b_3, b_4) + \bar{x}^2 se(b_4)^2}$, where $\widehat{cov}(b_3, b_4)$ is the estimated covariance between b_3 and b_4. In this example the resulting standard error of AME_{Ed} is 627, so the AME is highly statistically significant at significance level 0.05 as $t = 5773/627 = 9.21$.

15.5   Log-linear and Log-log Models

Remark 128 *Coefficients in models with dependent variable or regressor(s) in natural logarithms are most easily interpreted as semi-elasticities or elasticities; see Chapter 9.3.*

In this section we additionally present marginal effects that consider changes in y in levels, rather than elasticities and semi-elasticities that consider proportionate changes. Marginal effects obtained using the calculus method use the result that $\Delta \ln y = \Delta y / y$ for small proportionate changes in y (i.e., small $\Delta y/y$ or equivalently small $\Delta \ln y$).

These marginal effects depend in part on the predicted value of y. It is simplest to evaluate the marginal effects at the sample average $\bar{y}$. If instead evaluation is at predicted values of y, the predictions need to control for retransformation bias that arises due to predicting levels from a model in logs; see Chapter 15.6.

15.5.1   Log-linear Model

A fitted **log-linear model** is

$$\widehat{\ln y} = b_1 + b_2 x + b_3 z,$$

where $\ln y$ is the natural logarithm of y. This model can be used only if $y > 0$ since only then is $\ln y$ defined.

Remark 129 *For the log-linear model a one unit change in x is associated with a b_2 proportionate change or a $100b_2\%$ change in y. The marginal effect in this model equals $b_2\widehat{y}$ using calculus methods and equals $[\exp(b_2) - 1]\widehat{y}$ for a one-unit change using the finite difference method.*

The proportionate interpretation was derived in Chapter 9.3.

To obtain the marginal effect using calculus methods, note that for this OLS regression the slope b_2 gives the marginal effect on $\ln y$ of a change in x, that is $\Delta \ln y / \Delta x = b_2$. Now $\Delta \ln y = \Delta y / y$ for small $\Delta \ln y$, and making this substitution yields $(\Delta y / y)/\Delta x = b_2$. Rearranging yields the marginal effect $\Delta y/\Delta x = b_2 y$.

For the finite difference rewrite the fitted model as $\widehat{y} = \exp(b_1 + b_2 x + b_3 z)$. When x increases to $x + \Delta x$ we have $\widehat{y}_{new} = \exp(b_1 + b_2(x + \Delta x)b_3 z) = \exp(b_1 + b_2 x + b_3 z) \times \exp(b_2 \Delta x) = \widehat{y}\exp(b_2 \Delta x)$. Subtracting yields a change of $\widehat{y}\exp(b_2 \Delta x) - \widehat{y} = \widehat{y} \times [\exp(b_2) - 1]$. For b_2 close to zero $\exp(b_2) \simeq 1 + b_2$ so $\exp(b_2) - 1 \simeq b_2$ and the calculus and finite difference marginal effects are then similar.

Note that the marginal effect varies with the point of evaluation x since $\widehat{y}$ varies with x.

The log-linear model is sometimes called the **exponential model**, since taking the exponential of both sides yields $\widehat{y} = \exp(b_1 + b_2 x + b_3 z)$.

15.5.2   Log-Linear Example: Earnings and Age

For the earnings data the fitted log-linear model is

$$\ln \widehat{Earnings} = \underset{(59.63)}{8.96} + \underset{(3.83)}{0.0078} \times Age + \underset{(11.68)}{0.101} \times Education, \ R^2 = 0.190, \ s_e = 0.6164,$$

where t statistics based on heteroskedastic-robust standard errors are in parentheses. One year of aging, controlling for education, is associated with a 0.78 percent ($= 100 \times 0.0078$) increase in earnings.

The marginal effect of aging is $0.0078\widehat{y}$. The marginal effect is always positive, and increases with age since $\widehat{y}$ increases with age. It is simplest to evaluate at $\bar{y}$, in which case the marginal effect of a year of aging is a \$440 increase in earnings ($= 0.0078 \times 56369$).

15.5.3   Log-Log Model

The **log-log model** applies the natural logarithm transformation to both y and x, leading to fitted model

$$\widehat{\ln y} = b_1 + b_2 \ln x + b_3 z.$$

This model can be used only if both $y > 0$ and $x > 0$.

Remark 130 *For the log-log model a 1% change in x is associated with a b_2% change in y. For this model, the marginal effect equals $b_2 \widehat{y}/x$ using calculus methods.*

The proportionate interpretation was derived in Chapter 9.3.

To obtain the marginal effect, note that the slope b_2 gives the marginal effect on $\ln y$ of a change in $\ln x$, that is $\Delta \ln y / \Delta \ln x = b_2$. Now $\Delta \ln y = \Delta y / y$ for small Δy, and $\Delta \ln x = \Delta x / x$ for small Δx. Making these substitutions, $(\Delta y / y)/(\Delta x / x) = b_2$, and rearranging yields marginal effect $\Delta y / \Delta x = b_2 \times y/x$. The marginal effect varies with the point of evaluation x.

The log-linear model is sometimes called the **power model**, since taking the exponential of both sides and manipulating leads to $\widehat{y} = e^{b_1} x^{b_2} e^{b_3 z}$.

15.5.4   Log-Log Example: Earnings and Age

For the earnings data the fitted log-linear model is

$$\ln \widehat{Earnings} = \underset{(24.23)}{8.01} + \underset{(4.21)}{0.346} \times \ln Age + \underset{(11.67)}{0.100} \times Education, \ R^2 = 0.193, \ s_e = 0.6155,$$

where t statistics based on heteroskedastic-robust standard errors are in parentheses. A one percent increase in age, controlling for education, is associated with a 0.346 percent increase in earnings.

The marginal effect of aging is $0.346\widehat{y}/x$ and is always positive. It is simplest to evaluate at $\bar{y}$ and $\bar{x}$, in which case the marginal effect of a year of aging is a \$450 increase in earnings ($= 0.346 \times 56369/43.31$).

15.6   Prediction from Log-Linear and Log-Log Models

Prediction of y in levels requires transformation from a model in logs. For the log-linear model with $\widehat{\ln y} = b_1 + b_2 x + b_3 z$, the obvious prediction is $\widehat{y} = \exp(b_1 + b_2 x + b_3 z)$. However this prediction under-predicts y due to a retransformation bias presented in this section.

15.6.1   Prediction Controlling for Retransformation Bias

The population model for the log-linear model for regression of y on x is

$$\ln y = \beta_1 + \beta_2 x + u,$$

where z is dropped for simplicity and $\mathrm{E}[u|x] = 0$. This model specifies the conditional mean of $\ln y$ given x, but we need to predict the conditional mean of y (and not that of $\ln y$) given x.

The log-linear model implies $y = \exp(\beta_1 + \beta_2 x + u)$, so the conditional mean of y given x is

$$
\begin{aligned}
\mathrm{E}[y|x] &= \mathrm{E}[\exp(\beta_1 + \beta_2 x + u)|x] \\
&= \exp(\beta_1 + \beta_2 x) \times \mathrm{E}[\exp(u)|x].
\end{aligned}
$$

The log-linear model specifies $\mathrm{E}[u|x] = 0$. A mathematical result shows that this condition implies that $\mathrm{E}[\exp(u)|x] > 1$. So $\mathrm{E}[y|x] > \exp(\beta_1 + \beta_2 x)$ and the obvious prediction $\widehat{y} = \exp(b_1 + b_2 x)$ underpredicts on average by the multiple $\mathrm{E}[\exp(u)|x]$.

In the special case that errors are normally distributed and homoskedastic, so $u|x \sim N(0, \sigma_u^2)$, it can be shown with some difficulty that $\mathrm{E}[\exp(u)|x] = \exp(\sigma_u^2/2)$. It follows that in this special case

$$\mathrm{E}[y|x] = \exp(\sigma_u^2/2)\exp(\beta_1 + \beta_2 x).$$

Then $\mathrm{E}[y|x]$ is predicted using

$$\widetilde{y} = \exp(s_e^2/2)\exp(b_1 + b_2 x),$$

where s_e is the standard error of the log-linear regression.

For example, suppose $s_e = 0.4$. This means that the standard error of the residual is 0.4 on a log scale, which is quite large. Then $\exp(s_e^2/2) = \exp(0.08) = 1.083$ and we multiply $\exp(b_1 + b_2 x)$ by 1.083.

More generally for regression of $g(y)$ on x the fitted value $\widehat{g(y)} = b_1 + b_2 x$ leads to unbiased prediction of $g(y)$ but upon simple retransformation leads to biased (and inconsistent) prediction of y. For a model with $\ln y$ as the dependent variable and with normally distributed errors it is possible to provide a simple formula for a correct prediction. For other models, however, this is usually not the case.

Remark 131 *Retransformation bias arises whenever a model for $g(y)$ is estimated but prediction of y is desired. For a log-linear model a correction multiplies the obvious prediction $\widehat{y} = \exp(b_1 + b_2 x)$ by $\exp(s_e^2/2)$ where s_e is the standard error of the log-linear regression.*

This last result generalizes to log-linear models with more regressors. For $\widehat{\ln y} = b_1 + b_2 x + \cdots + b_k x_k$ we use prediction $\widetilde{y} = \exp(s_e^2/2)\widehat{y}$ where $\widehat{y} = \exp(b_1 + b_2 x + \cdots + b_k x_k)$. And for the log-log model $\widehat{\ln y} = b_1 + b_2 \ln x$, by similar argument use $\widetilde{y} = \exp(s_e^2/2)\exp(b_1 + b_2 \ln x)$, where s_e is the standard error of the residual in the log-log regression.

These corrections are exact if errors u are normally distributed and homoskedastic. In many applications where a log-linear or log-log model is appropriate, the original variable y is right-skewed, the transformed variable $\ln y$ is more symmetrically distributed and the assumption of homoskedastic normal errors may be a reasonable approximation.

15.6.2 Prediction with Retransformation Example: Earnings and Age

For the earnings data the fitted log-linear model is $\widehat{\ln y} = 8.96 + 0.0078x + 0.101z$ with $s_e = 0.6164$ and $\exp(0.6164^2/2) = 1.2092$. So we use as prediction $\widetilde{y} = 1.2092 \times \exp(8.96 + 0.0078x + 0.101z)$. This substantial correction by multiplication by 1.2092 relies on the assumption of normally distributed errors and is therefore not perfect, but it is much better than making no correction.

For these data the sample mean of variable *Earnings* is \$56,369, the average of the in-sample predictions without correction is \$45,838, a large under-estimate, while the average of the in-sample predictions with correction is \$55,427, within \$1,000 of \$56,369.

The correction does well here as in this example the residuals from the log-linear model appear to be approximately normally distributed, from visual inspection of their histogram and kernel density estimate, and because the skewness statistic is close to zero and the kurtosis statistics is close to 3.

For the log-log model $s_e = 0.6155$ and $\exp(0.6155^2/2) = 1.2085$. So we use as prediction $\widetilde{y} = 1.2085 \times \exp(8.96 + 0.0078 \ln x + 0.101z)$. The average of the consequent predictions is \$55,424, close to the sample average \$56,369, and much better than the average \$45,861 of predictions without the correction.

15.6.3 R-squared with Transformed Dependent Variable

Recall that R^2 in regression of y on x measures the fraction of the variation in y_i, around the mean $\bar{y}$, that is explained by the regressor. By contrast R^2 in regression of $g(y)$ on x explains the fraction of the variation in $g(y_i)$, around its mean $\overline{g(y)} = \frac{1}{n}\sum_{i=1}^{n} g(y_i)$, that is explained by the regressor. These two measures are not comparable.

Remark 132 *It is meaningless to use R^2 to compare the fit of models with different transformations of y as the dependent variable.*

For data y that are right-skewed, the model with $\ln y$ as dependent variable generally has higher R^2 than the model with y as dependent variable, since the logarithmic transformation brings in large outlying values that can lead to poor model fit.

For persistent time series data, such as GDP, there is much less variation in y_t around $\bar{y}$ than there is variation in the one-period change $\Delta y_t = y_t - y_{t-1}$ around its mean. So R^2 in a model in regression with Δy_t as the dependent variable can be much lower than R^2 in a model in regression with y_t as the dependent variable.

Recall that R^2 in the linear regression model equals the squared correlation coefficient between the fitted and actual values of y. More generally we can compare models with transformations of y as the dependent variable on the basis of the correlation between $\widehat{y}$ and y, provided it is possible to compute predictions $\widehat{y}$ that correct for retransformation bias.

15.7 Models with a Mix of Regressor Types

In practice regression models may have a mix of regressor types – levels, natural logarithm, indicator variables, polynomials and interactions. Two examples of regression models for annual earnings are presented – one with the dependent variable in levels and the other with dependent variable in logs.

15.7.1 Dependent Variable in Levels

It is natural to include age and education as regressors in levels, as interest lies in the effect on earnings of one more year of aging or one more year of education. If interest lies instead in the effect on earnings of a proportionate or percentage change in a variable then the variable can be included in natural logarithms, as the slope coefficient can then be interpreted as giving the result of a proportionate change.

We fit the following model for the level of earnings

$$
\widehat{Earnings} = \underset{(-5.38)}{-356632} - \underset{(-5.31)}{14330} \times Gender + \underset{(3.08)}{3283} \times Age - \underset{(-2.59)}{31.58} \times Agesq + \underset{(8.85)}{5399} \times Education
$$

$$
+ \underset{(1.07)}{9361} \times Dself - \underset{(-0.10)}{291} \times Dgovt + \underset{(4.34)}{69964} \times Lnhours, \qquad R^2 = .206, \quad s_e = 46102,
$$

where t statistics based on default standard errors are given in parentheses. The omitted category for type of worker is private worker ($Dpriv= 1$).

The coefficients of *Gender* and *Education* are interpreted in the usual way – women earn \$14,330 less than men on average and one more year of schooling is associated with an increase in earnings of \$5,399. Earnings increase with age to 51.9 years ($= -3283/(2\times(-31.58))$). Self-employed workers earn \$9,360 more than private sector workers and government workers earn \$291 less than private sector workers, after controlling for the other regressors. The coefficient of *Lnhours* (which equals ln(*Hours*)) can be most easily interpreted as a semi-elasticity. A 1% increase in usual hours worked is associated with an \$699 increase in annual earnings ($= 0.01 \times 69964$).

15.7.2 Dependent Variable in Natural Logarithms

It is common to model the natural logarithm of earnings, since earnings are right-skewed.

The fitted OLS regression with dependent variable *Lnearnings*, the natural logarithm of earnings, is

$$\widehat{LnEarnings} = \underset{(6.89)}{4.459} - \underset{(-4.88)}{0.193}\, Gender + \underset{(3.55)}{0.0561} \times Age - \underset{(-2.99)}{0.000549} \times Agesq + \underset{(11.17)}{0.0934} \times Education$$
$$- \underset{(-1.17)}{0.118} \times Dself + \underset{(1.53)}{0.070} \times Dgovt + \underset{(6.88)}{0.975} \times Lnhours, \qquad R^2 = .281, \; s_e = 0.5824,$$

where t statistics based on default standard errors are given in parentheses. The omitted category for type of worker is private worker (*Dpriv*= 1).

The coefficients of *Gender* and *Education* are most easily interpreted as semi-elasticities – women earn 19.3% less than men on average and one more year of schooling is associated with a 9.34% increase in earnings. Earnings increase with age to 51.1 years ($= -.0561/(2 \times (-.000549))$). Self-employed workers earn 11.8% more than private sector workers and government workers earn 7.0% more than private sector workers, after controlling for the other regressors. More precisely, since $\exp(-0.118) - 1 = -0.111$, self-employed workers earn 11.1% less than private sector workers. The coefficient of *Lnhours* can be most easily interpreted as an elasticity. A 1% increase in usual hours worked is associated with a 0.975% increase in earnings.

For the log-linear model if we form the obvious prediction $\widehat{y}_i = \exp(\widehat{\ln y_i})$ for each observation in the sample, then the sample average of $\widehat{y}$ equals \$46,906 which is much less than \$56,369, the sample average earnings. The log-earnings regression has $s_e = 0.5824$ so the correction factor $\exp(s_e^2/2) = 1.185$. Multiplying $\widehat{y}$ by this yields the corrected prediction $\widetilde{y}$ with sample average of \$55,576, much closer to the sample average of earnings.

For this log-linear model the in-sample correlation of earnings with the corrected prediction $\widetilde{y}$ regression is 0.474. This exceeds the corresponding correlation of 0.454 in the linear model (which can be obtained as $\sqrt{R^2} = \sqrt{0.206}$).

15.7.3 Standardized Regression Coefficients

An advantage of a log-log regression is that coefficients are scale-free. For example, a coefficient of 0.2 means that a 1% change in the regressors is associated with a 0.2% change in the dependent variable. By contrast, the interpretation of whether a coefficient of 0.2 in a linear regression measures a large or small effect varies with the scaling of variables.

Standardized regression coefficients are obtained by first standardizing the dependent variable and the regressors to have mean zero and standard deviation one. Thus the z-score $(y_i - \bar{y})/s_y$ is regressed on the z-scores $(x_{2i}-\bar{x}_2)/s_{x_2},...,(x_{ki}-\bar{x}_k)/s_{x_k}$. This can be shown to be equivalent to rescaling b_j, the coefficient of x_{ji} in the original OLS regression, by s_{x_j}/s_y.

For the current earnings regression the standardized coefficients are

$$\widehat{Earnings} = -0.138 \times Gender + 0.680 \times Age - 0.574 \times Agesq + 0.302 \times Education$$
$$+ 0.052 \times Dself - 0.002 \times Dgovt + 0.224 \times Lnhours, \qquad R^2 = .206, \; s_e = 0.895.$$

Consider the coefficient of *Education*. In the original OLS regression the coefficient of 5399 means that one more year of schooling is associated with earnings on average \$5,399. Whether this is a big or small effect depends on the scaling of *Earnings*. The standardized coefficient of 0.302 means that a one standard deviation change in years of schooling is associated with a 0.302 standard deviations change in earnings, which is a large effect. Note that the standard deviations of *Earnings* and *Education* are, respectively, 51,516 and 2.88, and $5399 \times 2.88/51516 = 0.302$.

Standardized regression coefficients are less useful for interpreting indicator variables. For example, it is less clear how to interpret a one standard deviation change in gender.

Standardized coefficients can be obtain in Stata using command `regress` with option `beta`, in R using the `lm.beta` function in the `QuantPsyc` R package, and in Gretl using the `sols` package.

15.8 Key Concepts

1. The marginal effect (ME) on the predicted value of the dependent variable of a change in a regressor is defined as the ratio of the change in $\widehat{y}$ to the change in x, so ME$= \Delta\widehat{y}/\Delta x$.

2. In a linear model the ME equals the slope coefficient and does not vary with x.

3. In a nonlinear model the ME varies with x.

4. The finite difference method calculates the ME for a discrete change Δx in x.

5. The calculus method calculates the ME for an infinitesimally small change Δx. It equals the ME from the finite difference method as $\Delta x \to 0$.

6. Three alternative measures of the marginal effect are the average marginal effect (AME), the marginal effect at the mean (MEM), and the marginal effect at a representative value (MER).

7. The marginal effect of x in the quadratic model $b_1 + b_2 x + b_3 x^2$ equals $b_2 + 2b_3 x$ using calculus methods.

8. The marginal effect of x in the interactions model $b_1 + b_2 x + b_3 z + b_4 xz$ equals $b_2 + b_3 z$.

9. A test of the statistical significance of a variable that additionally appears in an interaction term is an F test of the joint statistical significance of that variable and the interaction term. A t test of statistical significance of the interacted regressor is a test of whether the interaction term is needed.

10. The marginal effect in the linear-log model equals b_2/x using calculus methods.

11. The marginal effect in the log-linear model equals $b_2\widehat{y}$ using calculus methods, and equals $\widehat{y} \times [\exp(b_2) - 1]$ for a finite one-unit change.

12. The marginal effect in the log-log model equals $b_2\widehat{y}/x$ using calculus methods.

13. Coefficients with models in logs can be interpreted as elasticities and semi-elasticities; see Chapter 9.3.

14. Models with transformed dependent variable have the complication of retransformation bias.

15. It is meaningless to use R^2 to compare the fit of models with different transformations of y as the dependent variable.

16. Key Terms: nonlinear model; marginal effect; marginal effect; finite-difference method; one-unit change; calculus method; derivative; average marginal effect (AME); marginal effect at mean (MEM); marginal effect at representative value (MER); quadratic model; polynomial model; interacted regressor; joint F test; natural logarithm; linear-log model; log-linear model; log-log model; semi-elasticity; elasticity; retransformation bias.

15.9 Exercises

1. You obtain OLS estimates $\widehat{y} = 2 + 3x + 4x^2$ for a dataset with $\bar{y} = 30$ and $\bar{x} = 2$. Use the calculus method in obtaining marginal effects.

   (a) Give the marginal effect of a one unit change in x.
   (b) Give the AME of a one unit change in x.
   (c) Give the MEM of a one unit change in x.
   (d) Give the ME of a one unit change in x evaluated at $x = 3$.
   (e) Give the turning point for this parabola.

2. Repeat the previous exercise for a dataset with $\widehat{y} = 3 + 2x + x^2$ for a dataset with $\bar{y} = 20$ and $\bar{x} = 4$.

3. You obtain OLS estimates $\widehat{y} = 1 + 2x + 4d + 7d \times x$ for a dataset with $\bar{y} = 22$, $\bar{x} = 3$ and $\bar{d} = 0.5$.

   (a) Give the marginal effect of a one unit change in x.
   (b) Give the AME of a one unit change in x.
   (c) Give the MEM of a one unit change in x.
   (d) Give the ME of a one unit change in x evaluated at $d = 1$ and $x = 2$.
   (e) Give the marginal effect of a one unit change in d.

4. Repeat the previous exercise for $\widehat{y} = 4 + 3x + 2d + 5d \times x$ for a dataset with $\bar{y} = 20$, $\bar{x} = 2$ and $\bar{d} = 0.8$.

5. Use dataset HEALTH2009 detailed in Chapter 8.1. From Figure 8.1 the relationship between life expectancy (*lifeexp*) and health spending per capita (*hlthpc*) appears to be nonlinear. Here we add the quadratic term *hlthpcsq=hlthpc²*. Use heteroskedastic-robust standard errors.

   (a) OLS regress *lifeexp* on an intercept, *hlthpc* and *hlthpcsq* and use heteroskedastic-robust standard errors. Report the fitted model.

   (b) Is the quadratic term statistically significant at 5%?

   (c) Is health spending per capita statistically significant at 5%?

   (d) Compute the ME of health spending per capita on life expectancy at mean health spending per capita. Hence state the change in life expectancy if health spending per capita increases by $1,000.

   (e) Generate a variable equal to the ME of health spending per capita for each observation. Hence give the average marginal effect.

   (f) For what level of health spending per capita does the marginal effect of health spending per capita on life expectancy become negative.

   (g) Obtain predictions of *lifeexp* from the fitted model in part (b), plot these against *hlthpc* along with a scatterplot of *lifeexp* against *hlthpc* and comment.

   (h) Drop the observation for the US (*country_name is* United States). Does your answer in part (f) change much? Explain.

6. Repeat the previous exercise using dataset HEALTH2018.

7. Dataset ELECTRICITYPERCAP has annual data from 1990 to 2019 on variable *year* and US residential electricity consumption per capita in megawatt hours (*respcmwh*).

   (a) Plot *respcmwh* against *year*. Does the relationship appear to be linear? Explain.

   (b) OLS regress *respcmwh* on a quadratic in *year* with heteroskedastic robust standard errors. Do the results support a linear relationship? Explain.

   (c) Give the marginal effect of one more year on *respcmwh*. Evaluate this for the year 2000.

   (d) Give the average marginal effect of one more year on *respcmwh*.

   (e) Compute the residuals from part (b) and plot the residuals against *year*. Do the residuals appear to be correlated over time?

   (f) Given your plot in part (e) do you think it is correct to base inference on heteroskedastic robust standard errors for these time series data?

8. Repeat exercise 5 with regressor health spending as percentage of GDP (*hlthgdp*) and its square.

9. Use dataset HEALTH2009 introduced in Chapter 8.1. In Chapter 8.2 we regressed per capita health expenditures (*hlthpc*) on an intercept and per capita GDP (*gdppc*) for a sample of 34 OECD countries.

    (a) OLS regress ln(*hlthpc*) on an intercept and ln(*gdppc*). Report the fitted model.

    (b) Interpret the slope coefficient as an elasticity or semi-elasticity.

    (c) Give the marginal effect on *hlthpc* of increasing *gdppc* and evaluate at sample averages.

    (d) Compare your answer in part (c) to the ME from OLS in levels.

    (e) Obtain the prediction of ln(*hlthpc*) from part (a) and hence obtain a simple prediction of the level of *hlthpc*.

    (f) Obtain a prediction of the level of *hlthpc* that corrects for retransformation bias.

    (g) Compare the predictions in parts (e) and (f) with the actual data. Which prediction do you prefer? Explain.

10. Repeat the previous exercise using dataset HEALTH2018.

11. A detailed description of dataset SALARYSAT.DTA is given in exercise 3 of Chapter 7. We consider the relationship between salary (*salary*) and *satmath*, *satverb*, *age* and *highgrade*. Use heteroskedastic-robust standard errors.

    (a) Take natural logarithms to create variables *lnsatmath* and *lnsatverb*. If any observations are lost explain why.

    (b) Regress *lnsalary* on *lnsatmath*, *lnsatverb*, *age* and *highgrade*. Provide a meaningful interpretation of how salary changes as *satmath*, *satverb*, *age* and *highgrade* change.

    (c) Which variables are statistically significant at 5%?

    (d) Do any of the regressors have coefficients with unexpected sign? Explain.

12. Repeat the previous exercise restricting the sample to *age*= 28 and regressing *lnsalary* on *lnsatmath*, *lnsatverb*, *highgrade*, *height* and *weight*.

13. Consider the *lnsalary* regression of exercise 11.

    (a) Predict *lnsalary* for each observation. Verify whether or not the average of the predictions equals the average of *lnsalary*.

    (b) Obtain the naive prediction of *salary*. Compare the average of these predictions to the average of *salary*. Is there a problem?

    (c) Obtain the prediction of *salary* that corrects for retransformation bias. Compare the average of the predictions in part (e) to the average of *salary*. Comment.

14. Repeat the previous exercise but for the sample and model of exercise 12.

15. Using dataset SALARYSAT.DTA, consider regression of *salary* on *satmath, satverb, age, highgrade, height* and *weight*. Use heteroskedastic-robust standard errors.

    (a) Which variables are statistically significant at 5%?

    (b) Do any of the regressors have coefficients with unexpected sign? Explain.

    (c) Given the regression output in part (b), do you think that height is a more important determinant of salary than is the SAT Math score? Explain.

    (d) Now obtain the standardized regression coefficients for this regression using an appropriate statistical package command; see Chapter 15.7.3. Do you think that height is a more important determinant of salary than is the SAT Math score? Explain.

    (e) Manually obtain the standardized regression coefficient for *height* given its coefficient in the original OLS regression and the standard deviations of *salary* and *height*.

16. Repeat the previous exercise but for the sample and model of 12.

17. From the web obtain the article by Krueger (1994). Depending on access privileges you can obtain this via Google scholar or JStor (http://www.jstor.org). The basic model is: $\ln w_i = \beta_1 + \beta_2 x_{2i} + \cdots + \beta_k x_{ki} + \alpha c_i + \varepsilon_i$, where $\ln w_i$ is natural logarithm of wage and c_i is a dummy variable equal to one if the worker uses the computer at work and is zero otherwise. We focus on the October 1989 results in Table II (columns 4 to 6). Important: when determining the number of parameters in each model, also look at the footnote to the table.

    (a) Give the formula for the equation estimated in column (4) of table II.

    (b) It is claimed that computer use is associated with higher wages. Perform an appropriate one-sided test at $\alpha = .05$ of the statistical significance of the computer dummy variable in model (4) in table II.

    (c) What is the size of the estimated difference in wages between workers who use computers on the job and those who do not given the estimate in column (4) of table II.

    (d) Is computer use associated with higher wages after controlling for individual characteristics? Perform an appropriate one-sided test at $\alpha = .05$ of the statistical significance of the computer dummy variable in model (6) in table II.

    (e) What is the effect of education on wage given the estimates in column (6) of table II?

    (f) Perform an F test at $\alpha = .05$ of the overall goodness of fit of model (6) in table II. The standard errors are default standard errors, so the special result in Chapter 11.6 can be used.

    (g) According to the estimates in model (6) in table II, what is the difference between wages with and without use of computer, controlling for other regressors that might determine wages?

    (h) Which model do you prefer on the basis of adjusted R^2, model (5) or model (6)?

(i) According to the interviewers' instructions: 'Using a computer' refers only to respondent's 'DIRECT' or 'HANDS ON' use of a computer with typewriter like keyboards. The computer may be a personal computer, minicomputer or mainframe computer. Would workers using electronic cash registers at MacDonalds be counted as using computers at work?

(j) Do the results in Table II prove that using a computer at work causes higher wages? Explain.

Chapter 16

Checking the Model and Data

There are many potential pitfalls in using the regression methods presented in this text.

The first step is to ensure that there are no problems with the data. In particular the data should be free of error. And one should check whether key results would change greatly if just a few key observations were dropped. This important subject is deferred to the latter part of the chapter.

Ideally the data should have enough variation that coefficients of key variables can be estimated with sufficient precision. This may not be possible due to perfect collinearity or due to multicollinearity of the regressors.

The regression model should be correctly specified. For example, a log-linear model may be better than a linear model. And variables should perhaps be included as a quadratic function or interacted with each other.

The text to date has emphasized that regression estimates should be viewed as measuring association rather than causation. In order for a causal interpretation to be given to coefficient estimates it is essential that model errors are uncorrelated with regressors. This chapter presents examples where this assumption fails, and Chapters 17.4 and 17.5 summarize various methods that have been proposed to obtain estimates that can be given a causal interpretation.

Avoiding such pitfalls is difficult. To some extent econometric modelling is an art, not just a science, one that benefits greatly from personal experience and from the experience of others who have analyzed similar data. For example, to explain individual earnings it is standard to use log-linear models and include as regressors age and education (often as a quadratic in age and education), race, gender, region and other socioeconomic characteristics. And a standard starting point for modelling output as a function of production inputs is a Cobb-Douglas production function estimated as a log-log model.

Finally once a model is estimated, statistical inference relies on correct calculation of standard errors and the consequent t statistics and p-values. Modifications to the default OLS output for the complications of heteroskedastic errors or correlated errors are easily implemented in standard econometrics packages. For correlated errors, however, some judgement is required. From Chapter 12.1, cluster-robust standard errors require specifying the cluster units and HAC standard errors require determining the lag length at which autocorrelation disappears.

16.1 Multicollinear Data

OLS estimation requires that it is possible to compute all regression coefficients. This is not possible if there is perfect collinearity among regressors. Multicollinearity occurs when regressors are highly collinear but not perfectly collinear. In that case it is possible to compute all regression coefficients, but the individual coefficients of the multicollinear regressors can be very imprecisely estimated.

16.1.1 Perfect Collinearity

Perfect collinearity arises when one (or more) of the regressors can be expressed as an exact linear combination of the other regressors. A simple example was given in Chapter 10.8. A leading example is the dummy variable trap, see Chapter 14.4. With three mutually exclusive categories, for example, the three indicator variables satisfy $d1 + d2 + d3 = 1$, so $d1$ can be expressed as a linear combination of $d2$ and $d3$ since $d1 = 1 - d2 - d3$.

If regressors are perfectly correlated then one or more of the regressors needs to be dropped. Perfect collinearity effects estimation of only the coefficients of the regressors that are collinear, and usually these are just a subset of the regressors, such as in the dummy variable trap example.

16.1.2 Multicollinearity

Multicollinearity is the situation where the regressors are close to being linearly dependent. Then least squares regression is still valid, but it is difficult to separately identify the impact of each individual regressor. As a consequence individual coefficients may be statistically insignificant due to relatively large standard errors, and estimates of individual coefficients may be numerically unstable so that adding another observation can lead to quite different estimated coefficients.

Multicollinearity often arises with interacted regressors or with polynomials such as quadratics, an example is given below.

Multicollinearity can also arise is subtle ways. For example, in an earnings regression data may be available on a persons age (*Age*), years of education (*Education*) and years of work experience (*Experience*). For many individuals schooling begins around age six and work experience begins around the time that education ends, so approximately $Experience \simeq Age - Education - 6$. In this case it will be difficult to disentangle the separate roles of age, education and years of work experience.

A third example of multicollinearity is time series analysis of aggregate data series with regressors that tend to move together closely over time.

Signs of multicollinearity are large standard errors, low t statistics and "wrong" signs. But these are also indications of a poor model even in the absence of multicollinearity. How do we determine that our problems are those of multicollinearity? The problem is likely to be one of multicollinearity if joint F tests are statistically significant at the same time that individual t tests are statistically insignificant.

16.1.3 Multicollinearity Example

An example of multicollinearity was given in Chapter 15.4.3 and is repeated here.

OLS regression of *Earnings* on *Age* and *Education* yields estimates

$$\widehat{Earnings} = \underset{(-4.15)}{-46875} + \underset{(3.47)}{525} \times Age + \underset{(9.06)}{5811} \times Education, \; R^2 = 0.115,$$

where t statistics based on heteroskedastic-robust standard errors are given in parentheses. Both regressors are highly statistically significant and have economically meaningful coefficients.

Now add an interaction term *AgebyEduc* that equals *Age* times *Education*. The fitted model is now

$$\widehat{Earnings} = \underset{(-0.94)}{-29089} + \underset{(0.18)}{127} \times Age + \underset{(1.88)}{4515} \times Education + \underset{(0.52)}{29.04} \times AgebyEduc, \; R^2 = 0.115,$$

where t statistics based on heteroskedastic-robust standard errors are given in parentheses. All three coefficients are statistically insignificant at 5%. So at first glance it appears that now age and education have no statistically significant effect on earnings. A joint test of the statistical significance of the regressor *Age* and *AgebyEduc*, here a test of $H_0 : \beta_2 = 0$, $\beta_4 = 0$, has $F = 6.49$ with $p = 0.002$, so age is actually highly statistically significant. Similarly a joint test of *Education* and *AgebyEduc* yields $F = 43.00$ with $p = 0.000$, so education is highly statistically significant.

The pairwise correlation between *AgebyEduc* and *Age* is 0.73 and between *AgebyEduc* and *Education* is 0.64. These values are not high enough to suggest a multicollinearity problem. But what matters is the relationship between the three regressors. Regression of *AgebyEduc* on *Age* and *Education* yields $R^2 = 0.973$ which is very high and indicates a relationship between the three regressors that is close to linear.

16.1.4 Solutions to Multicollinearity

It is important to realize that multicollinearity is not always a problem. OLS is still unbiased and consistent and overall estimation is fine. The problem is just that the contribution of individual regressors may be imprecisely estimated. To be more precisely estimated we need more data.

There is no problem if multicollinearity is confined to regressors that are included only as controls, rather than the regressors of intrinsic interest. And it is not a problem if interest lies solely in predicting the dependent variable.

Solutions to multicollinearity include the following. If only a subset of regressors are highly correlated, do joint inference (F tests) on this subset. Put restrictions on the coefficients of variables, usually by dropping variable(s), in recognition that the data are being "pushed" too far. For experimental data, design the experiment to minimize the correlation of regressors.

Most fundamentally, if possible get more data. The problem with multicollinearity is not that OLS is biased or inconsistent. The problem is a lack of estimator precision, and precision improves with additional data.

Remark 133 *Multicollinearity makes it difficult to disentangle the influence of individual regressors. It is not a problem for those regressors that are not multicollinear, and it is not a problem for prediction.*

16.2   Model Assumptions Revisited

From Chapter 11.1, the following assumptions are made:

1. The population model is $y = \beta_1 + \beta_2 x_2 + \beta_3 x_3 + \cdots + \beta_k x_k + u$.

2. The error for the ith observation has zero mean conditional on the regressors.

3. The error for the ith observation has constant variance σ_u^2 conditional on the regressors.

4. The errors for different observations are statistically independent.

These model assumptions matter. In the most critical case, failure of assumptions 1 and/or 2 leads to the OLS estimator being biased and **inconsistent**. If instead just assumptions 3 and/or 4 fail then the OLS estimator remains unbiased and **consistent**, but appropriate robust standard errors should be used rather than default standard errors.

The practitioner needs to determine whether these assumptions are reasonable for their data and, if this is not the case, how to adapt analysis to obtain valid estimates and to perform valid statistical inference.

16.2.1   Why do the Assumptions Matter?

To see where each assumption is used, consider the simplest case of regression of y_i on x_i without an intercept. Appendix C.1 provides full details. Here just the key steps are given.

OLS regression of y_i on x_i without intercept yields $\widehat{y}_i = bx_i$ where $b = \left(\sum_{i=1}^{n} x_i y_i\right) / \left(\sum_{i=1}^{n} x_i^2\right)$. This can be written as

$$b = \sum_{i=1}^{n} w_i y_i, \quad \text{where } w_i = \frac{x_i}{\sum_{j=1}^{n} x_j^2}.$$

This is just a weighted average of the y's, where the weights depend only on the regressor x.

Clearly to make any progress we need to make an assumption about the model for y_i. If we assume that $y_i = \beta x_i + u_i$ (assumption 1) then $b = \sum_{i=1}^{n} w_i(\beta x_i + u_i)$ and some algebra (see Appendix C.1) shows that this simplifies to

$$b = \beta + \sum_{i=1}^{n} w_i u_i.$$

This representation is very useful as it makes clear that, given assumption 1, the OLS estimator b equals β plus a weighted sum of the error terms u. The properties of b as an estimator of β will therefore depend crucially on assumptions about the error terms.

For OLS to be unbiased, i.e. $E[b] = \beta$, the second term on the right-hand side must have expected value 0. This is the case under assumption 2, that $E[u_i|x_i] = 0$. Going the other way, the OLS estimator will be biased and inconsistent if either assumption 1 or assumption 2 fails.

Now consider the variance of the OLS estimator. Since b is unbiased for β, and given the preceding expression for β, it follows that

$$\text{Var}[b] = E[(b - \beta)^2] = E\left[\left(\sum_{i=1}^{n} w_i u_i\right)^2\right].$$

To evaluate this requires additional assumptions about u_i. From Appendix C.1, if we assume that $\mathrm{Var}[u_i] = \sigma^2$ for all observations (assumption 3) and that the u_i are independent across observations (assumption 4) then

$$\mathrm{Var}[b] = \frac{\sigma_u^2}{\sum_{i=1}^{n} x_i^2}.$$

If alternative assumptions to 3 and 4 are made then we get an alternative formula for $\mathrm{Var}[b]$, leading to the use of robust standard errors.

Finally, consider the distribution of the OLS estimator. From results above, b equals β plus a weighted sum of the u_i. If errors u_i are normally distributed, then the weighted sum is normally distributed and hence b is normally distributed. If instead errors are nonnormal, the usual case, we rely on a central limit theorem so that if the sample is large then the normal distribution still provides a good approximation. In finite practice the related t distribution is used.

We considers in turn the failure of assumptions 1 through 4.

16.3 Incorrect Population Model

Assumption 1 specifies that

$$y = \beta_1 + \beta_2 x_2 + \beta_3 x_3 + \cdots + \beta_k x_k + u.$$

This specification may be wrong due to omission of regressors, unnecessary inclusion of regressors, or incorrect functional form of the model.

16.3.1 Incorrect Functional Form

Suppose the true model is

$$y = f(x_2, x_3, ..., x_k) + u,$$

where this relationship need not be linear. Then the least squares estimator from regression of y on $x_2, ..., x_k$ is biased and inconsistent, since a model with **incorrect functional form** has been estimated.

As an example it may be that a linear regression of y on $x_2, ..., x_k$ is estimated when we should have instead estimated a log-linear model, regressing $\ln y$ on $x_2, ..., x_k$.

If the functional form $f(\cdot)$ is known, and is not so simple that it can be transformed to a linear-in-parameters model such as log-linear or linear-log, estimation is still possible using the method of nonlinear least squares mentioned briefly in Chapter 17.6.4.

16.3.2 Irrelevant Variables

Suppose the regressor x_k does not appear in the true population model, so that

$$y = \alpha_1 + \alpha_2 x_2 + \alpha_3 x_3 + \cdots + \alpha_{k-1} x_{k-1} + u,$$

where the error u satisfies population assumptions 1 and 2. If y is regressed on an intercept and $x_2, ..., x_k$, erroneously including the **irrelevant variable** x_k, then it can be shown that the least squares coefficient estimates $b_2, ..., b_{k-1}$ are unbiased and inconsistent but are not as precisely estimated. And $E[b_k] = 0$ as expected.

Thus the only problem is a loss of precision in estimation – the standard errors will be higher and the t statistics will be lower than in the model that correctly excludes irrelevant regressors.

16.3.3   Omitted Variables Bias

Suppose that the true model is

$$Earnings = \alpha_1 + \alpha_2 Education + \alpha_3 Ability + v,$$

where *Education* is years of schooling, *Ability* is a measure of raw ability and v is an error term that satisfies assumptions 1-2.

Studies usually regress *Earnings* on only *Education*, because a measure of ability such as an IQ score is not available. That is we estimate

$$Earnings = \beta_1 + \beta_2 Education + u.$$

Then the coefficient b_2 is capturing not only the effect of *Education* but is also picking up the effect of *Ability*. This will lead to b_2 overstating the effect of *Education*, since *Education* and *Ability* are positively correlated and *Earnings* also increase with *Ability*. This accords with intuition - people with more schooling on average have higher raw ability and this ability effect is being ascribed to length of time in school. Few datasets have data on individual ability and determining the causal effect of schooling on earnings is an active area of empirical research that uses methods presented in Chapters 17.4 and 17.5.

More generally the true population model has an additional regressor x_{k+1}, so that

$$y = \alpha_1 + \alpha_2 x_2 + \cdots + \alpha_k x_k + \alpha_{k+1} x_{k+1} + v,$$

while the estimated model with x_{k+1} omitted is

$$y = \beta_1 + \beta_2 x_2 + \cdots + \beta_k x_k + u.$$

The OLS estimates $b_2, ..., b_k$ are all inconsistent, unless the omitted variable x_{k+1} is uncorrelated with the included regressors $x_2, ..., x_k$. Inconsistency arises because the error in the estimated model is $u = \alpha_{k+1} x_{k+1} + v$ and this error will be correlated with the included regressors if x_k is correlated with the included regressors.

It can be shown that b_j is biased for α_j with expected value

$$E[b_j] = \alpha_j + \gamma_j \times \alpha_{k+1},$$

where γ_j is the coefficient of x_j from OLS regression of the omitted regressor x_{k+1} on the included regressors $x_2, ..., x_k$. For example, if x_j and x_{k+1} are both positively related with y and with each other, and $\alpha_j > 0$ and $\alpha_{k+1} > 0$, then the true effect α_j of x_j, is being overstated since $\gamma_j \alpha_{k+1} > 0$. This was the case in the earlier earnings, education and ability example.

The problem is called **omitted variables bias**, though OLS is not just biased but is also **inconsistent**. Omitted variables bias can even lead to the estimated OLS coefficient having the wrong sign; an example was given for the Phillips curve in Chapter 13.3.3-13.3.4.

Omitted variables bias is clearly a serious problem, unless the omitted variable is uncorrelated with the variables included. It is possible in some cases to know the direction of the bias, in which case we know whether b_2 provides an lower bound or upper bound for β_2. In the preceding earnings example if $b_2 = 500$, say, then we know that an extra year of schooling leads to at most an additional $500 of earnings.

16.3.4 Cures for Omitted Variables Bias

Inclusion of irrelevant variables leads to less precision in variable estimates, whereas omitted variables can lead to the much more serious problem of biased and inconsistent parameter estimates. It is best to be on the cautious side, including questionable regressors while bearing in mind that including too many regressors decreases the precision of estimates and may lead to problems with multicollinearity. Regression models for economics data tend to include many regressors, especially if the sample size is large. This is a departure from some other fields of applied statistics. For example, in biostatistics it is common to include regressors in a model only if they are statistically significant at significance level 0.05.

If it is not possible to include variables to avoid omitted variables bias then at least one should try to determine the likely direction of bias, by estimating for the example at hand the likely signs of γ_j and α_{k+1} in the previously given formula for $E[b_j]$. Better is to use methods presented in Chapters 17.4 and 17.5, such as instrumental variables, assuming that the data necessary for such methods are available.

Omitted variables bias is a serious concern for many regression studies that use observational data.

Remark 134 *To avoid the serious problems of incorrect functional form and omitted variables bias, provided the sample size is large enough economists use models with many regressors and, if necessary, flexible functional forms, such as quadratic terms, interactions and natural logarithm transformations.*

16.3.5 Model Misspecification Tests

A simple test of correct specification of the functional form is the Ramsey Regression Equation Specification Test (RESET). The **RESET test** adds powers of the OLS predictions as extra regressors. For example, let $\widehat{y}$ be the predicted value of y from regression of y on an intercept and $x_2, ..., x_k$. Then add $\widehat{y}^2$ and $\widehat{y}^3$ as regressors and estimate

$$y = \beta_1 + \beta_2 x_2 + \beta_3 x_3 + \cdots + \beta_k x_k + \alpha_1 \widehat{y}^2 + +\alpha_2 \widehat{y}^3 + u.$$

Rejection of $H_0 : \alpha_1 = 0, \alpha_2 = 0$ at, say, significance level 0.05 is interpreted as model misspecification.

The RESET test is an example of a **misspecification test**. There are several limitations of such tests.

First, as sample sizes get larger and larger then estimator precision gets better and better so that H_0 may be rejected even if the estimates of α_1 and α_2 are very close to zero. More generally, almost any test at a fixed significance level such as 0.05 will reject H_0 as the sample size gets very large.

Second, it is difficult to know how "big" is the extent of model misspecification.

Third, there can be several causes of the model misspecification. A misspecification test does not on its own indicate what is the best way to correct a misspecified model.

16.4   Regressors Correlated with Errors

Assumption 2 is that the errors are not correlated with the regressors, so

$$\mathrm{E}[u|x_2, ..., x_k] = 0.$$

Correlation of regressors with errors is the most serious problem. It leads to the OLS estimator being biased and **inconsistent**. Methods to control for this problem are presented in Chapter 17; see especially chapter 17.5. These methods require additional assumptions that in many potential applications are inapplicable, and in many instances cannot be tested, and have greater data requirements. So if errors are correlated with regressors then only in a subset of applications is it possible to use an alternative method or model to obtain consistent estimates.

It can be very difficult to determine that this problem exists since the model errors are not observed. The OLS residuals cannot be used to directly test this condition, since OLS regression by construction forces the OLS residuals to be unrelated with the regressors as the OLS normal equations imply $\sum_{i=1}^n x_{ji}e_i = 0$; see Chapter 10.4.2.

A general term for correlation of regressors with errors is **endogeneity** or **endogenous regressors**, where the term "endogenous" means caused by factors inside the system. Regressors that are uncorrelated with the error are instead called **exogenous regressors**, where "exogenous" means outside the system. The key notion is that while we may consider estimation of a single equation, the data generating process may be more complex than this single equation. Several leading examples follow.

First, **omitted variables** is an example of the endogenous regressor problem that has already been discussed. The error term will be correlated with regressors since the error term will include the omitted regressor and the omitted regressor is correlated with included regressors.

Second, **feedback** from the dependent variable to the regressors also leads to correlation between the regressors and error term. The leading example in econometrics is **simultaneous equations bias**. A simple example is the consumption-income relationship using national aggregate data. Increases in income lead to increases in consumption, but these increases in consumption in turn lead to an increase in income since income in a closed-economy is the sum of consumption, investment and government spending. A more complicated example of feedback is the estimation of a demand relationship, with price as a function of quantity demanded, using aggregate data.

An increase in demand leads to an increase in price, but an increase in price will then lead to an increase in supply which will then depress the price.

Third, if some regressors are measured with error then the error term can be shown to be correlated with the regressors leading to **measurement error bias** whereby OLS coefficients are biased downwards. More precisely, suppose that the true model includes variable x_j^* but we include x_j as a regressor. An example is to include SAT score (x_j) as a measure of ability (x_j^*). And suppose that $x_{ji} = x_{ji}^* + v_i$ where the **measurement error** $v_i \sim (0, \sigma_v^2)$. So on average x_j is correct for x_j^*, but x_j is a noisy measure with variance σ_v^2. Then it can be shown that OLS regression of y on an intercept, $x_2, ..., x_j, ..., x_k$ yields coefficient b_j that has expected value or limit value that is smaller in absolute value than the true parameter β_j.

Fourth, if the sample is selected on the basis of values taken by the dependent variable then it can be shown that the error term will be correlated with regressors. This is called **sample selection bias**.

Fifth, time series models with lagged dependent variable and autocorrelated error can be shown to have regressor correlated with the error; see Chapter 12.1.5.

Misspecification due to regressors correlated with error can occur in many regression applications. A distinguishing feature of econometrics is the concern about this possible misspecification, and the use of methods that are nonetheless valid, provided certain assumptions are satisfied. The most commonly-used methods are summarized in Chapter 17.5.

Remark 135 *It is difficult to detect that regressors are correlated with model errors and it is difficult to control for this problem.*

16.5   Heteroskedastic Errors

Assumption 3, the assumption that the error variance is constant for different observations and does not depend on regressors, is called the assumption of **homoskedastic errors**. When this assumption is not satisfied, i.e. the error variances differ across observations, the errors are said to be **heteroskedastic**.

As an example, if we regress earnings on schooling we expect more variability around the regression line for people with high levels of schooling, such as a postgraduate degree, than for people with low levels of schooling, such as a high school only education. Thus the errors are heteroskedastic, with variance that increases with the schooling regressor.

The least squares coefficient estimates are still unbiased. But they are not estimated as precisely as they would be if the heteroskedasticity was controlled for. And more importantly, the OLS standard errors and t statistics reported by the usual computer output will be incorrect, unless heteroskedasticity is controlled for.

Cross-section data regression applications with independent errors usually have heteroskedastic errors. It is possible to test whether heteroskedasticity is present. The standard practice is to not bother to perform such tests, but instead always use **heteroskedastic-robust standard errors** following OLS regression; see Chapter 12.1.2.

16.6   Correlated Errors

Assumption 4 is the assumption that the errors for different observations are uncorrelated. When this assumption fails, but assumptions 1 and 2, still hold the OLS estimator remains unbiased and consistent, but default standard errors and resulting statistical inference are incorrect.

Remark 136 *Provided assumptions 1-2 still hold, OLS remains consistent if assumptions 3 and/or 4 do not hold, but appropriate robust standard errors must be used.*

Different forms of error correlation lead to different robust standard errors. We consider the two most common ways that error correlation arises.

16.6.1   Clustered Errors

Errors are said to be **clustered** if errors are correlated for observations in the same cluster and are uncorrelated for observations in different clusters. This can arise with cross-section data where, for example, model errors for individuals in the same village or state or school are likely to be correlated. And this can arise in panel data where even if errors are uncorrelated across individuals they are usually correlated over time for a given individual.

The simplest solution is to continue to use OLS estimation and base inference on **cluster-robust standard errors**; see Chapter 12.1.4 for a detailed discussion. It is essential that such adjustment is made when errors are clustered as the erroneous use of default and heteroskedastic-robust standard errors can lead to great underestimation of the standard errors; see, for example, the application in Chapter 13.4.4.

Alternative random effects and fixed effects estimators are presented in Chapter 17.1 for cross-section data and Chapter 17.2 for panel data. Random effects estimators may be more efficient, and fixed effects estimators may be able to control for correlation between regressors and model errors.

16.6.2   Autocorrelated Errors

Consider time series regression, such as a regression model for U.S. gross domestic product (GDP) using quarterly data. If GDP is overpredicted in one quarter, i.e. actual GDP is unusually low, then it is likely that GDP will be overpredicted in the subsequent quarter. Similarly for underprediction. But then the error terms in different quarters are positively correlated, and assumption 4 on the error term no longer holds. Time series correlated errors are called **autocorrelated errors** or **serially correlated errors**.

The simplest solution is to continue to use OLS estimation and base inference on heteroskedastic and autocorrelation consistent (**HAC**) robust standard errors; see Chapters 12.1.5 and 17.7.

As an example, consider the model $y_t = 1 + 2x_t + u_t$ where the error $u_t = 0.8u_{t-1} + e_t$ and $e_t \sim N(0,1)$. A dataset with 10,000 observations was generated from this dataset, where the regressor $x_t = 0.8x_{t-1} + v_t$ and $v_t \sim N(0,1)$. So both the regressor and the error are autocorrelated.

Table 16.1: Democracy and growth: Variable definitions and summary statistics (n=131).

Variable	Definition	Mean	Standard Deviation	Min	Max
Democracy	500 year democracy change (1500-2000)	0.647	0.331	0.0	1.0
Growth	500 year income per capita change (1500-2000)	1.916	1.108	-0.089	4.253
Constraint	Constraint on the executive at independence	0.372	0.362	0.0	1.0
Indcent	Year of independence / 100	19.044	0.677	18.00	19.77
Catholic	Catholics proportion of population in 1980	0.306	0.355	0.0	0.969
Muslim	Muslim proportion of population in 1980	0.248	0.371	0.0	0.997
Protestant	Protestant proportion of population in 1980	0.127	0.213	0.0	0.978
Other	Other religion proportion of population in 1980	0.320	0.320	0.001	1.000
n	131				

Then OLS estimation of y_t on an intercept and x_t yielded coefficient of x_t equal to 2.0063 with HAC-robust standard error of 0.0202 compared to default standard error of 0.0101 and heteroskedastic-robust standard error of 0.0104.

Note, however, that if regressors include lagged values of the dependent variable, in addition to the errors being serially correlated, then assumption 2 no longer holds and OLS is inconsistent; see Chapter 17.6 for explanation. As an example, the data were instead generated from the model $y_t = 1 + 0.6y_{t-1} + 2x_t + u_t$, with u_t and x_t generated as before. Then OLS estimation of y_t on an intercept, y_{t-1} and x_t yielded slope coefficients of 0.7179 and 1.6421, quite different from the true values of 0.6 and 2.0.

16.7 Example: Democracy and Growth

The remainder of this chapter presents the use of various model diagnostics, illustrated using the dataset DEMOCRACY.

This dataset comes from the article by Acemoglu, Johnson, Robinson, and Yared (2008). The study investigates whether increased income in a country leads to increased democracy. The OLS regression analyzed is the regression for democracy in the very long run given in the fourth column of Table 8A of the article.

Table 16.1 presents variable definitions and summary statistics for the data on 131 countries. The original dataset had 173 observations. Only 135 observations had data on the dependent variable Democracy, and an additional four observations are lost due to missing data on other variables.

The level of democracy in 2000 is based on a Polity Composite Democracy Index that is normalized to be between zero and one, with higher values corresponding to greater democracy. The level of democracy in 1500 for many countries is zero, including those countries that did not exist in 1500, though some countries have non-zero democracy if there was some constraint on the executive. The variable Democracy, measuring the 500-year change in the level of democracy, is between zero and one as no country saw a reduction in the level of democracy (Qatar and Saudi

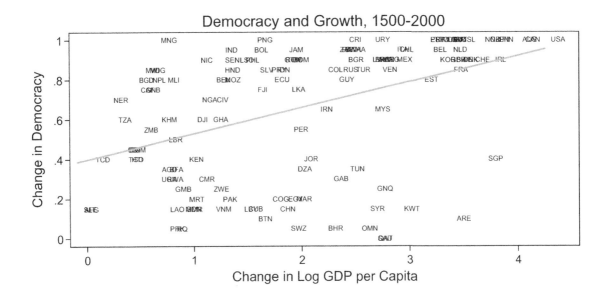

Figure 16.1: Democracy and growth: Scatter plot and fitted line.

Arabia remained at zero) while 20 countries went from zero to one.

The variable *Growth* measures the 500-year change in log GDP per capita. If the natural logarithm changes by amount g then the level has multiplied by amount e^g. For example, if variable *Growth* equals 2, close to the sample mean, then GDP per capita is $e^2 = 7.389$ times higher in 2000 than in 1500.

Bivariate OLS regression yields fitted model

$$\widehat{Democracy} = 0.397 + 0.131\,Growth, \quad R^2 = 0.192, \quad n = 131, \quad s_e = 0.299.$$
$$\underset{(0.046)}{} \quad \underset{(0.019)}{}$$

where heteroskedastic-robust standard errors are given in parentheses. Figure 16.1 presents a scatter plot with the fitted regression line.

The variable *Growth* is highly statistically significant, with $t = 0.131/0.019 = 6.89$. The magnitude of the coefficient is difficult to gauge as the variable *Democracy* is an index rather than an inherently measurable variable. One way to interpret the result is to note that R^2 is the squared correlation coefficient r^2 as this is a bivariate regression. Since $r^2 = 0.192$, a one standard deviation change in *Growth* is associated with a $\sqrt{0.192} = 0.44$ standard deviation change in *Democracy*, a large effect.

The multiple regression studied in this chapter includes five additional regressors, defined in Table 16.1. Variable *Constraint* takes a range of values between zero and one, with the most common values 0, 1/3 and 1 for, respectively, 38, 29 and 24 of the 131 observations. The four religious affiliation variables are proportions of population that sum to one for each observation so one variable, in this case variable *Other*, needs to be omitted.

The complete multivariate fitted model is

$$
\widehat{Democracy} = \underset{(0.975)}{3.031} + \underset{(0.025)}{0.047}\,Growth + \underset{(0.072)}{0.164}\,Constraint - \underset{(0.050)}{0.133}\,Indcent
$$
$$
+ \underset{(0.089)}{0.117}\,Catholic - \underset{(0.101)}{0.233}\,Muslim + \underset{(0.104)}{0.180}\,Protestant, \quad R^2 = 0.449, \quad n = 131,
$$

where heteroskedastic-robust standard errors are given in parentheses. Default standard errors are within twenty percent of the heteroskedastic-robust standard errors.

Now *Growth* is much less statistically significant, with $t = 0.047/0.025 = 1.88$. More importantly the coefficient of variable *Growth* is now one-third as large. Controlling for institutional features such as religion is important, the main point of the article. Here growth is higher for countries with greater proportions of Catholics and Protestants, and is lower for countries with greater proportions of Muslims, compared to the omitted category *Other*.

16.8 Diagnostics

There is no clearly best method to detect problematic data. The methods given in this section are the methods most commonly used. They are generally developed to identify one of the complications, but can also shed light on other complications. The graphs presented in this section can additionally aid in detecting that the functional form of the model may be misspecified.

16.8.1 Outliers and Influential Observations

An **outlier** or **outlying observation** is one whose value is unusual given the rest of the data. For a single variable an outlier can be detected using a box-and-whisker plot presented in Chapter 2.1. With data on several variables detection of an outlier is less straightforward. It can be more difficult to detect an outlier and, going the other way, what seems to be an outlier when one variable is considered in isolation may not be an outlier given data on the other variables. For example, someone with unusually high earnings might be viewed as an outlier given only earnings data. But if the person is a heart surgeon, and regressors include detailed occupation dummies, then the observation would not be viewed as an outlier. Going the other way, if the same heart surgeon had earnings similar to those of a fast food worker then the observation would be an outlier, but looking at earnings alone would not detect this.

It is important to screen data for outliers as these may be due to **erroneous data**. If an outlier can be determined to be due to miscoding then it should obviously be coded correctly or dropped if this is not possible.

A second reason for concern about an outlier is that it may have a very large impact on the results of OLS estimation. For bivariate OLS regression the estimated slope coefficient is

$$
b_2 = \frac{\sum_{i=1}^{n}(x_i - \bar{x})(y_i - \bar{y})}{\sum_{i=1}^{n}(x_i - \bar{x})^2}.
$$

An observation (x_i, y_i) that is a long way from both $\bar{x}$ and $\bar{y}$ will have a large influence as then $(x_i - \bar{x})(y_i - \bar{y})$ is large in magnitude. More generally for multiple regression an **influential**

observation is one that has a relatively large effect on the results of regression analysis, notably on predicted values of the dependent variable or on the estimated OLS coefficients.

Not all outliers are influential observations. In the bivariate case if y_i is a long way from $\bar{y}$, yet $x_i = \bar{x}$, then the observation would have no effect on the OLS slope coefficient since then $(x_i - \bar{x})(y_i - \bar{y}) = 0$ and $\sum_{i=1}^{n}(x_i - \bar{x})^2$ is unchanged. Going the other way, an outlier that has regressor value that is a long way from the sample mean $\bar{x}$ is said to have high **leverage**.

If the data include valid influential observation(s) then the standard procedure in economic data analysis is to still include the observation(s) in the analysis. As a robustness check results with the observation(s) excluded might additionally be reported.

Remark 137 *An outlier is an observation whose value is unusual given the rest of the data. An influential observation is one that has a relatively large effect on the results of regression analysis.*

16.8.2 Scatter Plots against the Fitted Values

For bivariate regression a useful diagnostic plot is a scatter plot of y against x superimposed with the fitted regression line, such as that given in Figure 16.1. Outliers are observations that are a long way from the bulk of the observation, and influential observations are those that are a long way from both $\bar{x}$ and $\bar{y}$.

For multiple regression such a plot is not particularly useful due to dependence on other regressors. Instead, one approach is to plot y (or the residual $y - \widehat{y}$) against the fitted value $\widehat{y}$ rather than against x.

The first panel of Figure 16.2 plots the actual value of *Democracy* against the fitted value of *Democracy* from the preceding OLS multiple regression that has six regressors. The solid line is obtained by OLS regression of y on $\widehat{y}$. The dashed line is obtained by nonparametric regression of y on $\widehat{y}$, using Lowess. There seem to be no outliers and the Lowess curve suggests that the relationship between actual and fitted values is linear, so there is no sign of misspecification of the conditional mean.

The second panel of Figure 16.2 plots the residual $e = y - \widehat{y}$ from the *Democracy* regression against the fitted value of *Democracy*. This scatter plot is a rotation of the scatter plot in the first panel, since it is a plot of $y - \widehat{y}$ against $\widehat{y}$ whereas the first panel is a plot of y against $\widehat{y}$. Since an intercept was included in the OLS regression the residuals are on average zero, and regressing e on $\widehat{y}$ yields a line with intercept zero and slope zero. The dashed line is obtained by nonparametric regression of e on $\widehat{y}$, using Lowess. The second panel suggests that the errors are heteroskedastic, with more variability for low values of $\widehat{y}$. It is best to use heteroskedastic-robust standard errors for this model; as noted earlier these are within twenty percent of default standard errors.

Remark 138 *Key diagnostic plots are plots of the dependent variable or of the residual against the fitted value.*

16.8.3 Scatter Plots for a Single Regressor

More advanced plots isolate the role of a single regressor in multiple OLS regression. Several such plots have been proposed.

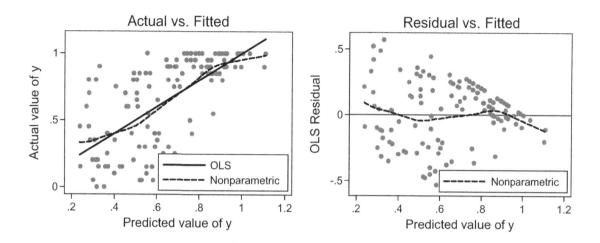

Figure 16.2: Diagnostics: Actual values and OLS residuals plotted against fitted values.

The most obvious plot is a **residual versus regressor plot** that plots the OLS residual from the multiple regression against one of the model regressors. That is plot e_i against x_{ji}. An OLS regression line fitted to this plot will always have slope zero and intercept zero as a consequence of the OLS normal equations that $\sum_{i=1}^{n} x_{ji} e_i = 0$; see Chapter 10.4. Any strong pattern in this plot around zero may suggest a problem with the model or a problem with outliers.

A **component plus residual plot** or **partial regression plot** is a variation of the residual versus regressor plot that rotates the plot by adding back the predicted role of the jth regressor, so that $p_{ji} = b_j x_{ji} + e_i$ is plotted against x_{ji}, where b_j is the OLS coefficient of x_j from the original multiple regression. It is felt that this plot makes it easier to detect nonlinearities.

An **added variable plot** or **partial regression plot** is a plot of the dependent variable y against the jth regressor x_j after purging both y and x_j of the effect of the other regressors. Specifically, define X_{-j} to be all regressors other than x_j, so $X_{-j} = (x_2, ..., x_{j-1}, x_{j+1}, ..., x_k)$. Let $\widetilde{x}_{ji}$ denote the ith residual from regressing x_j on an intercept and X_{-j}, and let $\widetilde{y}_i$ denote the ith residual from regressing y on an intercept and X_{-j}. Then a partial regression plot is a plot of $\widetilde{y}$ on $\widetilde{x}_j$. It can be shown that the slope coefficient from OLS regression on this scatter plot equals that of x_j from the original multiple OLS regression of y on an intercept and $x_2, ..., x_k$ (see Chapter 10.4.3), and that the residuals from the two regressions coincide. This plot is felt to be useful for detection of outliers.

Figure 16.3 presents these three plots for the regressor *Growth* following multiple regression of *Democracy* on *Growth*, *Constraint*, *Indcent*, *Catholic*, *Muslim* and *Protestant*. In practice such plots would be presented for all regressors – for space reasons they are given for only one of the regressors. The plots included an OLS regression line and a Lowess nonparametric regression curve fitted to the data in the scatter plot.

The first panel of Figure 16.3 presents a plot of the OLS residual from multiple regression

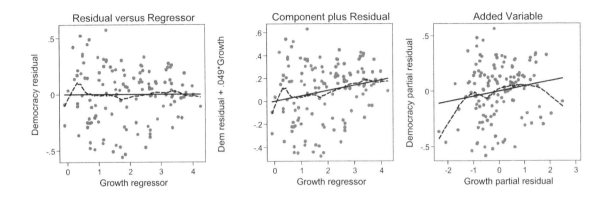

Figure 16.3: Diagnostics: Residual, component plus residual and added variable plots

on variable *Growth*. There is no sign of outliers or of nonlinearity. There is a suggestion of less variability in the residuals at higher levels of growth.

The second panel of Figure 16.3, a component plus residual plot, is just a rotation of the first panel obtained by adding $0.047 \times Growth$ to the y-axis variable.

The third panel of Figure 16.3 plots the partial residual for the dependent variable *Democracy* against that for the regressor *Growth*. Again this graph finds nothing fundamentally wrong.

Remark 139 *Diagnostic plots for a single regressor include residual versus regressor plots, component plus residual (or partial regression) plots, and added variable (or partial regression) plots.*

16.8.4   Detecting Influential Observations

Observations that have the greatest influence on the predicted value $\widehat{y}$ can be detected using a measure called DFITS. For the ith observation DFITS$_i$ equals the scaled difference between predictions of y_i with and without the ith observation included in the OLS regression (so **DFITS** means **difference in fits**). Large absolute values of DFITS indicate an influential observation. A rule of thumb is that observations with $|\text{DFITS}| > 2\sqrt{k/n}$, where k is the number of regressors including the intercept and n is the sample size, may be worthy of further investigation. This rule is conservative and can suggest that a considerable fraction of the observations are influential.

Observations that have the greatest influence on the coefficient of an individual regressor (b_j for regressor x_j) can be detected using a measure called DFBETA. For the jth regressor and i^{th} observation, DFBETA$_{ji}$ equals the scaled difference between b_j with and without the ith observation included in the OLS regression (so **DFBETA** means **difference in beta**). Large absolute values of DFBETA indicate an influential observation. A rule of thumb is that observations with $|\text{DFBETA}| > 2/\sqrt{n}$ may be worthy of further investigation. Again this rule is conservative and can suggest that many observations are influential.

For the OLS regression in this chapter $n = 131$ and $k = 7$. Five countries have $|\text{DFITS}| > 2/\sqrt{7/131} = 0.462$, with a maximum value of $|-0.704|$ for China. There are not so many unusually large values as to imply that there is a problem. When these five countries are dropped the coefficient of *Growth* changes very slightly from 0.0468 to 0.0480, while coefficients of the control variables change more substantially.

For the regressor *Growth* twelve observations have $|\text{DFBETA}| > 2 \times \sqrt{131} = 0.175$, with the largest value of 0.327 for Haiti. This is not so large as to imply a problem, though the twelve observations did tend to be poorer African and Asian countries. When these twelve countries are dropped the coefficient of *Growth* changes considerably from 0.0468 to 0.0627 (an even larger effect), while coefficients of the control variables change less than when countries with large values of $|\text{DFITS}|$ were dropped.

Stata and Eviews include a command to compute DFITS and DFBETA following OLS regression, in R one can use the `olsrr` package or the `car` package, and Eviews has a command to compute DFITS.

Remark 140 *DFITS and DFBETAs measure the influence of a particular observation on, respectively, the fitted values and estimated coefficients.*

16.8.5 Residual Distribution

Residuals that are unusually large in absolute value may indicate outliers, and an asymmetry of sample residuals may indicate that a nonlinear model needs to be estimated. So it can be useful to plot the histogram of the residuals, or to plot the quantiles of the residuals against the quantiles of the normal distribution (called a quantile-quantile plot or q-q plot).

It is important to bear in mind that regression residuals are not the same as model errors. For bivariate regression the OLS residual is

$$
\begin{aligned}
e_i &= y_i - b_1 - b_2 x_i \\
&= y_i - \beta_1 - \beta_2 x_i - b_1 + \beta_1 - b_2 x_i + \beta_2 x_i \\
&= u_i - (b_1 - \beta_1) - (b_2 - \beta_2) x_i,
\end{aligned}
$$

using $y_i = \beta_1 + \beta_2 x_i + u_i$. So the OLS residual e_i depends on x_i (and on the $x's$ of other observations through the estimates b_1 and b_2) even if the model error u_i does not. This dependence disappears as the sample size gets large, since the OLS estimates are consistent so $(b_1 - \beta_1) \to 0$ and $(b_2 - \beta_2) \to 0$. But in finite samples the residuals will be heteroskedastic and correlated even if the model errors are not.

16.9 Key Concepts

1. Multicollinearity makes it difficult to disentangle the influence of individual regressors. It is not a problem for those regressors that are not multicollinear, and it is not a problem for prediction.

2. To avoid the serious problems of incorrect functional form and omitted variables bias, provided the sample size is large enough economists use models with many regressors and, if neces-

sary, flexible functional forms, such as quadratic terms, interactions and natural logarithm transformations.

3. It is difficult to detect that regressors are correlated with model errors and it is difficult to control for this problem (the subject of Chapter 17.5).

4. Failures of assumption 3 and/or 4 lead to inconsistent OLS estimates in the special case of models with lagged dependent variables as regressors and serially correlated errors. Otherwise OLS is generally consistent, but appropriate robust standard errors need to be used.

5. An outlier or outlying observation is one whose value is unusual given the rest of the data.

6. An influential observation is one that has a relatively large effect on the results of regression analysis, notably on predicted values of the dependent variable or on the estimated OLS coefficients.

7. Key diagnostic plots are plots of the dependent variable against the fitted value, and of the residual against the fitted value.

8. Diagnostic plots for a single regressor include residual versus regressor plots, component plus residual (or partial regression) plots, and added variable (or partial regression) plots.

9. DFITS and DFBETAs measure the influence of a particular observation on, respectively, the fitted values and estimated coefficients.

10. Key Terms: perfect collinearity; multicollinearity; omitted variables bias; irrelevant variables; incorrect functional form; RESET test; misspecification test; endogenous variable; endogeneity; instrumental variables; feedback; simultaneous equations; measurement error bias; sample selection bias; heteroskedastic error; serially correlated error; lagged dependent variable; clustered error; robust standard error; outlier; influential observation; leverage; residual versus regressor plot; component plus residual plot; partial regression plot; added variable plot; partial regression plot; DFITS; DFBETA.

16.10 Exercises

1. We estimate by OLS the model $y_i = \beta_1 + \beta_2 x_{2i} + \beta_3 x_{3i} + u_i$ and obtain default standard errors. What problems arise when, in turn, each of the following occurs.

   (a) x_3 should not appear in the model.
   (b) x_3 is an indicator variable that takes only values 0 or 1.
   (c) $x_3 = 2x_2$.
   (d) x_4 should also have appeared in the model.
   (e) u_i does have mean zero but it is not independent of the other u_j.
   (f) u_i does have mean zero and is independent of the other u_j, but it is heteroskedastic.

2. For each of the following conditions state whether or not OLS estimates of β_1, β_2 and β_3 in the model $y_i = \beta_1 + \beta_2 x_i + \beta_3 z_i + u_i$ are likely to be biased.

   (a) The sample comprises six observations.

   (b) We should not have included variable z in the model.

   (c) We should have included variable z in the model.

   (d) We should have use $\ln y$ and not y as the dependent variable.

   (e) The correlation of x and z equals 0.9.

   (f) The error u is heteroskedastic.

3. A detailed description of dataset SALARYSAT is given in exercise 3 of Chapter 7. Use heteroskedastic-robust standard errors.

   (a) OLS regress *salary* on an intercept and *satmath, satverb, highgrade* and *age*. Are *highgrade* and *age individually* statistically significant at 5%?

   (b) Add as a regressor *highgradeXage* = *highgrade*×*age*. Are the individual regressors *highgrade* and *age* statistically significant at 5%? Comment.

   (c) Perform an appropriate test of whether highest grade is statistically significant at 5%.

   (d) Perform an appropriate test of whether age is statistically significant at 5%.

   (e) Find the correlations of *highgradeXage* with *satmath, satverb, highgrade* and *age*. Comment given your result in part (b).

   (f) Regress *highgradeXage* on an intercept and *satmath, satverb, highgrade* and *age*. Comment given your result in part (b).

4. For each of the following state whether multicollinearity or perfect multicollinearity is likely to be a problem in an OLS regression that includes an intercept.

   (a) The regression includes $x1$, $x2$ and $x3$ and $5x1 + 3x2 + 7x3 = 22$.

   (b) The regression includes $x1$ and $x2 = x1^2$ and $x1$ takes just the two values 10 and 20.

   (c) The regression includes $x1$, $x2$ and $x3$ where $x1$, $x2$ and $x3$ are a complete set of mutually exclusive indicator variables.

   (d) The regression includes $x1$, $x2$ and $x3 = x1 \times x2$ where $x1$ and $x2$ are indicator variables.

5. For a sample of size 1,000 generate in order the following variables: $x2 \sim N(0,1)$, $x3 = x2 + N(0,1)$, $x4 = x2 + N(0,1)$, $u \sim N(0,1)$ and $y = \beta_1 + \beta_2 x2 + \beta_3 x3 + u$ where $\beta_1 = \beta_2 = \beta_3 = 1$. See Chapter 3.8.1 for the relevant computer commands.

   (a) Obtain the various pairwise correlations of $x2$, $x3$, $x4$ and u.

   (b) Regress y on an intercept, $x2$ and $x3$. Do the OLS slope coefficients appear to be consistent? Explain your answer.

   (c) Regress y on an intercept and $x2$. Does the OLS slope coefficient appear to be consistent? Explain your answer.

   (d) Regress y on an intercept, $x2$, $x3$ and $x4$. Do the OLS slope coefficients appear to be consistent? Explain your answer.

6. Repeat the previous exercise where a sample of size 1,000 is generate in the following order: $x2 \sim N(0,1)$, $x3 = N(0,1)$, $x4 = x3 + N(0,1)$, $u \sim N(0,1)$ and $y = \beta_1 + \beta_2 x2 + \beta_3 x3 + u$ where $\beta_1 = \beta_2 = \beta_3 = 1$.

7. For a sample of size 1,000 generate in order the following variables: $u \sim N(0,1)$, $z \sim N(0,1)$, $x2 = z + u$, $x3 = z + N(0,1)$, and $y = \beta_1 + \beta_2 x2 + \beta_3 x3 + u$ where $\beta_1 = \beta_2 = \beta_3 = 1$. See Chapter 3.8.1 for the relevant computer commands.

   (a) Obtain the various pairwise correlations of $x2$, $x3$ and u.

   (b) Regress y on an intercept, $x2$ and $x3$ and report the results.

   (c) Do the OLS slope coefficients appear to be consistent? If not, explain why.

8. Repeat the previous exercise generating in order the following variables: $u \sim N(0,2^2)$, $z \sim N(0,1)$, $x2 = z + N(0,1)$, $x3 = z + 0.5u$, and $y = \beta_1 + \beta_2 x2 + \beta_3 x3 + u$ where $\beta_1 = 1$, $\beta_2 = 2$, and $\beta_3 = 1$.

9. Use dataset AUTOSMPG detailed in Chapter 13.4. Restrict attention to cars ($d\_truck=0$) in 1980 ($year=1980$). OLS regress $lmpg$ on an intercept, $lcurbwt$, lhp, d_manual and d_diesel.

   (a) Compare heteroskedastic-robust standard errors to default standard errors.

   (b) Compare cluster-robust standard errors, with clustering on manufacturer, to heteroskedastic robust standard errors.

   (c) Computations for this example find that the intracluster correlation of the OLS residual is 0.314 and the intracluster correlation of lhp is 0.430. Given this information, use the formula in Chapter 12.1.4 to calculate the approximate inflation in the standard error of lhp due to clustering.

   (d) Compare your answer in part (c) to the actual inflation in the standard error.

10. Repeat the previous exercise for trucks ($d\_truck=1$) in 1980.

11. This question entails more complicated recursive generation of autocorrelated time series and computation of HAC-robust standard errors. It is easiest to adapt the code for Chapter 16 provided at the book website. For a sample of size 1,000 generate in order the following variables: $e_t \sim N(0,1)$, $u_t = 0.9u_{t-1}+e_t$, $v_t \sim N(0,1)$, $x_t = 0.6x_{t-1}+v_t$, and $y_t = 2+4x_t+u_t$. For answers below ignore the intercept for brevity and just answer for the slope coefficients.

    (a) Regress y_t on an intercept and x_t. Do coefficients appear to be correctly estimated? Explain.

    (b) Compare heteroskedastic-robust to HAC-robust standard errors. Comment.

    (c) Generate $y_t = 2+0.8y_{t-1}+4x_t+e_t$ (note: e_t not u_t) where initially set $y_t = 10$. Regress y_t on an intercept, y_{t-1} and x_t. Do coefficients appear to be correctly estimated? Explain.

    (d) Compare heteroskedastic-robust to HAC-robust standard errors. Comment.

    (e) Generate $y_t = 2+0.8y_{t-1}+4x_t+u_t$ (note: now u_t) where initially set $y_t = 10$. Regress y_t on an intercept, y_{t-1} and x_t. Do coefficients appear to be correctly estimated? Explain.

12. Repeat the previous exercise where the coefficient of x_t is 2 in all models and the coefficient of y_{t-1} is 0.7.

13. Use dataset EARNINGS_COMPLETE on full-time year-round workers detailed in chapter 14.1 and restrict analysis to women (*gender*=1). OLS regress *lnearnings* on an intercept, *age*, *education*, and *lnhours*, using heteroskedastic-robust standard errors.

    (a) Are the regressors statistically significant with expected signs? Explain.

    (b) Plot the OLS residual against the fitted value. Comment on any unusual observations. Hint: use the standard deviation of the OLS residual as a basis for comparison.

    (c) Plot the OLS residual against *education* value. Comment on any unusual observations.

    (d) List *earnings, age, education* and *hours* for the four observations with the lowest education. Do you see any problems?

    (e) Obtain *dfits*. How many observations have |*dfits*| larger than the rule-of-thumb threshold.

    (f) List *dfits, lnearnings, age, education, hours*, the fitted value and the residual for the observations with the six largest values of |*dfits*|. Comment.

    (g) Drop observations with |*dfits*| larger than the rule-of-thumb threshold, re-estimate and compare coefficients, their standard errors, and model fit to that with all observations.

14. Repeat the previous exercise for men (*gender*=0).

Chapter 17

Special Topics

The simplest case of regression assumes a linear model with independent homoskedastic errors. Specifically, we make the following assumptions: (1) $y_i = \beta_1 + \beta_2 x_{2i} + \beta_3 x_{3i} + \cdots + \beta_k x_{ki} + u_i$; (2) $\mathrm{E}[u_i | x_{2i}, ..., x_{ki}] = 0$; (3) $\mathrm{Var}[u_i | x_{2i}, ..., x_{ki}] = \sigma_u^2$; (4) u_i and u_j are independent, for all $i \neq j$.

This chapter presents special considerations that arise with each of the three main types of data – cross-section, panel and time series data. Then usually one or more of the preceding assumptions no longer holds, and analysis needs to be adjusted appropriately. In the simplest cases the OLS estimator remains unbiased and consistent, but inference is based on appropriate robust standard errors and alternative more efficient estimators might be used.

The chapter first considers cross-section data (with independent or clustered observations) and panel data with estimation using OLS, random effects and fixed effects estimators. It then presents methods for establishing the causative effect of a treatment, such as a training program or further education, on an outcome, such as earnings, using observational data. To date this text has considered only measuring association, rather than causation. The methods are restricted to settings where the data at hand are likely to satisfy the additional assumptions that need to be made when assumption 2 no longer holds. The chapter then introduces the most commonly-used nonlinear models (logit, probit and Poisson). The chapter concludes with a discussion of time series, a discussion that is quite advanced in places.

The coverage here is very brief and just surveys commonly-used methods. A considerable number of applications are given in Chapter 13 and in the end-of-chapter exercises. Advanced undergraduate econometrics texts provide detailed coverage of methods for cross-section, time series and panel data. For causal analysis using observational data, references include Angrist and Pischke (2009, 2015), Cunningham (2021) and Cameron and Trivedi (2022b).

17.1   Cross-Section Data

Cross-section data are data on individual entities that, in the simplest case, are assumed to be independent. The most common extension to OLS with default standard errors is OLS with robust standard errors that control for heteroskedastic errors or clustered errors. When data are clustered the random effects estimator or the fixed effects estimator may be used instead of OLS.

17.1.1   Heteroskedastic-Robust Standard Errors

Consider OLS estimation of the model

$$y_i = \beta_1 + \beta_2 x_{2i} + \cdots + \beta_k x_{ki} + u_i,$$

where the error u_i has conditional mean zero, so $\mathrm{E}[u_i|x_{2i},...,x_{ki}] = 0$, and is uncorrelated over i. So OLS is unbiased and consistent.

Suppose model errors are independent but are heteroskedastic, so $\mathrm{Var}[u_i|x_{2i},...,x_{ki}] = \sigma_i^2$ where σ_i^2 varies with the values of the regressors. Then it is standard to base inference on heteroskedastic-robust standard errors; see Chapter 12.1 for a detailed discussion.

17.1.2   Cluster-Robust Standard Errors

It is not unusual for cross-section data to have model errors that are correlated, rather than independent. The leading example of correlation is one where observations are grouped into **clusters**, with model errors correlated for observations in the same cluster but uncorrelated for observations in different clusters. For example, if a regression model overpredicts (or underpredicts) for one individual in a household (or village or region) then it is also likely to overpredict (or underpredict) for other individuals in the same household (or village or region).

We again consider the model $y_i = \beta_1 + \beta_2 x_{2i} + \cdots + \beta_k x_{ki} + u_i$ with $\mathrm{E}[u_i|x_{2i},...,x_{ki}] = 0$, so OLS is unbiased and consistent. The change is to suppose that

$$\sigma_{ij} = \mathrm{Cor}[u_i, u_j|x_{2i},...,x_{ki}] \begin{cases} \neq 0 & \text{if } i \text{ and } j \text{ are in the same cluster} \\ = 0 & \text{if } i \text{ and } j \text{ are in different clusters} \end{cases}.$$

Additionally the errors may be heteroskedastic.

Then it is standard to base inference on cluster-robust standard errors. Furthermore it is essential as default and heteroskedastic-robust standard errors can be a fraction of the appropriate cluster-robust standard errors. The theory requires that the number of clusters should be large, say greater than 30; better alternative methods have been proposed when there are few clusters. For detailed discussion of these points see Chapter 12.1.4. Exercises 1-4 provide applications.

17.1.3   Cluster-Specific Random Effects

When errors are clustered OLS is no longer the best estimator as more efficient estimation is possible. We add a subscript g for the cluster; for example y_{gi} for the ith individual in cluster g.

An obvious model that accounts for clustered errors is to suppose that the model error u_{gi} has two components – a cluster-specific component, denoted α_g, and an individual-specific component, denoted ε_{gi}. Thus if individual i is in cluster g the error is

$$u_{gi} = \alpha_g + \varepsilon_{gi}$$

The **random effects model** assumes this error structure, and additionally assumes that the α_g are independently and identically distributed with mean 0 and variance σ_α^2, while ε_{gi} is independently and identically distributed with mean 0 and variance σ_ε^2. It can be shown that this model implies that the errors are homoskedastic, with $\text{Var}[u_{gi}] = (\sigma_\alpha^2 + \sigma_\varepsilon^2)$ For individuals i and j in different clusters the errors are uncorrelated. For individuals in the same cluster the error correlation coefficient is constant, equalling $\sigma_\alpha^2/(\sigma_\alpha^2 + \sigma_\varepsilon^2)$, and the errors are said to be equicorrelated.

The **random effects estimator** is the efficient (feasible GLS) estimator given these assumptions for the error. The formula in the panel data case is given section 17.2.5 and section 17.2.7 covers implementation in various statistical packages.

The error assumptions for the RE estimator are unlikely to hold exactly. Then the RE estimator is still consistent but one needs to use cluster-robust standard errors, rather than default standard errors. Furthermore, because the error assumptions are unlikely to be met exactly, in practice RE can even be less efficient than OLS.

It is common economics practice to just use OLS with cluster-robust standard errors. Examples of random effects for cross-section data are given in exercises 1-4; see also the closely-related panel application detailed in Chapter 17.3.

17.1.4 Cluster-Specific Fixed Effects

The **fixed effects model** also specifies that $u_{gi} = \alpha_g + \varepsilon_{ig}$, but relaxes the assumption that the α_g are purely random with mean 0 and variance σ_α^2. Instead the α_g are treated as being random (despite the term fixed effects) with unspecified distribution. Furthermore α_g may potentially be correlated with regressors. In that case OLS regression of y on an intercept and $x_2, ..., x_k$ in the model

$$y_{gi} = \beta_1 + \beta_2 x_{2gi} + \cdots + \beta_k x_{kgi} + \alpha_g + \varepsilon_{gi}$$

would be biased and inconsistent as $\text{E}[\alpha_g + \varepsilon_{gi}|x_{2ii}, ..., x_{kii}] \neq 0$ since $E[\alpha_g|x_{2ii}, ..., x_{kii}] \neq 0$.

An alternative consistent estimator is obtained as follows. Define $\bar{y}_g, \bar{x}_{2g}, ..., \bar{x}_{kg}$ and $\bar{\varepsilon}_g$ to be averages across all individuals in the gth cluster, and note that $\overline{\alpha}_g = \alpha_g$ since the average of a constant is the constant. Then

$$\bar{y}_g = \beta_1 + \beta_2 \bar{x}_{2g} + \cdots + \beta_k \bar{x}_{kg} + \alpha_g + \bar{\varepsilon}_g.$$

Subtracting the two equations

$$y_{gi} - \bar{y}_g = \beta_2(x_{2ii} - \bar{x}_{2g}) + \cdots + \beta_k(x_{kii} - \bar{x}_{kg}) + (\varepsilon_{ii} - \bar{\varepsilon}_g).$$

The **fixed effects estimator** is the OLS estimator in this transformed model. Because α_g has been eliminated this estimator is consistent for $\beta_2, ..., \beta_k$ even if in the original model $\text{E}[\alpha_g|x_{2gi}, ..., x_{kgi}] \neq 0$.

This estimator is also called the **within estimator** as it uses only **variation within** each cluster, as terms such as $x_{2gi} - \bar{x}_{2g}$ measure variation in cluster g of individual observations x_{2gi} around the cluster mean $\bar{x}_{2g}$. Decomposition of overall variation into within and between variation is presented in greater detail for the panel case in Chapter 17.2.2, while the chapter exercise 1 provides a clustered data example.

The fixed effects estimator is widely used in economics applications as it has the advantage of providing consistent parameter estimates when assumption 2 does not hold, provided the only part of the error term that is correlated with the regressors is one that is the same for all individuals in a given cluster. The estimator uses only variation within cluster, so there can be a loss of efficiency. And in the extreme case that a regressor, say x_j, takes the same values for all individuals in a cluster, $(x_{jgi} - \bar{x}_{jg}) = 0$ and we cannot identify β_j. The remaining coefficients can still be identified.

The default standard errors for the fixed effects estimator are correct if the errors ε_{gi} are homoskedastic and independent. In practice this is not the case, and it is standard to use cluster-robust standard errors for the fixed effects estimator, rather than default standard errors. Examples of fixed effects estimation for cross-section data are given in exercises 1-4; see also the closely-related panel application detailed in Chapter 17.3.

17.2   Panel Data

Panel data or **longitudinal data** are data on multiple individuals observed over multiple time periods. The observation y_{it} is that for the ith of N individuals in the tth period. We assume that individuals are observed at regular time periods. There are T time periods and, for simplicity, we assume that individuals are observed in all time periods.

We consider a **short panel** that has many individuals and a limited number of time periods. This type of panel is common for panel data on people and on firms. This type of data can be simply treated as similar to clustered data in Chapter 17.1, with the cluster unit being the individual and the different time periods providing the multiple observations per cluster.

A **long panel** has many time periods and relatively few periods and is more complicated to analyze as time series considerations need to be addressed to ensure valid statistical inference, an extension of Chapter 17.7. An example is macroeconomic data such as GDP on several countries over many time periods.

For the simplest models OLS is consistent and inference is based on panel-robust standard errors that are similar to cluster-robust standard errors. In that case more efficient estimation may be possible.

A commonly-used alternative estimator is the fixed effects estimator which has the advantage of controlling for a limited form of correlation between the model errors and regressors.

17.2.1   Pooled OLS with Cluster-robust Standard Errors

The **pooled OLS model** estimates by OLS a model where the parameters do not vary over individuals, so

$$y_{it} = \beta_1 + \beta_2 x_{2it} + \cdots + \beta_k x_{kit} + u_{it}.$$

The regressors x_{it} can control for variation over time by including, for example, a linear time trend or a quadratic time trend or, for a short panel, $(T - 1)$ indicator variables for each time period.

The error terms for a given individual in different periods may be correlated with each other. For example, consider regression of annual hours worked on wage rate using panel data on a number of people followed for several years. For a given person, it may be that hours worked are routinely overpredicted in each time period or underpredicted in each time period, due to unobserved propensities to work.

In the simplest case observations for different individuals are assumed to be independent, and inference should be based on cluster-robust standard errors that cluster on the individual and are also called **panel robust**. More generally independence may only hold at a higher level of aggregation, such as household, village or state. Then we cluster at that higher level.

For detailed discussion of cluster-robust standard errors see Chapter 12.1.4. In particular failure to use cluster-robust standard errors can lead to OLS standard errors that are greatly downwards biased, t statistics that are too large and p values that are too small. And the number of cluster units needs to be reasonably large.

17.2.2 Within and Between Variation

With panel data, dependent variables and regressors can potentially vary over both time and individuals. This variation can be decomposed as follows.

For panel data variation over time for a given individual is called **within variation**, and variation across individuals is called **between estimation**.

The **total variation** in a variable z_{it} is the variation around the overall mean $\bar{z} = \frac{1}{nT} \sum_{i=1}^{n} \sum_{t=1}^{T} z_{it}$. **Within variation** is the variation over time for a given individual, the variation of z_{it} around the individual mean $\bar{z}_i = \frac{1}{T} \sum_{t=1}^{T} z_{it}$. **Between variation** is variation across individuals, the variation of the individual mean $\bar{z}_i$ around the overall mean $\bar{z}$.

The corresponding decomposition for the overall variance is

$$
\begin{aligned}
\text{Within variance:} \quad & s_{\text{W}}^2 = \frac{1}{nT-1} \sum_i \sum_t (z_{it} - \bar{z}_i)^2 \\
\text{Between variance:} \quad & s_{\text{B}}^2 = \frac{1}{n-1} \sum_i (\bar{z}_i - \bar{z})^2 \\
\text{Overall variance:} \quad & s_{\text{O}}^2 = \frac{1}{nT-1} \sum_i \sum_t (z_{it} - \bar{z})^2.
\end{aligned}
$$

For unbalanced data replace NT in the formulas by $\sum_t T_i$. It can be shown that $s_{\text{O}}^2 \simeq s_{\text{W}}^2 + s_{\text{B}}^2$.

This distinction is important because different panel estimators differ in their use of within and between variation. OLS uses both within and between variation. The fixed effects estimator uses only within variation. The random effects estimator uses both within and between variation and is closer to OLS when the within variation is relatively small.

17.2.3 Random Effects and Related Estimators

OLS is no longer the most efficient estimator when errors are correlated over time for a given individual, as in order for OLS to be optimal the errors need to be independent over both i and t. More efficient estimation is possible by modelling the correlation over time for a given individual, while maintaining the assumption that individuals good model

The **random effects model** models this correlation over time by specifying that the error $u_{it} = \alpha_i + \varepsilon_{it}$ where α_i are independently and identically distributed with mean 0 and variance σ_α^2, while ε_{it} is independently and identically distributed with mean 0 and variance σ_ε^2. The **random effects estimator** is the efficient estimator given these assumptions for the error.

The random effects model imposes the restriction that the correlation between u_{it} and u_{is} equals $\sigma_\alpha^2/(\sigma_\alpha^2 + \sigma_\varepsilon^2)$, $s \neq t$, which is the same regardless of how many periods apart are the errors.

In practice we might expect that $Cor(u_{it}, u_{is})$ declines as the time difference $|t - s|$ increases (a consideration not relevant in the earlier discussion of cross-section data that is clustered). Various alternative estimators exist that allow for such correlation; a simple model specifies $u_{it} = \rho u_{i,t-1} + \varepsilon_{it}$ where ε_{it} is independently and identically distributed with mean 0 and variance σ_ε^2. For the random effects and related estimators one should use cluster-robust standard errors, to guard against misspecification of the assumptions made on u_{it}.

Despite the potential efficiency gains of random effects and related estimators most econometrics studies use OLS with cluster-robust standard errors, unless there is reason to used the fixed effects estimator.

17.2.4 Fixed Effects Estimator

The **fixed effects model** also specifies that $u_{it} = \alpha_i + \varepsilon_{it}$, but relaxes the assumption that the α_i are purely random with mean 0 and variance σ_α^2. Instead the α_i are treated as being random (despite the term fixed effects) with unspecified distribution. Furthermore α_i may potentially be correlated with regressors. In that case OLS regression of y on an intercept and $x_2, ..., x_k$ in the model

$$y_{it} = \beta_1 + \beta_2 x_{2it} + \cdots + \beta_k x_{kit} + \alpha_i + \varepsilon_{it}$$

would be biased and inconsistent as $\mathrm{E}[\alpha_i + \varepsilon_{it}|x_{2it}, ..., x_{kit}] \neq 0$ since $E[\alpha_i|x_{2it}, ..., x_{kit}] \neq 0$.

By algebra similar to that for the cluster-specific fixed effects model, manipulation yields the mean-differenced model

$$y_{it} - \bar{y}_i = \beta_2(x_{2i} - \bar{x}_{2i}) + \cdots + \beta_k(x_{kit} - \bar{x}_{ki}) + (\varepsilon_{it} - \bar{\varepsilon}_i),$$

where, for example $\bar{y}_i = \frac{1}{T} \sum_{i=1}^T y_{it}$ is the average over time for the ith individual. The fixed effects estimator is the OLS estimator in this model and inference should be based on cluster-robust standard errors.

The fixed effects estimator has the advantage of providing consistent parameter estimates when assumption 2 does not hold, provided the only part of the error term that is correlated with the regressors is one that is the same for all individuals in a given cluster.

For example suppose we regress earnings (y_{it}) on years of schooling (x_{it}) and other regressors. It is likely that individuals with high unobserved ability have both high years of schooling (x_{it}) and also earnings higher than the model predicts given their years of schooling, so a high u_{it} that is correlated with the regressor x_{it}. A fixed effects model controls for this by assuming that any such correlation between u_{it} and x_{it} is only due to the component α_i of u_{it} that is constant over time.

The fixed effects estimator uses only variation over time for each individual, so there is a loss of efficiency. Furthermore, in the extreme case that a regressor, say x_j, does not vary over time for each individual then $(x_{jit} - \bar{x}_{ji}) = 0$ and we cannot identify β_j. This would be the case for the regressor schooling in the earnings-schooling example if we only observe individuals in years after they have completed their schooling. The remaining coefficients can still be identified.

Fixed effects estimates can be obtained by standard OLS regression of y_{it} on $x_{2it}, ..., x_{kit}$ and a complete set of n indicator variables $d1_{it}, ..., dn_{it}$, where dj_{it} equals one if $i = j$ and equals zero if $i \neq j$. Then $d1_{it}, ..., dn_{it}$ are called individual dummies and the method is called least squares dummy variable regression. But it is better to use specialized software that estimates the mean-differenced model for two reasons. First it is computationally faster as there are fewer variables in the regression. Second, the degrees-of-freedom adjustment used following least squares dummy variable regression leads to over-estimation of cluster-robust standard errors.

17.2.5 Fixed Effects versus Random Effects

The random effects estimator can be shown to be equivalent to OLS estimation in the model

$$y_{it} - \widehat{\theta}_i \bar{y}_i = (1 - \widehat{\theta}_i)\beta_1 + \beta_2(x_{2i} - \widehat{\theta}_i \bar{x}_{2i}) + \cdots + \beta_k(x_{kit} - \widehat{\theta}_i \bar{x}_{ki}) + (\varepsilon_{it} - \widehat{\theta}_i \bar{\varepsilon}_i),$$

where $\theta_i = 1 - \sqrt{\sigma_\varepsilon^2/(T_i \sigma_\alpha^2 + \sigma_\varepsilon^2)}$ and there are T_i periods of data for the ith observation. It follows that the random effects estimator (1) lies between the OLS and fixed effects estimators, and (2) approaches the fixed effects estimator as the number of periods becomes large and/or as the within cluster correlation $\sigma_\alpha^2/(\sigma_\alpha^2 + \sigma_\varepsilon^2)$ approaches one.

Conceptually there is a big difference, however, as the fixed effects estimator allows regressors to be correlated with the error, provided the correlation is only with the time-invariant component α_i of the error.

17.2.6 Dynamic Models

For panel data the current value of the dependent variable y_{it} may be determined in part by past values of y_{it}. For example, individual earnings this period may depend in part on earnings in the previous period.

The pooled OLS model partially captures this dependence in part through the regressors $x_{2it}, ..., x_{kit}$. And the fixed effects model can additionally capture this through the fixed effect α_i whereby some individuals have high α_i (or low α_i) period after period, reflecting permanently higher (or lower) than expected earnings given the regressors $x_{2it}, ..., x_{kit}$.

An alternative approach is to directly include past values of the dependent variable as regressors. This brings in more complicated issues that arise for time series regression with a lagged dependent variable and serially correlated errors. In this brief review we merely note that the preceding methods generally lead to inconsistent parameter estimates when lagged dependent variables appear as regressors. Alternative estimation methods are needed.

17.2.7 Grouped Data Models Estimation using Different Statistical Packages

Analysis requires that the grouped data (either panel or clustered cross-section) are in the correct format. For concreteness consider panel data. Most often estimation commands assume the data are organized so that each observation is an individual-time pair. But the original data may be organized so that each observation has data for all individuals in a time period, or each observation has data for all time periods for an individual. In these latter cases the data may need to be reshaped to individual-time pairs.

The more specialized estimation commands for grouped data models require specification of the time variable for panel data or the grouping variable for clustered data. In Stata the xtset command specifies the grouping variable and the **xtreg** command estimates random and fixed effects models. In R use the **plm** function in the **plm** package; option **index** defines the grouping variable. In Gretl the **setobs** command specifies the grouping variable and the **panel** command estimates the models. In Eviews the grouping variable is defined in a panel workfile and estimation uses the **panel** command. Different packages can give slightly different random effects estimates of model coefficients as there are different ways to estimate the error variances σ_α^2 and σ_ε^2.

It can be useful to calculate the within and between standard deviations of key variables. The Stata command **xtsum** does this immediately, as does the **xtsum** function in the R **dplyr** package. In other statistical packages it can be necessary to compute these standard deviations manually. The key component is computing within group means; in Gretl use the **pmean** command and in Eviews use **@Statsby**.

17.3 Panel Data Example: NBA Team Revenue

Data on twenty-nine teams in the U.S. National Basketball Association (NBA) for the ten seasons 2001-02 to 2010-11 are in dataset NBA.We treat the data as being from a short panel.

The dataset is arranged so that each line contains all data for a team-season pair. Alternatively the dataset could have been arranged with each line containing all data for all seasons for a given team, or with each line containing all data for all teams in a given season. It may be necessary to rearrange data to get it into the format required by a statistical package. And the dataset should have a variable that identifies the team and a variable that identifies the season.

Table 17.1 presents variable definitions and summary statistics. The average team revenue was $96 million and the average number of wins was 41. There is considerable variation in both revenue and wins.

Table 17.1: NBA team revenue: Variable definitions and summary statistics (n=29, T=10).

			Standard deviation				
Variable	**Definition**	**Mean**	**Overall**	Between	Within	**Min**	**Max**
Revenue	Team revenue in millions of 1999 $	95.714	24.442	22.467	10.319	58.49	187.72
Lnrevenue	Natural logarithm of team revenue	4.532	0.236	0.213	0.108	4.069	5.235
Wins	Number of wins including playoff	41.04	12.438	7.044	10.356	9	67
Playoff	=1 if made playoffs in previous season	0.545	0.499	0.243	0.439	0	1
Champ	=1 if champion in previous season	0.035	0.184	0.094	0.159	0	1
Allstars	Number of players voted Allstars	0.860	0.871	0.524	0.704	0	4
Lncitypop	Log of city population in millions	1.301	0.801	0.807	0.098	-0.015	2.94
Teamid	Team identifier	14.86	8.355	8.515	0.000	1	29
Season	Season identifier	5.542	2.872	0.371	2.858	1	10

Table 17.1 includes a decomposition of overall variation into within variation and between variation. The within variation exceeds between variation for the various performance measures (*Wins*, *Playoff*, *Champ* and *Allstars*), so there is relatively large variation in how a given team performs from season to season. The within variation is less than between variation for the outcome

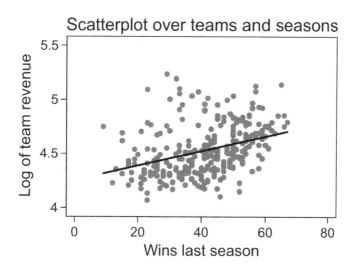

Figure 17.1: NBA team revenue: Scatterplot of natural logarithm against number of wins in previous season for 29 teams over 10 seasons.

of interest (*Lnrevenue*) and for the measure of market size (*Lncitypop*), which will lead to less precision, and possibly different estimates, for the fixed effects estimator that uses only within variation.

Figure 17.1 presents a scatter plot of the natural logarithm of team revenue (in millions of dollars) against number of wins last season. There is a positive relationship, with correlation coefficient of 0.36 and fitted OLS regression line with slope coefficient 0.00676. This coefficient in a log-linear model is a semi-elasticity, see Chapter 9.3, so one more win last season is associated with a 0.676% increase in team earnings.

The observed positive relationship may arise for several reasons. It may be that some teams are successful year after year, with both high revenue and high number of wins – like the New York Yankees in baseball – while others are unsuccessful year after year. Or it may be that there is a relatively level playing field, with teams enjoying higher revenues following seasons with more wins. Panel data analysis seeks to identify these different mechanisms

17.3.1 Pooled OLS

Table 17.2 presents OLS estimates from regression of the natural logarithm of team revenues on an intercept, *Wins*, and the variable *Season* which equals 1 in the first season, 2 in the second season, and so on. The variable *Season* acts as a linear time trend. The estimated slope coefficients indicate that team revenue increases by 0.68% with each extra win, and team revenue is increasing (in real terms) by 1.82% per year.

Three different standard errors and associated t statistics are reported in Table 17.2. The default and heteroskedastic robust standard errors are very similar. By contrast the preferred cluster-robust

Table 17.2: NBA team revenue: Various robust standard error estimates for pooled OLS.

Variable	Coefficient	Default		Het robust		Cluster robust	
		St. Error	t	St. Error	t	St. Error	t
Wins	.00681	.00102	6.65	.00099	6.88	.00190	3.59
Season	.01824	.00443	4.11	.00450	4.05	.00331	5.51
Intercept	4.15162	.05060	82.04	.05075	81.81	.09658	42.99
Observations	286						
R^2	.176						

Table 17.3: NBA team revenue: Pooled OLS, random effects and fixed effects estimates.

Variable	Estimator, coefficients and standard errors					
	Pooled OLS		Random Effects		Fixed Effects	
	Het-robust	Robust	Default	Robust	Default	Robust
Wins	.0049***	.0049***	.0024***	.0024***	.0027***	.0027***
	(.0014)	(.0015)	(.0008)	(.0008)	(.0007)	(.0007)
Season	.0180***	.0180***	.0188***	.0188***	.0200***	.0200***
	(.0035)	(.0033)	(.0017)	(.0033)	(.0017)	(.0029)
Playoff	.0306	.0306	.0385***	.0385*	.0362***	.0362*
	(.0359)	(.0447)	(.0176)	(.0200)	(.0167)	(.0209)
Champion	.1089***	.1089***	.0118	.0118	.0052	.0052
	(.0331)	(.0473)	(.0316)	(.0163)	(.0300)	(.0167)
Allstars	.0353***	.0353**	.0372***	.0372***	.0356***	.0356***
	(.0127)	(.0178)	(.0075)	(.0066)	(.0071)	(.0068)
Lncitypop	.1440***	.1440***	.0196	.0196	-.2021***	-.2021***
	(.0196)	(.0598)	(.0315)	(.0872)	(.0491)	(.0632)
Intercept	3.9945	3.9945	4.2477	4.2477	4.5222	4.5222
	(.0491)	(.0596)	(.0560)	(.1076)	(.0649)	(.0957)
Observations	286	286	286	286	286	286

standard error for the key variable, *Wins*, is 1.86 times as large (= .00190/.00102). Using these preferred standard errors variable *Wins* is nonetheless still highly statistically significant.

17.3.2 Random Effects and Fixed Effects Estimators

In this section we regress the natural logarithm of team revenues on an intercept and several regressors. Three estimators are given – pooled OLS, random effects and (discussed later) fixed effects. For each estimator two standard errors are given: heteroskedastic-robust and cluster-robust with clustering on the team. For cluster-robust inference with 29 clusters we use the $t(28)$ distribution with 10%, 5% and 1% critical values of, respectively, 2.76, 2.05 and 1.70. One, two and three asterisks are used to denote statistical significance of a variable at, respectively, 10%, 5% and 1%.

Columns 1 and 2 of Table 17.3 present the pooled OLS estimates. All coefficients have the expected positive sign and are economically significant. For example, one more win is associated with a 0.49% increase in earnings after correlation for the other variables. For all variables the cluster-robust standard errors are similar to or larger than heteroskedastic-robust standard errors.

Columns 3 and 4 of Table 17.3 give the random effects estimates. The coefficient for variable *Wins* falls from .0049 for pooled OLS to .0024 and the coefficients for *Champion* and *Lncitypop* are now much smaller and statistically insignificant at 5%. The big change in the coefficient for *Lncitypop* is because this variable varies little over time and is captured by the team random effect α_i. (When *Lncitypop* is dropped as a regressor there is considerable change in the pooled OLS estimates but very little change in the random effects and fixed effects estimates). The preferred cluster-robust standard errors in this example are generally larger than the default standard errors given in column 3. The random effects estimates are much more precise than the pooled OLS estimates in this example. The cluster-robust standard errors for variables *Wins*, *Playoff*, *Champion* and *Allstars* given in column 4 are generally less than half those given in column 2 for pooled OLS.

Columns 5 and 6 of Table 17.3 give the fixed effects estimates. The estimates, aside from the coefficient of *Lncitypop* are quite similar to the random effects estimates, and again the preferred cluster-robust standard errors in this example are sometimes larger and sometimes similar to the default standard errors given in column 5.

17.4 Instrumental Variables

For simplicity, begin with bivariate regression before generalization. The OLS estimator in the model $y = \beta_1 + \beta_2 x + u$ is inconsistent if $E[u|x] \neq 0$ (assumption 2 fails).

The instrumental variables estimator is a long standing method that enables consistent estimation of β_1 and β_2 provided there exists an **instrumental variable**, denoted z, that is correlated with z but does not directly determine y given x (so $E[u|z] = 0$).

17.4.1 Instrumental Variables Estimator

Figure 17.2 presents three path diagrams that illustrate the instrumental variables method for regression of y on x.

The first path diagram presents conditions under which OLS is consistent. Then the regressor x and the error u each determine the outcome y but there is no link between u and x.

The second path diagram additionally supposes that u is correlated with x. Then regression of y on x combines two effects on y of a change in x, namely the direct effect $(x \to y)$ and the indirect effect $(u \to x \to y)$ since x and u are correlated. More formally, now $y = \beta_1 + \beta_2 x + u(x)$ so that using calculus the total derivative of y with respect to x is $dy/dx = \beta_2 + du/dx$. The data give information on dy/dx, so OLS estimates the total effect $\beta_2 + du/dx$ rather than β_2 alone. The OLS estimator is therefore biased and inconsistent for β_2, unless there is no association between x and u.

The third path diagram introduces an additional variable z that has the property that changes in z are associated with changes in x but there is no direct path from z to u. Formally $E[u|z] = 0$. The general terminology is that x is an **endogenous** regressor and z is an **instrument** for x.

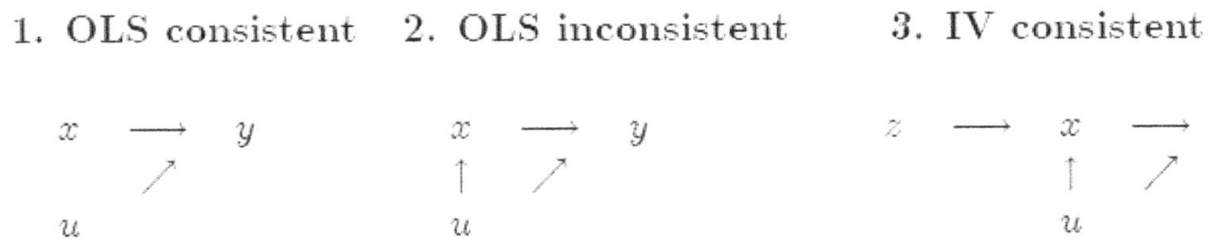

1. OLS consistent   2. OLS inconsistent   3. IV consistent

$$x \longrightarrow y \qquad\qquad x \longrightarrow y \qquad\qquad z \longrightarrow x \longrightarrow y$$

$$\nearrow \qquad\qquad\qquad \uparrow \quad \nearrow \qquad\qquad\qquad\qquad \uparrow \quad \nearrow$$

$$u \qquad\qquad\qquad\qquad u \qquad\qquad\qquad\qquad\qquad\qquad u$$

Figure 17.2: Instrumental variables: Path diagrams for OLS and for IV

Given these assumption, $\mathrm{Cov}[z,y] = \mathrm{Cov}[z, \beta_1 + \beta_2 x + u] = \mathrm{Cov}[z, \beta_1] + \mathrm{Cov}[z, \beta_2 x] + \mathrm{Cov}[z,u] = \beta_2 Cov[z,x]$, since the covariance of a random variable with a constant is zero, and the crucial assumption that $\mathrm{E}[u|z] = 0$ implies that $\mathrm{Cov}[z,u] = 0$. It follows that

$$\beta_2 = \frac{\mathrm{Cov}[z,y]}{\mathrm{Cov}[z,x]}.$$

The **instrumental variables (IV) estimator** of β_2 is the sample analog

$$b_{IV} = \frac{\sum_i (z_i - \bar{z})(y_i - \bar{y})}{\sum_i (z_i - \bar{z})(x_i - \bar{x})}$$

The properties of the IV estimator are given in Appendix C.3. It can be shown that the IV estimator $b_{IV} = b_{yz}/b_{xz}$ where b_{yz} is the slope coefficient from OLS of y on an intercept and z, and b_{xz} is the slope coefficient from OLS of x on an intercept and z. Intuitively $\frac{\Delta y}{\Delta x} = \frac{\Delta y}{\Delta z} / \frac{\Delta z}{\Delta x}$.

The instrument needs to satisfy the assumptions that (1) z is uncorrelated with the error u; and (2) z is correlated with the regressor x.

The first assumption excludes the instrument z from being a regressor in the model for y, since if instead y depended on both x and z and y is regressed on x alone then z is being absorbed into the error so that x will then be correlated with the error. This crucial assumption is not testable. In particular, the obvious approach of regressing y on both x and z and testing for statistical significance of z may well find that z is statistically significant, since it is correlated with x by the second assumption, even if the first assumption is satisfied. Instead the assumption needs to be justified by strong credible arguments and in many settings it is not possible to come up with a plausible instrument.

The second assumption requires that there is some association between the instrument and the variable being instrumented. The higher is this association the more precise will be the IV estimator.

17.4.2 Extensions

In practice additional regressors are included in the model. Most often these additional regressors are **exogenous regressors**, meaning that they are uncorrelated with the error. Exogenous variables can be used as instruments for themselves, and common terminology is to refer to a variable as an instrument only if it is an additional variable whose only use is as an instrument for the endogenous regressor.

Given a single endogenous regressor and a single instrument, we can use the preceding formula after first purging the effect of the other exogenous regressors. So $b_{IV} = \sum_i e_{zi} e_{yi} / \sum_i e_{zi} e_{xi}$ where e_{zi}, e_{yi} and e_{xi} are residuals from OLS regression of, respectively, z, y and x on an intercept and the additional regressors.

In many applications it requires considerable ingenuity to have even a single instrument. In some applications, however, there can be more than one instrument for the single endogenous regressor x. Then the **two-stage least squares (2SLS) estimator**, which includes IV as a special case, is used.

Much less frequently there can be more than one endogenous regressor. Then one needs at least as many instruments as there are endogenous regressors, and again the 2SLS estimator is used. The model is said to be **just identified** (or **over identified**) if there are as many (or more) instruments as there are endogenous regressors.

IV and 2SLS estimates can be much less precise than OLS estimates. Furthermore; conventional inference methods can break down if the instrument(s) are only weakly correlated with the endogenous regressor after controlling for the exogenous regressors. A diagnostic and alternative inference method are briefly presented in the application below.

17.4.3 Instrumental Variables Application: Returns to Schooling

An application of instrumental variables estimation is given in Chapter 13.8.

Here we give another application, measuring the average returns to a year of schooling. The basic model is

$$\ln w_i = \beta_1 + \beta_2 sch_i + \beta_3 x_{3i} + \cdots + \beta_{28} x_{28i} + u_i,$$

where w is the hourly wage and sch denotes years of schooling. The additional regressors $x_3, ..., x_{28}$ are 26 control variables that include race, geographic indicators and measures of parental education.

The concern is that individuals select their level of schooling in part due to the expected impact on their earnings, so higher (or lower) levels of schooling (sch) will be chosen by individuals with unusually high (or low) expectations of $\ln w$ even after inclusion of the 26 controls (this deviation is captured by the error u). As a result sch and u are correlated. Card (1995) proposed IV estimation using proximity to a college as an instrument for years of schooling. The key assumption is that college proximity can be excluded from the log-wage model.

Dataset RETURNSTOSCHOOLING has the same data from the NLS young men's cohort on $3,010$ males aged 24 to 34 years old in 1976 as that used to produce Table 1 of Kling (2001), and originally used by Card (1995). The dependent variable is the log hourly wage (*wage76*), the endogenous regressor is the highest grade completed (*grade76*), and the instrument is an indicator variable equal to one if there is a four-year college in the county of residence (*col4*).

Table 17.4 model 1 presents the key results, with heteroskedastic-robust standard errors reported in parentheses. The IV estimate of the return to an extra year of schooling is 12.0% compared to 3.5% using OLS. The IV estimate is much less precise, with standard error 0.053 compared to 0.003

Table 17.4: Rreturns to schooling: OLS and IV estimates in a log-wage regression

	Model 1		Model 2	
	OLS	IV	OLS	IV
schooling (sch)	0.035	0.120	0.073	0.133
	(0.003)	(0.053)	(0.004)	(0.048)
experience (exp)	-	-	0.039	0.038
	-	-	(0.002)	(0.003)
26 controls	Yes	Yes	Yes	Yes
R^2	0.219	0.032	0.292	0.194

for OLS. The reason for the great loss of efficiency is that the correlation between the instrument (*col4*) and the endogenous regressor (*grade76*) is only 0.144.

When IV estimation uses **weak instruments** the usual inference methods can be invalid. Here weak means that the instrument has little explanatory power for the endogenous regressor after inclusion of the exogenous regressors. A commonly-used diagnostic is to use the F statistic for test of joint statistical significance of instrument(s) in a regression of the endogenous regressor on the instrument(s) and exogenous regressors. This statistic is called the **first-stage F statistic**. The diagnostic is very imperfect – values less than 10 are strongly suggestive that there may be a weak instrument problem, but instruments can be weak even with values much greater than ten. For the current example, with only one instrument, first-stage regression of *grade76* on *col4* and the 26 exogenous regressors yields $t = 3.591$ for *col4*, so $F = 3.591^2 = 12.90$ and it is possible that the instruments are weak.

The IV estimates lead to standard 95% confidence interval, called a Wald confidence interval, for *grade76* of $0.120 \pm 1.96 \times 0.53$ or $(0.016, 0.224)$. An alternative confidence interval using the **Anderson-Rubin (AR) test** method is valid regardless of whether or not instruments are very weak. For the current example the 95% AR confidence interval is $(0.030, 0.286)$, similar to the Wald confidence interval.

Model 1 is limited as it does not include work experience or the closely related variable age as a regressor. Work experience is generally not observed, and following standard procedure it is assumed that work experience starts once schooling ends and schooling starts at age six. So experience is constructed as `exp76=age76-grade76-6`. The model then becomes

$$\ln w_i = \beta_1 + \beta_2 sch_i + \beta_3 exp_i + \beta_3 s_i + \beta_4 x_{4i} + \cdots + \beta_{29} x_{29i} + u_i,$$

There are two endogenous regressors, schooling (as before) and now experience since by construction it depends on schooling. We use as instruments college proximity (as before) and age (which is a good instrument for experience). The model is just identified as there are two endogenous regressors and two instruments. Estimation is by two-stage least squares.

Table 17.4 model 2 presents the results. Now the IV estimate of the returns to an additional year of schooling is 13.3%, and is statistically significant at 5%.

Standard arguments for the endogeneity of the schooling variable suggest that the OLS estimates will understate the returns to education, yet here the IV estimates are twice the OLS estimates.

An alternative interpretation of instrumental variables presented in Chapter 17.5.8 provides an explanation for why IV estimates can exceed the OLS estimates.

17.4.4 Instrumental Variables Estimation using Different Statistical Packages

Econometrics packages include commands for IV and 2SLS estimation. As an example consider estimation of $y = \beta_1 + \beta_2 x_2 + \beta_3 x_3 + \beta_4 x_4 + \beta_5 x_5 + u$ where x_2 is endogenous, $x_3, ..., x_5$ are exogenous and z_1 and z_2 are instruments for x_2. In Stata give command `ivregress 2sls y x3 x4 x5 (x2 = z1 z2)`. In R use the `ivreg` package and command `ivreg(y ~ x2+x3+x4+x5 | z1+z2+x3+x4+x5)`. In Gretl give command `tsls y 0 x2 x3 x4 x5; 0 z1 z2 x3 x4 x5`. In Eviews give command `tsls y x2 x3 x4 x5 @ z1 z2 x3 x4 x5`.

17.5 Causal Inference: An Overview

This section presents an overview of a range of methods that measure the causative average marginal effect of a treatment. It is important to note that while many of the methods presented here can be implemented using OLS regression, or using simple extensions of OLS, the topic is more recently developed and entails many subtleties. Further reading is recommended.

Each method is greatly reliant on assumptions that vary from method to method, results may be limited in their generalizability, and the method that can be employed depends very much on data availability. Several of the methods are restricted to the case where the treatment is binary. And we do not consider methods that look at measures of the effect of treatment effect that are more detailed than the average effect.

The presentation here is very brief. For application of several of these methods see the case studies in Chapters 13.5–13.8.

17.5.1 The Causality Problem

Let y_i denote earnings, and let d_i be an indicator variable equal to 1 if training is received and $d_i = 0$ otherwise. Then a very simple regression model is

$$y_i = \beta_1 + \gamma d_i + u_i,$$

where γ is "gamma", the third letter in the Greek alphabet.

Recall that consistency of the OLS estimator requires assumption 2 that $\mathrm{E}[u_i|d_i] = 0$, meaning that the error term has expected value zero for those with training ($d_i = 1$) and has expected value zero those with no training ($d_i = 0$). This is a reasonable assumption if training is randomly assigned through an experiment, such as a coin toss.

But for observational data where individuals chose whether to get training, it is likely that those who chose to be trained expected on average to receive a higher benefit from training than those who did not chose to get training. As a consequence comparing average earnings across the two groups will overstate the benefit of training. In terms of the current model $\mathrm{E}[u_i|d_i = 1] > 0$ and $\mathrm{E}[u_i|d_i = 0] < 0$.

In principle including additional regressors can partly control for this selection bias, but in many applications it is felt that treatment status is still correlated with the remaining error.

17.5.2   Potential Outcomes Model

The modern econometrics methods for estimating the causative effect of a treatment use as starting point the **potential outcomes model** or **Rubin causal model**. We present this model, along with the associated commonly-used terminology.

Consider a binary treatment D, with $D_i = 1$ for individual i if treated and $D_i = 0$ if individual i is not treated (a control). We are interested in the effect of treatment on the observed outcome Y_i.

For individual i there are two possible outcomes, denoted Y_{1i} if $D_i = 1$ and Y_{0i} if $D_i = 0$. Interest lies in estimating the treatment affect $\gamma_i \equiv Y_{1i} - Y_{0i}$. The problem is that we observe only one of the two outcomes, which can be expressed as $Y_i = D_i Y_{1i} + (1 - D_i) Y_{0i}$. Note that this expression implicitly assumes that the outcome of individual i is not affected by any treatment received by other individuals. This assumption of no spillovers is called the stable unit treatment value assumption (SUTVA).

Because the treatment effect is not observable for an individual we need to restrict attention to more aggregated measures. The most common aggregate measure is the **average treatment effect** (ATE). In the population this is

$$\text{ATE} = E[\gamma_i] = E[Y_{1i} - Y_{0i}].$$

A second measure is the **average treatment effect on the treated** (ATET)

$$\text{ATET} = E[\gamma_i | D_i = 1] = E[(Y_{1i} - Y_{0i}) | D_i = 1].$$

Common variations are to consider these quantities conditional on specific values of control variables, e.g. $\text{ATET}|x = E[(Y_{1i} - Y_{0i}) | X_i = x]$.

If assignment to treatment is purely random, such as through a coin toss, then we can estimate the ATE by the difference in the average outcomes for the treated and untreated.

In economic applications assignment to treatment is rarely purely random. This leads to a range of methods that vary with available data and assumptions about the **random assignment mechanism**. The **selection on observables** assumption is that treatment assignment can be viewed as purely random once we control for treatment assignment using observed variables. This assumption makes analysis much simpler, but the assumption is not testable. If the assumption is not viewed as reasonable then we have **selection on unobservables** and other very strong assumptions must be made to estimate a treatment effect.

A second important assumption is whether the treatment effect γ_i is assumed to be the same across all individuals or, at least, the same for all individuals with the same characteristics. This assumption of **homogeneous effects** makes analysis much simpler, but it is preferable to relax this assumption and allow for **heterogeneous effects**.

17.5.3 Experiments

The simplest **random experiment** has random assignment to treatment group or control group. The effect of treatment is measured using the **difference in means** in the two groups which from Chapter 14.2 is equivalent to the coefficient of d from OLS regression of outcome y on an intercept and treatment indicator d.

Experiments, especially for outcomes of interest in economics, are often not practical on ethical grounds or on grounds of expense. They may not be generalizable due to restriction to a subset of the population, such as a drug trial restricted to adult males who are unlikely to die from other causes.

Nonetheless experiments are increasingly used in economics. In particular, field experiments are run in less developed countries where the cost of running the experiment is relatively low. Chapter 13.5 provides an example of a leading large social experiment that is also used in exercises 11 and 12 below.

17.5.4 Difference-in-Differences Estimators

Suppose we have data on two groups over two periods of time. Both groups are untreated in the first period, while in the second period only one of the groups is treated. For example, one set of villages receive treatment in the second period while another set of villages do not. The complication is that the individuals in the two groups are not directly comparable, so treatment assignment is not truly random. For example, the treatment was given to a poorer group of villages.

A **difference-in-differences** estimate uses change over time for the untreated group to control for nontreatment changes over time. The treatment effect equals $\Delta \bar{y}$ for those treated less $\Delta \bar{y}$ for those not treated, where $\Delta \bar{y}$ is the change over time in the average outcome.

This method is an example of exploiting a **natural experiment**. It provides a treatment effect estimate that can be given a causal interpretation, under the key "**parallel trends**" assumption that the treated and untreated groups would have the same trend over time in the absence of treatment.

Given individual-level data, the differences-in-differences estimate can be obtained by an appropriate OLS regression. Chapter 13.6 provides further details and a substantive application.

17.5.5 Regression Adjustment Estimators

For observational data, individuals self select into treatment. A natural way to control for this self selection is to add regressors that potentially control for this self selection.

A simple approach estimates the average treatment effect to be the OLS coefficient of d_i in the model

$$y_i = \beta_1 + \gamma d_i + \beta_2 x_{2i} + \cdots + \beta_k x_{ki} + u_i.$$

A limitation of this model is that it assumes homogeneous effects, as the treatment effect is restricted to be the same for all individuals (so $\gamma_i = \gamma$).

The richer **regression adjustment model** estimates separate models for the subset of individuals that received each level of treatment, makes predictions from each fitted model for all individuals, and compares the average predictions. For binary treatment, $\widehat{\text{ATE}} = \frac{1}{n}\sum_{i=1}^{n}\widehat{y}_{1i} - \frac{1}{n}\sum_{i=1}^{n}\widehat{y}_{0i}$ where the coefficients used to predict y_{1i} (or y_{0i}) were based on regression only for those with $d_i = 1$ (or $d_i = 0$). This is equivalent to using all the sample to regress y on a model that fully interacts d with the regressors $x_2, ..., x_k$ and obtaining the difference in average predictions for $d_i = 1$ and $d_i = 0$.

The regression adjustment model allows for heterogeneous effects. But it does require the nontestable selection-on-observables assumption that the included regressors fully account for self selection into treatment. In most applications this assumption is not reasonable. For example, if the outcome is earnings and the treatment is obtaining a college degree, then selection into treatment will depend in part on inherent ability that in most datasets is unobserved or poorly observed. This weakness has led to the alternative methods presented below.

17.5.6   Fixed Effects Estimators

For panel data on individuals the **fixed effects** model presented in Chapter 17.2 and applied in Chapter 17.3 specifies

$$y_{it} = \beta_1 + \gamma d_{it} + \beta_2 x_{2it} + \cdots + \beta_k x_{kit} + \alpha_i + \varepsilon_{it},$$

where the error term has been decomposed into a "fixed effect" α_i and an idiosyncratic error ε_{it}. The average treatment effect estimate is the fixed effects estimate of the coefficient of the treatment d_{it}.

Fixed effects estimation of this model allows for individual selection into treatment, under the assumption that the treatment variable d_{it} is correlated only with the individual-specific component of the error α_i (which does not change over time). Any remaining error time-varying error ε_{it} needs to be uncorrelated with treatment. This is an untestable assumption that needs justification on a case-by-case basis. In the earnings-schooling example, unobserved ability needs to be time invariant.

The fixed effects estimator can also be applied to cross-section data with individuals grouped into identified clusters, such as villages, and different levels of treatment d chosen by each cluster; see Chapter 17.1. Then the key assumption is that after controlling for the other regressors, the selected treatment level d_{it} is correlated only with a cluster-specific component α_i of the error and is not correlated with an error term ε_{ig} that varies across individuals in the cluster.

17.5.7   Regression Discontinuity Design

Regression discontinuity design (RDD) is a setting where a threshold variable determines treatment status. For example, suppose admission into treatment is based on a score denoted s, with scores above 100, say, leading to treatment ($d = 1$). Then a simple RDD estimate compares the average value of y for individuals on either side of the threshold.

In most RDD settings the outcome variable varies with s at points other than just the threshold. For example there may be a linear relationship. Suppose that without treatment $y = \beta_1 + \beta_2 s + u$. Then a simple RDD estimate of the treatment effect of treatment is obtained as the coefficient of d from OLS estimation of the model

$$y_i = \beta_1 + \gamma d_i + \beta_2 s_i + u_i.$$

In practice more flexible models are used, such as different linear or quadratic trends on either side of the threshold, and estimates are focused on observations in the neighborhood of the threshold. Even more generally nonparametric methods are used either side of the threshold.

An application of the RDD model is given in Chapter 13.7.

17.5.8 Instrumental Variables and Local Average Treatment Effects

Instrumental variables estimation was presented in Chapter 17.4. One feature of the model in that section was that the treatment effects were assumed to be the same for all individuals, since the endogenous regressor appeared with a constant coefficient. One consequence is that for any choice of valid instrument we should obtain the same estimated effect, aside from estimator imprecision. Yet in practice different instruments can lead to quite different IV estimates. A second consequence is that IV estimates can differ in surprising ways from OLS estimates, as in the returns to schooling example of Chapter 17.4.3.

These puzzles can be explained by allowing for treatment effects to be heterogeneous, differing across individuals. In the returns to schooling example, the instrument college proximity is most likely to affect those who are financially constrained. An alternative instrument, the minimum age at which one can leave school is most likely to affect those who desire little schooling. The returns to schooling can be expected to be different for these different groups.

In general the effect of treatment on the outcome Y of treatment D is $\Delta Y/\Delta D$. Given instrument Z this effect can be decomposed as $(\Delta Y/\Delta Z)/(\Delta D/\Delta Z)$. Specialize to a binary instrument Z so, for example, $\mathrm{E}[\Delta Y/\Delta Z] = E[Y|Z=1] - E[Y|Z=1]$. Then the treatment effect is

$$\text{ATE} = \frac{\mathrm{E}[Y|Z=1] - \mathrm{E}[Y|Z=0]}{\mathrm{E}[D|Z=1] - \mathrm{E}[D|Z=0]}.$$

This can be shown to equal $\mathrm{Cov}[Z,Y]/\mathrm{Cov}[Z,D]$ so can be estimated by IV regression of y on d with instrument z.

To interpret the estimate, specialize to a binary treatment D and suppose for simplicity that the higher value of Z makes selection into treatment ($D=1$) more likely. Distinguish between four types of people: (1) **Always-takers** chose treatment ($D=1$) regardless of the value of Z; (2) **Never-takers** never chose treatment ($D=0$) regardless of the value of Z; (3) **Compliers** are induced into treatment so $D=1$ when $Z=1$ and $D=0$ when $Z=0$; and (4) **Defiers** are induced away from treatment so $D=0$ when $Z=1$ and $D=1$ when $Z=0$. Then under the crucial and nontestable assumption that there are no defiers, also called the monotonicity assumption, it can be shown that

$$\text{ATE} = \mathrm{E}[Y|Z=1, \text{Complier}] - \mathrm{E}[Y|Z=0, \text{Complier}].$$

So if the usual assumptions for instrumental variables are made, and the additional assumption of no defiers is made, the IV estimator gives the average treatment effect for compliers, a subgroup of the population. This is called a **local average treatment effect** (**LATE**) as it applies to a subgroup that varies with the instrument.

Analysis becomes more complicated in applications such as that in Chapter 17.4.3 where exogenous regressors are also present and the treatment (years of schooling) takes more than two values.

Then loosely the IV or 2SLS estimator is viewed as a weighted average of treatment effects across compliers, and again different instruments lead to different sets of compliers and hence different IV estimates.

17.5.9 Inverse Probability Weighting

Restrict analysis to a binary treatment, with $d_i = 1$ if treated and $d_i = 0$ if not treated. Define the **propensity score** to be the predicted probability of treatment, specifically $\widehat{p}_i = \widehat{\Pr}[d_i = 1 | x_{2i}, ..., x_{ki}]$. Then the inverse probability weighting computes the weighted average of the outcome with weights determined by the propensity score.

Specifically, we observe $d_i y_i$ if the individual is treated and $(1 - d_i)y_i$. The average treatment effect is then the weighted average $\frac{1}{N} \sum_{i=1}^{n} w_i \{d_i y_i - (1 - d_i)y_i\}$ where the weights $w_i = 1/\widehat{p}_i$ if treated and $w_i = 1/(1 - \widehat{p}_i)$ if untreated.

The essential assumption for interpreting the treatment effect is that, after conditioning on variables $x_2, ..., x_k$, selection into treatment is random. In practice a rich and flexible logit or probit model (see Chapter 17.6.1) for d_i is often used.

17.5.10 Matching

Again restrict analysis to a binary treatment d and suppose that after conditioning on variables $x_2, ..., x_k$ selection into treatment is random. The regression adjustment approach relies on the additional assumption of a correctly specified regression model, typically a linear model. Matching provides an alternative and potential richer model.

Assume an ideal world where for both treated and untreated groups we had many observations for each combination of values taken by $x_2, ..., x_k$. Then for each specific combination of values of $x_2, ..., x_k$ we could obtain the difference in the average outcome across treated and untreated groups, and then in turn aggregate over all combinations of $x_2, ..., x_k$ values. Such **matching** is not practical, however, unless there are very few combinations of values taken by $x_2, ..., x_k$.

Nearest neighbor matching is a variation where the outcome for each treated observation is compared to the average outcome of the K observations whose values of $x_2, ..., x_k$ are closest to those for the treated observation. Implementation requires specifying a measure of closeness and specifying a value for K such as $K = 10$.

Propensity score matching instead compares outcomes with similar probability of treatment. This uses the propensity score, the predicted probability of treatment obtain from logit or probit regression of the binary treatment variable d on a flexible function of $x_2, ..., x_k$.

The essential assumption for matching is that any differences between an observation and its matches is purely random and is unrelated to the decision to select into treatment.

17.6 Nonlinear Regression Models

In Chapter 14 we considered models that introduced nonlinearity through quadratic and logarithmic transformations. These models remained linear in the parameters $\beta_1, ..., \beta_k$, however, so that OLS estimation was still possible.

Now we present the most commonly-used nonlinear models. For these models there is no explicit solution for the estimates of $\beta_1, ..., \beta_k$. Instead the estimates are obtained by iterative methods, with sequential updating of initial estimates until convergence. Statistical packages automatically perform such computation, making estimation of standard nonlinear models as easy as OLS. Interpretation of the resulting estimates is more difficult than for a linear model, however, as the marginal effect on y of a change in regressor x_k is no longer simply β_k.

17.6.1 Logit and Probit Models for Binary Outcomes

The models presented so far in this text are best used when the dependent variable y is numerical and takes a continuous range of values. In empirical economic research the most common departure from this situation arises when y is categorical and takes only two possible values. Examples are whether a person is employed or not employed, or whether a worker commutes by car or commutes by other means.

For convenience binary outcome data are typically coded as y taking values of 1 or 0. However, the data are not intrinsically numerical. Instead they are categorical, see Chapter 1, and the obvious approach is to model the probability that y equals one (or zero), rather than model the mean of y.

In a regression context we model how this probability varies with regressors. For example, the probability of being employed may vary with age and education. The regression model should ensure that outcome probabilities are bounded between zero and one and sum to one. For this reason OLS is not the best estimation method. Instead the two commonly-used models are the logit model and the probit model.

The **logit model** specifies that

$$\begin{aligned} \Pr[y = 1 | x_2, ..., x_k] &= \frac{\exp(\beta_1 + \beta_2 x_2 + \cdots + \beta_k x_k)}{1 + \exp(\beta_1 + \beta_2 x_2 + \cdots + \beta_k x_k)} \\ \Pr[y = 0 | x_2, ..., x_k] &= 1 - \Pr[y = 1 | x_2, ..., x_k]. \end{aligned}$$

Equivalently $\Pr[y = 1 | x_2, ..., x_k] = \Lambda(\beta_1 + \beta_2 x_2 + \cdots + \beta_k x_k)$ where $\Lambda(\cdot)$ is the cumulative distribution function of the logistic distribution with $\Lambda(z) = e^z / (1 + e^z)$.

The **probit model** specifies that

$$\begin{aligned} \Pr[y = 1 | x_2, ..., x_k] &= \Phi(\beta_1 + \beta_2 x_2 + \cdots + \beta_k x_k) \\ \Pr[y = 0 | x_2, ..., x_k] &= 1 - \Pr[y = 1 | x_2, ..., x_k], \end{aligned}$$

where $\Phi(\cdot)$ is the cumulative distribution function of the standard normal distribution.

Estimation is by a method called **maximum likelihood** (see Chapter 17.6.4 and Appendix C.5), rather than by least squares regression. Specifically, the estimates of $\beta_1, \beta_2, ..., \beta_k$ maximize $\sum_{i=1}^{n} \{y_i \ln p_i + (1 - y_i)(1 - p_i)\}$ where, for example, $p_i = \Lambda(\beta_1 + \beta_2 x_{2i} + \cdots + \beta_k x_{ki})$ for the logit model.

The first panel of Figure 17.3 presents an example of logit regression of a binary outcome on a single regressor x using generated data. Each dot in the scatter plot is an observation on (y, x). Clearly the probability that $y = 1$ increases as x increases. The curve is the predicted probability that $y = 1$ given x, obtained from logit regression of y on x that is detailed next.

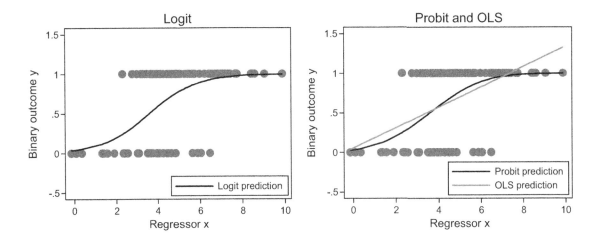

Figure 17.3: Nonlinear models: Predictions from logit, probit and OLS regression.

As expected the predicted probability that $y = 1$ increases as x increases, and as desired the predicted probabilities lie within zero and one. The second panel of Figure 17.3 presents predicted probabilities for the probit model that are very similar to those for the logit model. It also presents predicted probabilities from OLS regression that have the limitation of sometimes being negative or exceeding one.

Interest lies in $\widehat{p}$, the predicted probability that $y = 1$ given the regressors (replace $\beta_1, ..., \beta_k$ in the formula with $b_1, ..., b_k$), and how this changes as the regressors change.

The marginal effects (see Chapter 15.2) are no longer simply the coefficients. For the logit model it can be shown, using calculus methods, that for the jth regressor

$$\mathrm{ME}_j = \frac{\Delta \widehat{p}}{\Delta x_j} = \widehat{p}(1 - \widehat{p})b_j,$$

where $\widehat{p}$ is the predicted probability. Since $0 < \widehat{p} < 1$ it follows that $0 < \widehat{p}(1 - \widehat{p}) < 0.25$, so $|\mathrm{ME}_j| \leq 0.25 \times |b_j|$ and the sign of the coefficient gives the sign of the marginal effect. An approximation is that the average marginal effect equals $\bar{y}(1 - \bar{y})b_j$.

For the probit model it can be shown, using calculus methods, that

$$\mathrm{ME}_j = \phi(\widehat{p})b_j,$$

where $\phi(\cdot)$ is the standard normal density function with $\phi(z) = \frac{1}{\sqrt{2\pi}}e^{-z^2/2}$. Since $\phi(\cdot) \geq 0$ takes a minimum value of $1/\sqrt{2\pi} \simeq 0.40$, it follows that $|\mathrm{ME}_j| \leq 0.4 \times |b_j|$ and the sign of the coefficient gives the sign of the marginal effect. And probit coefficients are approximately $0.4/0.25 = 1.6$ times logit coefficients. An approximation is that the average marginal effect equals $1.6 \times \bar{y}(1 - \bar{y})b_j$.

For observations that are independent there is usually little difference between default and heteroskedastic-robust standard errors.

An alternative method is to perform OLS regression. When y is a binary outcome this is called the **linear probability model** as the probability that $y = 1$ is a linear function whereas the logit and probit models transform this linear function. If OLS is used then inference must be based on robust standard errors.

The OLS slope coefficients tend to be similar to the average marginal effects for the probit and logit models, and the t statistics for statistical significance of regressors are also similar. If interest lies in predictions and marginal effects at the individual level, however, a logit or probit should be used.

While logit and probit estimators were originally designed for binary data they can also be applied to proportions data, where the dependent variable takes continuous values between zero and one. In that case one needs to always use robust standard errors.

17.6.2 Logit Regression Example: High Earnings

As an example consider a logit model for whether or not someone has high earnings. We use dataset EARNINGS_COMPLETE already used in Chapters 14-16. The indicator variable *dhighearn* equals one if annual earnings exceed \$60,000 and equals zero otherwise; 27% of the sample have high earnings.

Logit regression of *dighearn* on *Age* and *Education* yields maximum likelihood estimates

$$\widehat{\Pr}[y = 1] = \Lambda \left(\underset{(-11.66)}{-8.065} + \underset{(4.84)}{0.0385 Age} + \underset{(10.22)}{0.3743 Education} \right), \quad n = 872,$$

where $\Lambda(z) = e^z/(1 + e^z)$ is the logistic function and heteroskedastic-robust t statistics are given in parentheses. Since the slope coefficients are positive, the probability of high earnings increases with age and with education, and the coefficients are highly statistically significant.

The marginal effect of a year of aging is positive, since $b_{Age} > 0$. The average marginal effect of a year of aging is an increase of approximately 0.0076 in the probability of having high earnings, using $\bar{y}(1 - \bar{y})b_j = 0.27 \times 0.73 \times 0.0385$. Using specialized software the average marginal effect is actually 0.0064 for a year of aging and is 0.0618 for an extra year of education. The effect of increased education is especially high. In this example, the average marginal effects are approximately one-sixth of the estimated coefficients.

Probit estimation using the same data yields slope coefficients of 0.0228 and 0.2217, leading to average marginal effects of 0.0064 and 0.0624. OLS estimation yields slope coefficients of 0.0064 and 0.0540. While the coefficients are scaled differently across logit, probit and OLS, the resulting average marginal effects are similar.

17.6.3 Quasi-Poisson Regression for Counts and Nonnegative Outcomes

The Poisson regression model specifies that the conditional mean is exponential, so that

$$E[y|x_2, ..., x_k] = \exp(\beta_1 + \beta_2 x_2 + \cdots + \beta_k x_k).$$

This model is applicable to nonnegative data as the conditional mean is guaranteed to be positive, since $\exp(x) > 0$ for all x.

Estimation is by a method called **quasi-maximum likelihood**, rather than by least squares regression. Specifically, the estimates of β_1, β_2,...,β_k maximize $\sum_{i=1}^{n} \{y_i \ln \mu_i - \mu_i\}$ where $\mu_i = \exp(\beta_1 + \beta_2 x_{2i} + \cdots + \beta_k x_{ki})$. Quasi-Poisson regression is also called **exponential regression**.

The marginal effects (see Chapter 15.2) are no longer simply the coefficients. For the exponential conditional mean it can be shown, using calculus methods, that for the jth regressor

$$\text{ME}_j = \frac{\Delta \widehat{y}}{\Delta x_j} = \widehat{y} b_j,$$

where $\widehat{y}$ is the predicted value of y. It can also be shown that the average marginal effect using Quasi-Poisson regression estimates equals $\bar{y} b_j$.

Some calculus shows that the coefficients can be directly interpreted as semi-elasticities. So if $b_j = 0.2$, for example, then a one unit change in x_j is associated with a 0.2 proportionate increase in $\widehat{y}$ or, equivalently, a 20% increase in $\widehat{y}$. Thus the model is suitable for models where regressors are expected to have a multiplicative effect on the outcome, rather than the additive effect of the linear regression model. Furthermore, the coefficient of x in Poisson regression of y on $\ln x$ is an elasticity.

The term Poisson regression is used as a simple model for count data is the Poisson. The Poisson restricts the conditional variance of y to equal the conditional mean of y. For most economics data, the conditional variance exceeds the conditional mean. Then the Poisson estimator remains consistent, provided the conditional mean is correctly specified, but default standard errors are too small and it is essential to base inference on robust standard errors.

Poisson regression was originally developed for count data, such as the number of doctor consultations. The model can more generally be applied to nonnegative data. In particular, the model can be especially useful for modelling right-skewed continuous data such as expenditure data that include zero values. In that case a log-linear model, which also gives semi-elasticities, cannot handle zero values.

17.6.4   Other Commonly-used Nonlinear Regression Models

The logit, probit and Poisson models are not the only commonly-used nonlinear regression models that are departures from the linear regression model. Different regression models are used for different types of dependent variable. Table 17.5 provides a summary of different data types commonly encountered in cross-section studies and the simplest regression models or estimators that are used for such data.

An example of multinomial data with three unordered categories is commuting to work by car, by bus or by train. An example of multinomial data with three ordered categories is health status assessed to be poor, good or excellent. An example of count data is the number of visits to a doctor in the past three months. An example of duration data is the length of time unemployed. An example of nonnegative data with bunching at zero is annual earnings for a sample that includes those who did not work at all during the year. An example of an incompletely observed dependent variable is the number of visits to a doctor where the sample is taken at a medical establishment so that people with no visits are not included in the sample.

Table 17.5: Nonlinear models: Leading examples for different data types.

Data Type for Dependent variable y	Model and/or Estimator
Continuous in interval $(-\infty, \infty)$	Ordinary least squares, nonlinear least squares
Binary (two categories)	Logit, probit
Multinomial (m unordered categories)	Multinomial logit
Multinomial (m ordered categories)	Ordered logit, ordered probit
Count taking values 0, 1, 2, ...	Poisson, negative binomial
Duration taking values in $(0, \infty)$	Cox proportional hazards, Weibull
Nonnegative continuous in interval $[0, \infty)$	Nonlinear least squares, Poisson
Nonnegative with bunching at zero	Tobit, two-part, selection
y is incompletely observed	Tobit, censored, truncation, selection

The **nonlinear least squares estimator** is a natural extension of OLS to nonlinear models. An example of a nonlinear model is one with exponential conditional mean, so that $y = \exp(\beta_1 + \beta_2 x_2 + \cdots + \beta_k x_k) + u$. Then the nonlinear least squares estimates $b_1, ..., b_k$ minimize the sum of squared residuals $\sum_{i=1}^{n} \{y_i - \exp(b_1 + b_2 x_2 + \cdots + b_k x_k)\}^2$. Unlike for linear regression there is no subsequent exact formula for $b_1, ..., b_k$. Instead the estimates are obtained by a numerical iterative method.

The other estimators are obtained using the quite different method of **maximum likelihood method**. This method specifies a particular model for the conditional probability of y_i given regressors $x_{2i}, ..., x_{ki}$, whereas least squares only specifies a model for the conditional mean of y_i given $x_{2i}, ..., x_{ki}$. An example of such conditional probabilities has already been given for the logit and probit models. The **likelihood function** is then the joint conditional probability of observing $y_1, ..., y_n$ given the regressors, and the estimates of model parameters are those values that maximize the likelihood function. So the parameter estimates are those values that maximize the probability that the dependent variables take the specific values $y_1, ..., y_n$ observed in the sample. As for nonlinear least squares, estimates are obtained by a numerical method. See Appendix C.5 for more detail.

The regression output from such models is similar to that for OLS regression, and includes a table of estimated coefficients, standard errors, t statistics and p-values (for test of statistical significance), and a 95% confidence interval, as well as a test of joint statistical significance of all regressors. Since these models are intrinsically nonlinear, like the logit and probit models, the marginal effects are no longer simply the estimated coefficients.

For grouped data (clustered or panel) one should base inference on cluster-robust standard errors. Random effects estimators are also generally available, but consistency then relies on the strong assumption that the random effects are normally distributed. Unlike for the linear model, fixed effects estimators are generally unavailable if there are few observations in each cluster or panel; the Poisson is a notable exception.

17.6.5   Nonlinear Models Estimation using Different Statistical Packages

The commonly-used nonlinear regression models - logit, probit and Poisson - are included in statistical packages and usually have similar format to the command for OLS regression. In Stata and in Gretl use commands `logit`, `probit` and `poisson`. In Eviews use commands `logit`, `probit` and `count`. In R these models are special cases within the `glm` package; for logit use `family=binomial`, for probit use `family=binomial(link="probit")` and for Poisson with heteroskedastic-robust standard errors use `family=quasipoisson`.

In these nonlinear models the estimated coefficients do not directly measure marginal effects. Marginal effects (and associated standard errors) following estimation can be computed in Stata using the `margins, dydx(*)` command, and in R using the `margins` package.

17.7   Time-Series Data

A **time series** is a collection of observations taken at different points in time that are assumed here to be equidistant in time. The observations are ordered by time, with y_t denoting the time series variable of interest. Then y_{t-1} denotes y in the preceding period and y_{t-j} denotes y **lagged** j periods. For example, for monthly data if y_t is the interest rate in March 2002 then y_{t-2} is the interest rate in January 2002. The first observed value of y is y_1 and the sample of size T is $y_1, y_2, ..., y_T$. At times **first differenced** data Δy_t, where $\Delta y_t = y_t - y_{t-1}$, are used. First differencing leads to loss of the first observation and the sample is $\Delta y_2, \Delta y_3, ..., \Delta y_T$.

Most time series are dependent, with current values depending on past values, so that observations are no longer independent. An important assumption in the first parts of this section is that this dependence eventually dies out; otherwise OLS estimates can be severely biased and inconsistent leading to spurious findings of association between variables where none exists.

If the dependence does eventually die out then inference still needs to control for the dependence over time. There are two broad classes of time series models. If the regression model does not include past values of the dependent variable as regressors, then estimation by OLS is fine (though is not fully efficient) and the only adjustment is to use HAC standard errors that correct for serial correlation in the model errors. If instead the regression model includes as regressors past values of y, then for OLS to be consistent sufficient lags of the dependent variable need to be included to ensure that the model errors are independent over time.

17.7.1   HAC Robust Standard Errors

Consider OLS regression in the model

$$y_t = \beta_1 + \beta_2 x_{2t} + \cdots + \beta_k x_{kt} + u_t, \quad t = 1, ..., T.$$

when the errors are serially correlated, so that u_t is correlated with past u_t and assumption 4 no longer holds.

It is standard to base inference on heteroskedastic and autocorrelation robust (HAC) standard errors; see Chapter 12.1.5 and Appendix C.2 for the formula and for discussion including the underlying assumptions. These assumptions rule out use of HAC standard errors if the regressors include lagged dependent variables, and require that errors are autocorrelated only up to m periods apart. Use of these robust standard errors is not as straightforward as for heteroskedastic-robust standard errors, however, as one needs to specify or estimate the number m of lagged periods after which errors are no longer correlated.

17.7.2 Stationary Processes and Data Transformation

Broadly speaking the application of standard statistical inference methods for regression analysis of time series data requires that the mean and variance of the error term are not changing over time.

A leading example with this property is a **covariance stationary process**. This greatly simplifies analysis by restricting the mean and (finite) variance of y_t to be the same regardless of the point in time t considered, and restricts the covariance between y_t and y_s to depend only on the time separation $|t - s|$. Briefly, $E[y_t]$, $Var[y_t]$ and $Cov[y_t, y_{t-s}]$ do not vary with the time period t, where covariance is defined in Appendix B.3. The simplest example of a stationary process is a **white noise process**, often denoted ε_t, which has mean zero, constant variance and is uncorrelated across time.

Time series data are often transformed to a stationary process before any analysis. In particular, many macroeconomic variables such as real GDP are trending upward over time. The series are nonstationary as the mean and variance are increasing over time. If such growth is exponential then the first step is to take the **natural logarithm** as then the growth is linear in natural logarithms; see Chapter 9.5.3.

Even after such transformation the data often have a time trend in the mean. A **linear time trend model** lets $y_t = \beta_1 + \beta_2 t + u_t$ where the error u_t is assumed to be stationary. Then on average y_t increases by β_2 each period, so the data are nonstationary. There are several ways to handle this nonstationarity. Regression analysis may be based on a model for y_t provided a linear trend is included in the model. Analysis may be based on **detrended data**. Thus regress y on an intercept and a time trend and analyze the residual $y_t - \widehat{\beta}_1 - \widehat{\beta}_2 t$. Analysis may be based on **first-differenced data** Δy_t, as the time trend model implies $\Delta y_t = \beta_2 + \Delta u_t$ which has eliminated the time trend.

In some applications the error term u_t may not be stationary. This complication is deferred to later in Chapter 17.7.9–17.7.11.

17.7.3 Sample Autocorrelations

Persistence in a stationary time series is gauged using sample autocorrelations that measure the correlation between the current value and lagged values.

The **population autocorrelation at lag j** is

$$\rho_j = \text{Cor}[y_t, y_{t-j}] = \frac{\text{Cov}[y_t, y_{t-j}]}{\text{Var}[y_t]}.$$

The **sample autocorrelation at lag** j is an estimate of ρ_j. This estimate can be computed in several ways, including

$$\widehat{\rho}_j = \frac{\frac{1}{T-j}\sum_{t=j+1}^{T}(y_t - \overline{y})(y_{t-j} - \overline{y})}{\frac{1}{T}\sum_{t=j+1}^{T}(y_t - \overline{y})^2}, \quad -1 \leq \widehat{\rho}_j \leq 1.$$

where $\overline{y} = \frac{1}{T-j}\sum_{t=j+1}^{T} y_t$. The sum in the numerator is only over $(T-j)$ terms as y_{t-j} can only be computed from time $t = j+1$ on (since $y_{t-j} = y_1$ when $t = j+1$).

If y_t are actually independent with constant variance, then it can be shown that the autocorrelation estimate $\widehat{\rho}_j$ has mean 0 and standard deviation equal to $1/\sqrt{T}$, while for an autocorrelated process the standard error is larger. So a 95% confidence interval for the population autocorrelation coefficient ρ_j is at least $(\widehat{\rho}_j - 1.96\sqrt{T}, \widehat{\rho}_j + 1.96\sqrt{T})$.

Specialized software such as Stata computes sample autocorrelations automatically, along with confidence intervals, for the first m, say, autocorrelations. Some computer packages use a refinement of the formula given above.

17.7.4   Tests for Autocorrelation

Throughout assume that y_t are actually independent, so $\rho_j = 0$ for all $j > 0$. Then in large samples $\widehat{\rho}_j \sim N(0, [1/\sqrt{T}]^2)$, so $\sqrt{T}\widehat{\rho}_j \sim N(0,1)$. A simple test based on the first m autocorrelations is the Box-Pierce statistic $T\sum_{j=1}^{m}\widehat{\rho}_j^2$ which is $\chi^2(p)$ distributed since it equals $(\sqrt{T}\widehat{\rho}_1)^2 + \cdots + (\sqrt{T}\widehat{\rho}_m)^2$ which is the sum of the squares of m independent standard normal variables.

In practice a variation, the **Ljung-Box portmanteau test statistic** $Q = T(T+2)\sum_{j=1}^{m}\frac{1}{T-j}\widehat{\rho}_j^2$, is used as it has better finite sample properties. We reject $H_0 : \rho_1 = 0, ..., \rho_m = 0$ at level 0.05 if $Q > \chi_{.05}^2(m)$.

The same test can be applied to the autocorrelations of OLS residuals, provided the regressors do not include lagged dependent variables. If lagged dependent variables are included then a variation, the **Breusch-Godfrey test** which for brevity is not detailed here, should be used. Specialized time-series software commands provide these tests.

17.7.5   Autoregressive Models

An autoregressive model is one where y is regressed on past values of itself.

The simplest model is an **autoregressive model of order 1 (AR(1)** model) that specifies

$$y_t = \alpha_0 + \alpha_1 y_{t-1} + u_t, \quad |\alpha_1| < 1, \ t = 2, ..., T.$$

The restriction $|\alpha_1| < 1$ is used to ensure that the process is not explosive.

If the error u_t in the AR(1) model is a white noise error then it can be shown that $\rho_j = \text{Cor}[y_t, y_{t-j}] = \alpha_1^j$. So the series y_t is very persistent if $|\alpha_1|$ is close to 1 and is not at all persistent if $|\alpha_1|$ is close to 0.

The more general **autoregressive model of order p (an AR(p)** model) specifies

$$y_t = \beta_1 + \alpha_1 y_{t-1} + \alpha_2 y_{t-2} + \cdots + \alpha_p y_{t-p} + u_t, \ t = p+1, ..., T,$$

where the error term u_t is white noise. To ensure stationarity the α coefficients need to satisfy a restriction, not given here, that generalizes the condition that $|\alpha_1| < 1$ in the AR(1) model.

Consistency of the OLS estimator requires that sufficient lags in y are included to ensure that u_t is serially uncorrelated. Computer packages with a time series component include a test of whether or not the error term u_t is serially correlated.

17.7.6 Finite Distributed Lag Models

A **finite distributed lag model** regresses y_t on current and lagged values of the regressor x_t to the regression. So

$$y_t = \alpha + \beta_0 x_t + \beta_1 x_{t-1} + \cdots + \beta_q x_{t-q} + u_t, \ t = q+1, ..., T.$$

Here the regressors do not include lagged dependent variables, so a serially correlated error is permitted. Inference is then based on HAC standard errors.

For a model with lags in x_t, distinction is made between the **initial impact** (β_0) on y_t of a change in x_t, and the **cumulative effect** $(\beta_0 + \beta_1 + \cdots + \beta_q)$ over all q time periods on y_t of a change in x_t.

17.7.7 Autoregressive Distributed Lag Models

The more general **autoregressive distributed lag model of orders p and q** (an **ADL(p,q)** model) includes lagged values of both y_t and x_t as regressors. Then

$$\begin{aligned} y_t = {} & \alpha_0 + \alpha_1 y_{t-1} + \alpha_2 y_{t-2} + \cdots + \alpha_p y_{t-p} \\ & + \beta_0 x_t + \beta_1 x_{t-1} + \cdots + \beta_q x_{t-q} + u_t, \ t = (\max(p,q)+1), ..., T. \end{aligned}$$

Since lagged dependent variables appear in this model, the error u_t needs to be serially uncorrelated to ensure that the OLS estimator is consistent. Computation of the effect on y_t of a change in x_t is now more complicated due to the presence of lagged terms in y_t. An example using impulse response functions is given in Chapter 17.8.11.

17.7.8 Autoregressive Error Models

Another way to allow for serial correlation is to specify an autoregressive process for the error u_t rather than for y_t.

Suppose $y_t = \beta_1 + \beta_2 x_t + u_t$ where $u_t = \rho u_{t-1} + \varepsilon_t$, $|\rho| < 1$ and ε_t is a white noise error. We could estimate this model by OLS and base inference on HAC robust standard errors.

A more efficient estimator is the following. Lagging the model by one period and multiplying by ρ we have $\rho y_{t-1} = \rho \beta_1 + \rho \beta_2 x_{t-1} + \rho u_{t-1}$. Subtracting from the original equation, and noting that $u_t - \rho u_{t-1} = \varepsilon_t$, we have $(y_t - \rho y_{t-1}) = \beta_1 (1 - \rho) + \beta_2 (x_t - \rho x_{t-1}) + \varepsilon_t$. The errors ε_t in this transformed model are homoskedastic and independent, so OLS is the most efficient estimator in this model. To operationalize this we need a consistent estimator of ρ.

The **Cochrane-Orcutt estimator** proceeds as follows. First, perform OLS regression of y on an intercept and x and obtain the OLS residual e_t. Second, estimate ρ by $\hat{\rho} = \Sigma_t e_t e_{t-1} / \Sigma_t e_{t-1}^2$.

Third estimate by OLS regression the transformed model $(y_t - \widehat{\rho}y_{t-1}) = \beta_1(1 - \widehat{\rho}) + \beta_2(x_t - \widehat{\rho}x_{t-1})$. Default standard errors can be used in this equation, assuming the AR(1) model is the correct model for the error process, even though $\widehat{\rho}$ is estimated. There are several variations of this method leading to estimates that differ by a small amount in finite samples.

While this method leads to efficiency gains it requires the assumption that the model error is indeed AR(1); also the efficiency gains need not be great. It is common practice to just use OLS with HAC standard errors (provided lagged dependent variables are not included as regressors).

17.7.9   Nonstationary Time Series and Unit Root Processes

To date we have assumed a stationary time series. When instead the series is **nonstationary** the usual properties of regression estimators no longer hold. As a result the methods of the previous chapters may be the wrong methods to use! We present a very brief discussion of this advanced topic.

A simple example of a nonstationary process is $y_t = 1.02 \times y_{t-1}$, where for simplicity there is no error. Then $y_t = 1.02 \times y_{t-1} = 1.02 \times (1.02 \times y_{t-2}) = \cdots = 1.02^t y_0$. This is explosive in levels (though not in logs, since $\ln y_t = \ln(1.02) + \ln y_{t-1}$).

A **random walk process** is the leading example of a nonstationary process. Then

$$y_t = y_{t-1} + \varepsilon_t, \quad t = 1, ..., T$$

where ε_t is a white noise process with zero mean and variance σ_ε^2. This is an obvious model for highly persistent data – this period's observation is simply last period's observation plus some purely random noise. By recursive substitution $y_t = y_{t-1} + \varepsilon_t = [y_{t-2} + \varepsilon_{t-1}] + \varepsilon_t = \cdots = y_0 + \sum_{j=0}^{t-1} \varepsilon_{t-j}$.

The nonstationarity arises because $\mathrm{Var}[y_t] = \mathrm{Var}\left[\sum_{j=0}^{t-1} \varepsilon_{t-j}\right] = \sum_{j=0}^{t-1} \mathrm{Var}[\varepsilon_{t-j}] = t\sigma_\varepsilon^2$, so the variance of y_t increases over time. Due to this complication standard inference methods no longer apply to models for y_t, but they still apply to the difference Δy_t since $\Delta y_t = \varepsilon_t$ is white noise.

More generally, a **random walk with drift** allows an increment of δ each period so that

$$y_t = \delta + y_{t-1} + \varepsilon_t, \quad t = 1, ..., T.$$

By recursive substitution $y_t = y_0 + \delta t + \sum_{j=0}^{t-1} \varepsilon_{t-j}$, so again y_t is nonstationary as $\mathrm{Var}[y_t] = t\sigma_\varepsilon^2$ which increases with t. A random walk with drift is often called a **stochastic trend model**, as the nonstationarity is now around the trend $y_0 + \delta t$. By contrast, the linear time trend model $y_t = \beta_1 + \beta_2 t + u_t$ with a stationary error is called a **deterministic trend model**.

A random walk model, with or without drift, is a special case of a **unit root process**. The term unit root is used as the random walk is the special case of the AR(1) model $y_t = \alpha_0 + \alpha_1 y_{t-1} + \varepsilon_t$ with $\alpha_1 = 1$ (**unity**).

The distinction between unit root and non-unit root processes is important for policy analysis, as the explosiveness of a random walk model means that a temporary shock can have a permanent effect. For example, if GDP follows a random walk (with or without drift), then a temporary one-period negative shock to GDP will permanently lower GDP, not just lower it in the next few periods.

The distinction is also important for inference. For example, if y_t is a unit root process then the slope coefficient from OLS regression of y_t on y_{t-1} (equivalent to the first-order autocorrelation of y_t) is biased and inconsistent and inference cannot be based on the usual standard normal or t distribution.

17.7.10 Spurious Regression

Suppose y_t and x_t are both unit root processes but are unrelated. If we nonetheless regress y_t on x_t, then conventional statistical inference methods are exceptionally likely to falsely discover a relationship between the two series.

In a simulation exercise we recursively generated samples of size 100 of $y_t = y_{t-1} + u_t$ and $x_t = x_{t-1} + v_t$, where u_t and v_t are independent draws from the standard normal distribution, and regressed y_t on an intercept and x_t to obtain fitted model $\widehat{y}_t = a + bx_t$. Repeating this exercise 1,000 times, the average R^2 was 0.235 (an average correlation between y and x of $\sqrt{0.235} = 0.48$), suggesting a relationship. And a standard test of statistical significance based on $t_b = b/se(b)$, where $se(b)$ is the default standard error, led to a finding of statistical significance at 5% in 778 samples, rather than 50 samples (5% of 1,000). This over-rejection cannot be solved by instead using HAC-robust standard errors. In fact in this setup it can be shown that rather than t_b having a normal distribution in large samples, the rescaled statistic $t_b/\sqrt{T}$ has a nonstandard distribution.

This is an example of a **spurious regression**, one that detects a relationship between series when in fact there is no relationship. A commonly-used example of a spurious regression is a time series regression of GDP of a country such as the U.S. on the cumulative rainfall in the country's capital. Rainfall is not driving GDP, but a strong statistically significant relationship will be found as both series are trending upwards over time. For stationary processes this could be controlled for by including a linear time trend in the model, but if the data are nonstationary including a time trend is still not enough.

When unit roots are present, one way to detect whether the relationship is spurious is to estimate by OLS the changes model $\Delta y_t = \beta_1 + \beta_2 \Delta x_t + u_t$, since Δy_t and Δx_t are stationary. A second method is to add first order lags of y_t and x_t as regressors in the levels model and estimate by OLS $y_t = \beta_1 + \beta_2 x_t + \beta_3 y_{t-1} + \beta_4 x_{t-1} + u_t$. In both cases if $H_0 : \beta_2 = 0$ is rejected than there is a relationship between y_t and x_t.

17.7.11 Regression with Nonstationary Data

Unit root processes that are actually related to each other are called **cointegrated series**. An example of cointegrated series is the price of a specific good in two different markets, where the price in each market follows a random walk. The prices should be equal in the two markets by the law of one price, but this equivalence will not be instantaneous due to practical complications such as transportation costs. Over time, however, they should be roughly the same.

How do we proceed in this case? The simplest thing to do is to regress Δy_t on Δx_t, since the first differences are stationary.

Better methods exist, but their application is an advanced topic typically taught at the graduate level. The econometricians Clive Granger and Robert Engle were awarded the Nobel Prize in

Economics for developing the relevant theory.

17.7.12   Forecasting

Forecasting is the prediction of future values of y_t on the basis of past data and a dynamic model linking variables observed over time. The model is estimated using the sample, and the forecasts are out-of-sample predictions.

If the purpose of regression is forecasting, rather than inference, then the regression model may be selected on the basis of its forecast performance. A commonly-used method is to choose lag length to minimize the Bayesian information criterion (BIC), defined in Chapter 10.6.

Forecasting from a dynamic model is not straightforward. Consider forecasting from an estimated AR(2) model, with $\widehat{y}_t = b_0 + b_1 y_{t-1} + b_2 y_{t-2}$. We wish to forecast in periods $T+1$, $T+2$, ... given model estimates using data available up to time T. These forecasts are denoted $\widehat{y}_{T+1|T}$, $\widehat{y}_{T+2|T}$, ... The forecast for period $T+1$ is a one-step ahead forecast that is straightforward as all necessary data are available. We obtain $\widehat{y}_{T+1|T} = b_0 + b_1 y_T + b_2 y_{T-1}$. The two-step ahead forecast for $T+2$ is more problematic, as data for y_{T+1} is not available. Instead we estimate y_{T+1} by the one-step ahead forecast $\widehat{y}_{T+1|T}$. We obtain $\widehat{y}_{T+2|T} = b_0 + b_1 \widehat{y}_{T+1|T} + b_2 y_T$. More generally, for an h-step ahead forecast from an AR(p) model, actual data are used for time period T and earlier, while forecast values are used after time period T. The forecast is called a **recursive forecast**.

The important distinction between predicting the conditional mean and predicting an actual value is presented in Chapter 12.2. In both cases the same predicted value is used, but the confidence intervals are wider for predicting the actual value as model errors need to be accounted for. For time series forecasting the goal is to predict the actual value. Furthermore if the forecast is for a nonstationary process the uncertainty in the forecast will blow up over time.

If the model is estimated in changes, then the forecast in changes can be converted to forecasts of levels. For example if $y_T = 3.2$ and the model yields forecast $\widehat{\Delta y}_{T+1|T} = 0.4$, then $\widehat{y}_{T+1|T} = y_T + \widehat{\Delta y}_{T+1|T} = 3.2 + 0.4 = 3.6$.

Forecasting from models with variables x_t other than lags of y_t is more problematic, as this requires forecasts of x_t. In some examples we may be willing to replace x_{T+1} by a forecast $\widehat{x}_{T+1}$ obtained as an educated estimate or from an econometric model. More often in this case a systems model is used that models both y_t and x_t.

Remark 141 *Forecasts of future values from a dynamic time series model are recursive forecasts.*

17.7.13   Time Series Analysis using Different Statistical Packages

Specialized software for time series analysis require declaring the data to be time series data and providing an identifier for the time series variable; note that handling different date formats can be tricky. Lagged variables and differenced variables are then easily constructed. Specific commands enable computation of HAC-robust standard errors (see also Chapter 12.1.9), calculation of autocorrelations, and tests for autocorrelation.

In Stata the time variable, say `time`, is identified with the command `xtset time`. For variable y the second-order lag (y_{t-2}) is `l2.y` and the first difference (Δy_t) is `d.y`. The `newey` command, rather than the `regress` command, is used to obtain Newey-West standard errors for OLS. The `corrgram` command provides autocorrelations and the Ljung-Box statistic, the `ac` command plots autocorrelations with confidence bands, and the `estat bgodfrey` command provides the Breusch-Godfrey statistic.

The R packages `zoo` and `xts` provide formats for saving and manipulating time series. The `sandwich` package `NeweyWest` function provides Newey-West standard errors and the `vcovHAC` function provides alternative HAC-robust standard errors. The `acf` function provides autocorrelation values and plots, the `Box.test` function provides the Ljung-Box statistic, and the `bgtest` function in the `lmtest` package provides the Breusch-Godfrey test.

In Gretl the `--time-series` option of the `set obs` command identifies the data as being time series. The `diff` command provides first differences in data, and for variable y the second-order lag (y_{t-2}) is `y(-2)`. The `corrgm` function provides autocorrelations and option `--plot-display` provides a plot with confidence bands. The `modtest --autocorr` command provides the Breusch-Godfrey test.

The Eviews package specialty is time series analysis. The workfile structure type `Dated-regular frequency` is used for time-series data. For variable y the second-order lag (y_{t-2}) is `y(-2)` and the first difference is `d(y)`. `Correlogram` provides autocorrelations. `View / Residual Diagnostics / Serial Correlation / LM Test` provides the Breusch-Godfrey test.

17.8 Time Series Example: U.S. Treasury Security Interest Rates

We analyze monthly data in dataset INTERESTRATES that are annualized percentage nominal interest rates on U.S. government securities, and are yields at constant maturity rate.

Table 17.6 summarizes the data. On average the 10-year rate exceeds the one-year rate by 1.5 percentage points, reflecting a reward for greater exposure to risk in holding longer term securities. The one-year rate is a little more volatile over this period, as *GS10* and *GS1* have standard deviations of, respectively, 2.88 and 3.28. Over this period there was considerable variation in interest rates, from a high of close to 15% per annum to as low as 0.10% for the one-year rate.

Table 17.6 additionally summarizes data on the monthly changes in the rates, in which case the first observation is lost. The sample means are negative because rates were on average declining over this period. For example, the ten-year rate was declining by around 0.4 percentage points per year ($\simeq 12 \times (-0.032)$).

The first panel of Figure 17.4 presents a time series plot of the levels data. There is strong persistence for both series, as the current period rates are closely related to those in the immediate preceding periods. Both rates show a pronounced downward trend for two reasons. First price inflation and inflationary expectations declined from highs in the 1970's and early 1980's to moderate levels beginning in the 1990's. Second the real interest rate has itself has declined over this period. Note that the one-year interest rate at the end of the sample period is very close to the zero interest rate lower bound – it is difficult, though not impossible, to have negative nominal interest rates. The two interest rates tend to move together, with the one-year rate fluctuating more.

The second panel of Figure 17.4 presents a scatterplot of the ten-year rate against the one-year rate. The relationship between the two rates appears to be linear with a slope of roughly

Table 17.6: US 10-year and 1-year Treasury securities monthly from January 1982 to January 2015: Variable definitions and summary statistics (T=297)

Variable	Definition	Mean	St. Dev.	Min	Max
GS10	10-year Treasury Note Constant Maturity Rate	6.186	2.878	1.53	14.59
GS1	1-year Treasury Note Constant Maturity Rate	4.691	3.283	0.10	14.73
$\Delta GS10$	Monthly change in 10-year Treasury Note Rate	-0.032	0.274	-1.43	0.78
$\Delta GS1$	Monthly change in 1-year Treasury Note Rate	-0.036	0.288	-1.81	0.76

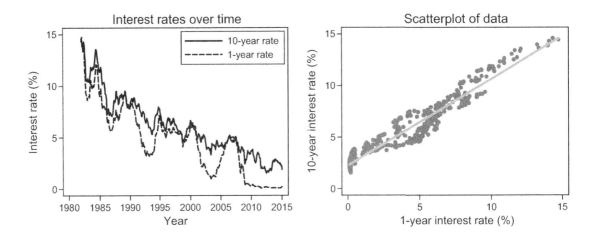

Figure 17.4: U.S. Treasury securities: Plot of 10-year and 1-year annualized returns from 1982 to 2015.

$(14-3)/(14-0) \simeq 0.8$.

Modelling of economic time series data should be guided by economic theory, in addition to the statistical properties of the data. Economic theory applies best to interest rates after correction for expected price inflation, liquidity of the asset, and expectations of default. For U.S. Treasuries the most important consideration is expected price inflation, which is unknown. We could instead model real interest rates, the nominal interest rate less the observed price inflation rate, rather than nominal rates. Price inflation did not vary enormously during this period (the inter-quartile range for the CPI was 2.3% to 3.9%). For bonds of different maturities the difference in real rates equals the difference in nominal rates, however, so that price inflation mostly nets out when modelling the relationship between bonds of different maturities. The various theories of the interrelationship between bonds of different maturity is not presented here.

Table 17.7: US Treasury securities: Autocorrelations and residual autocorrelations.

Variable	Autocorrelation at lag j ($\hat{\rho}_j$)							Ljung-Box	
	j=1	j=2	j=3	j=4	j=5	j=18	j=36	Q (m=12)	p-value
GS10	0.98	0.96	0.94	0.92	0.90	0.75	0.56	3797.6	0.000
GS1	0.98	0.96	0.94	0.92	0.90	0.69	0.42	3693.0	0.000
Residual: GS10 time trend model	0.95	0.87	0.80	0.72	0.65	0.10	0.03	1781.0	0.000
Residual: GS1 time trend model	0.97	0.92	0.87	0.82	0.76	0.18	-0.40	2432.9	0.000
Residual: GS10 AR(1) model	0.33	0.00	0.01	-0.01	-0.05	-0.07	0.01	-	-
Residual: GS1 AR(1) model	0.41	0.18	0.12	0.05	0.08	-0.02	-0.08	-	-
$\Delta GS10$	0.33	0.00	0.02	-0.01	-0.04	-0.07	0.01	51.6	0.000
$\Delta GS1$	0.42	0.18	0.13	0.05	0.09	-0.02	-0.08	97.1	0.000

17.8.1 A Simple Regression

We begin by regressing the ten-year rate on the one-year rate, with a time trend (a count of the month beginning with one in January 1982) included. Then

$$\widehat{GS10}_t = \underset{(8.88)}{5.910} - \underset{(-5.79)}{0.011} \times t + \underset{(6.28)}{0.508} \times GS1_t, \; s_e = 0.665, \; R^2 = 0.947,$$

where t statistics given in parentheses are based on HAC standard errors with 24 lags and it is assumed that there is no autocorrelation after 24 lags. A one percentage point increase in the one-year rate is associated with a 0.508 percentage point increase in the ten-year rate.

This analysis is valid if *GS10* and *GS1* are stationary series and model errors are uncorrelated after 24 lags. A possible complication here, however, is that *GS10* and *GS1* have very high persistence and may be nonstationary. The first five autocorrelations of the residuals are, respectively, 0.95, 0.89, 0.83, 0.77, and 0.71, and the autocorrelations at lags 18 and 36 are, respectively, 0.15 and 0.06. It is not clear whether the autocorrelations have died out sufficiently.

17.8.2 Autocorrelations

Table 17.7 presents autocorrelations for the two interest rate series, the residuals from some regression models, and changes in these series.

From the first two rows, there is extraordinarily high persistence for both the ten-year and one-year rates. Even 36 months or three years out the autocorrelation is 0.56 for *GS10* and 0.42 for *GS1*. From the subsequent two rows this persistence is reduced but not eliminated if we time detrend the series. For example, OLS yields $\widehat{GS10}_t = 10.858 - 0.023 \times t$ and the third row of Table 17.7 gives the autocorrelations for the residual $e_t = GS10_t - 10.858 + 0.023 \times t$.

The table also includes Ljung-Box test statistics of autocorrelation (see Chapter 17.7.4) out to 12 lags. In all cases $p = 0.000$ and so the null hypothesis of no autocorrelation is strongly rejected.

17.8.3   Autoregressive model

The sample autocorrelations for *GS10* given in the first row of Table 17.7 suggest that a good model for *GS10* is an AR(1) model $y_t = \alpha_0 + \alpha_1 y_{t-1} + u_t$ with $\alpha_1 \simeq 0.98$. This model predicts the autocorrelation at lag j to be 0.98^j which predicts first five autocorrelations of approximately 0.98, 0.96, 0.94, 0.92 and 0.90, $\rho_{18} = 0.98^{18} = 0.70$ and $\rho_{36} = 0.98^{36} = 0.54$. These autocorrelations are close to those in Table 17.7.

OLS regression yields estimated AR(1) model $\widehat{GS10}_t = 0.046 + 0.987 \times GS10_{t-1}$. This model has $s_e = 0.272$, so it fits these data much better than the linear time trend model that had much lower $s_e = 1.015$. The fifth row of Table 17.7 gives the autocorrelations of the residuals from this AR(1) regression. The residuals are essentially uncorrelated after the first lag. And from the sixth row of Table 17.7 the residuals from the AR(1) model for *GS1* are correlated for only the first two lags. The Ljung-Box statistic is not reported in Table 17.7 since the residuals are from a regression with a lagged dependent variable as a regressor. Instead one should use the Breusch-Godfrey test which here has $p = 0.000$ at 12 lags for both series.

Note that here the OLS coefficients are biased and inconsistent in these first-order autoregressive models since these regressions have both a lagged dependent variable as regressor and a serially correlated error. Consistent coefficient estimates can be obtained by adding enough additional lags to obtain an error that is serially uncorrelated.

17.8.4   Autocorrelations in Changes

The autocorrelations for the changes $\Delta GS10$ and $\Delta GS1$ are given in the final two columns of Table 17.7. The autocorrelations for the changes are very similar to those for the residuals from the AR(1) model since that model with $\alpha_1 = 1$ yields a first difference, and in this case the estimated AR(1) models had $\widehat{\alpha}_1$ very close to one.

17.8.5   Unit Roots and Nonstationary

A unit root process $y_t = \alpha_0 + y_{t-1} + u_t$, equivalent to an AR(1) process with $\alpha_1 = 1$, is a nonstationary process that complicates analysis because standard inference methods cannot be used. Furthermore, if standard inference methods are mistakenly used it is possible to mistakenly find relationships between series when none exist.

The empirical macroeconomic literature finds very high persistence in both nominal and real interest rates. Formal statistical tests provide mixed results on whether or not this persistence is high enough to be a unit root. At the same time economic theory does not support unit roots in interest rates. And if interest rates really were unit root processes then we would expect to find many more periods of very high interest rates than are observed historically.

If data are not highly persistent, then the possibility of a unit root can be ignored. One rule of thumb is that a unit root is very unlikely if the sample autocorrelation at lag one is less than 0.8 and autocorrelations after two or three lags are below 0.5. If instead a series has high persistence then it is important to test whether the persistence is so high that a unit root is present. For example, a unit root is likely to be present if low-order autocorrelations exceed 0.9 and are slow to

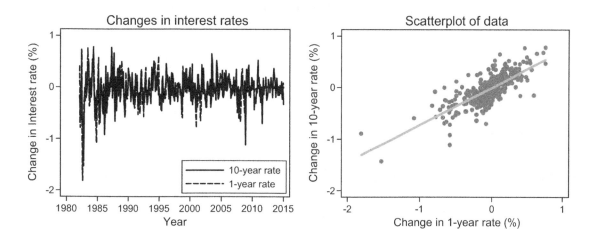

Figure 17.5: U.S. Treasury securities: Plots of monthly changes in 10-year and 1-year annualized returns from 1982 to 2015.

die out. The autocorrelation function provides only a guide, albeit a valuable one. Formal tests for a unit root, such as the **Dickey-Fuller test**, are based on nonstandard distributions and are beyond the scope of this text; their application here gives somewhat mixed results though leans towards rejecting the null hypothesis of a unit root.

17.8.6 Regression in Changes

The safest approach is to assume the possibility of a unit root in *GS10* and *GS1* and perform regression analysis in first differences. In the remainder of this section we illustrate various models specified in changes. With stationary series similar analysis could be conducted in levels.

Regression in changes yields

$$\widehat{\Delta GS10}_t = -0.006 + 0.720 \times \Delta GS1_t, \; s_e = 0.180, \; R^2 = 0.570,$$
$$\underset{(-0.62)}{} \quad \underset{(16.37)}{}$$

where t statistics given in parentheses are based on HAC standard errors with 3 lags. This lag length should be sufficient as the first three autocorrelations of the residuals are 0.25, −0.04 and 0.06. The estimates indicate a very strong relationship between the two rates, so the relationship between *GS10* and *GS1* is not spurious. The slope coefficient is large – a one percentage point change in *GS1* is associated with a 0.72 percentage point change in *GS10* – and the t statistic equals 16.37.

Figure 17.5 plots the monthly changes in the two interest rates over time (first panel) and provides a scatterplot of $\Delta GS10$ *against* $\Delta GS1$ (second panel). There does appear to be a relationship between the two series.

17.8.7   Finite Distributed Lag Model in Changes

For the interest rate data a finite distributed lag model for $\Delta GS10$ with up to two lags in $\Delta GS1$ yields

$$\widehat{\Delta GS10}_t = \underset{(-0.73)}{-0.008} + \underset{(15.23)}{0.759\times\Delta GS1_t} - \underset{(-1.42)}{0.058\times\Delta GS1_{t-1}}$$
$$- \underset{(-1.05)}{0.040\times \Delta GS1_{t-2}},\ s_e = 0.178,\ R^2 = 0.580.$$

where t statistics computed using HAC standard errors ($m = 3$) are given in parentheses. Since none of the regressors are lags of the dependent variable, OLS is consistent even if the error is serially correlated. Including lagged changes yields only a slight improvement in R^2, from 0.570 to 0.580, and a joint test finds that $\Delta GS1_{t-1}$ and $\Delta GS1_{t-2}$ are jointly statistically insignificant at 5% ($p = 0.31$).

The impact of a change in $\Delta GS1$ of one percentage point is a 0.759 percentage point change in $\Delta GS10$. The cumulative effect is a 0.661 percentage point change ($= 0.759 - 0.058 - 0.040$).

17.8.8   Autoregressive Model in Changes

An autoregressive model of order 2 for $\Delta GS10$ yields estimates

$$\widehat{\Delta GS10}_t = \underset{(-1.78)}{-0.023} + \underset{(6.27)}{0.374\times\Delta GS10_{t-1}} - \underset{(-1.96)}{0.121 \times \Delta GS10_{t-2}},$$
$$s_e = 0.256,\ R^2 = 0.125.$$

OLS is now inconsistent if the error is serially correlated, since lags of the dependent variable are regressors. A Breusch-Godfrey test with 12 lags finds no correlation in the error, so OLS estimates are consistent. The reported t statistics are based on heteroskedastic–robust standard errors.

Both lags of $\Delta GS10$ are statistically significant at level 0.05, and further analysis reveals that two lags are sufficient. The AR(2) model has much worse fit than the DL(2) model, as R^2 has fallen from 0.580 to 0.125.

17.8.9   Autoregressive Distributed Lag Model

An ADL(2,2) model that combines the previous two models has estimates

$$\widehat{\Delta GS10}_t = \underset{(-0.80)}{-0.007} + \underset{(5.17)}{0.283\times\Delta GS10_{t-1}} - \underset{(-1.86)}{0.102 \times \Delta GS10_{t-2}}$$
$$+ \underset{(17.10)}{0.740 \times \Delta GS1_t} - \underset{(-3.99)}{0.259 \times \Delta GS1_{t-1}} + \underset{(0.92)}{0.051 \times \Delta GS1_{t-2}},$$
$$s_e = 0.171,\ R^2 = 0.611.$$

The model errors are serially uncorrelated, as was the case for the AR(2) model. The model fit is improved somewhat compared to the DL(2) model, with R^2 increased from 0.580 to 0.611. The reported t statistics based on heteroskedastic–robust standard errors show that $\Delta GS1_{t-2}$ could be dropped from the model.

Further analysis shows that the ADL(3,3) provides a better fit on the basis of BIC. Since the ADL(3,3) drops an additional observation, due to computing an additional lag, the ADL(2,2) should also drop this observation when the models are compared using BIC.

17.8.10 Spurious Regression Check in Levels

The initial regression of $\Delta GS10$ on $\Delta GS1$ showed that the relationship between $GS10$ and $GS1$ is not spurious. Another way to establish is to fit a model in levels with first-order lags included as regressors. Then

$$\widehat{GS10}_t = \underset{(1.50)}{0.047} + \underset{(16.85)}{0.719} \times GS1_t + \underset{(110.37)}{0.978} \times GS10_{t-1} - \underset{(-16.41)}{0.701} \times GS1_{t-1}, \; s_e = 0.180, \; R^2 = 0.996,$$

where t statistics given in parentheses are based on HAC standard errors with 24 lags. The coefficient on $GS1_t$ remains highly statistically significant and meaningfully large, so we conclude that the relationship is not spurious. Note, however, that the t statistic can only be a guide here as the error is (mildly) serially correlated and the model includes a lagged dependent variable.

The relationship between $GS10$ and $GS1$ does appear to be real. In this section the interest rates were viewed as having unit roots, so regression analysis was in first differences. This procedure is valid, though there are better more advanced methods that enable richer modelling of the data.

17.8.11 Impulse Response Function

Interest often lies in the future responses of y_t over time to a change in the current period value of x_t. The collection of responses over time is called an **impulse response function**.

A simple way to obtain the impulse responses is to use the **local projection method**. To obtain the h-period ahead impulse response, one estimates the original model except the dependent variable is y_{t+h} instead of y_t. The impulse response is then the coefficient of x_t.

As an example consider the ADL(2,2) model in changes, with $\Delta GS10_t$ regressed on $\Delta GS10_{t-1}$, $\Delta GS10_{t-2}$, $\Delta GS1_t$, $\Delta GS1_{t-1}$ and $\Delta GS1_{t-2}$. The impulse response h periods later on $\Delta GS10$ of a one unit change in $\Delta GS1$ is the coefficient of $\Delta GS1_t$ from OLS regression of $\Delta GS10_{t+h}$ on $\Delta GS10_{t-1}$, $\Delta GS10_{t-2}$, $\Delta GS1_t$, $\Delta GS1_{t-1}$ and $\Delta GS1_{t-2}$.

For valid inference the ADL model must have enough lags so that the residuals in the are serially uncorrelated. The consequent regressions with $\Delta GS10_{t+h}$ as dependent variable will then have residuals that are correlated up to h lags, however, so for the subsequent impulse response estimates HAC standard errors with $m = h$ should be used.

For the current example, the initial regression yielded Breusch-Godfrey test statistic at 12 lags with $p = 0.232$ so the null hypothesis of no autocorrelation is not rejected. The subsequent impulse responses, with Newey-West HAC-robust standard errors using h lags given in parentheses, are 0.740 (0.049) initially, 0.293 (0.047) at one month, 0.088 (0.086) at two months, 0.021 (0.077) at three months and -0.053 (0.053) at four months. The impulse response function estimates are often presented as a graph, with 90% or 95% confidence intervals.

17.9   Further Reading

There are many undergraduate econometrics texts. At a level more advanced than this book two leading texts in the U.S. are Stock and Watson (2018) and Wooldridge (2019).

Books at the advanced undergraduate and masters level that cover quasi-experimental approaches to causal inference are Angrist and Pischke (2015), Cunningham (2021), and the more advanced book Angrist and Pischke (2009); see also Cameron and Trivedi (2022b). An introduction to machine learning methods is given in James, Witten, Hastie and Tibshirani (2021).

Standard graduate econometrics texts are Hansen (2022), Greene (2018), Wooldridge (2010), and Cameron and Trivedi (2005). These texts use matrix algebra extensively. The text by Greene includes time series analysis in addition to cross-section and panel data analysis.

17.10   Key Concepts

1. For cross-section data inference is usually based on heteroskedastic-robust standard errors if observations are independent or cluster-robust standard errors if observations are clustered.

2. Richer estimators than OLS for clustered cross-section data are random effects and fixed effects estimators.

3. For panel data inference should be based on panel-robust standard errors that cluster on the panel identifier, or even more broadly on a cluster if the panels are clustered.

4. Richer estimators than OLS for panel data are random effects and fixed effects estimators.

5. Common models for panel data are the pooled model, random effects model and fixed effects model.

6. There are many methods for obtaining causal estimates using observational data. Different methods rely on different assumptions, not all testable, and the availability of specific forms of data.

7. A logit model or probit model is used when the dependent variable is categorical with just two categories. They can also be used for proportions data that take values between zero and one.

8. A Poisson model is used when the dependent variable is a count. It can also be used for nonnegative dependent variable.

9. For logit, probit and Poisson models the interpretation of estimated coefficients is model specific; unlike a linear model a slope coefficient does not equal the marginal effect.

10. Time series analysis is complicated by persistence in the data.

11. The sample autocorrelation at lag j measures the correlation between y_t and y_{t-j}. Persistence is higher the closer the sample autocorrelations are to one.

12. For static regression OLS can be used if errors are serially correlated, with inference based on heteroskedastic and autocorrelation consistent (HAC) standard errors.

13. A regression is said to be dynamic if lagged dependent variables are included in the regression. In that case OLS can only be used if sufficient lags of the dependent variable are included to yield errors that are serially uncorrelated.

14. If time-series data have unit roots then standard methods need to be modified. This is an advanced topic.

15. Key terms: Clustered data; panel data; random effects; fixed effects; within variation; between variation; instrumental variables; experiments; regression adjustment; differences in differences; matching; inverse-probability weighting; regression discontinuity design; logit; probit; Poisson; marginal effect; time series; HAC robust standard errors; autocorrelation; autoregressive model; finite distributed lag model; autoregressive distributed lag model; autoregressive error model; impulse response function; nonstationary data; unit root; random walk; spurious regression; cointegration.

17.11 Exercises

1. Use dataset AUTOSMPG detailed in Chapter 13.4. Restrict attention to cars ($d\_truck=0$) in 1980 ($year=1980$). OLS regress $lmpg$ (log of miles per gallon) on an intercept, $lcurbwt$ (log of weight), lhp, d_manual and d_diesel. For clustered standard errors and cluster-specific fixed effects and random effects the cluster variable is $idmfr$ (manufacturer identifier).

    (a) Obtain OLS estimates with cluster-robust standard errors. Provide interpretation of the coefficient of $lcurbwt$.

    (b) For $lcurbwt$ compare cluster-robust standard errors with default standard errors.

    (c) Obtain random effects estimates with cluster-robust standard errors. What coefficients differ from those in part (a) by more than 10%? Has there been an improvement in the precision of estimates?

    (d) For the random effects estimates compare cluster-robust to default standard errors.

    (e) Obtain fixed effects estimates with cluster-robust standard errors. What coefficients differ from those in part (a) by more than 10%?

    (f) For the fixed effects estimates compare cluster-robust to default standard errors.

2. Repeat the previous exercise for pickup trucks ($d\_truck=1$) in 1980 ($year=1980$).

3. Dataset PHARVIS introduced in exercise 5 of Chapter 12 covers 27,753 people in 5,739 households and 194 communes (villages). We consider OLS regression of *pharvis* (number of direct pharmacy visits) on an intercept, *hhexp* (total household expenditure), *age* (age in years), *illness* (number of illnesses in past year) and *hlthins* (= 1 if have health insurance cover). We will cluster on *commune* (commune or village).

   (a) Obtain OLS estimates with cluster-robust standard errors. Are the signs of coefficients what you expect? Explain.

   (b) For *illness* compare cluster-robust standard errors with default standard errors.

   (c) Obtain random effects estimates with cluster-robust standard errors. What coefficients differ from those in part (a) by more than 10%? Has there been an improvement in the precision of estimates?

   (d) For the random effects estimates compare cluster-robust to default standard errors.

   (e) Obtain fixed effects estimates with cluster-robust standard errors. What coefficients differ from those in part (a) by more than 10%?

   (f) For the fixed effects estimates compare cluster-robust to default standard errors.

   (g) For the fixed effects estimates why is the coefficient for *hhexp* not estimated?

4. Repeat exercise 1 parts (a)-(f) with clustering on *hhid* (household).

5. Use dataset NBA, detailed in Chapter 17.3, for regression of *lnrevenue* (log of team revenue) on an intercept and *wins*.

   (a) Obtain OLS estimates and for *wins* compare heteroskedastic-robust to cluster-robust standard errors.

   (b) Obtain random effects estimates and for the coefficient of *wins* compare default to cluster-robust standard errors.

   (c) Obtain fixed effects estimates and for the coefficient of *wins* compare default to cluster-robust standard errors.

   (d) Compare the slope estimates obtained in parts (a)-(c).

   (e) Compare the cluster-robust standard errors obtained in parts (a)-(c).

6. Repeat the previous exercise using dependent variable *revenue* (log of team revenue).

7. Use dataset NBA, detailed in Chapter 17.3, and consider the following ways to obtain fixed effect estimates from regression of *lnrevenue* (log of team revenue) on an intercept and *wins*. In each case obtain cluster-robust standard errors with clustering on team.

   (a) Use a fixed effects estimation command.

   (b) OLS regress *lnrevenue* on *wins* and a full set of team indicator variables.

   (c) For *lnrevenue* (y_{it}) compute the individual team means $\bar{y}_i$ and hence generate the mean differences y_{it}. Do similar computations for *wins* (x_{it}) to generate $x_{it} - \bar{x}_i$. Then

   (d) Compare the slope coefficients of *wins* from parts (a)-(c).

   (e) Compare the cluster-robust standard errors of the slope coefficient of *wins* from parts (a)-(c).

8. Repeat the previous exercise using dependent variable *revenue* (log of team revenue).

9. Use dataset USMANUFACTURING that has data for 51 U.S. states (including D.C.) for each of the years 2014-2016 in 2014 on output (q), capital (k) and labor (l), measured in millions of dollars, and their natural logarithms (*lnq*, *lnk* and *lnl*). Cluster on state (variable *idstate*).

   (a) OLS regress *lnq* on an intercept and *lnk* and *lnl*. Compare default standard errors to cluster-robust standard errors.

   (b) Using cluster-robust standard errors, test at 5% whether returns to scale are constant, i.e. whether $\beta_{lnl} + \beta_{lnk} = 1$.

   (c) Now obtain random effects estimates for the model of part (a). Compare default standard errors to cluster-robust standard errors.

   (d) In this example has random effects estimation lead to improved efficiency compared to OLS? Explain.

10. Use dataset USMANUFACTURING described in the preceding exercise. Use cluster-robust standard errors with clustering on state.

   (a) OLS regress *lnq* on an intercept and *lnk* and *lnl*.

   (b) Now obtain fixed effects estimates.

   (c) For these data there is very little within variation. For example, for *lnq* the within standard deviation is 0.109 while the between standard deviation is 1.424. Use this information to explain key differences between the estimates and precision in parts (a) and (b).

11. Consider the Rand Health Experiment detailed in Chapter 13.5. Analyze total spending (*spending*) in all years and use cluster-robust standard errors that cluster on family (*idfamily*).

    (a) OLS regress *spending* on an intercept and the set of mutually exclusive coinsurance indicator variables, with *coins0* the omitted category. Does the coinsurance level appear to make a difference? Explain.

    (b) Are the indicator variables jointly statistically significant at 5%?

    (c) Is there a reason to consider fixed effects estimation here? Explain.

    (d) Are fixed effects estimates even possible here? Explain.

12. Consider the Rand Health Experiment detailed in Chapter 13.5. Analyze outpatient spending (*outpat*) in all years. Use cluster-robust standard errors that cluster on family (*idfamily*).

    (a) OLS regress *outpat* on an intercept and the set of mutually exclusive coinsurance indicator variables, with *coins0* the omitted category. Does the coinsurance level appear to make a difference? Explain.

    (b) Are the indicator variables jointly statistically significant at 5%?

    (c) Now add as regressors *age*, *gender*, *badhealth* and *goodhealth*. Do these additional variables have the expected signs? Are these additional variables jointly statistically significant at 5%.

    (d) Has inclusion of the additional variables improved the precision of estimation of the coefficients of the coinsurance indicator variables? Are the coinsurance indicator variables jointly statistically significant at 5%.

13. For a sample of size 1,000 generate in turn $v_i \sim N(0,1)$, $w_i \sim N(0,1)$, $u_i = 0.8v_i + 0.6w_i$, $z_i \sim N(2,1)$, $x_i = 0 + z_i + v_i$, $y_i = 0 + 0.5x_i + u_i$. We are interested in estimating the model $y = \beta_1 + \beta_2 x + u$. For this generating process errors are homoskedastic so default standard errors can be used.

    (a) Obtain the correlation between the regressor x and the error u. Do you expect a problem in OLS regression of y on x? Explain.

    (b) Regress y on an intercept and x. Has the slope coefficient been consistently estimated? Explain.

    (c) Is z a valid instrument for x? Explain.

    (d) Is z likely to be a good instrument for x? Explain.

    (e) Obtain the IV estimate of the model using z as a instrument for x. Has the slope coefficient been consistently estimated? Explain.

    (f) Regress y on an intercept and z, regress x on an intercept and z, take the ratio of the slope estimates and compare to the IV slope estimate from part (e).

(g) The name 2SLS is obtained because the IV estimate can be obtained as follows. First, regress x on an intercept and z and obtain predictions $\widehat{x}$. Second, regress y on an intercept and $\widehat{x}$. Do this and compare to your answer in part (e).

(h) Now compare the standard error of the slope estimate in part (g) with that in part (e). Comment.

14. Repeat the previous exercise with the changes that $u_i = 0.6v_i + 0.8w_i$ and $y_i = 1 + 2x_i + u_i$.

15. Use dataset RETURNSTOSCHOOLING presented in chapter 17.4.3. For this exercise see the code provided at the book website to obtain the names of the 26 exogenous regressors. Use heteroskedastic-robust standard errors.

(a) Create a binary treatment variable *dtreat* equal to one if *grade76* ≥ 18. What fraction of the sample is treated?

(b) OLS regress *wage76* on an intercept, *dtreat* and the 26 exogenous regressors. Report the coefficient of *dtreat*.

(c) Obtain the IV estimates of the model of part (b) with instrument *col4*. Report the coefficient of *dtreat*.

(d) The IV estimate is large. Is it plausible? (Hint: look at the difference in schooling by treatment status).

(e) Is the IV estimate for *dtreat* statistically significant at 5%?

(f) Obtain the correlation between *col4* and *dtreat*. Can this explain the difference in precision between OLS and IV estimates.

(g) Obtain the first-stage F statistic. Could *col4* be a weak instrument?

16. Use dataset RETURNSTOSCHOOLING presented in chapter 17.4.3. For this exercise see the code provided at the book website to obtain the names of the 26 exogenous regressors. Here we add as regressors a quadratic in experience. Use heteroskedastic-robust standard errors.

(a) OLS regress *wage76* on an intercept, *grade76*, *exp76* , *expsq76*, and the 26 exogenous regressors. Report the coefficient of *grade76*.

(b) Obtain IV estimates of the model in part (a) with instruments *col4*, *exp76* and *expsq76*. Report the coefficient of *grade76*.

(c) Is the IV estimate for *grade76* statistically significant at 5%?

(d) Do you think a quadratic in experience is necessary, or would a linear model in experience do? Explain.

(e) Which of the instruments of the coefficient of *col4*, *exp76* and *expsq76* seem to possibly be weak?

17. Consider a logit model with $\Pr[y=1|x] = \Lambda(1+0.5x)$ where $\Lambda(z) = e^z/(1+e^z)$.

    (a) Compute the probability when $x = 2$.

    (b) Compute the marginal effect of a change in x when $x = 2$.

    (c) Suppose the dependent variable y has sample mean 0.6. Compute the approximate average marginal effect of a change in x.

18. Consider a probit model with $\Pr[y=1|x] = \Phi(-1+x)$ where $\Phi(z) = \frac{1}{\sqrt{2\pi}}e^{-z^2/2}$.

    (a) Compute the probability when $x = 1.5$.

    (b) Compute the marginal effect of a change in x when $x = 1.5$.

    (c) Suppose the dependent variable y has sample mean 0.8. Compute the approximate average marginal effect of a change in x.

19. Use dataset EARNINGS_COMPLETE.

    (a) Create the binary variable *dhighearn* that equals one if earnings exceed \$60,000. Report the sample mean of *dhighearn*.

    (b) Perform OLS regression of *dhighearn* on an intercept and *education* and report the slope coefficient.

    (c) Compute predicted probabilities for each individual and produce a line plot of predicted probabilities against *education*. Do you see a problem? Explain.

    (d) Repeat part (b) using logit regression.

    (e) Repeat part (c) following logit regression.

20. Use dataset PHARVIS.

    (a) Create the binary variable *dpharvis* that equals one if make at least one pharmacy visit and equals zero otherwise.

    (b) Obtain the slope estimates from logit, probit and OLS regression of *dpharvis* on an intercept and *illness*. Probit slope coefficients can be shown to be approximately four times OLS slope coefficients. Is that the case here?

    (c) Using the approximations given in Chapter 17.6.1 compare the approximate average marginal effect of *illness* for the logit, probit and OLS model.

    (d) For logit regression of *dpharvis* on an intercept and *illness* compare default standard errors, heteroskedastic-robust standard errors and cluster-robust standard errors with clustering on *commune*.

21. Dataset DOCTORVISITS has individual level data from the 1977-78 Australian Health Survey. The sample here is only of single person households, so observations can be viewed as independent. One health outcome in the dataset is *visits*, the number of doctor visits in the past two weeks. As regressors we consider *female* (equals one if female), *age* (age in years), *income* (annual income in \$10,000's), *illness* (the number of illnesses in the past two weeks) and *levyplus* (equals one if have private insurance that is more generous than the basic universal government insurance).

    (a) Create an indicator variable *dvisit* that equals one if *visits*>0 and equals zero if *visits*=0. What fraction of the sample visited a doctor?

    (b) Obtain estimates from logit regression of *dvisit* on an intercept, *female*, *age*, *income*, *illness* and *levyplus*, using default standard errors. Do the coefficients have the expected sign?

    (c) Using $\bar{y}$, compute the approximate average marginal effect of one more illness on the probability of visiting a doctor.

    (d) Use a specialized command (see Chapter 17.6.5) to compute the average marginal effect of one more illness on the probability of seeing a doctor.

    (e) Now compute the average marginal effect manually as follows. First, for each observation compute $\widehat{p}_i$, the predicted value of the probability of a doctor visit. Second, obtain the marginal effect for each observation of one more illness, using the formula $\widehat{p}_i(1 - \widehat{p}_i)b_j$. Third, average the marginal effect for each observation. Does this equal your answer in part (d)?

    (f) Compare your answer in part (d) (or in part (e)) to the coefficient of *illness* from OLS regression of *dvisit* on an intercept, *female*, *age*, *income*, *illness* and *levyplus*.

22. Repeat the previous exercise for probit regression, where in part (e) use the formula $\phi(\widehat{p}_i)b_j$ where $\phi(z) = \frac{1}{\sqrt{2\pi}}e^{-z^2/2}$.

23. Consider a Poisson model with $E[y|x] = \exp(-1 + 0.2x)$.

    (a) Compute the conditional mean when $x = 2$.

    (b) What is the percentage change in the conditional mean when x changes by one unit?

    (c) What is the change in the conditional mean when x changes, evaluated at $x = 2$?

    (d) Suppose the dependent variable y has mean 0.6. What is the average marginal effect of a change in x?

24. Repeat the previous exercise for $E[y|x] = \exp(1 - 0.4x)$ at $x = 3$ and with $\bar{y} = 0.9$.

25. Use dataset DOCTORVISITS described in exercise 21. Here we model *visits*, the number of doctor visits in the past two weeks.

    (a) Obtain estimates from Poisson regression of *visits* on an intercept, *female, age, income, illness* and *levyplus* using heteroskedastic-robust default standard errors. Do the coefficients have the expected sign?

    (b) Now instead obtain default standard errors. Is there a substantial difference with those from part (a)?

    (c) Provide an interpretation of the coefficient of *illness* as a semi-elasticity.

    (d) Compute the average marginal effect of one more illness on the number of doctor visits using AME= $\bar{y} \times b_j$.

    (e) Use a specialized command (see Chapter 17.6.5) to compute the AME of one more illness.

    (f) Compare your answer in part (d) to the coefficient of *illness* from OLS regression of *visits* on an intercept, *female, age, income, illness* and *levyplus*.

26. Repeat the previous exercise for dependent variable *prescrib*, the number of prescribed medications used in the past two days.

27. Consider calculation of price elasticities for the Rand Health Insurance Experiment, detailed in Chapter 13.5.4. Use dataset HEALTHINSEXP and variables *spending* (total health spending) and *coinsrate* (coinsurance rate). Here use all years of data and cluster-robust standard errors that cluster on *idfamily*. A complication for using log-log OLS regression is taking logs when *spending* and *coinsrate* can take zero values.

    (a) Estimate the price elasticity by OLS regression of $\ln(spending+1)$ on $\ln(coinsrate)$ for the 13,363 observations with *coinsrate*>0. Give the estimate and a 95% confidence interval.

    (b) Estimate the price elasticity by Poisson regression of *spending* on $\ln(coinsrate)$ for the 13,363 observations with *coinsrate*>0. Give the estimate and a 95% confidence interval.

    (c) Which method do you think is better? Explain.

28. Repeat the previous exercise for *outpat* (outpatient spending).

29. This exercise contrasts an AR(1) process with a random walk. To recursively generate time series data see the code for the chapter 17.8 application posted at the book website.

    (a) Generate a sample of size 1000 with $y_t = \alpha y_{t-1} + u_t$ where $\alpha = 0.9$ and $u_t \sim N(0,1)$.

    (b) It can be shown that for this data generating process, $E[y_t] = 0$ and $Var[y_t] = 1/(1-\alpha^2)$. Does that appear to be the case for your sample? Explain.

    (c) It can be shown that for this data generating process, $\rho_j = \alpha^j$. Does that appear to be the case for your sample? Explain.

    (d) Provide a time series plot of y against t. Does the process often move between positive and negative values?

(e) Now generate a sample of size 1000 with $z_t = z_{t-1} + v_t$ where $v_t \sim N(0,1)$.

(f) It can be shown that for this data generating process, $E[y_t]$ and $\text{Var}[y_t]$ do not exist. Might this be the case for your sample? Explain.

(g) It can be shown that for this data generating process the autocorrelations are very slow to disappear. Obtain $\widehat{\rho}_{100}$ and comment.

(h) Provide a time series plot of z against t. Does the process often move between positive and negative values? Comment.

30. Repeat the previous exercise with $\alpha = 0.8$.

31. This exercise regresses a random walk on a random walk. To recursively generate time series data see the code for chapter 17.7 posted at the book website.

(a) Generate a sample of size 1000 with $y_t = y_{t-1} + u_t$ where $u_t \sim N(0,1)$ and $x_t = x_{t-1} + u_t$ where $v_t \sim N(0,1)$.

(b) Provide a time series plot of y and x against t. Does there appear to be a relationship?

(c) Provide a scatterplot of y against x. Does there appear to be a relationship?

(d) Regress y on an intercept and x and report the R^2. Does this suggest a relationship?

(e) Using default standard errors test statistical significance of the slope coefficient at 5%.

(f) Obtain the first 20 autocorrelations of the residual. Does the residual appear to be highly serially correlated?

32. Repeat the previous exercise with $y_t = 0.01 + y_{t-1} + u_t$, $x_t = x_{t-1} + u_t$, and regress y on an intercept, a time trend (t) and x.

33. Use dataset INTERESTRATES presented in Chapter 17.8. Consider the relationship between five-year rates ($gs5$) and one-year rates ($gs1$).

(a) Compare the sample means of $gs5$ and $gs1$. Are you surprised by the difference?

(b) Obtain the first 40 autocorrelations of $gs5$ and $gs1$. Comment.

(c) Provide a time series plot of $gs5$ and $gs1$ against *time*. Do the two series appear to move together over time?

(d) Provide a scatterplot of $gs5$ against $gs1$. Does there appear to be a close relationship between the two series?

(e) Regress $gs5$ on an intercept and $gs1$. Compare heteroskedastic-robust standard errors to Newey-West HAC-robust standard errors with 24 lags. Comment.

(f) Using the Newey-West standard errors, test at 5% the hypothesis that an increase in the one-year rate leads on average to the same magnitude increase in the five-year rate.

34. Repeat the previous exercise for the relationship between ten-year rates (*gs10*) and two-year rates (*gs2*).

35. Use dataset INTERESTRATES presented in Chapter 17.8. Consider the relationship between five-year rates (*gs5*) and one-year rates (*gs1*) with a time trend included. Use Newey-West HAC-robust standard errors with 24 lags.

    (a) Regress *gs5* on an intercept, *time* and *gs1*.

    (b) Provide an interpretation of the time trend term.

    (c) Test at 5% the hypothesis that an increase in the one-year rate leads on average to the same magnitude increase in the five-year rate.

    (d) Obtain the first 24 autocorrelations of the residual from this regression. Do you think the autocorrelations have died down after 24 lags?

36. Repeat the previous exercise for the relationship between ten-year rates (*gs10*) and two-year rates (*gs2*).

37. Use dataset INTERESTRATES presented in Chapter 17.8. Consider the relationship between monthly changes in five-year rates (*dgs5*) and monthly changes in one-year rates (*dgs1*).

    (a) Generate variable *dgs5*, obtain summary statistics and provide an interpretation of the mean.

    (b) Obtain the first 40 autocorrelations of *dgs5* and *dgs1*. Comment.

    (c) Provide a time series plot of *gs5* and *gs1* against *time*. Do the two series appear to move together over time?

    (d) Provide a scatterplot of *gs5* against *gs1*. Does there appear to be a close relationship between the two series?

    (e) Regress *dgs5* on an intercept and *dgs1* and use Newey-West HAC-robust standard errors with 12 lags. Is there an economically meaningful and statistically meaningful relationship between five-year rates and one-year rates? Explain.

38. Repeat the previous exercise for the relationship between monthly changes in ten-year rates (*dgs10*) and monthly changes in two-year rates (*dgs2*).

39. Use dataset INTERESTRATES presented in Chapter 17.8. Consider the relationship between five-year rates ($gs5$) and lags in five-year rates. Use heteroskedastic-robust standard errors.

    (a) Regress $gs5$ on an intercept and $gs5$ lagged one period. Do the residuals appear to be serially correlated? Explain.

    (b) Regress $gs5$ on an intercept and $gs5$ lagged one period and two periods. Do the residuals appear to be serially correlated? Explain.

    (c) Regress $gs5$ on an intercept and $gs5$ lagged one period, two periods and three periods. Does the residual appear to be serially correlated? Explain.

    (d) For which of the preceding models are the OLS coefficients consistent? Explain.

    (e) Would it be appropriate to use Newey-West HAC-robust standard errors here? Explain.

    (f) Test at 5% the hypothesis that the sum of the slope coefficients equals one in the part (c) model. (This requires a quite specialized hypothesis testing command).

    (g) Using a specialized command implement the Breusch-Godfrey test at the 5% level for the model in part (b) using twelve lags. State your conclusion.

40. Repeat the previous exercise for two-year rates ($gs2$) and lags in two-year rates.

41. Use dataset INTERESTRATES presented in Chapter 17.8. Consider the relationship between changes in five-year rates ($dgs5$) and current and lagged changes in one-year rates ($dgs1$). Use Newey-West HAC-robust standard errors with 6 lags.

    (a) Regress $dgs5$ on an intercept, $dgs1$, and $dgs1$ lagged one period and two periods. Do the lagged terms in $dgs1$ need to be included? Explain.

    (b) Do the residuals appear to be serially correlated? Explain.

    (c) Are the slope coefficients consistently estimated?

    (d) Now consider regression in levels. Regress $gs5$ on an intercept, $gs1$, and $gs1$ lagged one period and two periods. Do the residuals appear to be serially correlated? Explain.

    (e) Using a specialized command implement the Ljung-Box test at the 5% level for the model in part (a) using twelve lags. State your conclusion.

42. Repeat the previous exercise for changes in ten-year rates ($dgs10$) and two-year rates ($dgs2$).

43. Use dataset INTERESTRATES presented in Chapter 17.8. Consider the relationship between changes in five-year rates ($dgs5$) and changes in one-year rates ($dgs1$) using an ADL(1,1) model.

    (a) Regress $dgs5$ on an intercept, $dgs5$ lagged one period, $dgs1$ and $dgs1$ lagged one period.

    (b) Does the residual appear to be serially correlated? Explain.

    (c) Is it important that the residual be serially correlated? Explain.

    (d) Are the slope coefficients consistently estimated?

    (e) Now consider regression in levels. Regress $gs5$ on an intercept, $gs5$ lagged one period, $gs1$ and $gs1$ lagged one period. Does the residual appear to be serially correlated? Explain.

    (f) Using a specialized command implement the Breusch-Godfrey test at the 5% level for the model in part (a) using twelve lags. State your conclusion.

44. Repeat the previous exercise for changes in ten-year rates ($dgs10$) and two-year rates ($dgs2$).

45. Use dataset INTERESTRATES presented in Chapter 17.8. Consider the relationship between changes in five-year rates ($dgs5$) and changes in one-year rates ($dgs1$) using an ADL(1,1) model.

    (a) Regress $dgs5_t$ on an intercept, $dgs5_{t-1}$, $dgs1_t$ and $dgs1_{t-1}$.

    (b) Does the residual appear to be serially correlated? Explain.

    (c) Regress $dgs5_{t+1}$ on an intercept, $dgs5_{t-1}$, $dgs1_t$ and $dgs1_{t-1}$. Use Newey-West standard errors with 1 lag. Hence give an estimate of $\Delta gs5$ one period after a one unit change in $\Delta gs1$, and a standard error of this estimate.

    (d) Regress $dgs5_{t+2}$ on an intercept, $dgs5_{t-1}$, $dgs1_t$ and $dgs1_{t-1}$. Use Newey-West standard errors with 2 lags. Hence give an estimate of $\Delta gs5$ two periods after a one unit change in $\Delta gs1$, and a standard error of this estimate.

46. Repeat the previous exercise for changes in ten-year rates ($dgs10$) and two-year rates ($dgs2$).

Appendix A

Using Statistical Packages

This chapter begins with general issues that arise regardless of the statistical package used. It then introduces several statistical packages often used by economists and economics students: the commercial package Stata, the free packages R and Gretl, and the commercial package Eviews. The spreadsheet Excel is also considered. Python is not covered here; it can be used within Stata version 16 and later versions.

The statistical packages have graphical user interfaces that enable one to implement analysis by selecting relevant icons and then selecting or entering relevant information. For replicability and for lengthier and more advanced analysis, however, it is best to use commands collected into a script or program file.

Introductory examples of such scripts are provided in this appendix for each of the statistical packages. Additional package-specific details for some commonly-used methods are given in relevant parts of the main text; see the book index entry *statistical packages* for page references for ways to implement in Stata, R, Gretl and Eviews the following: random samples, histograms, kernel density estimates, nonparametric regression, robust standard errors, joint hypothesis tests, prediction, missing data codes, sets of indicator variables, marginal effects, fixed and random effects for clustered and panel data, and nonlinear models such as logit, probit and Poisson.

Finally, the book website provides chapter-by-chapter scripts in Stata, R and Gretl that reproduce the analysis for the entire book.

A.1 General Issues

This section addresses the following general issues that arise regardless of what statistical package is used.

- How to obtain help.

- How to input commands.

- How to write a script.

- How to stop command execution.

- How to use a working directory.

- How to read in data.

- How to check that the data are correctly read in.

- How to perform statistical analysis with missing data.

- How to save results.

- How to incorporate these results into a word processor.

A.1.1   Help

Statistical packages generally have built-in help that provides an overview of commands and a short description of specific commands. This can be obtained through the help menu. For some packages help on a specific command can also be obtained by directly typing in the command window.

Reference manuals for statistical packages can generally be downloaded as free pdf files through the help menu. Statistical package websites usually provide tutorials, often available as PowerPoint slides or short video clips. And web searches such as "OLS regression in R" can be useful.

A.1.2   Inputting Commands

Statistical packages have a **windowing interface** or **graphical user interface** (GUI) that enables inputting commands by using **drop-down menus**. For example, to obtain descriptive statistics in Stata, choose the menu for Statistics, the sub-menu for Summary, Tables, and Tests, the subsequent sub-menu Summary and Descriptive Statistics, the further sub-menu Summary Statistics, and within that choose the relevant variable(s), the range of observations, and additional options such as whether to display additional statistics beyond those reported by default. This is the best way to begin using a package.

Once you have familiarity with the package, however, it is often quicker to directly type in the relevant command in the statistical package's **command window**. In Stata, for example, the command `summarize price` gives descriptive statistics for the variable *price*. For highly customized graphs, however, it may be easier to use the windowing interface. Note that most statistical packages are case-sensitive – commands must use the correct case (usually lower case) and `price` and `PRICE` are different variables.

A.1.3   Scripts

For analysis requiring many commands, or lengthier commands, it is best to collect all the commands into a **script**, also called a **program**, that is then stored as a plain text file. Then execute or run the entire script. Double-clicking on the script file opens the package's editor, provided your computer recognizes that the extension used for your script file is associated with your statistical package. Alternatively enter the statistical package and read in the script from the File menu.

Table A.1: Statistical packages: File-name extensions for script files and data files.

Package	Script file	Data file	Results also in Data File?
Stata	.do or .ado	.dta	No
R	.R of .r	.Rdata or .rda	Yes
Gretl	.inp	.gdt and .gretl	Yes for .gretl
Eviews	.prg	.wf1	Yes
Excel	–	.xls or .xlsx	Yes

A script provides a permanent record of how results were obtained, and makes it easy to modify and redo the analysis if necessary. Placing comments in the script can greatly improve its readability. Script files can be created using a text editor or using an editor window within the statistical package. In the latter case one can run selected portions of the script by highlighting the desired part before execution.

Script files are given different file-name extensions by different packages. These are listed in Table A.1. An example script for each specific statistical package is presented in the relevant section below.

As already noted, the book website provides chapter-by-chapter scripts in Stata, R and Gretl that reproduce the analysis for the entire book.

A.1.4 Halting Commands

In some cases a command takes a long time to execute or produces so much output that you wish to break execution of the command, without having to exit the statistical package.

The command script window for most statistical packages includes a break or stop button to stop execution of the script. Additionally there may be a hot key that also stops execution. For example, in R one can use the escape key.

A.1.5 Working Directory

It is simplest to keep datasets, script files and result files in the same directory, called a **working directory**. This avoids the need to use lengthier filenames that include the complete directory path for the file.

If the statistical package is opened directly from the working directory, for example by double-licking a script file or dataset that is in the working directory, and your computer associates the file extension with the appropriate statistical package, then the statistical package may automatically open in the desired working directory.

In other cases, after opening your statistical package you may need to use drop-down menus or type a command to change to the desired working directory.

A.1.6 Reading in Data

It can be remarkably difficult to read in data as data come in many formats. A major distinction is between text files, sometimes called ASCII files, that can be read by a simple text editor such as Windows Notepad, and formatted files such as a Stata dataset or an Excel spreadsheet, that can only be read by more specialized software that can interpret that specific format.

For **text files** the standard format is to have all variables for one observation on the one line, and separate each variable by a character. It is most common to use a comma to separate the values, so such files are usually called **comma-separated values (csv)** files and given the extension **.csv**. Other characters can be used as a separator, though if a space is used then care is needed if the data include text data with spaces, such as a variable for street address. The first line of the csv file may give the names for each of the variables.

An alternative form for a text file is a **fixed-width file** where, for example, the first variable is stored in columns 1-3, the second in columns 4-7, and so on. In that case one needs to tell the statistical package the formatting used, along with the corresponding variable names. A commonly-used extension for such files is **.txt**, though other extensions are also used.

Formatted data files are specific to each statistical package. They have the advantage over text files of being immediately readable by the statistical packages and potentially including additional information beyond the data, such as descriptions of each of the variables in the dataset. The standard file-name extensions used for data files produced by the different statistical packages are given in Table A.1.

Some of these package-specific files, notably those with extension **.rda** or **.Rdata**, **.wf1**, **.gretl**, and **.xls** or **.xlsx** can additionally include the results from statistical analysis. Files with file-name extension **.dta** and **.gdt** contain only data.

The datasets for this book are provided in two formats. Files with **extension .DTA** are saved in Stata version 11 format (Stata 11 was introduced in 2008). These can be read in Stata (version 11 and higher), and with the appropriate command(s) can be imported into R, Gretl and Eviews. Note, however, that the latter three statistical packages will not necessarily be able to read Stata datasets saved in the most recent versions of Stata. The .DTA files for this book usually include variable descriptions, called variable labels. The same datasets are also saved as comma-separated values files with **extension .CSV**.

A.1.7 Checking Data

Once data are read in one should list some of the observations and obtain summary statistics to check that the data are successfully read in. This important step cannot be overemphasized.

A common pitfall is dealing successfully with **missing values**. A code such as -999 or 999 may be used to denote a missing value. In that case care is needed to not misinterpret this as being the actual value of the variable. If a missing value is left as a blank, then the statistical package may mistakenly interpret this value as being a zero. And if an asterisk is used for missing values, then problems may arise as this is a character whereas the remaining data are numerical.

The datasets used in this book generally do not have these complications. Many have less than 1,000 observations so that student versions of statistical packages can be used.

A.1.8 Analysis with Missing Data

Statistical packages assign a particular value for missing data and have a particular way of displaying the missing data. If any variables used in an OLS regression are missing for an observation then Stata, Gretl and Eviews automatically drop that observation from the analysis. In R, however, one needs to use the `na.action=na.omit` of the `lm` function.

A.1.9 Computer Precision

Computers convert data from decimal (base 10) to binary (base 2), perform calculations in binary, and then provide results that convert the binary back to decimal. This leads to rounding error in calculations. Single precision uses 32 bits (where a bit takes value 0 or 1) and has precision of approximately 10^{-7} while double precision uses 64 bits and has precision of approximately 10^{-16}. For example, OLS residuals may not sum to exactly zero, especially if single precision is used. For most purposes such rounding error is inconsequential, but if precision is required then programs should store data in double precision and perform calculations in double precision.

A.1.10 Basic Statistical and Regression Analysis

For univariate analysis all packages have a command that provides summary statistics. Not all packages have commands that directly provide 95% confidence intervals for the mean and hypothesis tests on the mean. Then some additional coding is needed using stored results from summary statistics. For histograms and smoothed histograms different packages have different defaults for bin width, for example, leading to some difference across packages.

For regression all packages have an OLS command that provides coefficients, default standard errors, t statistics and p-values, but not necessarily 95% confidence intervals, and standard measures of model fit including the overall F test. Different statistical packages can use different variants of robust standard errors so that, for example, HAC-robust standard errors may differ somewhat across packages; see Chapter 12.1.9. For nonparametric regression different packages have different defaults for bandwidth, for example, leading to some difference across packages.

Analysis of cross-section data is relatively straightforward. Methods specific to panel data and time series data require additional use of commands that define the structure of the data, and, for example, commands to lag variables.

Different packages use different random number generators, so any analysis that involves simulated datasets or simulation analysis will differ somewhat across statistical packages.

A.1.11 Saving Results

It is important to save results, along with the commands used to obtain these results.

Stata saves text results, though not graphs, in a results file, called a **log file**. For Stata create the log file as soon as you start analysis as only results from that point on are saved. For R, Gretl, Eviews and Excel both data and results can be saved in a special format file with filename extension, respectively, **.rda**, **.gretl**, **.wf1** and **.xls**. Results in these files can be cut and pasted into a word processor. For R, Gretl and Eviews, it is also possible to send results to a log file.

Statistical packages often store graphics internally in a special format that can only be read by that package. To read the graph into a word processor graphs need to be saved in an appropriate graphics file format. Common **graphics file formats** are Windows Metafile (extension **.wmf**) and extended Windows Metafile (extension **.emf**) if working in a PC Windows environment, Portable Network Graphics (extension **.png**) and Encapsulated Postscript (extension **.eps**). The format to save in will vary with the word processor and the computer platform that you use. For instance, for Microsoft Word use .wmf, and for Latex use .eps or .png formats.

A.1.12   Reporting Results in a Word Processor

Descriptive statistics and regression output are provided in a **monospace font** where each character takes up the same space, so that output table columns will be properly aligned. When such output is copied into a word processor or text editor one should therefore change to a monospace font, such as Courier New or Lucinda Console.

Output from a statistical package can be voluminous. For reports and assignment answers only the essential output should be included.

A.2   Stata Essentials

Stata is a commercial statistical package that is used mostly in economics and related social sciences, especially political science and sociology, and in biostatistics. For standard analysis of individual-level economics data Stata is the main statistical package used by economics researchers. Cheaper student versions are available and many universities provide free access to Stata. The Stata website `stata.com` provides the free *User's Guide*, many other free documents that run to over 15,000 pages, and video tutorials. A helpful website is `http://www.ats.ucla.edu/stat/stata/`.

Stata is programmable, leading to some **user-written commands** or **packages**. For this book no user-written commands are needed. For introductory analysis of economics data the most useful such command is the `freduse` command to obtain macroeconomic time series data. In Stata give command `findit freduse`, to locate the command and then click on the install button. Command `help freduse` then explains how to use the command.

Example datasets can be obtained within Stata by selecting File > Example Datasets ... A common Stata manual dataset to use is file `auto.dta`. To read in your own data and to save key output it is best to first use File > Change Working Directory ... to change to the directory that has the dataset.

One can begin to learn Stata by initially using the Stata drop-down menus. The resulting output is preceded by the actual Stata command, so one can potentially learn and remember the direct commands for future use. To save results, create a log file immediately upon opening Stata by choosing menu File > Log > Begin ... in the Results Window.

Basic Stata commands, such as those needed for this book, are relatively straightforward. Note that like many statistical packages, Stata is case sensitive. As an alternative to using the dropdown menus, commands can be directly typed in at the Command Window, a small window that is usually beneath the Results Window. Even better in the long run, a script can be stored in a file with file-name extension **.do**. The script file can be opened from outside Stata by double-clicking on the file, or within Stata by choosing menu File > Do... and selecting the desired file.

An example Stata script, with many of the key commands needed for this book, is the following.

```
* aed_example.do   Stata example script written 9/30/2020
* Create a plain text log file that contains commands and results
log using Stataresults.txt, text replace
* Read in Stata dataset HOUSE.DTA; first clear any existing data in memory
clear
use AED_HOUSE.DTA
* Example of help command - how to import datasets in different formats
help import
* Descriptive statistics for all variables
summarize
* List first five observations for all variables
list in 1/5
* More detailed descriptive statistics including skewness and kurtosis
summarize price, detail
* Example of creating a new variable
generate PriceperSqfoot = price/size
* Histogram
histogram price
* Kernel density plot (a smoothed histogram)
kdensity price
* Two-way scatterplot with regression line saved in .png graphic format
scatter price size || lfit price size, saving(graphstata.gph, replace)
graph export graphstata.png, replace
* Descriptive statistics for two variables
summarize price size
* More detailed descriptive statistics for one variable
summarize price, detail
* Confidence intervals for a single variable
mean price
* t test that population mean price = 250000
ttest price == 250000
* Multiple OLS regression - same as chapter 10
regress price size lotsize bedrooms bathrooms age monthsold
* Same regression with heteroskedastic-robust standard errors
regress price size lotsize bedrooms bathrooms age monthsold, vce(robust)
* Test subset of regressors equal to zero
test lotsize bedrooms bathrooms age monthsold
* Save the Stata dataset
save Stataexample.dta, replace
```

```
* Close the log file
log close results.txt
* Exit Stata
exit
```

Lines preceded by an asterisk (*) and any text after two forward slashes (//) are interpreted as comments. Stata commands include options, given after a comma. For example, in the first `log` command the option `text` means that the output is saved as a plain text file and the option `replace` permits any previous version of the same file to be overwritten. Unlike most other packages, many Stata commands and options can be abbreviated. For example, `summarize` can be shortened to `sum` or even `su`. The script requires that file `AED_HOUSE.DTA` is in the working directory, and not in some other directory. As already noted, graphs may be saved in several different graphics formats – the png format used here will not work in all word processors. The command `exit` results in automatically exiting Stata once the script is run.

Figure A.1 gives some of the output from Stata. This is the form that the output takes both on the screen and in the log file. Commands are preceded by a period, while results from the command are not.

The first set of results in Figure A.1 are descriptive statistics – the number of non-missing observations for each variable, the sample mean, the standard deviation, and the minimum and maximum sample values of the variable. More complete summary statistics, including the median, quartiles and skewness and kurtosis statistics, can be obtained by using option `detail` of the `summarize` command. For variable *price* this yields skewness statistic 1.5608 and kurtosis statistic 5.6127.

The second set of results in Figure A.1 gives a 95 percent confidence interval for the population mean price that is (239688, 268133). It also gives the standard error of the sample mean, which is the standard deviation 37390.71 divided by $\sqrt{29}$.

The third set of results in Figure A.1 are regression results that are identical to those given in Table 10.4 and discussed in Chapters 10.7 and 11.7. Additionally the top left-hand corner of the regression output includes an analysis of variance table that gives the explained sum of squares, which Stata calls the model sum of squares, the residual sum of squares and the total sum of squares. Note that Stata automatically includes an intercept, and this is reported as the final regression coefficient, not the first. Additional regression output, such as standardized regression coefficients, can be obtained as options to the `regress` command. And to learn how to obtain still further output give command `help regress postestimation`.

A.3 R Essentials

R is a free programming language that is used especially in the mathematical and physical sciences, including statistics, and is increasingly used in economics. The website http://www.r-project.org/ provides the R package for free download as well as links to manuals, and a helpful website is http://www.ats.ucla.edu/stat/r/.

The base installation of R is quite basic. R is programmable, however, leading to programs called **packages** that provide commands and functions for more detailed statistical and regression

```
. * Descriptive statistics for two variables
. summarize price size
```

Variable	Obs	Mean	Std. Dev.	Min	Max
price	29	253910.3	37390.71	204000	375000
size	29	1882.759	398.2721	1400	3300

```
. * Confidence intervals for a single variable
. mean price
```

```
Mean estimation                    Number of obs    =         29
```

	Mean	Std. Err.	[95% Conf. Interval]	
price	253910.3	6943.281	239687.7	268133

```
. * Multiple OLS regression - same as chapter 10
. regress price size lotsize bedrooms bathrooms age monthsold
```

Source	SS	df	MS			
				Number of obs	=	29
				F(6, 22)	=	6.83
Model	2.5466e+10	6	4.2444e+09	Prob > F	=	0.0003
Residual	1.3679e+10	22	621790812	R-squared	=	0.6506
				Adj R-squared	=	0.5552
Total	3.9146e+10	28	1.3981e+09	Root MSE	=	24936

price	Coef.	Std. Err.	t	P>|t|	[95% Conf. Interval]	
size	68.36942	15.38947	4.44	0.000	36.45361	100.2852
lotsize	2303.221	7226.535	0.32	0.753	-12683.7	17290.14
bedrooms	2685.315	9192.526	0.29	0.773	-16378.82	21749.45
bathrooms	6832.88	15721.19	0.43	0.668	-25770.88	39436.64
age	-833.0386	719.3345	-1.16	0.259	-2324.847	658.7699
monthsold	-2088.504	3520.898	-0.59	0.559	-9390.399	5213.392
_cons	137791.1	61464.95	2.24	0.035	10320.56	265261.6

Figure A.1: Stata: Sample output

analysis and easier to read output. Any package must be installed once in the **library** subdirectory of R on your computer. Additionally, any R script or interactive analysis that uses the commands must first call the library for the necessary package. There are thousands of R packages, and a given statistical procedure may be included in several different packages, with different command names. So there can be more than one way to implement a given procedure in R. Furthermore, better packages may supplant the packages used here.

It is easiest to begin by using **R Commander**, a free Windows interface front-end to R with drop-down menus that needs to be installed separately from installation of R. R Commander provides two windows. An output window lists the output from the commands. A script window provides the associated commands in the R programming language. This provides a convenient way to learn the commands, as is also the case for Stata and Gretl. And from the script window one can directly run (or submit) commands. So it is easy to modify an existing command, such as adding R options not made available through the drop-down menus, and execute the modified command. Note that R, like many packages, is case sensitive. R Commander provides only a subset of R through the Windows interface, so ultimately you need to program in R.

For direct programming in R a good free Windows interface to use is **R Studio**. R stores both data and output as objects in a file with file-name extension **.Rda**. The sink command in R creates a log file, but this does not list all commands and results. An alternative is to use no log file. Then a complete text listing of both commands and results is given in the Console Window of R Studio, after running the script. This output can be cut and pasted into a Word processor. Even simpler is to use the Teachingdemos package as shown below.

The following R commands install packages that are used in the R code below. This code should be executed if these packages are not already included in the R libraries for your installation of R.

```
# Once only - Install any needed packages in your version of R
install.packages("TeachingDemos")
install.packages("foreign")
install.packages("psych")
install.packages("MASS")
install.packages("sandwich")
install.packages("lmtest")
install.packages("car")
```

An example R script, with many of the key commands needed for this book, is the following:

```
# aed_example.R   R example script written 9/20/2020
# Clear the workspace
rm(list=ls())
# Create a log file with commands and results - requires package TeachingDemos
library(TeachingDemos)
txtStart("Rresults.txt")
# Read in the Stata data set - requires package foreign
library(foreign)
data.appxA <- read.dta(file = "AED_HOUSE.DTA")
```

```
# Allow variables in database to be accessed simply by giving names
attach(data.appxA)
# Example of help command
help(load)
# Summary statistics - very basic
summary(data.appxA)
# Detailed descriptive statistics for two variables - uses package pscyh
library(psych)
describe(cbind(price,size))
# List the first ten observations
head(data.appxA)
# Histogram
hist(price)
# Kernel density plot (a smoothed histogram)
plot(density(price))
# Two-way scatterplot with regression line and save as PNG file
png("graphr.png")
reg1 <- lm(price~size)
plot(size,price)
abline(reg1)
dev.off()
# Multiple OLS regression - same as chapter 10
model1.ols <- lm(price ~size+lotsize+bedrooms+bathrooms+age+monthsold)
summary(model1.ols)
# Confidence interval for model parameters - uses package MASS
library(MASS)
confint(model1.ols)
# Same regression with heteroskedastic-robust standard errors
# Package sandwich gives robust variance estimate and hence robust standard errors
# For heteroskedastic-robust the book has used variance type HC1
library(sandwich)
robvar <- vcovHC(model1.ols, type = "HC1")
# For individual tests and CI's use coeftest and coefci in package lmtest
library(lmtest)
coeftest(model1.ols, vcov = robvar)
coefci(model1.ols, vcov = robvar)
# For multiple hypothesis tests use linearHypothesis command in package car
library(car)
linearHypothesis(model1.ols,c("bedrooms=0","bathrooms=0"), vcov=robvar)
# Save workspace in .RData file
save.image(file="Rexample.Rdata")
# Close output file
```

```
txtStop()
# exit R
quit(save="no")
```

Lines preceded by a hash mark (#) are interpreted as comments. The package `TeachingDemos` command `txtStart` sends all commands and results to a text file and is better than the base installation command `sink`. The script requires that file AED_HOUSE.DTA is in the working (default) directory, and not some other directory. The package `foreign` command `read.dta` reads a file that is a Stata versions 5 to 12 formatted dataset. The package `psych` command `describe` gives much more detailed descriptive statistics than the command `summary`. The command for regression automatically includes an intercept. The package `MASS` command `confint` gives confidence intervals after OLS regression – these are not included in the basic summary of OLS results. The package `Sandwich` commands `vcovHC`, `vcovCL`, `vcovHAC` can be used to obtain, respectively, heteroskedastic-robust, cluster-robust and HAC standard errors; see Chapter 12.1.9 for further details. The package `lmtest` commands `coeftest` and `coefci` give resulting t-tests and confidence intervals. The package `car` command `linearHypothesis` enables tests of multiple hypotheses such as subsets of regressors. The command `save.image` saves all the results (objects and functions) in an Rdata file that can subsequently read into R using command `load("Rexample.Rdata")`.

Figure A.2 gives some of the output from R.

The first set of results in Figure A.2 provides a wide range of descriptive statistics. The symmetry and excess kurtosis statistics differ a little from those obtained using the other packages, due to use of slightly different formulae.

The second set of results in Figure A.2 are regression results that are identical to those given in Table 10.4 and discussed in Chapters 10.7 and 11.7. Unlike some of the other packages, the regression output does not include an analysis of variance table as econometrics analysis does not use this table.

A.4 Gretl Essentials

Gretl is a free statistical package developed specifically for students learning econometrics. It covers considerably more econometrics methods than those presented in this book. The Gretl website `gretl.sourceforge.net` provides the package for free download as well as documentation - the key references are a *User's Guide* and the *Command Reference*.

Gretl is programmable, leading to some **function packages** that provide additional commands and functions. For this book the only function package that is used is `lp-mfx` for marginal effects in logit and probit models. In interactive use, choose `File > Function Packages > On server` to open the list of available packages. To install `lp-mfx`, click on the diskette icon on the menu bar or right-click and choose install. Additionally, any R script or interactive analysis that uses the commands must first include the function; give command `include lp-mfx.gfn`.

In interactive use, example datasets can be obtained by selecting File > Open data > Sample File ... To read in your own data it is best to first use File > Working Directory ... to change to the directory that has the dataset.

```
                           .
> library(psych)
> describe(cbind(price, size))
      vars  n        mean        sd median trimmed       mad     min     max   range
price    1 29 253910.34 37390.71 244000  249296 22239.00 204000 375000 171000
size     2 29    1882.76   398.27   1800    1836   296.52    1400    3300    1900
      skew kurtosis       se
price 1.48     2.23 6943.28
size  1.64     3.29   73.96
> model.ols <- lm(price ~ size + lotsize + bedrooms + bathrooms +
+ age + monthsold)
> summary(model.ols)

Call:
lm(formula = price ~ size + lotsize + bedrooms + bathrooms +
    age + monthsold)

Residuals:
   Min    1Q Median    3Q    Max
-37613 -18463  -1215  16800  43130

Coefficients:
             Estimate Std. Error t value Pr(>|t|)
(Intercept) 137791.07   61464.95   2.242 0.035387 *
size            68.37      15.39   4.443 0.000205 ***
lotsize       2303.22    7226.54   0.319 0.752947
bedrooms      2685.32    9192.53   0.292 0.772932
bathrooms     6832.88   15721.19   0.435 0.668065
age           -833.04     719.33  -1.158 0.259254
monthsold    -2088.50    3520.90  -0.593 0.559114
---
Signif. codes:  0 '***' 0.001 '**' 0.01 '*' 0.05 '.' 0.1 ' ' 1

Residual standard error: 24940 on 22 degrees of freedom
Multiple R-squared:  0.6506,    Adjusted R-squared:  0.5552
F-statistic: 6.826 on 6 and 22 DF,  p-value: 0.0003424
```

Figure A.2: R: Sample output

Gretl stores data in a data file with extension .gdt. It also stores both data and output as objects in a container called a **session file** with file-name extension **.gretl**. In order for output to be saved in the session file, one selects File > Save to session from the relevant results window. Then before exiting from Gretl choose from the main Gretl window File > Sessions Files > Save session. Storing results in a session file is qualitatively similar to storing results in an Excel worksheet.

One can begin to learn Gretl by initially using such Gretl drop-down menus. The basic commands, though not necessarily subsequent options chosen through the Windows interface, can be viewed under Tools > Command log. This log file is called `session.inp` and can be saved, under a different name, by choosing the "Save as" option once viewing the log file.

Basic Gretl commands, such as those needed for this book, are relatively straightforward. Example Gretl scripts can be obtained by selecting File > Script Files > Practice file ... Note that like many other statistical packages, Gretl is case sensitive. Commands can be given from the command window, opened by choosing Tools > Gretl console. Or a script can be stored in a file with extension **.inp**. The script can be opened from outside Gretl by double-clicking on the file, or within Gretl by choosing menu File > Script Files > User file ... and selecting the desired file.

Output can be directed to a text file using command `outfile`. This output includes comments, commands and resulting text output.

Gretl does not automatically provide confidence intervals after regression. When using the Windows interface, after regression (menu Model > Ordinary Least Squares ...), within the regression output window select Analysis > Confidence intervals for coefficients. This method can also be used to obtain confidence intervals for a single variable – simply regress the variable on an intercept. When running Gretl using a script, however, there appears to be no way to obtain confidence intervals other than through saving coefficients and standard errors and writing code to compute the resultant confidence intervals.

An example Gretl script, with many of the key commands needed for this book, is the following.

```
# aed_example.inp   Gretl example script written 4/1/2014
# Set working directory which will contain any output and graph files
set workdir C:\Users\.....    # Give your directory here
# Output file that contains both commands and results
outfile Gretlresults.txt -- write
# Read in the Stata dataset AED_HOUSE.DTA
# Gretl treats a file ending with .DTA as being in Stata dataset format
open AED_HOUSE.DTA
# Example of help command - how to import datasets in different formats
help open
# Descriptive statistics for all variables
summary
# List data for a single variable
price
# Example of creating a new variable
genr PriceperSqfoot = price/size
# Two-way scatterplot with regression line saved in .png graphic format
```

```
graph1 <- gnuplot price size --output=graphgretl.png
# 95% Confidence interval for one variable
summary price
scalar lb = mean(price) - critical(t,$nobs-1,0.025) * sd(price)/sqrt($nobs)
scalar ub = mean(price) + critical(t,$nobs-1,0.025) * sd(price)/sqrt($nobs)
# Two-sided t test that population mean price = 250000
summary price
scalar tstat = (mean(price) - 250000) / (sd(price)/sqrt($nobs))
scalar p = 2*pvalue(t,$nobs-1,abs(tstat))
# Descriptive statistics for two variables
summary price size
# Multiple OLS regression - same as chapter 10
model1 <- ols price const size lotsize bedrooms bathrooms age monthsold
# 95% confidence interval for regressor size
scalar lb = $coeff(size) - critical(t,$df,0.025) * $stderr(size)
scalar ub = $coeff(size) + critical(t,$df,0.025) * $stderr(size)
printf "The 95%% confidence interval is (%.4f, %.4f)\n",lb,ub
# Same regression with heteroskedastic robust standard errors
model2 <- ols price const size lotsize bedrooms bathrooms age monthsold --robust
# Save in a Gretl data file the dataset
store Gretldata.gdt
# Close output file
outfile ---close
# Exit Gretl
quit
```

Lines preceded by a hash mark (#) are interpreted as comments. The script requires that file AED_HOUSE.DTA is in the working (default) directory, and not some other directory. Gretl treats a file with extension .DTA (or .dta) as a Stata format dataset, rather than as a Gretl dataset. This Gretl script includes examples of commands to manually perform a t test and to compute confidence intervals, since there is no Gretl command to do so. The command for regression requires the user to explicitly include the intercept, if one is desired, using the Gretl constructed variable called const. Leading text such as model1 <- is only necessary if you want to include the results in the session file, in this case as model1.

The output file includes results from running the script, aside from graphs, as well as the commands and comments. In principle a session file can be saved after running this script. But this seems possible only if commands are entered from the dropdown menus or from the Command Console, rather than through running an entire script.

Figure A.3 gives some of the output from Gretl. This is the form that the output takes in the script output window and in the corresponding text file if it is saved. Commands are preceded by a question mark, while results from the command are not.

The first set of results in Figure A.3 provides a wide range of descriptive statistics. The kurtosis statistic given is that for excess kurtosis.

```
Generated scalar p = 0.577792
# Descriptive statistics for two variables
? summary price size
```

	Mean	Median	Minimum	Maximum
price	2.5391e+005	2.4400e+005	2.0400e+005	3.7500e+005
size	1882.8	1800.0	1400.0	3300.0

	Std. Dev.	C.V.	Skewness	Ex. kurtosis
price	37391	0.14726	1.5608	2.6127
size	398.27	0.21154	1.7277	3.7428

	5% perc.	95% perc.	IQ range	Missing obs.
price	2.0800e+005	3.5750e+005	39500	0
size	1400.0	2950.0	450.00	0

```
# Multiple OLS regression - same as chapter 10
? model1 <- ols price const size lotsize bedrooms bathrooms age monthsold

model1: OLS, using observations 1-29
Dependent variable: price
```

	coefficient	std. error	t-ratio	p-value	
const	137791	61465.0	2.242	0.0354	**
size	68.3694	15.3895	4.443	0.0002	***
lotsize	2303.22	7226.54	0.3187	0.7529	
bedrooms	2685.32	9192.53	0.2921	0.7729	
bathrooms	6832.88	15721.2	0.4346	0.6681	
age	−833.039	719.335	−1.158	0.2593	
monthsold	−2088.50	3520.90	−0.5932	0.5591	

Mean dependent var	253910.3	S.D. dependent var	37390.71
Sum squared resid	1.37e+10	S.E. of regression	24935.73
R-squared	0.650553	Adjusted R-squared	0.555249
F(6, 22)	6.826098	P-value(F)	0.000342
Log-likelihood	−330.7412	Akaike criterion	675.4824
Schwarz criterion	685.0535	Hannan-Quinn	678.4799

```
Excluding the constant, p-value was highest for variable 4 (bedrooms)
```

Figure A.3: Gretl: Sample output

The second set of results in Figure A.3 are regression results that are identical to those given in Table 10.4 and discussed in Chapters 10.7 and 11.7. Unlike some of the other packages, the regression output does not include an analysis of variance table as econometrics analysis does not use this table. The regression output includes the Schwarz, Akaike and Hannan-Quinn criteria for model fit; see Chapter 10.6.

A.5 Eviews Essentials

Eviews is a commercial statistical package that is used mostly in economics, though is more broadly especially useful for its specialty of analysis of time series data. The Eviews website `eviews.com` provides the free documentation *Eviews Illustrated* for interactive use and *Command Reference* for writing scripts. **Eviews emphasizes interactive use.** For this reason scripts for each chapter of this book are not provided for Eviews; an example of and Eviews script is given below. A free student-lite version is available that uses an (adequate) older version of Eviews and, at the time of writing, is restricted to saving and exporting datasets with no more than 1,500 observations per variable and 15,000 total observations.

Eviews stores both data and output as objects in a container called a **workfile**, with file-name extension **.wf1**. Some output is automatically saved in the workfile, while other output such as that from regression needs to be explicitly named as an **object** in order for it to be saved in the workfile. Storing results in a workfile is qualitatively similar to storing results in an Excel worksheet. And if desired there can be more than one worksheet, which Eviews calls a **page**. As for Excel spreadsheet analysis, results are linked to the data. So if the data is changed then the results also change. If instead one wants the results to be permanent, the command `freeze` is used.

An example workfile can be obtained by selecting File > New > Workfile, going to the Eviews directory and within this selecting subdirectory Example Files / EV8 Manual Data / Chapter 2 - A Demonstration / and opening file demo.wf1. This includes dataset variables, which Eviews calls series, and results from two estimated OLS equations.

To read in your own data select File > Open, and then select either Foreign Data as Workfile or Eviews Workfile, depending on whether or not the data is already in an Eviews workfile. Once you have browsed to find the dataset or workfile check the option Update default directory to set the working directory. This will remain the working directory in subsequent uses of Eviews, until you elect to change it. The working directory can also be set using the `cd` command.

Eviews does not automatically create a log file. Instead the default is to store results in the workfile. These results can then be cut and pasted into a word processor. Additionally one can direct output to a log file, discussed after the script below.

Eviews does not provide confidence intervals and t tests in the univariate case. One can construct these manually, see the code below. Alternatively, a confidence interval for a single variable can be obtained following OLS regression of the variable on just an intercept and then using the confidence interval option within regression.

Eviews commands can be directly entered in the Command Window, located immediately below the menu bar. Eviews, unlike many other packages, is not case sensitive. Alternatively, an Eviews command script can be stored in a file with file-name extension **.prg**. Unlike Stata and Gretl, however, using the Eviews windows interface does not lead to a listing of the corresponding Eviews command. This makes it harder to learn the Eviews command language, and **Eviews is much easier to use interactively.** For this reason scripts for each chapter of this book are not provided for Eviews. The script can be opened from outside by double-clicking on the file, or within Eviews by choosing menu File > Run... and selecting the desired file. Chapter 12 of the Eviews 12 Command and Programming Reference summarizes Eviews basic commands.

An example Eviews script, with many of the commands needed for this book, is the following.

```
' aed_example.prg   Eviews example script written 09/30/2020
' Create a log file that contains just results in two steps
' First send all output to the printer - command pon
' Second redirect printer output to an RTF file - command output
pon
output(r) Eviewsresults.rtf
' Read in Stata dataset AED_HOUSE.DTA
open AED_HOUSE.DTA
' Create an object named gr0 that contains the variables price and size
group gr0 price size
' List the data for the two variables in object gr0
show gr0
' Descriptive statistics for the two variables
gr0.stats
' Example of creating a new variable
genr PriceperSqfoot = price/size
' Two-way scatterplot with regression line saved in .emf graphic format
freeze(grapheviews) gr0.scat(r)
grapheviews.save(t=wtf) grapheviews
' 95% confidence interval for one variable
scalar stderror = @stdev(price)/@sqrt(@obs(price))
scalar lb = @mean(price) - @qtdist(.975,@obs(price)-1)*stderror
scalar ub = @mean(price) + @qtdist(.975,@obs(price)-1)*stderror
show lb
show ub
' Two-sided t test that population mean Price = 250000
scalar tstat = (@mean(price)-250000) / (@stdev(price)/@sqrt(@obs(price)))
scalar p = 2*(1-@ctdist(tstat,@obs(price)-1))
show tstat
show p
' OLS regression - same as chapter 10 - results are not saved in an object
ls price c size lotsize bedrooms bathrooms age monthsold
' Same regression with results saved in equation object eq1
equation eq1.ls price c size lotsize bedrooms bathrooms age monthsold
' 95% confidence interval for parameters
```

```
eq1.cinterval(p) .95
' Same regression with heteroskedastic robust standard errors - saved as eq1rob
equation eq1rob.ls(cov-White) price c size lotsize bedrooms bathrooms age monthsold
' Save in an Eviews workfile the preceding analysis
save Eviewsexample.wf1
' Close output file
poff
' Exit Eviews
exit
```

Lines preceded by a single-quote (') are interpreted as comments, and command options appear in parentheses.

The command `output(r)` sends any text and graphics output that would normally be sent to the printer to instead be sent to a **rich text format** (**RTF**) file. Alternatively `output(t)` sends only text output, but not graph output, to a text file. Command `pon` sends output from each command to a printer. The commands `pon` and `poff` do not work in interactive use. If giving commands interactively, to send output to a file we again use the preceding `output` command, but now the option (`p`) needs to be used for each command that we want to obtain output for. For example the commands become `gr0.stats(p)`, `show(p)` and `eq1.ls(p)`. Output can also be sent to a **spool** file – this is not covered here. Note that if the file named in the `output` command already exists then Eviews appends the new output to the end of the file.

Eviews interprets a file with extension .DTA as a Stata dataset, rather than as an Eviews dataset. The script requires that file AED_HOUSE.DTA is in the working (default) directory, and not in some other directory. Command `freeze` preserves a graph or table as an object in the workfile. This Eviews script includes examples of commands to manually compute confidence intervals and perform a t test. The command `ls` leads to OLS regression, and option (`cov_White`) leads to heteroskedastic-robust standard errors. By defining the equation `eq.ls`, the OLS results will be preserved in the workfile as the object `eq1`. The command `exit` results in automatically exiting Eviews once the script is run.

The resulting workfile includes data on each variable, the computed scalars such as `ub`, and the results for the named objects such as `gr0.stats`, `grapheviews` and `eq1.ls`. The log file includes all results, but not the commands that produced the results.

Figure A.4 gives some of the output from Eviews. Note that the output file does not include the command that produced the output.

The first set of results in Figure A.4 are descriptive statistics. These include the Jarque-Bera test for whether the data are normally distributed with common mean and variance. Since $p < .05$ the null hypothesis of normality is rejected at significance level 0.05.

The second set of results in Figure A.4 are regression results that are identical to those given in Table 10.4 and discussed in Chapters 10.7 and 11.7. Unlike some of the other packages, the regression output does not include an analysis of variance table as econometrics analysis does not use this table. The regression output includes the Schwarz, Akaike and Hannan-Quinn criteria for model fit, where these criteria defined in Chapter 10.6 have been divided by the number of observations, here 29. The Durbin-Watson statistic is for test of whether the error term in a time

	PRICE	SIZE
Mean	253910.3	1882.759
Median	244000.0	1800.000
Maximum	375000.0	3300.000
Minimum	204000.0	1400.000
Std. Dev.	37390.71	398.2721
Skewness	1.560837	1.727665
Kurtosis	5.612707	6.742809
Jarque-Bera	20.02340	31.35374
Probability	0.000045	0.000000
Sum	7363400.	54600.00
Sum Sq. Dev.	3.91E+10	4441379.
Observations	29	29

Dependent Variable: PRICE
Method: Least Squares
Date: 01/22/14   Time: 12:02
Sample: 1 29
Included observations: 29

Variable	Coefficient	Std. Error	t-Statistic	Prob.
C	137791.1	61464.95	2.241783	0.0354
SIZE	68.36942	15.38947	4.442610	0.0002
LOTSIZE	2303.221	7226.535	0.318717	0.7529
BEDROOMS	2685.315	9192.526	0.292119	0.7729
BATHROOMS	6832.880	15721.19	0.434629	0.6681
AGE	-833.0386	719.3345	-1.158068	0.2593
MONTHSOLD	-2088.504	3520.898	-0.593174	0.5591

R-squared	0.650553	Mean dependent var	253910.3
Adjusted R-squared	0.555249	S.D. dependent var	37390.71
S.E. of regression	24935.73	Akaike info criterion	23.29250
Sum squared resid	1.37E+10	Schwarz criterion	23.62253
Log likelihood	-330.7412	Hannan-Quinn criter.	23.39586
F-statistic	6.826098	Durbin-Watson stat	1.259370
Prob(F-statistic)	0.000342		

Figure A.4: Eviews: Sample output.

series model is autocorrelated.

A.6 Excel and Google Sheets Spreadsheet Applications

Excel is a commercial spreadsheet package that is part of Microsoft Office. It has very limited statistical capabilities compared to the preceding statistical packages, as it is a spreadsheet package and not a statistical package. If at all possible, use a statistical package rather than Excel to implement the methods in this book. The free spreadsheet application **Google Sheets** can be used in place of Excel.

Excel includes single functions that compute some key statistical quantities. For example, typing in cell A31 the command =AVERAGE(A2:A30) sets cell A31 equal to the average of the values in rows 2 to 30 of column A. Excel is available in many different languages, and commands such as AVERAGE will differ with the language version.

It is much more convenient, however, to use the **Data Analysis ToolPak** in Excel as this automatically combines several commands at once, such as computing the several different quantities reported in a table of descriptive statistics. However, this toolpack provides very few statistical methods. Furthermore Excel's Data Analysis ToolPak is not available on Apple computers running under Apple's IOS as it is an Excel add-on that is written in visual basic, a programming language specific to Microsoft Windows. The **XLMiner Analysis Toolpack**, that essentially replicates the Excel Data Analysis Toolpack, is freely available for both Excel and Google Sheets.

For PC users the Data Analysis ToolPak appears at the right-end of the Data menu as Data Analysis in Excel 2007 and later versions, and appears in the Tools menu of earlier versions of Excel. Because the Data Analysis Toolpak is an Excel add-in, it may not be automatically loaded when you open Excel. If this is the case, an internet search on `install excel analysis toolpak` will provide instructions on how to do so.

Figure A.5 provides some essential output from Excel analysis of file HOUSE.CSV that includes variable names in the first row. The descriptive statistics output is obtained by choosing Descriptive Statistics in the Data Analysis Toolpak. Then choose input range \$A\$1:\$B\$30, data grouped by columns, labels in first row, summary statistics, confidence level for the mean (with default 95%) and set k^{th} largest and k^{th} smallest at 8, as this gives the upper and lower quartiles for a sample of size $n = 29$. The output can be placed in either the current worksheet at, say, column \$A\$32, or in a new worksheet. The entry confidence level (95%) gives the half-width of a confidence interval, so the 95% confidence interval is $253910.3 \pm 14222.60 = (239687.7, 268133.0)$. The symmetry and excess kurtosis statistics differ a little from those obtained using the other packages, due to use of slightly different formulae.

The multiple regression output in Figure A.5 is obtained by choosing Regression in the Data Analysis Toolpak. Then choose input Y range \$A\$1:\$A\$30, input X range \$B\$1:\$G\$30, labels data grouped by columns, labels in first row, and confidence level (with default 95%). Again the output can be placed in either the current worksheet at, say, column \$A\$52, or in a new worksheet. The Regression Statistics output is the usual summary statistics after regression. The ANOVA output is an analysis of variance table that gives the same sum of squares decomposition as the Stata output discussed in Appendix A.2, along with the resultant F statistic for the test of overall

Price		Size	
Mean	253910.34	Mean	1882.758621
Standard Error	6943.2807	Standard Error	73.95727789
Median	244000	Median	1800
Mode	235000	Mode	1600
Standard Deviation	37390.711	Standard Deviation	398.2721302
Sample Variance	1.398E+09	Sample Variance	158620.6897
Kurtosis	3.3656321	Kurtosis	4.717891678
Skewness	1.6472971	Skewness	1.823365476
Range	171000	Range	1900
Minimum	204000	Minimum	1400
Maximum	375000	Maximum	3300
Sum	7363400	Sum	54600
Count	29	Count	29
Largest(8)	270000	Largest(8)	2000
Smallest(8)	233000	Smallest(8)	1600
Confidence Level(95.0%)	14222.666	Confidence Level(95	151.4946142

SUMMARY OUTPUT

Regression Statistics	
Multiple R	0.8065686
R Square	0.6505528
Adjusted R Square	0.5552491
Standard Error	24935.734
Observations	29

ANOVA

	df	SS	MS	F	Significance F
Regression	6	25466429042	4244404840	6.826098	0.000342425
Residual	22	13679397855	621790811.6		
Total	28	39145826897			

	Coefficients	Standard Error	t Stat	P-value	Lower 95%	Upper 95%
Intercept	137791.07	61464.95187	2.241782699	0.035387	10320.55799	265261.573
Size	68.369419	15.38947183	4.44260984	0.000205	36.45360797	100.28523
Lotsize	2303.2214	7226.535205	0.318717242	0.752947	-12683.69529	17290.138
Bedrooms	2685.3151	9192.525674	0.292119404	0.772932	-16378.81621	21749.4465
Bathrooms	6832.88	15721.19154	0.434628635	0.668065	-25770.87557	39436.6356
Age	-833.0386	719.3345439	-1.1580684	0.259254	-2324.847132	658.769929
Monthsold	-2088.504	3520.897859	-0.59317359	0.559114	-9390.398837	5213.39159

Figure A.5: Excel: Sample output.

significance, and its associated p-value. The final regression output is the same as that given in Chapter 10. Note that Excel automatically includes a constant, and this is reported as the first regression coefficient. Additional regression diagnostics, included residual plots and line fit plots, are available as Regression options.

A.7   Critical values and p-values

In many cases output from statistical packages includes desired confidence intervals and p-values for hypothesis tests.

When this is not the case one needs to use tables or commands in a statistical package to obtain the necessary critical values for confidence intervals and to obtain either p-values or critical values for hypothesis tests.

Unfortunately, the commands are very arcane. Different packages use different function names, the degrees of freedom may be given as the first argument or the last argument of the function, and probabilities given may be in the upper tail, lower tail or both tails depending on the package used.

The first two columns of Table A.2 present commands in various packages to obtain critical values for 95% confidence intervals and for two-sided hypothesis tests at level 0.05 based on, respectively, the t_{22} distribution and the standard normal distribution. The last two columns present critical values for hypothesis tests based on, respectively, the $F_{5,22}$ distribution and the χ_5^2 distribution. The degrees of freedom chosen are those for the multiple regression of Chapter 10 with $n = 29$, $k = 7$ and, for the last two columns, a test of whether the five regressors other than *size* are statistically significant at 5%. In all cases the null hypothesis is rejected if the test statistic exceeds the critical value.

Table A.2: Statistical packages: Commands to calculate 5% critical values

	Distribution and command			
	Students t	Standard normal	F distribution	Chi-squared
	t_{22}	N(0,1)	$F_{5,22}$	χ_5^2
Stata	invttail(22,.025)	-invnormal(.025)	invFtail(5,.05)	invchi2tail(5,.05)
R	tcrit = qt(.975,22)	qnorm(.975)	qf(.95,6,22)	qchisq(.95,6)
Gretl	critical(t,22,.025)	critical(z,22,.025)	critical(F,5,22,.05)	critical(x,5,.05)
Eviews	@qtdist(.975,22)	@qnorm(.975)	@qfdist(.95,5,22)	@qchisq(.95,5)
Excel	TINV(.05,22)	NORMSINV(.975)	FINV(.05,5,22)	CHIINV(.05,5)
Value	$t_{22,.025}$ =2.07387	$z_{.025}$=1.95996	$F_{5,22,.025}$ =2.66127	$\chi_{5,.025}^2$ =11.07050

Table A.3 presents commands in various packages to obtain p-values for two-sided hypothesis tests based on respectively, the t_{22} distribution, the standard normal distribution, the $F_{5,22}$ distribution and the χ_5^2 distribution. For the first two columns the test statistic of .292 is the t statistic for test of statistical significance of the regressor *Bedrooms* in the multiple regression of Chapter 10. The F statistic of .417 is that for test of whether the five regressors other than *size* are statistically

Table A.3: Statistical packages: Commands to calculate p-values for a two-sided test.

| | Distribution and command | | | |
	Students t $\Pr[|T_{22}|>.292]$	Standard normal $\Pr[|Z|>.292]$	F distribution $\Pr[|F_{5,22}|>.417]$	Chi-squared $\Pr[\chi_5^2>5\times.417]$
Stata	2*ttail(22,.292)	2*(1-normal(.292))	Ftail(5,22,.417)	chi2tail(5,5*.417)
R	2*(1-pt(.292,22)	2*(1-pnorm(.292))	1-pf(.417,5,22)	1-pchisq(5*.417,5)
Gretl	2*pvalue(t,22,.292)	2*pvalue(z,.292)	pvalue(F,5,22,.417)	pvalue(x,5,5*.417)
Eviews	2*(1-@ctdist(.292,22))	2*(1-@cnorm(.292))	1-@cfdist(.417,5,22)	1-@cchisq(5*.417,5)
Excel	TDIST(.292,22,2)	2*(1-NORMSDIST(0.292))	FDIST(0.417,5,22)	CHIDIST(5*0.417,5)
Value	0.77302	0.77029	0.83181	0.83726

significant. For the chi-squared distribution the test value of .417 is multiplied by the degrees of freedom, here five, to make the χ^2 test comparable to the F test. For two-sided hypothesis tests be sure to use the absolute value of the test statistic.

Appendix B

Some Essentials of Probability Theory

Statistical inference extrapolates from sample estimates, notably the sample mean and regression coefficients, to their population analogs – the mean and the conditional mean. This extrapolation controls for the randomness of the sample using results from probability theory.

Appendix B.1 presents basic probability theory, Appendix B.2 presents results on the distribution of the sample mean, and Appendix B.3 presents material on conditional distributions that is the probability basis for the linear regression model.

B.1 Probability Theory for a Single Random Variable

A **random variable** is a variable whose value is determined by the outcome of an experiment, where an **experiment** is an operation whose outcome cannot be predicted with certainty. Standard notation is to denote the random variable in upper case, say X (or Y or Z), and to denote the values that the random variable can take in lower case, say x (or y or z).

The **probability distribution** of a random variable X describes the random behavior of X.

B.1.1 Discrete Random Variables

A **discrete random variable** is a random variable that can only take a finite number of values (or a countably infinite number of variables such as 0, 1, 2, 3, ...). As an example, X may measure whether or not a person is currently employed, so X may take values 1 (employed) or 0 (not employed). As a second example, X may be the number of consultations with a doctor over the past year; then X may take the values 0, 1, 2, ...

In general a discrete random variable takes values x_1, x_2, ... The **probability mass function** cumulative probability distribution function gives the probabilities for each value taken by the random variable:

$$\Pr[X = x], \quad x = x_1, x_2, ...$$

Probabilities lie between 0 and 1 and sum to one over all possible values of X, so

$$\sum_x \Pr[X = x] = 1,$$

where $\sum_x$ denotes summation over all possible values taken by X.

The **cumulative distribution function** gives the probability that the random variable X is less than or equal to a particular value:

$$\Pr[X \le x] \quad x = x_1, x_2, ...$$

The probability that X lies in a given range can be calculated using either the probability mass function or the cumulative distribution function. We have

$$
\begin{aligned}
\Pr[a \le X \le b] \; &= \Pr[X = a] + \cdots + \Pr[X = b] \\
&= \Pr[X \le b] - \Pr[X < a].
\end{aligned}
$$

The **expected value** of a function $g(X)$ of the random variable X is the long-run average value that we expect if we draw a value x_1 of X at random and compute $g(x_1)$, draw a second value and so on, and then obtain the average of these values. Equivalently, for each value that x might take, compute $g(x)$ and then calculate the probability-weighted average of these values by weighting this value by the probability of that value x occurring. Then the **expected value** of $g(X)$

$$
\begin{aligned}
\mathrm{E}[g(X)] \; &= \; g(x_1) \times \Pr[X = x_1] + g(x_2) \times \Pr[X = x_2] + \cdots \\
&= \; \sum_x g(x) \times \Pr[X = x].
\end{aligned}
$$

The two most commonly-used expected values are the **mean** $\mu \equiv \mathrm{E}[X]$ that sets $g(X) = X$ and the **variance** $\sigma^2 \equiv \mathrm{E}[(X - \mu)^2]$ that sets $g(X) = (X - \mu)^2$. Additionally the **standard deviation** σ is the square root of the variance. The expected value of a constant is the constant: $\mathrm{E}[a] = a$.

The discrete probability distributions analyzed in introductory probability courses are the **Bernoulli**, **binomial** and **Poisson** distributions. Basic analysis of economics data uses only the first of these, which is presented next.

B.1.2   Bernoulli Distribution

The **Bernoulli distribution** is the term used to describe the distribution of a random variable that takes just one of two values: 0 or 1. This is the simplest example of a discrete random variable.

Denote the probability that $X = 1$ by p. For example, $p = 0.5$ in the case of a coin toss if the the coin is fair. Then it must be the case that $X = 0$ with probability $1 - p$, since the probabilities over all possible outcomes must sum to one, and $p + (1 - p) = 1$. So

$$
\Pr[X = x] = \begin{cases} p, & x = 1 \\ 1 - p, & x = 0. \end{cases}
$$

The quantity p that determines the probability distribution is called a **parameter**. It is unknown, but can be estimated given a sample.

A Bernoulli random variable has mean $\mu = p$ and variance $\sigma^2 = p(1 - p)$.

These properties can be obtained using the following algebra. For the mean, $\mathrm{E}[X] = 0 \times \Pr[X = 0] + 1 \times \Pr[X = 1] = 0 \times (1 - p) + 1 \times p = p$. And the variance $\sigma^2 = \mathrm{E}[(X - \mu)^2] = (0 - p)^2 \times \Pr[X = 0] + (1 - p)^2 \times \Pr[X = 1] = p^2 \times (1 - p) + (1 - p)^2 \times p = p(1 - p)\{p + (1 - p)\} = p(1 - p)$.

B.1.3 Linear Transformation of a Random Variable

If we **add a fixed amount** a **to a random variable** then the mean is changed by the amount a and the variance is unchanged. If we **multiply a random variable by a fixed multiple** then the mean is multiplied by b and the variance is multiplied by b^2 (hence the standard deviation is multiplied by b). Combining, if X has mean μ and variance σ^2 then the random variable $Y = a+bX$, a **linear transformation** of X, has mean $\mathrm{E}[Y] = a + b\mathrm{E}[X]$ and variance $\mathrm{Var}[Y] = b^2\mathrm{Var}[X]$.

It follows that if X has mean μ and variance σ^2 then $X - \mu$ has mean $\mathrm{E}[X] - \mu = \mu - \mu = 0$ and variance σ^2. Subsequent division by σ leads to mean $0/\sigma = 0$ and variance $\sigma^2/\sigma^2 = 1$. Thus the random variable $Y = (X - \mu)/\sigma$ is a **standardized random variable** with mean zero and variance 1. So if we subtract the mean and divide by the standard deviation we transform the random variable X to the new random variable Y that necessarily has mean 0 and variance 1.

B.1.4 Continuous Random Variables

Not all random variables take just discrete values.

A **continuous random variable** X can take an uncountably infinite number of values, such as any real value, or any positive real value, or any real value between zero and one. As an example, X may be annual income of an individual. Or X may be the length of time that the individual has been employed at their current job.

Since X can take any value, the probability that it equals any particular value is infinitesimally small. So it is meaningless to consider the probability of X taking a particular value. Instead we evaluate the probability that X lies in a range of values.

A **continuous probability distribution** is defined by the **probability density function** $f(x)$. This function has the property that the probability that X lies between two values, say a and b, is given by the area under the function $f(x)$ between a and b. Since $\Pr[X = a] = 0$ for a continuous random variable, the following expressions yield equivalent probabilities

$$\Pr[a < X < b] = \Pr[a \le X \le b] = \Pr[a \le X < b] = \Pr[a < X \le b].$$

The total area under the probability density function curve, from the minimum to maximum value of X, equals one since probabilities sum to one.

The associated **cumulative probability distribution function**, denoted $F(x)$, is defined as $\Pr[X \le x]$ and is given by the area under the curve from the lowest value that X can take to x.

B.1.5 Standard Normal Distribution

The leading example of a continuous random variable is a standard normal random variable. The **standard normal distribution** is defined by its probability density function

$$f(x) = \frac{1}{\sqrt{2\pi}} \exp\left(\frac{-x^2}{2}\right), \quad -\infty < x < \infty.$$

The standard normal can be shown to have mean $\mu = 0$ and standard deviation $\sigma = 1$. The notation $N(0, 1)$ is used to denote the standard normal distribution. The standard normal density is the curve given in Figure B.1.

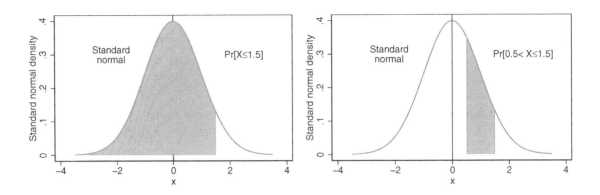

Figure B.1: Standard normal density: Graphs of $\Pr[X \leq 1.5]$ and $\Pr[0.5 \leq X \leq 1.5]$.

The shaded region in the left panel of Figure B.1 gives $\Pr[X \leq 1.5]$, since this is the area under the curve from $-\infty$ to 1.5. The total area under the curve is necessarily 1, and it appears visually that $\Pr[X \leq 1.5] \simeq 0.9$ since the shaded region is about 90% of the total area under the curve. From standard normal tables or a computer in fact $\Pr[X \leq 1.5] = 0.9332$.

The right panel of Figure B.1 gives $\Pr[0.5 < X \leq 1.5]$. This appears to be approximately equal to 0.2. From standard normal tables or a computer in fact $\Pr[0.5 < X \leq 1.5] = 0.2317$.

For those familiar with **integral calculus** the area under the curve is obtained by taking the integral. Thus, for example, $\Pr[X \leq 1.5] = \int_{-\infty}^{1.5} f(x)dx$. For the standard normal, where $f(x) = (1/\sqrt{2\pi}) \exp(-x^2/2)$, this integral has no exact solution. Instead one uses numerical approximations that are given in statistical tables or are calculated by the computer.

B.1.6   Other Continuous Distributions

The normal distribution is a generalization of the standard normal distribution that allows for a nonzero mean and a standard deviation other than one. In the more general case the **normal distribution**, with mean μ and standard deviation σ, has probability density function $f(x) = (1/\sqrt{2\pi\sigma^2}) \exp\left(-(x-\mu)^2/2\sigma^2\right)$ and is denoted $N(\mu, \sigma^2)$.

A powerful property of the normal, shared by few other distributions, is that linear combinations of normally distributed random variables are also normally distributed. If $X \sim N(\mu, \sigma^2)$ then $Y = a + bX \sim N(a + b\mu, b^2\sigma^2)$. One consequence of this result is that if $X \sim (\mu, \sigma^2)$ then $Y = (X - \mu)/\sigma \sim N(0, 1)$. In words, for a normally distributed random variable, subtracting the mean and then dividing by the standard deviation leads to a random variable that is standard normal distributed.

Aside from the normal, the continuous probability distributions most often used in econometrics are the t, F and chi-squared distributions, as these are used to obtain critical values and p-values for hypothesis tests. The probability density functions for these distributions are complicated and are not presented here, and probabilities need to be obtained from tables or be calculated by the computer. The t **distribution** is discussed in some detail in Chapter 4.2. The F **distribution** and the **chi-squared distribution** are introduced in Chapter 11.5. Appendix F gives tables.

B.2 Probability Theory for the Sample Mean

We provide in more detail results presented in Chapter 3 for the average $\bar{X}$ that is the sum of n independent random variables $X_1, ..., X_n$ divided by n.

B.2.1 Statistical Independence

The two random variables X and Y are **statistically independent** or, more simply, **independent** if the value taken by X is unrelated to the value taken by Y.

For example, let the two random variables X and Y represent the outcomes from two consecutive tosses of the coin. Then the two random variables are statistically independent if the result of the first toss, say a head, has no bearing on the result of the second toss. If the probability of heads on the first toss is p then, regardless of whether the first toss results in heads or tails, the probability of heads on the second toss is still p. (This is the case even if $p = 0.4$, say, so that the coin is not fair).

Random variables are not necessarily statistically independent. But under simple random sampling $X_1, ..., X_n$ are statistically independent.

B.2.2 Sums of Random Variables

The mean of a **weighted sum of random variables** equals the weighted sum of their means. That is,
$$\mathrm{E}[aX + bY] = a \times \mathrm{E}[X] + b \times \mathrm{E}[Y].$$

The variance of a sum of random variables is more complicated, as it depends on the statistical relationship between X and Y. Simplification occurs if the random variables are statistically independent. Then
$$\mathrm{Var}[aX + bY] = \mathrm{Var}[aX] + \mathrm{Var}[bY] = a^2 \times \mathrm{Var}[X] + b^2 \times \mathrm{Var}[Y].$$

This is a weighted sum of the individual variance, with weights that are the square of the original weights.

Applying this result, for statistically independent random variables the sum $X + Y$ has variance that is the sum of the variance of X and the variance of Y. Similarly, the difference $X - Y$ has variance that is the sum of the variance of X and the variance of Y.

B.2.3 Mean and Variance of the Sample Mean

The sample mean is the random variable $\bar{X}$ that equals the sum of X_1 to X_n divided by n. This can be written as a weighted sum of random variables
$$\bar{X} = \frac{1}{n}X_1 + \frac{1}{n}X_2 + \cdots + \frac{1}{n}X_n.$$

We first show that $E[\bar{X}] = \mu$ given common mean $E[X_i] = \mu$ (assumption A in Chapter 3.4). Then $E[X_i/n] = \mu/n$ and hence

$$E[\bar{X}] = \frac{1}{n}\mu + \frac{1}{n}\mu + \cdots + \frac{1}{n}\mu = \mu.$$

Next we want to show that $Var[\bar{X}] = \sigma^2/n$ given assumptions A–C in Chapter 3.4. The X_i are statistically independent by assumption C, so the variance of a sum is the sum of the variances and

$$
\begin{aligned}
Var[\bar{X}] &= Var\left[\tfrac{1}{n}X_1 + \tfrac{1}{n}X_2 + ... + \tfrac{1}{n}X_n\right] \\
&= Var\left[\tfrac{1}{n}X_1\right] + Var\left[\tfrac{1}{n}X_2\right] + \cdots + Var\left[\tfrac{1}{n}X_n\right] \\
&= \left(\tfrac{1}{n}\right)^2 Var\left[X_1\right] + \cdots + \left(\tfrac{1}{n}\right)^2 Var\left[X_n\right],
\end{aligned}
$$

where the third equality uses $Var[bX] = b^2 Var[X]$. Given assumption B of a common variance σ^2, $Var[\bar{X}] = \left(\tfrac{1}{n}\right)^2 \sigma^2 + \cdots + \left(\tfrac{1}{n}\right)^2 \sigma^2$, which equals n times $\left(\tfrac{1}{n}\right)^2 \sigma^2$, which equals $\tfrac{1}{n}\sigma^2$.

It follows that the standard deviation of $\bar{X}$ is $\sqrt{\sigma^2/n} = \sigma/\sqrt{n}$.

B.2.4   Law of Large Numbers

Now consider the behavior of $\bar{X}$ as the sample size gets large. Then $\bar{X}$ has mean μ and variance that goes to zero, since the variance $\sigma^2/n \to 0$ as $n \to \infty$.

So the distribution of $\bar{X}$ is centered on μ with very little variation around μ. The formal statistical term used is that $\bar{X}$ **converges in probability** to μ if the probability that $|\bar{X} - \mu| > \varepsilon$ goes to zero as $n \to \infty$, no matter how small $\varepsilon > 0$ is chosen to be.

A **law of large numbers** states that, under some assumptions on the individual X_i, an average of random variables converges in probability to its expected value; here that $\bar{X}$ converges in probability μ. The simplest law of large numbers assumes that X_i are statistically independent and identically distributed and that the mean μ exists. This is the case for simple random sampling.

B.2.5   Central Limit Theorem

The standardized variable $Z = (\bar{X} - \mu)/(\sigma/\sqrt{n})$ has mean zero and variance one.

A **central limit theorem** states that, under some assumptions on the individual X_i, Z is standard normally distributed as the sample size gets large. That is, as $n \to \infty$

$$Z = \frac{(\bar{X} - \mu)}{\sigma/\sqrt{n}} \sim N(0,1).$$

Note that this result does not require that X_i is normally distributed. It follows that in large samples $\bar{X} \sim N(\mu, \sigma^2/n)$.

There are many central limit theorems that vary with the assumptions made about the individual random variables X_i. The simplest central limit theorem is the Lindberg-Levy central limit theorem that assumes that X_i are statistically independent and identically distributed with mean μ and variance σ^2. This is the case for simple random sampling.

More general central limit theorems do not require a common mean, a common variance and/or statistical independence. Then $Z = (\bar{X} - E[\bar{X}])/\sqrt{Var[\bar{X}]} \sim N(0,1)$ where $E[\bar{X}]$ may no longer simplify to μ and $Var[\bar{X}]$ may no longer simplify to $\sigma/\sqrt{n}$.

B.3   Probability Theory for Two Related Random Variables

The bivariate regression model is a model of the conditional mean of Y given $X = x$. Here we define the conditional mean, conditional variance, covariance and correlation.

B.3.1   Joint Probabilities

Consider the statistical relationship between two random variables X and Y that are both discrete random variables. Their joint probability of occurrence is defined by the **joint probability mass function**

$$\Pr[X = x, Y = y], \quad x = x_1, x_2, ..., \quad y = y_1, y_2, ...$$

where upper case denotes the random variable and lower case denotes the values that the random variable might take.

Given knowledge of the joint probabilities of X and Y we can obtain the separate probabilities for X and for Y. For example, $\Pr[X = x]$ equals the sum over all possible values of y of the joint probability $\Pr[X = x, Y = y]$.

B.3.2   Example

Throughout this appendix we consider the following example:

$$\Pr[X = x, Y = y] = \begin{cases} 0.1 & \text{for } x = 1, \, y = 50 \\ 0.1 & \text{for } x = 1, \, y = 30 \\ 0.2 & \text{for } x = 0, \, y = 30 \\ 0.6 & \text{for } x = 0, \, y = 10. \end{cases}$$

Note that these probabilities sum to one.

For this example, $\Pr[X = 1] = \Pr[X = 1, Y = 50] + \Pr[X = 1, Y = 30] = 0.1 + 0.1 = 0.2$ and $\Pr[X = 0] = \Pr[X = 0, Y = 30] + \Pr[X = 0, Y = 10] = 0.2 + 0.6 = 0.8$. So $X = 1$ with probability 0.2 and $X = 0$ with probability 0.8. Thus

$$\Pr[X = x] = \begin{cases} 0.2 & \text{for } x = 1 \\ 0.8 & \text{for } x = 0. \end{cases}$$

By similar summation, now over the possible values of X, $\Pr[Y = 50] = 0.1$, $\Pr[Y = 30] = 0.1 + 0.2 = 0.3$, and $\Pr[Y = 10] = 0.6$. So

$$\Pr[Y = y] = \begin{cases} 0.1 & \text{for } y = 50 \\ 0.3 & \text{for } y = 30 \\ 0.6 & \text{for } y = 10. \end{cases}$$

B.3.3   Conditional Distribution

A very important result is **Bayes Theorem** that states that for any two events A and B, the probability that event A happens, given that event B happens, is the joint probability that A and B happen divided by the probability that B happens:

$$\Pr[A|B] = \frac{\Pr[A \cap B]}{\Pr[B]},$$

where $A \cap B$ means the intersection of events A and B.

For example, consider the probability of getting a three on the second toss of a six-sided die (event A), given that the combined sum of the first two tosses is five (event B). The only way that both A and B can occur is if the first toss was a 2 and the second was a 3. The two tosses can sum to five in four ways, with tosses $(1,4)$, $(2,3)$, $(3,2)$, and $(4,1)$. All these outcomes are equally likely, so the conditional probability of event A given B is one in four, or 0.25.

More generally, the **conditional probability** of Y given X

$$\Pr[Y = y|X = x] = \frac{\Pr[Y = y, X = x]}{\Pr[X = x]}.$$

Consider the earlier numerical example and condition on $X = 1$. Then $Y = 50$ or $Y = 30$ with $\Pr[X = 1, Y = 50] = 0.1$ and $\Pr[X = 1, Y = 30] = 0.1$. Also $\Pr[X = 1] = 0.2$. It follows that the conditional distribution of Y given $X = 1$ is $\Pr[Y = 30|X = 1] = 0.1/0.2 = 0.5$ and $\Pr[Y = 50|X = 1] = 0.1/0.2 = 0.5$. By similar reasoning, since $\Pr[X = 0] = 0.8$, the conditional distribution of Y given $X = 0$ is $\Pr[Y = 10|X = 0] = 0.6/0.8 = 0.75$ and $\Pr[Y = 30|X = 0] = 0.2/0.8 = 0.25$.

The conditional probabilities for Y given $X = 1$ are therefore

$$\Pr[Y = y|X = 1] = \begin{cases} 0.5 & \text{for } y = 50 \\ 0.5 & \text{for } x = 30, \end{cases}$$

and for Y given $X = 0$:

$$\Pr[Y = y|X = 0] = \begin{cases} 0.25 & \text{for } y = 30 \\ 0.75 & \text{for } y = 10. \end{cases}$$

If X and Y are **statistically independent** then the probability of Y taking a particular value is unaffected by the value taken by X. In that case the conditional probability $\Pr[Y = y|X = x]$ reduces to the unconditional probability $\Pr[Y = y]$.

In the example of this appendix X and Y are **not** statistically independent.

B.3.4   Conditional Mean

The **conditional expected value** of a function $g(Y)$ given $X = x$ is an extension of the usual unconditional expected value of $g(Y)$, except that the values $g(y)$ are weighted by the conditional probabilities of $Y|X = x$ rather than the unconditional probabilities of Y. Thus

$$\mathrm{E}[g(Y)|X = x] = g(y_1) \times \Pr[Y = y_1|X = x] + g(y_2) \times \Pr[Y = y_2|X = x] + \cdots$$

The **conditional mean** of Y given X is the mean of the conditional distribution. This is the weighted sum of the possible values of Y where the weighting is by the conditional probability of Y given x. So

$$E[Y|X = x] = \sum_y y \times \Pr[Y = y|X = x].$$

For the example of this appendix begin with the conditional mean of Y given $X = 1$. When $X = 1$, Y takes value 30 with $\Pr[Y = 30|X = 1] = 0.5$, and Y takes value 50 with $\Pr[Y = 50|X = 1] = 0.5$. It follows that $E[Y|X = 1] = 30 \times 0.5 + 50 \times 0.5 = 40$. By similar calculation $E[Y|X = 0] = 10 \times \Pr[Y = 10|X = 0] + 30 \times \Pr[Y = 30|X = 0] = 10 \times 0.75 + 30 \times 0.25 = 15$. So

$$E[Y|X = x] = \left\{ \begin{array}{ll} 40 & \text{for } x = 1 \\ 15 & \text{for } x = 0. \end{array} \right.$$

In this example the conditional mean of Y given X varies with the value of X.

For linear regression it is assumed that the **conditional mean** $E[Y|X = x]$ **is a linear function of** x. Then the population relationship between Y and X is a line with intercept denoted β_1 and slope denoted β_2, so

$$E[Y|X = x] = \beta_1 + \beta_2 x.$$

For example, suppose that $E[Y|X = x] = 3 + 2x$. Then when X takes the values 1, 2, and 3, for example, the corresponding conditional means are $E[Y|X = 1] = 5$, $E[Y|X = 2] = 7$, and $E[Y|X = 3] = 9$.

The conditional mean function is not necessarily linear. For example, suppose $E[Y|X = 1] = 5$, $E[Y|X = 2] = 7$, and $E[Y|X = 3] = 12$. Then the conditional mean function is nonlinear in X since it increases by 2 from $X = 1$ to $X = 2$ but increases by 5 from $X = 2$ to $X = 3$. Chapter 15 presents some more general models for linear regression that relax the assumption of a conditional mean for Y that is linear in X.

B.3.5 Conditional Variance

The **conditional variance** of Y given X measures the variation in Y around the conditional mean $E[Y|X = x]$, where the deviation is squared and is weighted by the conditional probabilities. Then

$$\text{Var}[Y|X = x] = E[(Y - E[Y|X = x])^2|X = x],$$

is the probability-weighted average of all possible values of $(Y - E[Y|X = x])^2$ when $X = x$.

For the example of this appendix, we have already calculated that $\Pr[Y = 50|X = 1] = 0.5$, $\Pr[Y = 30|X = 1] = 0.5$, and $E[Y|X = 1] = 40$. It follows that $\text{Var}[Y|X = 1] = (50 - 40)^2 \times .5 + (30 - 40)^2 \times .5 = 100$. Similarly, $\text{Var}[Y|X = 0] = (30 - 15)^2 \times .25 + (10 - 15)^2 \times .75 = 75$. Note that the conditional variance here differs according to whether we condition on $X = 0$ or on $X = 1$.

Assumption 3 (homoskedastic errors) that $\text{Var}[u|X = x]$ does not depend on x implies that $\text{Var}[Y|X = x]$ does not depend on x. Alternative assumptions regarding $\text{Var}[u|X = x]$ lead to different ways to estimate the precision of the least squares estimates; see Chapter 7.7.

B.3.6 Covariance

The **covariance** of Y and X measures the joint variation of X and Y around their respective means. Let μ_X denote $E[X]$ and μ_Y denote $E[Y]$. Then

$$
\begin{aligned}
\text{Cov}[X,Y] &= E[(X-\mu_x)(Y-\mu_Y)] \\
&= \sum_x \sum_y (X-\mu_x)(Y-\mu_Y) \times \Pr[Y=y|X=x].
\end{aligned}
$$

It can be shown that $\text{Cov}[X,Y] = E[XY] - \mu_x\mu_Y$.

For the example of this appendix, $\mu_X = 1 \times 0.2 + 0 \times 0.8 = 0.2$ and $\mu_Y = 50 \times 0.1 + 30 \times 0.3 + 10 \times 0.6 = 20$. Then $\text{Cov}[X,Y] = (1-0.2) \times (50-20) \times 0.1 + (1-0.2) \times (30-20) \times 0.1 + (0-0.2) \times (30-20) \times 0.2 + (0-0.2) \times (10-20) \times 0.6 = 4$. So $\text{Cov}[X,Y] = 4$.

The covariance between a random variable and a constant is zero. To see this, let a be a constant in which case $\mu_a = E[a] = a$. Then $\text{Cov}[X,a] = E[(X-\mu_x)(a-\mu_a)] = E[(X-\mu_x)(a-a)] = E[0] = 0$.

The law of iterated expectation states that the overall mean (more formally the unconditional mean) of a random variable is the expected value of the conditional mean, where the expectation is with respect to the conditioning variable. Thus

$$
E[Y] = E[E[Y|X=x]] = \sum_x E[Y|X=x] \times \Pr[X=x].
$$

One consequence is that if the regression error term has mean zero conditional on the regressors then it has unconditional mean zero, since $E[u|X=x] = 0$ implies that $E[u] = E[E[u|X=x]] = E[0] = 0$.

A second consequence is that if the regression error term has mean 0 conditional on regressors then it is uncorrelated with the regressors. To see this use $E[Xu] = E[E[Xu|X=x]] = E[X \times E[u|X=x]] = E[X \times 0] = 0$. So $\text{Cov}[X,u] = E[Xu] - \mu_x\mu_u = 0 - \mu_x \times 0 = 0$.

B.3.7 Correlation

The **correlation coefficient** of Y and X standardizes the covariance to lie between -1 and 1. We have

$$
\text{Cor}[X,Y] = \frac{\text{Cov}[X,Y]}{\sqrt{\text{Var}[X] \times \text{Var}[Y]}}.
$$

For the example of this appendix, $\text{Var}[X] = (1-0.2)^2 \times 0.2 + (0-0.8)^2 \times 0.8 = 0.16$ and $\text{Var}[Y] = (50-20)^2 \times 0.1 + (30-20)^2 \times 0.3 + (10-20)^2 \times 0.6 = 180$. So $\text{Cor}[X,Y] = 4/\sqrt{0.16 \times 180} = 0.745$. In this example X and Y are quite highly positively correlated.

The covariance and correlation coefficients are the population analogs of the sample covariance and sample correlation coefficient that are defined in Chapter 5.4.

Appendix C

Properties of OLS, IV and ML Estimators

This appendix sketches proofs of the key properties of the slope coefficient of the OLS estimator from regression of a single variable y on a single regressor x. It is simplest to consider the case where the regressor x is fixed, as in an experiment, rather than random, as with survey data. But the results extend to the case of random regressors.

In addition to considering inference with independent homoskedastic errors, results for independent heteroskedastic errors, clustered errors and autocorrelated errors are also presented. Instrumental variables estimation and maximum likelihood estimation are also presented.

These results with a single regressor use summation notation. Corresponding proofs for the case of many regressors entail the same concepts and assumptions, but require use of matrix algebra methods. A brief presentation of OLS with matrix algebra is provided.

C.1 OLS with Independent Homoskedastic Errors

We begin by obtaining the expressions for the mean and variance of the OLS slope coefficients given in Chapter 6.3 under assumptions 1-4.

C.1.1 A model without intercept

For simplicity we consider a model with no intercept, so $y = \beta x + u$. Then the OLS estimator b of β, obtained from regressing y on x without an intercept, is

$$b = \left(\sum_{i=1}^{n} x_i^2 \right)^{-1} \sum_{i=1}^{n} x_i y_i.$$

Throughout it is assumed that $\sum_i x_i^2 \neq 0$, since otherwise b is not defined.

There is no loss in generality in dropping the intercept if the data y and x are demeaned data. To see this, note that OLS regression of the demeaned variable $(y_i - \bar{y})$ on the demeaned variable $(x_i - \bar{x})$ using the above formula yields $b = \sum_{i=1}^{n} (x_i - \bar{x})(y_i - \bar{y}) / \sum_{i=1}^{n} (x_i - \bar{x})^2$. But this is just the usual formula for the OLS estimate of the slope. The algebra is much less unwieldy, however, in the demeaned case.

Additionally the regressor x_i is assumed to be fixed. In that case there is no need to take conditional expectations with respect to x, simplifying the notation.

The assumptions are:

1. Model: $y_i = \beta x_i + u_i$.

2. Zero error mean: $\mathrm{E}[u_i] = 0$.

3. Constant error variance: $\mathrm{Var}[u_i] = \sigma_u^2$.

3. Uncorrelated errors: $\mathrm{Cov}[u_i, u_j] = 0, \quad i \neq j$.

C.1.2   A convenient expression for b

Given assumption 1 it is always the case that

$$b = \beta + (\textstyle\sum_i x_i^2)^{-1}(\textstyle\sum_i x_i u_i).$$

Properties of the OLS estimator will therefore be determined primarily by assumptions made about the errors u_i.

To obtain this result, note that

$$
\begin{aligned}
b &= (\textstyle\sum_i x_i^2)^{-1}(\textstyle\sum_i x_i y_i) \\
&= (\textstyle\sum_i x_i^2)^{-1}(\textstyle\sum_i x_i(\beta x_i + u_i)) \\
&= (\textstyle\sum_i x_i^2)^{-1}(\textstyle\sum_i \beta x_i^2 + x_i u_i) \\
&= (\textstyle\sum_i x_i^2)^{-1}(\textstyle\sum_i \beta x_i^2) + (\textstyle\sum_i x_i^2)^{-1}(\textstyle\sum_i x_i u_i) \\
&= \beta + (\textstyle\sum_i x_i^2)^{-1}(\textstyle\sum_i x_i u_i),
\end{aligned}
$$

where the second equality uses assumption 1 that $y_i = \beta x_i + u_i$.

C.1.3   The Mean of b

Given the preceding result,

$$
\begin{aligned}
\mathrm{E}[b] &= \mathrm{E}\left[\beta + (\textstyle\sum_i x_i^2)^{-1}(\textstyle\sum_i x_i u_i)\right] \\
&= \mathrm{E}[\beta] + \mathrm{E}\left[(\textstyle\sum_i x_i^2)^{-1}(\textstyle\sum_i x_i u_i)\right],
\end{aligned}
$$

since the expected value of a sum is the sum of the expected values. For the first term, $\mathrm{E}[\beta] = \beta$ as the expected value of a constant is the constant. For the second term, with fixed regressor x_i, $(\sum_i x_i^2)^{-1}$ is a constant and the expected value of a constant times a random variable is the constant times the expected value of the random variable.

So

$$\mathrm{E}[b] = \beta + (\textstyle\sum_i x_i^2)^{-1} \times \mathrm{E}[\textstyle\sum_i x_i u_i].$$

It follows that $E[b] = \beta$ if $E[\sum_i x_i u_i] = 0$.

Now the expected value of a sum is the sum of the expected values:

$$E[\textstyle\sum_i x_i u_i] = \textstyle\sum_i E[x_i u_i].$$

So we need $E[x_i u_i] = 0$. This is the case under assumption 2 that $E[u_i] = 0$, and for fixed regressor x_i, since then $E[x_i u_i] = x_i E[u_i] = x_i \times 0 = 0$.

Thus $E[b] = \beta$ and the OLS estimator is unbiased under assumptions 1 and 2. (If the regressor x_i is instead random a modification of the above yields that OLS is unbiased if $E[u_i|x_i] = 0$, i.e. if the error has mean 0 conditional on the regressor.)

C.1.4 The variance of b

Given $b = \beta + (\sum_i x_i^2)^{-1}(\sum_i x_i u_i)$ and $E[b] = \beta$ it follows that under assumptions 1-2

$$b - E[b] = (\textstyle\sum_i x_i^2)^{-1}(\textstyle\sum_i x_i u_i).$$

Now $\text{Var}[b] = E[(b - E[b])^2] = \text{Var}[(b - E[b])]$. So

$$\text{Var}[b] = \text{Var}\left[(\textstyle\sum_i x_i^2)^{-1}(\textstyle\sum_i x_i u_i)\right].$$

The term $(\sum_i x_i^2)^{-1}$ is a constant while $(\sum_i x_i u_i)$ is a random variable. In general the variance of a constant times a random variable is the constant squared times the variance of the random variable.

Thus given just assumptions 1-2 we have

$$\text{Var}[b] = \left[(\textstyle\sum_i x_i^2)^{-1}\right]^2 \times \text{Var}[\textstyle\sum_i x_i u_i].$$

Next add in assumptions 3-4. Given assumption 4 that u_i are uncorrelated the terms $x_i u_i$ are uncorrelated. But the variance of a sum of uncorrelated random variables equals the sum of the variances. So

$$\text{Var}[b] = (\textstyle\sum_i x_i^2)^{-2} \times \textstyle\sum_i \text{Var}[x_i u_i].$$

In general $\text{Var}[x_i u_i] = x_i^2 \times \text{Var}[u_i]$, for x_i a fixed regressor. So given assumption 3 of homoskedastic errors, so that $\text{Var}[u_i] = \sigma_u^2$, we have $\text{Var}[x_i u_i] = x_i^2 \sigma_u^2$. It follows that

$$\text{Var}[b] = (\textstyle\sum_i x_i^2)^{-2} \times \textstyle\sum_i x_i^2 \sigma_u^2 = \sigma_u^2 (\textstyle\sum_i x_i^2)^{-1}.$$

Upon converting to data before demeaning, we replace x_i by $x_i - \bar{x}$ and obtain $\text{Var}[b_2] = \sigma_u^2 (\sum_i (x_i - \bar{x})^2)^{-1}$ as presented in Chapter 6.3. Replacing σ_u^2 by its estimate s_e^2 yields

$$\widehat{\text{Var}}_{def}[b_2] = \frac{s_e^2}{\sum_{i=1}^n (x_i - \bar{x})^2}.$$

C.1.5   Distribution of b

The OLS estimator is a weighted linear combination of the errors u_i, since we have shown that

$$b = \beta + \sum_i w_i u_i \text{ where } w_i = (\sum_j x_j^2)^{-1} x_i.$$

Suppose it is assumed that, in addition to assumptions 1-4, the errors u_i are normally distributed. Then it follows immediately that b is normally distributed because linear combinations of the normal are normal. So b is normally distributed with mean b and variance $\sigma_u^2 (\sum_i x_i^2)^{-1}$.

This result cannot be used directly because σ_u^2 is not known. An advanced result from statistics theory shows that if we replace σ_u^2 with s_e^2, where s_e is the standard error of the residual, then $T = (b - \beta)/s_b$, where $s_b^2 = s_e^2 (\sum_i x_i^2)^{-1}$, is t distributed under assumptions 1-4 and the assumption of normally distributed errors.

In practice the assumption of normally distributed errors is relaxed. Then the t distribution continues to be used for the t statistic but is now only an approximation, one that improves as the sample size gets larger.

C.1.6   Random Regressors

For simplicity it was assumed that the regressors x are fixed. This would be the case for an experiment where x is set by the experimenter. For example, x may be the amount of fertilizer applied to a field or the dosage level of a medicine given to a patient.

More often in social sciences such as economics the data are observational, in which case the regressors are random since the sample observation (y_i, x_i) is randomly chosen. Then we assume that assumptions on the errors are conditional on x_i, so $u_i | x_i$ must have mean zero and for statistical inference we may assume, for example, that $u_i | x_i$ is homoskedastic.

The preceding results still hold if analysis is viewed as being conditional on the value of the regressors. If instead the analysis is viewed as unconditional on the regressors, then we ultimately use the same methods as in the conditional case, though there are some changes in the intermediate results. In particular, $\text{Var}[b] = \sigma_u^2 (\sum_i \text{E}[x_i^2])^{-1}$ and the t statistic is no longer exactly t distributed, even if errors are normally distributed and assumptions 1-4 hold.

C.2   Robust Standard Errors

We consider in turn heteroskedastic-robust standard errors, introduced in Chapter 7.7, and cluster-robust and HAC robust standard errors introduced in Chapter 12.1.

C.2.1   OLS with Independent Heteroskedastic Errors

Replace assumption 3 with the assumption that errors are heteroskedastic.

3.*het* $\text{Var}[u_i] = \sigma_i^2$.

The proof for independent heteroskedastic errors is the same as that for independent homoskedastic errors up to

$$\text{Var}[b] = (\textstyle\sum_i x_i^2)^{-2} \times \sum_i \text{Var}[x_i u_i].$$

Now $\text{Var}[x_i u_i] = x_i^2 \text{Var}[u_i] = x_i^2 \sigma_i^2$ assuming heteroskedastic errors. So

$$\text{Var}[b] = (\textstyle\sum_i x_i^2)^{-2} \times \sum_i x_i^2 \sigma_i^2.$$

There is no further simplification. The result is usually written as

$$\text{Var}[b] = (\textstyle\sum_i x_i^2)^{-1} \times \sum_i x_i^2 \sigma_i^2 \times (\textstyle\sum_i x_i^2)^{-1},$$

as this form generalizes to that for the case of multiple regressors.

This result cannot be directly implemented, as σ_i^2 is unknown. Furthermore, it is difficult to estimate the n error variances σ_i^2 without making assumptions about the nature of the heteroskedasticity. However, this is not necessary as all we need to do is estimate the single scalar $\sum_i x_i^2 \sigma_i^2$. This can be done using $\sum_i x_i^2 \widehat{u}_i^2$ as proved by White (1980). So we use

$$\widehat{\text{Var}}_{het}[b] = (\textstyle\sum_i x_i^2)^{-1} \times \sum_i x_i^2 \widehat{u}_i^2 \times (\textstyle\sum_i x_i^2)^{-1},$$

where $\widehat{u}_i = y_i - \widehat{y}_i$ denotes the OLS residual (denoted e_i in the main text). The result requires the additional assumption that $\text{E}[u_i^4]$ and $\text{E}[x_i^4]$ are finite, an assumption that means that extreme outlying values of the data are unlikely, and that $n \to \infty$.

The variance estimate is called a heteroskedastic-consistent estimate of the variance of the OLS estimate, and the resultant standard errors and t statistics are called heteroskedastic-robust or, more simply, robust. It is valid in large samples. Converting to data before demeaning we obtain

$$\widehat{\text{Var}}_{het}[b_2] = \frac{\sum_{i=1}^n \widehat{u}_i^2 (x_i - \bar{x})^2}{\{\sum_{i=1}^n (x_i - \bar{x})^2\}^2}.$$

Most statistical packages modify this by the degrees of freedom adjustment $\frac{n}{n-k}$, leading to the formula for the standard error given in Chapter 7.7 with $k = 2$.

The t statistic is asymptotically normal in large samples. It is no longer exactly t distributed in finite samples (even if the error is normally distributed). But it is common to continue to use the t distribution in finite samples.

C.2.2 OLS with Clustered Correlated Errors

We suppose that observations can be grouped into clusters, where errors for observations in the same cluster are correlated, while errors for observations in different clusters are uncorrelated. Introduce an indicator variable that takes value 1 for observations in the same cluster and value 0 for observations in different clusters. Then

$$\delta_{ij} = \begin{cases} 1 & \text{if observations } i \text{ and } j \text{ are in the same cluster} \\ 0 & \text{otherwise.} \end{cases}$$

The errors may also be heteroskedastic. Then assumptions 3 and 4 are replaced by

3.*clu* $\text{Var}[u_i] = \sigma_i^2$ and nonzero $\text{Cov}[u_i, u_j] = \sigma_{ij}$.

4.*clu* $\text{Cov}[u_i, u_j] \neq 0$ if $\delta_{ij} = 1$ while $\text{Cov}[u_i, u_j] = 0$ if $\delta_{ij} = 0$.

From the previous section, in general

$$\sum_i \text{Var}[x_i u_i] = \sum_i \sum_j \text{Cov}[x_i u_i, x_j u_j] = \sum_i \sum_j x_i x_j \text{E}[u_i u_j].$$

$\text{Cov}[x_i u_i, x_j u_j] = x_i x_j \text{Cov}[u_i u_j]$ given fixed regressors and $\text{Cov}[u_i u_j] = \text{E}[u_i u_j]$ given $\text{E}[u_i] = 0$. Then assumption 4.*clu* implies that we can write

$$\text{Var}[b] = (\sum_i x_i^2)^{-1} \times \sum_i \sum_j \delta_{ij} x_i x_j \text{E}[u_i u_j] \times (\sum_i x_i^2)^{-1}.$$

Converting to data before demeaning, provided the number of clusters G is large this can be consistently estimated by

$$\widehat{\text{Var}}_{clu}[b_2] = \frac{\sum_i \sum_j \delta_{ij}(x_i - \bar{x})(x_j - \bar{x})\hat{u}_i \hat{u}_j}{\{\sum_{i=1}^n (x_i - \bar{x})^2\}^2}.$$

Statistical packages generally apply a degrees of freedom adjustment to the preceding formula. A common choice is to multiply by $G/(G-1)$; some packages additionally multiply by $(n-1)/(n-k)$.

This estimate is called a cluster-robust estimate of the variance of the OLS estimate, and the resulting standard errors and t statistics are called cluster robust; it also controls for heteroskedasticity. The theory requires that the number of clusters goes to infinity, while there can be as few as one observation in each cluster.

The t statistic is asymptotically normal if there are many clusters, though it is common to continue to use the t distribution with $G - 1$ degrees of freedom, where G is the number of clusters.

C.2.3 OLS with Serially Correlated Errors

For time series data with autocorrelated or serially correlated errors we use subscript t rather than i. We assume that the regressor x_t is not a lag of y_t, since with lagged y_t as a regressor OLS becomes inconsistent if errors are serially correlated.

We assume that errors are potentially correlated for observations up to m periods apart, and allow for heteroskedasticity, so assumptions 3 and 4 are replaced by

3.*hac* $\text{Var}[u_t] = \sigma_t^2$.

4.*hac* $\text{Cov}[u_t, u_s] \neq 0$ for $|t - s| \leq m$.

The proof for serially correlated errors proceeds the same as that for independent errors up to

$$\begin{aligned} \text{Var}[b] &= (\sum_t x_t^2)^{-2} \times \text{Var}[\sum_t x_t u_t] \\ &= (\sum_t x_t^2)^{-1} \times \text{Var}[\sum_t x_t u_t] \times (\sum_t x_t^2)^{-1}. \end{aligned}$$

The challenge is to find $\text{Var}[\sum_t x_t u_t]$ when errors are serially correlated.

Now for random variables that are correlated, the variance of the sum is not simply the sum of the variances. Instead, for example

$$\text{Var}[Y_1 + Y_2] = \text{Var}[Y_1] + \text{Var}[Y_2] + 2\text{Cov}[Y_1, Y_2].$$

To see this note that

$$
\begin{aligned}
\text{Var}[Y_1 + Y_2] &= E[\{(Y_1 + Y_2) - E[(Y_1 + Y_2)]\}^2] \\
&= E[\{(Y_1 + Y_2) - (\mu_1 + \mu_2)\}^2] \\
&= E[\{(Y_1 - \mu_1) + (Y_2 - \mu_2)\}^2] \\
&= E[(Y_1 - \mu_1)^2 + (Y_2 - \mu_2)^2 + 2(Y_1 - \mu_1)(Y_2 - \mu_2)] \\
&= E[(Y_1 - \mu_1)^2] + E[(Y_2 - \mu_2)^2] + 2E[(Y_1 - \mu_1)(Y_2 - \mu_2)] \\
&= \text{Var}[Y_1] + \text{Var}[Y_2] + 2\text{Cov}[Y_1, Y_2].
\end{aligned}
$$

More generally

$$
\begin{aligned}
\text{Var}[\textstyle\sum_t Y_t] &= [\textstyle\sum_t \sum_s \text{Cov}[Y_t, Y_s]] \\
&= \textstyle\sum_t \text{Var}[Y_t] + 2\sum_t \text{Cov}[Y_t, Y_{t-1}] + 2\sum_t \text{Cov}[Y_t, Y_{t-2}] + \cdots
\end{aligned}
$$

It follows that

$$\text{Var}[\textstyle\sum_t x_t u_t] = \textstyle\sum_t \text{Var}[x_t u_t] + 2\sum_t \text{Cov}[x_t u_t, x_{t-1} u_{t-1}] + 2\sum_t \text{Cov}[x_t u_t, x_{t-2} u_{t-2}] + \cdots$$

Under assumption 4.*hac*, the dependence disappears after m lags so

$$\text{Var}[\textstyle\sum_t x_t u_t] = \textstyle\sum_t \text{Var}[x_t u_t] + 2\sum_t \text{Cov}[x_t u_t, x_{t-1} u_{t-1}] + \cdots + 2\sum_t \text{Cov}[x_t u_t, x_{t-m} u_{t-m}].$$

Newey and West (1987) proposed estimating this by the weighted sums

$$\widehat{\text{Var}}[\textstyle\sum_t x_t u_t] = \textstyle\sum_{t=1}^{T} x_t^2 \widehat{u}_t^2 + 2\frac{m}{m+1} \sum_{t=2}^{T} x_t x_{t-1} \widehat{u}_t \widehat{u}_{t-1} + \cdots + 2\frac{1}{m+1} \sum_{t=m}^{T} x_t x_{t-m} \widehat{u}_t \widehat{u}_{t-m}.$$

So we use

$$
\begin{aligned}
\widehat{\text{Var}}_{clu}[b] &= (\textstyle\sum_t x_t^2)^{-1} \times \{\sum_{t=1}^{T} x_t^2 \widehat{u}_t^2 + \frac{2m}{m+1} \sum_{t=2}^{m} x_t x_{t-1} \widehat{u}_t \widehat{u}_{t-1} \\
&\quad + \cdots + \frac{2}{m+1} \sum_{t=m}^{T} x_t x_{t-m} \widehat{u}_t \widehat{u}_{t-m}\} \times (\textstyle\sum_t x_t^2)^{-1},
\end{aligned}
$$

This is called a heteroskedastic and serially correlated (HAC)-consistent estimate of the variance of the OLS estimate, and the resulting standard errors and t statistics are called HAC standard errors or, more simply, serial-correlation robust.

The resulting t statistic is asymptotically normal in large samples. It is no longer exactly t-distributed in finite samples (even if the error is normally distributed). But it is common to continue to use the t distribution in finite samples.

C.3 Instrumental Variables Estimation

The instrumental variable is introduced in Chapter 17.4. For simplicity we continue to consider a model with no intercept, so $y_i = \beta x_i + u_i$. Given a single instrument z_i, the instrumental variables estimator of β is

$$b_{IV} = (\textstyle\sum_{i=1}^n z_i x_i)^{-1} \sum_{i=1}^n z_i y_i.$$

By algebra similar to that used for OLS, we obtain

$$
\begin{aligned}
b_{IV} &= (\textstyle\sum_i z_i x_i)^{-1}(\sum_i z_i y_i) \\
&= (\textstyle\sum_i z_i x_i)^{-1}(\sum_i z_i(\beta x_i + u_i)) \quad \text{as } y_i = \beta x_i + u_i \\
&= (\textstyle\sum_i z_i x_i)^{-1}(\sum_i \beta z_i x_i) + (\sum_i z_i x_i)^{-1}(\sum_i z_i u_i) \\
&= \beta + (\textstyle\sum_i z_i x_i)^{-1}(\sum_i z_i u_i).
\end{aligned}
$$

with key result

$$b_{IV} = \beta + (\textstyle\sum_i z_i x_i)^{-1}(\sum_i z_i u_i).$$

We first assume for simplicity that both the instruments z_i and the regressor x_i are fixed, that the same assumptions 1-2 and 4 as used for OLS hold, and additionally that there is variation in the instrument z. Then $\mathrm{E}[b_{IV}] = \beta$ given assumptions 1-2 hold and

$$
\begin{aligned}
\mathrm{Var}[b_{IV}] &= \mathrm{Var}[(\textstyle\sum_i z_i x_i)^{-1}(\sum_i z_i u_i)] \\
&= (\textstyle\sum_i z_i x_i)^{-2} \times \mathrm{Var}[\textstyle\sum_i z_i u_i].
\end{aligned}
$$

Then $\mathrm{Var}[\sum_i z_i u_i] = \sigma_u^2 \sum_i z_i^2$ if additionally the errors are independent and homoskedastic (assumptions 3-4), $\mathrm{Var}[\sum_i z_i u_i] = \sum_i \sigma_i^2 z_i^2$ if the errors are independent and heteroskedastic (assumptions 3.*het* and 4), and so on.

For example, with independent and heteroskedastic errors the estimated variance of b_{IV} is

$$\widehat{\mathrm{Var}}_{het}[b_{IV}] = \frac{\sum_i z_i^2 \widehat{u}_i^2}{\{\sum_i z_i x_i\}^2},$$

where $\widehat{u}_i = y_i - b_{IV} x_i$. The estimator b_{IV} is normally distributed in large samples. Then $T = (b_{IV} - \beta)/se(b_{IV})$ is normally distributed in large samples, though usually we instead treat it as t distributed, as in the OLS case.

In practice the regressor x_i and instrument z_i are not fixed, as the rationale for IV estimation is that the regressor x is random and correlated with the error u so $\mathrm{E}[u_i|x_i] \neq 0$. Then assumption 2 is replaced with the assumption that $\mathrm{E}[u_i|z_i] = 0$. When x and z are random the IV estimator is no longer unbiased; indeed the mean does not even exist. [The reason is that in order for $\mathrm{E}[(\sum_i z_i x_i)^{-1}(\sum_i z_i u_i)] = 0$ we need $\mathrm{E}[u_i|x_i, z_i] = 0$ which is not possible if $\mathrm{E}[u_i|x_i] \neq 0$.]

Nonetheless the IV estimator can be shown to be consistent for β if $\mathrm{E}[u_i|z_i] = 0$. This result is obtained by noting that

$$b_{IV} = \beta + (\tfrac{1}{N}\textstyle\sum_i z_i x_i)^{-1}(\tfrac{1}{N}\sum_i z_i u_i) \to \beta + 0 \text{ as } N \to \infty$$

since the average of $\frac{1}{N}\sum_i z_i u_i$ can be shown to approach its expected value which is 0 since $\mathrm{E}[z_i u_i] = 0$ if $\mathrm{E}[u_i|z_i] = 0$. So the IV estimator is centered on β in large samples, though not exactly in small samples. For statistical inference with independent and heteroskedastic errors we continue to use the same estimated variance $\widehat{\mathrm{Var}}_{het}[b_{IV}]$ as given above for the case of fixed instruments and regressors.

C.4 OLS with Matrix Algebra

This section presumes familiarity with vectors and matrices.

The preceding results considered only one regressor (and no intercept) for notational simplicity. When there are several regressors, usually the case, it is no longer possible to express results simply using summation notation. Instead matrix notation is used. For completeness we present the matrix results.

C.4.1 Linear Model in Matrix Notation

Let the ith equation be

$$y_i = \beta_1 + \beta_2 x_{2i} + \beta_3 x_{3i} + \cdots + \beta_k x_{ki} + u_i.$$

In vector notation this can be written as

$$y_i = \begin{bmatrix} 1 & x_{2i} & \cdots & x_{ki} \end{bmatrix} \begin{bmatrix} \beta_1 \\ \beta_2 \\ \vdots \\ \beta_k \end{bmatrix} + u_i.$$

Stacking all n equations for the n observations into vectors and matrices yields

$$\begin{bmatrix} y_1 \\ \vdots \\ y_i \\ \vdots \\ y_n \end{bmatrix} = \begin{bmatrix} 1 & x_{21} & \cdots & x_{k1} \\ \vdots & \vdots & \vdots & \vdots \\ 1 & x_{2i} & \cdots & x_{ki} \\ \vdots & \vdots & \vdots & \vdots \\ 1 & x_{2n} & \cdots & x_{kn} \end{bmatrix} \begin{bmatrix} \beta_1 \\ \beta_2 \\ \vdots \\ \beta_k \end{bmatrix} + \begin{bmatrix} u_1 \\ \vdots \\ u_i \\ \vdots \\ u_n \end{bmatrix},$$

or

$$\underset{(n\times1)}{\mathbf{y}} = \underset{(n\times k)}{\mathbf{X}} \underset{(k\times1)}{\boldsymbol{\beta}} + \underset{(n\times1)}{\mathbf{u}},$$

defining the $n \times 1$ vectors $\mathbf{y}$ and $\mathbf{u}$, the $n \times k$ matrix $\mathbf{X}$, and the $k \times 1$ vector $\boldsymbol{\beta}$.

C.4.2 OLS Estimator in Matrix Notation

The OLS estimator minimizes the sum of squared residuals $\sum_{i=1}^{n} u_i^2 = \mathbf{u}'\mathbf{u}$, since

$$\mathbf{u}'\mathbf{u} = \begin{bmatrix} u_1 & \cdots & u_n \end{bmatrix} \begin{bmatrix} u_1 \\ \vdots \\ u_n \end{bmatrix} = u_1^2 + \cdots u_n^2.$$

It can be shown that the OLS estimator is the solution to the so-called normal equations $\mathbf{X}'\mathbf{u} = \mathbf{0}$ or, equivalently,

$$\mathbf{X}'(\mathbf{y} - \mathbf{X}\boldsymbol{\beta}) = \mathbf{0}.$$

Solving for $\boldsymbol{\beta}$ yields the following formula for the OLS estimator:

$$\mathbf{b} = (\mathbf{X}'\mathbf{X})^{-1}\mathbf{X}'\mathbf{y},$$

where $\mathbf{b}$ is a $k \times 1$ vector with entries $b_1, b_2, ..., b_k$. This step requires that the inverse of $\mathbf{X}'\mathbf{X}$ exists, which requires that the regressor matrix $\mathbf{X}$ has full column rank k.

Under assumptions 1-4, including the assumption of independent homoskedastic errors,

$$\text{Var}[\mathbf{b}] = \sigma_u^2 (\mathbf{X}'\mathbf{X})^{-1},$$

which is estimated by

$$\widehat{\text{Var}}[\mathbf{b}] = s_e^2 (\mathbf{X}'\mathbf{X})^{-1},$$

where $s_e^2 = \frac{1}{n-k} \sum_{i=1}^{n} \widehat{u}_i^2 = \frac{1}{n-k} \widehat{\mathbf{u}}'\widehat{\mathbf{u}}$ where $\widehat{\mathbf{u}} = \mathbf{y} - \mathbf{X}\mathbf{b}$.

C.4.3 Example of OLS Model in Matrix Notation

As an example, we apply these formulas to the data of Chapter 5.11. There are five sample observations with $y_1 = 1$, $y_2 = 2$, $y_3 = 2$, $y_4 = 2$ and $y_5 = 3$. The regressors are an intercept, equal to 1 for all five observations, and a variable that takes values of, respectively, 1, 2, 3, 4, and 5. Stacking these data yields

$$\mathbf{y} = \begin{bmatrix} 1 \\ 2 \\ 2 \\ 2 \\ 3 \end{bmatrix}; \quad \mathbf{X} = \begin{bmatrix} 1 & 1 \\ 1 & 2 \\ 1 & 3 \\ 1 & 4 \\ 1 & 5 \end{bmatrix}.$$

It follows that

$$\mathbf{X}'\mathbf{X} = \begin{bmatrix} 1 & 1 & 1 & 1 & 1 \\ 1 & 2 & 3 & 4 & 5 \end{bmatrix} \begin{bmatrix} 1 & 1 \\ 1 & 2 \\ 1 & 3 \\ 1 & 4 \\ 1 & 5 \end{bmatrix} = \begin{bmatrix} 5 & 15 \\ 15 & 55 \end{bmatrix}.$$

Matrix inversion yields

$$(\mathbf{X}'\mathbf{X})^{-1} = \begin{bmatrix} 5 & 15 \\ 15 & 55 \end{bmatrix}^{-1} = \frac{1}{275 - 225} \begin{bmatrix} 55 & -15 \\ -15 & 5 \end{bmatrix} = \frac{1}{10} \begin{bmatrix} 11 & -3 \\ -3 & 1 \end{bmatrix}.$$

Also

$$\mathbf{X}'\mathbf{y} = \begin{bmatrix} 1 & 1 & 1 & 1 & 1 \\ 1 & 2 & 3 & 4 & 5 \end{bmatrix} \begin{bmatrix} 1 \\ 2 \\ 2 \\ 2 \\ 3 \end{bmatrix} = \begin{bmatrix} 10 \\ 34 \end{bmatrix}.$$

Combining,

$$\mathbf{b} = \begin{bmatrix} \widehat{b}_1 \\ \widehat{b}_2 \end{bmatrix} = (\mathbf{X'X})^{-1}\mathbf{X'y} = \frac{1}{10}\begin{bmatrix} 11 & -3 \\ -3 & 1 \end{bmatrix}\begin{bmatrix} 10 \\ 34 \end{bmatrix} = \frac{1}{10}\begin{bmatrix} 8 \\ 4 \end{bmatrix} = \begin{bmatrix} 0.8 \\ 0.4 \end{bmatrix},$$

so the intercept is 0.8, the slope coefficient is 0.4, and the predicted value is $\widehat{y}_i = 0.8 + 0.4x_i$. Some algebra, not given, yields $\sum_{i=1}^{n}\widehat{u}_i^2 = 0.4$, so $s_e^2 = 0.4/3$. It follows that

$$\widehat{\mathrm{Var}}[\mathbf{b}] = s_e^2(\mathbf{X'X})^{-1} = \frac{0.4}{3} \times \frac{1}{10}\begin{bmatrix} 11 & -3 \\ -3 & 1 \end{bmatrix} = \begin{bmatrix} \frac{.44}{3} & -.04 \\ -.04 & \frac{.4}{30} \end{bmatrix}.$$

In particular, taking the square root of the $(2, 2)$ element of $\widehat{\mathrm{Var}}[\mathbf{b}]$, the standard error of the slope coefficient equals $\sqrt{.4/30} = 0.11547$, as given in Chapter 6.3.

C.5   Maximum Likelihood Estimation

The **maximum likelihood (ML) method** specifies a particular model for the conditional probability of the dependent variable given the regressors. This model depends on unknown parameters, and the ML method chooses as estimates of the parameters those values that make the aforementioned conditional probability of observing the data as high as possible.

We consider the case of independent observations with a single regressor and parameters(s) θ. Let $f(y_i|x_i,\theta)$ denote the specified conditional probability mass function or probability density function. Then the joint conditional probability of observing the n independent observations is given by

$$f(y_1, ..., y_n|x_1, ..., x_n, \theta) = f(y_1|x_1, \theta) \times \cdots \times f(y_n|x_n, \theta).$$

The **likelihood function** reframes this probability as a function of the parameter(s) θ given the data $(y_1, x_1), ..., (x_1, x_n)$. Then

$$L(\theta) = L(\theta|(y_1, x_1), ..., (y_n, x_n)) = f(y_1|x_1, \theta) \times \cdots \times f(y_n|x_n, \theta).$$

We estimate θ by the value that maximizes $L(\theta)$. Since $L(\theta)$ is positive we can equivalently use θ that maximizes the natural logarithm of $L(\theta)$. Since the log of a product is the sum of the logs, the **log-likelihood function** is

$$\begin{aligned} \ln L(\theta) &= \ln f(y_1|x_1, \theta) + \cdots + \ln f(y_n|x_n, \theta) \\ &= \sum_{i=1}^{n} f(y_i|x_i, \theta). \end{aligned}$$

The **maximum likelihood estimator** (MLE) of θ, denoted $\widehat{\theta}_{\mathrm{ML}}$, maximizes $\ln L(\theta)$

For standard problems the MLE has very desirable properties. Assuming $f(y_i|x_i, \theta)$ is correctly specified the MLE is consistent, has asymptotic distribution that is normal, and has the smallest variance among consistent and asymptotically normal estimators.

If inference is relaxed to allow for the possibility that $f(y_i|x_i, \theta)$ is incorrectly specified then the MLE is called the **quasi-MLE.** Then inference must be based on appropriate robust standard errors. In general the quasi-MLE is inconsistent for θ, though in the leading cases of logit, probit and Poisson regression, and the linear model with independent normally distributed errors, the quasi-MLE is still consistent for θ provided that the functional form for the conditional mean $\mathrm{E}[y_i|x_i]$ is correctly specified.

As an example, consider regression for a binary outcome. In general if $y_i = 1$ with probability p_i and $y_i = 0$ with probability $1 - p_i$, then the probability can be re-expressed as $f(y_i|p_i) = p_i^{y_i}(1-p_i)^{1-y_i}$, so $\ln f(y_i|p_i) = y_i \ln p_i + (1-y_i)\ln(1-p_i)$. The logit model specifies $p_i = \Lambda(\beta_1 + \beta_2 x_i)$, leading to log-likelihood function

$$\ln L(\beta_1, \beta_2) = \sum_{i=1}^{n} \{y_i \ln \Lambda(\beta_1 + \beta_2 x_i) + (1 - y_i)\ln(1 - \Lambda(\beta_1 + \beta_2 x_i))\}.$$

The ML estimates of β_1 and β_2 maximize this function.

C.6   Exercises

1. For the house price and size data

   (a) Compute demeaned price $(y_i - \bar{y})$ and demeaned size $(x_i - \bar{x})$.
   (b) Regress demeaned price on an intercept and demeaned size.
   (c) Compare the fitted slope coefficient and its standard error to that from regression of price on an intercept and size.
   (d) What do you conclude?

2. For the house price and size data

   (a) Compute demeaned price $(y_i - \bar{y})$ and demeaned size $(x_i - \bar{x})$.
   (b) Regress demeaned price on size without an intercept, using the no constant or no intercept option of your regression package.
   (c) Compare the fitted slope coefficient to that from regression of price on an intercept and size. What do you conclude?
   (d) Compare the standard error of the fitted slope coefficient to that from regression of price on an intercept and size. What do you conclude? Hint: Think about the degrees of freedom.

3. Adapt the analysis for OLS with heteroskedastic errors to suggest a formula for heteroskedastic errors for the IV estimator.

4. Suppose a sample of size 3 has observations on (x, y) equal to $(1, 2)$, $(2, 5)$ and $(3, 14)$. Calculate the least squares estimates from regression of y on an intercept and x using the matrix algebra formula. Then compute $\widehat{\mathrm{Var}}[\mathbf{b}] = s_e^2(\mathbf{X}'\mathbf{X})^{-1}$ and hence give the standard error for the slope coefficient.

Appendix D

Solutions to Selected Exercises

Usually for most odd-numbered questions.

D.1   Solutions: Analysis of Economics Data

1. (a) Numerical time series. (b) Numerical cross-section data. (c) Numerical panel data. (d) Categorical cross-section. data. (e) Numerical repeated cross-section.

3. (a) Observational. (b) Experimental. (c) Observational.

D.2   Solutions: Univariate Data Summary

1. (a) 1+1+1+1+1=5. (b) (1+2+3+4+5)=15. (c) 110. (d) 2.28333. (e) 55.

3. (a) $\sum_{t=1}^{3} x_{1t} = x_{11} + x_{12} + x_{13} = 15.$ $\sum_{t=1}^{3} x_{2t} = x_{21} + x_{22} + x_{23} = 18.$
   (b) $\sum_{i=1}^{2} x_{i1} = x_{11} + x_{21} = 5 + 8 = 13.$ $\sum_{i=1}^{2} x_{i2} = x_{12} + x_{22} = 9;$ $\sum_{i=1}^{2} x_{13} + x_{23} = 11.$

5. $\bar{x} = 2$; $s = \sqrt{8/3} = 1.633$; CV=$\frac{2}{1.663} = 1.225$; Skew= $0/(8/32)^{3/2} = 0$; Kurt= $(32/4)/(8/4)^2 = 2.$

7. Only the mean changes. It becomes 4.

9. $100 \pm 3 \times 14 = (58, 142)$ as 99.7% are within 3 standard deviations of the mean.

11. (a) Median. (b) Mean. (c) No. (d) 12.

13. (b) Data appear right-skewed: skewness $1.56 > 0$ (and mean= 253910 > median= 244000).
    (c) No. Histogram is clearly right-skewed. (d) No. Kernel density estimate is right-skewed.

15. (b) $\bar{x} = 13.033333$; $s = 1.991072$; interquartile range (12, 14).

17. (b) $\bar{x} = 2.7$; $s = 0.8932495$; interquartile range (2.1, 3.3).

21. (a) Somewhat right-skewed (1.01) and excess kurtosis (4.54>3). (b) Quite right-skewed.
(c) Quite volatile - big peak in 2000 (technology stocks bubble) plus other peaks including around 1929 (before the Great Depression) and 2018. (d) Yes - over twice the mean (and median) in 2020.

23. (b) Yes (aside from very small computational error). (c) No. Not normal and big spike at low value reflecting the early periods. (d) Yes, the three series appear to move together.

25. (a) Yes. (d) Estimate in (b) is much more volatile than that in (c).

D.3   Solutions: The Sample Mean

1. (a) $\mu = 1000 \times 0.8 + 4000 \times 0.2 = 1{,}800$.
   (b) $\sigma^2 = (1000 - 1800)^2 \times 0.8 + (5000 - 1800)^2 \times 0.2 = 2{,}560{,}000$. (c) $\sigma = 1{,}600$.

3. (a) $X + 3$ has mean $5 + 3 = 8$, variance 4 (and standard deviation $\sqrt{4} = 2$).
   (b) $E[2X] = 2 \times 5 = 10$, $\text{Var}[2X] = 2^2 \times 4 = 16$.   (c) $E[2X + 3] = 2 \times 5 + 3 = 13$, $\text{Var}[2X + 3] = 2^2 \times 4 = 16$. (d) $E[(X - 5)/2] = 0/2 = 0$, $\text{Var}[(X - 5)/2] = 4/2^2 = 1$.

5. (a) 200. (b) $\sigma^2 = 400/100 = 4$; $\sigma = \sqrt{4} = 2$. (c) Most likely given sample size of 100 is reasonably large.

7. (a) Yes. (b) 100. (c) Yes. (d) Data appear random. (e) Observations appear unrelated.

9. $E[\bar{X}]$ unchanged, $\text{Var}[\bar{X}]$ one-quarter as large, standard deviation of $\bar{X}$ one-half as large.

11. (a) $\mu = 1 \times \frac{1}{6} + 0 \times \frac{5}{6} = \frac{1}{6} \simeq 0.167$. (b) $\sigma^2 = (1 - \frac{1}{6})^2 \times \frac{1}{6} + (0 - \frac{1}{6})^2 \times \frac{5}{6} = \frac{5}{36} \simeq 0.139$. (d) Sample mean and variance should be quite close to 0.167 and 0.139. (e) No.

12. (a) Yes since $\bar{x} = 0.169975 \simeq \frac{1}{6}$ and $s = 0.037151 \simeq \sqrt{\frac{5}{36}/100} = 0.037268$. (b) Histogram is not exactly normal. With a larger sample size we would get closer to exactly normal.

15. (a) $E[\bar{X}] = 5{,}000$, $\text{St.Dev.}[\bar{X}] = 20000/\sqrt{10000} = 200$. (b) Low probability of 0.025 of making a loss this large since \$5,400 is two standard deviations higher than the expected average loss of \$5,000 and $\bar{X}$ is normally distributed given the large sample. $\Pr(X > 5400) = 0.0228$.

17. (a) $\bar{x} = 100.0564$ and $se(\bar{x}) = 7.97252$ are close to $\mu = 100$ and $\sigma/\sqrt{n} = 16/\sqrt{4} = 8$.
   (b) The mean of $se(\bar{x}) = 14.75808$ is close to $\sigma = 16$. (c) $(X - \mu)/(\sigma/\sqrt{n}) = (X - 100)/8$ is normal even in small samples as X is normal. (d) z has mean $0.007 \simeq 0$, standard deviation $0.997 \simeq 1$, skewness $0.028 \simeq 0$, kurtosis $3.177 \simeq 3$. (e) Yes, it appears standard normal.

19. (a) Representative. (b) Most likely unrepresentative. (c) Most likely unrepresentative.

21. (a) 7436390. (b) 467.099. (c) Unweighted mean is 446.66. (d) 32578.1.
   (e) $\sqrt{32578.1} = 180.49$ vs. 181.31. (f) In Stata `sum net_worth[weight=number]`.

23. (b) Yes, essentially 0 and 1. (c) No. They are very left skewed. (d) Yes.

25. (a) Yes. (d) The part (b) measure is much more variable than the part (c) measure.

D.4   Solutions: Statistical Inference for the Mean

1. (a) 0.028998. (b) 0.057996. (c) 1.717144. (d) 2.073873.

3. (a) 0.025. (b) 0.05. (c) 2.0 (or 1.96 more precise). (d) 2.0 (or 1.96).

5. (b) The $z's$ are draws of $Z = (\overline{X} - \mu)/\sigma$ where X_i's are normal so expect z has mean 0, variance 1 and standard normal distribution.
   (c) Similar as the 1,000 $z's$ have mean 0.00705 and standard deviation 0.996.
   (d) The $t's$ are draws of $Z = (\overline{X} - \mu)/se(\overline{X})$ where X_i's are normal so Z is t–distributed with $n - 1$ degrees of freedom and here $n - 1 = 3$. (e) The 1,000 $t's$ have mean 0.00415 and variance 2.197. (f) The density for t is squashed (lower peak and fatter tails) compared to density for z.

7. $\bar{x} \pm t_{30;.10} \times se(\bar{x}) = 40 \pm 1.3 \times 10 = (27, 53)$.

9. $\bar{x} \pm t_{24;.025} \times (20/\sqrt{25}) = 10 \pm 2.064 \times 4 = (1.744, 18.256)$.

11. (b) $(239688, 268133)$.
    (c) $\bar{x} \pm t_{28;.025} \times se(\bar{x}) = 253910.3 \pm 2.0484071 \times 37390.71/\sqrt{29} = (239688, 268133)$.

13. (a) Wider. (b) Narrower. (c) Similar width but larger values. (d) Wider.

15. (b) $H_0 : \mu = 270000$ against $H_a : \mu \neq 270000$. $p = 0.0280 < 0.05$ so reject H_0 at level 0.05.
    (c) $c = t_{28,.025} = 2.0484$. $|t| = 2.31730 > 2.0484$ so reject H_0 at level 0.05.
    (d) $t = (\bar{x} - \mu^*)/se(\bar{x}) = (253910.3 - 270000)/(37390.71/\sqrt{29}) = -2.31730$.
    $p = \Pr[|T_{28}| < |-2.31730|] = 0.0280 < 0.05$.

17. (a) $2.0/\sqrt{25} = 0.4$. (b) $1.2 \pm t_{24,.024} \times 0.4 = (0.3744, 2.0256)$.
    (c) $H_0 : \mu = 0$ vs. $H_a : \mu \neq 0$. $t = 1.2/0.4 = 3$. Reject H_0 as $|t| > t_{24;.025} = 2.064$ or as $p = 0.006 < 0.05$.
    (d) $H_0 : \mu < 0$ vs. $H_a : \mu \geq 0$. $t = 3$. Reject H_0 as $|t| > t_{24;.05} = 1.711$ or as $p = 0.003 < 0.05$. Support the claim.
    (e) Observations have common mean and variance and are independent (and for exact t distribution are normally distributed).
    (f) Observations are unlikely to be independent and are possibly (downward) biased.

19. (a) Less likely - $p > 0.05$ was given so $p > 0.01$. (b) More likely given more precise estimation.

21. (b) 951 of 1,000 or 95.1% of 95% confidence intervals included 100, close to 95% as expected.
    (d) 49 of 1,000 or 4.9% of tests rejected, close to 5% as expected.

23. Answers will vary with package. Stata gave the following.
    (b) 953 of 1,000 or 95.3% of 95% confidence intervals included 200.
    (d) 47 of 1,000 or 4.7% of tests rejected $H_0 : \mu = 200$.

25. (a) $19.73/\sqrt{109} = 1.890$. (b) $(29.06, 36.56)$. (c) $H_0 : \mu = 35$ against $H_a : \mu \neq 35$. $t = -1.159$.
    Do not reject H_0 as $|t| > t_{108;.025} = 1.982$ or as $p = 0.249 > 0.05$. (d) $H_0 : \mu > 35$ against
    $H_a : \mu < 35$. $t = -1.159$. Do not reject H_0 as $t > -t_{108;.05} = -1.659$ or as $p = 0.124 > 0.05$.

27. (a) Do not reject as $p = 0.0868 > 0.05$. (b) Reject as $p = 0.0434 < 0.05$.
    (c) $62.468 \pm t_{84,.05} \times 10.0796 = (45.70, 79.23)$.
    (d) $t = (62.468 - 35)/10.079 = 2.75$ has $p = 0.007 < 0.05$. So reject H_0.

29. (b) $(2.245, 2.515)$. (c) $H_0 : \mu = 2.5$ against $H_a : \mu \neq 2.5$, $t = (32.81 - 35)/1.89 = -1.758$,
    $p = 0.081 > 0.05$ so do not reject H_0 at level 0.05.
    (d) $H_0 : \mu \geq 2.5$ against $H_a : \mu < 2.5$, $t = -1.758$, $p = 0.040 < 0.05$ so reject H_0 at level 0.05.

31. (a) $25 \pm 2 \times 4 = (17, 33)$. (b) $2 \times 4 = 8$. (c) $t = (25 - 15)/4 = 2.5$. Reject H_0 at level 0.05.

33. (a) $\bar{x} = 550/1025 = 0.5366$ and $se(\bar{x}) = \sqrt{.5366 \times (1 - .5366)/1025} = 0.0156$.
    (b) $0.5366 \pm 1.960 \times 0.0156 = (0.506, 0.567)$. (c) $2 \times 0.0156 = 0.0312$.
    (d) $H_0 : \mu \leq 0.5$ vs. $H_a : \mu > 0.5$. $t = (0.5366 - 0.5)/0.0156 = 2.35$. Reject H_0 at level 0.05
    as $t = 2.35 > 1.645$ or $p = 0.0094 < 0.05$.

D.5   Solutions: Bivariate Data Summary

1. (a) Yes. (b) $\bar{x} = 4$, $\bar{y} = 14$; $\sum_{i=1}^{3}(x_i - \bar{x})(y_i - \bar{y}) = (2-4)(4-14) + (4-4)(10-14) + (6-4)(28-14) = 48$, so $\text{Cov}(x, y) = 48/2 = 24$. Unclear whether this means a strong relationship.
   (c) $\sum_{i=1}^{3}(x_i - \bar{x})^2 = (2-4)^2 + (4-4)^2 + (6-4)^2 = 8$. $\sum_{i=1}^{3}(y_i - \bar{y})^2 = (4-14)^2 + (10-14)^2 + (28-14)^2 = 312$; $\text{Cor}(x, y) = 48/\sqrt{8 \times 312} = 0.9608$. Yes, very strong as close to 1.

3. (a) It is not immediately obvious. It requires some calculation. e.g. *dvisits*=0 for 82%
   $(100 \times 3686/4491)$ with *hospadmi*=0 compared to only 68% with *hospadmi*=1.
   (b) Now clearer. e.g. if no relationship we expect *dvisits*=0 and *hospadmi*=0 for 3583.3 which
   is less than actual 3686. (c) Correlation is 0.2484 so clearly a positive relationship.

5. (a) $\bar{x} = 4$, $\bar{y} = 14$; $\sum_{i=1}^{3}(x_i - \bar{x})(y_i - \bar{y}) = (2-4)(4-14) + (4-4)(10-14) + (6-4)(28-14) = 48$.
   $\sum_{i=1}^{3}(x_i - \bar{x})^2 = (2-4)^2 + (4-4)^2 + (6-4)^2 = 8$. So $b_2 = 48/8 = 6$.
   (b) $b_1 = \bar{y} - b_2\bar{x} = 14 - 4 \times 6 = -10$.

7. (a)-(b) indicate a strong relationship. (c) Correlation $= 0.9315$. (d) $price = 82559 + 292 \times size$.
   (e) One more square foot is associated with a \$292 increase in house price.

9. (a) $10/(\sqrt{100} \times \sqrt{25}) = 0.2$. (b) $10/100 = 0.1$. (c) 0.2 standard deviations.

11. (c) 0.9949. (b) $realgdppc = 17024 + 169.7 \times quarter$. (e) Real GDP per capita rises on average
    by \$169.71 each quarter.

13. (a) $e_1 = 2 - 3 = -1$, $e_2 = 4 - 5 = -1$, $e_3 = 9 - 7 = 2$; yes as $\sum_{i=1}^{3} e_i = -1 + (-1) + 2 = 0$.
    (b) $\sum_{i=1}^{3} e_i^2 = (-1)^2 + (-1)^2 + 2^2 = 6$; $\bar{y} = 5$ so $\sum_{i=1}^{3}(y_i - \bar{y})^2 = (2-5)^2 + (4-5)^2 + (9-5)^2 = 26$;
    $R^2 = 1 - 6/26 = 0.769$.

15. (a) $\bar{x} = 2$, $\bar{y} = 3$; $\sum_{i=1}^{3}(x_i - \bar{x})(y_i - \bar{y}) = -6$; $\sum_{i=1}^{3}(x_i - \bar{x})^2 = 2$; $\sum_{i=1}^{3}(y_i - \bar{y})^2 = 24$.
    $\text{Cor}(x, y) = -6/\sqrt{2 \times 24} = -0.866$. (b) $b_2 = -6/2 = -3$, $b_1 = \bar{y} - b_2\bar{x} = 3 - (-3) \times 2 = 9$.
    (c) $\hat{y}_1 = 9 - 3 \times 1 = 6$, $\hat{y}_2 = 9 - 3 \times 2 = 3$, $\hat{y}_3 = 9 - 3 \times 3 = 0$; $e_1 = 7 - 6 = 1$, $e_2 = 1 - 3 = -2$,
    $e_3 = 1 - 0 = 1$. yes as $\sum_{i=1}^{3} e_i = 1 + (-2) + 1 = 0$.
    (d) $\sum_{i=1}^{3} e_i^2 = 1^2 + (-2)^2 + 1^2 = 6$. $s_e^2 = \frac{1}{3-2}\sum_{i=1}^{3} e_i^2 = 6$. $s_e = \sqrt{6} = 2.450$.
    (e) ExpSS$=\sum_{i=1}^{3}(\hat{y}_i - \bar{y})^2 = (6 - 3)^2 + (3 - 3)^2 + (0 - 3)^2 = 18$ and already computed
    TSS$=\sum_{i=1}^{3}(y_i - \bar{y})^2 = 24$, ResSS$=\sum_{i=1}^{3} e_i^2 = 6$, yes as $18 + 6 = 24$.
    (f) $R^2 = 1 - 6/24 = 0.75 = 0.866^2$. (g) Reverse regression: $b_2 = -6/24 = -0.25 \neq (1/-3)$.

17. (a) $R^2 = 81/300 = 0.27$. (b) $\sqrt{0.27} = 0.5196$. (c) $s_e = \sqrt{(300 - 81)/64} = 1.8498$.

19. (b) Summary statistics should give mean 0 and standard deviation 1. (c) $zprice = 0 + 0.7858 \times zsize$. (d) 0.7858. (e) Same. (f) Same R^2 but slope $0.00837 \neq 1/73.77$.

21. (a) Detroit (0.3308). (b) Los Angeles (0.9955). (c) Scatterplot is very strange - the lower curve shows the run up in prices to 2006 and the upper curve shows the decline and eventual increase in prices after 2006. (d) A one unit increase in index for Los Angeles is associated with a 0.205 increase in index for Cleveland. (e) $r^2 = 0.6005^2 = 0.3606 = R^2$.

23. (a) 2.291 times higher. (b) Yes, the slope of 1.769 is much greater than one.
    (c) Observations 66 and 154 appears furthest from the line. (d) $e_{66} = 60746$ and $e_{154} = -79080$. (e) slope increases to 1.951 as e_{154} was pulling the line down. (f) Slope decreases to 1.727 as e_{66} was pushing the line up (the two offset so we are close to original 1.769).

25. (d) The relationship appears linear. (e) Now the curve is more bumpy.

D.6 Solutions: The Least Squares Estimator

1. (a) $E[y_1|x_1] = 1 + 2 \times 1 = 3$, $E[y_2|x_2] = 5$, $E[y_3|x_3] = 7$.
   (b) $u_1 = y_1 - E[y_1|x_1] = 3.78 - 3 = 0.78$, $u_2 = 1.69$, $u_3 = 0.51$.
   (c) $\hat{y}_1 = 2.27 + 1.87 \times 1 = 4.12$, $\hat{y}_2 = 6.01$, $\hat{y}_3 = 7.90$.
   (d) $e_1 = y_1 - \hat{y}_1 = 3.78 - 4.12 = 0.34$, $e_2 = -0.68$, $e_3 = -0.32$.

3. (a) $E[y|x] = 3 + 5x$. (b) $\text{Var}[y|x] = 4$.

5. (a) $b_2 = 120/80 = 1.5$, $b_1 = 10 - 1.5 \times 2 = 7$. (b) $s_e^2 = \frac{1}{18} \times 450 = 25$, $se(b_2) = \sqrt{25/80} = 0.559$.

7. (a) 100. (b) 10. (c) 80.

9. (a) Yes as assumptions 1-2 are met. (b) Yes as assumptions 1-2 are met.
   (c) No, as the error variance is not constant.

11. (a) Yes as errors are homoskedastic. (b) No as errors are heteroskedastic. (c) No as errors are not independent.

13. (b) The true value is $\beta_2 = 2$ but with few observations this will be imprecisely estimated. Stata code gave $b_2 = -1.824$ (with a large standard error of 2.468). R code gave $b_2 = -0.396$ (with a large standard error of 2.248). Note that Stata and R results are expected to differ here as they use different algorithms to generate the random variables x and u.

15. (b) If unbiased the average of the 400 slopes should be close to 2. For Stata the average was 2.066 and for R the average was 1.974. These are close (and with more simulations we would get increasingly close to 2). (c) Close to normal. Some small skewness and excess kurtosis. (Aside: This is because different $x's$ were generated in each sample).

D.7 Solutions: Statistical Inference for Bivariate Regression

1. (a) House price increases by \$291.92 with each extra square foot.
   (b) (249.40, 334.44) from output.
   (c) Statistically significant at level 0.05 as $t = 14.02$ has $p = 0.000 < 0.05$.
   (d) $b_2 \pm t_{30,.025} \times se(b_2) = 291.9212 \pm 2.0422725 \times 20.81895 = (249.40, 334.44)$.
   (e) $t = b_2/se(b_2) = 291.9212/20.81895 = 14.02 < t_{30,.025} = 2.042$ or $p = \Pr[|T_{30}| < 14.02] = 5.2 \times 10^{-15} \simeq 0.000$.

3. (a) No. (b) 0.2184. (c) A one point increase in SAT math score is associated with a \$48.42 increase in earnings. (d) $R^2 = 0.0477 = 0.2184^2$. (e) Yes as $t = 6.62$ with $p = 0.00 < 0.05$.
   (f) $H_0 : \beta_2 = 30$ against $H_0 : \beta_2 \neq 30$. $t = (48.42 - 30)/7.31 = 2.52$ has $p = 0.012 < 0.05$ so reject H_0 at 5%.

5. (a) $7 \pm 2.0243 \times 3 = (0.927, 13.073)$.
   (b) $t = 7/3 = 2.333$. Reject as $|t| > 2.024$ or as $p = 0.025 < 0.05$.
   (c) $t = 2.333$. Reject as $t > 1.686$ or as $p = 0.0125 < 0.05$.
   (d) $t = (7 - 10)/3 = -1.0$. Do not reject as $|t| < 2.024$ or as $p = 0.3234 > 0.05$.
   (e) Assumptions 1-2 needed for b_2 unbiased; 3-4 needed if $se(b_2)$ is the default standard error. For t statistics to be exactly $t(n-2)$ distributed we need 1-4 and normally distributed errors.

7. (a) $39 \pm 1.96 \times 10 = (19.4, 58.6)$ or also okay more approximately $39 \pm 2 \times 10 = (19, 59)$.
   (b) $t = (39 - 20)/10 = 1.9$; do not reject H_0 at level 0.05 as $|t| \leq 1.96$ or approximately $t| \leq 2$.
   (c) $H_0 : \theta \leq 20$ against $H_a : \theta > 20$. Again $t = 1.9$. We reject at 5% if $t > z_{.05} = 1.645$ so do reject here. This supports at 5% the claim that $\theta > 20$.

9. (a) Yes. (b) A \$1 increase in income is associated with an increase of \$12.22 in assets (equals 0.01222 thousands of dollars).
   (c) Yes. $t = 20.96$ and $p = 0.00$. (d) $H_0 : \beta_2 = 0.012$ against $H_a : \beta_2 \neq 0.12$. $t = (.01222 - .012)/.000583 = 0.377$ and $p = 0.706$. Do not reject H_0 at 5%.
   (e) $H_0 : \beta_2 \leq 0.012$ against $H_a : \beta_2 > 0.12$. Same $t = 0.377$ and $p = 0.706/2 = 0.353$. Do not reject H_0 at 5%. Does not support initial claim that $\beta_2 > 0.12$.

11. (a) Yes. (b) $t = 13.65$ and $p = 0.000$. (c) $H_0 : \beta_2 = 2$ against $H_a : \beta_2 \neq 2$. $t = (1.7689 - 2)/0.1296 = -1.738$ and $p = 0.0763$. Do not reject H_0 at 5%.
(d) $H_0 : \beta_2 \geq 2$ against $H_a : \beta_2 < 2$ Same $t = -1.738$ and $p = 0.0763/2 = 0.0381 < 0.05$. Reject H_0 at 5%. Support initial claim that $\beta_2 < 0.12$.

13. (a) 360. (b) 1-90/360=0.75. (c) $\sqrt{90/19} = 2.176$. (d) 6/3=2. (e) $\Pr[|T_{19}| > 2] = 0.060$. (f, g) $6 \pm t_{19;.025} \times 3 = (-0.28, 12.28)$. (h) $t = b/se$ so $se = b/t = -8/(-1.6) = 5$.

D.8 Solutions: Case Studies for Bivariate Regression

1. (a)-(c) See section 8.1. (d) The relationship essentially disappears; it was driven by high infant mortality in the very poorest countries in the dataset (Mexico and Turkey).

3. (b) It falls by 0.518 per 1,000 live births. (b) Yes. $t = -2.13$ and $p = 0.040 < 0.05$.
(d) The relationship disappears.

5. (c) Life expectancy increases by 0.7149 years. (d) Actual value 78.6 is much less than the predicted value 85.1.

7. (a) Walmart is more variable than Coca Cola. (b) Slope is 0.748 with het-robust $se = 0.909$.
(c) Yes as intercept exceeds 0 with $t = 0.39$ and $p = 0/0085$ using a one-sided test.
(d) Yes. Claim is $\beta_2 > 0$ so test $H_0 : \beta_2 \leq 0$ against $H_a : \beta_2 > 0$ has $p = 0.000 < 0.05$ so reject H_0. (d) Yes. Claim is $\beta_2 < 1$ (and $\beta_2 > 0$) so test $H_0 : \beta_2 \geq 1$ against $H_a : \beta_2 < 1$ has $t = 2.775$ and $p = 0.003 < 0.05$ so reject H_0.

D.9 Solutions: Models with Natural Logarithm

1. (a) $a + bx$. (b) $\exp(c + dx)$. (c) $c \ln(a + bx)$. (d) $\ln x + \ln z$.

3. (a) $(520 - 500)/500 = 0.04$. (b) $\ln 520 - \ln 500 = 0.03922071$.
(c) Quite close as expected since $\frac{\Delta x}{x} \simeq \Delta \ln x$ for small $\frac{\Delta x}{x}$.
(d) Now $\frac{\Delta x}{x} = 1.00$ is quite different from $\Delta \ln x = 0.69314718$ as large $\frac{\Delta x}{x}$.

5. (a) IQ up by 1 point then earnings up by $200.
(b) IQ up by 1 point then earnings up by proportion 0.009 (or 0.9%).
(c) IQ up by 1 percent then earnings up by 0.8 percent.
(d) IQ up by proportion 0.01 (or 1%) then annual earnings up by $0.01 \times 15000 = \$150$.

7. (a) Semi-elasticity. (b) Neither. (c) Elasticity.

9. (a) An increase of one in *satmath* is associated with a 0.001254 proportionate increase or a 0.1254% increase in *salary*.
(b) A 1% increase in *satmath* is associated with a 0.6307% increase in *salary*.
(c) $t = (.6307 - 1.0)/.1233 = -2.995$ has $p = 0.0028$. Reject the null hypothesis at 5%.

(d) The two models have same dependent variable and number of regressors so choose model with highest R^2 which is (marginally) the first model.

11. (a) $\widehat{lifeexp} = 73.084 + 0.00111 Hlthpc$. (b) $\widehat{lifeexp} = 44.867 + 3.993 \ln(hlthpc)$. A 1% increase in health spending per capita is associated with a $0.01 \times 3.993 = 0.03993$ years greater life expectancy. c) Linear-log as $R^2 = 0.487 > 0.320$.
(d) Linear-log has a curved shape (with declining slope) that fits the scatterplot better.

13. (a) $\ln y \simeq \ln 0.09 + \ln x = -2.41 + 1 \times \ln x$. (b) Yes, though perhaps slight curvature for largest values of $hlthpc$. (c) $\ln(\widehat{hlthpc}) = -5.010 + 1.256 \ln(gdppc)$. Similar to (a).
(d) A 1% change in GDP pc is associated with a 1.256% increase in health spending pc.
(e) $t = (1.256 - 1)/0.174 = 1.472$; not statistically different from one at level 0.05.

15. (a) Exponential. (b) Latter half of the 2000's (precisely June 2007 to February 2009).
(c) Yes exponential growth since the log is approximately linear in time.
(d) The 1980's and 1990's had the highest proportionate growth.
(e) Approximately $(9.5 - 6.2)/670 = 0.00493$ so around 0.49% growth per month.
(f) OLS had slope 0.00549 so 0.55% growth per month.

17. (a) 72/9=8 so 8%. (b) Quadrupled in 16 years so doubled in 8 years so 72/8=9 so 9%.
(c) $\Delta \ln x / \Delta time = 0.50/20 = 0.020$ or 2.0%.

19. (a) Follows as y increased from $\ln x$ to $\ln(x + \Delta x)$. (b) Use $\ln a - \ln b = \ln(a/b)$.
(c) Divide by x. (d) Use $\ln(1 + r) \simeq r$ for small r. (e) Divide both sides by Δx.

D.10   Solutions: Data Summary with Multiple Regression

1. (a) *satmath* as it is more highly correlated with salary. (b) An increase in the verbal SAT score of one point is associated with a $23.92 increase in annual salary. (c) After controlling for the math SAT score, an increase in the verbal SAT score of one point is associated with a $11.25 reduction in annual salary. (d) The correlation of *satverb* and *satmath* of 0.62 is quite high and positive, so we expect a considerable change in the slope coefficient when *satmath* is added as a regressor, though not necessarily a sign change.

3. (a) One more bathroom is associated with a $36,147 higher price.
(b) Controlling for house size, one more bathroom is associated with a $9,892 higher price.
(c) A one standard deviation increase has bigger effect for size as $71.09 \times 398.3 = 28,315 > 9892 \times 0.341 = 3,373$.
(d) The slope coefficient of the residual is 9891.897, same as in part (b); see section 10.4.3.
(e) We have $9892 + 71.09 \times 369.3 = 36146$, same as in part (a); see section 10.5.3.

5. (a) TV (has the highest mean). (b) TV ($r = 0.78$). (c) Radio ($b = 202.5$).
(d) Radio ($b = 188.5$).

7. (a) 23,667.3. (b) 1,553, a big change. (c) 23,584, so little change. (d) Correlation of *bedrooms* with *size* is high (0.518) and with *age* is low (-0.026). Results change little when a variable is added that is essentially uncorrelated with the other regressors.

9. (b) Average of predictions equals the average *price*. (c) Essentially zero as residuals sum to zero. (d) Essentially zero as regressor orthogonal to residual.

11. (a) $\sqrt{500/19} = 5.129$. (b) $1 - 400/500 = 0.20$. (c) $\sqrt{400/16} = 5.0$. (d) $1 - \frac{400/16}{500/19} = 0.05$.
    (e) $\sqrt{0.20} = 0.447$.

13. The variable *bedrooms* is dropped. The problem is perfect collinearity with the intercept as for all observations the value of *bedrooms* (3) equals three times the intercept (1). Or can say that there is no variation across observations in the regressor *bedrooms*.

D.11 Solutions: Statistical Inference for Multiple Regression

1. (a) $E[y|x_2, x_3] = 1 + 2 \times 2 + 3 \times 4 = 17$. (b) $u = y - E[y|x_2, x_3] = 17.8 - 17 = 0.8$.
   (c) $\hat{y}_1 = 1.7 + 2.5 \times 2 + 1.7 \times 4 = 13.5$. (d) $e = y - \hat{y} = 17.8 - 13.5 = 4.3$.

3. (a) $E[y|x_2, x_3] = 3 + 5x_2 + 14x_3$. (b) $Var[y|x_2, x_3] = 9$.

5. (a) Yes as assumptions 1-2 hold. (b) Yes as assumptions 1-2 hold. (c) No as the error is heteroskedastic.

7. (a) *satmath* is most highly correlated (correlation $= 0.2184$. (b) *satmath*, *age*, and *highgrade*.
   (c) *satverb* has unexpected negative sign though is statistically insignificant at 5%.
   (d) Controlling for SAT verbal score, age and highest grade, a one point increase in the SAT math score is associated with a $52.33 increase in annual earnings.
   (e) Yes as $F = 15.49$ has $p = 0.000$. (f) Full model as $\overline{R}^2$ increases from 0.0466 to 0.0658.
   (g) Yes. Test of joint significance of *satverb*, *age*, and *highgrade* has $F = 7.31$ and $p = 0.0001$.

9. (b) Drop in order *sex*, *minority*, *satverb*, *highgrade*. Preferred model has regressors *satmath*, *age*, *height*, *weight* and *genhealth*. (c) None become statistically significant at 5%.

11. (a) Reject as $p = 0.0154$. (b) $F_{6,43,.05} = 2.318$. (c) Do not reject as $p = 0.06197$.
    (d) $\chi^2_{6,.05} = 12.592$.

13. Definitely statistically significant in parts (a) and (e) as $p = 0.04 < 0.05$.

15. (a) $t = 72/40 = 1.8$. (b) Not statistically significant as $|t| = 1.8 < z_{.025} = 1.96$.
    (c) $72 \pm 1.96 \times 40 = (-6.4, 150.4)$.

17. (a) Statistically significant as $|t| = 3 > z_{.025} = 1.96$.
    (b) Since $t = b/s_b$, $s_b = b/t = 72/3 = 24$. (c) $72 \pm 1.96 \times 24 = (24.96, 119.04)$.

D.12   Solutions: Further Topics in Multiple Regression

1. (a) Heteroskedastic robust. (b) Default. (c) HAC robust. (d) Cluster robust.

3. (a) Coeffs: -96520, 52.3, -13.1, 3577.2, 9684.4. Default se's: 27800, 9.33, 9.66, 994.3, 406.8.
   (b) Heteroskedastic-robust se's are 29525, 10.77, 9.48, 1058.2, 399.0. (c) Same OLS estimates.
   (d) The two are generally within 10% of each other, sometimes larger and sometimes smaller.
   (e) $F = 16.40$ in part (a) and $F = 15.49$ in part (b). Similar and both have $p = 0.0000$.

5. (a) The negative coefficient for *hlthins* may be surprising. An explanation is that people with
   health insurance are covered for a doctor visit so are less likely to visit the pharmacy.
   (b) The big change is that the standard error for *illness* increases from 0.01297 to 0.01825.
   (c) The standard error for *illness* increases from 0.01825 to 0.03435, while all others also
   increase.

7. (a) $\bar{x} = 0.5110$ and $se(\bar{x}) = 0.007879$. (b) $b_1 = 0.5110$ and $se(b_1) = 0.007879$. Same.
   (c) Same as (a) and (b). (d) $b_1 = 0.5110$ and $se(b_1) = 0.024967$. Much larger.

9. (a) $\hat{y} = 3.008 - 1.589x$ with slope standard error 0.163. (b) Yes as $\hat{\rho}_1 = 0.46$, $\hat{\rho}_2 = 0.42$,
   $\hat{\rho}_3 = 0.35$, $\hat{\rho}_4 = 0.31$, $\hat{\rho}_5 = 0.33$, $\hat{\rho}_6 = 0.25$ (answers here may vary a bit with software used).
   (c) Slope standard error has increased to 0.216.

11. (d) *gs1* and *gs20* have means 2.7101 and 4.6245.
    (e) Short-term rate *gs1* is more volatile as st. dev. is $2.18 > 1.59$ for long-term rate *gs20*.
    (f) The series move together for the first 7-8 years, then the relationship breaks down (first
    due to the early 2000's recession and second due to the 2008 on Great Recession). Both show
    a general downward trend.
    (g) Yes, aside from observations where *gs1* is close to zero.
    (h) Slope $= 0.605$ so a 1 percentage point increase in *gs1* is associated with 0.604 percentage
    point increase in *gs20*. The less than 1-to-one relationship is expected, since long-term rates
    fluctuate less than short-term rates. The relationship is reasonably strong with $R^2 = 0.688$.

13. (a) Using Stata, standard errors are in order, 29570.609, 10.809, 9.496, 1063.139, 399.126.
    (b) All are within 1% of each other.
    (c) Now a bigger difference, as much as 15% for *satmath* $(10.8090/9.3345 = 1.16)$.

15. (a) \$261,167. (b) 8,428. (c) (243842, 278492). (d) $\sqrt{8428^2 + 23981^2} = 25,419$.
    (e) (208917, 313417). (f) Now 8,448 in (b) and 25,624 in (d).

17. (a) Great variability as *perwt* ranges from 12 to 265 with standard deviation 75.6 that is large
    compared to the mean of 119.2. (b) Slope parameter equals 5270.7 with standard error 736.2.
    (c) Slope parameter equals 5012.4 with standard error 873.3. (d) The same results.

19. (a) 44,898 with standard error 2,041. (b) 44,062 with standard error 2,366.
    (c) 44,062. (d) Same as part (b).

21. (a) False. (b) True. (c) True.

23. (a) 0.05. (b) 0.05. (c) $\Pr(\text{not reject } H_0|H_a) = 1 - \Pr(\text{reject } H_0|H_a) = 1 - 0.20 = 0.80$.
    (d) 0.20.

D.13 Solutions: Case Studies for Multiple Regression

1. (c) API score rises by 54.29 points with each extra year of parental education.
   (d) yes as $p = 0.000$. (e) Predicted API $= -36.8585 + 54.287 \times 16.78 = 874.07$.
   (f) (867.3, 880.8). (g) (792.6, 955.5). (h) Davis API of 829 is lower than the prediction 874.

3. (a) A 1% increase in K is associated with a 0.946% increase in Q.
   (b) $t = (.945998 - 1)/.0365949) = -1.476$ has $p = 0.146$. Do not reject $H_0 : \beta_{lnk} = 1$.
   (c) Yes. $F = 1190.9$ with $p = 0.000$. (d) $b_{lnk} + b_{lnl} = 1.0457$. $F = 4.46$ with $p = 0.040$.
   Reject at 5% constant returns to scale $H_0 : \beta_{lnk} + \beta_{lnl} = 1$.
   (e) $\bar{R}^2$ only slightly increases from 0.9831 to 0.9834. (f) No. $F = 1.01$ with $p = 0.398$.

5. (a) Yes, there is a negative relationship. (b) Yes. $b = -1.101$ with $t = -2.62$ and $p = 0.017$.
   (c) 0.21, -0.14, 0.01. Not much autocorrelation. (d) Now $t = -2.83$ (using Stata) still
   statistically significant. (e) Plot does not suggest a relationship.
   (f) Now $b = 0.172$ with $t = 0.76$ and $p = 0.449$. So wrong sign and statistically insignificant.

7. (a) Yes. (b) Yes, the 2006 curve is further out. (c) Yes, it appears linear in logs.
   (d) Decline by 7.44%. (e) 6.77%. (f) The correct cluster-robust standard errors are almost
   4.4 times larger (.0440/.0100)! Due to errors correlated across years for a given manufacturer.
   (g) 4.67%.

9. (a) \$1,436, \$879, \$1,030, \$650, \$1,024, \$637. All plans have lower outpatient spending than
   the free plan, though spending does not drop uniformly with coinsurance rate.
   (b) Yes, $F = 26.85$ with $p = 0.000$. (c) Yes, expected signs. Yes, $F = 67.51$ with $p = 0.000$.
   (d) Little change in coefficients and $F = 31.35$ compared to 26.35. Little change is expected
   as due to random assignment the insurance indicators are essentially uncorrelated with any
   of these additional variables.

11. (a) Treated 1993: 0.271, untreated 1993: 0.489, treated 1998: 1.392, untreated 1998 0.568.
    (b) Before-after: $1.392 - 0.271 = 1.121$. Yes. (c) Treat-control: $1.392 - 0.568 = 0.824$. Yes.
    (d) Diff-in-diff $= (1.392 - 0.271) - (0.568 - 0.489) = 1.042$. Yes.
    (e) $b = 1.042$, $se = .381$, $t = 3.48.$, $.73p = 0.008$. Statistically significant at 5%.

13. (a) Yes. Democrats won 50.7% of past elections and had an average winning margin of 1.73%.
    (b) Yes. Graph suggests an incumbency advantage (the gap at 0) of around 10% of vote.
    (c) No. (d) Yes. $b = 11.52$, $t = 8.39$. (e) Yes. $b = 7.56$, $t = 4.52$. (f) Yes. $b = 9.04$, $t = 3.48$.

15. (a) Yes, a positive relationship. (b) Yes. $b = 0.487$, $t = 6.61$. (c) Yes. -0.36.
    (d) Yes. $b = 1.281$, $t = 3.19$. (e) Yes. Standard error of b rose from 0.074 to 0.402.

(f) A one standard deviation change in *avexpr* leads to a $1.281 \times 1.47 = 1.88$ increase in *logpgp95*, or a $100 \times (e^{1.88} - 1) = 655\%$ increase in GDP. This is an enormous effect!

D.14 Solutions: Models with Indicator Variables

1. (a) $\widehat{y}_i = 20 + 10d_i$. (b) $\bar{y} = 3$ for subsample with $d_i = 0$ and $\bar{y} = 8$ for subsample with $d_i = 1$.

3. $se = \sqrt{\frac{2000^2}{400} + \frac{3000^2}{300}} = 200$; $t = \frac{2800-2500}{200} = 1.5$; difference not statistically different at 5%.

5. (a) 0.448. (b) $247569.2 - 259062.5 = -11493.3$.
   (c) Slope is same as (b); $t = -0.88$ so statistically insignificant at 5%.
   (d) Same estimate; st. error 13092.79 vs. 13117.5 for OLS; degrees of freedom 21.89 vs. 27.
   (e) Now $t = -0.82$. (f) Same estimate as (e) with same $se = 14044.55$ and degrees 27.

7. (a) $\widehat{y}_i = 8 + 13x_i$ when $d_i = 1$ and $\widehat{y}_i = 3 + 6x_i$ when $d_i = 0$. (b) $\widehat{y}_i = 6 + 7d_i - 4x_i - 2dx_i$.

9. (a) $\overline{dlater} = 0.448$, $\overline{dlatersize} = 803.45$. (b) Yes, higher intercept, lower slope for *dlater*= 1.
   (c) $\widehat{y} = 76648 + 93.25size + 111183dlater - 59.92dlatersize$.
   (d) $H_0 : \beta_{dlater} = 0, \beta_{dlatersize} = 0$; $F = 6.17$ has $p = 0.0066$ so reject H_0- there is a difference.
   (e) $H_0 : \beta_{size} = 0, \beta_{dlatersize} = 0$; $F = 47.92$ has $p = 0.0000$, *size* is statistically significant.
   (f) Part (c) estimates give $\widehat{y} = 76647 + 93.25size$ when *dlater*= 1 and $\widehat{y} = (76648+111183.4) + (93.25 - 59.92)size = 187831 + 33.33size$; equals coefficients in the separate OLS regressions.

11. (a) $\widehat{y} = 1 + 2x + 4d1 + 7d2 = 1 + 2x + 4d1 + 7(1 - d1 - d3) = 8 + 2x - 3d1 - 7d3$. $R^2 = 0.5$.
    (b) $\widehat{y} = 5 + 2x + 3d2 - 4d3$. $R^2 = 0.5$. (c) $\widehat{y} = 1 + 2x + 4d1 + 7d2 = (d1+d2+d3) + 2x + 4d1 + 7d2 = 2x + 5d1 + 8d2 + d3$. R^2 changes in equation with no intercept.

13. (b) Tabulation shows *d1*, *d2*, and *d3* each only take values 0 or 1. Variable $tot = d1 + d2 + d3$ takes value 1 for all observations. (c) $\widehat{price} = 108720 + 73.07size + 3559lotsize$.
    (d) $\widehat{price} = 112078 + 72.18size + 6643d2 + 8040lotsize$. Test $H_0 : \beta_{d2} = 0, \beta_{d3} = 0$ has $F = 0.37$ and $p = 0.697$ so statistically insignificant at 5%.
    (e) Part (d) model is more flexible but favor part (c) model with lower $\bar{R}^2$ (0.593 > 0.578).
    (f) *size* has same slope coefficient and standard error, same R^2, same F statistic, different intercept and indicator coefficients. (g) One indicator variable is dropped as $d1 + d2 + d3 = 1$. (h) One of the indicator variables is dropped as $d1 + 2d2 + 3d3 = lotsize$.

D.15 Solutions: Models with Transformed Variables

1. (a) $\text{ME}_x = 3 + 8x$. (b) $\text{AME}_x = \frac{1}{n}\sum_{i=1}^{n}(3 + 8x_i) = 3 + 8 \times \frac{1}{n}\sum_{i=1}^{n} x_i = 3 + 8\bar{x} = 3 + 8 \times 2 = 19$.
   (c) $\text{MEM}_x = 3 + 8\bar{x} = 19$. (d) $\text{ME}_x = 3 + 8 \times 3 = 27$. (e) $-3/(2 \times 4) = 0.375$.

3. (a) $\text{ME}_x = 2 + 7d$. (b) $\text{AME}_x = \frac{1}{n}\sum_{i=1}^{n}(2 + 7d_i) = 2 + 7\frac{1}{n}\sum_{i=1}^{n} x_i = 2 + 7\bar{d} = 2 + 7 \times 0.5 = 5.5$.
   (c) $\text{MEM}_x = 2 + 7\bar{d} = 5.5$. (d) $\text{ME}_x = 2 + 7 \times 1 = 9$. (e) $\text{ME}_x = 4 + 7x$.

5. (a) $\widehat{lifeexp} = 67.97 + 0.00438 hlthpc + -4.33 \times 10^{-7} hlthpcsq$.
   (b) Yes, $t = -6.63$ and $p = 0.000 < 0.05$. (c) Yes. $F = 22.70$ has $p = 0.000$.
   (d) $0.004378 - 2 \times 0.000000433 \times 3255.6 = 0.00156$. 1.56 more years for \$1,000 higher $hlthpc$.
   (e) 0.00156. AME=MEM for quadratic. (f) $-0.0043781/(2 \times (-0.000000433)) = \$5,055$.
   (g) USA is past the turning point and is where life expectancy is predicted to decline with increased health spending. (h) Turning point is now 15% lower at \$4,369.

7. (a) The relationship does not appear to be linear. (b) Yes as $yearsq$ is highly statistically significant with $t = -7.64$ and $p = 0.000$. (c) ME $= 9.0827 + 2 \times (-.022592) = 0.046$ in year 2000. (d) AME $= 0.256$. (e) yes as there are periods of positive residual followed by periods of negative residual. (f) No. The scattering of residuals does not trend with year.

9. (a) $\widehat{lnhlthpc} = -5.0096 + 1.256 lngdppc$.
   (b) A 1% increase in GDP pc is associated with a 1.256% increase in health spend pc.
   (c) ME$= 1.256 \times 3255/33054 = 0.124$. (d) 0.00124 is similar to 0.089 from levels OLS.
   (g) Averages for $hlthpc$ and predictions in parts (e) and (f) are 3255, 3232 and 3297. In this example the usually preferred corrected prediction overpredicts by more than the naive prediction underpredicts.

11. (a) No observations are lost as $satmath$ and $satverb$ are greater than zero for all observations.
    (b) Holding the other variables constant, a 1% change in $satmath$ (or $satverb$) is associated with a 0.577% (or 0.009%) higher salary, and being one year older (or having one more year if schooling) is associated with a 0.122% (or 0.024%) higher salary.
    (c) $lnsatmath$ and age. (d) No, all have the expected positive sign.

13. (a) Both $lnsalary$ and its prediction have average 10.264. (b) The average naive prediction is 29,119, much less than the average salary of 36,767. Yes, there is a problem.
    (c) The average corrected prediction is 39,986, still different from the average salary of 36,767, but closer than the naive prediction of part (b).

15. (a) All variables except $satverb$ are statistically significant at 5%. (b) The negative coefficient of $satverb$ is surprising, though it is statistically insignificant at 5% ($p = 0.155$). (c) It's difficult to say - it is not enough to say one coefficient is bigger than the other. One more inch of height is associated with the same change in salary as $b_{satmath}/b_{height} = 862.1/48.78 = 17.7$ higher SAT math score. (d) The standardized coefficient of $satmath$ is 0.220 compared to 0.146 for $height$, so a one standard deviation change in SAT math score is associated with a bigger change in salary than a one standard deviation change in height.

D.16 Solutions: Checking the Model and Data

1. (a) Irrelevant regressor included causes no problem, though estimation less precise.
   (b) Indicator variable causes no problem.
   (c) Perfect collinearity so cannot estimate both β_2 and β_3.
   (d) Omitted variable so biased and inconsistent (unless x_4 is uncorrelated with x_2 and x_3).

(e) Correlated errors so need to use appropriate robust standard errors.

(f) Heteroskedastic errors so need to use heteroskedastic-robust standard errors.

3. (a) Yes. (b) No. t statistics are much smaller. Multicollinearity may be the reason.

(c) $H_0 : \beta_{highgrade} = 0, \beta_{highgradeXage} = 0$, $F = 3.13$, $p = 0.044$, statistically significant at 5%.

(d) $H_0 : \beta_{age} = 0, \beta_{highgradeXage} = 0$, $F = 5.88$, $p = 0.003$, statistically significant at 5%.

(e) Cor($highgrade,highgradeXage$)= 0.9755 is very high so multicollinear.

(f) $R^2 = 0.9993$, exceptionally high so very strong multicollinearity.

5. Answers will vary but will approximately equal the following.

(a) Cor($x2, x3$) $\simeq$ Cor($x2, x4$) $\simeq \sqrt{0.5} = 0.707$, Cor($x3, x4$) $\simeq 0.5$, Cor($u, x2$) $\simeq$ Cor($u, x3$) $\simeq$ Cor($u, x4$) $= 0$. (b) Yes. Estimated correct model with error uncorrelated with regressors.

(c) No. $b_2 \simeq 2 \neq 1$. Omitted regressor $x3$ which is correlated with $x2$.

(d) Yes. Here the variable $x4$ is not part of the model generating y. Irrelevant regressor.

7. Answers will vary but will approximately equal the following.

(a) Cor($x2, x3$) $\simeq$0.5, Cor($u, x2$) $\simeq \sqrt{0.5} = 0.707$, Cor($u, x3$) $= 0$.

(b) $b_2 \simeq 5/3 = 1.667 \neq 1$ and $b_3 \simeq 2/3 = 0.667 \neq 1$.

(c) No. The regressor $x2$ was correlated with the error (and this affected both b_2 and b_3).

9. (a) The two are within 30% of each other for all regressors.

(b) Cluster-robust standard errors are 2 to 4 times the heteroskedastic-robust standard errors.

(c) $\tau_{lhp} \simeq \sqrt{1 + 0.430 \times 0.314 \times ((22/507) - 1)} = 1.99$.

(d) The actual inflation is larger: $0.0839/0.0289 = 2.90$ compared to heteroskedastic-robust and $0.0839/0.0230 = 3.64$ compared to default standard errors.

11. Your answers will vary somewhat from these due to different seed, different package, ...

(a) Yes. The coefficient of x is 3.91, close to 4.

(b) HAC standard error of b_x is 0.097 is much different from the heteroskedastic-robust standard error of 0.058. This is because the error u_t is autocorrelated.

(c) Yes. The slope coefficients are 0.801 and 3.953, close to 0.8 and 4.

(d) HAC standard errors of 0.0027 and 0.0291 are close to the heteroskedastic-robust standard errors of 0.0024 and 0.0273. This is because the error e_t is independent.

(e) No. The coefficients are 0.862 and 3.597, more than four standard errors away from 0.8 and 4. This is because we have both a lagged dependent variable and an autocorrelated error.

13. (a) Yes. (b) The standard deviation of the OLS residual is 0.53, so the residual of around 2 and three residuals of around -2 are suspicious. The four residuals for $\hat{y} \simeq 9.2$ may be suspicious. (c) The four observations with 0 or 1 years of education have large residuals.

(d) Observations with 0 or 1 years of education are surprising and suggest coding error. One person has only \$4,000 in annual earnings despite working all year for 40 hours per week.

(e) 22 observations had $|dfits| > 2\sqrt{4/378} = 0.206$. (f) Four of the six observations were those with *education* equal to 0 or 1. Another had the largest OLS residual of 2.218.

(g) The coefficients are within 15% of each other, the standard errors are roughly 30% smaller with the outliers dropped due to better fit (higher R^2 and lower standard error of the regression).

D.17 Solutions: Special Topics

1. (a) A 1% change in weight is associated with a 0.61% reduction in miles per gallon (or more precisely $100 \times (e^{.614} - 1) = 0.85\%$).
   (b) Cluster-robust standard errors are $0.1366/0.0331 = 4.13$ times the default.
   (c) *d_manual* has coefficient $0.0353/0.0296 = 1.19$ times larger. No gain in efficiency as cluster-robust standard errors are larger for all but *d_manual*.
   (d) Cluster-robust standard errors are two to five times the default.
   (e) *d_manual* has coefficient that is $0.0336/0.0296 = 1.13$ times larger.
   (f) Cluster-robust standard errors are two to five times the default.

3. (a) No. The negative coefficient for *hlthins* is surprising. An explanation is that for poor uninsured people in low income countries it is cheaper to see a pharmacist than a doctor.
   (b) Cluster-robust standard error is $0.0183/0.08 = 2.29$ times the default standard error.
   (c) *hhexp* changes a lot (with a sign reversal) and *hlthins* changes from -0.0135 to -0.0102. No improvement as cluster-robust standard errors are actually larger for RE.
   (d) Cluster-robust are around 10% larger except $0.0334/0.0081 = 4.1$ times higher for *illness*.
   (e) Similar to part (c) as fixed effects estimates are very close to random effects estimates.
   (f) Similar to part (d) as fixed effects estimates are very close to random effects estimates.

5. (a) $b = 0.0068$ with $se_{clu} = 0.00191$ substantially greater than $se_{het} = 0.00102$.
   (b) $b = 0.0046$ with $se_{clu} = 0.00083$ greater than $se_{def} = 0.00059$.
   (c) $b = 0.0045$ with $se_{clu} = 0.00084$ greater than $se_{het} = 0.00059$.
   (d) FE and RE slopes are two-thirds of OLS. (e) se_{clu}'s lower for RE and FE than for OLS.

7. (d) $b_{wins} = 0.004505$ all methods. (e) $se_{wins} = 0.000842$ in (a),(c) and 0.000886 in (b). (As stated at the end of Chapter 17.2.4 use cluster-robust standard errors from (a) or (c).)

9. (a) Cluster-robust standard errors are larger; e.g. 0.0841 versus 0.0445 for $\ln k$.
   (b) $b_{\ln l} + b_{\ln k} = 1.0247$, $F = 1.17$, $p = 0.284 > 0.05$. Do not reject constant returns to scale.
   (c) Cluster-robust standard errors are larger e.g. 0.0831 versus 0.0506 for $\ln k$.
   (d) Compare cluster-robust se's. For RE they are smaller for b_{lnk} but larger for b_{lnl}.

11. (a) Yes. In general spending decreases with increased coinsurance, though the effect is not uniform. The coefficients for 25%, mixed, 50%, individual and 95% are respectively -559, -364, -514, -489 and -805 compared to a base of 2153 with 0% coinsurance.
   (b) Yes. $F(5, 2204) = 8.83$ with $p = 0.00 < 0.05$.
   (c) A reason for fixed effects is concern that regressors are correlated with the error. But this is an experiment with the regressors (the coinsurance levels) randomly assigned.
   (d) No as there is no within variation in the coinsurance indicator variables.

13. Exact answers will vary with seed, random number generator, etc.
   (a) $\widehat{\text{Cor}}[x, u] = 0.568$ so problems for OLS as regressor x is correlated with error u.
   (b) No as $b_2 = 0.893$ with $\text{se}(b_2) = 0.018$ is a long way from $\beta_2 = 0.5$.
   (c) Yes as $\widehat{\text{Cor}}[z, u] = 0.015 \simeq 0$ so instrument z is uncorrelated with error u.
   Note that it in practice this test can't be performed as with real data we do not know u.
   (d) Yes as $\widehat{\text{Cor}}[z, x] = 0.579 \simeq 0$ so instrument z is highly correlated with regressor x.
   (e) Yes as $b_{2,IV} = 0.5147$ with $\text{se}(b_{2,IV}) = 0.030$ is close to 0.5.
   (f) Here $0.5069/0.9488 = 0.5147 = b_{2,IV}$. (g) We obtain $0.5147 = b_{2,IV}$.
   (h) The standard errors differ (0.047 versus correct 0.030). We need to use part (e) method.

15. (a) 0.505. (b) $b_{OLS} = 0.106$. (c) $b_{IV} = 0.619$. (d) This seems very high, an 85.6% increase
   ($e^{.619} - 1 = .857$). But there is a $15.37 - 11.12 = 4.25$ years difference in average schooling.
   (e) Yes. $t = 2.18$. (f) $r = 0.114$ is quite low so there will be a big loss in precision.
   (g) $F = 13.04$ is low, so *col4* might be a weak instrument.

17. (a) $\Pr[y = 1|x = 2] = e^{1+0.5\times2}/(e^{1+0.5\times2}) = 0.8808$. (b) ME$= 0.8808 \times (1 - 0.8808) \times 0.5 = 0.210$. (c) ME$\simeq 0.6 \times (1 - 0.6) \times 0.5 = 0.12$.

19. (a) $\bar{y} = 0.273$. (b) $b_{ols} = 0.053$. (c) Problem - some predicted probabilities are negative.
   (d) $b_{logit} = 0.358$. (e) Now all predicted probabilities are positive (and less than one).

21. (a) 20.21%. (b) b_{income} is surprisingly negative, though it is very imprecisely estimated.
   (c) $\bar{y}(1 - \bar{y})b = 0.202 \times 0.798 \times 0.0654 = 0.0603$. (d) AME$= 0.05547$. (e) Yes.
   (f) 0.0654 is about 20% higher than 0.05547.

23. (a) $\exp(-1+0.2\times2) = 0.5488$. (b) 0.2%. (c) $0.5488\times0.2 = 0.1098$. (d) $b\bar{y} = 0.2\times0.6 = 0.012$.

25. (a) Yes, except $b_{income} < 0$ though is statistically insignificant at 5%.
   (b) Yes. Robust se's are about 1.7 times the default se's. (c) Controlling for the other
   variables, one more illness is associated with a 31% increase in doctor visits.
   (d) AME$= 0.31190.3017 = 0.0941$. (e) 0.0941. (f) $b_{ols} = 0.1169 \simeq 1.25\times$AME.

27. (a) $b = -0.606$ and 95% CI is (-0.843, -0.369). (b) $b = -.142$ and 95% CI is (-0.281, -0.003).
   (c) Poisson regression is better as it avoids problems with zero spending.

29. Answers will vary due to different seeds, data generating processes, ...
   (b) Yes. I had $\bar{y} = 0.032$ and $s = 2.336 \simeq \sqrt{1/.19} = 2.294$.
   (c) Yes. e.g. I had $\hat{\rho}_{12} = 0.279 \simeq 0.9^{12} = 0.282$. (d) Yes. At least 50 times.
   (f) It is difficult to say with just one sample - we can always calculate a sample mean but
   this does not mean that E$[z]$ exists.
   (g) I found $\hat{\rho}_{100} = 0.300$ which is still quite large. (h) Many simulations will find zero crossings.

31. Answers will vary due to different seeds, data generating processes, ...
   (b) No. (c) Perhaps a positive relationship. (d) $R^2 = 0.066$, so perhaps.
   (e) $t = 8.46$ so highly statistically significant. (f) Yes as $\hat{\rho}_{20} = 0.675$.
   Note: with an alternative seed I got $R^2 = 0.151$, $t = 13.32$ and $\hat{\rho}_{20} = 0.797$.

33. (a) No. *gs5* mean is 0.988 higher and we expect higher interest rates for a longer term.
(b) The series are very highly autocorrelated e.g. $\widehat{\rho}_1 > 0.98$.
(c) Yes, though with larger fluctuations in *gs1*. (d) Yes. (e) Newey-West standard error of 0.0329 is 3.7 times the HAC-robust standard error of robust standard error of 0.0089.
(f) $H_0 : \beta_{gs1} = 1$ against $H_a : \beta_{gs1} \neq 1$ has $t = \frac{0.9365-1}{0.0329}/0.0329 = 1.930$ with $p = 0.054$. Do not reject H_0. This may be surprising as may expect more fluctuation in the one-year rate.

35. (b) Every month the gap between the rates is narrowing by 0.0082 (so by 0.0987 per year).
(c) $H_0 : \beta_{gs1} = 1$ against $H_0 : \beta_{gs1} \neq 1$ has $t = (0.6811 - 1)/.0562 = -5.67$. Reject H_0.
(d) Yes. By 14 lags the autocorrelations are less than 0.1.

37. (a) Every month the five-year rate was declining on average by 0.0335 (so by 0.426 per year).
(b) The autocorrelations die out very quickly: $|\widehat{\rho}_4| < 0.10$ for both. (c) Yes. (d) Yes.
(e) Yes. A one percentage point change in *gs1* is associated with a 0.858 percentage point change in *gs5*, with $t = 17.88$ and $p = 0.000$.

39. (a) Yes. $\widehat{\rho}_1 = 0.37$. (b) No. First twelve $|\widehat{\rho}_j| < 0.11$. (c) No. First twelve $|\widehat{\rho}_j| < 0.09$.
(d) The models in parts (b) and (c) as the errors there are serially uncorrelated.
(e) No, as lagged dependent variables are included.
(f) $t = (b_{l1gs} + b_{l2gs} + b_{l3gs} - 1)/se = (0.9901 - 1)/.005557 = -1.78$. Do not reject H_0.
(g) Breusch-Godfrey statistic $= 13.47$ with $p = 0.33 > 0.05$. Do not reject H_0 : no correlation.

41. (a) Based on 5% tests, no. Individually $p > 0.05$. Joint test $F = 1.84$ with $p = 0.16$.
(b) Yes, though only $\widehat{\rho}_1 = 0.24$ is large. (c) Yes, an autocorrelated error is fine here as the regressors are not lagged dependent variables. (d) Yes, very autocorrelated. e.g. $\widehat{\rho}_{12} = 0.46$.
(e) Ljung-Box $\chi^2(12)$ statistic $= 33.26$ with $p = 0.002 < 0.05$. Reject H_0 : no correlation.

43. (b) Yes. $|\widehat{\rho}_j| < 0.10$ for all $j \leq 12$.
(c) Yes, if error is serially correlated then OLS with lagged dependent variables is inconsistent.
(d) Yes as error is serially uncorrelated. (e) Yes as $\widehat{\rho}_1 = 0.25$.
(f) Ljung-Box $\chi^2(12)$ statistic $= 9.87$ with $p = 0.57 > 0.05$. Do not reject H_0 : no correlation.

45. (b) Yes. $|\widehat{\rho}_j| < 0.10$ for all $j \leq 12$. (c) Impulse response is coefficient of $dgs1_t$: 0.365 with standard error 0.063. (d) Impulse response is coefficient of $dgs1_t$: 0.100 with se 0.093.

Appendix E

Tables for Key Distributions

We give tables for the following distributions

1. Standard normal distribution: probabilities in the left tail for many values.

2. Student $T(v)$ distribution: selected critical values for various degrees of freedom.

3. $F(v_1, v_2)$ distribution: critical values at the 10% significance level for various degrees of freedom.

4. $F(v_1, v_2)$ distribution: critical values at the 5% significance level for various degrees of freedom.

5. $F(v_1, v_2)$ distribution: critical values at the 1% significance level for various degrees of freedom.

6. $F(v_1, \infty)$ distribution and $\chi^2(v)$ distributions: critical values at the 10% significance level for various degrees of freedom.

The first two tables apply to tests of a single hypothesis. The remaining tables can be used for tests of multiple hypotheses.

z	0	1	2	3	4	5	6	7	8	9
				Second decimal value of z						
0.0	0.5000	0.5040	0.5080	0.5120	0.5160	0.5199	0.5239	0.5279	0.5319	0.5359
0.1	0.5398	0.5438	0.5478	0.5517	0.5557	0.5596	0.5636	0.5675	0.5714	0.5753
0.2	0.5793	0.5832	0.5871	0.5910	0.5948	0.5987	0.6026	0.6064	0.6103	0.6141
0.3	0.6179	0.6217	0.6255	0.6293	0.6331	0.6368	0.6406	0.6443	0.6480	0.6517
0.4	0.6554	0.6591	0.6628	0.6664	0.6700	0.6736	0.6772	0.6808	0.6844	0.6879
0.5	0.6915	0.6950	0.6985	0.7019	0.7054	0.7088	0.7123	0.7157	0.7190	0.7224
0.6	0.7257	0.7291	0.7324	0.7357	0.7389	0.7422	0.7454	0.7486	0.7517	0.7549
0.7	0.7580	0.7611	0.7642	0.7673	0.7704	0.7734	0.7764	0.7794	0.7823	0.7852
0.8	0.7881	0.7910	0.7939	0.7967	0.7995	0.8023	0.8051	0.8078	0.8106	0.8133
0.9	0.8159	0.8186	0.8212	0.8238	0.8264	0.8289	0.8315	0.8340	0.8365	0.8389
1.0	0.8413	0.8438	0.8461	0.8485	0.8508	0.8531	0.8554	0.8577	0.8599	0.8621
1.1	0.8643	0.8665	0.8686	0.8708	0.8729	0.8749	0.8770	0.8790	0.8810	0.8830
1.2	0.8849	0.8869	0.8888	0.8907	0.8925	0.8944	0.8962	0.8980	0.8997	0.9015
1.3	0.9032	0.9049	0.9066	0.9082	0.9099	0.9115	0.9131	0.9147	0.9162	0.9177
1.4	0.9192	0.9207	0.9222	0.9236	0.9251	0.9265	0.9279	0.9292	0.9306	0.9319
1.5	0.9332	0.9345	0.9357	0.9370	0.9382	0.9394	0.9406	0.9418	0.9429	0.9441
1.6	0.9452	0.9463	0.9474	0.9484	0.9495	0.9505	0.9515	0.9525	0.9535	0.9545
1.7	0.9554	0.9564	0.9573	0.9582	0.9591	0.9599	0.9608	0.9616	0.9625	0.9633
1.8	0.9641	0.9649	0.9656	0.9664	0.9671	0.9678	0.9686	0.9693	0.9699	0.9706
1.9	0.9713	0.9719	0.9726	0.9732	0.9738	0.9744	0.9750	0.9756	0.9761	0.9767
2.0	0.9772	0.9778	0.9783	0.9788	0.9793	0.9798	0.9803	0.9808	0.9812	0.9817
2.1	0.9821	0.9826	0.9830	0.9834	0.9838	0.9842	0.9846	0.9850	0.9854	0.9857
2.2	0.9861	0.9864	0.9868	0.9871	0.9875	0.9878	0.9881	0.9884	0.9887	0.9890
2.3	0.9893	0.9896	0.9898	0.9901	0.9904	0.9906	0.9909	0.9911	0.9913	0.9916
2.4	0.9918	0.9920	0.9922	0.9925	0.9927	0.9929	0.9931	0.9932	0.9934	0.9936
2.5	0.9938	0.9940	0.9941	0.9943	0.9945	0.9946	0.9948	0.9949	0.9951	0.9952
2.6	0.9953	0.9955	0.9956	0.9957	0.9959	0.9960	0.9961	0.9962	0.9963	0.9964
2.7	0.9965	0.9966	0.9967	0.9968	0.9969	0.9970	0.9971	0.9972	0.9973	0.9974
2.8	0.9974	0.9975	0.9976	0.9977	0.9977	0.9978	0.9979	0.9979	0.9980	0.9981
2.9	0.9981	0.9982	0.9982	0.9983	0.9984	0.9984	0.9985	0.9985	0.9986	0.9986
3.0	0.9987	0.9987	0.9987	0.9988	0.9988	0.9989	0.9989	0.9989	0.9990	0.9990

Example: The probability that standard normal is less than 0.65 equals 0.7422.
Example: The probability that standard normal is greater than 0.65 equals 1-0.7422 = 0.2378.

Figure E.1: Standard normal distribution: Probabilities in the left tail

		Significance Level			
Degrees	20% (2-sided)	10% (2-sided)	5% (2-sided)	2% (2-sided)	1% (2-sided)
of Freedom	10%(1-sided)	5%(1-sided)	2.5%(1-sided)	1%(1-sided)	0.5%(1-sided)
1	3.078	6.314	12.706	31.821	63.657
2	1.886	2.920	4.303	6.965	9.925
3	1.638	2.353	3.182	4.541	5.841
4	1.533	2.132	2.776	3.747	4.604
5	1.476	2.015	2.571	3.365	4.032
6	1.440	1.943	2.447	3.143	3.707
7	1.415	1.895	2.365	2.998	3.499
8	1.397	1.860	2.306	2.896	3.355
9	1.383	1.833	2.262	2.821	3.250
10	1.372	1.812	2.228	2.764	3.169
11	1.363	1.796	2.201	2.718	3.106
12	1.356	1.782	2.179	2.681	3.055
13	1.350	1.771	2.160	2.650	3.012
14	1.345	1.761	2.145	2.624	2.977
15	1.341	1.753	2.131	2.602	2.947
16	1.337	1.746	2.120	2.583	2.921
17	1.333	1.740	2.110	2.567	2.898
18	1.330	1.734	2.101	2.552	2.878
19	1.328	1.729	2.093	2.539	2.861
20	1.325	1.725	2.086	2.528	2.845
21	1.323	1.721	2.080	2.518	2.831
22	1.321	1.717	2.074	2.508	2.819
23	1.319	1.714	2.069	2.500	2.807
24	1.318	1.711	2.064	2.492	2.797
25	1.316	1.708	2.060	2.485	2.787
26	1.315	1.706	2.056	2.479	2.779
27	1.314	1.703	2.052	2.473	2.771
28	1.313	1.701	2.048	2.467	2.763
29	1.311	1.699	2.045	2.462	2.756
30	1.310	1.697	2.042	2.457	2.750
60	1.296	1.671	2.000	2.390	2.660
90	1.291	1.662	1.987	2.368	2.632
120	1.289	1.658	1.980	2.358	2.617
Infinity	1.282	1.646	1.962	2.330	2.581

Example: For one-sided test at 10% the area to the right of the critical value is 0.10.
Example: For two-sided test at 10% the area to the right of the critical value is 0.05
and the area to the left of minus one times the critical value is also 0.05.

Figure E.2: Student t distribution: Key critical values

| Second Degrees | First Degrees of Freedom (v1) | | | | | | | | | |
of Freedom (v2)	1	2	3	4	5	6	7	8	9	10
1	39.86	49.50	53.59	55.83	57.24	58.20	58.91	59.44	59.86	60.19
2	8.53	9.00	9.16	9.24	9.29	9.33	9.35	9.37	9.38	9.39
3	5.54	5.46	5.39	5.34	5.31	5.28	5.27	5.25	5.24	5.23
4	4.54	4.32	4.19	4.11	4.05	4.01	3.98	3.95	3.94	3.92
5	4.06	3.78	3.62	3.52	3.45	3.40	3.37	3.34	3.32	3.30
6	3.78	3.46	3.29	3.18	3.11	3.05	3.01	2.98	2.96	2.94
7	3.59	3.26	3.07	2.96	2.88	2.83	2.78	2.75	2.72	2.70
8	3.46	3.11	2.92	2.81	2.73	2.67	2.62	2.59	2.56	2.54
9	3.36	3.01	2.81	2.69	2.61	2.55	2.51	2.47	2.44	2.42
10	3.29	2.92	2.73	2.61	2.52	2.46	2.41	2.38	2.35	2.32
11	3.23	2.86	2.66	2.54	2.45	2.39	2.34	2.30	2.27	2.25
12	3.18	2.81	2.61	2.48	2.39	2.33	2.28	2.24	2.21	2.19
13	3.14	2.76	2.56	2.43	2.35	2.28	2.23	2.20	2.16	2.14
14	3.10	2.73	2.52	2.39	2.31	2.24	2.19	2.15	2.12	2.10
15	3.07	2.70	2.49	2.36	2.27	2.21	2.16	2.12	2.09	2.06
16	3.05	2.67	2.46	2.33	2.24	2.18	2.13	2.09	2.06	2.03
17	3.03	2.64	2.44	2.31	2.22	2.15	2.10	2.06	2.03	2.00
18	3.01	2.62	2.42	2.29	2.20	2.13	2.08	2.04	2.00	1.98
19	2.99	2.61	2.40	2.27	2.18	2.11	2.06	2.02	1.98	1.96
20	2.97	2.59	2.38	2.25	2.16	2.09	2.04	2.00	1.96	1.94
21	2.96	2.57	2.36	2.23	2.14	2.08	2.02	1.98	1.95	1.92
22	2.95	2.56	2.35	2.22	2.13	2.06	2.01	1.97	1.93	1.90
23	2.94	2.55	2.34	2.21	2.11	2.05	1.99	1.95	1.92	1.89
24	2.93	2.54	2.33	2.19	2.10	2.04	1.98	1.94	1.91	1.88
25	2.92	2.53	2.32	2.18	2.09	2.02	1.97	1.93	1.89	1.87
26	2.91	2.52	2.31	2.17	2.08	2.01	1.96	1.92	1.88	1.86
27	2.90	2.51	2.30	2.17	2.07	2.00	1.95	1.91	1.87	1.85
28	2.89	2.50	2.29	2.16	2.06	2.00	1.94	1.90	1.87	1.84
29	2.89	2.50	2.28	2.15	2.06	1.99	1.93	1.89	1.86	1.83
30	2.88	2.49	2.28	2.14	2.05	1.98	1.93	1.88	1.85	1.82
60	2.79	2.39	2.18	2.04	1.95	1.87	1.82	1.77	1.74	1.71
90	2.76	2.36	2.15	2.01	1.91	1.84	1.78	1.74	1.70	1.67
120	2.75	2.35	2.13	1.99	1.90	1.82	1.77	1.72	1.68	1.65
Infinity	2.71	2.30	2.08	1.94	1.85	1.77	1.72	1.67	1.63	1.60

Note: The area to the right of the critical value is 0.10.
Example: The probability that F(3,20) exceeds 2.28 is 0.10

Figure E.3: F(v1,v2) distribution: Critical values for a 10% significance test

Second Degrees	First Degrees of Freedom (v1)									
of Freedom (v2)	1	2	3	4	5	6	7	8	9	10
1	161.45	199.50	215.71	224.58	230.16	233.99	236.77	238.88	240.54	241.88
2	18.51	19.00	19.16	19.25	19.30	19.33	19.35	19.37	19.38	19.40
3	10.13	9.55	9.28	9.12	9.01	8.94	8.89	8.85	8.81	8.79
4	7.71	6.94	6.59	6.39	6.26	6.16	6.09	6.04	6.00	5.96
5	6.61	5.79	5.41	5.19	5.05	4.95	4.88	4.82	4.77	4.74
6	5.99	5.14	4.76	4.53	4.39	4.28	4.21	4.15	4.10	4.06
7	5.59	4.74	4.35	4.12	3.97	3.87	3.79	3.73	3.68	3.64
8	5.32	4.46	4.07	3.84	3.69	3.58	3.50	3.44	3.39	3.35
9	5.12	4.26	3.86	3.63	3.48	3.37	3.29	3.23	3.18	3.14
10	4.96	4.10	3.71	3.48	3.33	3.22	3.14	3.07	3.02	2.98
11	4.84	3.98	3.59	3.36	3.20	3.09	3.01	2.95	2.90	2.85
12	4.75	3.89	3.49	3.26	3.11	3.00	2.91	2.85	2.80	2.75
13	4.67	3.81	3.41	3.18	3.03	2.92	2.83	2.77	2.71	2.67
14	4.60	3.74	3.34	3.11	2.96	2.85	2.76	2.70	2.65	2.60
15	4.54	3.68	3.29	3.06	2.90	2.79	2.71	2.64	2.59	2.54
16	4.49	3.63	3.24	3.01	2.85	2.74	2.66	2.59	2.54	2.49
17	4.45	3.59	3.20	2.96	2.81	2.70	2.61	2.55	2.49	2.45
18	4.41	3.55	3.16	2.93	2.77	2.66	2.58	2.51	2.46	2.41
19	4.38	3.52	3.13	2.90	2.74	2.63	2.54	2.48	2.42	2.38
20	4.35	3.49	3.10	2.87	2.71	2.60	2.51	2.45	2.39	2.35
21	4.32	3.47	3.07	2.84	2.68	2.57	2.49	2.42	2.37	2.32
22	4.30	3.44	3.05	2.82	2.66	2.55	2.46	2.40	2.34	2.30
23	4.28	3.42	3.03	2.80	2.64	2.53	2.44	2.37	2.32	2.27
24	4.26	3.40	3.01	2.78	2.62	2.51	2.42	2.36	2.30	2.25
25	4.24	3.39	2.99	2.76	2.60	2.49	2.40	2.34	2.28	2.24
26	4.23	3.37	2.98	2.74	2.59	2.47	2.39	2.32	2.27	2.22
27	4.21	3.35	2.96	2.73	2.57	2.46	2.37	2.31	2.25	2.20
28	4.20	3.34	2.95	2.71	2.56	2.45	2.36	2.29	2.24	2.19
29	4.18	3.33	2.93	2.70	2.55	2.43	2.35	2.28	2.22	2.18
30	4.17	3.32	2.92	2.69	2.53	2.42	2.33	2.27	2.21	2.16
60	4.00	3.15	2.76	2.53	2.37	2.25	2.17	2.10	2.04	1.99
90	3.95	3.10	2.71	2.47	2.32	2.20	2.11	2.04	1.99	1.94
120	3.92	3.07	2.68	2.45	2.29	2.18	2.09	2.02	1.96	1.91
Infinity	3.84	3.00	2.60	2.37	2.21	2.10	2.01	1.94	1.88	1.83

Note: The area to the right of the critical value is 0.05.
Example: The probability that $F(3,20)$ exceeds 2.92 is 0.05

Figure E.4: $F(v1,v2)$ distribution: Critical values for a 5% significance test

Second Degrees	First Degrees of Freedom (v1)									
of Freedom (v2)	1	2	3	4	5	6	7	8	9	10
1	4052.18	4999.50	5403.35	5624.58	5763.65	5858.99	5928.36	5981.07	6022.47	6055.85
2	98.50	99.00	99.17	99.25	99.30	99.33	99.36	99.37	99.39	99.40
3	34.12	30.82	29.46	28.71	28.24	27.91	27.67	27.49	27.35	27.23
4	21.20	18.00	16.69	15.98	15.52	15.21	14.98	14.80	14.66	14.55
5	16.26	13.27	12.06	11.39	10.97	10.67	10.46	10.29	10.16	10.05
6	13.75	10.92	9.78	9.15	8.75	8.47	8.26	8.10	7.98	7.87
7	12.25	9.55	8.45	7.85	7.46	7.19	6.99	6.84	6.72	6.62
8	11.26	8.65	7.59	7.01	6.63	6.37	6.18	6.03	5.91	5.81
9	10.56	8.02	6.99	6.42	6.06	5.80	5.61	5.47	5.35	5.26
10	10.04	7.56	6.55	5.99	5.64	5.39	5.20	5.06	4.94	4.85
11	9.65	7.21	6.22	5.67	5.32	5.07	4.89	4.74	4.63	4.54
12	9.33	6.93	5.95	5.41	5.06	4.82	4.64	4.50	4.39	4.30
13	9.07	6.70	5.74	5.21	4.86	4.62	4.44	4.30	4.19	4.10
14	8.86	6.51	5.56	5.04	4.69	4.46	4.28	4.14	4.03	3.94
15	8.68	6.36	5.42	4.89	4.56	4.32	4.14	4.00	3.89	3.80
16	8.53	6.23	5.29	4.77	4.44	4.20	4.03	3.89	3.78	3.69
17	8.40	6.11	5.18	4.67	4.34	4.10	3.93	3.79	3.68	3.59
18	8.29	6.01	5.09	4.58	4.25	4.01	3.84	3.71	3.60	3.51
19	8.18	5.93	5.01	4.50	4.17	3.94	3.77	3.63	3.52	3.43
20	8.10	5.85	4.94	4.43	4.10	3.87	3.70	3.56	3.46	3.37
21	8.02	5.78	4.87	4.37	4.04	3.81	3.64	3.51	3.40	3.31
22	7.95	5.72	4.82	4.31	3.99	3.76	3.59	3.45	3.35	3.26
23	7.88	5.66	4.76	4.26	3.94	3.71	3.54	3.41	3.30	3.21
24	7.82	5.61	4.72	4.22	3.90	3.67	3.50	3.36	3.26	3.17
25	7.77	5.57	4.68	4.18	3.85	3.63	3.46	3.32	3.22	3.13
26	7.72	5.53	4.64	4.14	3.82	3.59	3.42	3.29	3.18	3.09
27	7.68	5.49	4.60	4.11	3.78	3.56	3.39	3.26	3.15	3.06
28	7.64	5.45	4.57	4.07	3.75	3.53	3.36	3.23	3.12	3.03
29	7.60	5.42	4.54	4.04	3.73	3.50	3.33	3.20	3.09	3.00
30	7.56	5.39	4.51	4.02	3.70	3.47	3.30	3.17	3.07	2.98
60	7.08	4.98	4.13	3.65	3.34	3.12	2.95	2.82	2.72	2.63
90	6.93	4.85	4.01	3.53	3.23	3.01	2.84	2.72	2.61	2.52
120	6.85	4.79	3.95	3.48	3.17	2.96	2.79	2.66	2.56	2.47
Infinity	6.64	4.61	3.78	3.32	3.02	2.80	2.64	2.51	2.41	2.32

Note: The area to the right of the critical value is 0.01.
Example: The probability that F(3,20) exceeds 4.51 is 0.01

Figure E.5: $F(v1,v2)$ distribution: Critical values for a 1% significance test

	F(v1,infinity) Significance Level				Chi-squared(v1) Significance Level		
v1	10%	5%	1%		10%	5%	1%
1	2.71	3.84	6.64		2.71	3.84	6.63
2	2.30	3.00	4.61		4.61	5.99	9.21
3	2.08	2.60	3.78		6.25	7.81	11.34
4	1.94	2.37	3.32		7.78	9.49	13.28
5	1.85	2.21	3.02		9.24	11.07	15.09
6	1.77	2.10	2.80		10.64	12.59	16.81
7	1.72	2.01	2.64		12.02	14.07	18.48
8	1.67	1.94	2.51		13.36	15.51	20.09
9	1.63	1.88	2.41		14.68	16.92	21.67
10	1.60	1.83	2.32		15.99	18.31	23.21
11	1.57	1.79	2.25		17.28	19.68	24.72
12	1.55	1.75	2.18		18.55	21.03	26.22
13	1.52	1.72	2.13		19.81	22.36	27.69
14	1.50	1.69	2.08		21.06	23.68	29.14
15	1.49	1.67	2.04		22.31	25.00	30.58
16	1.47	1.64	2.00		23.54	26.30	32.00
17	1.46	1.62	1.97		24.77	27.59	33.41
18	1.44	1.60	1.93		25.99	28.87	34.81
19	1.43	1.59	1.90		27.20	30.14	36.19
20	1.42	1.57	1.88		28.41	31.41	37.57
21	1.41	1.56	1.85		29.62	32.67	38.93
22	1.40	1.54	1.83		30.81	33.92	40.29
23	1.39	1.53	1.81		32.01	35.17	41.64
24	1.38	1.52	1.79		33.20	36.42	42.98
25	1.38	1.51	1.77		34.38	37.65	44.31
26	1.37	1.50	1.76		35.56	38.89	45.64
27	1.36	1.49	1.74		36.74	40.11	46.96
28	1.35	1.48	1.72		37.92	41.34	48.28
29	1.35	1.47	1.71		39.09	42.56	49.59
30	1.34	1.46	1.70		40.26	43.77	50.89

Note: First three columns are for F distribution.
Note: Ssecond three columns are for chi-squared.

Figure E.6: F(v1,infinity) and chi-squared(v1) distributions: Key critical values

Appendix F

References

Arone-Dine, Aviva, Lirun Einav, and Amy Finkelstein (2013), "The RAND Health Insurance Experiment, Three Decades Later," *Journal of Economic Perspectives*, Vol.27(1), pages 197-222.

Acemoglu, Daron, Simon Johnson, and James A. Robinson (2001), "The Colonial Origins of Comparative Development: An Empirical Investigation," *American Economic Review*, Vol. 91(5), pages 1369-1401.

Acemoglu, Daron, Simon Johnson, James A. Robinson, and Pierre Yared (2008), "Income and Democracy," *American Economic Review*, Vol. 98(3), pages 808-42.

Angrist, Joshua D., and Jörn-Steffen Pischke (2009), *Mostly Harmless Econometrics: An Empiricist's Companion*, Princeton University Press.

Angrist, Joshua D., and Jörn-Steffen Pischke (2015), *Mastering Metrics*, Princeton University Press.

Calonico, Sebastian, Matias Cattaneo, Max Farrell, and Rocío Titiunik (2017), "Rdrobust: Software for Regression-discontinuity Designs," *The Stata Journal*, Vol.17(2), pages 372–404.

Cameron, A. Colin, and Pravin K. Trivedi (2005), *Microeconometrics: Methods and Applications*, Cambridge University Press.

Cameron, A. Colin, and Pravin K. Trivedi (2022a), *Microeconometrics using Stata: Volume 1: Cross-section and Panel Regression Models*, Second Edition, forthcoming, Stata Press.

Cameron, A. Colin, and Pravin K. Trivedi (2022b), *Microeconometrics using Stata: Volume 2: Nonlinear Models and Causal Inference Models*, Second Edition, forthcoming, Stata Press.

Card, David E. (1995), "Using Geographic Variation in College Proximity to Estimate the Return to Schooling," in *Aspects of Labor Market Behavior: Essays in Honor of John Vanderkamp*, L.N. Christofides, E.K. Grant and R. Swidinsky (Eds.), 201-222, University of Toronto Press.

Cobb, Charles W. and Paul H. Douglas (1928), "A Theory of Production," *The American Economic Review*," December, pages 139-165.

Cunningham, Scott (2021), *Causal Inference: The MixTape*, Yale University Press.

Greene, William H. (2018), *Econometric Analysis*, Eighth Edition, Pearson.

Hansen, Bruce E. (2022), *Econometrics*, Princeton University Press, forthcoming.

James, Gareth, Daniela Witten, Trevor Hastie, and Robert Tibshirani (2021), *An Introduction to Statistical Learning: with Applications in R*, Second Edition, Springer.

Kling, Jeffrey R. (2001), "Interpreting Instrumental Variables Estimates of the Returns to Schooling," *Journal of Business and Economic Statistics*, Vol.19(3), 358-364.

Knittel, Christopher R. (2012), "Automobiles on Steroids: Product Attribute Trade-offs and Technological Progress in the Automobile Sector," *American Economic Review*, Vol.101(7), pages 3368-3399.

Krueger, Alan (1993), "How Computers have Changed the Wage Structure: Evidence from Micro-Data, 1984-1989," *Quarterly Journal of Economics*, Vol.108(1), pages 33-60.

Manning, Willard G., Joseph P. Newhouse, Naihua Duan, Emmet B. Keeler, Arleen Leibowitz, and M. Susan Marquis, (1987), "Health Insurance and the Demand for Medical Care: Evidence from a Randomized Experiment," *American Economic Review*, Vol. 77(3), pages 251-277.

Newey, Whitney K. and Kenneth D. West, "A Simple, Positive Semi-definite, Heteroskedasticity and Autocorrelation Consistent Covariance Matrix," *Econometrica*, Vol. 55(3), pages 703-708.

Nollenberger, Natalia , Núria Rodríguez-Planas, and Almudena Sevilla (2016), "The Math Gender Gap: The Role of Culture," *American Economic Review*, Vol. 106(5), pages 257-261.

Phillips, A. W. (1958), "The Relation Between Unemployment and the Rate of Change of Money Wage Rates in the United Kingdom, 1861–1957," *Economica*, Vol. 25(10), pages 283-299.

Stock, James H. and Mark K. Watson (2018), *Introduction to Econometrics*, Fourth Edition, Pearson.

Tanaka, Shinsuke (2014), "Does Abolishing User Fees Lead to Improved Health Status? Evidence from Post-Apartheid South Africa," *American Economics Journal: Economic Policy*, Vol. 6(3), pages 282-312.

White, Halbert A., "A Heteroskedasticity-consistent Covariance Matrix Estimator and a Direct Test for Heteroskedasticity," *Econometrica*, Vol. 48(4), pages 817-838.

Wooldridge, Jeffrey M. (2010), *Econometric Analysis of Cross Section and Panel Data*, Second Edition, MIT Press.

Wooldridge, Jeffrey M. (2019), *Introductory Econometrics: A Modern Approach*, Seventh Edition, Cengage.

Index

Acemoglu, A., 301, 365, 501
added variable plot, 369
adjusted R-squared, 208
    and overall F test, 234
    compared to t test, 224
Akaike information criterion, 208
analysis of variance table, 108, 210
Angrist, J. D., 416, 501
ANOVA, 327
Aron-Dine, A., 292, 501
assumptions
    for causal methods, 391
    for regression, 126, 133, 146, 218, 358, 464
    for sample mean, 41
    relaxing for regression, 137, 158, 222
asymptotic properties, 43, 48, 136, 139, 222, 250
asymptotically normal, 43, 136, 222, 242, 467
autocorrelated errors, 173, 247, 364
autocorrelation, 100, 403, 411
    tests for, 404, 411
    using a statistical package, 404
autoregressive distributed lag model, 405, 414
autoregressive error model, 405
autoregressive model, 404, 414
average absolute deviation, 11
average marginal effect, 335, 398, 400

bar chart, 19
basis point change, 28
Bayesian information criterion, 208, 408
Bayesian methods, 265
    posterior distribution, 265
    prior information, 265
    uninformative prior, 266
before-after comparison, 295

Bernoulli distribution, 81, 454
bootstrap standard errors, 249
    pairs bootstrap, 249
box-and-whisker plot, 12
Breusch-Godfrey test, 404

Calonico, S., 298, 501
Cameron, A. C., 416, 501
Card, D. E., 389, 501
case study
    automobile efficiency, 288–291
    capital asset pricing model, 170–173
    cleaning data, 303–308
    Cobb-Douglas production function, 280–284
    gains from political incumbency, 298–300
    health and access to health, 295–298
    health expenditures across countries, 170
    health insurance experiment, 291–295
    health outcomes across countries, 165–168
    health spending across countries, 168
    institutions and country growth, 301–303
    output and unemployment, 173–176
    Phillips curve, 284–288
    school academic performance, 275–280
categorical data, 2, 96, 315, 397
categorical variables, see indicator variables
Cattaneo, M., 298, 501
causal methods, 391–396
    applications, 291–303
    difference-in-differences, 295–298, 393
    experiments, 291–295, 393
    instrumental variables, 301–303, 387–391
    inverse probability weighting, 396
    local average treatment effect, 395
    matching, 396

propensity score, 396
  regression adjustment, 393
  regression discontinuity design, 298–300, 394
causation, 112–113, 206
  and correlation, 112
Census example, 45–46, 131–132
central limit theorem, 43, 61, 136, 146, 220, 458
charts, 15–22
Chebychevs inequality, 12
chi-squared distribution, 232, 451
  compared to F distribution, 232
  tables of critical values, 500
cluster-robust standard errors, 245–246, 364, 378, 380, 467
  degrees of freedom, 246
  using a statistical package, 250–251
clustered data, 378–380
  using a statistical package, 383
clustered errors, 245, 364
Cobb, C. W., 280, 501
Cochrane-Orcutt estimator, 405
coefficient of variation, 11
coin toss example, 36, 40, 50, 454
cointegrated series, 407
collinear variables, *see* multicolliearity
column chart, 19
complier, 395
component plus residual plot, 369
compounding, 187
  continuous compounding, 191
conditional mean, 125, 126, 218
  definition, 461
  prediction, 252–258
conditional probability, 460
conditional variance, 461
confidence interval
  best confidence intervals, 261
  critical value, 66, 148, 223
  derivation, 66
  for actual value forecast, 254
  for conditional mean, 254
  for proportions data, 81

for slope parameter, 148–150, 222–223
for the mean, 65–69
generalizations, 79
interpretation, 68, 149
margin of error, 80, 82
two standard error interval, 68, 149
what level of confidence, 67, 148
consistent estimator, 48, 139, 221, 358
convergence in probability, 458
correlation, 97–100, 200, 201, 462
  and causation, 112
  and covariance, 98
  and R-squared, 107, 207
  and regression, 111
  and tests of statistical significance, 152
  autocorrelation, 100, 403, 411
  definition, 97
  strength of correlation, 99
covariance, 98, 462
covariate, 101, 201
critical value, 64, 72, 151, 224, 230
  F distribution, 228
  tables, 493–500
  using a statistical package, 451
cross tabulation, 95
cross-section data, 3, 377–402
  fixed effects, 379, 394
  random effects, 378
cumulative distribution function, 454
Cunningham, S., 416, 502

data analytics, 264
data cleaning, 303–308
data collection methods, 3
data science, 264
data transformation, 22–28, 307, 333–353, 403
data types, 2–3
dataset in main text
  API99, 275
  AUTOSMPG, 288
  CAPM, 170
  CENSUSAGEMEANS, 46
  CENSUSREGRESSIONS, 132

COBBDOUGLAS, 280
COINTOSSMEANS, 40
DEMOCRACY, 365
EARNINGS, 7, 59, 185
EARNINGS_COMPLETE, 315, 333, 399
EARNINGSMALE, 74
FISHING, 22
GASPRICE, 73
GDPEMPLOY, 174
GENERATEDDATA, 129
GENERATEDREGRESSIONS, 131
HEALTH2009, 165
HEALTHACCESS, 296
HEALTHCATEGORIES, 19
HEALTHINSEXP, 292
HOUSE, 94, 145, 197, 223, 244
INCUMBENCY, 298
INSTITUTIONS, 301
INTERESTRATES, 409
MONTHLYHOMESALES, 25
NBA, 384
PHILLIPS, 284
PSID raw data, 303
REALGDPPC, 19, 26, 75, 249
RETURNSTOSCHOOLING, 389
SP500INDEX, 188
default standard errors, 158, 241, 465
degrees of freedom, 39, 63, 105, 206, 227, 242
    cluster-robust standard errors, 246
dependent variable, 101, 201
descriptive statistics, *see* summary statistics
DFBETA, 370
DFITS, 370
diagnostics, 367–371
    influential observation, 368, 370
    outlying observation, 367
    plots, 368
Dickey-Fuller test
    in first differences, 413
difference in means, *see* indicator variables
difference in means tests, 317–318
    using a statistical package, 318

difference-in-differences, 295–298, 393
disturbance term, *see* error term
Douglas, P. H., 280, 501
Duan, N., 292, 502
dummy variable, 315
dummy variable trap, 323
dummy variables, *see* indicator variables

economic significance
    versus statistical significance, 151, 225
Einav, L., 292, 501
elasticities, 181–187, 342–344, 400
endogenous regressor, 362, 387
error sum of squares, 107, 207
error term, 126, 218
    autocorrelated, 247, 468
    clustered, 245, 467
    compared to residual, 127, 371
    correlated with regressor, 362
    definition, 126, 218
    heteroskedastic, 159, 243, 466
    homoskedastic, 134, 219, 465
estimate
    defined, 47
estimator
    best linear unbiased, 139, 221
    best unbiased, 139, 222
    consistent, 48, 221, 361, 362
    defined, 47
    efficient, 47
    minimum variance, 47, 139, 221, 260, 473
    unbiased, 47, 138, 221
Eviews, *see also* statistical packages
    essentials, 445–449
    robust standard errors, 251
Excel, 449–451
exogenous regressor, 362, 388
expected value, 36, 454
experimental data, 3
experiments, 291–295, 393
explained sum of squares, 106, 207
explanatory variable, 101, 201
exponential function, 190

continuous compounding, 191
exponential growth
    linearizing, 188

F distribution, 227–228, 451
    compared to chi-squared distribution, 232
    critical value, 228
    degrees of freedom, 227
    inverse probabilities, 228
    mean, 227
    probabilities, 228
    tables of critical values, 493
F statistic, 229
F tests, 229–234
    and adjusted R-squared, 234
    compared to t test, 231
    complete model, 229
    computation in a statistical package, 231
    of exclusion restrictions, 230, 234
    of overall significance, 230, 233
    of statistical significance, 231
    of subsets of regressors, 230, 234
    reduced model, 229
    restricted model, 229
    under assumptions 1-4, 232–234
    unrestricted model, 229
Farrell, M., 298, 501
feasible generalized least squares, 260
finite distributed lag model, 405, 414
Finkelstein, A., 292, 501
fitted value, 101, 201
fixed effects estimator, 379, 382, 386, 394
    using a statistical package, 383
forecast, 254
    confidence interval, 254
    with time-series data, 408

Gauss-Markov theorem, 221
generalized least squares, 260
Gini coefficient, 11
Google sheets, 449–451
Greene, W. H., 416, 502
Gretl, *see also* statistical packages

essentials, 440–445
    robust standard errors, 251
grouped data, *see* clustered data
growth rate, 28
    rule of 72, 187

HAC-robust standard errors, 247–249, 402, 468
    using a statistical package, 250–251
Hansen, B. E., 416, 502
Hastie, T., 416, 502
heteroskedastic errors, 159, 243–245, 363
    and estimator properties, 466
heteroskedastic-robust standard errors, 159–160, 243–245, 466
    using a statistical package, 250–251
histogram, 16–18
    smoothed histogram, 17
    using a statistical package, 18
homoskedastic errors, 134, 219
    and estimator properties, 463, 466
hypothesis tests
    best tests, 262
    critical value, 72, 155, 230
    examples for the mean, 73–76
    F tests, 227–234
    for proportions data, 81
    for slope parameter, 158, 223–225
    for the mean, 69, 80
    generalizations, 80
    joint hypothesis tests, 227–234
    most powerful test, 263
    multiple testing, 232
    of autocorrelation, 404
    of exclusion restrictions, 230
    of overall significance, 230
    of statistical significance, 150, 224, 231
    of subsets of regressors, 230
    on interacted indicator variables, 320
    on sets of indicator variables, 324
    one-sided, 76–79, 156–158
    p-value, 71, 155, 230
    rejection using critical region, 72, 155, 224
    rejection using p-values, 71, 155, 224

relationship with confidence interval, 73, 155
significance level, 70, 153, 263
test power, 263
test size, 70, 153, 263
two-sided, 76, 153–156
type I error, 69, 153, 262
type II error, 262
which significance level, 72, 151

impulse response function, 415
inconsistent estimator, 358–363
independence, *see* statistical independence
independent variable, 101, 201
indicator variables, 315–329
    and additional controls, 319–320
    ANOVA, 327
    as dependent variable, 322, 397–399
    base category, 323
    creating in statistical package, 327
    difference in means, 104, 316, 393
    difference in several means, 327
    dummy variable trap, 323
    hypothesis tests, 324
    interacted, 320, 322
    mutually exclusive, 323
    omitted category, 323
    reference category, 323
    sets of indicator variables, 322–328
    single indicator variable, 315–318
inequality measures, 11
influential observation, 368
    DFBETA, 370
    DFITS, 370
information criteria, 208
instrument, 387
instrumental variables, 301–303, 387–391, 470
    Anderson-Rubin test, 390
    complier, 395
    local average treatment effect, 395
    two-stage least squares estimator, 389
    using a statistical package, 391
    weak instruments, 390
interacted variables, 340–342

with indicator variables, 322
intercept coefficient, 101, 102, 201
intercept-only regression, 104, 248
interquartile range, 11
inverse probability weighting, 396
irrelevant variables, 359

James, G., 416, 502
jitter, 97
Johnson, S., 301, 365, 501
joint hypothesis tests, *see* F tests

Keeler, E. B., 292, 502
kernel density estimate, 17
    using a statistical package, 18
Kling, J. R., 389, 502
Knittel, C., 288, 502
Krueger, A., 352, 502
kurtosis statistic, 15

law of large numbers, 48, 458
least squares regression, *see* regression
Leibowitz, A., 292, 502
likelihood function, 473
line chart, 18
linear probability model, 399
linear-log model, 183
Ljung-Box test
    of autocorrelation, 404
local average treatment effect, 395
local constant regression, 115
local linear regression, 116
local projection method, 415
loess regression, 116
log-likelihood function, 473
log-linear model, 183, 342
    prediction, 345
log-log model, 183, 280, 343
    prediction, 344
logit regression, 397–399, 474
    marginal effects, 398
longitudinal data, 3, *see* panel data
lower quartile, 10

machine learning, 264
Manning, W. G., 292, 502
margin of error, 80, 82
marginal effect at a representative value, 335
marginal effect at the mean, 335
marginal effects, 333–337
    average marginal effect, 335
    calculus method, 334
    computing in a statistical package, 336, 402
    computing in astatistical package, 402
    finite difference method, 334
    for logit regression, 398
    for Poisson regression, 400
    for probit regression, 398
Marquis, M. S., 292, 502
matching estimators, 396
matrix algebra for regression, 471–474
maximum likelihood estimator, 401, 473
mean of a random variable
    conditional mean, 461
    definition, 36, 454
    estimator for, 47–48
mean of sample, see sample mean
measurement error bias, 363
median of sample, 9
mid-range, 9
missing data, 305
    codes in statistical packages, 305
misspecification tests, 361
mode of sample, 9
model sum of squares, 106, 207
moving average, 24
multicollinearity, 210, 356–357

Nadaraya-Watson estimator, 115
natural logarithm, 23, 179–196
    and elasticities, 181–187, 342–344
    and semi-elasticities, 181–187, 342–344
    approximating, 187
    approximating percentage change, 180
    approximating proportionate change, 180
    Cobb-Douglas example, 280–284
    defined, 179

    linearizing exponential growth, 188
    regression models, 181–187, 342–348
    rule of 72, 187
Newey, W. K., 469, 502
Newhouse, J. P., 292, 502
Nollenberger, N., 313, 502
nominal data, 26
nonlinear least squares estimator, 401
nonlinear regression models, 397–402
nonparametric regression, 115–117
    using a statistical package, 116
nonrepresentative sample, 48, 258, 272
nonstationary time series, 406–408
normal distribution
    fraction within k standard deviations, 12
    in large samples, 43, 61, 136, 147, 220, 458
    needed for exact t distribution, 62, 147, 220
    standard normal distribution, 455
    table of critical values, 493
numerical data, 2

observational data, 2
omitted variables, 360
ordinary least squares regression, see regression
outlying observation, 11, 12, 111, 367–371

p-value, 71, 155, 224, 230
    using a statistical package, 451
panel data, 3, 380–387
    dynamic models, 383
    example, 384–387
    fixed effects, 382, 386, 394
    long panel, 380
    pooled OLS, 385
    random effects, 381, 386
    short panel, 380
    special considerations, 380–384
    using a statistical package, 383
    within variation, 381
panel-robust standard errors, 381
parameters
    defined, 47, 454
    of linear regression model, 126, 218

partial regression plot, 369
per capita data, 27
percentage change, 28
percentage point change, 28
percentiles, 9
Phillips, A. W., 284, 502
pie chart, 22
Pischke, J.-S., 416, 501
plots, *see* charts
    diagnostic, 368
Poisson regression, 399
    marginal effects, 400
pooled data, 3
population mean, 47, 243
population model for regression, 126, 218, 464
power of test, 263
predicted value, 101, 201
prediction, 110, 252–258
    average versus actual, 252, 257
    bivariate regression, 256
    bivariate regression example, 257
    for log-linear model, 345
    for log-log model, 344
    multiple regression example, 255
    of actual value, 254
    of average outcome, 253
    of conditional mean, 253
    using a statistical package, 255
    using big data, 264
probability density function, 455
probability mass function, 453
probit regression, 397–399
    marginal effects, 398
propensity score, 396
proportions data, 81
    using a statistical package, 81

quadratic model, 337–340
quartiles, 9
quasi-maximum likelihood estimator, 473

R, *see also* statistical packages
    essentials, 436

robust standard errors, 251
R-squared, 105–108, 207–208
    adjusted R-squared, 208
    alternative definition, 107, 207
    and correlation, 107, 207
    definition, 105, 207
    interpretation, 108
    with transformed dependent variable, 345
random effects estimator, 379, 381, 386
    using a statistical package, 383
random number generator, 50
random sample
    definition, 38
    generation in a statistical package, 50–52
    nonrepresentative, 48, 258
    simple random sample, 41
random variables, 35–39, 453–462
    conditional mean, 126, 461
    conditional probability, 460
    conditional variance, 461
    continuous, 455
    correlation, 462
    covariance, 462
    cumulative probability distribution function, 454
    discrete, 453
    expected value, 454
    joint probability, 459
    linear transformation of, 455
    mean, 36, 454
    probability density function, 455
    probability mass function, 453
    standard deviation, 37, 454
    standardized, 455
    statistical independence, 457, 460
    sums of, 457
    variance, 37, 454
random walk process, 406
range of sample, 11
real data, 26
regression
    a brief history, 266

adjusted R-squared, 208
and correlation, 111
and difference in means, 104, 318
and sample mean, 104, 243, 248
assumptions, 126, 133, 146, 218, 358, 464
best linear unbiased estimator, 139, 221
causal methods, *see* causal methods
Census example, 131–132
commonly-used models, 400
computation by hand, 113
computer output, 108–110, 209–210
conditional mean, 125, 126, 218
conditional mean of the error, 127
confidence interval, 148–150, 222–223
consistent estimator, 139, 221
cross-section data, 377–402
degrees of freedom, 105, 206, 227
derivations of estimator properties, 463–470
diagnostics, *see* diagnostics
estimated coefficients, 102, 133, 203, 472
experiment example, 128–131
F tests, 229
hypothesis tests, 150, 158, 223–234
in first differences, 407, 413
inadequate variation in regressor, 210
incorrect model, 359
indicator variables, 315–329
inestimable models, 210, 356
influential observation, 368, 370
information criteria, 208
instrumental variables, 301–303, 470
intercept-only, 104, 248
interpretation of slope coefficient, 103, 204, 206
least squares, 102, 202
linear-log model, 183
log-linear model, 183, 342
log-log model, 183, 343
marginal effects, 333–337
matrix algebra, 471–474
mean of slope coefficient, 134, 219, 464
minimum variance estimator, 138, 260

model fit, 105–108, 206, 209
multicollinearity, 210, 356–357
nonparametric, 115–117
nonrepresentative sample, 258
normal distribution in large samples, 136, 147, 220
not identified, 211
ordinary least squares, 102, 202
outlying observation, 11, 111, 367
panel data, 380–387
parameters, 126, 218
partial effect, 204
perfectly collinear regressors, 210, 323, 356
population line, 126, 218
population model, 126, 218
prediction, *see* prediction
R-squared, 105–108, 207–208
regression line, 101, 201
regressor orthogonal to residual, 202
relaxing assumptions, 137, 222
residual, 101, 202
residual sum of squares, 102, 202
robust standard errors, *see* robust standard errors
spurious regression, 407
standard error of slope coefficient, 135, 220
standard error of the regression, 105, 135, 206, 219
standardized coefficients, 347
t statistic, 146–147, 220
tests of statistical significance, 150, 224
time-series data, 402–415
total effect, 204
transformed variables, 333–353
unbiased estimator, 138, 221, 465
variance of slope coefficient, 134, 219, 465
weighted least squares, 259
regression adjustment, 393
regression analysis, 4
regression discontinuity design, 298–300, 394
regression sum of squares, 106, 207
regressor, 101, 201

correlated with error term, 362
repeated cross-section data, 3
RESET test, 361
residual, 101, 202
    compared to error term, 127, 371
    standard error of the residual, 105, 206
residual sum of squares, 102, 107, 202, 207
residual versus regressor plot, 369
right-skewed data, 13
Robinson, J. A., 301, 365, 501
robust standard errors, 158, 160, 241–252, 466–469
    bootstrap, 249
    cluster-robust, 245–246, 364, 378, 380, 467
    for sample mean, 243, 248
    HAC-robust for time series, 247–249, 364, 402, 468
    heteroskedastic-robust, 160, 243–245, 363, 466
    panel-robust, 381
    using a statistical package, 250–251
    when to use, 252
Rodríguez-Planas, N., 313, 502
rolling average, 24
root mean squared error of the residual, 105, 135, 206
rule of 72, 187

sample correlation coefficient, *see* correlation
sample covariance, 98
sample mean, 8
    and intercept-only regression, 104, 243, 248
    as outcome of random variable, 39
    assumptions, 41
    Census example, 45–46
    coin toss example, 40
    mean, 41, 458
    normal distribution in large samples, 43
    robust standard error, 243, 248
    standard deviation, 42, 458
    statistical properties, 41–45, 457
    variance, 42, 458
sample selection bias, 363
sample standard deviation, 10, 39

sample variance, 10, 39
scatterplot, 96, 199
seasonal adjustment, 25
seed for random number generator, 50
semi-elasticities, 181–187, 342–344, 400
sets of indicator variables, *see* indicator variables
Sevilla, A., 313, 502
simple random sample
    computer generation, 50–52
    definition, 41
simultaneous equations bias, 362
skewness, 13
skewness statistic, 13
slope coefficient, 101, 102, 201
    consistent estimator, 139, 221
    derivation of mean, 358, 464
    derivation of variance, 359, 465
    economic significance, 151, 225
    interpretation, 103, 204, 206
    mean, 134, 219
    minimum variance estimator, 138
    standard error, 135
    statistical significance, 150–153, 224
    unbiased estimator, 138, 221
    variance, 134, 219
smoothed histogram, 17
spatial map, 21
spurious regression, 407, 415
standard deviation of a random variable
    definition, 37, 454
    estimator for, 44
standard deviation of sample
    definition, 10
    interpretation, 11
standard error
    default, 158
    of slope coefficient, 135, 220
    of the regression, 105, 135, 206
    of the residual, 105, 206
    of the sample mean, 44
    robust, 160, 241–252, 466–469
standard normal distribution, 451, 455

standardized random variable, 455
standardized regression coefficients, 347
standardized score, 23
Stata, *see also* statistical packages
  essentials, 434–436
  robust standard errors, 251
stationary process, 403
statistical independence, 457, 460
statistical learning, 264
statistical packages, 429–452
  autocorrelations, 404
  computer precision, 433
  computing marginal effects, 336
  critical values, 451
  difference in means tests, 318
  Eviews, 445–449
  Excel, 449–451
  fixed effects estimator, 383
  generating a random sample, 50–52
  Gretl, 440–445
  grouped data, 383
  histogram, 18
  hypothesis tests, 231
  indicator variables creation, 327
  instrumental variables estimation, 391
  intercept-only regression, 104
  kernel density estimate, 18
  local linear regression, 116
  loess regression, 116
  missing data codes, 305
  multicollinearity, 210
  nonlinear model estimators, 402
  nonparametric regression, 116
  p-values, 451
  prediction, 255
  proportions data, 81
  R, 436–440
  random effects estimator, 383
  regression output, 108–110, 209–210
  robust standard errors, 250–251
  standardized regression coefficients, 347
  Stata, 434–436

time series data, 408
statistical significance, 150–153, 224
  based on correlation, 152
  of subsets of regressors, 230
  overall significance, 230
  versus economic significance, 151
Stock, J. H., 416, 502
Student's t distribution, *see* t distribution
summary statistics, 7–15
survey data, 49, 272
symmetric distribution, 13

t distribution, 62–65, 147, 451
  critical value, 64
  exact if data are normally distributed, 62
  exact if errors are normally distributed, 147
  inverse probabilities, 64
  mean and variance, 63
  probabilities for, 63
  table of critical values, 493
t statistic
  for slope parameter, 146–147, 220, 242
  for the mean, 62
tables of critical values, 493–500
  chi-squared distribution, 500
  F distribution, 493
  normal distribution, 493
  t distribution, 493
tabulation, 22, 95
Tanaka, S., 295, 502
tests, *see* hypothesis tests
Tibshirani, R., 416, 502
time-series data, 3, 402–415
  autocorrelation, 100, 403
  autoregressive error model, 405
  autoregressive model, 404
  differenced, 402
  finite distributed lag model, 405
  forecasting, 408
  impulse response function, 415
  lagged, 402
  nonstationary process, 406–408
  random walk process, 406

regression, 402–415

spurious regression, 407

stationary process, 403

transformations for, 24–28, 403

using a statistical package, 408

Titiunik, R., 298, 501

total sum of squares, 105, 207

transformed variables in regression, 353, 333 –
−353

treatment-control comparison, 295

Trivedi, P. K., 416, 501

two-stage least squares estimator, 389

two-way scatterplot, 96, 199

unbiased estimator

definition, 47

unit root process, 406, 412

upper quartile, 10

variance of a random variable

conditional variance, 461

definition, 37, 454

estimator for, 43

variance of sample, 10

Watson, M. K., 416, 502

weighted least squares, 259, 272

weighted mean, 49

West, K. D., 469, 502

white noise process, 403

White, H. A., 467, 502

Witten, D., 416, 502

Wooldridge, J. M., 416, 502

Yared, P., 365, 501

z-score, 24, 111, 347

Made in United States
North Haven, CT
19 August 2023

40480605R00291